PRENTICE HALL'S
ILLUSTRATED
DICTIONARY OF
COMPUTING

2ND EDITION

On Earth, I endure.
It's my dreams wherein we live.

If you could see what we do there,
you'll agree that it's best kept that way.

This book is dedicated to those who see,
and to the few who know.

0125871

Books are to be returned on or before
the last date below.

PRENTICE HALL'S
ILLUSTRATED
DICTIONARY OF
COMPUTING

2ND EDITION

JONAR C. NADER

PRENTICE HALL

SYDNEY   NEW YORK   TORONTO   MEXICO   NEW DELHI
LONDON   TOKYO   SINGAPORE   RIO DE JANEIRO

1 2 3 4 5 99 98 97 96 95

National Library of Australia
Cataloguing-in-Publication Data

Nader, Jonar C.
    Prentice Hall's illustrated dictionary of computing.

    2nd ed.
    ISBN 0 13 205725 5.

    1. Computers - Dictionaries. 2. Electronic data processsing -
    Dictionaries. I. Title. II. Title: Illustrated dictionary of
    computing

004.03

Library of Congress
Cataloging-in-Publication Data

Nader, J. (Jonar).
    Prentice Hall's illustrated dictionary of computing /
    Jonar C. Nader. -- 2nd ed.

    p.   cm.
    ISBN 0 13 205725 5.
    1. Computers -- Dictionaries. I. Title.
QA76.15.N33   1995   94–47617
005.1'4—dc20   CIP

Prentice Hall of Australia Pty Ltd, *Sydney*
Prentice Hall, Inc., *Englewood Cliffs, New Jersey*
Prentice Hall Canada, Inc., *Toronto*
Prentice Hall Hispanoamericana, *SA, Mexico*
Prentice Hall of India Private Ltd, *New Delhi*
Prentice Hall International, Inc., *London*
Prentice Hall of Japan, Inc., *Tokyo*
Prentice Hall of Southeast Asia Pty Ltd, *Singapore*
Editora Prentice Hall do Brasil Ltda, *Rio de Janeiro*

 PRENTICE HALL

A division of Simon & Schuster

PREFACE

Readers might expect me to support the notion that 'computers have advanced the world'. Instead, I suggest that computers have become the haven for inefficiency and failure; and a burden unto businesses and individuals.

The fact the you are using this book leads me to suspect that you belong to the 'immediate-response' society that we have all been guilty of establishing. The error does not lie in our fine technological achievements, but in the little training and lack of standards.

In a recent court case between two computer giants over the technical implications of the use of the term 'IBM compatible', a senior judge (from the United States District Court from the Southern District of New York) determined that it is imperative for practitioners within the computer industry to take extra care when using common terms, particularly when this industry is primarily concerned with, and depends upon, accuracy. The judge concluded that it would be an anomaly for responsible organizations to exercise anything other than precision.

HEAD OR TAILS

On a wet Sunday morning you can keep the whole family bemused by looking up three simple words in three different dictionaries.

Dust *The World Book Dictionary*, *Webster's International Dictionary*, and the good old *Funk & Wagnalls*, and search for the meaning of the words *billion, giga*, and *milliard*.

By comparing notes and trying to make head or tails out of it all, you will notice that, like the modern computer, the revered dictionary is subject to the forces of GIGO (garbage in, garbage out), even to the point of contradiction within the same text.

If you fancy more confusion, consult the faithful *Oxford* or *Encyclopædia Britannica*, and for a little more spice, have a French dictionary on standby.

You may be surprised to learn that most people, even experts within the computer industry, are not aware of the fact that the part-Latin word *billion* in an American dictionary (10^9) is vastly different in meaning to the British *billion* (10^{12}).

Similarly, many cannot define the meaning of the Greek word *giga*, or are totally unfamiliar with the French word *milliard* which, in most parts of the world except America, means 10^9.

It is complex enough trying to understand the origins and definitions of such words, yet the computer industry further complicates the issue by merging unofficial, obscurely-derived, words such as *byte* (<u>bi</u>nary di<u>git</u> <u>e</u>ight), with SI units (Système International d'Unités) to form commonly-used measures such as *kilobyte, megabyte,* and *gigabyte.*

Overnight we saw buzzwords, abbreviations, and acronyms created by industry professionals who are themselves inconsistent — adopting up to 20 variations for even the most common of words. For example, in computer-related publications and associated literature, *megabyte* is sometimes expressed as: m; mb; M; mB; MB; MBs; M-byte; M-Bytes; Meg; MEG; M-B; and in many other similarly-creative ways — all of which are incorrect. It is even harder trying to differentiate these from the word *megabit* (<u>bi</u>nary di<u>git</u>), where mb, mB, MB, and M-B are also used. A leading publication that erroneously uses 'MB' for mega<u>byte</u>, also writes 'MBps' to mean, quite confusingly, mega<u>bits</u> per second.

To add fuel to the fire, consider this: *kilo* (10^3) is a metric term meaning 1000; so 1 kilogram of sugar is 1000 grams of sugar. However, in computer jargon, 256 kilobytes of RAM does not mean 256 000 bytes (256×10^3) of random access memory. It means 262 144 bytes (256×2^{10}), because a *kilo* in this case equals 1024 (binary), not 1000 (decimal).

Although *mega* (10^6) means million, it is 2^{20} when used to refer to computer storage capacity; hence, a file comprising 20 megabytes does not contain 20 000 000 bytes, but $20 \times 1\,048\,576$, which equals 20 971 520 bytes. Furthermore, a *giga* (10^9) takes on a new form in computing to mean 2^{30}, which equals 1 073 741 824.

It is already common to hear professionals speaking in terms of billions. Some day it may be common to compare computer capacity by the centillion (10^{600}), but woe betide the one who gets this wrong; the American system states that a centillion is 10^{303}, not 10^{600}. So, compared to the international standards, that is a difference of 297 decimal points.

USING THIS DICTIONARY

Unlike most of the dictionaries on the market, this one dares to be 'prescriptive'. It also offers explanations as to *why* certain abbreviations and acronyms are used, and draws on real-life examples to help you understand the entries. The diagrams, tables, and photographs which support an entry are drawn to your attention by arrows (▲ ▼).

Entries in this dictionary take into account the Greek, Latin, Arabic, French, and English origins of words, and incorporate mathematical and scientific considerations. Where appropriate, the correct pronunciation of a word is shown and the etymology is given to help you understand its usage. In addition, interesting snippets of information have been included to make its reading more enjoyable.

Prentice Hall's Illustrated Dictionary of Computing was the first and only book to recognize the need for international standards, and to work closely with International Organization for Standardization (ISO) by including official terms defined by ISO and the International Electrotechnical Commission — both of whom form the specialized system for worldwide standardization. To complement these, respect and consideration was given to other standards authorities, including the American National Standards Institute (ANSI) and the Comité Consultatif International de Télégraphique et Téléphonique (CCITT).

This is also the first and only book of its kind to incorporate a Style Manual for correct usage of computer terminology, and to cover a wide cross-section of the industry — explaining the past and present, while exploring the future.

If you have comments and/or suggestions to make, please write to me at PO Box 15, Pyrmont NSW 2009, Australia.

POINT OF ORDER

There are two schools of lexicography: one that mimics the confused society and merely reports the jargon at hand, and one that defines, shapes, determines, and investigates terms as a judge would.

To some people, words may seem insignificant, and dictionaries may seem to be unimportant. However, our words are our definition; they determine our thoughts. We are what we think, we think what we know, and we know what we can articulate. Treat words with contempt, and we stand to lose the point of order.

Jonar C. Nader

STANDARDS

Standardized terms appearing in *Prentice Hall's Illustrated Dictionary of Computing*, and distinguished by [definitions appearing in square brackets] are terms defined by ISO (International Organization for Standardization) and IEC (International Electrotechnical Commission) which form the specialized system for worldwide standardization.

National bodies that are members of ISO or IEC participate in the development of international standards through technical committees. Standardization of terminology is an essential part of standardization activity because it is needed to define the technical terms contained within international standards. In the field of information technology, ISO and IEC have established a joint technical committee (ISO/IEC/JTC1) which has prepared the series of international standards (ISO/IEC 2382 'Information processing systems — Vocabulary').

Terms and definitions appearing in the ISO/AFNOR *Dictionary of computer science* are included here with the permission of ISO and AFNOR. These terms and definitions are the only International Standard terms and definitions resulting from an agreement among experts in the industry.

Copies of the ISO/AFNOR *Dictionary of computer science*, and copies of the book *ISO Member Bodies* can be obtained from the publishers: ISO, Case postale 56, CH–1211 Genève 20, Switzerland; and from: AFNOR, Tour Europe, Cedex 7, 92049 Paris La Défense, France; or from any ISO member body including: the American National Standards Institute (ANSI); Amt für Standardisierung, Messwesen und Warenprüfung (ASMW); the British Standards Institute (BSI); the Standards Association of Australia (SAA); the Standards Association of New Zealand (SANZ); the Standards Council of Canada (SCC); and the Singapore Institute of Standards and Industrial Research (SISIR).

RESEARCH

INTERNATIONAL DATA CORPORATION

Accurate research figures and up-to-date industry analysis were essential ingredients in the preparation of *Prentice Hall's Illustrated Dictionary of Computing*.

Valuable information was afforded by the consultants and from the archives and libraries of International Data Corporation (IDC), which provided the author with a wealth of industry-specific intelligence gathered from the United States, Australia, and Europe.

IDC is part of the International Data Group (IDG), whose subsidiary, IDG Communications, is one of the world's largest publishers of books and periodicals on information technology. The Group has a combined revenue in excess of US$800 million, and it employs over 5000 people in 60 countries. Its exposition management subsidiary, World Expo Corporation, runs more than 60 computer-related exhibitions and conferences in 21 countries.

Since its formation in Framingham, Massachusetts, in 1964, IDC has specialized in monitoring and reporting on all aspects of the rapidly-expanding information-technology industry. IDC has more than 40 offices in North America, Europe, the Middle East, Africa, and the Asia/Pacific region.

Market intelligence gathered by IDC for *Prentice Hall's Illustrated Dictionary of Computing* is reprinted with the permission of IDC.

PRODUCTION TEAM

AUTHOR	*Jonar C. Nader*
ACQUISITIONS EDITOR	*Kaylie Smith*
MANUSCRIPT EDITOR	*Philip A. Bennett*
TECHNICAL EDITOR	*Paul Zucker*
COPY EDITOR	*Robyn Flemming*
EDITORIAL MANAGER	*Fiona Marcar*
PRODUCTION MANAGER	*David Weston*
PRODUCT MANAGER	*Liz Guthrie*
MARKETING MANAGER	*Gillian May*
RETAIL SALES MANAGER	*Paul Summers*
INDUSTRY ANALYST	*Graham W. Penn*
	IDC Australia Pty Ltd
ARCHIVIST	*Mona Bennett*
ETYMOLOGIST	*Philippa Nader*
EDITORIAL ASSISTANT	*Fiona Brown*
CAD ARTIST	*Max Ervin*
COVER DESIGNER	*Randall Alexander*
	Go Man Go Productions
TYPESETTER	*Keyboard Wizards*
PRINTERY	*McPherson's Printing Group*
QUOTATIONS	*Exclamations by the author*
	© Jonar C. Nader

RESEARCHERS:

UNITED STATES	*Julie Ewers*
	Ken Ewers
AUSTRALIA	*Josie D'Arino*
	Tatiana Nader
FRANCE	*Hoda Abdallah*
	Najwa Barakat
GERMANY	*Stefan Föehrdes*
	Andreas Piefke
NEW ZEALAND	*Linley Hughes*

ACKNOWLEDGMENTS

The author wishes to thank the following people
for their invaluable contribution to this publication.

UNITED STATES

ALABAMA
Kathy Morelock
Michael Spalding

ARIZONA
Kate Daly
Julie A. Scholl

CALIFORNIA
V. Steven Arnaudoff
Sonja Bachus
Dave Becker
Nan Borreson
Nancy H. Coolman
Terrence E. Dooher
Alan Doyne
Todd Elvins
Christopher Escher
Beth A. Featherstone
Nancy Guittard
Tony Hampel
Bill Keegan
Anne Killingsworth
David R. Lawson
Karen Logsdon
Jeannie Low
Yazmin Martinez
Don McDonell
Anthony F. Miller
Kevin A. O'Connor
Carol Parcels

Lee W. Payne
Mark Pivan
John Putman
Mark Reiten
R. Rweirs
Kristy Sager
Greg Shandel
Dianne Sheppard
Janet Susich
Jessica Switzer
Sally Vandershaf

COLORADO
Heather Collaton

CONNECTICUT
Michael M. Danchak

FLORIDA
Patty Bates

ILLINOIS
Colleen M. Burke
Lauri M. Hamilton
Lauri Lentz
Nicholas B. Morris
Bruce Newburger
Karen J. Novak

KENTUCKY
John Connolly

MASSACHUSETTS
Ray Boelig
Hanne Herwick
Elizabeth Jewett
Colin Murphy

NEW JERSEY
Kent Ekberg
Diane Varga

NEW YORK
Scott Blau
Chuck Boyer
Barbara J. Henninger
Lisa Katz

OHIO
Bernie Thiel

OREGON
Michael E. Bernhardt
John Haynes

TEXAS
John Ahearne
Martha Brounoff
Donna Burke
Rena Cannon
Bill Cool
Cindy Henderson
Alicia Jansen
Ted Jernigan

Mary Kuna
The late Sally L.
Merryman
Dave Parker
Alison Peoples Golan
Mike Reising
Roger P. Rydell
Krystal Williams
Melody Wolfe

WASHINGTON D.C.
Dan Clemensen
Tony A. Trujillo Jr

WISCONSIN
Phil Katz
David Siebenaller

AUSTRALIA

NEW SOUTH WALES
Nick Angelucci
Paul Antonievich
Trish Arlidge
Robert Baker
Jackie Barnett
Davis Bass
Andrew Binnie
Jeff Bird
Tony Blackie
Sue Bone
Yvonne Borg
Derek Boughton
Shani Brownstein
Suzanne Burmeister
Michele Burn
Maxwell M. Burnet
Joe Cartwright
Heather Caulfield
Pam Chain
Chris Chaseling
Phil Cohen

Rosanna Cordova
John Costella
Melanie Cox
Peter Cunningham
Michael Czajka Jnr
Patricia Del Favero
Melissa Dempsey
Patricia Duffy
Georges Dussek
Amanda Easton
Anne Eckert
Leighton Farrell
Sean Ferguson
Camilla Fiorini
Marie Florian
Martin Fogarty
Bill Ford
Janet Forrester
Charlotte Franklin
Tony Fraser
Roger Frauman
Katrina Ganin
Janet George
Vance Gledhill
Bella Glenny
Ros Gordon
Suzanne Green
Malcolm Gurney
Belinda Hanna
David Henderson
Karen Hillerman
Chris Howells
Ken Hungerford
Ivan Hurwitz
Sarah Jackson
Alan Jones
Robert Kaye
Phillip Kerrigan
Paul Kitchin
Anne Love
Aviva Lowy
Fiona Lucas
Merri Mack

Ian MacArthur
Lesley MacLennan
Jim Macnamara
Nodas Madas
Gregory Madden
Teresa Marinovich
Stephen Marshall
Maria Mastro
Andrew Matherson
Jenny McDonald
Michael McGrath
Barbara Mede
Philip Meyer
Katie Millar
Michael Milne Home
Katrine Mooney
Camille Nader
Odette Nader
Carmela Naval
Fran Newberry
Carmel Nola
Deborah O'Brien
John Parselle
John C. Paterson
Karen Paterson
Harry Pears
Claire Peterson
David Petryca
Maria Pradzynski
Mark Priebatsch
Jeffrey J. Reeves
Chris Richardson
Meredith Rigney
Neville J. Roach
Ivan Roberts
Belinda Robinson
Lisa Robinson
Prue Robson
John Rogers
Souad Sader
Catena Salvia
Sue Sara
Greg Schwarzer

Ruth Sleeman
William E. Smith
Paul Solski
John Stanton
Ray Stuckey
Liz Thomas
Jenny Thurgate
Rebecca Torrens
Derek Twilley
Cait Tynan
Gordon Undy
Derek Walker
Denise Walsh
James Wang
Alan Watt
Hannah Watterson
Don Weatherman
Kim Webber
Dion Weisler
Jo Williams
Naomi Wilson
Steve Wood
Frank Wroe
Lindy Yarnold
Moshe Yerushalmy
Janice Young
Cheanne Yu
Jennifer Zanich

VICTORIA
Peter Coleman
Jackie Finn
Clinton Graham
Jonathan Graham
Graham Ham
Robert McGuirk

Melissa Pope
Mark Webley

QUEENSLAND
Joan M. Roach
Ronda B. Weidmann

CANADA

ONTARIO
Shannon Urie

GERMANY

SALZKOTTEN
Brigit Buschhorn

INDIA

NEW DELHI
Andrew Binnie

ISRAEL

TEL AVIV
D.W. Riker

LEBANON

BERUIT
Najee Barakat

Julia Kayrouz

MALAYSIA

PETALING JAYA
Choong Chong Yew

SINGAPORE

SINGAPORE
Ian M. Churton
Michele Greer

SWITZERLAND

GENÈVA
Jacques-Olivier Chabot

UNITED KINGDOM

BRISTOL
Gill Brown

MIDDLESEX
Michele Fitzpatrick

SURREY
Ronan P. McDonald

XIII

ORGANIZATIONS

*The author wishes to acknowledge the following organizations
for freely providing vast amounts of information,
and for giving permission to reproduce copyright material including
photographs, diagrams, and tables.*

A.S.K. Solutions
Acer Computer Australia
Acer, Inc
Adaptive Research Corporation
Adaptive Solutions, Inc
Advanced Micro Devices
Allison Thomas Associates
Amdahl
Amdahl Pacific Services
Apple Computer Australia
Apple Computer, Inc
Ashton–Tate
Association for Computing
Machinery, Inc
Association for Systems Management
AT&T EasyLink Services
Australia Ltd
AUSSAT Pty Ltd
Azonic Pty Ltd

Bay Networks, Inc
Bio-Recognition Systems
Blackie McDonald Pty Ltd
Borland
Borland Pacific
British Aerospace
Broderbund Software, Inc
Burton–Taylor Communications
Pty Limited
Business Software Association
of Australia

Canadian Information Processing
Society
Candle Corporation of Australia
Canon Australia Pty Ltd
Com Tech Communications
Pty Ltd
Communication Solutions
Compaq Computer Australia
Compaq Computer Corporation
Compaq Computer New Zealand
Computamart Pty Ltd
Convex Computer Corporation
Cooper Associates Pty Ltd
Corel Corporation

Data General
Datacap, Inc
Dauphin Technology, Inc
Dell Computer Corporation
Dell Corporate Services Corporation
Digital Equipment Corporation

Encore Computer Corporation
Evolution Computing
Exabyte Corporation

France Telecom
Franson, Hagerty and
Associates, Inc
Fujitsu America, Inc
Fujitsu Australia

Go Man Go Productions
GRiD Systems Corporation
GTCO Corporation

Hard Copy
Hartford Graduate Center
Hendale Pty Ltd
Hewlett–Packard Company

IBM Archives
IBM Australia Limited
IBM Corporation
ICL
IDC
IDG
Ideal Hardware Limited
Ink Magazine
Integrated Information Technology
Intel Australia Pty Ltd
Intel Corporation
International Organization for
Standardization
International Telecommunications
Satellite Organization

JVC Information Products Company
of America
Kalman Communications

Lexmark International (Australia)
Pty Limited
Loadplan Australasia Pty Ltd
Logitech
Lotus Development Corporation
LucasArts Entertainment Company

Macro Communication
Marketing Directions
Marshall Cutting Pty Ltd
MasPar Computer Corporation
Pty Limited
Mass Optical Storage Technology
Maxis

Megahertz Corporation
Megatec Pty Ltd
Micropolis Corporation
Microsoft Australia
Microsoft Corporation
MITAC Australasia Pty Ltd

NCR Australia Pty Ltd
NCR Corporation
NetComm
NeXT Computer, Inc

Object Management Group
Odyssey Development Pty Limited
Olivetti Systems
Oracle Systems
OTC

Palo Alto Research Center
Paterson Creighton & Associates
Photonics Corporation
Pick Systems
Pioneer Communications
of America, Inc
Pioneer Electronics Australia Pty
PK Ware, Inc
Protechno Card GmbH

Quarter-Inch Cartridge
Drive Standards
Readmore

San Diego Supercomputer Center
SANYO Icon
Scitec Communication Systems
Siemens Nixdorf
Silicon Graphics
Software Suppliers
Sony (Australia) Pty Ltd
SynOptics Communications, Inc

Technical Computing and Graphics
Tektronix Australia Pty Limited

THE WHOLE PURPOSE OF TECHNOLOGY
IS TO CREATE AN ADVANTAGE.

IF YOU PUT TECHNOLOGY IN THE HANDS OF
ALL PEOPLE, IT LOSES ITS VALUE.

THIS IS THE BLESSING AND THE CURSE
OF MY INDUSTRY.

a Atto-. An SI unit prefix for 10^{-18} expressed in decimal notation as 0.000 000 000 000 000 001, as in 'attosecond' (as) or 'attometer' (am).

A 1. See **ampere**. 2. The hexadecimal symbol for binary 1010 (which is equal to the decimal number 10). $A_{16} = 10_{10} = 12_8 = 1010_2$.

Å See **Ångstrom**.

AA A descriptive code given to common 1.5-volt batteries, weighing 23 grams, with a volume of 7.5 cubic centimeters. IEC designation 'LR6'.

AAA A descriptive code given to common 1.5-volt batteries, weighing 12 grams, with a volume of 3.5 cubic centimeters. IEC designation 'LR03'.

AAS Authorized application specialist.

A0, A1, A2 ... A10 Some of the international paper sizes specified by the International Organization for Standardization (ISO). See **paper sizes**.

abacus An ancient calculating device still being used in China, Russia, and the Far East. It consists of a series of beads strung on wires. The five beads on the lower right-hand side are valued at one unit each, while the upper two beads are each worth five units. Moving to the left, the next string of beads are each worth 10, while the upper two are worth 50 each. For each string to the left, the value increases by 10 so that the next string has five beads each worth 100, while the upper beads are valued at 500. Skilled abacus users can calculate very high figures at speeds equal to, or sometimes faster than, the average user of a modern calculator.

abandon To irrevocably clear a document from a computer's memory without first saving it to a file. The word 'abandon' comes from the French words *a bandon*, meaning 'under control'.

A–B box A switchbox that allows the user to switch one computer between two alternate peripherals, or two computers between one peripheral. Usually, the peripherals are printers or modems.

abbr-add Abbreviated addressing. Shorter forms of computer address words are used in order to provide faster computer language decoding.

abbreviation The shortening of a word, command, or phrase. Standard English abbreviations are derived by various means, including the use of the initial letter of a word ('b' for 'byte'), the initial letters from each word in a phrase ('RAM' for 'random-access memory'), the first and last letters of a word ('Dr' for 'doctor'), and the first part of a word ('Mac' for 'Macintosh'). Some computer languages allow the use of symbols to represent a word or command (such as '?' instead of 'PRINT'). Sometimes a letter followed by a full stop is used (such as 'L.' instead of 'LIST'). Such abbreviations can save time, but if non-standard abbreviations are used, communications and transfer of data may be unsuccessful. The word 'abbreviate' come from the Latin word *abbreviare*, meaning 'shorten'.

ABC 1. Arbitration bus controller. 2. Atanasoff–Berry Computer; the first digital computer to work by electronic means — developed in the late 1930s by Dr John Vincent Atanasoff (professor of mathematics and physics at Iowa State University), assisted by Clifford Berry, a part-time student-assistant employed from the proceeds of a US$650 university grant. Atanasoff wanted to build a machine that would assist his graduate students with the calculation of simultaneous linear equations. The computer they produced had 300 vacuum tubes, and was powerful enough to solve a set of simultaneous equations with 29 variables. This level of technology rendered IBM's Mark I obsolete. Atanasoff was born in 1903. He pursued academic life at Florida State University where he received a Bachelor of Science in 1925. He obtained a Master of Science in 1926 from Iowa State University, and received his doctorate in 1930 from the University of Wisconsin. 3. Automatic brightness control. To compensate for changes in ambient light levels, an ABC circuit is used to adjust (automatically) the luminance level of a display screen.

ABCA America, Britain, Canada, and Australia Standard; a committee formed by representatives of the four governments to agree on military and industry supplies standards.

abend See abnormal end.

aberration A movement away (wandering) from the standard, such as the failure of a lens (or reflective object) to bring to focus the rays of light (image) due to defects in the optical system. Spherical aberration is the distortion of an image (straight lines become curved), while chromatic aberration causes an image to be seen with a colored fringe (typical when a television picture is distorted due to incorrect adjustment or a bad signal). The word 'aberration' comes from the Latin words *aberratio* and *errare*, meaning 'to stray'.

ABI Application binary interface.

ABIST Autonomous built-in self-test; the ability of very-large-scale integration devices to automatically run a built-in self-test software program.

ABL Atlas BASIC language; a form of the BASIC computer language designed exclusively for use on an Atlas computer.

ABM Asynchronous balanced mode, as used in the IBM token ring logical link control (LLC). ABM operates at the SNA data link control level and allows devices on a token ring to send data link commands at any time (and to initiate responses independently of each other).

abnormal end The halting of a program due to a fault or power loss, or intervention by an operator. Abbreviation 'abend'.

ABNT Associação Brasileira de Normas Técnica; Brazil's standards body formed in 1940.

abort To bring a computer program, command, or procedure to a premature halt. This is often done for convenience, or when an error is detected, and may be done automatically by the application program or the system or may be generated by the user. The word 'abort' comes from the Latin words *orriri*, meaning 'being born', and *ab*, meaning 'away from'.

ABR Automatic baud recognition; the automatic recognition by a receiving device of the data rate of an incoming call and its adjustment to that speed. See **baud rate**.

absolute address The location number (referring to the real address) of a piece

of data, or a code for this location which can be interpreted by a control unit. The absolute address may also be referred to as a 'machine address'.

absolute value The value of a number regardless of its mathematical (algebraic) sign. For example, both –55.7 and +55.7 have an absolute value of 55.7.

AC Alternating current; an electric current often represented by a sine wave. The mains electricity supply in most countries is AC.

ACARD Advisory Council for Applied Research and Development; a UK body that provides advice on research and development policies to the British Government.

ACC See **accumulator**.

accelerator board An additional board that enables a computer with older hardware to upgrade so that processing speed can be brought closer to the current processing standards. There are many accelerator boards on the market, with most using either an Intel 80386 or 80486 chip. Installation is performed by removing the older chip from its socket, sliding the accelerator board into an empty expansion slot, and then connecting it to the empty socket with a special plug. With some boards, additional system software may also be required. Compare **OverDrive**.

accent Any of a number of marks used to form accented characters, such as: ´ (acute), ¸ (cedilla), ^ (circumflex), ` (grave), and ~ (tilde). These marks are also called 'diacritical marks'.

A

acceptable quality level A figure used by component manufacturers to describe the level of quality of each component. In some cases, components from a batch are tested randomly, and then graded to a certain percentage.

access To retrieve information (data) from a storage device such as a diskette, or to gain entry to a computer system or peripheral.

access arm The mechanism which houses a read/write head for reading or writing data on a magnetic or optical disk. The arm acts like the needle arm of an audio stereo system, except it does not touch the disk. It comes close enough to detect the magnetized data. A series of access arms may be used to read a disk pack (multiple disks stacked on top of each other), but only one read/write head may operate at one time. Head switching occurs when a different read/write head is activated so that data on different disks can be accessed. A modern disk drive positioner must be capable of bringing a head to the center of a track less than a thousandth of an inch wide for signal recovery. For an average disk drive, this means moving a 3.5-inch- (9-cm-) long access arm to within less than three-thousandths of an inch of the target position in an average time of 17 milliseconds, and maintaining this position indefinitely. Scaled up, this is roughly equivalent to one holding a 4-foot- (1.2-meter-) long pointer with one's arm extended, swinging it as fast as possible, and stopping suddenly with the tip pointing directly at a point of a needle. Access arms retract so that disk packs may be changed. To enhance seeking performance, more powerful positioner mechanisms have been com-bined with such optimization techniques as controller-based seek ordering. Average seek times can be reduced by mounting multiple heads on each access arm. A sealed data module is a unit in which the access arms and the data disks are enclosed in one unit (a fixed disk) — this is referred to as 'Winchester' technology. See **head switching** and **Winchester**.

access charge The cost of gaining entry (access) to a computer system such as a public or industry bulletin board. This may be accompanied by a charge for the time that a user is connected to the bulletin board, or for the data that is copied (transferred).

access code A form of security check which requires a sequence of letters or symbols to be keyed-in before entry (access) is allowed into the computer system. See **password**.

access control Any form of security device or entry system which is designed to restrict hackers or unauthorized users from entering certain sections of a computer room, computer network, or file. Control methods may include the use of passwords, magnetic entry keys, and electronic/photographic identification checks. See **biometric security devices**, **hacker**, and **password**.

access control system A system of security checks (such as passwords) which allow only authorized users to enter (log in to) a computer. Abbreviation 'ACS'. See **biometric security devices** and **password**.

access gate See **access slot**.

access line A communications line which

is permanently connected between a terminal and a 'data switching exchange'.

access method 1. The way in which different devices on a network gain entry to that network so that they can transmit data. Two standard access methods are CSMA/CD and token passing. See **CSMA/CD, time slot,** and **token passing**. 2. The way by which data is transferred from the main memory of a computer to input/output devices, including the monitor. Incompatibility is sometimes caused by differing access methods.

access slot The opening in a diskette that allows the read/write heads of a disk drive to make near-contact with the magnetic disk. In 5.25-inch disks, the access slot is open at all times and is susceptible to damage from dust, smoke, and fingerprints. In 3.5-inch disks, the access slot is covered by a metal 'access gate' which is spring-loaded, and automatically opens when the disk is inserted into the drive. See **diskette**.

access speed See **access time**.

access time The interval of time between the moment data is called from memory/storage and the moment the transmission to the requesting device is completed. Some of the many factors which govern this speed for disk drives are the time (seek time) it takes the read/write heads to get into position over a particular track of a magnetic or optical disk, the time it takes to stabilize (settle time), and the time it takes for the required track or sector to rotate under the heads (latency). The total of these is usually measured in milliseconds (ms), with 9 ms being fast and 100 ms being slow

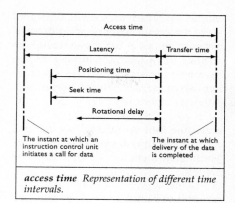

access time Representation of different time intervals.

for a disk drive. In a typical time-sharing application, it is common for 95–99% of total access time to be spent locating the data, and only 1–5% transferring it to host computer memory. Seeking alone can amount to as much as 60–80% of total access time, depending upon average seek distance. In transaction processing applications, where data transfers typically are smaller and more frequent, seek performance is of even more importance. Access speed in a modern disk drive such as the Digital RAxx is dependent upon the speed of the positioner (the mechanism which moves the access arms to effect seeking). The positioner is able to move the access arm assembly between any two tracks in an average of 17 ms, and from the outermost track to the innermost (or the reverse) in approximately 40 ms. This level of performance requires substantial acceleration and deceleration, with sufficient control to stop precisely at track center. This acceleration is about the equivalent of a car going from zero to 100 miles (160 kilometers) per hour in less than half a second. ⋀

accessory Any optional device which

can be connected to another device to make it function better or perform extra tasks, such as a car cigarette-lighter adapter for a laptop computer. Other computer accessories include a protective carry-case, fast battery charger, and external numeric key pad.

accordion fold A method of folding continuous paper for easier storage and printing; sometimes referred to as a 'fanfold'.

accounting package A set of software programs designed to automate the accounting process of a business. Point-of-sale equipment may be connected to the accounting package in order to capture inventory information at the time of sale. A knowledge of accounting principles is still essential for those who use the package.

accumulator A type of 'register' which collects the results of computations within the central processing unit. Once a calculation is made, it sends the data back to memory or outputs it to a peripheral device. The word 'accumulator' comes from the Latin word *cumulare*, meaning 'heap'. Abbreviation 'ACC'.

Accunet Data-oriented digital services from AT&T, including: Accunet T1.5 terrestrial wideband at 1.544 megabits per second; Accunet Reserved T1.5 satellite-based channels at 1.544 megabits per second, used primarily for video teleconferencing applications; Accunet packet-switching services; and Accunet dataphone digital services (DDS).

ACE 1. **See Advanced Computing Environment**. 2. Automatic Computing Engine; a very fast computer built by the National Physics Laboratory in 1950. The London Science Museum still has parts of it on display.

Acer Group Since its founding in 1976 with 11 employees, The Acer Group has grown into a major computer, peripherals, and component supplier. With annual revenues exceeding US$4200 million, Acer employs over 9000 employees operating in 100 countries. In 1991, Acer designed the world's first single-chip CPU upgrade technology, called 'ChipUp'. Its products range from high-end multi-user systems to PCs, notebooks, peripherals, and through a joint venture with Texas Instruments, Acer manufactures DRAM chips. Co-founder Stan Shih's mission for Acer is to expand the company into a US$10 000 million organization by the year 2000, and to rewrite the business textbooks in relation to business globalization and localization. Shih expects his client/server organization philosophy to place Acer at the forefront of business flexibility and practice. Other companies under The Acer Group include Ambit Micro-systems Corporation, Acer Laboratories, Acer Software, Acer TWP Corporation, Acer America Corporation, Acer Sertek Incorporated, and Fora International Corporation. Acer also owns Acer Investment Inc., a non-technical business investment firm; Multiventure Investment Inc., a venture-capital company specializing in high- tech business investments; and Acer Property Development Inc., a firm responsible for real estate ventures. See **Shih, Stan**.

acetate Transparent plastic sheets used for making overhead transparencies or graphic overlays. Acetate is available in many colors, and some may be fed through a photocopier or laser printer so that an image may be copied onto them.

ACIA Asynchronous communications interface adapter; a device that provides data formatting — as used between a microprocessor and a modem.

ACID test A set of software tests that are used to ensure hardware and software stability. For example, in transaction processing (TP), a computer transaction is said to provide integrity of operation and data when the transaction passes the ACID (atomicity, consistency, isolation, durability) test. A transaction has 'atomicity' if the operations that make up the transaction either all execute to completion, or can be made to appear never to have occurred at all. If some operations succeed and others fail, there is no atomicity. For example, in a money transfer transaction, one account is debited while another is credited with the same amount. Should a failure occur between the debit and the credit, the TP system aborts the transaction and does not update the database, so that no change takes place. The system can then automatically resubmit the transaction for processing at a later stage. A transaction has 'consistency' when it successfully transforms the system and the database from one valid state to another. Consistency in a TP system stems mainly from correct application programming (for example, always debiting and crediting the same amount). Because the TP system provides atomicity for the transaction, the application programmer can concentrate on the consistency of the application programs from a business standpoint. A transaction has 'isolation' if it is processed concurrently with other transactions and

still behaves as if it were the only transaction executing in the system. Transactions must not interfere with each other's database updates. A transaction has 'durability' if all the changes that it makes to the database become permanent when the transaction is committed. The ACID properties and the ability to recover (after a failure) make TP a distinct style of computing for which unique software products have been developed (such as the VAX ACMS and DECintact systems from Digital Equipment Corporation, and the CICS system from IBM). The term 'acid test' comes from the days when alchemists subjected metal samples to a strong acid in order to isolate the gold content. Today, the term generally refers to the process of stringent testing. See **transaction processing**.

ACK See **acknowledge**.

acknowledge (Of a receiving device) to signal during data communications to the sending (transmitting) device that the message has been received and that it is ready for another message. Abbreviation 'ACK'.

ACL Advanced CMOS logic; the further development of complementary metal-oxide semiconductors (CMOS) which offer low power-consumption, making them suitable for many computer and telecommunications devices. See **CMOS**.

ACM Association for Computing Machinery; an association devoted to the advancement of knowledge about computing and related fields. ACM supports many special-interest groups (SIG), such as SIGGRAPH (special interest group for computer graphics) and

SIGSMALL (special interest group for small computers).

ACOMPLIS A Computerised London Information Service; an information service run by the library department of the Council of Greater London.

acoustical feedback The effects of a microphone 'hearing' the loudspeaker which it is feeding. There is a closed loop with a gain >1, so the system 'runs away'. Feedback occurs at the frequency which has the highest gain, and usually causes a howl. When a system is just on the point of feedback, it is said to be 'ringing'.

acoustic coupler A type of modem to which a standard telephone receiver (handset) can be attached (coupled). Data is then sent via the telephone, through the receiver, and transmitted via the modem in digital signals using serial transmission. Two different tones are used to transmit zeros and ones. These are only used where access to the telephone wiring is not available. See **modem**.

acoustic delay line A special-effects device used to delay an audio signal (sound). Abbreviation 'ADL'.

acoustic hood A soundproof cabinet in which a noisy device (such as a printer) is placed to reduce the noise it releases into the work environment.

acoustics The branch of science that studies sound waves. The word 'acoustic' comes from the Greek word *akoustikos*, where *akoud* means 'to hear'.

ACR Audio cassette recorder; a device

used with earlier personal computers for storing data onto audio cassettes.

ACRE Automatic call-recording equipment; developed by British Telecom to record the details of operator-assisted telephone calls such as emergency calls.

ACRI Audio cassette recorder interface; used to connect a cassette recorder to a computer.

acronym A set of letters (word) formed by taking the first letter of a series of words to simplify communications. For example, 'BASIC' is the acronym formed from the words 'Beginners' All-purpose Symbolic Instruction Code', and it is pronounced 'bay-sick'. Note that 'IBM' is an abbreviation (not an acronym) because it is not spoken or pronounced like a word. IBM is pronounced 'eye-bee-em'. Other examples of acronyms include 'RAM', 'ROM', 'WYSIWYG', 'RISC', and 'radar'. The word 'acronym' comes from the Greek word *akrononum*, where *akron* means 'end' and *onum* means 'name'.

ACROS Accuse, convict, retrench, or sack; an electronic folder created to store files that may be drawn upon by the user to retrieve information that can be utilized for political purposes. Files may contain incriminating information about another person, or data that can be used against an enemy or opponent in an office. Traditionally, such folders were called 'ammunition'. The term 'ACROS' was coined in 1994 by D.W. Riker, an industry hacker. Not to be confused with Acer's trademark for its range of personal computers. Pronounced 'ack-ross'.

ACS 1. Access control system; a system

of security checks (such as passwords) which allows only authorized users to enter a computer. See **biometric security devices** and **password**. 2. Australian Computer Society.

actinic light Any light which can cause a chemical reaction, such as in photographic film or bromide within an electronic typesetting machine. The word 'actinic' comes from the Greek word *aktisinos*, meaning 'ray'.

active cell In a spreadsheet software application, the active cell is the field where the cursor is positioned.

active database The database file which is in use (active) or one which has been 'opened'.

active I/O An input/output process that is in execution (not in the queue).

active partition See **partition**.

active window Certain application programs and operating systems allow several programs or sub-programs to be displayed on the screen, each appearing in a frame (window) of its own. The user can switch between windows to perform a variety of tasks. The active window is the one which is ready for data input, or on which a command will act.

activity light The small colored light (usually red, yellow, or green) positioned on the front panel of the computer or the disk drives, which lights up to indicate that data is being read from or written onto the disk. Similar activity lights are also found in printers, modems, and other peripheral devices.

ACTP Advanced Computer Technology Project; funded by the British Government to improve computers and their applications for industry.

ACU Automatic calling unit.

acute An accent which slopes upwards to the right (´). See **accent**.

A

Ada A high-level block structuring computer programming language sponsored by the United States Department of Defense (DoD) in 1980. It was enforced as a military standard in 1983 (based primarily on Pascal) in order to reduce software obsolescence and the cost of software maintenance. In Directive 3405.1, issued 2 April 1987, and Directive 3405.2, issued 30 March 1987, the DoD reiterated its long-range goal of establishing Ada as the primary higher-order computer language for new weapons systems and major software upgrades of existing weapons systems. According to Directive 3405.1, signed by Deputy Secretary of Defense William H. Taft IV, 'The Ada programming language shall be the single, common, computer programming language for Defense computer resources used in intelligence systems, for the command and control of military forces, or as an integral part of a weapon system.' Ada is a registered trademark of DoD, named in honor of Ada Augusta Byron (later known as the 'Countess of Lovelace'), the only child of the English poet Lord Byron. She collaborated with computer inventor Charles Babbage and preserved his work after his death in 1871. She is dubbed the world's first programmer. Programs written in the Ada language are highly portable and can be moved from one platform to another easily if a compiler is available. See **Babbage, Charles**, **portability**, and **programming language**.

ADAPSO A̲ssociation of D̲a̲ta P̲rocessing Service O̲rganizations.

adapter In computing, this usually refers to a circuit board that plugs into a computer's expansion bus to offer greater capability. Common adapters for personal computers include display adapters, memory expansion adapters, input/output adapters, and other devices such as internal modems. Each station in a communications network must contain an adapter. The adapter's circuits may be on a separate board within the terminal or processor, or the circuits may be located on a common board with other logic. The adapter serves several functions which are required to allow the processor or terminal to interface with a modem. It converts the data from the byte parallel format used internally by the processor to the bit serial format required for transmission over a data communication channel. At the receiving end, the adapter performs the opposite function, converting the digital bit serial information received from a modem to a byte parallel format. It is important to emphasize that all data handled by the adapter is in digital form. The adapter also accommodates the speed mismatch which exists between a processor and a modem. A processor is capable of moving data at very high speeds, compared to the relatively slow speed with which data can be transferred over modems and telephone lines. The output transmission speed of the data (rated in bits per second) is typically controlled by a clock on the adapter. Also, in response to instructions received from the processor or terminal, the adapter controls the modem through an industry-standard interface called an 'RS-232-C' interface. Adapters are also classified according to how they interrupt a processor or terminal for data exchange. Older adapters used a character-level interrupt, but modern adapters use a message-level interrupt where data is exchanged through a direct memory access. The processor is interrupted only at the beginning and end of each message (these adapters contain random-access memory which allows buffering of the data). The last factor to consider in classifying adapters is the 'communication protocol' support (these being the rules to be followed in controlling the communication channel, and the format of the data to be exchanged). Adapters support three common communications protocols: asynchronous, synchronous, and data link control. Most adapters are designed to work with only one of these protocols, although some (through software) may support several. See **video adapter**.

Adaptive Research Corporation A software and consulting organization based in Huntsville, Alabama, specializing in the computer modeling of processes involving fluid flow, heat transfer, chemical reaction, and combustion. When first established, the company's name was CHAM of North America. The London office was established in 1974 by Professor D. Brian Spalding, and it serves as the technical development center of the corporation. The company developed 'Phonetics' — a computational fluid dynamics code that simulates fluid-flow phenomena by solving the finite-volume versions of the differential equations which govern mass, momentum, and energy. These include the Navier-Stokes equations, supplemented by others describing the balances of thermal energy, chemical concentration, properties of turbulence, and any other entities which may be relevant in particular cases. Also developed by Adaptive, EasyFlow was the industry's first full-capability computational fluid dynamics software package for personal computers. EasyFlow can be applied to a wide range of industrial and engineering disciplines including aerospace, architecture, automotive studies, electronics, environment, and other marine and nuclear applications.

ADB Apple Desktop Bus; an interface standard for connecting input devices (such as keyboards and mice) to the Apple Macintosh family of personal computers. To each ADB port, 16 input devices can be connected, each offering a data transfer rate of 4.5 kilobits per second.

ADC Analog-to-digital converter. See **A/D converter**.

ADCCP Advanced Data Communications Control Procedures; a communications standard controlled by the American National Standards Institute.

ADCON Ad<u>d</u>ress <u>con</u>stant.

A/D converter Analog-to-digital converter; a device which converts an analog (continuously varying) signal to a signal represented by a series of numbers (digital). For example, in a computer-controlled central heating system, the temperature (analog) is monitored several times per second and this value is converted into digits so that

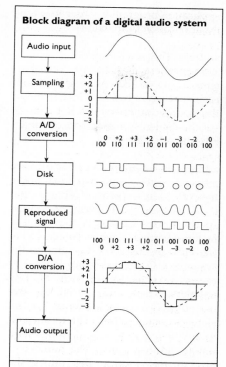

Block diagram of a digital audio system

A/D converter A device that translates analog signals to digital signals. Analog sound must first be converted to digital (sampled) sound. Music on compact disks is often digitized at 48 000 samples per second (16 bits per sample). This diagram shows how sound waves are converted from analog to digital, and then from digital to analog.

the computer can process the data within its program. [ISO A functional unit that converts data from an analog representation to a digital representation.] ⚠

ADDCL Ad<u>d</u> <u>cl</u>ause.

add-in program A software program designed to work in conjunction with an application program in order to extend the application's capabilities.

address The exact location in primary storage where an instruction or data is temporarily stored. Address locations each have a number. As with a mailbox, the address number does not change, yet the contents of each address (mailbox) may change.

addressable memory A part of primary memory, divided into two equal areas: memory address space and input/output (I/O) address space. Memory address space is used to access the primary memory hardware, which contains all of the software currently executing in the systems. I/O address space is used to access I/O hardware such as I/O adapters, buses, and special registers used by I/O devices, known as 'control status registers' (CSR). The location of each byte in memory is identified by a unique address value. The number of bits in the address determines the number of bytes in memory that can be accessed by the hardware. For example, in a typical 32-bit address, bit 0 is the lowest bit, while bit 31 is the highest. Bit numbers 31 and 30 of the address are used to determine the access mode, which can be user, supervisor, executive, or kernel. The 29th bit can have a value of either 0 or 1. If bit 29 = 0, then it is used to select memory address space. If bit 29 = 1, then it is used to select the I/O address space. Bits 28 through to 0 are used to locate the byte in memory. A 32-bit address therefore has 29 bits (0–28 inclusive) available to access up to 2^{29} (512 megabytes) of memory.

address bus The electronic channels along which the addresses (whereabouts)

of memory storage locations are trans-mit-ted internally from one system component to another — for example, from the microprocessor to the random-access memory (RAM). The size of the computer's main memory is determined by the width (number of wires) of the address bus. The bus can be likened to a motor freeway — the wider the freeway, the more cars that can travel at any one time. So an address bus 20 wires wide can transmit 20 bits in parallel. However, because computers use binary numbers internally (0 and 1), an address bus of 20 bits can identify and use a maximum of 2^{20} memory locations — better known as '1 megabyte of RAM'. This same equation applies to an address bus 24 bits wide, giving a maximum RAM of 16 megabytes (2^{24}).

address register A type of 'register' which holds the address of a location containing an item of data called for by an instruction. See **address**.

ad hoc query A read-only reference to a file or database not using a transaction predefined by the system manager. Ad hoc queries are typically constructed using a query language as part of the decision support activities.

ADL See **acoustic delay line**.

ADLC Advanced data link controller.

Adobe Illustrator A software program introduced in 1987, designed for professional illustrators. It produces object-oriented images, and formats them ready for printing on PostScript laser printers. Pronounced 'uh-<u>doe</u>-bee'. ▼

Adobe Systems Incorporated Head-

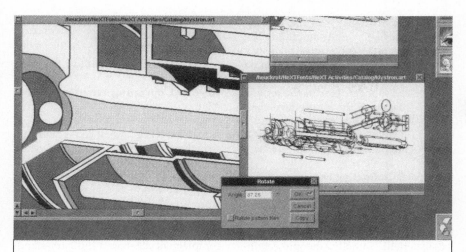

Adobe Illustrator Adobe Illustrator is a graphic design and illustration program for generating high-quality artwork. Because it uses Display PostScript, high-quality text and graphics can be created on the screen. Complex illustrations can be created in a number of ways. Adobe Illustrator's multiple zoom levels allow users to examine illustrations from the big picture to the smallest detail.

quartered in Mountain View, California, Adobe Systems (now part of Aldus Corporation) was founded in 1982 by Dr John Warnock and Dr Charles Geschke. Adobe Systems is the developer of PostScript (the industry-standard page description language for electronic printing and publishing) and Display PostScript (a device-independent graphics software component for computer displays). In addition, the company develops and markets a line of application software programs, including Adobe Illustrator, Adobe Type Manager, Adobe Type Library, and Adobe Streamline. Pronounced 'uh-<u>doe</u>-bee'.

ADP 1. Automatic data processing. 2. Automatic die positioner. A robotic piece of equipment which is used to select suitable dies and then place them on silicon wafers for bonding.

ADPCM Adaptive differential pulse code modulation; an encoding format for storing audio information in a digital format. Especially used in cordless telephones for coding and decoding.

ADPE Automatic data processing equipment.

ADPS Automatic data processing system.

ADRC <u>A</u>dvanced <u>d</u>ynamic <u>r</u>andom-access memory <u>c</u>ontroller. See **Intel 80286**.

ADRS 1. Automatic Document Request Service; a British Library lending service giving subscribers an online document request and reservation facility. This is provided by the <u>B</u>ritish <u>L</u>ibrary <u>A</u>uto-mated <u>I</u>nformation <u>Se</u>rvice (BLAISE). 2. A Departmental Reporting System.

ADSR Attack, decay, sustain, and release. These make up the amplitude of a sound generated by a musical instrument or a computer with music/sound facilities. 'Attack' refers to the immediate rise of a sound; 'decay' is the settling down; 'sustain' is the steady level; and 'release' is the reduction to silence.

ADU Automatic dialing unit.

Advanced Computing Environment An initiative announced 9 April 1991 by 21 leading computer companies who are committed to a non-proprietary, standards-based advanced computing environment. Initially, the project included a unified UNIX System (Open Desktop) from The Santa Cruz Operation; an advanced operating system (OS/2 version 3.0) from Microsoft Corporation; full support for Intel x86-based industry-standard personal computers and personal computer systems; and a new standard specification for microprocessor-based computers operating MIPS Computer System's reduced instruction set computing (RISC). The corporations that participated in the initial project were Acer, Compaq (who resigned in May 1992), Control Data Corporation, DEC, Kubota Computer Inc., Microsoft Corporation, MIPS Computer Systems Inc., NEC Corporation, NKK Corporation, Olivetti Systems and Networks, Prime Computer Inc., Pyramid Technology Corporation, The Santa Cruz Operation Inc., Siemens AG/Automation, Siemens Nixdorf Information–systeme AG, Silicon Graphics Computer Systems, Sony Corporation, Sumitomo Electric Industries Ltd, Tandem Computers Inc., Wang Laboratories Inc., and Zenith Data Systems (a Groupe Bull company). Acronym 'ACE'. See **ARC**.

advanced DRAM controller See **Intel 80286**.

Advanced Interactive Executive See **AIX**.

advanced operating environment See **AOE**.

Advanced RISC Advanced reduced instruction set computing; a specification for MIPS Computer System's RISC microprocessor-based computer platforms to provide products that scale from the laptop to the data center, providing binary compatibility for application software. This specification was designed to complement x86-based industry-standard personal computers, and to give existing users a wide range of non-proprietary, standards-based computing alternatives. Acronym 'ARC'. See **Advanced Computing Environment**.

Advanced RISC Machines Limited A joint-venture company formed in November 1990 between Acorn Ltd, Apple, and VLSI Technology to develop a RISC-based (reduced instruction set computing) processor. By November 1991, the new company, which is based in Cambridge, England, had created the world's smallest RISC processors, called the 'ARM6' family, of which the ARM610 was used in the first Newton PDA (personal digital assistant) from Apple. Abbreviation 'ARM'. See **ARM610**.

Ae See **aerial**.

AEC Atomic Energy Commission.

AEN Asynchronous event notification.

AENOR Asociación Española de Normalización y Certificación; Spain's standards body formed in 1985.

aerial A part of a radio system that actively radiates or receives electromagnetic waves, commonly used in radios and cordless telephones. Abbreviation 'Ae'. See **antenna**.

AES 1. Application Environment Specifications. See **OSF**. 2. Autoelectronic selector.

AF See **audio frequency**.

AFC Automatic frequency control.

AFIPS American Federation of Information Processing Societies, which represents the interests of a consortium of professional organizations and societies such as the American Statistical Association (ASA), and the Institute of Electrical and Electronics Engineers (IEEE).

AFNOR Association française de normalisation; a French standards authority, and member of the International Organization for Standardization (ISO). See **SI**.

AFSK Audio frequency-shift keying; mainly used in telecommunications. AFSK modulates a carrier wave by using audio frequency (AF) tones in order to convey a digital signal.

aftermarket To sell specific software and peripherals to purchasers of a particular type of computer once a large number of those computers have been sold.

AGC Automatic gain control. Commonly used in amplifiers, AGC is the process of maintaining a constant level of volume output, despite fluctuations in the input.

AGS Advanced graphics system.

AI See **artificial intelligence**.

AIA 1. Artificial intelligence application. See **artificial intelligence**. 2. Application Integration Architecture. AIA is a set of software standards that provide a framework for application interoperability and portability. AIA provides the architectural specification (blueprint) for programming interfaces, while the network application support (NAS) provides the actual code (such as toolkits and libraries) that implements the architecture and is used to build applications. See **NAS**.

AIIA Australian Information Industry Association.

Aiken, Howard Hathaway See **Mark I**.

AIM 1. Avalanche-induced migration; a process of permanently short circuiting a diffused junction in a programmable read-only memory (PROM) based on aluminum migration through silicon. 2. Australian Institute of Management.

AIO Action Information Organization. This is a control room on a warship that monitors inputs from aircraft radar, sonar, computerized missile controls, and other internal and external communications, for the purpose of evaluating the need for possible human or computer intervention for defense purposes.

AITS Australian Information Technology Society; an industry body formed in

A

1992 to meet the demand for a professional society that represents the users of information technology. AITS is a professionally-managed organization that collectively provides a forum to maximize the use of technology through sharing and cooperative work practices. AITS addresses a broad section of the industry, serving people in systems, manufacturing, software, hardware, and product development. Its committee focuses on issues and events that mold the computer industry. AITS works closely with government and educational institutions to make submissions relevant to the industry. The Society has become known for its controversial debates which it hosts on a regular basis. The founding members were Julian Day, Peter Kostantakis, Alan Manly, and Jonar C. Nader.

AIX Advanced Interactive Executive; a version of the UNIX operating system, specifically designed by IBM in 1985 to run on PCs, workstations, minicomputers, and mainframes. Pronounced 'ay-eye-ex'.

Alameda virus A variant of the Yale virus. See **Yale virus**.

ALC Automatic level control.

ALD Automatic location device.

Aldus PageMaker The first page-layout program designed for personal computers. This product was launched in 1985 by Aldus Corporation. It helped to establish the Apple Macintosh as a graphics-application and desktop publishing computer.

alert box A window which appears in graphical user interface (GUI) systems to warn the user of an error, or danger of possible error, unless the problem is attended to.

ALGOL Algorithmic-Oriented Language; a high-level programming language introduced in 1960 for mathematical and scientific programming where numeric procedures may be presented to a computer in a precise manner. In 1968, a more useful and powerful version called 'ALGOL-68' was developed. Its qualities are reflected in Pascal, C, and other languages.

algorithm A rigid mathematical (or logical) relationship which has only one starting point and one finishing point. For example, $X + Y = Z$. Each algorithm must have a finite list of executable instructions which must eventually come to an end. The British mathematician Alan Turing proved that an algorithmic approach can be used to solve any mathematical or logical problem for which a solution is known to exist. This means that one can deduce that any solvable problem can be handled by a computer, provided the correct algorithm is used. In computing, an algorithm is the plan, routine, or process of defining a set of instructions so that a computer program can be written to find the answer/solution to a given problem or task. Compare **heuristic**.

Algorithmic-Oriented Language See **ALGOL**.

Algorithmic/Procedural Language See **APL**.

aliasing 1. The rough or jagged edges which undesirably appear around images on the screen when using computer-generated graphics packages. Aliasing is especially noticeable when a diagonal line is drawn, showing the stepped (staircase) appearance. The automatic reduction or removal of the jagged edges is called 'anti-aliasing'. 2. The distortion of an audio signal when a digitized audio signal is replayed with a bandwidth that is too wide. The rule is that the audio should not extend above one-third of the sampling frequency. That is, if a signal is sampled at 8 kilohertz (kHz) and replayed with a bandwidth of up to 4 kHz, then there will be aliasing distortion in the top 1 kHz or so.

alignment The adjustment of a device to certain tolerances to ensure that it operates successfully. For example, the read/write head on a disk drive may require alignment to ensure that it is correctly positioned to read a disk. Once a diskette is formatted on a disk drive which is out of alignment, other disk drives may reject that disk. The word 'alignment' comes from the French word *aligner*, meaning 'into line'.

ALOFT Airborne Light Optic Fiber Technology; used in the American A-7 aircraft to analyze the economy of its internal fiber optics technology.

Alpha Released in 1992, the world's first 64-bit, super-pipelined, superscalar RISC microprocessor.

alphabetical order The strict order of appearance of the alphabet from A to Z. Some programs cannot follow this strict order because they use the ASCII code which lists capital letters first, followed by lowercase letters. For example, 'Z' is ASCII code 90 and 'a' is ASCII code 97.

alphabetic characters The uppercase and lowercase letters of the English alphabet.

alphabetic word [ISO A coded set whose elements are formed from an alphabetic (numeric) (alphanumeric) (binary) character set.]

alphameric See **alphanumeric**.

alphanumeric Referring to all the characters in the standard alphabet, the numerals 0–9 plus all punctuation marks, mathematical symbols, and conventional symbols.

alphanumeric character set [ISO A character set that contains both letters and digits and may contain control characters and special characters.]

alphanumeric data [ISO Data represented by letters and digits, perhaps together with special characters and the space character.]

alpha test The in-house testing of a new software package before it is commercially released. A second stage of testing is usually conducted outside the factory, and this is known as a 'beta test'.

ALS TTL Advanced lower-power Schottky transistor–transistor logic; an advancement on TTL enabling even smaller geometry on an integrated circuit slice, providing higher speeds at little or no power consumption above 1.5 milliwatts. The propagation delay is approximately 4.5 nanoseconds.

Alt key See alternate key.

alternate key On most personal com-

A

puters, a key on the keyboard which enables another to have several functions. For example, in Microsoft Word, the key that produces the letter 'B' may take on a new programmed function if used in conjunction with the alternate key. By depressing the alternate key and then typing the letter 'B', the selected text will be shown as bold. In Word-Perfect, the entire set of function keys (F1 to F12) take on a new function when used in conjunction with the alternate key. Abbreviation 'Alt'.

alternate route In data communications, a secondary (alternate) communications channel which is used when the primary channel is inadequate or unavailable.

alternate track (alternative track) [ISO A spare track used in place of a normal track in the event that the latter is damaged or inoperable.]

alternating current See **AC**.

ALU Arithmetic/logic unit; one of two parts of the central processing unit that contains the electronic circuits which control all arithmetic and logical operations.

am 1. Ante meridien. 2. Attometer. 'Atto-' is an SI unit prefix for 10^{-18}.

AM Amplitude modulation.

AMACUS Automated Microfilm Aperture Card Update System.

Amber An open architecture designed by Apple in 1994 to support solutions that not only cross applications and media, but also multiple heterogeneous

platforms to provide flexibility and ease-of-use to users and software developers. Most software applications (including word processors, spreadsheets, databases, or specialized tools) include text-editing capabilities. Some rely heavily on text editing, such as MacWrite, More, and HyperCard. Some use text only incidentally, such as MacDraw, MacProject, and Microsoft Excel. A person using all of these products would need to learn about each of their text-editing functions because some allow text styles and tab stops, and others do not. With Amber, a text paragraph becomes a software component, usable wherever text is needed. The user can choose the preferred text editor and use its functionality on any or all of the text items within a file. This means that a user need only learn how to use one text editor instead of six. Amber is available on the Macintosh and Windows platforms.

AMBIT <u>A</u>lgebraic <u>m</u>anipulation <u>bit</u>; a computer programming language used to manipulate algebraic symbols.

Amdahl Amdahl Corporation designs and manufactures large-scale, high-performance data processing systems. The company's product line includes large, general-purpose mainframe computers, data storage subsystems, data communications products, and software. Amdahl Corporation was formed 19 October 1970 by Dr Gene Amdahl (previously an employee of IBM). Amdahl shares a unique relationship with Fujitsu Limited of Japan. Fujitsu was an early investor in Amdahl and is now its largest shareholder, owning approximately 45% of the common stock. Fujitsu offers a complete line of data processing equipment and is a designer and manufacturer of highly sophisticated semiconductor components. The two companies share research and development efforts in several product areas, and Fujitsu supplies semiconductors, components, subassemblies, and in some cases, complete products built to Amdahl specifications. Fujitsu also distributes Amdahl processors in Japan, Brazil, Spain, and South Korea.

American National Standard COBOL See **CODASYL**.

American National Standard Hollerith punched card code A punched card code of 256 characters. The first 128 characters of the American National Standard Hollerith punched card code correspond to the 128 characters of the ASCII character set.

American National Standards Institute See **ANSI**.

American Standard Code for Information Interchange See **ASCII**.

American Telephone and Telegraph Company See **AT&T**.

AM/FM Amplitude modulation/frequency modulation; this usually refers to any radio receiver capable of detecting signals which are modulated either by their amplitude or their frequency. See **amplitude, frequency,** and **modulation. ▼**

A

Amiga A home computer developed by Commodore International. It is based on the Motorola 68000 microprocessor, and offers exceptional color graphics and multivoice stereo sound, making it well suited for playing computer games and composing music. While they have found good acceptance as home and niche business machines, they have not been considered as a general business computer. Pronounced 'uh-me-gah'.

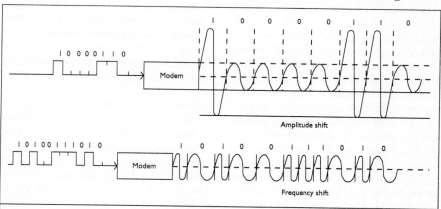

AM/FM Digital signals can be sent by either changing the height (amplitude) of the carrier wave, or by changing the number of times a carrier wave pulses per second (frequency). In other words, amplitude modulation is a method of encoding which enables the frequency of the radio (carrier) wave to remain constant, while the information it carries (wave) changes in strength. Frequency modulation measures the number of waveforms that are repeated per second. This cycle is expressed in hertz.

AMLCD Active matrix liquid crystal display; used in notebook computers.

ampere An SI unit of electric current named after the French scientist André Marie Ampère (1775–1836). A current of 1 ampere would produce a force equal to 2 x 10⁻⁷ newton per meter of length (if maintained in two parallel rectilinear conductors of infinite length and of negligible circular cross-section), in a vacuum at a distance of 1 meter apart. Abbreviation 'amp'.

ampersand The character '&', originally used as the ligature for *et*, the Latin word for 'and'. In English, it is used to mean 'and'.

Ampex A company formed in the United States in 1944 to pioneer magnetic recording systems, including magnetic tape for data storage.

amplifier A device which increases the magnitude (voltage) of an electrical signal. To ensure that a data signal is intelligible when it reaches the receiver, various corrective circuits must be used to compensate for distortion factors which are always present. Corrective circuits are found in both the telephone company facilities and modems. Amplifiers are employed at various points to compensate for the attenuation caused by line resistance. The amplifiers are adjusted by the telephone company to maintain an acceptable signal power level. On a dedicated line, amplifiers are installed to hold the typical signal power loss to approximately 16 decibels per milliwatt (dBmW). For example, if the transmit level is referenced at 0 dBmW (which is the maximum allowable), amplifiers will tolerate the level at the receiver to about –16 dBmW.

amplitude A measure of the strength (size) of an analog signal, pictured as a wave from the base line to one of the peaks. The higher the voltage, the higher the wave. Amplitude can measure an acoustic signal (loudness), electrical signal, light signal (brightness), or any other signal shaped like a wave. The amplitude of a digital signal is fixed, although a small margin (variation) is allowed. For example, if the binary 0 is represented by zero volts, and binary 1 is represented by 5 volts, then a level of 0 to 1.2 volts is still recognized as binary 0 and a level of 3.5 to 5 volts is still recognized as binary 1. Compare **frequency**.

amplitude modulation A method of encoding which enables the frequency of the radio (carrier) wave to remain constant, while the information it carries varies. This system changes the strength (size) of an analog signal (wave) from the zero line, to a positive peak, then to an equal negative peak. The stronger the voltage, the higher the wave. Abbreviation 'AM'. See **modulation**.

AMPS Advanced Mobile Phone Service; one of the original cellular radio systems developed for trial in 1978 by the Bell Telephone Company.

AMSAT The Radio Amateur Satellite Corporation formed in the United States in 1969 to coordinate a range of national and international space projects by amateur radio enthusiasts. One of the first group of satellites it launched was called 'OSCAR' (Orbital Satellite-Carrying Amateur Radio).

analog 1. 'Analog' comes from the Greek word *analogos*, meaning anything that is proportional to something else. Hence, an analog computer has an exact relationship between the object being represented and the computer representation. 2. [ISO Pertaining to data that consist of means of continuously variable physical quantities.] Compare **digital**.

analog biochips See **biochips**.

analog computer 1. A device that calculates data that changes continuously — for example, wind movement, speed, time, temperature, or features of a car's suspension. 2. [ISO A computer that processes analog data.]

analog data [ISO Data represented by a physical quantity that is considered to be continuously variable and whose magnitude is made directly proportional to the data or to a suitable function of the data.]

analog divider [ISO A functional unit whose output analog variable is proportional to the quotient of two input analog variables.]

analogical reasoning The process by which a phenomenon or a system is studied using only a model of that phenomenon or system.

analog input channel [ISO The analog data path between the connector and the analog-to-digital converter in the analog input subsystem. *Note:* This path may include a filter, an analog signal multiplexer, and one or more amplifiers.]

analog input channel amplifier [ISO An amplifier, attached to one or more

analog input channels, that adapts the analog signal level to the input range of the succeeding analog-to-digital converter.]

analog multiplier [ISO A functional unit whose output analog variable is proportional to the product of two input analog variables. *Note:* This term may also be applied to a device that can perform more than one multiplication — for example, a servo-multiplier.]

analog output channel amplifier [ISO An amplifier, attached to one or more analog output channels, that adapts the output signal range of the digital-to-analog converter to the signal level necessary to control the technical process. *Note:* If there is a common digital-to-analog converter in the subsystem, the amplifier performs the function of a sample-and-hold device.]

analog representation [ISO A representation of the value of a variable by a physical quantity that is considered to be continuously variable, the magnitude of the physical quantity being made directly proportional to the variable or to a suitable function of the variable.]

analog signal An electronic signal that can represent a range of frequencies, such as voice or radio waves. An analog signal commonly forms a wave pattern (sine wave) as it changes from the high voltage, back to zero voltage, and down to a maximum negative voltage. Each complete wave forms a cycle, and can be measured by its amplitude (strength), frequency, or wavelength.

analog-to-digital converter See **A/D converter**.

analog transducer See **transducer**.

Analytical Engine A mechanical computer invented in 1833 by Charles Babbage to carry out arithmetic calculation using punched cards. See **Babbage, Charles**.

analytical graphics Automatically produced charts and graphs used by professionals in the interpretation and presentation of data. See **presentation graphics**.

anamorphic A graphic equally scaled in vertical and horizontal dimensions.

ancestor See **nested transaction**.

Ångstrom A unit of length equal to 10^{-10} meters often used to express the wavelength of a very-high-frequency signal such as light. Symbol 'Å'.

animation The use of graphics, often computer-generated, to generate moving objects (motion graphics). Animation is an illusion produced by generating and recording a series of images, each one slightly different from the previous one. When these incrementally different images are played back at a higher speed, the eye perceives a smooth movement. The word 'animation' comes from the Latin word *animatus*, meaning 'give life'.

anisochronous transmission [ISO Data transmission process in which there is always an integral number of unit intervals between any two significant instants in the same group; between two significant instants located in different groups, there is not always an integral number of unit intervals. *Note:* In data transmission the group is a block or a character.]

ANL Automatic noise limiter; a circuit widely used in communications transceivers and receivers to reduce impulse noise and other external interference. In particular, an ANL can limit the amount of interference caused by motor-vehicle ignition systems and other external sources, including lightning.

ANOVA Analysis of variance.

ANS-COBOL The American National Standards Institute's version of COBOL, first standardized in 1968, and then again in 1974 in an effort to make COBOL machine-independent.

ANSI American National Standards Institute; a group of committees formed to establish voluntary commercial and government standards. The committee with specific responsibilities for computing, data processing, and information technology is called 'ANSI-X3'. Its former name was 'USASI' (United States of America Standards Institute). ANSI is a member of ISO. Pronounced 'an-see'.

ANSI.SYS A DOS device-driver that defines system attributes such as screen and keyboard characters.

ANSI X12 American National Standards Institute — Accredited Standards Committee X12. This committee develops and maintains generic standards for electronic data interchange (EDI).

answering [ISO The process of responding to a calling station to complete the establishment of a connection between data stations.]

antenna A device used for receiving or transmitting radio communications. The British term is 'aerial'.

anti-aliasing See **aliasing**.

anticipatory fetching [ISO A procedure in which stored instructions are read from memory by the central processing unit prior to the moment of need.]

anticipatory paging [ISO The transfer of a page from auxiliary storage to real storage prior to the moment of need.]

antistatic mat An earthed mat or pad which dissipates static electricity when a static-prone computer device is placed on or near it. If such mats are not used, the device may receive static shocks from handling, thereby causing loss of data or damage to the circuits of the device. Human handling is the greatest cause of static damage, and to prevent this, technicians are sometimes required to wear antistatic wrist bands. These are also earthed to ensure that the wearer does not develop a charge.

antivirus program A computer program written to search for unusual disk and memory activity, or search for text strings characteristic of viruses, and report any presence of a disk infection such as a virus. Known viruses can be detected quickly, but authors of computer viruses are constantly designing new viruses with which to cause malicious and widespread computer damage. See **virus**.

A-O Acousto-optic; an abbreviation used to refer to the interaction between acoustic and optical waves.

AOE Advanced operating environment; typically, an operating environment that is 32-bit, multitasking, portable across hardware architectures, and available unbundled from the system. In addition, AOEs support most features such as kernel multithreading and multiprocessing.

AP Analyst/programmer.

APA All points addressable.

aperture card [ISO A processable card of standard dimensions into which microfilm frames can be inserted.]

API Application Program Interface; used where proprietary application programs have to talk to communications software, or conform to protocols from another vendor's product. It also provides a standardized method of 'vertical' communications. The first computer to use the API concept was the Apple Macintosh.

APL A Programming Language; a high-level programming language developed by Kenneth Iverson, and introduced by IBM for its mainframe computers in 1968 for scientific and mathematical applications. A special keyboard with Greek characters is required when using APL. It is a compact and highly interactive program, sometimes known as an 'Algorithmic/Procedural Language'. See **algorithm** and **programming language**.

APPC Advanced Program-to-Program Communications; a set of protocols designed by IBM for its Systems Network Architecture. It enables applications to interact directly with each other on a peer-to-peer basis, even when

NEWSFLASH

Worldwide Macintosh unit shipments will more than double, from 2.7 million in 1992 to 5.5 million in 1997, for a compound annual growth rate (CAGR) of 15%. These sales will exceed the growth rate of the overall PC market, currently projected to grow at a CAGR of 11%. Macintosh market share will thus increase from 9% in 1992 to 11% in 1997. The US market will shrink slightly as a percentage of Apple's sales, going from 55.3% in 1993 to 52.5% in 1997.

Product	1993	1994	1995	1996	1997
Portables	508 000	640 000	725 000	810 000	900 000
Low-end	1 975 000	2 375 000	2 635 000	2 830 000	3 005 000
Midrange	775 000	925 000	1 050 000	1 125 000	1 200 000
High-end	235 000	300 000	340 000	375 000	405 000
Total	3 493 000	4 240 000	4 750 000	5 140 000	5 510 000

the programs are on separate and remote processors.

append To add a new record or data to the end of a file, database, character string, or list. From the Latin word *appendere*, meaning 'to hang'.

Apple Computer Corporation A major American manufacturer of personal computers, based in Cupertino, California. The company was started by Steven Jobs (former Atari employee) and Stephen Wozniak (former Hewlett-Packard employee) in 1976 in Silicon Valley. The first Apple computer was built in a garage from the proceeds (US$1300) of the sale of an old Volkswagen motor car, and other personal items. In the early years, Jobs convinced the former marketing manager for Intel, A.C. 'Mike' Markkula, to act as a de facto chief executive. Markkula invested US$91 000 and assisted Jobs and Wozniak to formulate business plans. Apple Computer was registered as a public company in December 1980. By 1983, the Apple Lisa

Apple Computer Corporation *This Apple I is one of only 60 machines built by Steve Wozniak and Steven Jobs in 1976.*

appeared and was the first personal computer to feature a graphical user interface. In 1984, the Macintosh was released. The first model only offered 128 kilobytes of random-access memory, and a single disk drive. More successful products were the Macintosh SE featuring a hard disk, and the Macintosh II (pronounced 'Macintosh two') which offered open architecture. See **Macintosh.** ⚠

Apple Desktop Bus See **ADB**.

Apple Macintosh See **Macintosh**.

AppleTalk The AppleTalk Personal Network; Apple Computer's proprietary local area network architecture, used primarily for networking up to 32 Macintosh or Apple II computers, laser printers, and other peripherals, including DOS-based personal computers. Although AppleTalk is very easy to connect (via LocalTalk boxes), it transmits data at 320 kilobits per second. This is very slow compared to an Ethernet network, which can transmit data at 20 megabits per second.

Apple II Produced by Apple Computer for home and educational use, the Apple II (pronounced 'Apple two') personal computer was first released in 1977, based on the MOS (metal oxide silicon) Technology 6502, 8-bit microprocessor. It featured 4 kilobytes (kb) of random-access memory (RAM); screen lines of 40 characters; a cassette recorder for secondary storage; plus a read-only memory (ROM) chip encoded with an integer version of the BASIC programming language. In 1979, the Apple II Plus was launched, offering up to 64 kb of RAM. In 1983, the Apple IIe offered 128 kb of RAM. A transportable version of this computer, the Apple IIc, was launched in 1984. To compete with 16-bit technology, Apple released its 16-bit computer in 1986, called the 'Apple IIGS', offering 256 kb of RAM (expandable to 8.25 megabytes), a clock speed of

2.8 megahertz, plus improved graphics with up to 16 colors per scan line, and up to 256 colors on screen — chosen from a palette of 4096 colors. See **Macintosh**.

application A computer program (or suite of programs) used for a specific task, such as accounting purposes, medical or scientific analysis, or word processing. This may be for common accounting applications, or uncommon poultry farm management. The term 'application' refers to the entire set of programs that collectively implement a specific business process. Individual programs that implement part of this business process are known as 'application programs', 'package', or 'application software'. See **vertical application**.

application designer The person with the overall responsibility for translating a set of business requirements into a computing system. An application designer may also be called a 'TP (transaction processing) system designer'.

Application Environment Specifications See **OSF**.

application growth Refers to any computer environment that is capable of expanding smoothly to support future application demands. Application growth is only possible if the system architecture is well structured, enabling the system to be divided into a small number of basic functional components. This separation of function allows for growth in four dimensions which are described in terms of: length (distributing the basic functions of a transaction to different processing nodes); width (partitioning the work performed by one or more different components to allow parallel processing of multiple transactions); depth (replicating functions to the level of redundancy necessary to achieve the system's availability goals); and time (dividing the application into pieces that can be scheduled independently to maximize the use of scarce resources). See **growth in depth, growth in length, growth in time**, and **growth in width**.

application layer The seventh (and highest) layer of the OSI (Open Systems Interconnection) model. The application layer is the only layer not transparent to the user, supplying network services such as password checks, document transfers, directory service, print service, and electronic mail. This layer should not be confused with the application program running on the station, which may in fact be requesting the communications service. Some OSI services include FTAM (file transfer, access, and management), MHS (message handling system), and CASE (common application service element). Services in this layer are tailored to the industry being served. See **OSI reference model**.

application problem [ISO A problem submitted by an end user and requiring information processing for its solution.]

Application Program Interface An interface for use when it is necessary for proprietary application programs to talk to communications software, or conform to protocols from another vendor's product. It also provides a standardized method of 'vertical' communications. The first computer to use the API concept was the Apple Macintosh.

application software See **application** and **vertical application**.

application software (program) [ISO Software (program) that is specific to the solution of an application problem.]

A Programming Language See **APL**.

AQL Acceptable quality level; a figure which is mainly used by component manufacturers to describe the level of quality of each component. In some cases, components from a batch are tested randomly, and then graded to a certain percentage.

ARC Advanced RISC (reduced instruction set computing); a specification for MIPS Computer System's RISC microprocessor-based computer platforms to provide products that scale from the notebook to the data center, providing binary compatibility for application software. The ARC specification was designed to complement x86-based industry-standard personal computers, and give existing users a wide range of non-proprietary, standards-based computing alternatives. See **Advanced Computing Environment**.

ARC500 A shareware program created by Systems Enhancement Associates, designed to compress (then decompress) data before (or after) it is archived. A similar program, called 'Stuffit', was designed by Raymond Lau specifically for the Apple Macintosh environment. The two common archive formats for the PC are ZIP and LHARC.

architecture The specific design and construction of a computer, usually referring to the hardware make-up of the central processing unit, and the size of the byte (or set of bytes) it processes; such as 8-bit, 16-bit, or 32-bit architecture. The design of the computer may need to take into account how the software will be used, and the primary purpose for which the computer was designed. For example, a computer may be designed to take into account one or more of the following: cost; system security; processing speed; system reliability; multitasking; or how easy it is to maintain. How the three basic elements (processing unit, storage, and input/output) of a computer interact determines the complexity of the architecture. Data moves around the computer through buses (circuits which form channels of communication), and the way in which these buses are linked determines the computer's architecture. For example, in the Intel 80386 and 80486 high-performance 32-bit microprocessors, 32-bit architecture provides the programming resources required to directly support 'large' applications — those characterized by large integers, large data structures, large programs (or large numbers of programs), and so on. The 80386's physical address space is 64 terabytes (2^{46} bytes). The 80386's eight 32-bit general registers can be used interchangeably both as instruction operands and addressing mode variables. Data types include 8-, 16-, and 32-bit integers and ordinals, packed and unpacked decimals, pointers, and strings of bits, bytes, words, and double-words. The 80386 has a complete set of instructions for manipulating these types, as well as for controlling execution. The 80386 addressing modes support efficient access to the elements of the standard data structures: arrays, records, arrays of records, and records containing arrays.

A 32-bit architecture does not guarantee high performance. To deliver the potential of the architecture requires leading-edge semiconductor technology, careful partitioning of functions, and attention to off-chip operations, particularly the interaction of processor and memory. Many 32-bit applications, such as reprogrammable multi-user computers, need the logical-to-physical address translation and protection provided by a memory management unit (MMU), yet other applications such as embedded real-time control systems do not. Most 32-bit microprocessor architectures respond to this dichotomy by implementing the memory management unit in an optional chip. The 80386 MMU, by contrast, is incorporated on the processor chip as two of the processor's pipelined functional units. The operating system controls the operation of the MMU, allowing a real-time system, for example, to forgo page translation. Implementing memory management on-chip produces better performance for applications that use the MMU and no performance penalty for those that do not. This achievement is made possible by shorter signal propagation delays, use of the half-clock cycles that are available on-chip, and parallel options. The word 'architecture' comes from the Greek words *arkhi*, meaning 'arch', and *tekton*, meaning 'builder'. See **Micro Channel Architecture**.

archive bit A DOS attribute bit that shows if a file has been achieved since the bit was last reset. This is normally used to indicate to a backup program that a file needs to be backed-up.

archive file 1. [ISO A file out of a collection of files set aside for later research or verification, for security or for any other purposes.] 2. Also called 'archived file'. Any computer file which is stored on magnetic tape or disk, and loaded onto the computer storage area only when it is required.

archiving [ISO The storage of backup files and any associated journals, usually for a given period of time.]

ARCnet The first commercially available local area network introduced in 1977 by Datapoint Corporation. ARCnet is a high-speed baseband network that uses the token-passing access method, running at 2.5 megabits per second, using either a star or bus topology. Although originally developed for thin coaxial cable, ARCnet can now be adapted for use with twisted pair wire and fiber optic cable.

area (In programming languages.) [ISO A space together with a mechanism for inserting data objects into it, and for accessing and for deleting data objects from it.]

areal density The number of data bits that can be recorded per unit of media area, such as on a magnetic disk. It is commonly measured by multiplying the number of bits per inch (along the innermost track where the bit density is greatest) by the number of tracks per inch. The areal density computed in this way is the disk drive's physical storage density. Higher areal density tends to enhance the properties of a disk drive, such as allowing more data capacity for a given media surface area. See **track density**.

argument 1. [ISO An independent vari-

able.] 2. [ISO Any value of an independent variable. *Examples:* A search key; a number identifying the location of an item in a table.]

arithmetic expression In a programming language such as COBOL, an expression which can be an identifier of a numeric elementary item; a numeric literal; such identifiers and literals separated by arithmetic operators; two arithmetic expressions separated by an arithmetic operator; or an arithmetic expression enclosed in parentheses.

arithmetic/logic unit See **ALU**.

arithmetic operation Any of the operations executed by the central processing unit that perform mathematical calculations — usually addition, subtraction, multiplication, and division.

arithmetic operator A symbol used to represent an arithmetic operation to the central processing unit. It is common to represent addition by a plus sign (+), subtraction by a hyphen (-), multiplication by an asterisk (*), and division by a slash (/).

arithmetic register [ISO A register that holds the operands or the results of arithmetic operations or logic operations.]

arithmetic shift [ISO A shift, applied to the representation of a number in a fixed radix numeration system and in a fixed-point representation system, in which only the characters representing the fixed point part of the number are moved. *Notes:* (a) An arithmetic shift is usually equivalent to multiplying the number by a positive or a negative integral power of the radix, except for the effect of any rounding. (b) Compare the logical shift with the arithmetic shift, especially in the case of floating point representation.]

arithmetic unit [ISO In a processor, the part that performs arithmetic operations. *Note:* The term 'arithmetic unit' is sometimes used for a unit that performs both arithmetic and logic operations.]

ARM See **Advanced RISC Machines Limited**.

ARM6 See **ARM610**.

ARM610 A general-purpose 32-bit microprocessor produced by Advanced RISC Machines Limited. On a single chip, it contains a 4-kb cache, a write buffer, and a patented Memory Management Unit (MMU) that was specified by Apple for the Newton MessagePad. The ARM610 chip supports a conventional two-level page-table structure and a number of extensions that make it suited for object-oriented systems. The chip is fully static, meaning that it consumes zero power when the clock is stopped. When operating, it consumers less than 0.5 watts of power, and it is capable of detecting interrupt responses at less than 1 microsecond. The CMOS (complementary metal-oxide semiconductor) chip has a die size of 71 mm² at 1 micron, and 46 mm² at 0.8 micron — both with two layers of metal. Each chip uses 366 000 transistors and is available in a 144-pin TQFP (thin quad flat package) plastic unit with a thickness of 1.4 mm. The ARM610 is manufactured by VLSI Technology in the US, GEC Plessey Semiconductors in the UK, and Sharp Corporation in Japan. A smaller member

of the ARM family is the ARM6 — a CPU macro cell that offers high performance from a die size of 5.9 mm² on a 0.8-micron CMOS process. The ARM6 consumes low levels of power (54 milliwatts @ 20 MHz @ 3 volts) with high code density and low interrupt latency. It combines both RISC and CISC (complex instruction set computing) techniques. See **Advanced RISC Machines Limited**.

ARPA Advanced Research Projects Agency; an agency of the United States Department of Defense.

ARPANET <u>A</u>dvanced <u>R</u>esearch <u>P</u>rojects <u>A</u>gency <u>Net</u>work; a wide area packet-switching network developed by the United States Department of Defense to link facilities in government agencies and universities.

array (In programming languages.) [ISO An aggregate that consists of data objects, with identical attributes, each of which may be uniquely referenced by subscripting.]

array processor 1. A special type of computer designed to calculate mathematical procedures at very high speeds — once numbers are grouped together and made ready for mass calculations. Their processing speeds are in the range of 5 to 100 MFLOP (million floating point operations per second) and they are priced from a few thousand dollars, up to US$300 000. Array processors became widely used in the 1980s, and today are used for applications such as CAT scanning. The more common computer (vector processor) can only handle one-dimensional items of data. Supercomputers are known as 'scalar processors'. 2. [ISO A processor capable of executing instructions in which the operands can be arrays of data and not only single elements. *Note*: In a special case where the array processor works on single elements, such elements are called 'scalars'.]

arrow-keys See **cursor-movement keys**.

ARS Automatic route selection; the capability of a switchboard, typically a private branch exchange (PBX), to determine automatically an optimal route establishing a circuit. This is also called 'least-cost routing' (LCR).

artefact An unintended, unwanted aberration or component in a signal, image, or sound.

artificial intelligence The capability of a computer system to learn from its experiences and simulate human intelligence in areas of judgment, reason, and learning. This branch of computer science began in the 1950s with attempts to write programs to challenge human thinking such as when playing chess or checkers. Early attempts at computerized chess were unsuccessful because programmers instructed the computer to think several steps ahead and to evaluate every possible move. This process failed because at that time, the processing power of computers was relatively low, and a computer would often be disqualified for taking too long to make the next move. Programmers later discovered that chess professionals often make judgments on rules-of-thumb called 'heuristics'. Areas where artificial intelligence is being trialed include the medical profession, robotics, expert systems, natural languages, vision systems, speech recognition, and computer imaging. Abbreviation 'AI'. See **expert systems**, **heuristic**, and **vision systems**.

artificial life Life forms based on elements other than those that are only carbon-based. Artificial-life researchers prefer to expand the definition of 'life' to include life forms based on elements such as silicon, bringing a new dimension to the meaning of 'alive'. Artificial-life technologies and techniques can be used in business or entertainment applications to simulate life on a computer by giving the computer simple rules via the software program, and observing what happens (emergent behavior). Often, through the use of genetic algorithms, the behavior will be unexpected and surprisingly lifelike. Emergent behavior is the part of a simulation that goes beyond the rules that were originally programmed into the software. Genetic algorithms are based on strings of computer data (much like DNA) that describe the appearance and behavior of an artificial life form. Such a string of data can be divided into two sections and combined with a segment of another divided string, to create a third data string. This new string will act like the offspring of the first two strings — a genetically unique artificial life form. Abbreviation 'AL'.

artificial satellite See **satellite transmission**.

ARU Audio response unit. See **voice output device**.

ASA 1. American Standards Association, formerly known as the 'United States of America Standards Association' (USASA). 2. American Statistical Association.

ASCC Automatic Sequence Controlled Calculator. See **Mark I**.

ascender In typography, the height of letters is determined from the lowercase letter 'x'. An ascender is any part of a lowercase letter which rises (ascends) above that 'x'. Hence, the letters b, d, f, h, k, l, and t all have ascenders. From the Latin word *ascendere*, meaning 'to climb'.

ascending order When sorting information in ascending (increasing) order, items are arranged from the smallest to the largest (1,2,3,4) or from the first to the last (a,b,c,d). Depending upon the software, other characters including punctuation marks and symbols may interfere with a 'dictionary' sort, causing words like 'A/D converter' to be placed before 'abacus'. When sorting data in ASCII, all capitalized words are placed before lowercase letters. See **ASCII character set**. Compare **descending order**.

ASCII American Standard Code for Information Interchange; a code that changes letters, numbers, and symbols into a 7-bit code, with an eighth bit acting as a check bit. ASCII, devised in 1968, is used for the purpose of standardizing the transmission of data to achieve hardware and software compatibility. ASCII permits a total of 96 visible characters (including the space) and 32 hardware control characters (such as sounding a bell or advancing the page on a printer). Computer graphics can be achieved by an extended version of ASCII (called 'ASCII-8') which makes use of an eighth bit, allowing a total of 256 characters to be used. For example, A = 65, Z = 90, a = 97, z = 122. Pronounced 'ass-key'. See **ASCII character set**.

ASCII character set American Standard Code for Information Interchange; translation of text data into binary form is usually based on ASCII. The ASCII character set assigns a unique pattern of 8 bits to every letter of the alphabet, each of the digits 0 through 9, every punctuation mark, and a variety of special characters. For example, E is designated as 01000101 in binary form. A group of 8 bits is called a 'byte', and ASCII values actually use only 7 of the 8 bits. ▼

ASCII collating sequence The sequence in which the characters of the ASCII character set are ordered for comparison purposes. The bit configuration determines which position a character has in the collating sequence. In the ASCII collating sequence, the lowest character is NUL, with a bit configuration of 0000 0000; and the highest character is DEL, with a bit configuration of 0111 1111.

ASCII-8 See **ASCII**.

Ashar virus A boot-sector virus that infects 5.25-inch diskettes. Its presence can be detected by the volume label '(c) Ashar' on the diskette which also shows 3 kilobytes of bad sectors. In addition, 7 kilobytes of RAM becomes unavailable to DOS, thereby slowing the operation of the diskette drive. Ashar is a variant of Brain, a virus rumored to have been written in 1986 by two brothers, Basit and Amjads, from Lahore, Pakistan. For this reason, the virus is sometimes referred to as the 'Pakistani virus' or 'Lahore virus'. See **boot-sector virus**.

Character	ASCII Code	Character	ASCII Code	Character	ASCII Code	Character	ASCII Code	Character	ASCII Code
.	0100000	4	0110100	G	1000111	[	1011011	o	1101111
!	0100001	5	0110101	H	1001000	\	1011100	p	1110000
"	0100010	6	0110110	I	1001001	]	1011101	q	1110001
#	0100011	7	0110111	J	1001010	^	1011110	r	1110010
$	0100100	8	0111000	K	1001011	_	1011111	s	1110011
%	0100101	9	0111001	L	1001100	'	1100000	t	1110100
&	0100110			M	1001101	a	1100001	u	1110101
		0100111	:	0111010	N	1001110	b	1100010	v	1110110
(	0101000	;	0111011	O	1001111	c	1100011	w	1110111
)	0101001	<	0111100	P	1010000	d	1100100	x	1111000
*	0101010	=	0111101	Q	1010001	e	1100101	y	1111001
+	0101011	>	0111110	R	1010010	f	1100110	z	1111010
,	0101100	?	0111111	S	1010011	g	1100111		
-	0101101	@	1000000	T	1010100	h	1101000	{	1111011
.	0101110	A	1000001	U	1010101	i	1101001			1111100
/	0101111	B	1000010	V	1010110	j	1101010	}	1111101
0	0110000	C	1000011	W	1010111	k	1101011	~	1111110
1	0110001	D	1000100	X	1011000	l	1101100	DEL	1111111
2	0110010	E	1000101	Y	1011001	m	1101101		
3	0110011	F	1000110	Z	1011010	n	1101110		

ASCII character set *These are 96 of the ASCII keyboard characters. There are another 32 control codes (not shown above) used to control computer functions such as 'carriage return' (cr) and 'form feed' (ff).*

AS/IAS Application Specialist/Industry Application Specialist.

ASIC Application-specific integrated circuit; computer chips developed for specific functions. These may be used in devices such as video machines, microwave ovens, and security alarms.

ASIMD Autonomous single instruction multiple data.

ASM Association for Systems Management; an international organization whose members include business and government systems professionals.

aspect ratio In computer graphics, the relationship between the vertical and the horizontal size of an image or shape. In television, the aspect ratio is 3:4, and in high definition television (HDTV), the recommendation is 9:16.

assemble [ISO To translate an assembly language program into an object program.]

assembler 1. [ISO A translator that can assemble.] 2. See **assembly language**.

assembly language A low-level first-generation computer language, popular between 1959 and 1964, that uses abbreviations or mnemonic codes. For example, 'A' is used for 'add', 'C' for 'compare', and 'MP' for 'multiply'. Assembly language was an improvement on the original machine language which used ones and zeros to represent 'on' or 'off'. An assembler program is used to translate assembly language codes into machine language, because computers can only execute instructions issued in machine language. See **programming language**. 2. [ISO A programming language that provides symbolic forms for machine instructions. *Note:* Assembly languages usually also provide macro calls.]

assertion [ISO A statement that a particular condition holds at a specified point in a program. *Note:* Assertions may be used for debugging, verification, or as comments.]

assignment [ISO A mechanism to give a value to a variable or to an aggregate. *Note:* This term also applies to the use of the mechanism.]

assignment by name [ISO An assignment of a record value to a record variable pertaining only to those components with matching identifiers.]

associative cache See **fully associative cache** and **set associative cache**.

associative storage [ISO A storage device whose locations are identified by their contents, or by part of their contents, rather than by their names or positions.]

assumed-size aggregate [ISO An aggregate formal parameter that takes some or all of its subscript ranges from a corresponding actual parameter.]

astable Referring to an electronic device of two states (as used in electronic watches) which continually switches (oscillates) from one to the other.

asterisk In DOS, OS/2, and other applications, the asterisk (*) may be used as a wildcard, replacing a series of unknown characters (such as when searching for a word or file for which only the first few characters are known).

The asterisk can be typed after the first few characters; and when the search is complete, a list of files matching this pattern is displayed. For example, when searching for all words beginning with comp*, the result may be 'compact', 'company', and 'comparison'.

asymmetrical multiprocessing Systems built around asymmetric processors are designed to split the overall program workload among multiple processors based upon the function. The primary CPU typically handles the operating system software, applications programs, and interrupt servicing, while input/output tasks such as LAN and file management are handled by one or more specialized satellite processors.

asynchronous communication adapter See **serial port**.

asynchronous modem A modem which cannot supply timing signals. All of the timing information must be supplied by the associated data terminal equipment (DTE). See **modem**.

asynchronous procedure [ISO A procedure that can be executed concurrently with the calling part of the program.] The word 'asynchronous' comes from the Greek and means 'not together in time'.

asynchronous transfer mode See **ATM**.

asynchronous transmission In computer communications, data (binary digits) can be transmitted in asynchronous mode or synchronous mode. When sending in asynchronous mode, the binary digits are not orderly — meaning they are out of synchronization and sent

A

at irregular intervals in characters, words, or blocks. In order to ensure that the receiving device is ready, a special 'start bit' is sent ahead of each character, and a 'stop bit' at the end of each character. This process continues until the final character is sent. In ASCII, where 8 bits form a character (byte), a total of 10 bits must be sent for each character. Asynchronous transmission is sometimes known as 'start–stop transmission'. The difference between asynchronous and synchronous communications can be compared to the difference between motor-car traffic on a freeway and a train. Asynchronous data is like the cars, all going in the same direction and at about the same speed but with different distances between them. Each car must be driven on its own. On the other hand, the train (synchronous data) has one engine and all the carriages are closely coupled, all traveling at the same speed, precisely and closely synchronized. Asynchronous is a little more error-prone and less efficient, but it uses a simpler technology. It was the first form of data communication and was originally designed for the telex service. Synchronous communication is more sophisticated, more accurate, and more efficient. It is more complex and is mainly used when connecting mainframe computers. Other types of transmission are half duplex and full duplex. To continue the car/train analogy, half duplex describes a one-way street (or train track) where the traffic can only 'turn around' if the way is clear. Full duplex is a two-way lane system where data can flow freely in both directions at the same time. Half duplex is used only in specialized mainframe applications (such as point-of-sale and electronic funds transfer terminals). Full duplex links can support higher traffic throughput, where the sender and receiver can be processing different applications. Some modems (such as NetComm's M-Series) can switch from asynchronous to synchronous communications as required. [ISO Data transmission in which the time of occurrence of the start of each character, or block of characters, is arbitrary; once started, the time of occurrence of each signal representing a bit within the character, or block, has the same relationship to significant instants of a fixed time base.] See **parity bit**.

AT Advanced Technology. Introduced in 1984 by IBM, the AT personal computer was based on the Intel 80286 microprocessor, and a 16-bit data bus. It offered up to 75% faster processing power than its previous model, the XT. Compare **XT**.

Atanasoff-Berry Computer See **ABC**.

Atanasoff, John Vincent See **ABC**.

AT bus The bus used in the IBM Personal Computer AT (Advanced Technology), or compatible machines, which use a 16-bit expansion bus, or contain AT-compatible slots. With the introduction of IBM's PC/AT personal computer, a broadening of the industry-standard bus structure occurred. The AT bus was just an extension of the original PC bus (62-pin bus connectors with eight data lines used to pass a byte of data at a time). The AT bus contains exactly the same connection lines plus some additional ones that were required for the Intel 80286 microprocessor. It can accommodate most option boards that were designed for the PC bus. The major change with the AT bus involved the addition of another eight lines for data transfer, bringing the total to 16. This meant faster processing speed, since 2 bytes of data could now be exchanged at a time. Most personal computers which use the AT bus have at least two connectors that are physically identical to those used on the older PC bus. The remaining connectors (option slots) are longer to accommodate option boards that require the full 16-bit-wide data bus.

AT&T American Telephone and Telegraph Company; the world's largest common carrier (communications service provider). In 1982, the Justice Department and AT&T settled a seven-year-old antitrust suit. In the settlement, AT&T divested itself of its 22 Bell Operating Companies (BOC). AT&T now consists of NCR, its computer products company; Western Electric, its manufacturing facilities; Bell Labs, its research facilities; the Long Lines Department, which is responsible for operating long-distance interstate lines; and several other subsidiaries, many of which had been formed to compete in the worldwide data communications market.

ATC Authorization to copy.

AT command set See **Hayes command set**.

ATE Automatic test equipment.

Atlas A well-known second-generation computer which was built using transistors. First-generation computers used thermionic valves.

ATM 1. Adobe Type Manager. Pronounced 'uh-<u>doe</u>-bee'. 2. Asynchronous transfer mode. A standard transport protocol that specifies a method of packaging data into cells. An ATM cell is 53 bytes in length, with 48 bytes of data and a 5-byte header. By comparison, an Ethernet data package can range in length from 64 bytes to 1518 bytes. The ATM standard was developed within ANSI X3T.3 in the late 1980s as a transport protocol for broadband ISDN. 3. Automatic telling machine; a computerized banking terminal which performs common banking transactions, including deposits and withdrawals. ▼

A to D converter See **analog-to-digital converter**.

atomicity In transaction processing (TP), a computer transaction is said to provide integrity of operation and data when the transaction passes the ACID (atomicity, consistency, isolation, durability) test. A transaction has 'atomicity' if the operations that make up the transaction either all execute to completion, or can be made to appear never to have occurred at all. If some operations succeed and others fail, there is no atomicity. For example, in a money transfer transaction, one account is debited while another is credited with the same amount. Should a failure occur between the debit and the credit, the TP system aborts the transaction and does not update the database, so that no change takes place. The system can then automatically resubmit the transaction for processing at a later stage. See **ACID test** and **transaction processing**.

atomicity, consistency, isolation, durability See **ACID test**.

ATM *This automatic telling machine (manufactured by NCR) is a self-service financial terminal that features a television-like screen on which instructions appear to guide customers through most routine financial transactions. Terminals can be installed through the outside walls of financial institutions, at shopping malls, supermarkets, and other retail locations. It is now common for financial institutions to extend their services to new areas such as office lobbies and airline terminals.*

atomic layer epitaxy See **molecular beam epitaxy**.

attachment unit interface [ISO In a data station on a local area network, the interface between the medium attachment unit and the data terminal equipment.]

attenuation Signal reduction in amplitude. A 'repeater' is used at certain points across a communications network to regenerate communications signals to their original strength and form. Attenuation distortion refers to the amplitude of one frequency being reduced more than the amplitude of another frequency. There are two types of attenuation distortion: high-frequency attenuation distortion and low-frequency attenuation distortion. High-frequency attenuation distortion is caused by the capacitance and inductance found in all telephone lines. When an analog signal is present, the capacitance causes the high frequency to be shorted across the cable pair more than the low frequency. The word 'attenuation' comes from the Latin word *attenuatus*, meaning 'made thin'. See **distortion**.

atto- An SI unit prefix for 10^{-18} expressed in decimal notation as 0.000 000 000 000 000 001, as in 'attosecond' (as) or 'attometer' (am). SI symbol 'a'.

attrib A DOS command used to set file attributes. An attribute has four single bits stored with a file under DOS which indicates the following four file attributes: read-only; system; archive; hidden. The attribute is either set to 'yes' or 'no'.

audio frequency Any frequency that can be heard by the human ear, when transmitted as a sound wave. A human's maximum audibility range is 16 hertz to 20 000 hertz. Due to the fact that the most audible part of speech lies between 300 and 3000 hertz, communications systems such as telephones are normally limited to this range in order to conserve bandwidth.

audio response unit See **voice-output device**.

audiotex A service that allows a database host to pass data to a voice-mail computer, where it is interpreted and delivered over the telephone as a natural, spoken-voice message.

audio video interleaved See **AVI**.

audit-review file [ISO A file created by executing statements for the explicit purpose of providing data for auditing.]

audit trail [ISO Data, in the form of a logical path linking a sequence of events, used for tracing the transactions that have affected the contents of a record.]

AUI Attachment unit interface.

Austpac A gateway, operated and maintained by Telecom Australia, to which private videotext and electronic mail systems are connected. Austpac allows connection at 300 bits per second (Bps), 1200 Bps, 1200/75 Bps, or 2400 Bps from anywhere in Australia, for the cost of a local phone call plus connection charges.

Australian Information Technology Society See **AITS**.

Australian virus A variant of the Stoned virus. See **Stoned virus**.

Austrian virus A variant of the Vienna virus. See **Vienna virus**.

author language A very-high-level programming language used to develop such applications as computer-assisted instruction packages. It does not require the user to have any programming experience. HyperCard for the Apple Macintosh is a typical example. See **programming language**.

auto-answer modem A modem capable of automatically answering an incoming telephone call from another modem. See **modem**.

AutoCAD A professional software program developed by Autodesk for computer-aided design. See **Autodesk**.

Autodesk An international supplier of computer-aided design software for personal computers and workstations. Founded in the United States in 1981, Autodesk is one of the largest software companies in the world. The company's flagship product, AutoCAD, is recognized as the industry standard, with more than a 63% share of the personal computer-based CAD market (with over 500 000 installations worldwide). All Autodesk products are designed to perform across industry-standard operating systems and hardware platforms. The company has branches in Austria, Australia, England, France, Germany, Holland, Italy, Japan, Spain, Sweden, Switzerland, and the US where it is headquartered. Other Autodesk products include Advanced Modeling Extension, AutoShade, Autodesk RenderMan, AutoFlix, AutoSketch, and Autodesk Animator — the first real-time animation desktop video program for personal computers, and the first of Autodesk's range of multimedia products. ▼

auto-dial modem A modem capable of automatically dialing a telephone number, and transmitting data from one computer to another. See **modem**.

AUTOEXEC.BAT When a DOS-based computer system boots, it automatically looks for a file called 'AUTOEXEC.BAT'.

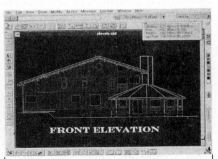

Autodesk More akin to an illustration program, AutoSketch for Windows is a computer-aided design program that is useful for architectural drawings. Using mathematical tables, re-sizing an image can be done automatically, either via a mouse, or for greater accuracy, through the data entry box.

This 'automatically executing' file contains many of the start-up parameters and programs which must be run to set-up the system for use.

automate [ISO To convert a process or equipment to automatic operation.]

automated office See **office automation**.

automatic [ISO Pertaining to a process or device that, under specified conditions, functions without human intervention.]

automatic answering [ISO Answering in which the called data terminal equipment (DTE) automatically responds to the calling signal. *Note:* The call may be established whether or not the called DTE is attended.]

automatic baud recognition The automatic recognition by a receiving device of the data rate of an incoming call and its adjustment to that speed. Abbreviation 'ABR'. See **baud rate**.

automatic brightness control An automatic brightness control circuit used to adjust (automatically) the luminance level of a display screen to compensate for changes in ambient light levels. Abbreviation 'ABC'.

automatic calling (In a data network.) [ISO Calling in which the elements of the selection signal are entered into the data network contiguously at the full data signalling rate. *Note:* The selection signal is generated by the data terminal equipment. A limit may be imposed by the design criteria of the network to prevent more than a permitted number of unsuccessful call attempts to the same address within a specified period of time.]

automatic constant function [ISO The function that allows a number automatically held in a calculator to be used repeatedly.]

automatic function [ISO A machine function or series of machine functions controlled by the program and carried out without the assistance of an operator.]

automatic noise limiter See **ANL**.

Automatic Sequence Controlled Calculator See **Mark I**.

automatic storage allocation [ISO A mechanism for allocating space to data objects only for the duration of the execution of their scope. *Note:* Automatic storage allocation is one form of dynamic storage allocation; another form is program controlled storage allocation.]

automatic telling machine See **ATM**.

automation [ISO The implementation of processes by automatic means.]

autonomous built-in self test The ability of very-large-scale integration devices to automatically run a built-in self-test software program. Acronym 'ABIST'.

auto recalc The ability of a spreadsheet program to automatically recalculate some or all of its cells when a cell value or formula is changed. If the spreadsheet is not recalculated, it may accidentally be printed or used with old (and therefore incorrect) results displayed.

Autumn virus A variant of the Cascade virus. See **Cascade virus**.

AUUG Australian UNIX User Group.

A/UX A derivative of AT&T's UNIX operating system specifically used with the Apple Macintosh. A Motorola 68020 microprocessor plus 4 megabytes of random-access memory are minimum requirements.

AV Audio/visual.

availability See **system availability**.

available time [ISO From the point of view of a user, the time during which a functional unit can be used.]

avalanche-induced migration A permanent process of short circuiting a diffused junction in a programmable read-only memory (PROM) based on aluminum migration through silicon. Acronym 'AIM'.

Avant Garde Developed by Herb Lubalin and Tom Carnase in 1970 for International Typeface Corporation (ITC), Avant Garde has proved to be a very successful contemporary sans serif

Aa	Bb	Cc	Dd	Ee
Ff	Gg	Hh	Ii	Jj
Kk	Ll	Mm	Nn	Oo
Pp	Qq	Rr	Ss	Tt
Uu	Ww	Xx	Yy	Zz
1	2	3	4	5
6	7	8	9	0

Avant Garde Some of the characters that form Avant Garde normal.

typeface. Usually supplied as a built-in font with most PostScript laser printers, it is more geometrical than any other sans serif faces (such as Helvetica), with the capitals 'G', 'O', and 'Q' being formed from perfect circles. In 1977, ITC commissioned a Swiss team to expand the family and design the oblique (italic) version of Avant Garde. ▲

average seek time The time required to do all possible unique seeks divided by the number of such seeks. A disk drive's average seek time specification usually results from laboratory measurement. A synthetic workload consisting of all possible seeks is performed on a sample of drives, and the elapsed time is divided into the number of seeks in the workload. The result is the drive's average seek time. See **access time**. Compare **single-cylinder seek time**.

average transfer rate See **data transfer rate**.

AVI Audio video interleaved; a file format for digital video and audio under Microsoft Windows. This file format is cross-platform compatible, allowing *.AVI video files to be played under other operating systems.

AViiON See **Data General**.

AWG American wire gauge.

axis One of the reference lines on a two-dimensional or three-dimensional co-ordinate system.

AZERTY A type of computer or type-writer keyboard layout used by the French. The first row of alphabet keys (positioned under the row of numeric keys) starts with the letters A, Z, E, R, T, Y. Overall, the layout closely resembles the QWERTY keyboard, with the home row letters being QSDFGHJKLM. Compare **QWERTY**. ▼

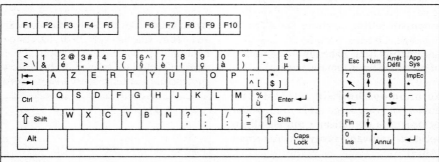

AZERTY The AZERTY keyboard is designed to facilitate the use of diacritical marks. It is used mainly by the French.

THERE IS NOTHING MORE BEWILDERING
THAN THE AMBIGUITY OF CONTRADICTION

b Symbol for byte (<u>b</u>inary digi<u>t</u> <u>e</u>ight). See **byte**.

B 1. The hexadecimal symbol for binary 1011 (which is equal to the decimal number 11). $B_{16} = 11_{10} = 13_8 = 1011_2$. 2. The symbol for bit (<u>b</u>inary digi<u>t</u>). See **bit**.

Babbage, Charles Born in Devonshire, England, in 1791, Babbage (dubbed the father of the modern computer) was an English inventor and mathematician. He became aware of the need for an accurate calculator after studying mathematics at Trinity College, Cambridge, where he was involved in compiling very large astronomical and nautical tables. During the early 1820s, he developed a calculating machine (the Difference Engine) capable of processing figures with 20 decimal places. By 1834, he had designed what could be called the world's first digital computer. He called it the Analytical Engine, and it was to be controlled by a set of punched cards — an idea he got from Joseph-Marie Jacquard who developed the punched card system for his silk-weaving looms. Babbage was a prolific inventor who had a reputation for not completing his projects. Nonetheless, he was responsible for the invention of the speedometer, the railway cow-catcher, and the oscillating lighthouse. Babbage was helped by Ada Augusta Byron (probably the world's first computer programmer) who preserved his work after his death in 1871. See **Ada** and **Jacquard, Joseph-Marie**.

background image [ISO That part of a display image, such as a form overlay, that is not changed during a particular sequence of transactions.]

background processing The processing of low-priority tasks such as printing. Processing only occurs when the computer does not have higher priorities such as those associated with real-time user interaction. Systems that are unable to perform multiple tasks (multitasking) carry out background processing during brief pauses in the system's primary (foreground) operations. The processing of high-priority tasks such as those associated with real-time user interaction on a multitasking computer is called 'foreground processing'. See **multitasking**.

backout 1. The act of removing the updates done by a transaction that has either aborted, or that was in-flight at the time the system failed. 2. The act of retracting from a multilevel software program so as to return to the base application screen or main menu. 3. In a windows environment, the act of closing all the windows as one is retracting back to the base application screen, or main menu.

backplane The section of a computer system board into which other boards are plugged.

backslash On most computer systems, the symbol (/) is referred to as the 'slash', while the symbol (\ ) is referred to as the 'backslash'. The backslash is also called the 'slosh'.

backspace The deletion of a character immediately to the left of the cursor. 2. To backspace (a data medium). [ISO To move a data medium backwards a specified distance. *Example:* To move a punched tape backwards by one tape row; to move a magnetic tape backwards by one block.] 3. To backspace (a position). [ISO To move the print or display position backwards one position along the printing or display line.]

backup 1. The disk or tape on which

important data is duplicated for the purpose of safety. Should the original stored information become corrupt (or be accidentally lost), the information can be retrieved from the backup. [ISO A copy of a file made for possible later reconstruction of the file.] 2. To copy data to a secondary storage unit, so as to end up with an archival copy. Some software packages like WordPerfect allow for timed automatic backups of the file being used. Should a power failure cause the buffer to lose the data, a backup file which contains the most recent version of the file can be retrieved. Some backup utility programs only update files which have changed since the last backup. This feature saves time, and is only available on more sophisticated programs. Backup of online files provides both disaster-protection (from destruction of media or its contents), and protection against system and application failures which might result from external events, such as fire or flood. Failures may also occur from the destruction of a volume's logical structure by inadvertent or malicious programming errors, or by operating system failure, or from equipment failure such as a disk head crash. Abbreviation 'B/U'. Compare **differential backup**, **image backup**, and **incremental backup**. 3. Of a backup. [ISO Pertaining to a procedure, technique, or hardware used to help recover lost or destroyed data or to keep a system operating.] ▼

backward chaining A commonly-used method of deduction to draw inferences in an expert system, using IF ... THEN rules. Such a system starts with a question such as 'How much is this car worth?', and then searches through the

B

backup *Being inserted in a tape drive of a computer, this backup tape contains 600 foot (182.9 meters) of magnetic tape ¼-inch wide.*

system backwards to determine which of the rules in the knowledge base must be answered before a conclusion can be made. The user is prompted to answer several questions such as, 'Does the car have a factory-fitted air conditioner?' Backward chaining continues until all IF ... THEN rules are answered and compared to the knowledge base. In this example, the knowledge base may have been programmed to increase the value of the car by $1000 if an air conditioner was fitted. The opposite to this is forward chaining, which requires the user to supply all the data before the question can be asked, or before inferences can be made. See **expert systems**.

backward channel [ISO A channel associated with the forward channel, used for supervisory or error control signals, but with a direction of transmission opposite to that of the forward channel in which user information is being transferred. *Note:* In case of simultaneous transfer of information in both directions, this definition applies with respect to the data source under consideration.]

backward compatibility The compatibility of files written using an older version of the software. With new software or hardware being introduced onto the market, manufacturers are mindful that users of earlier models/versions may still wish to use some of the applications they have used in the past. For example, WordPerfect version 5.1 is backwardly compatible, meaning files written using earlier versions of

WordPerfect (like version 5.0) can still be read and used on version 5.1 (although 100% compatibility cannot always be guaranteed). The term may also be used to describe the connectivity of hardware devices with older models.

backward (file) recovery [ISO The reconstruction of an earlier version of a file by using a newer version and data recorded in a journal.]

backward LAN channel [ISO In a broadband LAN, the channel assigned for uplink data transmission from the data stations to the headend.]

bad block See **self-test**.

bad sector An area on a hard or floppy disk which cannot store information accurately due to a manufacturing defect or damage caused by dust, scratches, fingerprints, and the like. Having bad sectors on a floppy disk may mean the entire disk cannot be used. However, the operating system has the capacity to ignore bad sectors on hard disks. See **sector** and **self-test**.

BAEC British Amateur Electronics Club; an international club formed in the United Kingdom in 1966.

balanced circuit Refers to a two-wire circuit in which the voltages and currents on the wires are electrical opposites.

balanced error [ISO A set of errors whose mean value is zero.]

BallPoint mouse A Microsoft pointing device that incorporates both mouse and trackball technology, designed to be attached to laptop and notebook computers, enabling the user to work with a pointing device in areas where space is limited. Launched in March 1991, the product was under development for two and a half years. BallPoint was the first portable pointing device that attached to the keyboard of most of the popular laptop and notebook computers, including models from Compaq, GRiD, NEC, Toshiba, and Zenith. The BallPoint comes with a universal clamp that fits onto the side of the keyboard, and a positioner that allows the user to adjust the angle of the mouse relative to the keyboard. When used with a computer-generated presentation, the mouse also slides off the positioner to be used like a standard trackball on the desktop, or held in the hand, offering a resolution of 400 points-per-inch. The unit has four user-programmable buttons arranged in two sets on either side of the ball. ▼

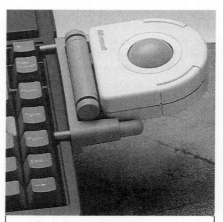

BallPoint mouse *Microsoft's BallPoint mouse, incorporating both mouse and trackball technology, has been designed especially for laptop and notebook computers. Here it is shown attached to a Toshiba laptop.*

BALUN Ba̲lanced to un̲balanced transformer; a device that converts a balanced signal to an unbalanced signal, and vice versa.

band 1. The full range of frequencies between two limits. The band which carries telephone voice messages ranges from approximately 300 to 3300 hertz (cycles per second). Attempts at sending information outside the nominated band will result in distortion, loss, and corruption of data. The CCITT recommends that public telephone systems should operate in the voice band of 300 to 3300 hertz. This is by no means a perfect bandwidth, but one capable of sufficiently and economically transmitting voice signals. In comparison, high-quality music systems require a bandwidth of 15 000 to 20 000 hertz. See **bandwidth**. 2. [ISO A group of tracks on a magnetic drum or on a magnetic disk all of which are read or written in parallel.]

band printer An impact printer that uses a horizontally-rotating band (belt) that contains characters (letters, numbers, and symbols). Hammers strike the ribbon and paper, hitting different characters on the band (which can be changed for different fonts). Print speeds may exceed 600 lines per minute. [ISO An impact printer in which the character set available for printing is carried on a flexible band (on a belt).] See **impact printer**.

bandwidth The range of frequencies that can pass along a cable or communications link. Signals may be carried along different forms of energy, including (electrical) alternating current (AC), radio waves, and light waves. The transmission medium (such as wire, optic fiber, or radio) determines the form of energy required, because each energy form can carry a different range of frequencies (measured in hertz). Telephone lines carry voice signals at a bandwidth of approximately 3 kHz (3000 hertz). This is determined by subtracting the low end of the frequency scale from the high end (3300 − 300 = 3000). This bandwidth is very narrow when compared to visible light, which has a bandwidth of 300^{12} hertz. Each bandwidth can be subdivided into smaller (narrower) bandwidths, as can be done with visible light — producing a different color as seen in a rainbow or through a prism. The lowest quality bandwidth is called 'narrowband'. It is capable of transmitting between 45 and 150 bits per second (Bps) and is used for low-speed data terminals, or telegraph lines. For direct data transfer from one computer to another, a wideband is used to transmit over 230 000 Bps. When transmitting computer data via a communications channel, the information can be sent across either the entire bandwidth, or only a portion of that bandwidth. Naturally, more information can be transmitted when the entire bandwidth is used — this is called 'baseband transmission'. When a number of messages must be sent simultaneously, broadband transmission is used. This technique allows many different messages to be sent via different channels, but at a slower rate. Telephone lines, using broadband transmission, are capable of carrying voice messages and other information along different bandwidths. This division is called 'multiplexing'. In a multiplexed system, a bandwidth of 60 megahertz is capable of carrying

B

approximately 10 800 telephone channels. A satellite system can offer extremely wide bandwidths, allowing thousands of signals to be transmitted simultaneously. See **multiplexer**.

bar code 1. Vertical marks (bars) printed on products or tags since the early 1970s. Each set of marks (bar code) represents data that can be sensed and read by a wand (light pen) or non-contact laser reader which recognizes the marks and converts them to electrical signals which are sent to the computer for processing. Bar codes can also be used for other purposes, such as on library books and identification cards, or general data applications involving repetitive typing. The four major bar code systems are known as 'the big four': Universal Product Code (UPC); Code 39; Interleaved Two of Five (ITF); and Codabar. UPC is used in the United States and Canada, while the European Article Number (EAN) is used in Western Europe, and Japanese Article Number (JAN) is used in Japan. UPC, ITF, and EAN are compatible coding systems. 2. [ISO A code representing characters by sets of parallel bars of varying thickness and separation which are read optically by transverse scanning.]

bar code reader See **bar code scanner**.

bar code scanner A non-contact optical recognition unit (laser scanner) as used in supermarkets to read Universal Product Code symbols (bar codes) which appear on most grocery items. Scanners register the item purchased, the price, and other important inventory management information which assist the store manager to keep track of stock levels. Error rates are as low as one-in-three-million characters. Point-of-sale scanner performance is determined by the scanning pattern of the laser beam. International bar codes (UPC, EAN, and JAN) can be read with two scanning lines, perpendicular to each other, regardless of the bar code's direction; for that reason, crossline patterns are widely used. Conventional scanners use complex optics with rotating or vibrating mirrors to generate these scanning patterns. Because some scanners are bulky, expensive to produce, and require complicated optical systems, holographic scanners are gaining popularity. (They also provide a better reading performance.) Abbreviation 'BCS'. See **bar code**. ▼

bar code scanner Bar codes are used almost universally to tag groceries and general merchandise. The prism and lens contained in the scanner direct a laser beam horizontally, vertically, and diagonally across bar codes as they pass over the window, thereby instantly reading and confirming the information.

bar printer [ISO An impact printer in which the type slugs are carried on a type bar.]

barrel distortion In monitor technology, the screen or image distortion where the sides bow out in the middle, making the image barrel-shaped. Compare **keystone distortion** and **pincushion distortion**.

base [ISO In a numeration system, the number that is raised to the power denoted by the exponent and then multiplied by the mantissa to determine the number represented. *Example:* The number 5 in the expression $2.8 \times 5^2 = 70$. *Note:* The term 'radix' is deprecated in this sense because of its use in the term 'radix numeration system'.]

base address [ISO An address used as the origin in the calculation of addresses.]

base (address) register [ISO A register that holds a base address.]

baseband A technique for transmitting a message at high line-speeds along a medium (such as a cable) only one signal at a time. Information is represented by changes in voltages. Baseband transmission cannot support video conferencing and is only able to support limited graphics facilities through either twisted pair, coaxial, or fiber optics cables. See **bandwidth**. Compare **broadband**.

baseband LAN [ISO A local area network in which data is encoded and transmitted without modulation of a carrier.]

baseband modem A modem which transmits a modified digital signal, rather than modulating and demodulating a carrier signal. It is also called a 'short haul' or 'limited distance' modem. Compare **modem**.

baseline In typography, the lowermost point of letters like 'x' and 'm' (not the lowest point of letters like 'p' and 'q').

base memory The portion of memory set aside for general use in a computer's random-access memory. Most personal computers running under DOS have a base memory of 640 kilobytes. The usable amount is much less because the operating system is also contained in the base memory.

BASIC Beginners' All-purpose Symbolic Instruction Code; a high-level programming language devised in 1965 by John Kemeny and Thomas Kurtz at Dartmouth College, in the United States. BASIC uses simple instruction codes similar to the English language (such as RUN, LOAD, and LIST). Some other forms of BASIC are: BASIC-PLUS (by Digital Equipment Corporation); UBASIC (by Sperry Univac); and True BASIC, which was designed in 1983 by the original creators of BASIC to take advantage of modern hardware and software techniques. See **programming language**.

Basic Input/Output System See **BIOS**.

basic mode link control [ISO Control of data links by use of the control characters of the ISO/CCITT seven-bit character set for information interchange.]

BASIC-PLUS See **BASIC**.

batch file A DOS file consisting of a sequence of one or more DOS commands and rudimentary programming constructs.

batch-header document [ISO A document that accompanies and identifies a batch of input documents and that may be used to validate them. *Example:* A document that includes balances, control totals, hash totals, or checksums.]

batch processing A technique in which transactions are collected into groups so that they can be processed or updated as a single job. Where large databases are involved, batch processing saves on computer time and avoids unnecessary computer interruption. Sometimes this technique is called 'dripfeed'. In contrast, real-time transactions are made by the computer fast enough so that records can be activated or updated immediately. [ISO The processing of data or the accomplishment of jobs, accumulated in advance, in such a manner that the user cannot further influence its processing while it is in progress.] Compare **real-time**.

Baudot code A special set of binary characters which use only 5 bits per character, forming 32 combinations (2^5). This was increased to 62 through the use of two special shift characters. The Baudot code was mainly used to handle telex messages by common communications carriers such as Western Union. Its main disadvantage is the lack of an error-checking bit. The code is named after its inventor, J.M. Emile Baudot (1845–1903).

baud rate The number of electronic signals or data symbols that can be transmitted along a communications channel every second. It was named after the French inventor J.M. Emile Baudot (1845–1903), and was originally used to measure the speeds of Morse code transmission. A modern facsimile machine transmits data at 9600 bits per second (Bps). Satellites transfer data at 7 million Bps, while fiber optics can transmit at approximately 1000 million Bps. Unlike the 'hertz', which is interchangeable with 'cycles per second', the baud rate (signals per second) is not always equal to bits per second. It was coincidental that early modems operating at 300 baud were transmitting 300 Bps, but in fact both the 1200-Bps and the 2400-Bps modems operate at 600 baud. This is because electronic signals and data symbols can each carry more than one bit of information. This can be likened to a highway with cars on it, where each car is a baud, and each passenger is a bit. The highway (communications channel) can only carry a limited number of cars per second, but each of the cars can have either one passenger (bit) or many passengers. Pronounced 'board'. See **modem**.

BB See **bulletin board**.

BBS Bulletin board system. See **bulletin board**.

BC 1. Broadcast. 2. Before Christ. 3. A Silicon Valley joke referring to anything which is old and has been around since before computers.

BCC Block check character; a control character that is appended to blocks in character-oriented protocols. It is used for determining if the block was received error-free.

BCD See **binary-coded decimal**.

BCS 1. British Computer Society. 2. See **bar code scanner**. 3. Bar code system. See **bar code**.

Because It's Time Network A wide area network developed by a non-profit education consortium (EDUCOM) to link over 1000 colleges and universities in the United States, Canada, and Europe. It provides electronic mail capabilities, plus file transfer and query applications. Acronym 'BITNET'.

beeper 1. Any device which can emit a 'beeping' sound when activated. Beepers are generally used to alert a computer operator to an error. 2. A small electronic radio signal receiver (pager) which can be activated to alert the carrier that a message awaits. More sophisticated pagers are used as alternatives to cellular radios (portable phones) because messages (data) can be sent in digitized format and viewed on liquid crystal display screens. Also called 'pager'.

Beginners' All-purpose Symbolic Instruction Code See **BASIC**.

beginning-of-file label [ISO An internal label that identifies a file, marks its location, and contains data for use in file control.]

beginning-of-tape marker [ISO A marker on a magnetic tape used to indicate the beginning of the recordable area. *Examples:* A photo-reflective strip; a transparent section of tape.]

beginning-of-volume label [ISO An internal label that identifies the volume and indicates the beginning of its data.]

Bell Operating Company One of the 22 United States local telephone companies spun off from AT&T as a result of divestiture, now reorganized into seven regional Bell holding companies. These are among the largest of the 1600 independent local telephone companies in the United States. Acronym 'BOC'.

Bell 103 A standard for 300 bits per second full duplex communications using the AT&T Bell protocol over the public switched telephone network (PSTN).

Bell 212 A standard for 1200 bits per second full duplex communications using the AT&T Bell protocol over the public switched telephone network (PSTN).

Bell 208 A standard for 4800 bits per second for modems that are mainly used on older mainframe computers using the AT&T Bell protocol over the public switched telephone network (PSTN).

belt printer An impact printer. See **band printer**.

benchmark A standard by which to compare computer systems or programs, usually in relation to processing speed, reliability, and accuracy. These include the Whetstone (speed of arithmetic operations); Khornerstone (overall system performance including the processor, memory access, and disk drive access speeds); and the Dhrystone (microprocessor and memory performance of a computer system). LIPS (logical interferences per second) is a benchmark used to measure the processing speeds of computers designed to handle artificial intelligence applications. One of the most important aspects of performance evaluation is choosing the right benchmark. For best results, users should evaluate system performance by comparing the execution time of their workload, the mixture of programs, and the operating system commands that the user runs on the machine. Unfortunately, this is time-consuming, costly, and often impractical for the average user. There are, however, a number of industry-standard benchmarks that have been developed to predict performance. The important issue is to identify the correct workload and draw a meaningful correlation between workload and the proper benchmarks. For example, in a scientific and engineering environment, floating point instructions contain a significant portion of the processor instructions, whereas in a business-oriented environment, the majority of processor instructions are of integer type. Therefore, if the system is to be used as a business-oriented productivity tool, for tasks such as online transaction processing, database manipulation, word processing, or spreadsheet applications, a meaningful benchmark program would consist of integer instructions. There are many factors other than the central processing unit that affect the overall system performance. For example, the rate at which the system communicates with the outside world (input/output rate) greatly affects the overall performance. In such business applications as database management and online transaction processing, it is imperative that the input/output subsystem delivers fast and reliable

performance. In many of today's corporate and government environments, price/performance may also be of interest to the user. See **SPEC**, **SPEC Rating**, and **TP1**.

benchmark test [ISO A test that uses a representative set of programs and data designed to evaluate the performance of computer hardware and software in a given configuration.]

BER Bit error rate; the ratio of received bits that are in error (relative to a specific number of bits received). Bit error rate is usually expressed as a number referenced to a power of ten.

Berkeley UNIX Berkeley Software Distribution derivative of UNIX developed at the University of California at Berkeley. It provided network support for UNIX, further support for peripherals, and an extensive software development environment which helped UNIX gain commercial acceptance. Also called 'BSD UNIX'.

Bernoulli box A trademark of Iomega Corporation, a Bernoulli box resembles a hard disk drive, but the magnetic media is removable. Each removable cartridge can hold up to 44 megabytes of data offering access times of approximately 22 milliseconds.

BERT Bit error rate test (or tester).

bespoke Custom-built. A product that is constructed especially for one user or organization. Typically, these include finance software programs.

beta site The place where beta test software is sent for use. See **beta test**.

beta test A second-stage test of a new software package, outside the factory, before its commercial release. The first-stage test is conducted in-house and is called an 'alpha test'.

BGI Borland Graphic Interface; a set of core graphics modules which have been incorporated into a number of Borland products. There are two main parts to the BGI: a graphical engine which includes instructions for producing various graphics, and a user interface which can be customized for use in various situations.

bias [ISO A systematic deviation of a value from a reference value.]

bias distortion Refers to a condition where an analog signal loses its ground reference at the receiving modem. This can be seen on an oscilloscope as an analog signal shifted either above or below the ground reference line. Bias distortion is sometimes encountered on telecommunications links which utilize T-carrier systems. See **distortion** and **T-carrier services**.

bias error [ISO An error due to bias. *Examples:* (a) The error caused by a shrunken measuring tape. (b) In computation, an error caused by truncation.]

bicimal point See **binary system**.

Big Blue A slang term used to refer to International Business Machines Corporation (IBM) whose corporate color is blue. See **IBM**.

Big Four, the The four major bar code systems: Universal Product Code (UPS); Code 39; Interleaved Two of Five (ITF); and Codabar. See **bar code**.

Big Italian virus See **Italian virus**.

billion See **exponent**.

BINAC See **Mauchly, John William**.

binary arithmetic operation [ISO An arithmetic operation in which the operands and the result are represented in the pure binary numeration system. *Note:* The term 'binary operation' is deprecated to avoid confusion with 'dyadic operation' and with 'Boolean operation'.]

binary cell [ISO A storage cell that can hold one binary character.]

binary character [ISO Each character of a binary character set. *Examples:* T (true) or F (false); Y (yes) or N (no).]

binary character set [ISO A character set that consists of two characters.]

binary-coded decimal Computers use binary numbers, and some use 8-bit chunks (bytes) to process data. Using this method, the largest number which can be represented using 8 bits is the number 256. Decimal numbers larger than 256 must first be coded, and a quick way of doing this is not to translate a decimal into binary, but to code the decimal number in binary form. For example, the decimal 370 can be broken down so that the numbers 3, 7, and 0 are each represented by 1 byte. In this way, 3 bytes of storage are needed for a three-digit decimal. Abbreviation 'BCD'. Compare **EBCDIC**.

binary-coded notation [ISO A binary notation in which each character is represented by a binary numeral.]

binary digit See **bit**.

binary digit eight See **byte**.

binary notation [ISO Any notation that uses two different characters, usually the digits 0 and 1.]

binary search [ISO A dichotomizing search that processes sets of an equal number of data elements, or in case of an odd number of elements in the initial set, allows for one set to contain one additional element.]

binary system An arithmetic system using a base of 2. Whereas the decimal system has a base of 10 (0, 1, 2, 3, 4, 5, 6, 7, 8, and 9), only two digits, 0 and 1, are used to correspond to 'off' and 'on', whether it be in the form of light bulbs, vacuum tubes, transistors, silicon chips, or bubble memory. Combinations of these zeros and ones are used to represent larger numbers. For example, the decimal number '3' is written as '0011' in the binary system, while '4' is written as '0100'. Binary fractions are signified by the use of bicimal points (just as decimal points are used in the decimal system). When different bases are being discussed, the number base is used as a subscript — for example, $4_{10} = 0100_2$. Letters and symbols can also be represented in binary. Also called 'binary numeration system'. [ISO The fixed radix numeration system that uses the digits 0 and 1 and the radix 2. *Example:* In this numeration system, the numeral 110.01 represents the number '6.25' — that is, $(1 \times 2^2) + (1 \times 2^1) + (1 \times 2^{-2})$.] See **bit**. ▼

bind 1. [ISO To relate an identifier to another object in a program. *Examples:* To relate an identifier to a value, an

Decimal	Binary	Decimal	Binary	Decimal	Binary	Decimal	Binary	Decimal	Binary
0	0	26	11010	52	110100	78	1001110	104	1101000
1	1	27	11011	53	110101	79	1001111	105	1101001
2	10	28	11100	54	110110	80	1010000	106	1101010
3	11	29	11101	55	110111	81	1010001	107	1101011
4	100	30	11110	56	111000	82	1010010	108	1101100
5	101	31	11111	57	111001	83	1010011	109	1101101
6	110	32	100000	58	111010	84	1010100	110	1101110
7	111	33	100001	59	111011	85	1010101	111	1101111
8	1000	34	100010	60	111100	86	1010110	112	1110000
9	1001	35	100011	61	111101	87	1010111	113	1110001
10	1010	36	100100	62	111110	88	1011000	114	1110010
11	1011	37	100101	63	111111	89	1011001	115	1110011
12	1100	38	100110	64	1000000	90	1011010	116	1110100
13	1101	39	100111	65	1000001	91	1011011	117	1110101
14	1110	40	101000	66	1000010	92	1011100	118	1110110
15	1111	41	101001	67	1000011	93	1011101	119	1110111
16	10000	42	101010	68	1000100	94	1011110	120	1111000
17	10001	43	101011	69	1000101	95	1011111	121	1111001
18	10010	44	101100	70	1000110	96	1100000	122	1111010
19	10011	45	101101	71	1000111	97	1100001	123	1111011
20	10100	46	101110	72	1001000	98	1100010	124	1111100
21	10101	47	101111	73	1001001	99	1100011	125	1111101
22	10110	48	110000	74	1001010	100	1100100	126	1111110
23	10111	49	110001	75	1001011	101	1100101	127	1111111
24	11000	50	110010	76	1001100	102	1100110		
25	11001	51	110011	77	1001101	103	1100111		

binary system *This table shows how the value of each column increases by the power of two: 1, 2, 4, 8, 16, 32, and 64.*

address or another identifier, or to associate formal parameters and actual parameters.] 2. (Of an address.) [ISO To associate an absolute address, virtual address, or device identifier with a symbolic address or label in a computer program.]

biochips A type of chip technology (still in its experimental stages) which can be used in place of silicon chip technology. It is proposed that biochips will use organic molecules or genetically-engineered proteins for their main circuits, thereby allowing microscopic chips to be built which consume virtually no power. Two types of biochips are being researched: the digital biochip, which will use organic molecules to turn the flow of electrons on and off to represent binary digits in the same way as silicon chips; and analog biochips, in which protein enzymes would be used for graded responses to represent variable data (not based on the binary system). Compare **silicon**.

biometric security devices A device which only allows access (to a computer file, or a room) to a person after certain unique physical characteristics (physical signatures) of that person are entered into a computer system for verification. For example, a person's voice can be used to gain entry; a retinal scan verifier can be used to measure the eye's blood vessel pattern; a hand geometry verifier can be used to measure the length and width of fingers and their webbing; or a signature verifier can be used to store the dynamic characteristics of a hand-written signature. Modern systems use a person's fingerprints for speed and convenience because card-based systems may be the subject of fraud,

especially if cards are lost or stolen. Some biometric security devices are based on digital holography, involving a small reading device about the size of a thumb-print which reads three-dimensional data from the finger such as skin undulations, ridges and valleys, reflections, and other living characteristics. On enrollment, the fingerprint image is scanned, and up to a quarter of a million pieces of information are digitized and converted to a mathematical characterization called a 'template'. This data is stored in ASCII code, against which all future scans are compared. Such a method of security is designed to prove that a person is who they claim to be. The ASCII data can also be integrated into existing card systems or into smart cards, enabling users to carry their template with them to access, for example, automatic telling machines. For example, using the patented TouchLock system (by Identix Inc.), each authorized user is assigned a personal identification number, authority level, restrictions for access time and location, and an expiry date at the time of enrollment. A typical enrollment sequence takes less than one minute, and thereafter, identity verifications take less than two seconds. Some systems also offer a time-stamped transaction log, providing irrefutable audit trails. This form of security can also be used for staff clocking, door access, and computer access. Major security areas such as restricted defense areas and bank vaults can use high-security revolving checkpoints where a revolving door is divided into four parts with a fingerprint reader in one compartment. When anyone enters, the door automatically revolves a quarter turn and locks. The user enters his or her

B

personal identification number and places a finger on the reader. If identification is verified, the door continues its revolution and allows access to the computer room. If access is denied, the user is gently reversed out of the compartment. The revolving door is equipped with sensors that detect whether more than one person has entered the compartment. All occupants must be identified within 20 seconds or the door reverses. See **fingerprint sensor**.

BIOS Basic input/output system. In computers using DOS, BIOS is contained in read-only memory and controls access to devices that are connected to the computer, such as the monitor, or the serial communications port. These are support routines needed by the central processing unit (CPU) to work with its disk drives, keyboard, monitor, and other hardware devices. The BIOS routines are stored in ROM but transferred into RAM when the system is booted-up because they need to be accessed frequently, and as quickly as possible. For example, every time a key is pressed, one or more of the BIOS routines are needed to move the data from the keyboard to the CPU. The BIOS also provides services to set the computer's 'time-of-day' clock and keep it updated. The contents of ROM are in binary machine language which is easily recognized by the CPU, but difficult and tedious for humans to work with. The machine-language programs which make up the BIOS are written to take advantage of the features of a specific CPU. These routines are written (burned) into the ROM chip at the factory and are considered permanent (they are then referred to as 'firmware').

Since firmware routines are considered to be a type of software, they are subject to copyright laws. Pronounced 'buy-os'. See **firmware**.

biquinary code [ISO A notation in which each number from 0 to 9 is represented by a pair of numerals, a and b; a being 0 or 1, b being 0, 1, 2, 3, or 4, and 5a + b being equal to that number. *Note:* Generally, each of the two numerals is represented in binary.]

bis Second version. See **V.xbis**.

BIS Bureau of Indian Standards; India's standards body formed in 1986. Standards activities were previously handled by the Indian Standards Institution which was formed in 1947.

B-ISDN Broadband integrated services digital network. See **ISDN**.

bistable (Of an electronic device) capable of having two stable states where, for example, one state can be used to represent a 0 (zero) and the other state a 1 (one).

bistable (trigger) circuit [ISO A trigger circuit that has two stable states.]

Bisync Binary synchronous communications control; a type of synchronous communications control procedure set up by IBM as a line control procedure in which the sending and receiving stations are synchronized before a message is sent. The synchronization is checked and adjusted during the transmission, using a defined set of control characters.

bit 1. Binary digit; a name coined by Claude Shannon of Bell Telephone

Laboratories to describe the fundamental unit of information. A bit is either a 0 (zero) or a 1 (one). It is the basic unit for storing data in primary storage; 0 for 'off' and 1 for 'on'. Groups of bits are needed to represent other symbols, such as letters of the alphabet. For example, the letter 'A' is represented in the EBCDIC coding scheme by a special sequence of eight ones and zeros: 11000001. This sequence of 8 bits is called a 'byte' (binary digit eight). The transfer of data is usually measured in bits per second (Bps). A simple burglar alarm signal may require 50 bits of information; a simple memorandum may require 3000 bits; a newspaper-quality photograph may require in excess of 100 000 bits; whilst a very-high-quality color photograph (the size of a postcard) would require a minimum of 8 million bits. When dealing with very large numbers, the prefixes 'kilo', 'mega', and 'giga' are used. The use of such prefixes only serves as a representation, not as an accurate meaning. For example, in the metric system, 'kilo' literally means 1000, but 1 kilobit (kB) refers to 2^{10}, or 1024 bits. 'Mega' means 1 million, but a megabit refers to 2^{20}, or 1 048 576 bits. Other uses include gigabit (GB) 2^{30} and terabit (TB) 2^{40}. When abbreviating the term 'bit' (B), do not confuse it with 'byte' (b). The 'bit' came before the 'byte'; hence, to abbreviate 'megabit', the capitals of the first two letters were joined to form 'MB'. Since this usage was taken up, 'megabyte' had to be abbreviated to 'Mb' using a lowercase 'b'. Abbreviation 'B'. See **binary system**. 2. [ISO Either of the digits 0 or 1 when used in the pure binary numeration system.]

bit density 1. [ISO A measure of the number of bits recorded per unit of length or area.] 2. See **linear density**.

bit error rate The ratio of received bits that are in error to a specific number of bits received. Bit error rate is usually expressed as a number referenced to a power of ten. Acronym 'BER'.

bit map A group of bits (binary digits) stored in a computer's memory which represents an image. A bit map monochrome image has a one-to-one correspondence between the pixels and the image.

bit-mapped font A font (complete set of characters of a typeface) whose characters are composed of a pattern of picture elements (pixels). Large amounts of memory are required for bit-mapped fonts because a full representation of each character must be stored in either the printer or the computer. Bit-mapped fonts are not designed for flexibility. Each font must be used as mapped, so that a Palatino 12 point (normal) font cannot be italicized, nor scaled up or down. Attempts to do so will result in ragged-edged type causing staircase distortions called 'aliasing'. Compare **outline font**.

bit-mapped graphics Graphics (sometimes called 'raster graphics') using picture elements (pixels) to form complex, artistic patterns on the screen using paint programs such as MacPaint, PC Paintbrush, and SuperPaint. Attempts to re-size these images will cause distortion. Compare **object-oriented graphics**.

bit-oriented Referring to a communications protocol or transmission procedure in which control information is encoded in fields of one or more bits, each oriented toward full duplex link operations. This protocol uses less overhead, and is therefore more efficient than character-oriented or byte-oriented protocols.

bit position [ISO A character position in a word in a binary notation.]

bit slice processor [ISO A central processing unit constructed of an array of identical units, each of which operates simultaneously upon one or more adjacent bits.]

bits per inch The number of bits (binary digits) a tape is capable of storing per inch of length. Abbreviation 'Bpi'. See **bit**.

bits per second The number of bits (binary digits) which can be transmitted (or transferred) each second. Abbreviation 'Bps'. See **bit**. Compare **baud rate**.

Bitstream Headquartered in Cambridge, Massachusetts, Bitstream Inc. develops and licenses typefaces and related software to more than 500 hardware manufacturers and software developers in 19 countries. Bitstream offers these manufacturers a library of over 1300 typefaces, and a variety of font scaling technologies for incorporation in many different products, including laser printers, typesetters, broadcast video systems, and a wide range of software packages (for Macintosh and PC) such as FaceLift — a font scaling and special effects utility for WordPerfect. When the company was established in 1981, it was the first independent digital type foundry. Since then, it has grown into a prominent supplier of OEM, retail, and

networking software products, with several patents for font processing technologies to its credit. In 1992, the company entered the network print services software market with MOSAIC, the print management software package developed by Insight Development Corporation. Pronounced 'bit-stream'.

bit-stuffing A process in bit-oriented data communications protocols where a string of 'one' bits is broken by an inserted 'zero'. This 'zero' is added by the sender and removed by the receiver. This is done to prevent user data containing a series of 'one' bits from being interpreted as a flag control character.

Blackjack virus A variant of the Cascade virus. See **Cascade virus**.

blackout The term commonly used to refer to a total failure of the electrical mains supply. Compare **brownout**.

BLAISE See British Library Automated Information Service.

blanking [ISO The suppression of the display of one or more display elements or segments.]

blank medium [ISO A data medium in or on which neither marks of reference nor user data have been recorded.]

blinking [ISO An intentional periodic change in the intensity of one or more display elements or segments.]

BLOB Basic large object. All database management systems handle structured data such as part numbers and color with ease, but they must go back to the file system for unstructured data such as text, graphics, and digitized data. Interbase Software Corporation has produced the BLOB, which holds arbitrary pieces of data. A BLOB is a field in a record, like any other data element. It is subject to concurrency and transaction control. However, unlike other fields, a BLOB has no size limit. BLOB data is stored in the database, so it cannot be lost through a misguided file copy or backup. Most applications address data which is unstructured, or structured in ways that do not match the relational model. BLOBs are useful in applications such as computer-aided design (CAD), computer-assisted software engineering, and office automation. For example, before BLOBs, CAD databases could only hold the names of files; component descriptions and graphics were kept in the files. Putting graphics data directly in the database as BLOBs reduces the number of files to open or close, and gives the benefits of transaction and concurrency control.

block 1. In communications, a unit of information that is passed from one device to another. The size of a block may depend upon the protocol used. For example, 128 bytes is considered a block when using XModem, while 512 bytes is considered a block in DOS. 2. In word processing, a block is any set of figures, words, or records which the program treats as a single unit of data for the purpose of effecting change, such as copying, deleting, or moving text. 3. [ISO A sequence of elements recorded or transmitted as a unit. *Note:* The elements could be characters, words, or records.] 4. (In programming languages.) [ISO A compounded statement that coincides with the scope of at least one of the declarations contained within it. *Note:* A block may also specify storage allocation or segment programs for other purposes.]

block check [ISO That part of the error control procedure used for determining that a data block is structured according to given rules.]

block diagram [ISO A diagram of a system, a computer, or a device in which the principal parts are represented by suitably annotated geometrical figures to show both the basic functions of the parts and their relationships.]

blocking The inability of a network, switch, or access node to grant service to a requesting user due to the unavailability of the transmission channel. Blocking occurs mainly in private branch exchanges and central-office switches that lack the ability to provide circuits for all potential users all of the time.

blocking factor [ISO The number of records to be contained in a block.]

block size [ISO The number of bytes, or any other appropriate unit, in a block.]

block transfer [ISO The process of transferring one or more blocks of data in one operation. *Note:* A block transfer can be done with or without erasing data from the original location.]

B-mail An electronic mail utility provided by Banyan. See **electronic mail**.

BNC Bayonet coaxial.

board See **PC board**.

BOC See **Bell Operating Company**.

body copy See **body type**.

body type In typography, the font used for the main body of the text. The words on the page are known as 'body copy'. The body copy is usually set in a smaller font than those used for headlines, captions, and other elements. Studies show that body type, when set in a serif font, is much easier to read. Serif fonts have small 'feet' which guide the eye across the page. In Roman masonry, typographers used to chisel the letters in the stone and then cut a small perpendicular piece (a serif) at the end of every straight line to stop the crack from spreading. Palatino, Times, Garamond, and Century are common serif fonts. Examples of sans serif (non-serif) fonts are Helvetica and Gill Sans.

BOF Beginning of file.

boilerplate Pieces of often-used text, stored for incorporation into various documents. For example, boilerplate may be used in a standard contract where only minor details (such as name and address) are added. In word processing software, macros can be written to retrieve regularly-used passages automatically. Also called 'boilerplate text'.

boldface 1. (In typography) referring to a font which is darker/thicker than the normal text. 2. To make darker or thicker through the use of special commands. 3. A boldface font.

bomb To undergo an unexpected system failure.

Bookman A thick serif typeface origi-

A a	B b	C c	D d	E e
F f	G g	H h	I i	J j
K k	L l	M m	N n	O o
P p	Q q	R r	S s	T t
U u	W w	X x	Y y	Z z
1	2	3	4	5
6	7	8	9	0

Bookman *Some of the characters that form Bookman normal.*

nally produced as a bold face. It is often included as a built-in font with PostScript laser printers. In 1976, Ed Benguiat of International Typeface Corporation (ITC) completely revised Bookman, providing a range of weights in both Roman and italic. The x-height was increased and changes were made to a number of letters, with the swirling tail of the 'Q' being the most flamboyant. The cross bar of the lowercase 'e' was raised, and the width of the capital 'M' was reduced. ◣

Boolean algebra A set of rules which allow logical programming statements (rather than numeric ones) to be represented using algebra. Devised in 1847 by English mathematician George Boole (1815–64).

Boolean function [ISO A switching function in which the number of possible values of the function and of each of its independent variables is two.]

Boolean operation 1. [ISO Any operation in which each of the operands and the result take one of two values. *Notes:* (a) The term 'binary operation' is deprecated to avoid confusion with 'dyadic operation' and 'binary arithmetic operations'. (b) In order to simplify the definitions of individual Boolean operations and to simplify the table of monadic Boolean operations, the two Boolean values are referred to as 'Boolean value 0' and 'Boolean value 1'. Other pairs of values might be used without being in contradiction with the definitions.] 2. [ISO An operation that follows the rules of Boolean algebra. *Note:* The term 'binary operation' is deprecated to avoid confusion with 'dyadic operation' and 'binary arithmetic operations'.] ▼

Boolean operation table [ISO An operation table in which each of the operands and the result take one of two values.]

Boolean operator [ISO An operator each of whose operands and whose result take one of two values.]

Boole, George A mathematician and doctor of philosophy who, in 1847, devised a set of algebraic rules which allowed logical (rather than numeric) programming statements to be represented using algebra. This branch of algebra is called 'Boolean algebra'. Boole was born in England in 1815, and died in 1864.

BOOM Binocular omni-oriented monitor; a head-mounted display (similar to data-glasses) used in virtual reality systems.

boot Short for 'bootstrap'. 1. The loading of the operating system of a computer into the random-access memory from a storage device such as a floppy disk (in the case of a personal computer). This is generally an automatic loading procedure issued by the read-only memory chip. During the boot, several diagnostic tests are performed to check the working order of internal and external devices such as printers or disk drives. See **cold start**. 2. To perform a boot.

BOOTP Bootstrap protocol.

Operation number	Complementary operation	Result for:		Entry	Meaning	Examples for representation	
		$P = 0$	$P = 1$			Symbolic representation	Representation using Venn diagram
0	3	0	0	Zero constant	Zero constant	0	
1	2	0	1	Variable	P P		
2	1	1	0	Negation	Not P	–	
3	0	1	1	One constant	One constant	1	

Boolean operation Table of monadic Boolean operations. Note that the variable P is represented by the circle. The defined set is represented by the shaded area.

boot-sector virus Any computer virus capable of replacing the original code of the boot sector found on either a diskette or hard disk. The first sector of a DOS partition found on a hard disk, or the very first sector on a diskette, is called the 'boot sector'. This contains important information about the medium, such as the number of sectors that can be found in a logical volume. In most cases, when a personal computer is turned on, it first turns to drive A to read the boot sector. If a diskette is not present in drive A, it turns to the hard disk (usually drive C) and loads what it finds into memory and proceeds to run the program. A boot-sector virus moves the original boot-sector program to another area on the disk and replaces it with its own code (usually the virus), and then proceeds to complete the boot process, thereby placing the virus into memory before any software can be activated, making it impossible for antivirus programs to eliminate the boot-sector virus because a boot-sector virus would always become memory-resident long before the antivirus program can be activated. One way of preventing a boot-sector virus from getting in is to make the virus think that it is already memory-resident so that it does not try again. This process of inoculation is suitable for diskettes, but can be damaging to hard disks. Once a boot-sector virus secures its position on the boot sector of a disk, it runs automatically every time the computer is turned on (booted). A virus may develop its own hooks to some of the computer's common interrupt signals, such as the read/write interrupt (known as '13h'), so that every time the computer reads from, or writes to, a diskette or disk, the virus runs first. Some of the

better-known boot-sector viruses are Ashar, Brain, Italian, Ogre, and Typo. Abbreviation 'BSV'. See **virus**. Compare **partition-sector virus**.

bootstrap 1. [ISO A sequence of instructions whose execution causes additional instructions to be loaded and executed until a complete computer program is loaded into storage.] 2. [ISO To execute a bootstrap. *Note:* The term 'bootstrapping' is also used for translating a compiler by using itself or a previous version as the translator.]

Borland Borland International, Incorporated; a leading developer and marketer of high-performance microcomputer software products, including Paradox, Turbo Pascal, and Turbo C++. The company's corporate headquarters are in Scotts Valley, California. European headquarters are in Paris with European subsidiaries operating in London, Munich, and Scandinavia. Borland was founded in 1983 by Philippe Kahn with the introduction of the original Turbo Pascal programming language. It was the first company to market an object-oriented programming language, called 'Turbo Pascal 5.5'. Borland employs more than 600 people worldwide. Its products are marketed through a national sales organization, subsidiaries, and resellers. Borland products are available worldwide and are translated into many languages including French, German, and Spanish.

borrow digit [ISO A digit that is generated when a difference in a digit place is arithmetically negative and that is transferred for processing elsewhere. *Note:* In a positional representation system, a borrow digit is transferred to the digit place with next higher weight for processing there.]

bottom-up [ISO Pertaining to a method or procedure that starts at the lowest level of abstraction and proceeds toward the highest level.]

Bouncing Ball virus A variant of the Italian virus. See **Italian virus**.

bpc Bytes per centimeter; usually the number of bytes (letters, numbers, or symbols) a magnetic tape is capable of storing per centimeter of length.

Bpc Bits per centimeter; usually the number of bits (letters, numbers, or symbols) a magnetic tape is capable of storing per centimeter of length.

bpi Bytes per inch; usually the number of bytes (letters, numbers, or symbols) a magnetic tape is capable of storing per inch of length.

Bpi Bits per inch; usually the number of bits (binary digits) a tape is capable of storing per inch of length.

BPP Bits per pixel; the number of bits used to represent the color value of each pixel in a digitized image.

bps Bytes per second; usually the number of bytes which can be transmitted (or transferred) each second.

Bps Bits per second; usually the number of bits (binary digits) which can be transmitted (or transferred) each second. Compare **baud rate**.

BPS Bureau of Product Standards; Philippines' standards body formed in 1946.

brain See **human brain**.

brain scan The use of a computerized brain scanner which allows researchers to see a color-coded 'map' of brain activity. This procedure can help to identify manic-depressive or schizophrenic patients.

B

Brain virus A boot-sector virus that infects any 360 kilobyte (kb) 5¼-inch diskette. Its presence can be detected by the volume label '(c) Brain' on the diskette, which also shows 3 kb of bad sectors. In addition, 7 kb of random-access memory becomes unavailable to DOS, thereby slowing the operation of the diskette drive. It is rumored that two brothers, Basit and Amjads, from Lahore, Pakistan, wrote this virus in 1986. The virus is sometimes referred to as the 'Pakistani virus' or 'Lahore virus'. Once written to the boot sector, the first line of the text reads 'Welcome to the Dungeon'. See **boot-sector virus**.

branch [ISO In a network, a path that connects two adjacent nodes and that has no intermediate nodes.]

branch construct [ISO A language construct specifying a choice between different execution sequences by means of label references.]

break An interrupt signal initiated by a user to halt the processing of a program or a communication process.

breakout box A device placed in a circuit (such as between a computer and a modem) to provide terminal connections for testing purposes. This is done to ensure that communications cables are tested independently.

breakpoint [ISO A point in a computer program where execution may be halted. *Note:* A breakpoint is usually at the beginning of an instruction where halts, caused by external intervention, are convenient for resuming execution.]

bridge A device in a local area network (LAN) which will receive, regenerate, and retransmit packets that are addressed to stations other than those attached to the same local network. Bridges are like routers in that they are used to interconnect LANs that are using the same media and a common protocol. This approach assumes that the networks to be interconnected define a consistent addressing scheme. They do not support protocol conversion or code conversion. Bridges are implemented within both the physical layer (layer one) and the medium access control (MAC) sublayer of the data link layer (layer two) of the OSI model. Bridges are capable of supporting speed conversion or flow control. A bridge monitors all traffic on the two subnetworks that it links, and allows two networks to communicate, even though they may have different topologies or communications protocols. Bridges are designed to comply with IEEE data link protocols and are able to support higher-level protocols such as Xerox network systems, TCP, and DECnet. For example, a bridge might link an IEEE 802.3 CSMA/CD LAN with an IEEE 802.4 token-passing bus LAN. Some bridges are capable of automatically detecting and adjusting to changes in the configuration of the attached LANs. There are three primary types of bridges: simple, learning, and source routing. The simple bridge has a fixed table of addresses for all stations on the

network, as determined at installation time. This bridge is simple and fast, but it is useful only to networks which rarely add or move stations and in which the topology is fairly constant. The learning bridge, or transparent spanning tree bridge, forwards data by use of an address table that can be dynamically modified based upon the information gathered from received packets. Information on station location relative to the bridge is also gathered and fed into a 'spanning tree' algorithm resident in each bridge. The algorithm calculates a loop-free (although not necessarily optimal) route between any two stations in the network. This bridge is self-configuring and tolerant of link failures, station movements, and changes in topology. Its implementation requires no changes in existing IEEE 802-compatible products. The source routing bridge, developed by the IEEE 802.5 Committee, is primarily used with token-ring networks. In this scheme, the originating station specifies the route the data must take across multiple token-ring LANs. Routes are determined by sending out a special frame which is replicated and distributed throughout the entire network. Frames which reach the destination station are returned, containing a record of the route they took. The source station then chooses from among them the optimal route for all future correspondence with that particular destination station. At the same time, the sending station discovers and stores alternative routes that could be used in the event of route failure for load sharing. [ISO A functional unit that interconnects two local area networks that use the same logical link control protocol but may use different medium access control protocols.] See **topology**.

bridge input circuit (In process control.) [ISO An analog input circuit in which the sensing component of the technical process is in one branch of the bridge circuit and the reference components are in another branch.]

brightness The difference between light and dark shades of a color, assuming they have the same hue and saturation. Some graphics programs allow the user to specify color using the traditional terms: hue, saturation, and brightness. Brightness, sometimes called 'value', is similar to lightness (not whiteness). The ratio of brightest to darkest parts of the screen is called the 'contrast'. See **color** and **color monitor**.

British Library Automated Information Service A British library lending service giving subscribers an online document request and reservation facility. Acronym 'BLAISE'. Also known as 'ADRS' (Automatic Document Request Service).

British Standards Institute See **BSI**.

broadband A technique for transmitting analog signals along a medium (such as a radio wave). Broadband signaling works the way radio and television work, by splitting up the available frequencies into different channels. The data is transmitted simultaneously and is represented by changes in amplitude, frequency, or phase of the signal. Messages are carried at lower line speeds than baseband lines. Broadband transmission can be used to transmit different combinations of data, voice, and video information along one physical cable (normally with a bandwidth of 300 megahertz) with multiple communication channels of different frequencies. Many communication channels are created through frequency division multiplexing (FDM) which allows multiple devices to share one cable. Signals from each channel are multiplexed on and off the cable using sophisticated, and usually expensive, RF (radio frequency) modems. However, the necessary coaxial cable, taps, couplers, splitters, and repeaters are readily available because they are identical to those used for cable television. Although their initial cost is higher, broadband networks enable users to lay down a network cable once and then continually upgrade and expand the services it provides. This expendability makes these networks attractive to larger companies that are willing to pay the higher entry fee in order to be assured of a growth path. Baseband networks, on the other hand, are usually implemented in situations where a straightforward, data-only network is required. See **bandwidth**. Compare **baseband**.

broadband LAN [ISO A local area network consisting of more than one channel, in which data is encoded, multiplexed, and transmitted with modulation of carriers.]

Brøderbund Software, Inc. Headquartered in Novato, California, Brøderbund was established in 1980 by Doug and Gary Carlston. The company is a developer and publisher of personal computer software for the home, school, and small-business markets. Employing over 350 people, Brøderbund has sold over 15 million units of software. Its titles include 'The Print Shop', 'TypeStyler', 'Living Books' series, and the 'Carmen Sandiego' series.

B

Brooklyn Bridge A file transfer utility used to link laptop personal computers and desktop personal computers.

brownout A temporary period of low mains voltage, usually caused by a sudden high demand for electricity within the building, or entire city. Brownouts may cause computers to lose data, or crash. To avoid sudden power fluctuations, uninterruptible power supplies (UPS) are used in critical computer environments. The term 'blackout' is commonly used to refer to a total electrical failure.

brush reader A machine that translates the meaning of the holes in punched cards into electrical pulses which in turn are fed into the computer as data for processing. A brush reader has metal brushes that pass over the cards. When the brushes find a hole, an electrical connection is made and the signal is sent to the computer as data.

brush style In typography, a typeface whose characters are shaped as if they had been drawn freehand using a brush.

BSA Business Software Alliance. Headquartered in Washington, DC, BSA was formed 11 October 1988 by Aldus, Ashton-Tate, Autodesk, Lotus Development, Microsoft, and WordPerfect. BSA's objectives are to combat international software piracy, strengthen intellectual property protection, and review other barriers to software trade. In June 1989, BSA became a member of the International Intellectual Property Alliance (IIPA).

BSAA Business Software Association of Australia Ltd. To combat the increasing problem of software theft and piracy in Australia, BSAA was formed in September 1989 by Ashton-Tate, Autodesk Australia, Lotus Development, Microsoft, and WordPerfect Pacific. BSAA aims to: (a) increase awareness of those aspects of the Australian Copyright Act 1968 which protect the intellectual property of the software developer and copyright owner; (b) develop and implement nationwide education and awareness programs for the detection and prevention of software theft; and (c) communicate the benefits of using authorized software. Where necessary, BSAA is also aggressively committed to strong and well-publicized legal action, to the full extent of the law, against persisting offenders, and to continuing investigations to identify organizations or individuals engaged in software theft or piracy.

BSD Berkeley Software Distribution. See **BSD UNIX**.

BSD UNIX Berkeley Software Distribution derivative of UNIX developed at the University of California at Berkeley. It provides network support for UNIX, further support for peripherals, plus an extensive software development environment which helped UNIX to gain commercial acceptance.

BSI British Standards Institute. Established in 1901, BSI was the world's first national standards body to be formed. Its original name was the 'Engineering Standards Committee'. Its present title was adopted in 1931.

BSV See **boot-sector virus**.

BTL Backplane transceiver logic.

B/U See **backup**.

bubble memory Magnetic bubble memory storage introduced by Bell Laboratories in 1966. A bubble memory chip can have 10 to 100 times the capacity of the current generation of integrated circuit silicon chips. Intel has already produced a bubble memory chip capable of storing over 4 megabits. Although currently much more expensive to produce than integrated circuits, bubble memories are non-volatile, meaning they do not lose their data if the electrical current is turned off. Bubble memory consists of a chip of garnet coated with a thin layer of magnetic film on which a microscopic 'bubble' is formed when a magnetic field is applied. Using the basic principles of the binary system, the presence of a bubble represents a 1 (on), whereas its absence represents a 0 (off). A magnetic bubble memory stores data in the form of cylindrical magnetic domains in a thin film of magnetic material. An external rotating magnetic field propels these cylindrical domain bubbles through the film. Metallic patterns (or chevrons) deposited on the film steer the domains in the desired directions. Transfer rates, once started, are in the tens of thousands of bits per second, but because the data circulates past a pickup point at which it becomes available to the user, there is a latency averaging tens of milliseconds before data transfer can begin. In these respects, magnetic bubble memories are serial high-density storage devices like electromechanical disk memories. However, in a disk, the stored bits are stationary on a moving medium, whereas in the magnetic bubble memory the medium is stationary and the bits

move. Unlike disk memories, bubble memories are quiet and very reliable, because they have no moving parts. They are compact, dissipate very little power, and their support circuits are compatible with microprocessor systems. The production process resembles semiconductor manufacturing in many ways. Manufacturing begins with a non-magnetic garnet wafer on which a magnetic film is deposited, using conventional techniques. An ion implantation process alters the magnetization of the top surface of the film, discouraging the formation of abnormal bubbles with undesirable dynamic properties. Then non-magnetic conductors, bubble-steering patterns of magnetic metal, insulation, passivation, and bonding pads are deposited in

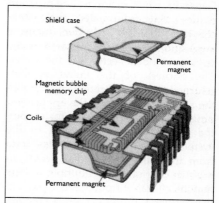

bubble memory *A magnetic bubble memory chip consists of permanent magnets which produce the magnetic field appropriate to hold the magnetic bubbles, coils to generate the rotating magnetic field, and a magnetic shield case that forms the magnetic bubble memory device. The capacity of a magnetic bubble memory device depends upon the size of the chip and that of the magnetic bubbles. A 10 x 10 millimeter chip in which the magnetic bubbles are 3 micrometers in diameter can store 300 kilobits.*

much the same way as successive layers on semiconductor integrated circuits, where patterns in each layer are defined photolithographically. [ISO A magnetic storage that uses cylindrically-shaped magnetized areas in thin film that are movable, non-volatile, and changeable.]. See **integrated circuit**. ◢

bubble storage See **bubble memory**.

buffer A temporary data-storage area. For example, a file sent to the printer is held in the printer's buffer because the printing speed is much slower than the data transfer speed. A disk buffer is an important element in advanced disk input/output strategies. It is simply a memory area containing the same amount of data as a disk-sector contains. Generally, when an application program requests data from a disk, the system software allocates a buffer (memory area) and transfers the data from the appropriate disk sector into the buffer. The address of the buffer is then returned to the application software. In the same manner, after the application program has filled a buffer for output, the buffer address is passed to the system software, which writes data from the buffer into a disk sector. In multitasking systems, multiple buffers may be allocated from a buffer pool. In these systems, the disk controller is often requested to read ahead and fill additional data buffers while the application software is processing a previous buffer. Using this technique, system software attempts to fill buffers before they are needed by the application programs, thereby eliminating program waits during input/output transfers. ▼

buffer storage [ISO A special-purpose storage or storage area allowing, through temporary storage, the data transfer between two functional units having different transfer characteristics. *Note*: A buffer storage is used between non-synchronized devices, or where one is serial and the other is parallel, or between those having different transfer rates.]

bug A logic error in a computer program. Diagnostic routines are performed to locate the error, which can often be removed (debugged). The term became popular after a programmer, Grace Murray Hopper, found a moth (bug) lodged in the circuits of Mark I, causing the computer to malfunction. Hopper wrote in her log book, 'Relay #70 Panel F (moth) in relay. First actual case of bug being found'.

bug fix An in-line release of software which is only intended to correct some of the known bugs.

built-in [ISO Pertaining to a language object that is declared by the definition of the programming language. *Examples:* The built-in function 'SIN' in PL/1, the pre-defined data type 'INTEGER' in FORTRAN.]

built-in font Any font which is encoded in a printer's read-only memory so that it is always available (resident) when the printer is switched on. Other fonts may be downloaded from the computer, but once the printer is switched off, these font configurations are lost.

bulk storage A form of secondary storage used to store extremely large amounts of data. Bulk storage is usually measured in gigabytes. Also called 'mass storage'. See **secondary storage**.

B

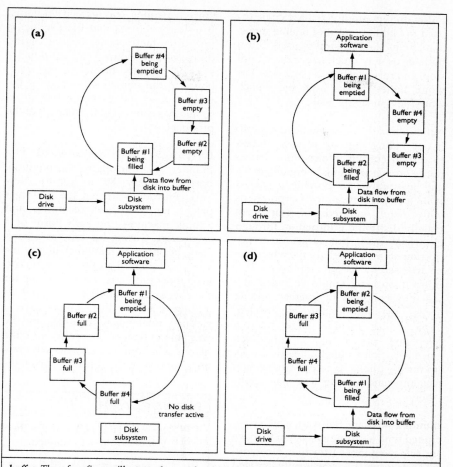

buffer *These four figures illustrate the use of multiple buffers in a ring configuration. (a) The first disk read request by the application software causes the disk subsystem to begin filling the first empty buffer. The application software must wait until the buffer is filled before it may continue execution. (b) After the first buffer is filled, the disk system continues to transfer disk data into the next buffer while the application software begins operating on the first full buffer. (c) When all empty buffers have been filled, disk activity is stopped until the application software releases one or more buffers for re-use. (d) When the application software releases a buffer (for re-use), the disk subsystem begins a disk sector read to re-fill the buffer. This strategy attempts to anticipate application software needs by maintaining a sufficient number of full data buffers in order to minimize data transfer delays. If disk data is already in memory when the application software requests, no disk transfer delays are incurred.*

bullet In typography, a filled circle (•) used to highlight a list of related items. Sometimes the full stop is used, but a bullet is usually much larger than a full stop, and raised above the baseline. The word 'bullet' comes from the French word *boule*, meaning 'ball'.

bulletin board A communications utility providing a group of users access to certain current information, just as notice boards are hung in organizations and institutions to provide a central point for communications. Corporations with many hundreds of employees usually distribute information through electronic mail, but larger reference documents are placed in a file which can be accessed by certain employees. This utility allows each employee to decide if the information is of interest, and to access the information as needed. Typical files include large internal telephone lists or frequently-updated price lists. Some bulletin boards are set up for the public to access. Connection fees and data transfer fees may apply. Abbreviation 'BB'.

bundled software Software which is included with a computer system to make the sale seem more attractive. A computer system which is specifically targeted to a profession (such as medical) is usually bundled with application-specific software suited to that profession.

burn-in A part of a testing process which engages the computer system in a series of checks and operations to ensure that semiconductor components are stable and error-free. Most computer manufacturers burn-in (test) all new products which come off a production line. When a product is relatively new,

burn-in periods may exceed 90 hours. If testing confirms that the product is free from failures, the testing period decreases to 24 hours. Once a product is shipped from the factory or the warehouse to the remote subsidiary or the reseller, a second round of burn-in is sometimes conducted to ensure that the product is still stable.

Burroughs, William Seward The founder of Burroughs Corporation. Born 28 January 1855 in Auburn, New York, Burroughs lodged the first ever patent for a key-set recording and adding machine (the early form of a calculator). During his time as a bank clerk, he observed that much of his time was spent guarding against errors, and even more time was wasted looking for the causes of errors. He conceived an adding machine that would give a running total when required, and he was able to finance his project with the help of a St Louis store owner who was impressed with the concept. Burroughs

---

NEWSFLASH

The number of PCs in use at the end of 1994 was 169 million.

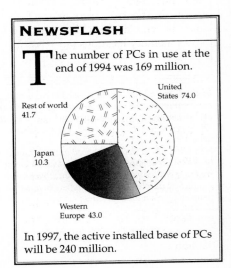

Rest of world 41.7

United States 74.0

Japan 10.3

Western Europe 43.0

In 1997, the active installed base of PCs will be 240 million.

started the American Arithmometer Company in 1886, and after the success of his machine, he renamed the company 'Burroughs Corporation', which continued to pioneer computer equipment. Today the company is known as 'Unisys'.

bursting The separation of continuous stationery paper at the perforated edge. This is often done by flicking one's finger at the perforated edge, causing the paper to break away (burst) very quickly. See **continuous stationery**.

burst transmission [ISO Data transmission at a specific data signaling rate during controlled intermittent intervals.]

bus 1. Any of the internal control paths which travel from the central processing unit to any of the adapters, the input/output ports, and to the random-access memory of the computer. A personal computer has four pathways. The first is a 'data bus' which sends data from memory to the microprocessor. The second is an 'address bus' which allocates memory locations (addresses).

FUN FACT

Imagine a microprocessor as a highway crammed with cars moving along at a certain speed. In 1981, personal computers were like eight-lane highways with cars moving at 5 miles (8 kilometers) per hour. In 1995, the fastest Intel processor had 32 lanes with cars moving at 500 miles (805 kilometers) per hour.

The third is the 'control bus' which carries the signals from the control unit. The fourth carries voltages from the power supply. Binary numbers travel along the data bus or the address bus simultaneously (in parallel). For example, sixteen-bit bus architectures enable central processing units to send and receive 16 binary digits simultaneously. See **architecture**. 2. [ISO A facility for transferring data between several devices located between two end points, only one device being able to transmit at a given moment.] 3. [ISO A common path along which signals travel from one of several sources to one of several destinations.]

bus arbitration [ISO A procedure that resolves priorities among units contending for control of a common bus and that passes control to the selected unit.]

bus architecture The way in which the address bus and data bus connect components, and the speed at which the bus operates.

business graphics The use of computer graphics to represent information in a readily understandable form. Sophisticated systems can analyze data and display the results in three-dimensional form. See **presentation graphics**.

Business Software Alliance See **BSA**.

Business Software Association of Australia See **BSAA**.

bus mouse A mouse that connects to the computer bus via a dedicated socket or a dedicated adapter card. The advantage is that the mouse does not occupy a serial port.

bus network [ISO A local area network in which there is only one path between any two data stations and in which data transmitted by any station is concurrently available to all other stations on the same transmission medium. *Note:* A bus network may be a linear network, a star network, or a tree network. In the case of a tree or star network, there is a data station at each endpoint node. There is no data station at an intermediate node. However, one or more devices such as repeaters, connectors, amplifiers, and splitters are located there.] See **bus topology**.

bus quiet signal [ISO In a token-bus network, a signal indicating that the transmission medium is inactive.]

bus topology In a local area network, a bus topology consists of one continuous cable to which devices are connected. Each device is considered to be connected to every other device, and can communicate directly along the network to any device. A bus topology is one of the easiest to set up. Unlike star and ring topologies, a bus topology is not interrupted when one of the devices (nodes) fails. Popular examples of local area networks capable of using a bus topology are Ethernet and AppleTalk. In a bus network, a message from the originating node is broadcast along the bus to all attached devices. The message is addressed so that the intended receiver will recognize its address and respond to the message. Bus networks commonly employ coaxial cable or optic fiber for their high-speed and information carrying capacities as well as their facility to carry data, voice, and video. See **topology**. Compare **ring topology** and **star topology**. ▼

bypass technology A method of transmitting data without the use of the local telephone lines for the benefit of reliability, added security, reduced cost, and increased technical advantages such as wider bandwidths. Techniques include microwave or infrared light for relatively close (line-of-sight) transmissions, optical fiber links, and two-way satellite communications for longer distances.

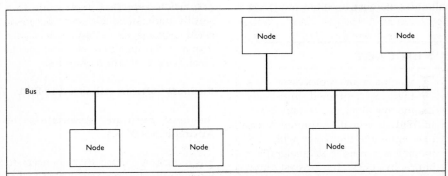

bus topology *Information flows along a bus topology via one single channel generally called the 'bus'. All of the nodes connected to the bus have unique addresses. When one node wishes to communicate with another, it sends a message along the bus tagged with that unique destination address. Each node sees the message, and if it realizes that the address is not its own, ignores it.*

Byron, Ada Augusta Born in 1816, Byron was later known as the 'Countess of Lovelace'. She was the only child of the English poet Lord Byron. At the age of 27, she collaborated with computer-inventor Charles Babbage and preserved his work after his death in 1871. She is dubbed the world's first programmer. In her honor, a high-level computer programming language called 'Ada' was sponsored and registered in 1980 by the United States Department of Defense (DoD), based primarily on Pascal. It was enforced as a military standard in 1983. See **Babbage, Charles** and **programming language**.

byte 1. Binary digit eight; a unit of information consisting of (usually) 8 bits. Notice that byte is spelt with a 'y' instead of an 'i' to eliminate any possible confusion between 'bit' and 'bite'. Each byte usually represents a character, letter, or symbol. For example, the letter 'A' is represented in the EBCDIC coding scheme by a special sequence of eight ones and zeros: 11000001. A file or potential storage capacity is measured in bytes, but when dealing with very large numbers, the prefixes 'kilo', 'mega', and 'giga' are used. The use of such prefixes only serves as a representation, not as an accurate meaning. For example, in the metric system, 'kilo' literally means 1000, but 1 kilobyte (kb) refers to 2^{10} or 1024 bytes. 'Mega' means 1 million, but a megabyte refers to 2^{20} or 1 048 576 bytes. Other uses include gigabyte (Gb) 2^{30} and terabyte (Tb) 2^{40}. When abbreviating the term 'byte' (b), do not confuse it with 'bit' (B). The 'bit' came before the 'byte'; hence, to abbreviate 'megabit', the capitals of the first two letters were joined to form 'MB'. Since this usage was taken up, 'megabyte' had to be abbreviated to 'Mb' using a lowercase 'b'. Pronounced 'bite'. Abbreviation 'b'. [ISO A string that consists of 8 bits.] See **metric system**.

bytes per centimeter The number of bytes (letters, numbers, or symbols) a magnetic tape is capable of storing per centimeter of length. Abbreviation 'bpc'.

bytes per inch The number of bytes (letters, numbers, or symbols) a magnetic tape is capable of storing per inch of length. Abbreviation 'bpi'.

bytes per second The number of bytes which can be transmitted (or transferred) each second. Abbreviation 'bps'.

INNOVATION DOES NOT COME FROM CONFORMITY.
GENIUS IS NOT HARNESSED BY MEDIOCRITY.

---

c Centi-. An SI unit prefix for 10^{-2} expressed as 0.01 in decimal notation, as in 'centimeter' (cm).

C 1. A programming language which can be written at either a low level or a high level. It is mainly used for operating systems and general business software offering flexible, modular, and open-ended programming on most types of computers, from personal computers to mainframes. C was developed in conjunction with UNIX (also written in C) in 1972 at AT&T's Bell Laboratories by Dennis Ritchie, and was the descendant of earlier languages called 'A' and 'B'. See **programming language**. 2. The hexadecimal symbol for binary 1100 (which is equal to the decimal number 12). $C_{16} = 12_{10} = 14_8 = 1100_2$. 3. One of the two types of telephone line conditioning. The operating characteristics of a basic telephone channel are guaranteed by the telephone company in terms of maximum allowable attenuation,

attenuation distortion, and delay distortion. When these characteristics are not adequate for a particular application, the line quality may be further improved by having the telephone company provide line conditioning to improve the quality of the line by adding corrective circuits. Two types of line conditioning are available: 'C' type and 'D' type. When 'C' type line conditioning is provided, attenuation distortion and delay distortion are minimized by adding additional amplitude equalizers and delay equalizers to the circuit. Five types of 'C' line conditioning are available (specified as C-1 through C-5). Two grades of 'D' type (D-1 and D-2) conditioners improve the signal-to-noise ratio on the circuit.

CA Computer-aided. Wherever a computer is used, the completion of the task can be deemed to have been aided by the computer. More specifically, sophisticated computer-aided hardware and software tools are being used to assist with areas such as design (CAD), engineering (CAE), and manufacturing (CAM). Such applications may be written in high-level programming languages such as FORTRAN or APL.

CAA Computer-aided administration.

cache A temporary buffer (storage area) within a computer's random-access memory (RAM) chip specially set aside to store information which is most frequently accessed in a computer application. Cache memory is controlled by the cache controller chip (such as the Intel 82385), and makes the computer operate at a much faster speed. Cache memory is different from disk cache — an area in the RAM chip which temporarily stores information frequently requested from the disk drives. Disk cache improves the speed of disk-intensive applications such as database management programs. When a program issues a 'read' for an instruction or an item of data, the processor first looks in its cache memory. If the requested data resides in the cache, a cache hit is said to have occurred and there is no need to read from primary memory. However, if the requested data is not available in the cache, a cache miss is said to have occurred and the processor must access primary memory to retrieve the data. Data retrieved from primary memory is written to the cache, where it is then read by the processor. Any data modified by the processor is also written to the cache. The cache has very limited storage, so a replacement strategy is used to determine what existing data to replace from the cache when new data is read from primary memory. Cache memory design takes advantage of a principle known as 'locality'. Programs tend to exhibit temporal locality and spatial locality. The word 'cache' comes from the French word *cacher*, meaning 'to hide' or 'put aside'. Pronounced 'cash'. See **cache memory, direct mapped cache, disk cache, fully associative cache, RAM cache, set associative cache, spatial locality,** and **temporal locality**. ▼

cache memory A section of fast memory assigned for temporary storage of data that has been retrieved from other slower storage devices, such as main memory or disk drives. In the case of a 386 personal computer running at 25 megahertz, the access time of the 64 kilobytes of static random-access memory (SRAM) is 25 nanoseconds versus the 100 nanoseconds access time of the main dynamic RAM. Data is algorithmically selected and stored in the cache in anticipation of future use by the system, to avoid subsequent accesses to the slower devices. As a result of the combination of the cache memory's speed, size, and cache algorithm, over 85% of the data requests are performed with zero wait states. The basic steps to cache memory involve the microprocessor which sends out a request for data. The cache memory controller intercepts it and checks the cache memory to see if the information is there so that it can be immediately accessed (this is known as a 'cache hit'). If the information is not there, it is called a 'cache miss', and the cache memory controller reads the data from the slower system memory. The information is then copied into cache memory as it is sent to the processor so that all subsequent requests for that information can be read from cache memory, at zero wait states.

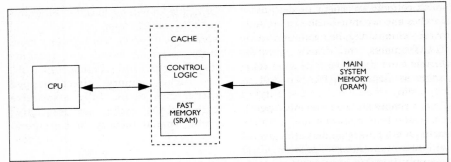

cache This figure shows a block diagram of a cache system design. Cache is a very fast local storage memory (usually made up of fast, expensive static random-access memory) that is used by the microprocessor. Cache fits into a system between the microprocessor and main system memory. It operates as a 'turbocharger' to the slower main system memory by holding copies of code and data that are frequently requested from the main system memory by the microprocessor.

[ISO A special-purpose buffer storage, smaller and faster than main storage, used to hold a copy of instructions and data obtained from main storage and likely to be needed next by the processor.] See **cache, look aside cache,** and **look through cache**.

cache miss An unsatisfied request by the microprocessor for code or data in a cache. Upon a cache miss, the cache requests from the main system memory not only the code or data requests by the microprocessor, but several additional bytes of code or data as well. This is called a 'line'. A line is a string of bytes that is moved from main system memory to the cache when the cache memory is updated. It is the basic unit or minimum amount of code or data transferred between the main system memory and cache. A larger line size increases the number of bytes of code and data copied from main system memory into the cache memory on an update. Increasing line size can increase cache performance by taking advantage of a software's locality of code principle.

Since program code and data is mostly sequential, it is very likely that the next item requested by the microprocessor will be within the line of the previous memory request. As a general rule, increasing line size increases hit rate. However, increasing line size is a trade-off with other system factors. If the line size exceeds the system data bus width, then multiple memory accesses will be required. This will take time and monopolize the memory bus. The processor will have to add wait states if it requires the memory bus when the bus is not available. 'Replacement policy' refers to how the cache memory is updated upon a cache miss. This is important when the cache already contains data. Replacing data that will be needed later will cause a lower hit rate and decreased microprocessor performance. See **cache**.

CACP Central arbitration control point.

CAD 1. Computer-aided drafting. 2. Computer-aided design; specialized industrial hardware and software tools which convert an artist's or designer's sketches into accurate finished diagrams, thereby eliminating the need for calculators, T-squares, and drawing boards. CAD is extensively used by such companies as General Motors for designing, testing, modifying, and specifying motor vehicles and components. Special high-resolution monitors and printers are required, plus large data storage and computer memory. Until recently, CAD was only possible on expensive mainframe or minicomputer systems, but since the introduction of the Intel 80386 and Motorola 68030 microprocessors, CAD has migrated to personal computers. Pronounced 'cad'. ▼

CADD Computer-aided design and drafting; specialized hardware and software tools which produce drawings

C

conforming to engineering conventions. Pronounced 'cad'. See **CAD**. ▼

caddy A protective cassette that holds a CD–ROM. The caddy that houses the compact disk is then placed in the appropriate disk drive. ▼

CAE 1. Computer-aided engineering; specialized hardware and software tools which help develop products faster by assisting designers and engineers with

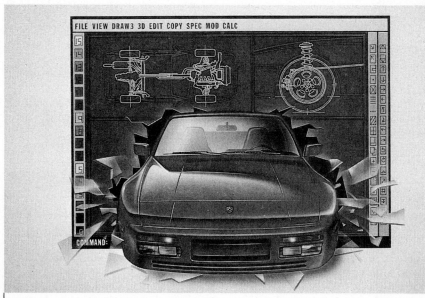

FILE VIEW DRAW3 3D EDIT COPY SPEC MOD CALC

COMMAND:

CAD Using a CAD software package, a designer can make alterations very quickly. Changing the basic shape of a car at its design stage can be done in a matter of minutes.

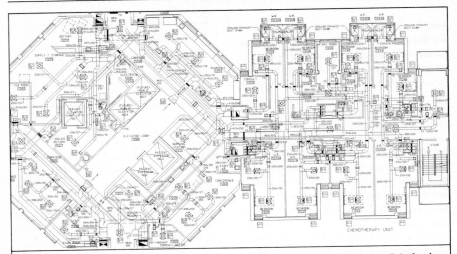

CADD *This two-dimensional drawing was designed with the help of a CADD program. It is the plan view of a ducting system for a chemotherapy unit. It provides the builder with exact specifications and measurements. The same program can be used to generate the electrical, plumbing, and other specifications at varying scales.*

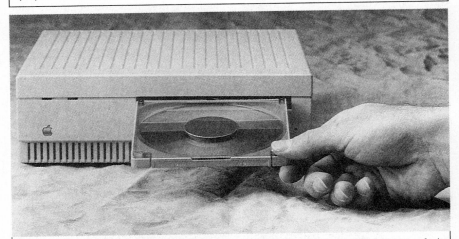

caddy *The caddy, being inserted into an Apple CD–ROM drive, holds the CD–ROM to make it easier to handle and to protect.*

the design, development, calculation, analysis, testing, and experimenting of new products. 2. College of Advanced Education. 3. See **Common Applications Environment** and **X/Open**.

CAFA Computer-aided financial analysis.

CAI 1. Common air interface. 2. Computer-assisted instruction. CAI is a learning tool for students, which takes the student through the subject while monitoring the learning and success rates. More interesting versions of CAI packages include the use of color monitors, video, sound, and graphics-intensive compact disks. See **interactive video disk**.

CAL Computer-aided learning. See **CAI**.

CALC Customer access line charge; the rate paid by a private organization to a telephone company for the connection of a private branch exchange (PBX) to the central exchange (centrex) through trunk lines.

calculator A machine used for arithmetic operations such as adding, subtracting, multiplying, and dividing. Today, sophisticated calculators can be readily found in small devices such as wrist watches. In his 1896 *Dictionary of the English Language,* lexicographer Joseph E. Worcester defined the word 'calculate' as '... a more generic term than compute, reckon or count. Calculate, reckon and count respect mostly the future; compute the past. The astrono-

mer, mathematician and statesman calculate, the chronologist computes; the accountant reckons. Calculate an eclipse; compute the time; compute or reckon the profit and loss; count or number the minutes or stars. This word is often improperly used in the US, in the sense of to expect; as, "I calculate to leave town tomorrow." (Pickering)'. [ISO A device that is especially suitable for performing arithmetic operations but that requires human intervention to alter its stored program, if any, and to initiate each operation or sequence of operations. *Note:* A calculator performs some of the functions of a computer but does not usually operate without frequent human intervention.] ▼

call-accepted signal [ISO A call control signal that is sent by the called data terminal equipment to indicate that it accepts the incoming call.]

callback The ability of a modem to dial and connect to a remote modem that has previously dialed it. Callback is used to ensure that the person originating a call

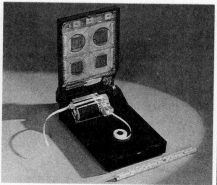

calculator (a) This was the first electronic held-held calculator. It was invented in 1967 at Texas Instruments by Jack St Clair Kilby, Jerry D. Merryman, and James H. Van Tassel. (b) Interior view.

to the modem is an authorized caller, connected to a recognized phone line.

call control procedure [ISO The implementation of a set of protocols necessary to establish and release a call.]

call-detail recording A feature that logs each telephone call, typically by time, number dialed, and charges. The details are then retrievable by the network operator for cost charging by department. Call-detail recording is sometimes called 'SMDR' (station message detail recording). Abbreviation 'CDR'.

call forwarding A PABX feature that lets a user direct calls to another extension. Modern public telephone networks also offer this option to their users. When subscribers leave their home or office, the telephone can be programmed to forward all calls to another number within the suburb.

calling [ISO The process of transmitting selection signals in order to establish a connection between data stations.]

calling sequence [ISO A sequence of instructions together with any associated data necessary to execute a call.]

call-not-accepted signal [ISO A call control signal sent by the called data terminal equipment to indicate that it does not accept the incoming call.]

call waiting A PABX or PSTN feature that lets a user know that another call is stacked.

CAM Computer-aided manufacturing; specialized industrial hardware and software tools which automate the entire

manufacturing process while coordinating the production line/robots, inventory, testing, quality control, and reporting.

Cambridge ring See **time slot**.

camera ready Artwork that is ready to be used for printing. High-end laser printers are capable of producing camera-ready artwork for newsletter-quality publications.

cap height In typography, the height of a capital letter in a font. This is measured in points (a point being 1/72 inch).

CAR Computer-assisted retrieval system.

carbon-based A term used jokingly to refer to situations or errors that were caused by humans.

card 1. An electronic printed circuit board designed to slot into a computer's expansion bus. 2. Any small, wafer-like set of circuits which can be plugged in (or inserted into) a device. Printers have font cards, and new laptop computers offer memory expansion through small, credit-card sized memory cards.

card column [ISO A line of punch positions parallel to the shorter edges of a punch card.]

card deck [ISO A group of punched cards.]

card hopper [ISO The part of a card-processing device that holds the cards to be processed and makes them available to the card feed.]

card path [ISO In a card-processing

device, the path along which cards are moved and guided.]

card punch A typewriter-like machine which punches holes in specially designed 80- or 96-column cards. A card reader can read data which is coded by the combination of holes. [ISO An output unit that produces a record of data in the form of hole patterns in punch cards.]

card reader A machine that translates the pattern of the holes found on punched cards into electrical pulses which in turn are fed into the computer as data for processing. Card readers can operate at speeds of over 1000 cards per minute. [ISO An input unit that reads or senses the holes in a punched card, transforming the data from the hole patterns to electric signals.] See **brush reader** and **photoelectric reader**.

card row [ISO A line of punch positions parallel to the longer edges of a punch card.]

card sorter [ISO A device that deposits punched cards in pockets selected according to the hole patterns in the cards.]

card stacker [ISO The part of a card-processing device that receives the cards after they have been processed.]

caret On most industry-standard keyboards, the caret is the symbol (^) found over the '6' key. It is sometimes used to denote a control function or used as a circumflex accent. Pronounced 'carrot'. See **accent**.

carriage return [ISO The movement of

the print or display position to the first position on the same line.] This should not be confused with a 'carriage return and line feed'.

carrier See **carrier wave**.

carrier band A single-channel, bi-directional transmission medium that can be used as an alternative to broadband in local area networks.

carrier sense [ISO In a local area network, an ongoing activity of a data station to detect whether another station is transmitting.]

carrier sense multiple access See **CSMA**.

carrier signal See **carrier wave**.

carrier wave A continuous signal which can be modulated for the purpose of transmitting a signal (information), as in the case of telegraphy, radio, television, or digital communications. The carrier wave actually carries (through imprint) low-frequency signals which, without the help of the carrier wave, cannot be radiated through space. The oldest and most basic form of modulation is the starting and stopping of a radio wave (as with Morse code, where the carrier is switched on or off). Carrier waves with high frequencies are capable of carrying more information because higher frequencies produce more cycles per second.

carry [ISO The action of transferring a carry digit.]

carry digit [ISO A digit that is generated when a sum or a product in a digit place exceeds the largest number that can be represented in that digit place and that is transferred for processing elsewhere. *Note:* In a positional representation system, a carry digit is transferred to the digit place with next higher weight for processing there.]

carry-save adder [ISO An adder which has, for each digit place, three inputs, one sum output, and one carry output and which does not propagate the carry digits by itself within one cycle of operation.]

cartridge Also called 'magnetic tape cartridge'. [ISO A container holding magnetic tape, driven by friction, that can be processed without separating it from the container. *Note:* When the driving mechanisms are not of concern, the words 'cassette' and 'cartridge' are sometimes used interchangeably.]

CAS 1. Computer-aided selling. 2. Computer-aided surgery.

cascaded carry [ISO In parallel addition, a procedure in which the addition results in a partial sum numeral and a carry numeral which are, in turn, added; this process is repeated until a zero carry is generated.]

Cascade virus An indirect-action file virus that adds 1701 bytes to any .COM file. This virus spreads without detection until a pre-set date (first activated in 1988 between October and December) which triggers what appears to be an entertaining cascade of all the characters on the screen in a rain fashion. This 'dropping' of characters continues until all the characters fall to the bottom of the screen in a heap. Because of the way that Cascade was

programmed, it is unlikely that it will appear again unless someone takes the trouble to reset the time-bomb to a more current or future date. Cascade is sometimes called 'Autumn', 'Blackjack', '1702', or 'Waterfall'. See **indirect-action file virus**. Compare **Traceback virus**.

CASE Computer-aided software engineering; a set of graphic–text tools designed to implement software engineering from formal specifications, through rigorous testing, to highly-automated code generation. Typical CASE applications include module management, project management, and compilers.

case-sensitive Some programs and application software are sensitive to the use of uppercase or lowercase letters. In DOS, one can type commands in either uppercase or lowercase without error, yet in some word processing software, for instance, performing a 'search' function may be case-sensitive. If searching for the name 'Jones', then typing in 'jones' will not find the required field. 'C' source code is also case-sensitive.

cassette Also called 'magnetic tape cassette'. [ISO A container holding magnetic tape, driven on axes, that can be processed without separating it from the container.] The word 'cassette' comes from the Latin *capsa*, meaning 'hold'.

cassette tape The common audio cassette tape which was used (instead of a disk) on some microcomputers as a cheap form of storage. Data transfer is very slow (between 300 and 1200 bits per second).

CAST Computer-aided software testing.
CAT 1. Computer-aided testing. 2. Computer-aided tomography; used in the field of medicine for the image processing (scanning) of body tissues through the analysis of X-ray data.

catalog 1. [ISO A directory of files and libraries, with reference to their locations. *Note:* A catalog may contain other information such as the types of devices in which the files are stored, passwords, blocking factors, etc.] 2. [ISO To enter information about a file or a library into a catalog.]

CATCH Computer-Assisted Terminal Criminal Hunt; an early form of criminal identification. CATCH was first implemented by the New York Police Department in 1978 to help witnesses quickly identify suspects.

cathode-ray tube An output device consisting of a screen (like that used in a television) on which the letters, numbers, or graphics output of a computer can be displayed. Most personal computers use a monitor based on cathode-ray tube technology. Inside the glass tube, an electron beam rapidly and repeatedly traces several hundred closely-spaced horizontal lines on the inside of the screen, which is coated with phosphor. Each individual dot on the display screen is called a 'pixel' (picture element). The more pixels per unit area, the more detail that can be portrayed, and the greater the resolution. Instead of one beam, a color monitor uses three electron beams which scan together. These three beams respectively strike red, green, and blue phosphor dots on the inside of the cathode ray tube. With color monitors,

cathode-ray tube One of the earlier Apple Macintosh computers showing the large cathode-ray tube which formed the user's viewing screen. Known only to a few Apple employees was the fact that on the inside of the first production run of Apple Macintosh was inscribed all the signatures of the design and manufacturing teams.

each triad grouping of red, green, and blue phosphor dots represents one pixel. The word 'cathode' comes from the Greek word *kathodos*, where *kata* means 'down' and *hodos* means 'way'. Abbreviation 'CRT'. See **video adapter**. ⚠

CAT scanning Computer-aided tomography; as used in the field of medicine for scanning (image processing) parts of the body through the analysis of X-ray data. The CAT scanner was invented in 1973 by British research scientist Godfrey Hounsfield.

CATV Community Antenna Television; involves broadband data communications based on radio frequency transmission, generally using 75-ohm coaxial cable as the transmission medium. See **broadband**.

CAV Constant angular velocity; one technique used with most magnetic disks for determining the bit density on a disk. If a disk rotates at constant angular velocity, bit density is lower at the outer diameter than at the inner. See **linear density**.

CBEMA Computer and Business Equipment Manufacturers' Association.

CBL Computer-based learning.

CBM Commodore Business Machines; a Pennsylvanian calculator company that entered the personal computer market with a personal computer model called 'PET' (Personal Electronic Transactor) — offering 8 kilobytes of random-access memory and 14 kilobytes of read-only memory.

CBMS Computer-based message system.

CBT Computer-based training. Using computer-assisted instruction (CAI) techniques, CBT is used to train adults for specific skills such as operating a piece of complex machinery.

CCD Charged coupled device.

CCIR Consultative Committee on International Radio; a permanent group of the International Telecommunications Union (ITU) that deals with the coordination of long-distance radio telecommunications. The other two permanent groups of ITU are the International Frequency Registration Board (IFRB), which regulates the allocation of radio frequencies; and the Consultative Com-

---

NEWSFLASH

In the United States, for each year until 1997, the information technology training and education industry will grow at a compound annual growth rate of 15.3%.

As a result, the education and training market will grow from US$4800 million in 1992 to US$9900 million by year-end 1997.

By 1997, multimedia training will become a US$492 million market in the United States.

Nontraditional course delivery methods such as multimedia and distance learning will outpace the instructor-led format, with growth rates of more than 20% until 1997.

---

mittee on International Telegraphy and Telephony (CCITT), which is the primary group responsible for the development of standards for telephone and data communication systems among participating governments.

CCITT Comité Consultatif International de Télégraphique et Téléphonique; an international body that develops communications standards. It is an advisory committee established under the United Nations, within the International Telecommunications Union (ITU) to recommend worldwide standards. Study groups are set up and assigned a series of technical questions to investigate during a four-year period. Draft recommendations are drawn up for approval by the CCITT. Approval recommendations are classified by a letter and a number published in the CCITT book. The letter relates to a series of recommendations. X.25 and X.400 are examples of CCITT standards. CCITT is a permanent group of the ITU. The other two permanent groups of the ITU are the Consultative Committee on International Radio (CCIR), which deals with the coordination of long-distance radio telecommunications; and the International Frequency Registration Board (IFRB), which regulates the allocation of radio frequencies. The CCITT V series is a set of standards that define modem operations and error correction/data compression, as well as diagnostic tests for modems. See **V.x.**

cc:Mail Microsoft's electronic mail software. See **electronic mail**.

CCP Command control program; a file which contains a series of instructions (commands), used primarily by an operator working in a real-time environment. The command control program is used to save the operator from the time-consuming function of typing lengthy computer codes to issue simple instructions such as logging in, printing, or sorting a file in a particular way.

CCTV Closed circuit television.

CCU 1. See **communications control unit**. 2. Card controller unit.

CD 1. See **compact disk**. 2. Change directory; a DOS command that changes the current directory to a specified directory.

CDB Command descriptor block.

CDC Control Data Corporation; initially a mainframe computer manufacturer.

CD–E A compact disk optical storage

system which allows the user to write, erase, and re-write data to or from the disk — as is possible with a diskette. See **compact disk** and **optical disk**.

CD–G Compact disk–extended graphics; the extended standard established in 1991 that records pictures, photographs, or words in the subcode area of a compact disk, and then displays them to the accompaniment of a tune. The conventional CD–G (as used in older karaoke systems) covered only 16 colors at a time. CD–EG allows 256 colors to be displayed, and picture images can be switched instantaneously by storing two screens in memory.

CDEV Control panel device. Pronounced 'see-dev'.

CD–I Compact Disk–Interactive; a standard for interactive compact disk systems used, for example, in interactive training systems which involve music, video, animation, and speech. This standard was established in 1986 by manufacturers of home electronic equipment to standardize CD–ROMs in the same manner as music-only CDs in order to promote their spread. The CD–I player is designed to use a TV set as a display and to retrieve video information interactively. A computer is incorporated in the CD–I player but the user is not conscious of it. Some home electronic equipment devices, such as a remote controller or a mouse, can be used instead of a keyboard. The CD–I standard provides detailed rules for the central processing unit, the operating system, integrated circuits, data processing systems, and recording systems. Therefore, hardware and software that conform to the CD–I standard are compatible even if the manufacturer is different. However, the strict standardization has caused another problem, that being the apprehension that the CD–I standard may not keep up with the rapid technological innovation of computers. The CD–ROM XA is provided to standardize the CD–ROM data processing system for existing personal computers and game machines using the CD–I audio/video processing system. However, not all software conforming to the CD–ROM XA standard can be reproduced on CD–I players. For this reason, a method called 'CD Bridge' was developed so that even CD–ROM software such as games or electronic publishing can be reproduced on CD–I players. In this method, the CD–I program is pre-written into the software which conforms to the CD–ROM XA standard. The method has begun to be used with EB–XA (electronic book), which is the standard for electronic publishing, photo CDs, and some game machines. Pronounced 'sea-dee-eye'. See **compact disk**.

CD–I FMV Compact Disk–Interactive Full Motion Video; a CD–ROM reproduction standard, based on MPEG1, for the reproduction of animation. CD–I FMV was introduced after manufacturers found it difficult to digitally record (onto CD–ROM) full-motion video such as video cassette recorder images and TV broadcast signals, both of which are composed of 30 frames per second (except for PAL, which broad-casts at 25 frames per second). CD–I's main attraction is the small size of the players, making them portable. See **CD–I**.

CDP Centralized data processing; data processing in which all data collection and computer management is done at a central location, providing a single point of control and security. Typically, large minicomputers or mainframes act as hosts, with a series of nodes which act as the collection points.

CDR See **call-detail recording**.

CD–R A compact disk storage system synonymous with WORM (write once, read many times) systems. See **compact disk**.

CD–ROM Compact disk–read-only memory; an optical secondary storage device that uses compact disk technology to store up to 700 megabytes of data on a single compact disk (4.7 inches in diameter). CD–ROM technology is used to store encyclopedias and dictionaries, because up to 300 000 pages of information may be condensed onto one disk. Some compact disks can only be read, while others can be written on. Although CD–ROM is a read-only technology, its large storage capacity and low price make it an effective way to distribute large-capacity database reference material. Data on a magnetic hard disk is stored in concentric circles, called 'tracks', with each track divided into a given number of sectors. The sectors near the center are physically shorter than those on the outside. A CD–ROM, on the other hand, stores data in a single spiral-shaped track. This one track is divided into many segments, each of equal length. To properly read data, the rotational speed of the optical disk must increase when the read head gets closer to the center, and decrease as the head moves back out. Typical data access time is approximately 0.5 to 1.5 seconds (much slower than a hard disk, at a typical 0.03 seconds). Pronounced

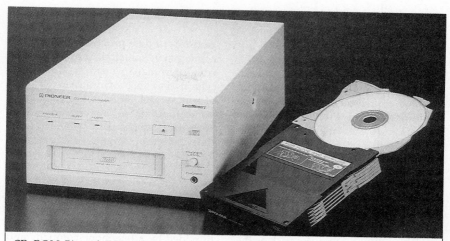

CD–ROM *Pioneer's DRM-604X CD–ROM minichanger allows users to access up to six CD–ROM disks in a single, removable magazine — a technology first introduced by Pioneer. In this model, the disks are loaded into the magazine cartridge, which is then placed into the minichanger. Data can be quickly retrieved, with a maximum change time of five seconds. The minichanger flips from disk to disk, and typical data access time is 300 milliseconds from a single disk. The DRM-604X has a data transfer rate of 614 kbps, with a 128 kb look-ahead cache. The CD–ROM minichanger can also act as a CD–audio juke-box, playing audio compact disks at 153 kbps — the standard speed for music or speech. Output to amplifiers, speakers, and headphones is provided.*

'see-dee-rom'. See **compact disk** and **secondary storage**. ⚠

CD–ROM density The advantage of CD–ROM disks is the high areal density with which they can be recorded. With a linear density of about 25 000 pits per inch (about 25% greater than the highest magnetic bit density achievable today), CD–ROM disks have a raw areal density of about 400 million pits per square inch. Adjusting for encoding, sector overhead, and for very elaborate error correction code mechanisms to cope with a higher raw media error rate than is common in magnetic recording, net user data density is about 320 megabits per square inch, or about 15 times as high as the highest-density magnetic disk products available today.

CD–ROM XA Compact disk–read-only memory extended architecture; an extension of the CD–ROM standard, billed as a hybrid of CD–ROM and CD–I and promoted by Sony and Microsoft. The extension adds ADPCM audio to permit the interleaving of sound and video data to animation (with sound synchronization). See **CD–I**.

CDTV Commodore Dynamic Total Vision; consumer multimedia system from Commodore that included a CD–ROM/CD audio player, Motorola 6800 processor, and infrared remote control.

CDV Compact disk video.

cedilla An accent which is shaped like a small tail (˛) to indicate pronunciation, generally beneath the letter 'c'. See **accent**.

cell The basic unit of a spreadsheet, referenced by its row and column address. A single cell can contain anything from one digit to an entire accounting system, limited only by the program and system memory.

cell animation An animation technique which uses a fixed background, over which clear sheets of celluloid are changed to produce the illusion of movement. This is commonly used in television cartoons. The same effect can be derived from a computer such as the Macintosh, using an animation program (such as MacroMind Director) to produce cell animation. In the same way that cell animation saves the cartoonist from having to re-draw the background with every frame, MacroMind Director saves on disk storage space.

cellular radio The common portable telephone uses cellular radio technology to transmit voice signals via a wireless telephone. This service was first developed in 1971 by AT&T's Bell Laboratories to enhance IMTS (improved mobile telephone service), which limited the number of remote telephone conversations to less than 30 per city the size of New York. Cellular radio technology uses low power frequencies (such as non-operational UHF TV channels), thereby permitting neighboring base stations (cells) to use the same frequencies.

centi- An SI unit prefix for 10^{-2} expressed as 0.01 in decimal notation, as in 'centimeter' (cm). SI symbol 'c'.

centillion See **exponent**.

central exchange See **centrex**.

centralized data processing Data processing in which all data collection and computer management is done at a central location, providing a single point of control and security. Typically, large minicomputers or mainframes act as hosts, with a series of nodes which act as the collection points. Abbreviation 'CDP'.

central processing unit See **CPU**.

centrex Central exchange; generally any telecommunications switching facility provided by a telephone company and made available to organizations through a subscription service. Most private branch exchanges (PBX) are connected through a centrex system via trunk lines.

Centronics The standard parallel printer interface used on PCs. It was named after the Centronics company. Being 8 bits wide and bi-directional, the Centronics port is used for other purposes such as external backup devices, dongles, and controllers.

Century Schoolbook See **New Century Schoolbook**.

CEPT Conference of European Postal and Telecommunications Administrations.

CES Commercial expert system.

C4 An abbreviation used to refer to the collection of activities performed by CAD (computer-aided design), CAM (computer-aided manufacturing), CAE (computer-aided engineering), and CIM (computer-integrated manufacturing).

C4 applications are usually processor-intensive, often requiring math co-processors to help speed-up numeric calculations, and high-resolution graphics for faster image visualization. For quick response times, large amounts of random-access memory are required. C4 applications can work on many different computer platforms, but the most popular include powerful personal computers, and engineering/technical workstations.

C4I Command, control, communications, computers, and Intelligence.

CGA 1. Computer-generated art. 2. Color Graphics Adapter; introduced in 1981, capable of displaying four colors simultaneously (from a possible selection of 16) with a horizontal resolution of 320 pixels (picture elements), and a vertical resolution of 200 pixels. A higher resolution of 640 x 200 can be achieved, but in this way, only one color can be shown at a time. Superior graphics adapters have since been produced, including the Enhanced Graphics Adapter (EGA) developed by IBM in 1984. Characters are formed in an 8 x 8 pixel matrix. See **video adapter**.

CGG Computer-generated graphics.

CGM Computer Graphics Metafile; a file format recognized internationally and used to store and transport object-oriented graphics from one system (or program) to another. Harvard Graphics, Ventura Publisher, Microsoft Windows, and OS/2 are four common programs capable of reading and writing to CGM formats.

CGMA Color/Graphics/Monochrome

Adapter; a graphics adapter introduced in 1985 with the NCR family of personal computers which used split board architecture. This was not a new standard, but a combination of two established standards, functioning as the standard IBM Color Graphics Adapter, as well as the Hercules Monochrome Adapter. See **video adapter**.

CGPM Conférence Générale des Poids et Mesures (General Conference of Weights and Measures). See **SI**.

CGSA Cellular geographic service area.

chad [ISO The material separated from a data medium when punching a hole.]

chained list [ISO A list in which the data elements may be dispersed in storage but in which each data element contains information for locating the next one.]

chained list search [ISO A search that uses a chained list.]

chained printing A word processing function which directs a series of files to print one after the other. This is achieved by placing a command at the end of the first file, instructing the program to automatically print the second file, and so on.

chain printer An impact printer consisting of characters on a chain that rotates past all the print positions. Hammers are aligned behind each character position, and when appropriate characters go by at high speed, each hammer strikes the paper and ribbon, hitting the characters to make an impression. Print speeds may exceed 3000 lines per minute. [ISO An impact printer in which the type slugs are carried by the links of a revolving chain.] See **impact printer**.

CHAM Refers to CHAM of North America, Incorporated — a software and consulting organization based in Huntsville, Alabama, specializing in the computer modeling of processes involving fluid flow, heat transfer, chemical reaction, and combustion. The company changed its name to Adaptive Research Corporation. See **Adaptive Research Corporation**.

change dump [ISO A dump of those storage locations whose contents have changed during a specified period.]

change-over system [ISO A temporary information processing system used to facilitate the transition from an operational system to its successor.]

channel 1. A communication path capable of transmitting data. Channels are derived from multiplexing, and generally do not correspond to physical circuits. Several channels can be multiplexed onto a single physical link. 2. [ISO A means of one-way transmission. *Note:* A channel may be provided, for example, by frequency or time division multiplexing.]

channel access In local area networks, the method of gaining access to the communications channel that links all the devices. Common channel access methods are polling, token ring, and connection.

channel capacity 1. A term that expresses the maximum bit rate that can be handled by the channel (communications path). 2. [ISO The measure of the ability of a given channel subject to specific constraints to transmit messages from a specified message source expressed either as the maximum possible mean transinformation content per character or as the maximum possible average transinformation rate, which can be achieved with an arbitrary small probability of errors by use of an appropriate code.]

character A single letter, number, punctuation mark, or special symbol that can be produced on screen, or printed.

character code Any of several standard sets of binary representations for the alphabet, numerals, and common symbols, such as ASCII, BCD, and EBCDIC. See **ASCII**, **binary-coded decimal**, and **EBCDIC**.

character display device [ISO A display device that provides a representation of data only in the form of graphic characters.]

character generator [ISO A functional unit that converts the coded representation of a character into the graphic representation of the character for display.]

character-oriented Referring to a communications protocol or transmission procedure that carries control information encoded in fields of one or more bytes.

character printer A device similar in concept to a typewriter. It prints one character at a time across the page. Typical character printers are the daisy-wheel and golf-ball printers/typewriters. [ISO A printer that prints a single character at a time. *Note*: A serial printer in this sense may have either a serial or parallel interface.]

character reader [ISO An input unit that performs character recognition.]

character recognition [ISO The identification of characters by automatic means.]

character set The set of acceptable and recognizable characters used by a particular computer system or software package. These are binary-coded, and often follow a standard such as ASCII or EBCDIC. [ISO A finite set of different characters that is complete for a given purpose. *Example:* The international reference version of the character set of ISO 646.] See **ASCII** and **EBCDIC**. ▼

character user interface An interface which displays only characters on the screen, rather than icons and windows. Compare **graphical user interface**.

charge corona A component in a laser printer using a tungsten wire electrode in a reflective shield. When a high DC (direct current) voltage is applied, the electrode ionizes the surrounding air, which in turn transfers charges to the surface of the drum. This corona is used in the charging step of the print cycle. See **laser printer**.

charged atom An atom in which the number of electrons is different from the number of protons. In electricity, a neutral atom (one with a zero charge) has as many electrons as it has protons. That is, the number of electrons in its orbits equal the number of protons in its nucleus. If there is an excess or a deficiency of free electrons in the outer orbit, the atom is said to be 'charged'. However, if there is an excess of electrons (which carry a negative charge), the atom will be negatively charged. If there is a deficiency of electrons, there will be more protons in

•	Bullet	¶	Paragraph sign	≈	Approximately equal
¢	Cent	‰	Per thousand	*	Asterisk
©	Copyright	₧	Pesetas	\	Backslash (Set minus)
c_R	CR (Carriage return)	£	Pound/Sterling	⋈	Bowtie
†	Dagger	℞	Prescription (Rx)	⸱	Centre dot
‡	Double dagger	®	Registered trademark	o	Degree
—	Em dash	»	Right double guillemet	=	Equivalent
...	Em leader (Ellipsis)	"	Right double quote	∞	Infinity
–	En dash	'	Right single quote	∫	Integral
c_E	European currency symbol	§	Section sign	≤	Less than or equal
F_F	FF (Form feed)	SM	Servicemark	◊	Lozenge
ƒ	Florin/Guilder	TM	Trademark	μ	Micro
o	Hollow bullet	¥	Yen	≠	Not equal
H_T	HT (Horizontal tab)	V_T	VT (Vertical tab)	±	Plus or minus
"	Inverted double quote			μ	Proportional
'	Inverted single quote		Common mathematical and	∟	Right angle
•	Large bullet		scientific characters not found	→	Right arrow
«	Left double guillemet		in the ASCII character set.	/	Slash (Fraction)
L_F	LF (Line feed)			Σ	Summation
£	Lire (Italian currency symbol)	|	Absolute value (Divides)	∴	Therefore
N_L	NL (Newline)	Å	Angstrom		

character set *Common typographic symbols not found in the ASCII character set.*

the atom than electrons, so the atom will be positively charged.

charging The first step in the electro-photography process in laser printers. A device called a 'charge corona' is used to ionize the air around the photoreceptor. This ionized air in turn applies a uniform layer of charges over the photoreceptor's surface. See **laser printer** and **photoreceptor**.

chastity lock A device that is the size of a floppy disk that is inserted into the computer's diskette drive. The chastity lock has a key-based locking mechanism that enables the user to affix it inside the drive in order to prevent other users from inserting their own diskettes into the computer. This safeguards the computer against data thieves or unauthorized users, and ensures that viruses cannot be loaded onto the computer by casual users.

Cheapernet A cheaper version of Ethernet. Soon after the introduction of Ethernet, it became apparent that the system was too expensive for many applications in the personal workstation tier of a local area network. International Computers Limited, Hewlett-Packard, and 3Com Corporation proposed a less expensive variant of the basic Ethernet specifications designated by IEEE 802.3, type 10base2 (sometimes called 'Thinnet' or 'Thinwire ENET'). Cheapernet uses more-readily available and less expensive 0.2-inch, 50-ohm coaxial cable with BNC (bayonet nut coupling) connectors. It also dispenses with the transceiver cable by mounting its transceiver on the controller board within each station, with the main cable connecting directly to the board using an 'off-the-shelf' BNC T-connector. The network topology is thus a simple daisy chain, like that used to connect laboratory instruments. Cheapernet maintains the same 10-megabits per second data rate and baseband Manchester signaling as Ethernet, but the lower quality RG58AU cable and BNC connectors decrease the maximum segment length to 600 foot (185 meters) and the maximum number of stations per segment to 30. Whilst the system offers lower wiring and installation costs than Ethernet, its wiring flexibility is decreased. Since Cheapernet is completely compatible with Ethernet, the two can be mixed in the same network, with Cheapernet serving at the subnetwork tier level. Cheapernet is used extensively for laboratory settings and CAD/CAE (computer-aided design and/or computer-aided engineering) workstation clusters where high performance is important and the exposed cabling is acceptable. See **Ethernet** and **10base2**.

check Also called 'data check'. [ISO An operation used to verify data quality or data integrity.]

check bit A bit (zero or one) which is added to a byte so that when transmitted, all bytes will have the same parity. For example, EBCDIC letter 'A' is represented by 11000001. Note that this has three ones, and is therefore an odd number. If using odd parity, the check bit would have to be a '0' so that the quantity of ones remain an odd number (110000010). Should the byte be received at the other end showing an even number of ones (110100010), then the computer knows that the information was corrupted during transmission. Errors could still occur if the incorrectly-transmitted byte contained two reversing errors which coincidentally and erroneously resulted in an odd number of ones. However, the probability of this occurring is very low. The same principles apply when the sending and receiving devices are configured to accept even parity, where the number of ones must always be even.

check box In a graphical user interface like that used in the Macintosh or Windows, the check box is a small box which can be accessed by the mouse for the purpose of selecting or de-selecting an option on the screen.

check digit Also called 'check character'. [ISO A check key consisting of a single digit (character).]

checking program [ISO A diagnostic program that examines source programs or data for errors in syntax, semantics, or conformity to other constraints.]

check key [ISO One or more characters, derived from and appended to a data item, that can be used to detect errors in the data item.]

checkpoint [ISO A sequence of instructions in a computer program for recording the status of execution for re-starting. *Note:* The term 'checkpoint' is also used for the recorded status of execution and for 'executing a checkpoint'.]

check problem [ISO A problem with a known solution used to determine whether a functional unit is operating correctly.]

checksum A number used in data communications to monitor the number of

bits being transmitted between communications devices by means of a simple mathematical algorithm. It is used to ensure that the full complement of bits is received successfully by the receiving device. [ISO The sum of a group of data associated with the group and used for checking purposes. *Note:* The data is either numeric or other character strings regarded as numeric for the purpose of calculating the checksum.] See **check bit**.

checksummer A program which detects changes in executable files by calculating a unique 'signature' for each executable file that it is protecting to prevent widespread damage by quickly detecting computer viruses. In order for a virus to be effective (cause damage as intended), it has to reproduce. On demand, the checksummer program scans through a particular file to see if its 'signature' has been altered (through tampering or scrambling of data by unauthorized users or a virus). In this way, if a virus changes (damages) the file in any way, the checksummer will alert the operator to a variance of the original 'signature'. See **virus**.

chevron A 'V'-shape; one of many possible shapes for a magnetic pattern deposited on a thin film to steer bubbles in a desired direction. Asymmetric chevrons are used in Intel memories. See **bubble memory**.

child transaction See **nested transaction**.

chip An integrated circuit; made from a semiconducting material, usually silicon which is a very common substance in the Earth's crust. It is etched photographically into electrical circuits which act as either transistors, resistors, or capacitors. Modern mass-production techniques have made chips quite inexpensive. Today, a simple microprocessor chip worth only a few dollars is many times more powerful than ENIAC — the first electronic digital calculator which cost the United States Government almost half a million dollars and weighed over 30 tons. The flow of electrons in chips is controlled by the transistors which form switches or gates. Chips are categorized by the number of logic gates available. For example, small-scale integration (SSI) chips each containing up to four logic gates were the first to replace vacuum tubes usually associated with second-generation computers. These developed to medium (MSI), large (LSI), very large (VLSI), and super-large-scale integration (SLSI) which exceeds several hundred thousand logic gates. See **integrated circuit**.

ChipUp A term coined by Acer Incorporated in 1991 when it designed the world's first single-chip CPU upgrade technology. ChipUp allows an owner of an Acer computer (or one that licenses this technology) to upgrade the CPU without having to change the motherboard. ChipUp is a cost-effective way of upgrading a computer to new processor levels. See **Acer Group**.

CHKDSK A simple DOS command for checking the integrity of files on a disk.

choice device [ISO An input device providing one value from a set of alternatives. *Example:* A function keyboard.]

chooser A desk accessory used on Apple Macintosh computers for selecting devices such as printers.

Christensen Protocol A communications protocol developed in the late 1970s by Ward Christensen to perform error checking on data being sent between two data transmission devices. The Christensen Protocol is sometimes known as the 'XModem' protocol. Compare **YModem** and **ZModem**.

chromatic aberration The failure of a lens (or reflective object) to bring to focus the rays of light (image) due to defects in the optical system causing an image to be seen with a colored fringe (typical when a television picture is distorted due to incorrect adjustment or a bad signal). Spherical aberration is the distortion of an image (straight lines become curved).

CICS Customer Information Control System; an IBM program, and mainframe operating environment, designed to enable transactions entered at remote terminals to be processed concurrently by user-written application programs. CICS includes facilities for building and maintaining databases. Pronounced 'kicks'.

CIE 1. Computer-integrated engineering. 2. Commission International de l'Eclairage. The standard reference for color measurement since 1931 has been the CIE Chromaticity Diagram. See **color** and **color monitor**.

CIM Computer-integrated manufacturing; a complete manufacturing control system which incorporates product design and analysis, quality control, inventory control, cost accounting, purchasing, and order entry. It is used to improve the productivity of the entire manufacturing enterprise, not just to integrate the manufacturing process. In a manufacturing company, it affects every department including manufacturing, factory automation, and information services. Controlling this entire process is a centralized database which is shared by all departments.

circuit 1. A communications path (channel) between two points. A circuit is a 'complete' path for electrical current flow, including the voltage source. An open circuit is one which prevents current flow. There are two types of circuits: series circuits, and parallel circuits. In a series circuit, there is only one path through which current can flow to complete the circuit, meaning

that all electrical current must flow through every component in the circuit. In a parallel circuit, there are as many paths for current to flow as there are parallel legs in the circuit. A series-parallel circuit is simply a combination of series and parallel circuits. See **integrated circuit**. 2. A collection of electronic components connected in such a way that they perform a task. ⚠

circuit board A sheet of non-conducting fiberglass or plastic that serves to support and interconnect a collection of chips and other devices which may be used in a computer. Modern boards are covered with copper which is etched with acid, leaving conducting pathways for microprocessors or other chips to be affixed. ▼

circuit-switched network The method used in the Public Switched Telephone Network (PSTN) to interconnect all telephone equipment in the huge public

circuit This is a much-expanded photograph of a modern silicon chip. The connections to the other circuits can be seen around the edges. The processor logic is at the top, and the memory circuits are on the rest of the chip. The memory appears very uniform to the eye because it consists of an enormous number of identical circuits.

circuit board A bird's-eye view of a circuit board. The main Motorola microprocessor can be seen at the top.

telephone system. All telephones are connected through a hierarchy of switching centers, commonly called the 'dial-up' system. The dial-up system connects only two points and is known as a 'point-to-point connection'. The caller dials the number of the destination telephone, and the PSTN assigns a specific physical circuit to the call. The telephones have exclusive use of this circuit for the duration of the call. The entire public telephone system is a complex network of switching centers. Because of the many switching centers and the manner in which they are organized, nearly all telephones can communicate with all other telephones. When circuit switching is used for data transmission, a specific physical channel is selected for the users. Data is transmitted over a 'local loop' between the customer's site and the associated switching center. Data is transmitted between switching centers over 'trunk' channels. These trunks are furnished by the local telephone company for local calls, or by a long-distance carrier for long-distance calls. In some local and most long-distance connections, signals are digitized and routed through a high-speed digital transmission trunk (which may use microwave, satellites, or fiber optics). In older switching equipment, the call setup procedure would take over ten seconds. Digital circuit-switching equipment that is now used in modern exchanges is capable of setting up calls in milliseconds. The primary advantages of a switched connection are that it is relatively inexpensive, and it provides a transparent path for transmitting data between the communications stations, which means that connected stations can use their own data formats, synchronization schemes,

and protocols without consideration for those in use at the receiving end. The primary disadvantage of the switched telephone network is the limitation on transmission speed. The maximum transmission speed on dial-up lines is 19 200 bits per second. The practical limitation is 2400 bits per second. Also, because of the number of possible routes, the transmission speed will vary at different points of the route.

circuit switching The temporary direct electrical connection of two or more channels between two or more points in order to provide the user with exclusive use of an open channel with which to exchange information. This is also called 'line switching'. [ISO A process that, on demand, connects two or more data terminal equipment and permits the exclusive use of a data circuit between them until the connection is released.] See **circuit-switched network**. Compare **packet-switched data network**.

circular reference Usually refers to an error in a spreadsheet program where two or more cells are logically connected such that they are dependent upon each other in a closed loop. In such a situation, calculation may never reach a stable solution.

circumflex An accent which is shaped like an upside down 'v' (^) to indicate pronunciation. See **accent**.

CISC Complex instruction set computing. Most personal computers have a CISC-based central processing unit capable of recognizing over 100 instructions for immediate computation. A faster technology commonly used in professional workstations, and more recently in personal computers, is a reduced instruction set computing (RISC) which reduces the number of instructions as much as possible. RISC is cheaper to produce and debug, and is designed to run up to 75% faster than complex instruction set computing. MISC (minimal instruction set computing) is another form of RISC produced by Teraplex of Illinois, in the United States. CISC is pronounced 'sisk'.

CKD See **Count Key Data format**.

CL Command language. See **job control language**.

clear [ISO To cause one or more storage locations to be set in a prescribed state, usually that corresponding to zero or that corresponding to the space character.]

clear all function [ISO The function that allows the cancelation of data in the working registers and storage devices.]

clear entry function [ISO The function that allows the cancelation of data entered into a calculator but not yet processed.]

clear memory function [ISO The function that allows the cancelation of data in the storage devices to which the keys refer. *Note:* There may be other 'clear' keys on the calculator used to cancel specified functions.]

client In a local area network, a node with processing capabilities such as a computer that can request information or applications from the file server. The word 'client' comes from the Latin *cluere*, meaning 'hear, obey'.

client-based application In a local area network, any application that resides exclusively on a user's (client's) workstation. This is useful when the workstation is a portable personal computer which may need to be disconnected and taken off site. The application therefore is not dependent on the server nor the network.

client/server architecture Architecture which splits an application into a 'front-end' client application and a 'back-end' server component as the basis for distributed applications. On the front end, the client applications running on a workstation gather data from the user, prepare it for the server, and then issue a request to the server. On the back end, the server waits for requests from its clients. When it receives a request, the server processes it and returns the requested information to the client. The client then presents the data to the user through its own user interface. Client/server architecture also makes it possible for a wide range of front-end client applications such as databases, spreadsheets, accounting packages, word

NEWSFLASH

On a platform basis, UNIX will continue to dominate the operating system market throughout the world, but NetWare and Windows NT will make significant strides. In 1997, UNIX will still account for 69.7% of market revenues.

Client/server environments will make up 77% of the advanced operating environment database server software revenues in 1997, up from 49.1% in 1992.

processors, and others to simultaneously share the same data. This provides a high level of data integrity, concurrency control, and improved performance. Client/server architecture allows each worker to use the application best suited to the particular job — order entry can be performed with dBASE, sales analysis with Microsoft Excel, and so on — each sharing the same data and services provided by Microsoft SQL Server. In addition, since applications are able to access data from various server-based applications directly, they need not be concerned with translating data from one application's data format to another (as is generally the case) in order to share information with other products. If an application is compatible with a server-based application, it can exchange data with any other front-end application that runs on that server.

client/server computing Networking in which many different networks and databases may be accessed from a single personal computer. User demand is rapidly driving the direction of personal computer communications toward sophisticated systems that link many types of networks. A securities salesperson, for example, may require access to three types of information from three different computer sources. First, current stock prices, which may require a tie to a private database service in another city. Second, an order entry system, which may be maintained on a company mainframe in another state. And third, current customer accounts, which may be maintained on a local area network (LAN). Through proper network integration and the use of multitasking operating systems, the salesperson can access all three func-

tions quickly from a single personal computer. For computers in LANs to access other wide area networks, one personal computer in the LAN must be configured using special hardware and software to function as a gateway. 'Gateway' is a generic term that refers to a device that allows different networks using different protocols to be connected.

clip art A collection of presentation graphics images available on paper for an artist to re-size and paste on artwork for the purpose of printing. There are clip art subscription services which mail topical and seasonal images. These same images can be digitized and sold on disk. Once accessed by a computer, the clip art images may be re-sized, rotated, or re-touched, then output to a high-resolution laser printer for photocopying or offset printing. ▼

clipboard (In a software application) a buffer (temporary storage area) for text and graphics which may have been cut, or copied from a file. Information in the clipboard is available to be pasted in another area, or moved to another application. If the contents of the clipboard are not saved, they will be lost once the power is switched off.

clipping [ISO Removing those display elements that lie outside a given boundary.]

CLNP Connectionless Network Protocol; a protocol used in the network layer of the OSI reference model.

clock 1. An electronic circuit which regulates the synchronization of the flow of information through a compu-

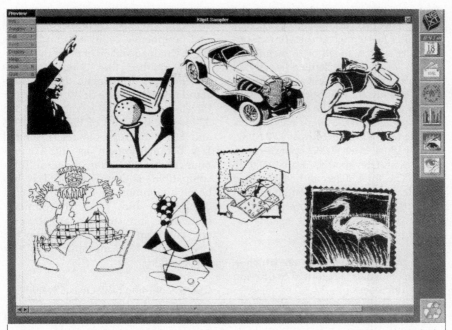

clip art *Drawings shown here are from the Klip It collection containing nearly 400 images in both EPS and TIFF formats. Klip It can usually be imported to word processing, publishing, or drawing applications, allowing the addition of illustrations to letters, documents, newsletters, and presentations.*

ter's internal communications channel. This clock generates evenly-spaced pulses at speeds of millions of cycles per second. [ISO A device that generates periodic, accurately-spaced signals used for such purposes as timing, regulation of the operations of a processor, or generation of interrupts.] 2. Another circuit on the motherboard that tracks real time in hours, minutes, and seconds. The word 'clock' comes from the Latin word *clocca*, meaning 'bell'.

clock/calendar board An add-on board that keeps track of real time in hours, minutes, and seconds. The built-in battery ensures the clock and calendar

remain active while the power is switched off.

clock cycle [ISO The time period, generally derived from an oscillator, that is used for sequencing data flow and synchronizing one or more functions.]

clock signal [ISO A periodic signal used for synchronization or for measuring intervals of time.]

clock speed Computer manufacturers often tag their personal computer with a model number plus the clock speed number. For example, the number 66 which appears in the name 'Compaq

ProLinea 486/66' actually refers to the clock speed, meaning this particular computer has a microprocessor that operates at a clock speed of 66 megahertz (MHz). Tasks which depend heavily on the central processing unit are performed more quickly by microprocessors with higher clock speeds. The original microprocessor used in IBM personal computers, the Intel 8088, operates at 4.77 MHz. The original Intel 80286 operates at 6 MHz, with later models available at 25 MHz. The Intel 80386 and 80486 chips operate at clock speeds ranging from 16 to 100 MHz. The Pentium microprocessor is available in clock speeds exceeding 100 MHz. See **hertz**.

clock track [ISO A track on which a pattern of signals is recorded to provide timing references.]

clone Software or hardware which is almost identical to an original. (Biologically, a clone is any individual produced asexually from only one ancestor. The word also refers to an identical copy of a person or thing.) The term 'IBM clone' usually refers to a personal computer which performs and functions in the same way as an IBM personal computer. Although Compaq Computer Corporation is now setting standards in the industry, it started out as a company that manufactured clones — personal computers which were compatible with, and in some cases superior to, the original IBM model. To protect its investment after several companies started manufacturing clones of the IBM Personal Computer, IBM relaunched its personal computer range in 1986 with a closed-architecture series called 'PS/2' (Personal System 2). The PS/2 was designed using a new bus architecture called

'Micro Channel Architecture' (MCA) which meant existing industry software and peripherals could not function on PS/2. Compaq and eight other manufacturers (dubbed the 'Gang of Nine') joined forces to maintain the industry-standard architecture (ISA), and further developed it to take advantage of the 32-bit bus structure of the Intel 80386 and 80486 microprocessors. Extended ISA became known as 'EISA', pronounced 'e-sah'. Today, the term 'IBM-compatible' is confusing, and it has become common to refer to personal computers, and personal computer systems, as industry-standard computers. The term 'clone' comes from the Greek word *klou*, meaning 'twig' (for propagation).

CLOS Common LISP Object System.

closed architecture An architecture that is compatible only with hardware and software produced from a single vendor. Compare **open architecture**.

closed user group [ISO A group of specified users of a data network that is assigned a facility which permits them to communicate with each other but precludes communication with all other users of the service or services. *Note*: A user data terminal equipment may belong to more than one closed user group.]

closed user group with outgoing access [ISO A closed user group that has a user to whom a facility is assigned which enables that user to communicate with other users of a data network transmission service where appropriate, that has users having a data terminal equipment connected to any other switched network to which interworking facilities are available, or both.]

cluster A group of data stored together on one or more sectors of a floppy disk or hard disk (a sector usually contains 512 bytes of data). When DOS stores data on a disk, it usually breaks the data into smaller sections which it writes at various places on the disk as appropriate. The location of each cluster is recorded in a file allocation table (FAT).

CLV Constant linear velocity; a technique used for increasing the capacity of optical disks by keeping the linear (bit) density constant. This requires the disk to spin more slowly when the outer tracks are being accessed, and more rapidly when the inner tracks are being accessed. If a disk rotates at constant angular velocity, bit density is lower at the outer diameter than at the inner. See **linear density**.

cm Centimeter. See **meter**.

CM Central memory.

CMI Computer-managed instruction.

CMIP Common Management Information Protocols; a group of network management standards defined by ISO.

CMIS Common Management Information Services; a group of network management standards defined by ISO.

CMISL Carnegie-Mellon's Intelligent Systems Laboratory.

CML Computer-managed learning.

CMOS Complementary (symmetry)

metal-oxide semiconductor; a microprocessor (memory chip) that permits many components to be packed together in a very small area. CMOS uses a very small electric current, thereby generating very little heat, making it suitable for very-large-scale integration. CMOS chips are nonvolatile, meaning they retain their information even after the power is switched off. They can be found in digital computers, operational amplifiers, calculators, watches, analog-to-digital converters, telecommunications, and data communications. The main characteristics of CMOS technology are low power consumption, high noise immunity, and slow speed. The low power consumption is inherent to the nature of the CMOS circuit. The noise immunity is due partly to the CMOS logic levels, and (in older versions) partly to the slowness of the circuits. The slow speed was due to the technology used to construct the transistors in the circuit. This technology is called 'metal-gate CMOS', because the transistor gates are formed by metal deposition. More importantly, the gates are formed after the drain and source regions have been defined, and must overlap the source and drain somewhat to allow for alignment tolerances. This overlap, plus the relatively large size of the transistors, results in high electrode capacitance; this is what limits the speed of the circuit. An even more advanced technique which requires even less power is a variation of this technology called 'high-speed CMOS' (HSCMOS). HSCMOS became feasible with the development of the self-aligning silicon-gate technology. In this process, polysilicon gates are deposited before the source and drain regions are defined. Then the source and drain regions are formed by ion implantation using the gate itself as a mask for the implementation. This eliminates most of the overlap capacitance. In addition, the process allows smaller transistors, resulting in a significant increase in circuit speed. The size reduction that contributes to the higher speed also demands an accompanying reduction in the maximum supply voltage — HSCMOS is generally limited to 6 volts. See **MOS**.

CMOS RAM C̲omplementary (symmetry) m̲etal-o̲xide s̲emiconductor r̲andom-access m̲emory; a type of random-access memory (used in newer personal computers) which uses special low-powered chips with battery backup, allowing information to be saved after the power is turned off. The batteries can last up to three years. Along with memory size and type of peripheral devices, CMOS RAM also keeps track of the time and date. One of the main reasons for using CMOS is to conserve power, but this does not just relate to reducing electricity consumption, nor does it necessarily relate to minimizing battery operation. The main reason for conserving power is to be able to put more functionality into a smaller space. Reduced power consumption allows the use of smaller and lighter power supplies. With less heat generated, denser packaging of circuit components is possible, and expensive fans and blowers can usually be eliminated. A cooler-running chip is also more reliable, since most random and wear-out failures relate to high temperature. Also, the lower power dissipation allows more functions to be integrated onto the chip. See **CMOS**.

CMYK C̲yan (blue), m̲agenta (dark pink), y̲ellow, and black̲; the main colors used in the printing process.

CNE Certified Network Engineer; a qualification implemented by Novell for its authorized resellers and education and service providers.

coarse-grain parallel processing See **parallel processing**.

coax See **coaxial cable**.

coaxial cable This is a relatively inflexible cable that consists of an inner cylindrical conductor (usually copper) surrounded by an insulator and then encased in a wire mesh or metal sheath. Coaxial cable is used for baseband and broadband communications networks, including local and wide area networks. It is used for cable television (RF and video) and in computer networks (such as Ethernet), because the cable is relatively free from external interference and permits very high transmission rates (maximum 300 million bits per second). Coaxial cable has a relatively high bandwidth and a moderate to high cost, and offers a wide choice of splitters, taps, and connectors. High-quality double-shielded coaxial cable is thick, heavy, and expensive, with segment length limited to 1640 foot (500 meters) in a 10-megabits-per-second Ethernet LAN due to signal degradation. A thinner coaxial cable that is lighter and less expensive will also support 10-megabits-per-second data rates, but is limited in length to 607 foot (185 meters). Abbreviation 'coax'.

COBOL C̲ommon B̲usiness-O̲riented L̲anguage; a high-level programming language developed in 1959 for business and commercial applications. ANSI first standardized COBOL in 1968, then later in 1974 standardized its own version called 'ANS-COBOL' (revised in 1985). COBOL programmers often criticize the language as being cumbersome and inefficient, yet it is easy to learn, using English words such as 'add', 'terminate', and 'move'. COBOL must be translated to serve as communication between the programmer and the computer. The COBOL program (the source program) written by a programmer is input to a COBOL compiler program which translates the COBOL program into a machine-language program called the 'object program'. Since each machine language varies from computer to computer, each computer would need its own COBOL compiler program to perform the translation from the COBOL language to the specific machine-language program. The smallest element in the COBOL language is the 'character'. A character is a digit, a letter of the alphabet, or a symbol. A COBOL word is one possible result obtained when one or more COBOL characters are joined in a sequence of contiguous characters. Just as English words are determined by rules of spelling, COBOL words are formed by following a specific set of rules. Using the COBOL rules of grammar, the COBOL words and COBOL punctuation characters are combined into statements, sentences, paragraphs, and sections. Pronounced 'coe-boll'. See **CODASYL** and **programming language**.

COBOL word A character-string of not more than 30 characters which forms a user-defined word, a system-name, or a reserved word.

CoCom Coordinating Committee for Multilateral Export Controls; a committee in the United States that regulates trade practices for the sale of supercomputers. Currently, only the following 23 member countries can purchase supercomputers from manufacturers in the United States: Australia, Austria, Belgium, Canada, Denmark, Finland, France, Germany, Greece, Iceland, Italy, Ireland, Japan, Luxembourg, Netherlands, New Zealand, Norway, Portugal, Spain, Sweden, Switzerland, Turkey, and the United Kingdom. See **supercomputer**.

Codabar A bar code system used for industrial applications which require only numeric labeling, such as those used in a library circulation system or a parcel tracking system. Codabar offers relatively wide inter-character spacing. It can also encode the following extra six characters: '$ - : / . +'. See **bar code**.

CODASYL Conference on Data System Languages; a committee of government and private-sector representatives which was formed in 1959 at the request of the United States Department of Defense. Its aim was to develop a high-level business-oriented computer programming language. In 1959, CODASYL introduced COBOL. CODASYL is also responsible for proposing standard data definition and data manipulation languages for databases conforming to the network model. The Forms Interface Management System (FIMS) standard was also initiated by CODASYL. In September 1962, the American National Standards Institute (ANSI) set up a committee to work on the definition of a standard COBOL programming language. This standardization effort was based on the technical content of COBOL as defined by the CODASYL COBOL Committee. In August 1968, American National Standard COBOL X3.23-1968 was approved. Pronounced 'coe-da-sil'. See **COBOL**.

CODASYL-compliant (Of a network database) complying with and conforming to standards issued by the Conference on Data Systems Languages, which has been active in developing network database specifications. See **network database**.

Codd, Edgar See **RDBMS**.

code 1. Usually refers to the type of language used to write a particular program. See **programming language**. 2. [ISO A collection of rules that maps the elements of one set onto the elements of a second set. *Notes:* (a) The elements may be characters or character strings. (b) The first set is the coded set and the second is the code element set. (c) An element of the code element set may be related to more than one element of the coded set but the reverse is not true.] 3. (Colloquial) All or part of a computer program. 4. To write code.

CODEC 1. Coder–decoder. Pronounced 'ko-dek'. 2. Compression/decompression (typically of video).

code converter [ISO A functional unit that changes the representation of data by using one code in place of another or one coded character set in place of another.]

coded character set [ISO A coded set whose elements are single characters. *Example*: The characters of an alphabet

when they are mapped onto a set of, for example 7-bit binary string.]

coded element [ISO The result of applying a code to an element of a coded set. *Examples*: (a) 'CDG' as the representation of Paris-Charles-De-Gaulle in the code for three-letter representation of airport names. (b) The seven binary digits representing the delete character in ISO 646.]

coded image [ISO A representation of a display image in a form suitable for storage and processing.]

coded set [ISO A set of elements which is mapped onto another set according to a code. *Examples:* A list of the names of airports which is mapped onto a corresponding set of three-letter abbreviations.]

code element set [ISO The result of applying a code to all elements of a coded set. *Example:* All the three-letter international representations of airport names.]

code extension character [ISO A control character used to indicate that one or more of the succeeding coded elements are to be interpreted according to a different code. *Note:* Code extension characters are described in ISO 646 and ISO 2022.]

code-independent data communication [ISO A mode of data communication that uses a character-oriented protocol that does not depend on the character set nor code used by the data source.]

Code 39 A bar code system adopted by the American National Standards

Institute (ANSI) in 1983, which is used for industrial applications which require alphanumeric labeling such as transaction documentation, medical records, and court records. Code 39 can also encode the following four extra characters: '$ / + %'. See **bar code**.

code-transparent data communication [ISO A mode of data communication that uses a bit-oriented protocol that does not depend on the bit sequence structure used by the data source.]

coefficient unit [ISO A functional unit whose output analog variable is equal to the input analog variable multiplied by a constant.]

COF Common object format.

coincident-current selection [ISO In an array of magnetic storage cells, the selective switching of one cell in the array by the simultaneous application of one or more currents such that the resultant magneto-motive force exceeds a threshold value only in the selected cell.]

Col. Column.

cold boot See **cold start**.

cold start The resetting of all functions in a computer by switching the electrical power off, then on again. Sometimes a cold start is required when a computer system crashes during its processing cycle, and all previous unsaved processing is lost. If processing is interrupted in a minor way, then a warm start is sometimes sufficient to resume from where an operator left off. Also known as 'cold boot'. See **boot**.

collate [ISO To arrange two or more sets of data into a single one according to a predetermined order.]

collator [ISO A device that collates, merges, or matches sets of punched cards or other documents.]

collision The simultaneous transmission of data by two or more workstations on a network to the same cable, resulting in a bad transmission which cannot be used. Some networks have an in-built checking device which detects collision and re-directs the traffic. [ISO An unwanted condition that results from concurrent transmissions on a channel.] See **CSMA/CA** and **CSMA/CD**.

collision enforcement [ISO In a CSMA/ CD network, the transmission of a jam signal by a data station after it has detected a collision, to ensure that all other data stations become aware of the collision.]

color 1. In word processing and typography, the distribution of word spacing in a large block of text. For example, text which has too many obvious hyphenations, bad word breaks, bad inter-character spacing, displeasing inter-word spacing, and 'rivers of white' is said to be 'off color'. 2. Color cards and color monitors available from companies like RasterOps can use a 19-inch color monitor to display 3000 times more color than can be found in an average photograph. Some 24-bit color boards allow the user to select from a palette of over 16.7 million colors and display 786 432 of them at any one time. In theory, one can create an infinite variety of colors by combining various intensities of red, green, and blue light

Light	Approximate wavelength in nanometers (nm)
Violet	420
Blue	460
Blue-green	490
Green	530
Yellow-green	550
Yellow	590
Orange	620
Red	660
Deep red	740

color The human retina is sensitive to a portion of the electromagnetic spectrum. This is considered to extend from 400 to 800 nanometers (nm). The visual spectra produces color when white light, through dispersion, is broken down into its wavelength components. The frequency band which corresponds to this is between 3.5×10^{14} and 7.5×10^{14} Hz.

which are called 'additive primaries' because, added together, they produce white light. In contrast, the primary colors of reflected light are magenta (dark pink), yellow, and cyan (blue). These are the principal colors human eyes pick up off objects such as walls, shirts, and trees, and these are known as 'subtractive primaries' because each absorbs (subtracts) one of the primaries from white light and reflects the others. For example, yellow paint is so because the paint absorbs blue light, reflecting red and green; hence, the eyes see this as yellow. Similarly, mixing all three subtractive primaries produces black, because all light is absorbed and none reflected. Since 1931, the standard reference for color measurement has been the CIE (Commission International de l'Eclairage) Chromaticity Diagram. See **color monitor**. ⋀

color cycling A technique that simulates motion in a video by changing colors.

Color Graphics Adapter Refers to a graphics adapter introduced in 1981, capable of displaying four colors simultaneously (from a possible selection of 16), with a horizontal resolution of 320 pixels (picture elements) and a vertical resolution of 200 pixels. A higher resolution of 640 x 200 can be achieved, but in this way, only one color can be shown at a time. Superior graphics adapters have since been produced, including the Enhanced Graphics Adapter (EGA) developed by IBM in 1984. Characters are formed in an 8 x 8 pixel matrix. Abbreviation 'CGA'. See **video adapter**.

Color/Graphics/Monochrome Adapter A graphics adapter introduced in 1985 with the NCR family of personal computers which used split-board architecture. This was not a new standard, but a combination of two established standards. It supports the function of the standard IBM Color Graphics Adapter, as well as the Hercules Monochrome Adapter. Abbreviation 'CGMA'. See **video adapter**.

color keying To superimpose one image over another to produce special effects on a video.

color monitor A computer display screen capable of displaying several colors, unlike a monochrome monitor which can only display one color such as amber or green. Color monitors (and television sets) employ light to create screen images using only red, green, and blue phosphors. A monitor creates different colors by varying the intensities of its electron gun. If all three guns fire at full (100%) intensity, the three phosphors add up to white (glows white). The video board codes all other colors as percentages of the full intensity. For example, '0.3R 0.9G 0.4B' means 30% red, 90% green, and 40% blue (hence the term 'RGB'), forming green light. To simplify matters, some graphics programs allow the user to specify color using the traditional terms: hue, saturation, and brightness. 'Hue' is the wavelength of light, determining whether one sees red or yellow, for example. Hues include all the colors of the spectrum plus magentas and purples. 'Saturation' refers to vividness, or the absence of white in a color; it is the difference between pink and red or between lavender and purple. 'Brightness', sometimes called 'value', is similar to lightness (not whiteness). It is the difference between light and dark shades of a color, assuming they have the same hue and saturation. See **color** and **video adapter**.

color separation Output which splits the original artwork into separate colors for printing in accordance with the specifications required by the color printing process.

COM Computer output microfilm; rolls or sheets of film (sometimes called 'microfiche') on which very small images are photographed, and later read using a microfilm reader. On one 10 x 15 centimeter sheet of microfilm, 200 quarto or A4 pages can be stored, thereby saving paper and storage space.

comb [ISO In a magnetic disk unit, an assembly of access arms that moves as a unit.]

combinational circuit [ISO A logic device whose output values, at any given instant, depend on the input values at that instant. *Note:* A combinational circuit is a special case of a sequential circuit whose internal state is not taken into account.]

combinatorial explosion See **combinatorics**.

combinatorics A branch of higher mathematics which studies, through analysis, all the permutations and elements in finite sets. In computing, a combinatorial explosion occurs when these sets and their possibilities are too large and too numerous for the computer to solve.

combined station [ISO In high-level data link control (HDLC), the part of a data station that supports the combined control functions of the data link and that generates commands and responses for transmission and interprets received commands and responses. *Note:* Specific responsibilities assigned to a combined station include initialization of control signal interchange, organization of data flow, interpretation of received commands, and generation of appropriate responses and actions regarding error control and error recovery functions at the data link level.]

COMDEX Computer Dealers' Exposition; a large annual computer trade show / exhibition which includes a series of seminars and product announcements.

comma-delimited file Any data file (though usually in ASCII) which separates each data item (or field) by a comma (,). When converting files from one application (or environment) to another, the comma acts as a guide. For example, if a database of names and addresses is being copied from Paradox to WordPerfect, the comma-delimited file might read: Mr,John,Smith,124, East, Provo,Utah,84606.

command Any signal issued by a user to the computer in order to initiate an action, calculation, termination, or otherwise control a specific operation or device. In command-driven programs and environments (such as DOS), the user must remember the command statements and type them in. Menu-driven programs offer the user on-screen menus from which commands may be chosen. Compare **graphical user interface**.

command control program A file which contains a series of instructions (commands), used primarily by an operator working in a real-time environment. The command control program is used to save the operator from the time-consuming function of typing lengthy computer codes to issue simple instructions such as logging in, printing, or sorting a file in a particular way. Abbreviation 'CCP'.

command language 1. [ISO A set of procedural operations with a related syntax, used to indicate the functions to be performed by an operating system.] 2. See **job control language**.

command-line operating system Any operating system (such as DOS) which relies upon the entry of user-initiated commands via the keyboard. Compare **graphical user interface**.

comment [ISO A language construct for the inclusion of text in a program and having no impact on the execution of the program. *Note:* Comments are used to explain certain aspects of the program.]

Commodore See **CBM**.

Common Applications Environment The formation of the X/Open Company saw an international group of computer systems suppliers and software developers establish a Common Applications Environment (CAE) to the mutual advantage of users, independent software vendors, and computer suppliers. Applications written to operate in this environment are portable at the source-code level to a wide range of machines. CAE thereby releases the user from dependence on a single supplier, reduces the necessary investment in applications, considerably increases the market for independent software, and opens up the market for systems suppliers. The technical foundations of CAE are the interfaces specified in the IEEE 1003.1-1988 POSIX standard. See **X/Open**.

common carrier A government-approved communications service provider, offering switched lines (as used for telephone connection) and private (leased) lines. These can be dedicated to a particular destination. For example, COMSAT (Communications Satellite Corporation) is a private United States' satellite carrier, established by Congress in 1962 for the coordination and construction of satellite communications and facilities for international voice and data communications. It is a member of the International Telecommunications Satellite Consortium (INTELSAT). A special carrier, on the other hand, offers high-capacity data transmission lines in competition with public telephone companies. These may be fiber optics, coaxial cables, or microwaves, before they finally connect to the standard telephone lines.

Common LISP See **LISP.**

common mode rejection [ISO The capability of a differential amplifier to suppress the effects of the common mode voltage.]

common mode voltage [ISO In a differential amplifier, that unwanted part of the voltage, between each input connection point and ground, that is added to the voltage of each original signal.]

Common Open Software Environment See **COSE.**

comm port The serial (communications) port in a personal computer.

Comm Server A communications software program from Microsoft which provides a gateway between various industry-standard personal computers and networks. In 1983, Digital Communications Associates (DCA) introduced the IRMA card which enabled a personal computer to emulate an IBM 3270-style terminal while providing a direct connection to the IBM host network. Terminal emulations made it possible for mainframe data to be sent to the personal computer, but only one screenful at a time. This evolved into file transfer, which allowed entire files to be sent to and from the mainframe. Later, gateway communications was devel-

oped, which enabled one personal computer on a network to connect to the mainframe and provide connectivity support for the other personal computers on a local area network (LAN).

communication channel Generally refers to the telephone network which carries the analog signal from the primary station to the secondary station, or vice versa. Several other terms that are frequently used to refer to the communication channel include communication 'link', 'facility', and 'circuit'. The communication channel itself may use various combinations of transmitting media in series. Microwave links and satellite links are also rapidly increasing in popularity. Although most communication channels consist of public telephone lines, user-owned links are installed and maintained by the user. These are usually installed on the user's property and use four wire circuits where one pair of wires is used for transmitted data and another pair for received data. These adapters are designed to transfer serial data within a building complex at high speed — 48 000 bits per second or higher. There is a distance limitation of 2500 foot (762.5 meters) to 12 000 foot (3660 meters), depending upon the particular design.

communications adapter A hardware feature on most processors and terminals that permits telecommunications lines to be attached. It converts data from parallel to serial for output, and from serial to parallel for input.

communications control unit A device used to maintain control over a communications network by handling a variety of functions such as converting code and directing communications 'traffic'. Such a device is sometimes called a 'concentrator'.

communications parameters In serial printing and telecommunications, the settings that customize serial communications for the hardware being used.

communications processor A processor and multiplexer combination that can function as a communication controller for a central processing unit (CPU). Used in this way, it is called a 'front-end', and the objective is to remove the communication processing burden from the CPU. It can also be used at a remote location to concentrate many low-speed lines onto one or two high-speed lines to the CPU. Used in this way, it is called a 'line concentrator'. It can also function as a message switcher in a large network and would then be called a 'node switch'.

communications protocol For computers engaged in telecommunications, the protocol (settings and standards) must be the same for both devices when receiving and transmitting information. A communications program (such as PC-Talk and QModem) can be used to ensure that the baud rate, duplex, parity, data bits, and stop bits are correctly set.

Communications Satellite Corporation Established by the United States Government in 1962, the Communications Satellite Corporation (COMSAT) is now a privately-owned corporation that launches and operates communications satellites. COMSAT is a member of the International Telecommunications Satellite Consortium (Intelsat). See **Intelsat**.

communication theory [ISO The mathematical discipline dealing with the probabilistic features of the transmission of messages in the presence of noise and any other disturbances.]

comp Composite. In desktop publishing, a comp is a complete, true-to-size page mock-up. It is used like a proof sheet to show what the finished page will look like once printed (including color shadings, typefaces, and sizes).

compact disk A plastic disk introduced in 1982 and used for optical storage. A disk 4.75 inches in diameter can store approximately 72 minutes of music, or 700 megabytes of digital data (this is equivalent to almost 2000 low-density floppy disks or up to 300 000 pages of typed information). The data is stored in both microscopic pits and smooth areas with differing reflective properties. The reflections of laser light which shine on the disk are detected and translated into digital data. The majority of applications use disks which cannot be erased. WORM (write once, read many times) is a particular technology which allows a disk sector to be written over only once. If a file is updated, then the new information is written on new tracks. The old information cannot be erased, but becomes inaccessible. WORM is popular for transaction logging because the sequence of data entry can be audited. A WORM disk can also be called a 'CD–R disk'. Another type of optical disk technology is CD–E, which allows writing, erasing, and re-writing — as is possible with a floppy disk. CD–I is a standard for interactive compact disk systems used in interactive training systems which involve music, video, animation, and speech. CD–I can quickly respond to a command from the user. Although compact disks are almost 20 times slower in access speeds than magnetic disks, they are removable, and offer high-capacity and high-quality storage relatively inexpensively when produced in large quantities. With CD, the original analog signals are divided into 44 100 blocks per second, then each block is coded (quantized) according to its dynamic range. The quantized information recorded in a CD is 16 bits — that is, $2^{16} = 65\,536$. The CD recording system has a standard that requires signals over 20 kHz to be cut off at recording because it was believed at that time that human beings cannot hear sounds above 20 kHz. This limitation of information by standards for amplitude and signal bandwidth is one of the conditions that maintain compatibility in CD digital recording. Although information outside the limits is dropped, one of the most important advantages with digital recording is that information within the limits can be accurately recorded and reproduced without being affected by noise or distortion. Abbreviation 'CD'. See **CD–ROM**. ▼

compact disk *Most personal computers equipped with CD–ROM disk drives can accept both compact disks (for audio playback) and CD–ROM disks for edutainment.*

compact disk–interactive See **CD–I**.

compact disk–read-only memory See **CD–ROM**.

company network A wide area network implemented by a large corporation to support its worldwide operations. Use of these networks is usually confined to employees of the companies which own and fund the networks. Examples of company networks include: (1) EASY-NET which was introduced by Digital Equipment Corporation in 1978. It is now used to interconnect over 60 000 users of approximately 10 000 hosts worldwide. (2) VNET is used by IBM to interconnect almost 3500 hosts worldwide. (3) INTERNET was developed by Xerox to link approximately 24 000 global users. (4) SWIFT supports the electronic transfer of funds between banks in over 18 countries. (5) SITA is one of the first worldwide networks which was set up to provide a message-switching and packet-switching service for the airline industry.

company WAN See **company network**.

Compaq Compaq Computer Corporation; a Houston-based manufacturer of industry-standard personal computers, and personal computer systems including a full range of tower, desktop, and portable computers. Compaq set a United States record in 1983 by becoming the first computer company to sell (in its first year) over US$100 million worth of computers. Later Compaq was the first to manufacture a desktop computer based on the Intel 80386 microprocessor. Compaq started out as a company which manufactured clones (personal computers which were compatible with the original IBM Personal Computer model). To protect its investment after several companies started to manufacture clones of the IBM Personal Computer, IBM re-launched its personal computer range in 1986 with a closed-architecture series called 'PS/2' (Personal System 2). The PS/2 was designed using a new architecture called 'Micro Channel Architecture' (MCA), which meant that existing industry software and peripherals could not function on PS/2. Compaq and eight other manufacturers (dubbed the 'Gang of Nine') joined forces to maintain the industry-standard architecture (ISA), and further developed it to take advantage of the 32-bit bus structure of the Intel 80386 and 80486 microprocessors. Extended ISA became known as 'EISA', pronounced 'e-sah'.

comparator 1. [ISO A functional unit that compares two items of data and indicates the result of the comparison.] 2. (In analog computing.) [ISO A functional unit that compares two analog variables and indicates the result of that comparison.]

compare [ISO To examine two items to discover their relative magnitudes, their relative positions in an order or in a sequence, or whether they are identical in given characteristics.]

compatibility Ease of transfer of data from one device to another, or from one software program to another.

compile [ISO To translate all or part of a program expressed in a high-level language into a computer program expressed in an intermediate language, an assembly language, or a machine language.]

compiler A program that translates a high-level computer language into machine language. There are different compilers for different computers, and one for each language, such as a FORTRAN compiler, or COBOL compiler. Unlike an interpreter, which converts then immediately executes each statement line by line, a compiler translates the complete program before any execution takes place. [ISO A translator that can compile.]

complementary metal-oxide semiconductor See **CMOS**.

complementary operation [ISO Of a Boolean operation, another Boolean operation whose result, when it is performed on the same operands as the first Boolean operation, is the negation of the result of the first Boolean operation. *Example:* Disjunction is the complementary operation of non-disjunction.]

complementer [ISO A functional unit whose output data is a representation of the complements of the numbers represented by its input data.]

complete carry [ISO In parallel addition, a procedure in which each of the carries is immediately transferred.]

completeness check [ISO A check to determine whether data is present where data is required.]

complex instruction set computing See **CISC**.

complex number [ISO A number consisting of an ordered pair of real numbers, expressible in the form $a + bi$, where a and b are the real numbers and $i^2 = -1$.]

compose sequence A series of special keystrokes used when an unusual character is required, and is not readily available as a key on the keyboard. For example, in Lotus 1-2-3, a lowercase 'e' with an acute accent can be generated by typing Alt-F1 followed by the numbers 233 to form (é). In WordPerfect, the compose sequence begins by pressing the control key and the number 2, followed by the table number, then the character number.

composite In desktop publishing, a complete, true-to-size page mock-up. It is used like a proof sheet to show what the finished page will look like once printed (including color shadings, typefaces, and sizes). Abbreviation 'comp'.

composite color monitor By today's standards, this is a low-quality display monitor which accepts a standard analog video signal. The image is produced by mixing the red, green, and blue signals together. The three colors are mixed together electrically so that the signal can be sent on one wire, not three or more. However, when the signal reaches the monitor, it is split back into three. See **color monitor**.

composite head See **read/write head**.

composite video A single video signal format that includes the complete visual waveform, including chrominance (color), luminance (brightness), blanking pedestal, field, line, color synchronization pulse, and field equalizing pulses.

compound document A file that contains more than one element (such as text, graphics, voice, and video).

compound statement [ISO A statement constructed by sequencing statements. *Note:* Most often the statements are grouped together by some syntactic device.]

compress [ISO To reduce the space taken on a data medium by encoding or removing repetitive characters.]

compressed video A digital video image or segment that has been processed using a variety of computer compression algorithms and other techniques to reduce the amount of data required to accurately represent the video content.

compression Any of several techniques that reduce the number of bits required to represent information in data transmission or storage. Compression is used for conserving bandwidth and/or memory. Compressed data must be decoded at the receiving end of the communications path in order to extract the original information. In modem data transmission, data compression allows modems to increase throughput without increasing the baud rate (transmission speed). With data compression, the sending modem compresses the data into a compact form. The receiving modem decompresses the data back to its original form. This process saves time and money because the information is transmitted much more quickly. International data compression standards exist. The V.42bis is a data compression standard specified by CCITT for modems that transmit 9600 bits per second (Bps). V.42bis compresses data by as much as 4:1, depending upon the type of file being sent, enabling a 9600-baud modem to transmit data at up to 38 400 Bps. Another method of data compression is the de facto standard known as MNP (Microcom Networking Protocol) class 5. MNP 5 provides up to 2:1 data compression, giving a 2400-baud modem an effective through-put of up to 4800 Bps, and a 9600-baud modem as much as 19 200 Bps. Data compression can occur only when the two communicating modems support the same compression techniques. If modems support more than one type of compression, the communicating modems will use the most powerful technique common to both.

CompuServe A large public subscription-based bulletin board which offers users online information. Other functions include electronic mail, downloadable files, current news, special interest groups, and an online encyclopedia service. CompuServe has a character-based command-line, making it a little difficult to use without tuition. A front-end program called 'CompuServe Navigator' was written to address this issue, giving users greater flexibility when using the service.

compute To perform a calculation — for example, to add, subtract, multiply, or divide numbers. The word 'compute' comes from the Latin word *putare*, meaning 'reckon'.

compute mode [ISO That operating mode of an analog computer during which the solution is in progress.]

computer Any machine capable of receiving input, processing, storing, and outputting data in the form of text, graphics, symbols, numbers, and sound. Digital computer systems of widely varying designs all have four functional elements in common: a central processing unit (CPU) with the control, timing, and logic circuits needed to execute stored instructions; a memory to store the sequence of instructions making up a program or algorithm; data memory to store variables used by the program; and some means of communicating with the outside world. The CPU usually includes one or more accumulators or special registers for computing or storing values during program execution. The instruction set of such a processor generally includes, at the minimum, operation classes to perform arithmetic or logical functions on program variables; move variables from one place to another; cause program execution to jump or conditionally branch based upon register or variable states; and call and return from subroutines. The program and data memory functions sometimes share a single memory space, but this is not always the case. When the address spaces are separated, program and data memory need not even have the same basic word width. A digital computer's flexibility comes in part from its ability to combine simple, fast operations to produce more complex (albeit slower) ones, which in turn link together to solve the problem at hand. A four-bit CPU executing multiple precision subroutines can, for example, perform 64-bit addition and subtraction.

The subroutines could in turn be building blocks for floating point multiplication and division routines. Eventually, the 4-bit CPU can simulate a far more complex 'virtual' machine. In fact, any digital computer with the above four functional elements can (given time) complete any algorithm.

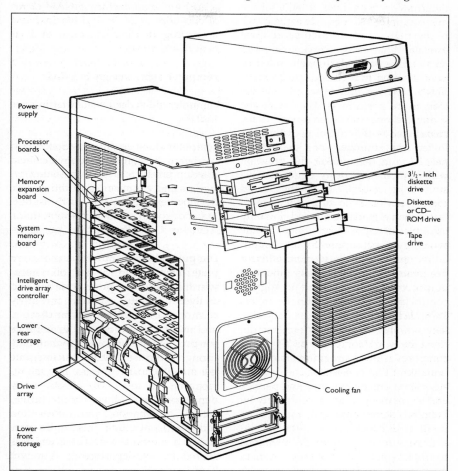

Power supply

Processor boards

Memory expansion board

System memory board

Intelligent drive array controller

Lower rear storage

Drive array

Lower front storage

3½ - inch diskette drive

Diskette or CD–ROM drive

Tape drive

Cooling fan

computer *Available in varying shapes and sizes, computers are becoming much more powerful, delivering an unprecedented combination of performance and expendability with each new model. Above is an illustration of a high-end personal computer system which can expand to address the requirements of network servers and multi-user hosts in connected-user environments. This Compaq model is 23.8 inches (60.5 centimeters) high and weighs 36.3 lb (16.4 kilograms). Such a system is capable of meeting the demands of advanced connectivity applications, including local area networking, communications bridges, and gateways. This computer can also support two system processor boards, up to 11 mass storage devices, and 11 full-sized expansion slots.*

However, the time needed in this instance would be so large that the computer would not in any way be productive or efficient. One of the factors determining how long it will take a microcomputer to complete a given task is the number of instructions it must execute. What makes a given computer architecture particularly well suited or poorly suited to a class of problems is how well its instruction set matches the task to be performed. The better the 'primitive' operations correspond to the steps taken by the control algorithm, the lower the number of instructions needed, and the quicker the program will run. All else being equal, a CPU supporting 64-bit arithmetic could clearly perform floating point math faster than a machine bogged down by multiple-precision subroutines. In the same way, direct support for bit manipulation naturally leads to more efficient programs handling the binary input and output conditions inherent in digital-control problems. Interestingly, in his 1896 *Dictionary of the English Language*, lexicographer Joseph E. Worcester defined the word 'computer' as 'One who computes'. [ISO A programmable functional unit that consists of one or more associated processing units and peripheral equipment, that is controlled by internally stored programs, and that can perform substantial computation, including numerous arithmetic operations or logic operations, without human intervention during a run. *Note:* A computer may be a stand-alone unit or may consist of several interconnected units.] ⋀

computer-aided Wherever a computer is used, the completion of the task can be deemed to have been aided by the computer. More specifically, sophisticated computer-aided hardware and software tools are being used to assist with areas such as design (CAD), engineering (CAE), and manufacturing (CAM). Such applications may be written in high-level programming languages such as FORTRAN or APL.

computer-aided design See **CAD**.

computer-aided design and drafting See **CADD**.

computer-aided engineering Specialized hardware and software tools which help develop products faster by assisting designers and engineers with the design, development, calculation, analysis, testing, and experimentation of new products. Acronym 'CAE'. Pronounced 'kay'.

computer-aided manufacturing A complete manufacturing control system which incorporates product design and analysis, quality control, inventory control, cost accounting, purchasing, and order entry. It is used to improve the productivity of the entire manufacturing enterprise, not just to integrate the manufacturing process. In a manufacturing company, it affects every department, including manufacturing, factory automation, and information services. Controlling this entire process is a centralized database which is shared by all departments. Acronym 'CAM'.

computer-aided software engineering A set of graphic–text tools designed to implement the discipline of software engineering that spans from formal specifications, through rigorous testing, to highly automated code generation.

Typical computer-aided software engineering applications include module management, project management, and compilers. Acronym 'CASE'.

computer-aided tomography Image processing (scanning) of body tissues through the computer analysis of X-ray data. Acronym 'CAT'.

computer-assisted instruction A learning tool for students which takes the student through the subject while monitoring the learning and success rates. More interesting versions of CAI packages include the use of color monitors, video, sound, and graphics-intensive compact disks. Abbreviation 'CAI'. See **interactive video disk**.

computer-based training The use of computer-assisted instruction (CAI) techniques to train adults for specific skills such as operating a piece of complex machinery. Abbreviation 'CBT'.

computer etiquette Refers to the way in which users communicate with other users on a local area network, or across a wide area network. For example, simple etiquette techniques for electronic mail would include placing one's full name and the date at the bottom of all electronic messages. Failure to do so will make it difficult for the recipient to respond. The recipient of a message from 'John' may be left wondering about who sent the message, especially if it had traveled around the world to four different people for comment before reaching the person who has to action it. Other simple rules suggest that users should not write messages in capital letters, because this makes it harder to read. Network etiquette may include company policy in relation to the handling and issuing of passwords to colleagues or strangers. Printer etiquette suggests that it is impolite to read other people's printed pages or facsimile messages even though they may be lying around waiting for the owner to collect them. The tone of messages should not be any more severe across a network than what would normally be considered courteous across a telephone. Sending copies of mail messages to a recipient's superior is considered in bad taste if it is politically motivated. This is known a 'CYA' (covering your ass). Computer network etiquette is also known as 'netiquette'.

computer graphics The use of computers to design/display graphics such as charts, diagrams, art, and industrial designs. Used also in scientific research to plot complex chemical compounds such as DNA (deoxyribonucleic acid) coils each containing over 7000 atoms where different colors are used to differentiate oxygen, hydrogen, carbon, nitrogen, and phosphorous. [ISO Methods and techniques for converting data to or from graphic displays via computers.] ▼

computer instruction code [ISO A code for representing the machine instructions of a computer.]

computer-integrated manufacturing Manufacturing using a complete control system which incorporates product design and analysis, quality control, inventory control, cost accounting, purchasing, and order entry. It is used to improve the productivity of the entire manufacturing enterprise, not just to integrate the manufacturing process. In a

computer graphics *Apart from scientific applications, computer graphics can be used for motion pictures and art. This illustration demonstrates the many textures that can be used to bring life to a still image. Although the illustration looks simple, behind it are thousands of lines of code that can be manipulated to enable the artist to animate the image. Every part of the image can be controlled separately. What now takes just a few hours to complete, five years ago would have taken an experienced computer artist weeks of work.*

manufacturing company, it affects every department, including manufacturing, factory automation, and information services. Controlling this entire process is a centralized database which is shared by all departments. Acronym 'CIM', pronounced 'sim'.

computerization [ISO Automation by mean of computers.]

computerize [ISO To automate by means of computers.]

computer micrographics [ISO Methods and techniques for recording on microforms data produced by a computer or for transforming data recorded on microforms into a form suitable for computer use.]

computer network [ISO A network of data processing nodes that are interconnected for the purpose of data communications.] See **network**.

Computer Ogre virus A variant of the Ogre virus. See **Ogre virus**.

computer output microfilm Rolls or sheets of film (sometimes called 'microfiche') on which very small images are photographed, and later read using a microfilm reader. On one 10 x 15 centimeter sheet of microfilm can be stored 200 quarto or 200 A4 pages, thereby saving paper and storage space. Acronym 'COM'.

computer output microfilmer [ISO A device for computer output microfilming.]

computer output microfilming [ISO A technique for converting and recording data from a computer directly onto a microform.]

computerphobia The feeling of intimidation when in contact with computers; human anxiety/fear of computers. Computerphobia is sometimes referred to as 'technophobia' or 'cyberphobia'.

computer science [ISO The branch of science and technology that is concerned with methods and techniques relating to data processing performed by automatic means.]

computer sex See **teledildonics**.

computer system A set of interrelated objects and processes that are used together to achieve a set of goals. For example, in a transaction processing system, the following elements make up a computer system: hardware, software (such as the operating system, layered software products, and applications), people (including the users, and main-

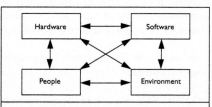

computer system A computer system is a set of interrelated objects and processes that are used together to achieve a set of goals. The hardware may consist of all machinery and associated peripherals. The software may include the operating system, layered software products, and applications. People are needed to configure the systems, and to operate and maintain them. The environment refers to the electrical power, air conditioning, and communications links.

tenance personnel), and environment (such as electrical power, air conditioning, and communications). All of the elements of a transaction processing system interact with each other in the process of performing work.

computer-system audit [ISO An examination of the procedures used in a computer system to evaluate their effectiveness and correctness, and to recommend improvements.]

computer vision An artificial intelligence application which focuses on converting images into digital data by creating symbolic descriptions of the image. Abbreviation 'CV'. See **vision systems**.

computer word [ISO A word, usually treated as a unit, that is suitable for processing by a given computer.]

COMSAT See **Communications Satellite Corporation**.

concatenation (In computing) the joining together of two or more units of information so that they form one unit. These may include text, graphics, and data files. Concatenation is also the linking of transmission channels such as end-to-end telephone lines, coaxial cable, and optic fiber. The word 'concatenation' comes from the Latin word *catena*, meaning 'chain'. Pronounced 'con-cat-ten-ay-shun'.

concentrator A small programmable device which acts as a communications control unit used to maintain control over a communications network by handling a variety of functions such as converting code. Concentrators are also used for combining signals from many terminals, then re-transmitting these signals over a single channel. Other functions include directing communications 'traffic', buffering, multiplexing, and polling.

conceptual system design [ISO A system design activity concerned with specifying the logical aspects of the system organization, its processes, and the flow of information through the system.]

concurrent Two or more activities operating or occurring within a given interval of time. For example, satisfying multiple requests for information simultaneously. [ISO Pertaining to processes that take place within a common interval of time during which they may have to alternately share common resources. *Example:* Several programs, when executed by multiprogramming in a computer having a single instruction control unit, are concurrent.]

concurrent processing The sharing of resources when two or more programs are operating under the same operating system. Concurrent processing is not simultaneous, yet because the processing speed is much faster than input/output speed, calculations can be taking place while data is being manipulated, giving the appearance of simultaneous processing.

condensed type In typography, a typeface which is narrower than normal. It is used to fit more characters in a given space, or for visual effect. Some typesetting equipment can electronically condense any font on file.

conditional construct [ISO A language construct that specifies several different execution sequences. *Example:* A CASE statement; an IF statement; a conditional expression in ALGOL.]

condition code register [ISO A register containing the indicators that result from the operation of the arithmetic and logic unit. *Note:* The register may also contain other indicators.]

condom See **keyboard condom**.

conductor A material which will conduct an electrical current. A good conductor is a material which contains many free electrons which are readily released and made to flow when a voltage is impressed across the material. Some commonly used conductors are copper, aluminum, silver, and gold. Material such as glass, plastic, and air have very few free electrons and will not conduct electricity. These materials are called 'insulators'. The conductivity of some material can be controlled so that it will slow or resist the flow of current in a circuit, thereby controlling the voltage and current in the circuit. Electrical components of this type of material are called 'resistors'. Compare **semiconductor**.

Conference on Data System Languages See **CODASYL**.

CONFIG.SYS An automatically-executing file.

configuration [ISO The arrangement of a computer system or network as defined by the nature, number, the interconnection, and chief characteristics of its functional units. *Note:* This term may refer to a hardware configuration or a software configuration.]

configuration control board [ISO Qualified personnel who evaluate, for approval or disapproval, all proposed changes to the current developmental baseline.]

conjunction [ISO The Boolean operation whose result has the Boolean value 1 if and only if each operand has the Boolean value 1.]

connection 1. [ISO An association established between functional units for conveying information.] 2. [ISO A mechanism that enables interaction among modules, particularly procedure calls to asynchronous procedures. *Note:* In COBOL, an ENABLE statement establishes a communication connection, an OPEN statement establishes an input/output connection.] The word 'connection' comes from the Latin word *nectere*, meaning 'bind'.

connectivity The ability of devices to successfully transmit data to each other.

connector [ISO A flowchart symbol that represents a break in a flowline and that indicates where the flowline is continued.]

consecutive [ISO In a process, pertaining to two events that follow one another without the occurrence of any other event between them.]

consistency In transaction processing (TP), a computer transaction is said to provide integrity of operation and data when the transaction passes the ACID (atomicity, consistency, isolation, durability) test. A transaction has 'consistency' when it successfully transforms the system and the database from one valid state to another. Consistency in a TP system stems mainly from correct application programming (for example, always debiting and crediting the same amount). Because the TP system provides atomicity for the transaction, the application programmer can concentrate on the consistency of the application programs from a business standpoint. See **ACID test** and **transaction processing**.

console [ISO A functional unit containing devices that are used for communications between a computer operator and a computer.]

constant [ISO A language object that takes only one specific value.]

constant angular velocity An unchanging speed of rotation. If a disk rotates at constant angular velocity, bit density is lower at the outer diameter than at the inner. Acronym 'CAV'. See **linear density**.

constant function [ISO The function that allows a number to be entered and held in a calculator for repeated use.]

constant linear velocity Unchanging speed of a disk as it passes the read/write head. A technique used for increasing the capacity of optical disks is to keep the linear (bit) density constant. This requires the disk to spin more slowly when the outer tracks are being accessed, and more rapidly when the inner tracks are being accessed. Abbreviation 'CLV'.

Consultative Committee on International Radio See **CCIR**.

contact bounce [ISO An unwanted

making and breaking of the connection while opening or closing a contact.]

contact input [ISO A binary input to a device generated by opening or closing a switch. *Note:* The switch could be either mechanical or electronic.]

contact interrogation signal [ISO A signal whose value indicates whether a contact is open or closed.]

contact protection [ISO Protection of a mechanical contact against overcurrent or overvoltage.]

contention 1. [ISO A condition arising when two or more data stations attempt to transmit at the same time over a shared channel, or when two data stations attempt to transmit at the same time in two-way alternate communication.] 2. [ISO In a local area network, a situation in which two or more data stations are allowed by the medium access control protocol to start transmitting concurrently and thus risk collision.]

contention access A channel access method in a local area network operating on a first-come, first-served basis. Contention access is a method of line control in which each terminal requests permission to transmit. If both devices bid for the line at the same time, contention occurs and both terminals would receive a negative response to the request. Contention access, also called 'carrier sense multiple access' (CSMA), greatly reduces the chance that two stations will try to use the channel simultaneously. But in networks with any substantial number of stations, it is likely that another node will try to

transmit at the same time and the two messages will collide. In networks using just CSMA, there is no immediate way to detect that the collision took place. If, after a fixed amount of time, an acknowledgment is not received, then a collision can be inferred. A collision can also be inferred if the messages are inspected upon receipt and found damaged. CSMA with collision avoidance (CSMA/CA) tries to avoid collisions by reserving specific time slots for each of the stations during which they may transmit without threat of collision. Although this works well for small networks with few stations, the performance is quickly degraded as the network size and station number increase. A more widely used contention access method is CSMA with collision detection (CSMA/CD), where the emphasis is on fast detection and recovery of collisions. Stations detect collisions as soon as they occur by either monitoring the signal level on the cable or comparing received signals with their own transmitted signals. If a collision is detected, both stations send a short 'jamming' signal to ensure that the entire network has 'heard' the collision, then both stations wait a random length of time before attempting to transmit again. CSMA/CD networks are termed 'probabilistic', meaning that access cannot be guaranteed within a given time limit. See **time slot** and **token passing**.

context-sensitive help Most software applications offer on-screen help messages to guide the user through the different tasks. Normally, a special help command will display an index of all the help functions available, and the user is expected to nominate in which area help is required. However, context-sensitive help immediately identifies the type of query being made, and displays help relative to where the user is at a particular point in the operation. For example, if a WordPerfect user (version 5.1 onwards) is having difficulty setting tabs and help is sought, the context-sensitive nature of the program will detect this requirement and immediately display all the tab-related options. In this way, the user need not navigate through hundreds of options, thereby minimizing keystrokes and wasted time.

context switching The immediate switching from one program to another, without first closing the files. This allows users to operate several programs concurrently, such as a graphics program and a word processing program. Data can be interchanged as required, but unlike the situation with multitasking, when one program is being used, the other halts. The advantages include rapid switching, exchange of clipboard files, and fast data transfer. In a multiple loading operating system like the Macintosh (equipped with MultiFinder), the programs are held in random-access memory.

contiguous Referring to a file containing elements which are placed one after the other. In contrast, a fragmented file is one where the groups of data are on various parts of a disk. From the Latin word *contiguus*, meaning 'touching'.

contingency procedure [ISO A procedure that is an alternative to the normal path of a process if an unusual but anticipated situation occurs. *Note:* A contingency procedure may be triggered by events such as an overflow or an operator intervention.]

continuous stationery Stationery in which each page is attached to the next and which comes in continuous 'Z-folds', often with sprocket holes along the side which help the printer to feed the paper quickly and accurately without slippage. Continuous stationery may be plain paper, or special pre-printed forms, company letterheads, invoices, or checks. A fine perforation runs along the sprocket holes and between each page so that the pages may be easily torn (burst) for better presentation.

continuous tone An image that has all the values (0 to 100%) of gray (black and white) or color in it. For example, a photograph is a continuous tone image.

control area [ISO A storage area used by a computer program to hold control information.]

control ball [ISO A ball, rotatable about its center, that is used as an input device, normally as a locator.]

control-break A user-initiated keyboard command whereby the control key and the break key are depressed together, causing the program to halt at the next available break point. This is common for DOS and OS/2. Abbreviation 'CTRL-BRK'.

control bus See **bus**.

control character Any one of 32 special hardware-control characters and symbols available in ASCII (sometimes having no printable or displayable character) which are used to control a communications process, or a peripheral device such as a printer. Control characters may be used to instruct the printer to advance paper, ring a bell, or move one line. They can also be used to signify the start and finish of a data transmission. [ISO A character whose occurrence in a particular context specifies a control function. *Notes:* (a) A control character may be recorded for use in a subsequent action. (b) A control character is not a graphic character but may have a graphic representation in some circumstances. (c) Control characters are described in ISO 646 and ISO 6429.]

control code See **control character**.

control flow [ISO An abstraction of all possible paths that the execution sequence may take through a program. *Note:* The control flow can be represented by a control flow graph.]

control frame [ISO A frame sent by a layer or a sublayer to an entity of the same layer or sublayer in another system, but not passed to higher layers or sublayers. *Example:* A medium access control frame.]

control key A key which is pressed in conjunction with other keys to activate a program command to minimize keystrokes when using an application. For example, in WordStar, a whole line can be deleted by placing the cursor anywhere on the line and pressing the control key together with the 'Y' key. In other programs, the control key acts in a similar way to the Alt (alternate) key to maximize the use of the keyboard. In WordPerfect, pressing the first function key (F1) allows the user to restore information recently deleted. Shift F1 activates the setup screen; Alt F1 activates the thesaurus; while control F1

enables the user to exit to the DOS shell. Abbreviation 'Ctrl'.

controller [ISO A functional unit that controls one or more input/output channels.]

controller duplexing Two storage controllers each have their own drive arrays that contain identical data. In the event of a drive or controller failure, the remaining array and controller service all requests.

control panel (In Windows, Windows NT, OS/2, and within the Macintosh system) a utility menu (desk accessory) which allows the user to set the parameters when using the computer and its peripheral devices. For example, the control panel allows the user to adjust the volume, colors on the screen, cursor speed, and mouse movement speed.

control program [ISO A computer program designed to schedule and to supervise the execution of programs in a computer system.]

Control Program for Microprocessors See **CP/M**.

control station [ISO In basic mode link control, the data station that nominates the master station and supervises polling, selecting, interrogating, and recovery procedures.]

control status register See **addressable memory**.

control structures See **structured flowchart**.

control unit 1. (Instruction control unit.)

[ISO In a processor, the part that retrieves instructions in proper sequence, interprets each instruction, and applies the proper signals to the arithmetic and logic unit and other parts in accordance with this interpretation.] 2. One of two parts of the central processing unit (CPU). The control unit contains circuits that, with electrical signals, direct and coordinate the entire computer system.

conventional programming A method of programming, using procedural languages such as BASIC and FORTRAN, in which the programmer must pay attention to the sequence of events as they occur within the computer. In contrast, nonprocedural programming languages give the programmer the flexibility to solve the problem at hand, rather than worrying about the way the program will be executed. See **programming language**.

convergence In an RGB monitor, where red, green, and blue signals all converge in one pixel. At full brightness, the RGB pixel in convergence would be white.

conversational mode [ISO A mode of operation of a computer system in which a sequence of alternating entries and responses between a user and the system takes place in a manner similar to a dialogue between two persons.]

conversion (In programming languages.) [ISO The transformation between values which represent the same data item but belong to different data types. *Note:* Information may be lost due to conversion, since accuracy of data representation varies among different data types.]

convert [ISO To change the representation to data from one form to another, without changing the information conveyed. *Example:* Code conversion; radix conversion; analog-to-digital conversion, media conversion.]

converter [ISO A functional unit that transforms data from one representation to a different, but equivalent, representation.]

Convex Computer Corporation An international supplier of high-performance computing technologies. It markets its products in 45 countries to scientific, engineering, and technical users for a wide variety of applications in areas such as seismic processing, reservoir simulation, computational chemistry, and molecular biology. Convex is a member of the Precision RISC Organization, an association of industry-leading companies that promote the use of HP's PA–RISC technology.

coordinate graphics [ISO Computer graphics in which display images are generated from display commands and coordinate data.]

coprocessor A microprocessor chip which supports the main chip. A personal computer may use a math coprocessor to more efficiently handle specialist mathematics-intensive applications, or a video coprocessor optimized for faster video imaging. For computations using binary-coded decimals, and floating point calculations, a microprocessor can perform at speeds of up to 100 times faster when a numeric coprocessor is used (handling approximately 80 bits at a time). Floating point operands are large, and the useful set of operations on them is quite complex; many thousands of transistors are required to implement a standard set of floating point operations such as those defined by IEEE standard 754. Consequently, a microprocessor such as the Intel 80386 provides hardware support for the numerics in a separate numeric coprocessor chip. The numeric coprocessors are invisible to application software; they effectively extend the 80386 architecture with IEEE 754-compatible registers, data types, and instructions. The combination of an 80386 microprocessor and an 80387 coprocessor can execute 1.8 million Whetstones per second. Intel numeric coprocessors are numbered to match the microprocessor, but ending with the number '7'. For example, the co-processor designed for the Intel 80286 microprocessor is called the 'Intel 80287'. The Intel 80486 microprocessor has an in-built numeric coprocessor. The Intel math coprocessor instruction set in-cludes 68 numeric functions for extended precision, floating point trigo-nometric, logarithmic, and exponential functions. While a program is running, the central processing unit (CPU) con-trols overall program execution. When it encounters a floating point operation, it generates an 'escape' instruction to the math coprocessor. The math coprocessor operates independently from the time it receives the instruction to the time it is ready to pass the result back to the CPU. While the coprocessor is working, the CPU can be either wait-ing for the result or processing other tasks. In addition to performing many calculations considerably faster than the CPU, the Intel math coprocessor can often provide much more accurate an-swers than software subroutines. The

Intel math coprocessor can perform arithmetic on integers with 64-bit preci-sion in the range of $\pm 10^{18}$, and can process decimal numbers up to 18 dig-its without round-off errors. [ISO A processing unit that extends the capa-bilities of its main processor, directly accesses the memory of that processor, and does not operate autonomously.]

coprocessor registers Registers in a co-processor which are used to improve the performance of numeric applica-tions. For example, connecting an Intel 80287 or 80387 numeric coprocessor to an 80386 microprocessor effectively adds these registers to the 80386. While a numeric coprocessor recognizes integers, packed decimals, and floating point formats of various lengths, inter-nally it holds all values in an eight-deep, 80-bit-wide floating point 'register stack'. Numeric instructions may implicitly refer to other registers. The 'status register' maintains the top of stack pointers with flags that identify exceptions (for example, overflow) and condition codes that reflect the result of the last instruction. The 'control register' contains option and mask bits which the programmer can set to select the rounding algorithm, decide how infinity is to be modeled, and decide whether exceptions are to be handled by the coprocessor or by the software. As personal computer application pro-grams become more sophisticated, they also get larger, more cumbersome, and slower. Even if an application does not involve mathematics explicitly, it may use mathematics behind the scenes to perform its work. For example, graph-ics and font manipulation, spreadsheet calculations, and even chart creation, all involve mathematical operations. There are two types of graphics software: bit-mapped and vector-oriented. Bit-mapped graphics use patterns of dots to make up lines, letters, boxes, and other shapes, and do not take advantage of coprocessor registers. However, vector-oriented graphics use a formula to represent what the user draws or writes and can benefit from a math coprocessor. For example, when the user draws a circle, the software actually calls up the formula for a circle. When the user saves the circle to disk, the formula is also stored, and when the user changes the size or location of the circle, the software simply has to change its formula and re-calculate it.

copy 1. In file handling, a duplicate of a particular file, image, or block of text. 2. In DOS, Windows NT, and OS/2, a command which duplicates files or directories. 3. In typography, the 'words' being used to make up a document. 4. [ISO To read data from a source data medium, leaving the source data unchanged, and to write the same data on a destination data medium that may differ from that of the source. *Example:* To copy a file from a magnetic tape onto a magnetic disk.]

copy protection A physical barrier or a set of hidden instructions and commands embedded into a software program by the manufacturer. Copy protection is designed to prevent unauthorized duplication of the software contained on a diskette. See **software piracy**.

copyright See **intellectual property**.

core Magnetic core. [ISO A flat circular plate with a magnetizable surface layer on one or both sides of which data can be stored.]

Corel Corporation A developer of graphics and SCSI software established in Canada in November 1989. The company's products include CorelDRAW, CorelSCSI, CorlRAID, and Ventura Publisher.

core memory The memory of a computer that is directly addressable by the central processing unit.

co-routine [ISO A subroutine which, when called again after an execution, resumes at the return point of its previous execution.]

Corporation for Open Systems Founded in 1985, a non-profit organization of networking vendors and users designed to promote OSI (Open Systems Interconnection) and ISDN (Integrated Services Digital Network) standards in the United States, and to advance interoperability certification. Acronym 'COS'.

corruption 1. Unwanted changes (impairment) of data (or a program) as it is being transmitted, such as the loss of data codes from a message when it is being read from a disk. This may be caused by the accidental loss of power during disk access, or because of noise, faulty equipment, program failure, or a virus. See **virus**. 2. Data corruption. [ISO A violation of data integrity.]

COS Corporation for Open Systems; founded in 1985, a non-profit organization of networking vendors and users designed to promote OSI (Open Systems Interconnection) and ISDN (Integrated

Services Digital Network) standards in the United States, and to advance interoperability certification.

COSE Common Open Software Environment. Announced in March 1993 by vendors Hewlett-Packard, IBM, The Santa Cruz Operation, Sun Microsystems, Univel, and UNIX System Laboratories, COSE is a new software environment that will allow users to mix products from different vendors to create solutions that not only have a common look and feel, but also interoperate across multiple hardware and software platforms, thereby protecting their investments in systems, data, applications, and training. The COSE agreement targets a common desktop environment that will give end users a standard graphical user interface with a consistent 'look and feel'. COSE will also give software developers a single set of application programming interfaces to create networked graphical applications. The controlling body for COSE is X/Open — the industry-wide standards group that publishes all standards to enable other organizations to develop their own open systems products that will comply with the XPG (X/Open Portability Guide). Participating companies will adopt common networking technologies, making it easier for end users to connect and integrate diverse systems. In addition, the companies will adopt specifications, standards, and technologies in the areas of graphics, multimedia, and object technology. COSE establishes OSF/Motif as the standard graphical user interface for open systems by making it a key component of the common desktop environment. This includes the X Window System that provides the underlying windowing technology for OSF/Motif, and desktop management specifications that provide menus, movable objects, and other elements to help users to run applications in a common fashion across different platforms. The common desktop environment will provide developers with a single set of application programming interfaces to create networked graphical applications. This will reduce costs for developers, enabling them to target multiple open systems platforms with the same graphical application. Pronounced 'cosy'.

COSQC Central Organization for Standardization and Quality Control; Iraq's standards body formed in 1979.

Count Key Data format The most popular technique for storing variable-length blocks on disks. Count Key Data format (KCD format) is an alternative to Fixed Block Architecture. This technique permits more efficient use of media, because it is possible to write a single block covering an entire track, eliminating interblock gaps. Also, overheads such as headers and error-correcting codes are incurred once per track instead of once per block. However, in practice, the complexity of allocating and managing storage space in a variable-length block format often means that capacity is less effectively used. Blocks written in CKD format can be overwritten only by blocks of identical or lesser length. If a block of greater length must be written, its entire track must be re-written. In practice, most randomly accessible files on CKD drives are actually written in fixed-size blocks. See **interblock gap**.

Countess of Lovelace See **Byron, Ada Augusta**.

A a	B b	C c	D d	E e
F f	G g	H h	I i	J j
K k	L l	M m	N n	O o
P p	Q q	R r	S s	T t
U u	W w	X x	Y y	Z z
1	2	3	4	5
6	7	8	9	0

Courier *Some of the characters that form Courier normal.*

Courier A square serif typeface style usually included as a built-in font in laser printers. Courier is a monospaced font which is used to simulate the output of old-fashioned office typewriters. It was originally designed in 1956 by Howard G. Kettler specifically for IBM's Model B electric typewriter. ◢

courseware Special software and associated literature written exclusively for computer-based training or computer-assisted training courses.

CPC Characters per centimeter; usually refers to the number of characters (letters, numbers, or symbols) a printer can output to a space of 1 centimeter; or the number of characters a magnetic tape is capable of storing per centimeter.

CPI Characters per inch; usually refers to the number of characters (letters, numbers, or symbols) a printer can output to a space of 1 inch; or the number of characters a magnetic tape is capable of storing per inch.

CPI-C Common Programming Interface for Communications; a layer of IBM's SAA that defines APIs for distributed processing applications.

CP/M Control Program for Microprocessors; an operating system written by Gary Kildall in 1973, and published by Digital Research (California) for personal computers with as little as 16 kilobytes of random-access memory, using the 8-bit Zilog Z-80, and Intel 8080 microprocessors. MS-DOS (originally a clone of CP/M) was designed by Seattle Microcomputer to ensure that business software would run on the new 16-bit IBM Personal Computer environment. Originally, CP/M was designed for 8-bit microcomputers, but CP/M 86 was later developed for 16-bit microcomputers. Before it was purchased by Bill Gates, it was called QDOS (quick and dirty operating system).

CPM Critical path method.

CPS 1. Characters per second; often used to measure the speed of a printing or communications device. 2. Cycles per second, properly expressed in hertz. See **hertz**.

CPU Central processing unit; a highly complex set of electrical circuits that executes stored program instructions. The CPU consists of the control unit and the arithmetic/logic unit (ALU). In a personal computer, the CPU is typically a single, powerful microprocessor chip. There are several different chips, including those from Intel (as used in IBM, Compaq, and Olivetti computers) and those from Motorola (as used in Apple computers). CPUs can be measured by the amount of data they can read from memory in one access, the number of operations per second, the total amount of memory supported, and whether more than one job can be run at one time. Sophisticated computer systems

C

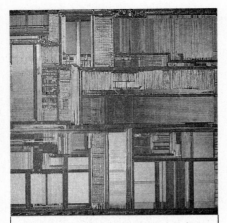

CPU *The developments in semiconductor design and manufacturing have made it possible to produce increasingly more powerful microprocessors in smaller packages. CPU designers are now working with CMOS (complementary metal-oxide semiconductor) process technology, with components measuring less than one micron (one-millionth of a meter) in size. Implemented in 0.8 micron CMOS technology, this Intel Pentium processor has 3.1 million transistors. The increase in the number of transistors has made it possible to integrate components that were previously external to the CPU (such as math coprocessors and cache memory) and place them on-board the chip. Another way to decrease the distance between components (and therefore increase the speed of communication between them) is to provide multiple levels of metal for interconnection. This CPU utilizes three layers of metal.*

such as Acer's AcerAltos 17000 servers can have more than one CPU operating within the same system. Λ

CR 1. Card reader. 2. Carriage return. 3. Credit.

CRA Computer-rendered artwork. Used in computer-aided design technology, CRA allows engineers and designers to easily sketch complex three-dimensional designs, and then rotate the designs to view them from any angle.

crash A program or power failure that renders the computer inoperative and requires that it be reset. See **cold start**.

Cray, Seymour See **Cray-1**.

Cray-1 A powerful mainframe computer capable of executing over 80 million operations per second. Cray-1 is known as a 'supercomputer'. It was developed by former Control Data Corporation employee, Seymour Cray. See **supercomputer**.

CRC 1. Camera-ready copy. 2. Cyclic redundancy check. A method of checking for data transmission errors between communications equipment by means of a mathematical algorithm. Information recorded on a floppy disk is subject to both hard and soft errors. Hard (permanent) errors are caused by media defects. Soft errors are temporary errors caused by electromagnetic noise or mechanical interference. Disk controllers use a standard error checking technique known as a 'cyclic redundancy check' (CRC). As data is written to a disk, a CRC character (usually 16-bit) is computed and also stored on the disk. When the data is subsequently read, the CRC character allows the controller to detect data errors. Typically, when CRC errors are detected, the controlling software retries the failed operation (attempting to recover from a soft error). If data cannot reliably be read or written after a number of re-tries, the system software normally reports the error to the operator. Multiple CRC errors normally indicate unrecoverable media error on the current disk track. Subsequent recovery attempts must be defined by the system designers and tailored to meet system interfacing requirements.

critical section [ISO In an asynchronous procedure, a part that cannot be executed simultaneously with a certain part of the same or another asynchronous procedure. *Note:* That part of the same or other asynchronous procedure is also a critical section.]

CR/LF Carriage return/line feed.

CRN Cellular radio network. See **cellular radio**.

cropping In desktop publishing and printing, the removal of unnecessary images around the edge of a photograph or piece of graphics for aesthetic reasons, or so that the image may fit a given area.

crossfooting [ISO Checking in which individual columns are totaled and the sum of these totals is compared to the sum of the totals of the individual rows.]

cross-modulation Interference between two or more modulated signals on the same channel. Cross-modulation mainly occurs in wideband and audio circuits. This is also known as 'inter-modulation'. See **modulation**.

crosstalk Interference which occurs when cables are too close to each other, resulting in loss or corruption of data. On telephone lines, hearing distant noises or entire conversations may be caused by crosstalk. This distortion is frequently the result of signals being transmitted at too strong a power level. The most common noise found on telephone company lines is 'random'

noise, or as it is frequently called, 'white' noise. White noise is made up of many different frequencies but maintains a fairly constant amplitude. Random noise 'riding' on a data signal generally does not cause a problem unless the amplitude is unusually high. Another source of distortion is 'impulse' noise. This is made up of short-duration, high-amplitude spikes generally two to three milliseconds in length. If severe enough, this type of distortion will destroy data. The major source of impulse noise is telephone company switching equipment. See **noise**. [ISO The disturbance caused in a circuit by an unwanted transfer of energy from another circuit.]

CRT See **cathode-ray tube**.

crunchy caffeine Instant coffee, apocryphally eaten by the spoonful (without water) to keep programmers awake.

cryptographic checksummer A virus detection program usually attached to a network to alert the administrators to any changes in executable files. The program calculates the number of bytes in executable files such as .EXE or .COM files. Given that viruses replicate and make changes to executable files, running checksummers on a regular basis (sometimes continuously) helps administrators to detect the presence of a virus and to isolate it. Cryptographic checksummers are not virus-specific. They do not look for viruses, but detect changes in the number of bytes in executable files. This makes detection faster, because the checksummer does not have to look for a particular string, nor increase the checking time with the increase in the number of viruses. The only disadvantage with using a checksummer is that it must be re-calculated every time a new version of software is installed on the network. Used as an early-warning system, a checksummer is only effective if the network administrator acts quickly to prevent the virus from spreading. To assist with this early detection, a checksummer can be connected to the electronic mail system to send a warning to the network administrator. Additionally, a siren and flashing light can also be attached for immediate warning. See **virus**.

CSBS China State Bureau of Standards; China's standards body formed in 1975.

CSMA Carrier sense multiple access; a contention method of operating a network, whereby multiple nodes 'listen to' or sense the communications medium and transmit when the medium is free from transmissions (when it is silent). This technology greatly reduces the chance that two stations will try to use the channel simultaneously, but in networks with a substantial number of stations, it is likely that another node will try to transmit at the same time and the two messages will collide. In networks using just CSMA, there is no immediate way to detect that the collision took place. If, after a fixed amount of time, an acknowledgment is not received, then a collision can be inferred. A collision can also be inferred if the messages are inspected upon receipt and found damaged. Compare **CSMA/CA**, **CSMA/CD**, and **CSMA/DCR**.

CSMA/CA Carrier sense multiple access with collision avoidance. In local area networking (LAN), whenever a single resource is to be used by multiple entities, some control method is required to regulate the use of the resources. There are several ways by which each station can gain access to the LAN when it needs to send a message. The three main categories of LAN access methods are token passing, contention access, and time slot. CSMA/CA tries to avoid collisions by reserving specific time slots for each of the stations during which they may transmit without threat of collision. Although this works well for small networks with few stations, the performance is quickly degraded as the network size and station number increase. A more widely used contention access method is CSMA with collision detection (CSMA/CD) where emphasis is on fast detection and recovery of collisions. See **token passing**. Compare **CSMA/CD** and **CSMA/DCR**.

CSMA/CD Carrier sense multiple access with collision detection. Because different devices on a network may try to communicate at any one time, access methods need to be established. Using the CSMA/CD method, a device first checks that the cable is free from other carriers, and then transmits, while continuing to monitor the presence of another carrier. If a collision is detected, the device stops transmitting and tries later. Networks not exceeding 40 nodes work particularly well with CSMA/CD — these include Ethernet and Apple-Talk. In a CSMA network with collision detection, all stations have the ability to sense traffic on the network. When a station wishes to transmit, it 'listens' on the main data channel for traffic. If the station senses traffic, it defers its transmission for a random interval and then resumes listening. When the station senses no traffic on the channel, it transmits. One weakness in CSMA 'without' collision detection is that two stations may sense a clear channel at the same time and transmit simultaneously, resulting in a collision. The IEEE 802.3 CSMA/CD bus access method offers high transmission speeds of up to 10 megabits per second. See **token passing**. Compare **CSMA/CA** and **CSMA/DCR**.

CSMA/DCR Carrier sense multiple access with deterministic collision. Developed by Intel Corporation, this is an offshoot of CSMA. In this scheme, network access is by CSMA/CD (collision detection) until a collision occurs and is reinforced. At this point, rather than have the two stations involved back off, wait, and re-transmit, the entire network switches to a time-slot arrangement. Each station has an assigned slot number and a slot time counter. As each station's slot comes up, it may transmit a frame. Slot times are separated by standard Ethernet interframe spaces. After the programmed number of slots have timed out, the network reverts to CSMA/CD. All nodes on the network have equal priority. The worst-case access time is easily calculated with a formula based upon the bit rate, number of stations, maximum frame size, interframe spacing, jamming time, collision detect time and round-trip propagation delay. CSMA/DCR also differs from Ethernet in that each station must be programmed with an assigned station number. Address discovery is performed at initialization. See **time slot**. Compare **CSMA/CA** and **CSMA/CD**.

CSP Cooperative Software Program.

CSR 1. Common sense reasoning; a branch of artificial intelligence. 2.

Control status register. See **addressable memory** and **self-test**.

CT Cordless telephone.

CTE Carrier terminal equipment; the multiplexing and demultiplexing equipment, owned and operated by a telephone company or common carrier, that combines the channels for transmission and separates channels after transmission.

Ctrl See **control key**.

CTS 1. Clear to send; an RS-232 signal used to tell the communications equipment that communications may commence. 2. Computer tomography system.

C2 The security standard set by the United States Government. Class C2 provides discretionary (need-to-know) protection through the inclusion of audit capabilities for accountability of subjects and the actions they initiate. US Government security levels range from Level D (least stringent) to Level A (most stringent), with levels B and C each containing sublevels. Most packaged software conforms to Level C2, allowing the owner of the computer system to set the security levels in accordance with the company's requirements, and to monitor who is accessing the software. For software programs that offer Level A and Level B security, the manufacturer must obtain government approval before that product can be sold.

CU Control unit.

CUG See **closed user group**.

CUI Character user interface. Compare **graphical user interface**.

current cell In a spreadsheet program, the active cell where the pointer/cursor is positioned, ready for the next entry.

current directory In DOS and many other operating systems, the directory to where the operating system would write a file unless directed otherwise. This is easily changed by the user with a command such as 'cd' (change directory). Many applications use a 'default directory' which is different from the 'current directory' and to which all files will be written by that application.

current drive In DOS or other computer applications, the current drive is the one from which all files are retrieved (or written to). Compare **default drive**.

cursor A marker on the screen of a computer that shows where the information will next appear when information is entered or retrieved. [ISO A movable, visible mark used to indicate the position at which the next operation will occur on a display surface.]

cursor-movement keys The keys on the

Insert	Home	Page Up		Num Lock	/	*	−
Delete	End	Page Down		7 Home	8 ↑	9 PgUp	+
				4 ←	5 −	6 →	+
↑				1 End	2 ↓	3 PgDn	Enter
←	↓	→		0 Ins		• Del	Enter

cursor-movement keys Special arrow keys are shown at the bottom left. Used in conjunction with the directional keys above, a user may move the cursor about the screen, or quickly relocate to another part of the document. The numeric keypad on the right can also be used for cursor movement if the Num (number) lock key is not active. These features increase productivity by enabling faster cursor and page navigation.

computer keyboard which direct the movement of the cursor. Often, these keys are incorporated in the numeric keypad, but expanded keyboards have special arrow keys. The cursor may be moved by the mouse, or by holding an arrow key in a particular direction, or in conjunction with other keys (which speed up the process). In WordPerfect, to automatically move the cursor to the beginning of the document, the 'home' key is pressed twice, followed by the 'up' arrow key. ⚑

curve follower [ISO An input unit that reads data represented by a curve.]

curve generator [ISO A functional unit that converts a coded representation of a curve into the graphic representation of the curve for display.]

Customer Information Control System An IBM program product and mainframe operating environment, designed

PLAY ON WORDS

Cursor The person whose mouse you've just broken.

Ethernet The tool used to catch and anaesthetize butterflies.

Execution time The time taken to kill the salesman who sold you a faulty computer.

to enable transactions entered at remote terminals to be processed concurrently by user-written application programs including facilities for building and maintaining databases. Abbreviation 'CICS'.

cutover [ISO The transfer of functions of a system to its successor at a given moment.]

cut-sheet feeder In both dot matrix and laser printers, a mechanism that carries single sheets of paper and automatically passes (feeds) them one sheet at a time through the printer.

CV See **computer vision**.

cybernetics The study of the automatic control systems of the nervous systems of the brain. This term may also be applied to the study of communications and control systems within mechanical or electronic systems (such as computers). Those who study cybernetics are called 'cyberneticists'. Those who modify control systems as a result of such studies are called 'cyberneticians'. The word 'cybernetics' comes from the Greek word *kybernetes*, meaning 'steersman or governor' (one who steers).

cyberphobia See **computerphobia**.

cybersex See **teledildonics**.

Cyberspace The name of a 'virtual reality' research project into cybernetics being conducted by several organizations including Autodesk and NASA. Using a motion-sensing glove and stereoscopic goggles linked to a personal computer, Cyberspace lets the user view and control three-dimensional models from all perspectives as if inside the computer. Cyberspace users can 'fly' through space in any direction and orientation, and turn their heads in any direction, with the view corresponding in the head-mounted display screen. A virtual laser beam pointer allows the user to move, stretch, rotate, or transform objects in the virtual environment. Whilst it currently has very few commercially-viable applications, in the future, Cyberspace technology will have applications for architects, designers, surveyors, and engineers, as well as a broad range of applications in education and entertainment.

cycle time [ISO The minimum time interval between the starts of successive read/write cycles of a storage device.]

cyclic redundancy check 1. See **CRC**. 2. [ISO A redundancy check in which the extra digits or characters are generated by a cyclic algorithm.]

cylinder On a magnetic hard disk, the vertical column of tracks which occupy the same relative position on the disk pack, but on different disks (one above the other). On a double-sided disk, a cylinder includes track 'X' on one side and track 'X' on the other side. The surface of a disk is divided logically into concentric circles radiating from the center, where each concentric circle is called a 'track'. The group of same tracks on all cylinders is collectively called a 'cylinder'. [ISO In an assembly of magnetic disks, the set of all tracks that can be accessed by all the magnetic heads of a comb in a given position.] The word 'cylinder' comes from the Greek word *kulindo*, meaning 'to roll'.

cylinder method A method of writing

data onto a magnetic disk pack wherein the read/write heads commence reading or writing on a sector (say track 3) then move to continue the process on the lower disk, while remaining on track 3, and so on. In this way, the access arms need not move until all the tracks are used on all disks, thereby decreasing access time.

Cyrix A manufacturer of processor and ancillary chips. Some of these are work-alikes to Intel microprocessors, while some are functionally similar but with different features and characteristics.

C0, C1, C2 ... C8 Some of the international paper sizes specified by the International Organization for Standardization (ISO). See **paper sizes**.

d Deci-. An SI unit prefix for 10^{-1} expressed as 0.1 in decimal notation, as in 'decibel' (dB).

D 1. Depth. 2. The hexadecimal symbol for binary 1101 (which is equal to the decimal number 13). $D_{16} = 13_{10} = 15_8 = 1101_2$.

da See **deka-**.

DA See **desk accessory**.

DAA Data access arrangement; the interface between a modem and the telephone line. It contains some of the primary modem components, and in some countries it contains the RJ-11 phone jack.

daemon A machine or program that performs a task on behalf of the operator.

DAFV See **direct-action file virus**.

daisy-wheel A sectored wheel (resembling a daisy) with characters (letters, numbers, and symbols) protruding from the tips of each sector. It is used in type-writers and printers to strike a ribbon, which in turn hits the paper to make high-quality impressions at speeds of up to 55 characters per second. Daisy-wheels are interchangeable, and available in different font styles. See **impact printer**.

daisy-wheel printer An impact printer that uses a daisy-wheel. See **daisy-wheel**.

Dark Avenger virus An indirect-action file virus that adds approximately 1800 bytes to any .COM file or .EXE file using MS-DOS version 3.0 or higher. Programmed in late 1988, Dark Avenger writes several sentences to a random sector, overwriting any information that may have been previously stored there. See **indirect-action file virus**.

DASD Direct access storage device; a secondary storage device on which data can be stored sequentially (in a particular order) or randomly. Access is available by going directly to the required record without having to read every preceding record (as is the case with magnetic tape reels). Pronounced 'dazdee'.

DASS Digital access signaling system.

DAT Digital audio tape; a consumer recording and playback medium for high-quality audio.

data Information such as letters, numbers, colors, symbols, shapes, temperatures, sound, or other facts suitable for processing. 'Data' is the plural; datum is singular, although there is an increasing trend toward the use of 'data' to mean 'information'. Only when data becomes meaningful to a person does it become 'information'. Computerized data is created and stored in codes such as ASCII and EBCDIC. [ISO A representation of facts, concepts, or instructions in a formalized manner suitable for communication, interpretation, or processing by human beings or by automatic means.]

data analysis [ISO A systematic investigation of the data and their flow in a real or planned system.]

data authentication [ISO A process used to verify the integrity of transmitted data, especially a message.]

data bank [ISO A set of data related to a given subject and organized in such a way that it can be consulted by users.]

database A collection of interrelated or nonrelated data stored together. A simple example would be the set of cards that a dentist would keep, each detailing the patient's name, address, date of birth, and other relevant information. A computerized database makes it easier to search for and sort information in a particular order, say by age. Interestingly, the *Guinness Book of Records* lists the 'Deutsches Worterbuch' as the largest dictionary (database of words). It was started by Jacob and Wilhelm Grimm in 1854, and was completed in 34 519 pages and 33 volumes in 1971. [ISO A data structure for accepting, storing, and providing on demand data for multiple independent users.]

database definition Database management systems allow users to define entries, such as fields and indexes, that are used to describe and work with data. These are collectively referred to as 'metadata', which is 'data about actual data'. Database definition is normally the responsibility of a trained database administrator. For example, if a database contains several sub-databases, where each sub-database assumes a postal code field of five numeric characters, then the database administrator can change each of those fields to accommodate longer postal codes simply by changing the master stored in the central data dictionary. See **data dictionary**.

database management system See **DBMS**.

database manipulation The changing of information in a database, such as adding, changing, and deleting data.

data bus See **bus**.

data circuit [ISO A pair of associated transmit and receive channels that provides a means of two-way data communication.]

data circuit transparency [ISO The capability of a data circuit to transfer all data without changing the data content or structure.]

data collection [ISO The process of bringing data together from one or more points for use in a computer. *Example:* To collect transactions generated at branch offices by a data network for use at a computer center.]

data collection device An input device, usually hand-held, used by warehouse personnel and couriers to ensure accuracy when recording labels or shipping documents. Once data has been collected (for example, at the end of the day), the data collection device is attached to a reader which transmits the information to the computer center for processing.

data communication The transfer of data from one device to another via direct cabling, or telecommunications links involving modems, a telephone network, or other connection methods. [ISO Transfer of information between functional units by means of data transmission according to a protocol.]

data communications equipment Equipment that is used to access a communications network. With RS-232 connections, the modem is generally 'data communications equipment', while the computer or terminal connected to a modem is generally the 'data terminal equipment' (DTE). Abbreviation 'DCE'.

data compression See **compression**.

data concentrator [ISO A functional unit that permits a common transmission medium to serve more data sources than there are channels currently available within the transmission medium.]

data corruption See **corruption**.

Datacrime virus A direct-action file virus that adds 1168 (or 1280) bytes to any .COM file (on drives A, B, C, and D) except for the COMMAND.COM file. Datacrime is time-bombed to 13 October of any year, when it displays the message 'DATACRIME VIRUS RELEASED 1 MARCH 1989'. The virus then proceeds to perform an automatic low-level format of the hard disk's cylinder zero, usually wiping the file allocation table, making the disk totally inoperable. Trying to change the clock on the computer will not always help because the virus is programmed to trigger every day between 13 October and 31 December. In addition, string searches for the Datacrime message will not find a match because the message is encrypted. Datacrime is sometimes called '1168'. Another virus that operates along similar lines is 'Datacrime II'. It adds 1514 bytes to any .COM file, and 400 bytes to any .EXE file on 13 October of any year, when it displays the message '*DATACRIME II VIRUS*'. See **direct-action file virus**.

data definition See **database definition**.

data density See **density**.

data dictionary A central master file, often used in conjunction with a database management system, containing data descriptions (metadata) that can be used in multiple databases and shared by multiple software applications and products. Storing data definitions in a data dictionary keeps programmers and database administrators from having to make dozens of changes throughout the entire database. Abbreviation 'DD'. See **database definition** and **DBMS**.

data diddling Computer crime which involves the unauthorized alteration or manipulation of data. A data diddler is one who, to his or her advantage, falsifies information such as bank transaction records and university grades.

data element [ISO A unit of data that, in a certain context, is considered indivisible. *Example:* The data element 'age of a person' with values consisting of all combinations of three-decimal digits.]

data encryption standard See **DES**.

data entry [ISO The process of putting data onto a machine-readable medium. *Example:* To enter data to a payroll file on a flexible disk from a terminal.]

data flow [ISO The transfer of data between constants, variables, and files accomplished by the execution of statements, procedures, modules, or programs.]

data flow control layer One of the layers of IBM's Systems Network Architecture (SNA). Each layer has its own set of rules for communicating with its peer layer in the other node. The layers communicate with each other by adding header information to user data. The data flow control layer (fifth layer) synchronizes the data flow between end points of a session, correlates exchange of data, and groups related data into units. See **SNA layers**.

Data General In 1968, Edson de Castro and two engineers, all in their twenties, left Digital Equipment Corporation and joined forces with Herb Richman and incorporated Data General. The company started its operation in rented space in what had previously been a beauty parlor, in the former mill town of Hudson, Massachusetts. The four men enlisted the help of a lawyer from a large New York firm, and managed to raise capital of US$800 000 which enabled them to build their first minicomputer, called 'NOVA'. At its unveiling at the National Computer Conference in 1969, Data General commenced its campaign by securing a picture of NOVA on the front cover of a trade magazine. At the time of the event, it featured a picture of NOVA on rented billboards on the road from the airport to the Conference. At the hotel where most of the delegates and visitors were staying, Data General arranged to have bellboys distribute free copies of the *Wall Street Journal* with a Data General advertising flier inside. When it came to pricing the NOVA, they announced extraordinary discounts for those customers buying a quantity of machines. Within ten years, Data General's name appeared in the list of the Fortune 500 — the 500 largest industrial corporations in the United States. Today, with annual revenue exceeding US$1300 million, Data General has installed over 300 000 computer systems worldwide, operating on a mixture of proprietary and industry-standard open systems for high-performance computing, distributed data processing, and client/server environ-

Data General Edson de Castro, founder of Data General Corporation.

ments. The company's product line includes what they call the '5th Generation' Eclipse MV/Family, plus the AViiON Open Systems range of high-performance RISC systems, suited to commercial, industrial, scientific, and technical applications. Data General also offers a family of industry-standard personal and portable computer systems. Abbreviation 'DG'. ⚠

datagram Like a letter or telegram, a datagram is a set of data which is transmitted as an isolated unit across a network. It is a finite-length packet with sufficient information to be independently routed from source to destination without reliance on previous transmissions. Datagram transmission typically does not involve end-to-end session establishment and may entail delivery-confirmation acknowledgment. [ISO In packet switching, a self-contained packet, independent of other packets, that carries information sufficient for routing from the originating data terminal equipment (DTE) to the destination DTE, without relying on earlier exchanges between the DTEs and the network.]

datagram service [ISO In packet switching, a service that routes a datagram to the destination identified in its address field without reference by the network to any other datagram. *Note:* Datagrams may be delivered to a destination address in a different order from that in which they were entered in the network.]

data highway The integration of computing, multimedia, telecommunications, and storage technologies on the one channel. Data highways are an extension of existing mini-highways such as the telephone network. The trend behind the construction of data highways was born out of a need to integrate the best of existing technologies in order to deliver more useful computer functionality. There exists several pockets of mini-highways. Electricity, water, gas, and other utilities delivered to the home are all considered to be mini-highways. Although these cannot be integrated as easily, other existing mini-highways such as radio, telephone, television, and satellite technologies can be integrated to deliver improved global communication for social, business, education, and entertainment.

data input station [ISO A user terminal primarily designed for entering data into a computer.]

data integrity [ISO The data quality

that exists as long as accidental or malicious destruction, alteration, or loss of data does not occur.]

data interchange format See **DIF**.

data inventory [ISO In an information processing system, all the data and their characteristics, including inter-dependencies.]

data leakage The term used to identify computer crime which involves the output (leakage) of confidential information. This can be done by employees who copy files onto floppy disks and sell these to interested parties. Usually, the data is encrypted (coded) so that it is not recognized as being confidential information, should the criminal be searched.

data link An assembly of terminal installations and the interconnecting circuits (which operate to specific standards) which permit information to be exchanged between the terminal installations. The standards relate to the transmission codes, transmission modes, and controls to be used. [ISO The assembly of parts of two data terminal equipment that are controlled by a link protocol, and the interconnecting data circuit, that enable data to be transferred from a data source to a data sink.]

data link control layer One of the layers of IBM's Systems Network Architecture (SNA). Each layer has its own set of rules for communicating with its peer layer in the other node. The layers communicate with each other by adding header information to user data. The data link control layer (second layer) governs the transmission of data on a single link. This is where the synchro-

nous data link control (SDLC) protocol resides. It initializes and disconnects logical links between adjacent nodes and controls the transfer of data over the logical links. See **SNA layers**.

data link layer The second layer of the OSI (Open Systems Interconnection) reference model. The data link layer deals with the composition of the frames of data sent out on the network, the error-free transmission of those frames between two network nodes, and the protocols for getting those transmissions onto the network medium. In its definitions for local area networks, the IEEE 802 Committee divided the data link layer into two sublayers: logical link control (LLC), and medium access control (MAC). The current relevant standards are IEEE 802.2 (LLC), IEEE 802.3 (CSMA/CD), IEEE 802.4 (token bus), and IEEE 802.5 (token ring). See **OSI reference model**.

data manipulation operation In most software applications, an operation such as data retrieval, data insertion, data deletion, or data modification.

data medium [ISO The material in or on which data may be recorded.]

data medium protection device [ISO A movable or removable device that allows only reading of a data medium.]

data module [ISO A removable and hermetically sealed disk pack that incorporates a read/write assembly and magnetic disks.]

data multiplexer [ISO A functional unit that permits two or more channels to share a common transmission medium.]

data network [ISO An arrangement of data circuits and switching facilities for establishing connections between data terminal equipments.]

data over voice A frequency division multiplexing technique that combines data and voice on the same line by assigning a portion of the unused bandwidth to the data. Abbreviation 'DOV'.

data processing The writing and manipulating of information within a computer system. Abbreviation 'DP'. [ISO The systematic performance of operations upon data. *Examples:* Handling, merging, sorting, computing, assembling, compiling. *Note:* Data processing may be performed by human beings or automatic means; in the latter case, it is often referred to as 'automatic data processing' or 'ADP'.] Compare **document processing**.

data processing node [ISO In a computer network, a node at which data processing equipment is located.]

data processing station [ISO At a data processing node, data processing equipment, and associated software.]

data processing system [ISO A system, including computing equipment and associated personnel, that performs input, processing, storage, output, and control functions to accomplish a sequence of operations on data. *Notes:* (a) In the English usage, 'data processing system' is a preferred term for those systems which include personnel. (b) A data processing system usually consists of one or more computers and associated software, that uses common storage for all or part of a program and also for all or part of the data necessary for the execution of the program; executes user-written or user-designated programs; performs user-designated data manipulation, including arithmetic operations and logic operations; and that can execute programs that modify themselves during their execution.]

data processing system security [ISO The technological and administrative safeguards established and applied to a data processing system to protect hardware, software, and data from accidental or malicious modifications, destruction, or disclosure.]

data protection [ISO The implementation of appropriate administrative, technical, or physical means to guard against the unauthorized interrogation and use of procedures and data.]

data quality [ISO The correctness, timeliness, accuracy, completeness, relevance, and accessibility that make data appropriate for their use.]

data-sensitive fault [ISO A fault that is revealed as a result of the processing of a particular pattern of data.]

data signaling rate [ISO The aggregate of the number of binary digits (bits) per second in the transmission path of a data transmission system.]

data sink [ISO The functional unit that originated data for transmission.]

data station [ISO The data terminal equipment (DTE), the data circuit-terminating equipment, and any intermediate equipment. *Note:* The DTE may

D

be connected directly to a data processing system, or may be part of it.]

data striping The act of distributing data across the drives of an array.

data switching exchange [ISO The equipment installed at a single location to perform switching functions, such as circuit switching, message switching, and packet switching.]

data terminal equipment 1. Generally, devices such as terminals or computers which connect to data communications equipment. Abbreviation 'DTE'. 2. [ISO That part of a data station that serves as a data source, a data sink, or both.]

data terminal ready A signal which indicates to the modem that the data terminal equipment is ready to begin communications. Abbreviation 'DTR'.

data transfer phase [ISO That phase of a call during which user data may be transferred between data terminal equipment that are interconnected via the network.]

data transfer rate The time taken to transfer data between primary storage (such as hard disk or CD–ROM) and secondary storage or system memory. Speed is measured in bytes per second (bps), or millions of bytes (megabytes) per second (Mbps). The data transfer rate of a disk drive is often quoted as the measure of its performance. The disk industry universally uses 'instantaneous transfer rate' — the rate at which data is delivered to or by a head while it is passing the data area of a sector. Instantaneous transfer rate is determined by bit density and rotational

speed. It is desirable for high-density drives to maintain a relatively high rotational speed in order to minimize rotational latency. However, a drive's instantaneous transfer rate is not a realistic determinant of performance for most applications. More significant in most cases is average transfer rates over different periods of time. The simplest average transfer rate for a drive is the track average. A drive can absorb or deliver no more than one track of data in one revolution. The track average transfer rate is therefore the number of user-visible sectors on a track divided by the revolution time. [ISO The average number of bits, characters, or blocks, per unit time passing between corresponding equipment in a data transmission system. *Notes:* (a) The rate is expressed in terms of bits, characters, or blocks per second, minute, or hour. (b) Corresponding equipment should be indicated, such as modems, or intermediate equipment, or source and sink.]

data transmission [ISO The conveying of data from one place for reception elsewhere by telecommunication means.]

datum The smallest amount of information which can be joined together to form letters, numbers, or facts suitable for processing. The plural 'data' is now used to mean both singular and plural. See **data**.

dB See **decibel**.

dBASE A database management program designed for personal computers and marketed by Borland. dBASE II was designed by C. Wayne Ratliffe, an engineer at the NASA Jet Propulsion Laboratory, who worked with data manipulation software for space probes. Needing something to help him to calculate the odds for his football results, he adapted a software program that was used in the laboratory and came up with a microcomputer program that his colleagues thought to be useful. He advertised it as 'Vulcan' (after *Star Trek*) in *Byte* magazine. Mr Tate, of Ashton Tate, bought the program and launched it as dBASE II to suggest that it was better than a first-generation product. dBASE II included advanced database management systems (DBMS) features, including relational database management. In 1984, dBASE III was introduced for IBM and industry-standard personal computers, and two years later, dBASE III Plus provided an easy-to-use menu-driven system. In 1988, Ashton-Tate released dBASE IV which included a Structured Query Language (SQL), an improved menu-driven interface, and new report-generation capabilities. Many bugs were found in the first version, damaging the company's credibility. Version IV.1 solved these problems, and established dBASE as a leading database program. The latest version is dBASE V.

DBMS Database management system; a collection of software programs (such as dBASE) designed to manage and maintain a collection of records (database) by providing facilities for storing, organizing, and retrieving related information as required. Database management systems provide mechanisms to ensure data integrity in the event of any failure. Other features of DBMS include distributed data access which allows users at different sites to access data which is physically stored at different locations yet to each user appears to be available locally. Each local site has control over its own data in the distributed database, although the end user accessing a piece of data is not aware of where or how that data is stored. The term 'DBMS' should not be confused with 'VAX DBMS', which is a specific database management software product developed by Digital Equipment Corporation. There are three main types of database management systems, distinguished by the way they logically organize data. These three types are hierarchical, network, and relational. See **hierarchical database**, **network database**, **RDBMS**, and **relational database**.

dBmW See **decibels per milliwatt**.

DB2 IBM's relational database system that runs on System 360-compatible mainframes under the MVS operating system.

DCC Digital compact cassette.

DCE 1. Data circuit-terminating equipment; a functional unit in a data communications system that performs some or all of the line interfacing functions, such as signal conversion and synchronization between a unit of data terminal equipment (DTE) and a data transmission line. In the case of an RS-232-C connection, the modem is usually regarded as DCE, while the user's device is a DTE. In a CCITT X.25 connection, the network access and packet-switching node is viewed as the DCE. 2. See **data communications equipment**.

D connector A series of connectors used in computers and communications devices. The name stems from the D-shaped shell of the connector. The code for the connector may be abbreviated to 'DB', plus the number of pins. Common types in use are the DB9 and DB25.

DCS Data communications system; a computer system that uses communications lines to transmit data. This is usually done over long distances, using telephone lines, coaxial cables, or fiber optic cables.

DCT Discrete cosine transform; a popular form of coding for bit rate reduction, used in compression systems.

DD Double density; refers to the recording technique that enables a floppy or hard disk to store twice the amount of data as a single-density medium allows. In personal computing, this is now known as 'low density'. See **density**, **diskette**, and **high density**. 2. See **data dictionary**.

DDCMP Digital Data Communications Message Protocol; a communications protocol used by Digital Equipment Corporation in computer-to-computer communications over public or leased transmission lines.

DDE 1. Direct data entry. 2. Dynamic data exchange.

DDL Data definition language; the language for modeling the structure (as opposed to the contents) of a database.

DDP 1. Decentralized data processing. This is the opposite of centralized data processing and involves the gathering, storing, and processing of data at various remote locations of a large computer environment. This became popular in the 1970s when minicomputers were decentralized (distributed away from the central computer) and could process data independently, yet still had access to the host. 2. See **distributed data processing**.

DDS Digital dataphone service. Many carriers have evolved their networks from leased analog lines to integrated digital networks (IDN) which are designed to provide a single digital network to integrate a variety of services such as telex, teletext, and data communications. The IDN is referred to as an 'integrated text and data network' because it accommodates both text and data services. DDS is offered by many common carriers. It is designed for the transmission of synchronous data at speeds of up to 65 kilobits per second (kBps), and is typically at 56 kBps. A device such as a digital service unit (DSU) and/or channel service unit (CSU) must be used as an interface to the network. A DSU replaces a modem on a digital transmission channel. The DSU is not actually a modem, since no modulation of the terminal's digital signal takes place. The DSU strengthens the terminal's signal for transmission over long distances. DSU rates via RS-232-C interfacing are 2.4, 4.8, and 9.6 kBps. A CSU terminates the digital line at the customer premises. The CSU also performs other functions, including amplification.

DE Dynamic environment; environments in which data changes continuously, such as during an emergency situation on an aircraft where data changes by the second. Expert systems are being developed to handle such dynamic environments.

deadlock 1. In transaction processing, a situation in which two or more transactions are simultaneously waiting, each one unable to proceed without access to resources already held by the other. It occurs when two users each have a lock on a separate object. Each wants to acquire a lock on the other user's object. When this happens, the first user is waiting for the second user to release the lock, but the second user will not let go until the lock on the first user's object is freed. Microsoft's SQL Server detects deadlocks and eliminates the bottleneck by aborting one of the two contending transactions. In this way, the remaining transaction obtains the lock it needs and is free to continue. The user with the aborted transaction resubmits the transaction at a later date when it is likely to proceed without incident. 2. [ISO A situation in which two or more activations of asynchronous procedures are incapable of proceeding because of their mutual dependencies.]

dead time In satellite communication, transmission to and from the satellite to the Earth station could take a quarter of a second. This delay (dead time) is also known as 'propagation delay' or 'satellite delay'. These unusually long delays require special equipment to ensure that the channel is not interrupted or broken, because the receiving device may assume a termination of the link.

dead zone unit [ISO A functional unit whose output analog variable is constant over a particular range of the input analog variable.]

debug [ISO To detect, to locate, and to eliminate errors in computer programs.]

debugging Detecting, locating, and correcting logic errors (bugs) found in a computer program. Diagnostic routines are performed to locate the error, which can often be removed (debugged). The term became popular after a programmer, Grace Murray Hopper, found a moth (bug) lodged in the circuits of Mark I, causing the computer to malfunction. Hopper wrote in her log book, 'Relay #70 Panel F (moth) in relay. First actual case of bug being found'.

debug registers On-chip registers which can significantly reduce program debugging time. These registers operate independently of the protection system and can therefore be used by all applications, including those that will run in production without protection. More importantly, they provide the ability to set data breakpoints in addition to the more familiar instruction breakpoints. The Intel 80386 microprocessor, for example, has a breakpoint instruction that can be used to invoke a debugger when it is executed. Data breakpoints can save hours of debugging time by pinpointing, for example, exactly when a data structure is being overwritten.

DEC Digital Equipment Corporation. Pronounced 'deck'. Also known as 'Digital'.

de Castro, Edson See **Data General**.

DECdta Digital's distributed transaction architecture; a blueprint for the evolution of Digital's transaction-based information systems for this decade. It enables its users to distribute both processing and data, and provides for the integration of transaction processing system components from multiple vendors. See **transaction processing**.

decentralized data processing See **DDP**.

DECforms Digital's forms management package. This is Digital's implementation of the Form Interface Management System (FIMS) ANSI/ISO standard prepared by the CODASYL Form Interface Management System Committee. It integrates text and simple graphics into forms and menus that application programs use as an interface to users. See **video form**.

deci- An SI unit prefix for 10^{-1} expressed as 0.1 in decimal notation, as in 'decibel' (dB). SI symbol 'd'.

decibel Equal to one-tenth of a bel. A unit for measuring the 'power' of a signal or the 'strength' of a sound. A decibel usually measures the strength of the received signal in relation to the strength of the signal originally sent by the standard source. In relation to the human ear, 20 decibels would constitute the sound of a whisper, 40 decibels would be the sound level of a normal conversation, while sounds above 150 decibels are considered to be painfully loud and damaging to an unprotected ear. In electronic circuits, the power is extremely low and is normally measured in milliwatts. From the American physicist Alexander Graham Bell, 1847–1922. Abbreviation 'dB'.

decibels per milliwatt Electrical power (watts) referenced to 1 milliwatt, in decibels. It is used to compare power levels in telephone and signal distribution systems. Since distortion factors will degrade the quality of a transmitted signal,

it is important that the signal power leaving the transmitter be set for the maximum allowable. 'Signal power' refers to the effective amplitude of the analog signal. Telephone companies measure signal power in decibels per milliwatt (dBmW). Zero dBmW is referenced as 1 milliwatt of power developed when a 1000-hertz signal is transmitted through a circuit of 600-ohms impedance. The power level of a signal in dBmW can easily be determined using an oscilloscope, or by using a digital voltmeter. See **impedance**.

decillion See **exponent**.

decimal 1. Referring to the number ten, or to tenths. 2. A decimal point. 3. Base 10.

decimal digit [ISO A digit used in the decimal numeration system. *Example:* The Arabic digits 0 through 9.]

decimal notation [ISO A notation that uses ten different characters, usually the decimal digits. *Examples:* (a) The character string 196912312359 (YYYYMMDDTTTT) may be construed to represent the date and time one minute before the start of the year 1970. (b) The representation used in the Universal Decimal Classification (UDC). *Note:* These examples use decimal notation but neither satisfies the definition of the decimal numeration system.]

decimal (numeration) system [ISO The fixed radix numeration system that uses the digits 0, 1, 2, 3, 4, 5, 6, 7, 8, and 9 and the radix ten and in which the lowest integral weight is 1. *Example:* In this numeration system, the numeral 576.2

represents the number $(5 \times 10^2) + (7 \times 10^1) + (6 \times 10^0) + (2 \times 10^{-1})$.]

decimal point [ISO The radix point in the decimal numeration system. *Note:* The decimal point may be represented, according to various conventions, by a comma, by a period, or by a point at the mid-height of the digits.]

decision content [ISO A logarithmic measure of the number of decisions needed to select a given event among a finite number of mutually exclusive events; in mathematical notation, this measure is: $(H_0 = \log n)$ where n is the number of events.]

decision table [ISO A table of conditions that are to be considered in the analysis of a problem, together with the action to be taken for each condition.]

decision tree A tree-like graphical presentation of a decision table.

declaration [ISO The mechanism for establishing a language object. *Note:* A declaration normally involves attaching an identifier, and allocating attributes, to the language object concerned.]

declarative language 1. A programming language, such as Structured Query Language, designed to assist the programmer to seek information from a computer by telling the computer what is required, rather than how to go about accomplishing the task. See **programming language** and **structured language**. 2. [ISO A programming language for expressing declarations. *Example:* A data description language.]

decode [ISO To convert data by revers-

ing the effect of some previous encoding.]

decoder [ISO A functional unit that has a number of input lines such that any number may carry signals and a number of output lines such that no more than one at a time may carry a signal and such that the combination of input signals serves as a code to indicate which output line carries the signal.]

decollating The automatic or manual separating of sheets, and the removal of carbon paper from continuous stationery or other multipart documentation.

decompression To reverse the procedure conducted by the compression software algorithm to return data to its original size and condition.

decryption The process of decoding information so that it can be read and manipulated. Compare **encryption**.

DECtp Digital Equipment Corporation's transaction processing. A transaction processing systems environment that integrates the capabilities necessary to build transaction processing applications such as databases, storage systems, data interoperability products, transaction processing monitors, and support programs. Digital products have been used in transaction processing systems since the early 1970s. Transaction processing monitors provide eight major functions, including terminal management, file/data management, transaction integrity, security, and productivity. See **transaction processing**.

dedicated file server In a local area network, a file server which only functions as a file server and cannot be used for any other purpose. Unlike a peer-to-peer network where all the computers are potential file servers, a dedicated file server's sole role is to run the network operating system and service the users on the network.

deep etch To remove the unwanted detail around the subject in a photograph. The term comes from the days when photographs were printed from metal blocks, and all unwanted metal was etched away.

de facto Referring to unofficial standards. These standards are not set by an agency, but are set over a period of time by users.

default 1. One of a set of operating conditions that is automatically used when a device (such as a printer or computer) is first switched on, or after it is re-set. 2. (Adjective.) [ISO Pertaining to an attribute, value, or option that is assumed when none is explicitly specified.]

default directory In DOS or other computer applications, the directory which is automatically available when the application is first switched on. The default directory may be changed; when this is done, the new directory becomes the 'current' directory.

default drive The drive which first becomes available when an application is switched on. The default drive may be changed; when this is done, the new drive from which all files are retrieved (or written to) becomes the 'current' drive.

deference [ISO A process by which a

data station delays its transmission when the transmission medium is busy in order to avoid a collision with ongoing transmission.]

defragmentation The rewriting of all the parts of a file on contiguous sectors (one after the other). When files on a hard disk are being updated, the information tends to be written all over the disk. This fragmentation causes delays in file retrieval. Defragmentation is the reversal of this process. Special defragmentation programs like Disk-Express and DOS Rx perform automatic defragmentation, providing up to 75% improvement in the speed of disk access and retrieval.

degradation Unwanted loss or corruption of signal quality. This hinders data interpretation unless the signal can be re-generated. See **distortion** and **repeater**.

de jure Referring to official standards developed by official organizations. They often represent a consensus of computer-industry leaders.

deka- An SI unit prefix for 10^1 expressed as 10 in decimal notation, as in 'dekameter' (dam). SI symbol 'da'.

delay element [ISO A device that yields, after a given time interval, an output signal essentially similar to a previously introduced input signal.]

delay line [ISO A line or network designed to introduce a desired delay in the transmission of a signal.]

DELCL Delete clause.

delete key A keyboard key that erases

the character directly at the cursor, unlike the backspace key which erases the character immediately to the left of the cursor. In the case of an insertion-tool cursor, the delete key erases the character to the right of the cursor. Abbreviation 'Del'.

delimiter A symbol such as a comma (,) which is used to mark the end of one section of information, and the beginning of another. This is especially used when transferring or converting files from one application (or environment) to another. The delimiter (in this example, the comma) acts as a guide. For example, if a database of names and addresses is being copied from Paradox to WordPerfect, the comma-delimited file might read: Mr,John,Smith,124,East, Provo,Utah,84606. [ISO One or more characters used to indicate the beginning or the end of a character string.]

Dell Computer Corporation A manufacturer and direct marketer of personal computers. Founded in 1984 in Austin, Texas, Dell has offices in over 15 countries, with combined sales exceeding US$2000 million per year. See **Dell, Michael S**.

Dell, Michael S. Founder of Dell Computer Corporation, Michael Dell started the company in 1984 with US$1000 with an idea to sell computers direct to the end user, bypassing the traditional approach of selling computers via resellers and retail stores. Dell attended the University of Texas at Austin where he is now an advisor to the Innovative Technology Management Association at the University. ▼

delta frame A method of storing only

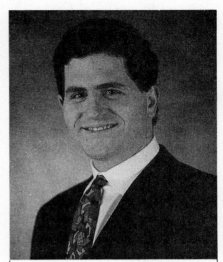

Dell, Michael S. Founder of Dell Computer Corporation, Michael Dell earned the title of Entrepreneur of the Year from Inc. Magazine (1989) and from the Association of Collegiate Entrepreneurs.

the pixels that are different to the previous frame of a video image. This is used to reduce the overall storage requirement of memory-intensive video clips. Also called 'difference frame'. See **key frame**.

demand paging [ISO The transfer of a page from auxiliary storage to real storage at the moment of need.]

demand reports Computer-generated reports produced at the request of the user. These are unscheduled reports, generated only when needed.

demo disk Demonstration diskette. Demo disks show some of the attractive features of a particular program or computer and are usually distributed for marketing and advertising purposes.

demodulation The decoding of modulated analog signals after being received from a carrier wave, so that they can be converted back to digital signals, such as the demodulation (extraction) in a television receiver of a video signal from a UHF carrier. See **modem** and **modulation**.

demodulator Any device or integrated circuit (detector) capable of receiving a carrier wave, then converting the analog signals to digital signals. [ISO A functional unit that converts a modulated signal into the original signal.] See **modem** and **modulation**.

denary notation The name given to the common numbering system using the digits 0 to 9. The word 'denary' comes from the Latin word *denarius*, meaning 'contains ten'. Also called 'decimal notation'. Compare **binary system**.

density The amount of data a tape or disk is capable of storing per centimeter or inch of length. May be expressed in characters, bits, or bytes. See **diskette**. [ISO The number of data characters stored per unit of length, area, or volume. *Notes:* (a) The data density is generally expressed in characters per millimeter (cpmm) or characters per radian (cprad). (b) On disks, the total storage capacity of the disk, recorded on one or both sides, is generally specified rather than the data density.] Also called 'data density'. See **track density**. ▼

Denzuk virus A boot-sector virus that infects diskettes by moving the data in the boot sector and overwriting it to track 40, and at the same time, overwriting the boot sector with that of a 360 kb diskette, thereby making 1.2 Mb

density Forty-five tracks on an average modern hard disk surface (such as the IBM 9355 disk drive) can fit between two lines of a fingerprint. This equates to 26 million bits (binary digits) per square inch. Incidentally, IBM's blue laser can store 2500 million bits of information in a square inch of optical disk space.

diskettes unreadable. Denzuk exposes itself by presenting a special color logo on a color monitor just before a reboot. There are two interesting features about this virus. One is its ability to annihilate the Brain virus (if it were present on the same diskette), and the other is the fact that it is impossible to intentionally make a full copy of Denzuk to another diskette using the usual DOS copy commands. One way of finding out if this virus is active in a computer is to press Control-Alt-F5. If the computer reboots, then it can be assumed that Denzuk is present. Denzuk is sometimes called 'Venezuelan', 'Search', or 'Ohio'. See **boot-sector virus**.

dependent compilation [ISO The compilation of a source module using all the necessary interface and context information from related source modules. *Note:* Interface and context information is used by the compiler to check validity and to resolve differences.]

DES Data encryption standard; a cryptographics algorithm designed by the American National Bureau of Standards to encipher and decipher data using a 65-bit key, as specified in the Federal Information Processing and Standard Publication 46, dated 15 January 1977.

descendant See **nested transaction**.

descender In typography, the section of a lowercase letter that hangs below the baseline. There are five letters in the English alphabet which have descenders: g, j, p, q, and y.

descending order When sorting information in descending (decreasing) order, items are arranged from the largest to the smallest (4,3,2,1) or from the last to the first (d,c,b,a). Depending upon the software program, other characters, including punctuation marks and symbols, may interfere with a 'dictionary' sort, causing words like 'A/UX' to be placed before 'abacus'. When sorting data in ASCII, all capitalized words are placed before lowercase letters. Compare **ascending order**.

descending sort The arranging of data in a way that places the highest value first, and the least last. For example, a descending sort of the numbers 1 to 10 will result in: 10, 9, 8, 7, ... 1; the letters A to Z will result in: Z, Y, X, W, ... A. See **descending order**.

descriptor 1. Registers on a microchip that act as a programmer-controlled

cache that eliminates selectors from most instructions and permits most logical addresses to be translated on-chip without consulting a descriptor table. The address references of most programs cluster in a few small address ranges (this is the 'locality of reference' principle that makes virtual memory practical). For example, if a procedure is stored in a segment, many instructions are likely to be fetched from the segment before control passes to another procedure in another segment. An Intel 80386 segment can be any size from 1 byte to 4 gigabytes. For every segment, the operating system maintains an architecture-defined descriptor that specifies the attributes of the segment. These attributes include a 32-bit base address and limit, and protection information that can guard a segment against incorrect use. Application programs deal only indirectly with descriptors, referring to segments by means of logical addresses. 2. A common field or search string. In database management, records with similar features can be tagged so that all records sharing a common subject may be retrieved as a group. For example, in a hospital, the descriptor 'heart' may be used to retrieve files on all patients with a heart-related condition.

desk accessory A 'mini-application' available on a graphical user interface, which can be used to assist with general tasks such as loading fonts, performing quick calculations on the screen, and displaying an on-screen clock. The control panel is a typical desk accessory. It allows the user to set the parameters when using the computer and its peripheral devices. For example, the control panel allows the user to adjust the volume, colors on the screen, cursor speed, and mouse movement speed. Abbreviation 'DA'.

desk checking 1. The manual examination of a program. As a computer program is being written, desk checking (like proofreading) allows the programmer the opportunity to mentally examine the logic of the program, without actually running it electronically. 2. [ISO The manual simulation of program execution to detect faults through step-by-step examination of the source program for errors in function or syntax.]

desktop computer Any personal computer or workstation small enough to fit on an office desk. A desktop computer may be connected to the local area network, and configured with sufficient memory and storage to perform standard or specialist business computing tasks. Portable computers are taking over from desktop computers because they allow users to take the computer away for off-site usage. Current technology offers full-function desktop computers which can be turned into portable notebook computers. This is done with a powerful battery-operated notebook computer which has a 'docking station', or desktop expansion base. When in the office, the small computer sits in the docking station for access to the local area network and peripherals. The first and smallest full-function computer to offer these features was the Compaq LTE 386s/20. See **laptop computer**. ▼

Desktop Management Interface See **DMI**.

Desktop Management Task Force A group of leading vendors that created a desktop management standard that can be integrated into a variety of management environments. The group includes DEC, HP, IBM, Intel, Microsoft, Novell, SunConnect, and SynOptics. They identified two primary goals: to establish a simple method for defining and managing desktop components; and to design a set of open application programming interfaces that enable the components to be managed in a common and consistent manner. Abbreviation 'DMTF'.

desktop publishing The production of reports, brochures, and manuals using personal computers and other peripherals. Desktop publishing has been one of the fastest growing sectors of personal computing applications. Text and graphics images may be combined with word processing features like spell checking and pagination to produce high-quality output, often used as camera-ready art. Several key innovations were instrumental in the proliferation of desktop publishing: the introduction of inexpensive personal computers (like the Apple Macintosh) which allowed the display and editing of text and graphics simultaneously; the development of page layout programs like Ventura Publisher; the development of PostScript and similar page description languages; and the introduction of affordable laser printers which offered a selection of typefaces. Common resolution on laser printers is 300 dots per inch (DPI), but a much higher output (above 2400 DPI) can be achieved by using professional laser typesetters like those offered by Linotype. Unfortunately, untrained office staff are usually given the task of writing, editing, and designing general corporate stationery and literature. The skills associated with page layout and

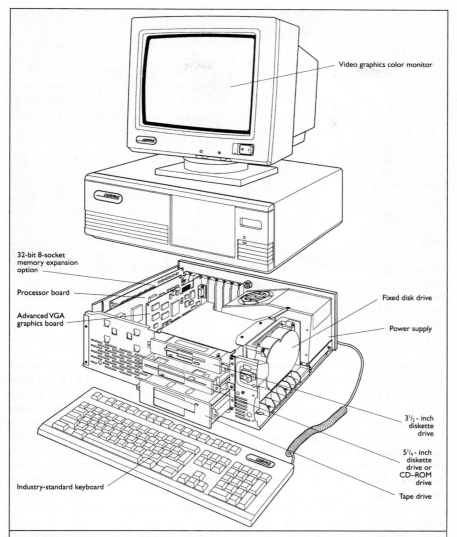

D

Video graphics color monitor

32-bit 8-socket
memory expansion
option

Processor board

Advanced VGA
graphics board

Fixed disk drive

Power supply

3¹/₂ - inch
diskette
drive

5¹/₄ - inch
diskette
drive or
CD–ROM
drive

Industry-standard keyboard

Tape drive

desktop computer *This modular system provides flexibility to upgrade the processor, video, and memory to meet the requirements of demanding applications while protecting the users' investment as applications become more complex. Modern desktop computers can offer integrated cache memory controllers to improve the average data access time and system performance. Sophisticated high-security devices prevent unauthorized users from tampering with the software or hardware. For example, a special password may be set to prevent unauthorized access when the computer is turned on. Additional security features include keyboard lock, screen blank, disk drive lock, and cable lock provision, allowing the system to be physically secured to the desk to prevent theft.*

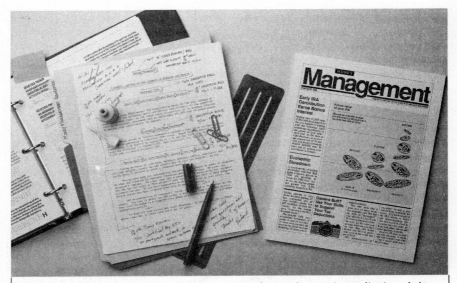

desktop publishing One of the faster growing sectors of personal computing applications, desktop publishing enables users to publish reports and documents much more quickly and accurately than was ever possible before computerization. The total number of software packages expected to be shipped for all segments of the desktop publishing software markets for PC/MS–DOS/Windows and Macintosh environments in 1997 is 1 375 000.

typography still require the attention of professionals for maximum visual communication. Ⱶ

DESQview A DOS program providing a user interface with the capability of loading more than one program at a time and processing several tasks simultaneously. Developed by Quarterdeck Office Systems, DESQview can take full advantage of Intel's 80386 (or above) microprocessor when running under DOS, making it a popular alternative to upgrading to OS/2 or Windows NT.

DeSRA Defense Supercomputer Research Alliance.

destructive read [ISO Reading that erases the data in the source location.]

detack corona An electrode contained within a sealed cartridge in some laser printers. When a high AC (alternating current) voltage is applied in a laser printer, the detack corona generates a field that neutralizes the electrostatic forces on the paper and photoreceptor, thus allowing the paper to be separated or 'detacked'. The detack corona is sometimes called a 'separation corona'. See **laser printer** and **photoreceptor**.

detail reports Computer-generated reports in which every record or transaction detail is printed for verification or archival.

detectable element (segment) [ISO A display element (segment) that can be detected by a pick device.]

developer 1. In laser printer technology, there are two types of development processes: positive and negative. To first explain the positive process, imagine a stationary laser beam striking an unmoving photoreceptor in a single spot. If this image were developed using a positive process, the result would be a single white dot in the center of a black page. In other words, the toner would be attracted to the area not exposed to the laser. When an actual image is formed and developed, the objective is to produce black characters on a white background. With a positive development process, this means that the laser beam must be turned on when scanning the background or non-image areas. The toner is then attracted to the unexposed areas, which correspond to the image. In a negative development process, the laser beam is turned on when scanning the image areas. Since the objective is still to form black characters on a white background, a different charge is then placed on the toner which causes it to adhere to the areas exposed to the laser, which in this case is the image areas. The terms 'positive' and 'negative' should not be thought of as they pertain to the development of photographic film. In electrophotography, these terms deal with the internal process used to create and develop the latent image, and regardless of which process is used, the final result is the same. See **laser printer**. 2. A person who produces or publishes software systems. Also called 'software developer'.

developmental baseline [ISO The specifications that are in effect at a given time for a system under development.]

device Any computer peripheral or hardware component capable of receiving and/or sending data. For example, a printer, a mouse, a monitor, or a disk drive.

device control character [ISO A control character used to specify a control function for peripheral devices associated with a computer system.]

device controller An expansion board used to control devices which were not connected to the original computer configuration. For example, if a second disk drive is later added to a personal computer, a device controller may be required to manage it. See **device driver**.

device coordinate [ISO A coordinate specified in a coordinate system that is device dependent.]

device driver Software that tells the computer how to connect to a peripheral device such a printer. The software acts as an interface between the operating system and the hardware attached to a computer to allow applications to communicate with hardware in a controlled, orderly fashion. A device driver is installed when the system is initialized, either by the operating system (a base device driver) or through an installable device driver. Examples of installable device drivers include a mouse driver, graphical/video monitor driver, communications port driver, printer driver, and network adapter card driver. See **device controller**.

device space [ISO The space defined by the complete set of addressable points of a display device.]

DFD Data flow diagram.

DG See **Data General**.

DGN Dirección General de Normas; Mexico's standards body formed in 1943.

Dhrystone benchmark A standard by which to test and compare the microprocessor and memory performance of a computer system, obtained by running the Dhrystone program (version 1.1) and comparing the Dhrystone rating to that of the VAX 11/780. It is also an indicator of raw central processing unit power and compiler efficiency. Other benchmarks include the Whetstone (speed of arithmetic operations), and the Khornerstone (overall system performance including the processor, memory access, and disk drive access speeds). The Dhrystone MIPS (million instructions per second) rating is a popular performance evaluator based on the Dhrystone benchmark. It has been used by companies such as IBM and SUN Microsystems to place MIPS ratings on their systems. The benchmark was developed in 1984 by R. Weicker. It is a single-program, integer benchmark with a heavy representation of integer constructs that can be found in many business-oriented application programs. Pronounced 'dry-stone'. See **benchmark**.

DIA Document Interchange Architecture; developed by IBM to aid in file transfer among dissimilar IBM devices. DIA provides logical addressing information. Documents which follow DIA are sent via the Systems Network Architecture Distribution Services.

diacritical mark A small typographic sign placed over or under (or attached

á	a Acute	ċ	c Dot Above
ą	a Ogonek	č	c Caron
å	a Ring		(Hachek)
à	a Grave	ꓹ	Cedilla
ā	a Macron	^	Circumflex
ä	a Dieresis	ß	German
	(Umlaut)		Double s
ă	a Breve	`	Grave
â	a Circumflex	–	Macron
´	Acute	ñ	n Tilde
æ	ae Digraph	œ	oe Digraph
Æ	AE Digraph	Œ	OE Digraph
˘	Breve	~	Tilde

diacritical mark A list of common multinational characters and diacritical marks.

to) a character to indicate pronunciation or accent, or to represent a phonetic value of a foreign language. Diacritical marks include an acute accent which slopes upwards to the right (´), a circumflex accent which is shaped like an upside down 'v' (^), and a grave accent which slopes upwards to the left (`). ⚠

diagnostic function [ISO The capability of a functional unit to detect problems and to identify the type of error.]

diagnostic program A program which is run to test components and report on errors or possible problems in order to check that computer hardware and/or software is operating correctly. Such programs can be configured so that a check can be conducted automatically at every operating session. There are two main categories of diagnostics commonly available for personal computers (PCs): level 0 diagnostics, which are contained in ROM (read-only memory), and level 1 diagnostics, which are contained on a diskette. Level 0 diagnostics are executed automatically every time a PC is turned on, and before any other activity takes place. These diagnostics are also referred to as 'start-up' diagnostics or 'POST' (for power-on self-test). Located in system ROM, the purpose of these routines is to verify that the major hardware components are capable of performing their basic functions. Level 0 diagnostics typically perform in three phases. First, the main processor board is checked, testing components which include the memory control circuits, interrupt controllers, and timer circuits. The second phase tests and initializes other system hardware such as RAM, disk drives, ROM, the keyboard, and coprocessor installations. The third phase verifies the system configuration so that the actual hardware found is compared to the definition of expected hardware as set up during system configuration. If actual hardware does not match the expected definition, a message is displayed advising the user to run a 'setup' program (usually ROM resident) to establish the system definition. As level 0 diagnostics are executing, text messages are displayed on the monitor. Audio beeps are also used. Level 1 diagnostics are used to thoroughly test specific components, such as memory, various controllers, and communications ports. These routines are contained on a diskette which must be inserted into the default drive before the system is turned on. After the 'power up' tests are complete, the level 1 routines are loaded from diskette into memory, and menus are displayed for test selection. [ISO A computer program that is designed to detect, locate, and describe faults in equipment or errors in computer programs.]

diagnostics The identification (by a compiler) of errors in source code so that the programmer may correct the fault. For example, when programming in FORTRAN, the use of an odd number of parentheses will result in the diagnostic message 'UNMATCHED PARENTHESES'. The word 'diagnostic' comes from the Greek word *giguosko*, meaning 'recognize'.

dialog box A message box which appears in a graphical user interface environment, perhaps asking the user to select certain options or answer questions before a requested function can proceed. For example, when printing a document, a dialogue box may ask the user to nominate the paper size, document orientation (landscape or portrait), and output quality.

dibit modem Phase shift modulation is an increasingly popular method for encoding digital data on an analog signal for transmission over the public telephone network. Frequently called 'phase shift keying' (PSK), this method uses an actual carrier frequency that is modulated through phase changes. PSK is generally used on synchronous modems. Modems that use PSK encode not one, but several bits at a time. This means that each group of bits is assigned a particular phase angle. With a modem that encodes two bits at a time, for example, '00' may be assigned to 0 degrees, '01' may be assigned to 90 degrees, '10' may be assigned to 180 degrees, and '11' may be assigned to 270 degrees. Since each unique phase angle represents two bits, modems that use this encoding scheme are called 'dibit modems'.

dichotomizing search [ISO A search in which an ordered set of data elements is

D

partitioned into two mutually exclusive parts, one of which is rejected; the process is repeated on the accepted part until the search is completed.]

DIF Data interchange format; a standard file format developed by Software Arts (the creators of VisiCalc) to enable database and spreadsheet programs, which are able to support data interchange files, to exchange files successfully.

difference frame See **delta frame**.

differential amplifier [ISO An amplifier that has two input circuits and that amplifies the difference between the two input signals.]

differential backup Unlike an incremental backup in which the volume's structure is scanned for all files created or modified since the date of the last backup (copying only those that have changed), a differential backup records only the differences between a baseline version of a file and an updated version. This mode of backup (also known as 'journaling') is most useful in applications which make relatively small numbers of random changes to a large file. Compare **global backup**, **image backup**, and **incremental backup**. See **backup**.

differential SCSI The less common SCSI logic encoding scheme. It uses the difference between two lines to indicate whether a logic '1' or a logic '0' is being encoded. The benefits of differential SCSI include longer maximum cable lengths and greater immunity from noise, allowing faster transfer rates.

digit [ISO A character that represents a non-negative integer. *Example:* One of the characters 0 through F in the hexadecimal numeration system.]

digital Referring to devices which represent data in the form of digits, based on the binary system where the binary digits (bits) are either zero or one. Compare **analog**. 2. [ISO Pertaining to data that consist of digits.] 3. Digital; 'Digital Equipment Corporation'.

digital biochips See **biochips**.

digital computer Any computer that can process information and perform computations using digits or other symbols which can represent binary notation.

Digital Darkroom A program developed by Silicon Beach Software for Macintosh computers, which uses computer techniques to modify and enhance the appearance of scanned photographs or images.

digital data [ISO Data represented by digits, perhaps together with special characters and the space character.]

Digital Data Communications Message Protocol A communications protocol used by Digital Equipment Corporation in computer-to-computer communications over public or leased transmission lines. Abbreviation 'DDCMP'.

digital monitor A visual display unit whose display adapter can convert digital information to analog signals. The cathode-ray tube then displays this information according to its adapter type — for example, Monochrome Display Adapter (MDA), Color Graphics

Adapter (CGA), or Enhanced Graphics Adapter (EGA). Unlike analog monitors, digital monitors cannot display continuously variable colors — only on and off. However, they do have several pre-defined states for each pixel. For example, off, on normal, and on bright. Video Graphics Array (VGA) monitors are analog, and can display continuously changing images. See **video adapter**.

digital representation [ISO A discrete representation of a quantized value of a variable — that is, the representation of a number by digits, perhaps together with special characters and the space character.]

digital signal processor In February 1991, Texas Instruments announced the world's fastest 32-bit floating point digital signal processor (DSP) which can deliver a peak performance of 40 million floating point operations per second (MFLOP). Called the 'TMS320', it provides increased performance for new designs requiring floating point capability and allows existing designs to see substantial performance increase. Texas Instruments' TMS320-C30-50 operates from a 40-megahertz clock and has a 50-nanosecond instruction cycle. Its 40 MFLOP is equivalent to 230 million operations per second (230 MOPS) or 20 million instructions per second (20 MIPS). Floating point arithmetic provides greater computational accuracy and a wider dynamic range, and does not require users to scale their numbers like fixed-point formats. High-performance floating point DSPs are used in a variety of applications such as graphics (to perform 3D transformations and object rendering), imaging (to perform image

recognition, filtering, enhancement, and compression), speech (to perform synthesis, recognition, and low-bit-rate/high-quality coding), audio (to perform filtering, music synthesis, mixing, and equalization, sound effects and compression/decompression), and numerical processing (to perform high-performance number processing in a wide range of arithmetic applications). Also in February 1991, Texas Instruments announced the first military high-performance floating point DSP. The 883C-compliant Class B qualified SMJ320-C30 is offered with execution speeds of 70 or 80 nanoseconds, with a 60-nanosecond version planned. The SMJ320-C30 is fabricated in 1-micron CMOS technology with a

D

digital signal processor *This digital signal processor chip from Texas Instruments contains almost 700 000 transistors and is designed to operate at 33 million floating point operations per second.*

highly parallel, pipelined architecture which supports 25–28 MFLOP. Two external buses (parallel and expansion) are built around a 32-bit data capability and a 24-bit address capability. This dual bus design provides up to 138 megabytes per second and eases memory resources in a single cycle. The wide address bus gives the SMJ320-C30 a combined internal/external address space of 16 million 32-bit words. Other features include separate program, data, and DMA (direct memory access) buses, CPU block, peripheral bus containing two serial ports and timers, and a DMA controller. ⚠

digital speech interpolation To handle both telephone and non-telephone services in a communications system, digital-based networks such as ISDN have been developed in various telecommunications organizations, providing the stimulus to develop high-capacity, long-distance digital communications systems. They have also made it necessary to develop and implement new transmission media, such as optical fibers and satellites. The result has been a widening range for digital communications systems and significantly lower circuit costs. However, the search is still on for new ways to increase channel capacity. Two techniques to emerge from this search are low-bit-rate encoding (LRE) and digital speech interpolation (DSI). LRE is based upon the principle that voice signals do not change fast; DSI is based upon the principle that when people talk, no signals are sent about half the time. When people talk on the telephone, one party usually listens as the other speaks. When the phone is off the hook, the telephone circuit is typically idle about half the time. For a

system of 100 channels or more, there will always be some channels idle in the pauses (silent periods) of conversation. As early as the 1950s, a method was developed to effectively use these pauses and silent periods in conversation. It is called 'time-assignment speech interpolation' (TASI). With this method, users are assigned a channel when they begin to speak. As soon as they stop speaking, the channel is assigned to another user. Detection and switching are done on an analog basis. If there are no free channels when a user begins to speak, speech will be clipped. This is called 'freeze-out'. The design objective of TASI systems is to achieve a freeze-out of 0.5%, a level at which most users will not recognize any degradation in speech quality. Freeze-out depends upon the number of input channels (trunks) connected to the system, the number of physical channels operated by the system, and the ratio between the two. Since the 1950s, several generations of TASI have been developed. Because speech detection and switching are done digitally in transmission systems, the method that provides these functions is called 'DSI'. Digital technology has improved speech detection ability and switching speed, making it possible for DSI systems to operate using fewer channels than was possible with previous analog systems.

Digital Storage Architecture See **DSA**.

digital transmission The transfer of encoded information using on and off pulses.

digitize [ISO To express or represent in a digital form data that is not discrete data. *Example:* To obtain a digital representation of the magnitude of a physical quantity from an analog representation of that magnitude.]

digitizer A device that scans pictorial material such as photographs, diagrams, or maps, and converts them into digital data which can be stored by a computer and represented on a computer screen. ▼

digit place [ISO In a positional representation system, each site that may be occupied by a character and that may be identified by an ordinal number or by an equivalent identifier.]

diminished radix complement [ISO In a fixed radix numeration system, a com-

plement that can be derived from a given number by subtracting it from one less than a specified power of the radix. *Note:* A diminished radix complement may be obtained by subtracting each digit of the given number from a digit that is one less than the radix.]

DIN Deutsche Industrie Norm; Germany's national standards organization that sets the standards for a system of plugs, cables, and sockets used for audio signaling equipment.

DIN connector A type of connector sometimes used in computer and audio connections. The most common is the PC keyboard connector. Macintosh

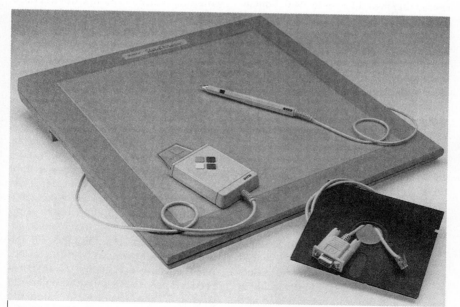

digitizer This digitizer has a 1000 lines-per-inch drawing resolution. Its low power consumption enables it to be powered by the RS-232-C port of the host computer. This digitizer comes with a tablet, a four-button cursor (sometimes called 'puck'), and a stylus. It operates with portable and desktop computers, as well as workstations and mainframes.

computers use a much smaller DIN connector.

dingbat See **Zapf Dingbats**.

diode As a non-linear two-terminal device, a diode is the simplest and most fundamental semiconductor used in electronics. It acts as a one-way valve letting current flow through it in one direction, while blocking current flow in the other. Light-emitting diodes (LEDs) are produced from semiconducting material. They emit light when an electric current flows through them. They were widely used as indicator lights, but their relatively high power consumption has led to the development of more energy-efficient liquid crystal displays (LCDs). In 1990, Fujitsu developed the world's first diode to exhibit rectifying functions under ultra-low voltage (a few millivolts) conditions. The device uses a new principle, employing the phenomenon of tunneling between the metal electrode and the high-permittivity dielectric. The new diode uses $SrTiO_3$ doped with Nb, which is an n-type high-permittivity semiconductor, a tunnel barrier made of silicon or silicon dioxide, and an Nb electrode. Fujitsu's experimental results revealed high non-linearly under a low bias voltage of 2 millivolts (approximately ten times that of a p–n junction diode) at room temperature. The rectifier operating at millivolt levels is significant for two reasons. It would permit, for the first time, use of rectifiers in a Josephson integrated circuit which operates at these voltages. It would also be a basic element in constructing a low-voltage transistor compatible with both Josephson integrated circuits and logic level voltages. The research to develop this diode was carried out by Fujitsu on contract from the New Energy and Industrial Technology Development Organization (NEDO). See **p–n junction**.

DIP switch Dual in-line package switch; a switch which might be used to select the operating parameters of a device. DIP switches are usually found on internal circuit boards. However, new devices are designed to give faster and easier access to the switch. They can be used to control such things as the amount of memory the operating system should recognize, or to identify the printer file format the printer should use. See **SMT**.

direct access [ISO The capability to obtain data from a storage device, or to enter data into a storage device, in a sequence independent from their relative position, by means of addresses indicating the physical position of the data.] See **random access**.

direct access storage device See **DASD**.

direct-action file virus Any computer virus capable of attaching itself to an executable file such as a .COM or .EXE file, or a system file with any extension. A direct-action file virus often copies its instructions to the end of an executable file, thereby enabling the virus to jump to the main virus code, activate itself, and jump back to the end of the executable file without being detected. Although any executable file that has been tampered with will show a new file date and time, some direct-action file viruses have been written to restore the file to its original date and time. Contrary to popular belief, a read-only file can still be infected because the virus can tamper with the file's attributes, infect the file, and change the attributes back to their original status. A read-only file on a network is better protected because of the sophisticated security and access limitations it can impose via a login code. However, if the user's access privileges permit changes to file attributes, then the virus can still append itself onto the file. Every time a direct-action file virus is run, it searches for an uninfected file and proceeds to infect it. Some of the better-known direct-action file viruses are Fumble, Virdem, and Virus-B. Abbreviation 'DAFV'. Compare **indirect-action file virus**.

direct address [ISO An address that identifies a location without reference to a storage location containing another address.]

direct call facility [ISO A facility that permits calling without requiring the user to provide address selection signals; the network interprets the call request signal as an instruction to establish a connection to one or more predetermined data stations. *Note:* This facility may permit a faster call setup than usual. No special priority is implied over other users of the network establishing a connection. The designated addresses are assigned for an agreed period of time.]

direct conversion A method of transferring to a new computer system or software program, whereby an organization chooses to immediately discard the old system and implement the new one. This may create problems if the new system fails or does not meet expectations. Other methods include: (1) Parallel conversion, which involves

the use of the old and new system side by side. Once the new system proves itself to be stable and satisfactory, the old system is either phased out or immediately abandoned. Although this procedure is much more expensive than other methods, it is the safest. (2) Pilot conversion, which involves a conversion by only one division of an organization. Once a system proves that it works satisfactorily, then all divisions convert. (3) A phased conversion method which slowly implements the new system and slowly relinquishes the old system. This process takes the longest, but allows staff time to train and become familiar with the new system.

direct mapped cache For a given cache size, direct mapped (one-way set associative) caches are lower in performance than either fully associative caches or set associative caches. Direct mapped caches are often subject to 'thrashing' and therefore have lower performance in multitasking and multi-user environments. The benefits of direct mapped caches are that they are simple to implement and can usually be done in discrete logic for lower system costs. A direct mapped cache organization uses the entire data cache RAM (random-access memory) as one bank of memory. The cache sees main system memory as logically broken up into pages, each page the size of the data cache RAM. The limitation of direct map is seen when the microprocessor crosses page boundaries in main system memory (such as from page x to page x + 1). If the microprocessor enters a software/data loop that repeatedly accesses both pages, the cache could end up constantly updating the same location in cache memory from main system memory. This is called cache 'thrashing'. A direct mapped cache consists of simpler logic than fully associative or set associative caches. When the microprocessor makes a memory request, the direct mapped cache will compare the memory request with the tag entry at that page location to determine if the information is in the cache (a hit). Only a single comparison needs to be done to determine if the information requested is stored in the cache. As a result of such simple logic, direct mapped caches are typically designed in discrete components to minimize system cost. See **cache**.

direct memory access A method of transferring blocks of data directly between a mass-storage device and memory, with no intervention from the processor. In order to transfer data between non-storage devices (such as terminals) and memory, the processor must intervene in the transfer of each byte. The direct memory access (DMA) interface is typically incorporated into the device controller. When a DMA read or write command is given by the processor, the processor loads information about the transfer into special registers in the device controller. This information includes the number of bytes to be moved, the target location in memory, the target device, and the location of the information on that device. After the special registers in the device controller have been loaded, the device controller handles the memory transfer operation independently of the processor, thus freeing the processor for other tasks. When the data transfer is complete, the device controller prepares a status message and interrupts the processor. The processor then reads the status message to confirm that the transfer was completed successfully. [ISO A technique for moving data directly between main storage and peripheral equipment without requiring processing of the data by the processing unit.]

directory A list of all the files (and groups of files) stored on a disk. This list acts like an index and displays the type and names of the files, the date stored (or last modified), and the size each file occupies on a disk. See **file allocation table**.

direct percentage function [ISO The function that directly calculates a percentage markup or discount value.]

dirty bit See **write-through caching**.

discrete [ISO Pertaining to data that consist of distinct elements such as characters, or to physical quantities having distinctly recognizable values.]

discrete data [ISO Data represented by characters.]

discrete representation [ISO A representation of data by characters, each character or a group of characters designating one of a number of alternatives.]

disjunction [ISO The Boolean operation whose result has the Boolean value 0 if and only if each operand has the Boolean value 0.]

disk See **disk drive**, **diskette**, and **hard disk**.

disk address The location of each record written on a magnetic/optical disk.

Often this is grouped by cylinder number, surface number, then record number. See **file allocation table**.

disk cache Random-access memory which temporarily stores information that is frequently requested from the disk drives. Disk caching improves the speed of disk-intensive applications such as database management programs. Disk cache should not be confused with memory cache. It is a software utility that manages hard-disk intensive operations by copying data from the hard disk into the much faster system memory, and functions as an interface between the system and the hard disk. It is based upon the principle that, most of the time, data is requested sequentially rather than randomly. Conceptually, the process of utilizing the system random-access memory as a buffer is similar to the way in which cache memory works. Disk cache allows the data read from a sector on the hard disk (and a number of the next logical sectors) to be accessed at the access speed of system memory (which can be up to 500 times greater than that of the hard disk). See **cache** and **RAM cache**.

disk cartridge [ISO An assembly of one or more magnetic disks that can be removed as a whole from a disk unit, together with the associated container from which it cannot be separated.]

diskcomp Disk comparison; a DOS and OS/2 command that checks all the information contained on two different disks so as to compare and report on whether the contents and disk structure are identical.

disk controller The electronics responsible for converting high-level disk commands (normally issued by software executing on the system processor) into disk drive commands that typically manage the operations of multiple diskette drives. A disk subsystem consists of four functional electronic units: disk controller electronics; disk drive electronics; controller/disk interface (cables, drivers, terminators); and controller/microprocessor system interface. The controller function permits the system processor to specify which drive is to be used in a particular operation. The controller issues a timed sequence of step pulses to move the head from its current location to the proper disk cylinder from which data is to be read or to which data is to be written. The controller stores the current cylinder number and computes the stepping distance from the current cylinder to be specified. The controller also manages the head select signal to select the correct side of the floppy disk. For correct sector selection, the controller monitors the data on a track until the requested sector is sensed. It also determines the times at which the head assembly is to be brought above the disk surface in order to read or write data. The controller is also responsible for waiting until the head has settled before reading or writing information. Often the controller maintains the head loading condition for up to 16 disk revolutions (approximately two seconds) after a read or write operation has been completed. This feature eliminates the head load time during periods of heavy disk input/output activity. Information recorded on a diskette is subject to both hard and soft errors. Hard (permanent) errors are caused by media defects. Soft errors are temporary errors caused by electro-

D

magnetic noise or mechanical interference. Disk controllers use a standard error-checking technique known as a 'cyclic redundancy check' (CRC).

diskcopy Unlike the copy command which duplicates only the specified files, diskcopy is a DOS, Windows NT, and OS/2 command which makes a complete and identical copy from one disk to another, including all hidden files.

disk drive A peripheral mass-storage device on which floppy disks or disk packs can be mounted for the purpose of magnetically storing and retrieving data and programs. In some cases, disks are fixed to the drives, and are called 'fixed-disk drives' or 'hard disks'. Disks may rotate at speeds of up to 60 revolutions per second. Most microcomputer systems in use today use low-cost, high-density removable magnetic media for non-volatile information storage. Since disk drives permit random access to stored information, they are significantly faster than tape units. For example, locating information on a disk requires less than a second, while tape movement (even at the fastest rewind or fast-forward speed) can take from two minutes up to an hour. This random-access ability permits the use of floppy disks in online storage applications (where information must be located, read, and modified/updated in real-time under program or operator control). Tapes, on the other hand, are ideally suited to archival or backup storage due to their large storage capacities. See **diskette** and **hard disk**. ▼

disk drive *This one-third height disk drive is used with 5¼-inch 1.2-megabyte diskettes. Its internal mechanism rotates at 360 revolutions per minute to transfer 500 kilobits per second to 15 sectors per track (512 bytes per sector and 80 tracks per side). It has two read/write heads capable of addressing 80 cylinders per diskette at the speed of three milliseconds (ms) from track to track. Its average access time is 80 ms, while its settling time is 15 ms.*

Disk Eater virus A variant of the Icelandic virus. See **Icelandic virus**.

diskette A magnetically-sensitive flexible disk used as a secondary storage medium. The two most common sizes are the 3½-inch disk which is fully enclosed in a rigid plastic casing, and the 5¼-inch floppy disk. The 3½-inch disk was developed by Sony Corporation and introduced by Apple Computer Corporation in its Apple Macintosh range. IBM, Compaq, and other leading computer manufacturers followed suit. As yet, 3½-inch disks have not entirely replaced 5¼-inch disks, but they do offer several advantages. For example, 5¼-inch disks have an exposed section which can be easily damaged by dust, fingerprints, and other particles, whereas 3½-inch disks employ an automatic aluminum gate which only opens after the disk has been inserted into the disk drive. Another advantage with the smaller disk is the ease of write-protecting. This is done simply by moving a plastic device located at the back — unlike the 5¼-inch disks which require a piece of adhesive tape to cover the notch on the side. When double density 3½-inch disks are formatted for Macintosh computers, they have a storage capacity of 800 kilobytes, while high-density disks store 1.44 megabytes. When formatting for DOS, double-density 3½-inch disks offer a storage capacity of 720 kilobytes, whilst high-density disks offer 1.44 megabytes. [ISO A small magnetic disk enclosed in a jacket. *Note:* Sometimes, the words 'diskette' and 'floppy disk' are used interchangeably.] See **access slot** and **hard disk**.

disk file system Part of the 'disk interface software' used by application programs. It is designed to treat the disk as a collection of named data areas (known as 'files'). These files are cataloged in the disk directory. File system interface software permits the creation of new files and the deletion of existing files under software control. When a file is created, its name and disk address are entered into the directory; when a file is deleted, its name is removed from the directory. Application software requests the use of a file by executing an 'open' function. Once opened, a file is normally reserved for use by the requesting program or task and cannot be re-opened by other tasks. When a task no longer needs to use an open file, the task closes the file, releasing it for use by other tasks. Most file systems also support a set of file attributes that can be specified for each file. File attributes may be used to protect files (such as the 'write protect' or 'read only' attribute which ensures that an existing file cannot accidentally be overwritten) and to supply system configuration information (such as a 'format' attribute) which may specify that a file should be automatically created on a new disk when the disk is formatted. Other typical file system functions include open, close, read, write, create, delete, re-name, and load.

disk interface software Software which sets the working parameters between an application program and the floppy disk controller (FDC). This is a major contributor to the efficient and reliable operation of a floppy disk subsystem. This software must be a well-designed compromise between the needs of the application software modules and the capabilities of an FDC. In an effort to meet these requirements, the implementation of disk interface software is often divided into several levels of abstraction. The software interface level closest to the FDC hardware is referred to as the 'physical interface level'. At this level, interface modules (often called 'disk drivers' or 'disk handlers') communicate directly with the FDC. Disk drivers accept floppy disk commands from other software modules, control and monitor the FDC execution of the commands, and finally return operational status information (at command termination) to the requesting modules. In order that these functions may be performed, the drivers must support the bit/byte-level FDC interface for status and data transfers. In addition, the drivers must field, classify, and service a variety of FDC interrupts. System and application software modules often specify disk operation parameters that are not directly compatible with the FDC. This software incompatibility is typically caused by one of the following: (1) The change from an existing FDC to a functionally equivalent design. (2) The upgrade of an existing FDC sub-system to a higher capability design. An expansion from a single-sided, single-density system to a double-sided, double-density system in order to increase data storage capacity is an example of such a system change. (3) The abstraction of the disk software interface to avoid redundancy. Many FDC param-eters (in particular, the density, gap size, number of sectors per track, and number of bytes per sector) are fixed for a floppy disk (after formatting). In many systems, these parameters are never changed during the life of the system. (4) The requirement for support of a software interface

that is independent of the type of disk attached to the system. In this case, a system-generated (logical) disk address (drive, head, cylinder, and sector numbers) must be mapped into a physical floppy disk address. (5) The necessity to support a bad track map. Since bad tracks depend upon the disk media, the bad track mapping varies from disk to disk. The key to logical interface software design is the mapping of the 'logical disk interface' (as seen by the application software) into the 'physical disk interface' (as implemented by the floppy disk drivers). This logical to physical mapping is tightly coupled to system software design, and the mapping serves to isolate both applications and system software from the peculiarities of the FDC.

Disk Killer virus A variant of the Ogre virus. See **Ogre virus**.

disk optimizer A program used to re-write all the parts of a file on contiguous sectors (one after the other). When files on a hard disk are being updated, the information tends to be written noncontiguously on the disk. This fragmentation may cause delays with file retrieval. Defragmentation is the reversal of this process. Special disk optimizer programs like DiskExpress and DOS Rx perform automatic defragmentation, providing up to 75% improvement in the speed of disk access and retrieval. Also called 'disk saver'.

disk pack [ISO An assembly of magnetic disks that can be removed as a whole from a disk unit, together with a container from which it must be separated when operating.] See **magnetic disk**.

disk saver See **disk optimizer.**

disk spanning The act of using more than one drive to store information contiguously, while making the drives appear as a single logical drive to the operating system. Subsequent disk drives will not be written to until the preceding drive has no more space to store data. For example, a database might have a file larger than a single disk drive and would be able to occupy more than one disk drive.

disk storage Also called 'magnetic disk storage'. [ISO A magnetic storage in which data is stored by magnetic recording on the flat surfaces of one or more disks which, in use, rotate around a common spindle.]

disk unit Also called 'magnetic disk unit'. [ISO A device that contains magnetic disks, a disk drive, one or more magnetic heads, and associated controls.]

dispatch [ISO To allocate time on a processor to jobs or tasks that are ready for execution.]

dispatcher [ISO That program in an operating system, or another functional unit, the purpose of which is to dispatch.]

display 1. [ISO To present data visually.] 2. [ISO A visual presentation of data.]

display and printing calculator [ISO A calculator that provides the data output facilities of a display calculator and, if selected by the operator, of a printing calculator.]

display calculator [ISO A calculator in which the data output is shown in the form of non-permanent characters.]

display command [ISO A command that changes the state or controls the action of a display device.]

display console [ISO A console that includes at least one display surface and may also include one or more input devices.]

display device [ISO An output unit that gives a visual representation of data. *Note:* Usually the data is displayed temporarily. However, arrangements may be made for producing a hard copy of this representation.]

display element [ISO A basic graphic element that can be used to construct a display image. *Examples:* A dot; a line segment.]

display image [ISO A collection of display elements or segments that are represented together at any one time on a display surface.]

Display PostScript The benefits of industry-standard Adobe PostScript as a page description language for output devices have been accepted for some time. NeXT Computer Incorporated, working in conjunction with Adobe, helped develop Display PostScript and was the first company to introduce a computer that featured it. Display PostScript is the same as industry-standard (regular) PostScript, except that the same language that controls printed images also controls how those images appear on the display screen. For users, this unified imaging model means

D

that images on the screen look just as they will when printed, which greatly reduces the guesswork and number of 'trial' versions the user must print. In Release 2.0 of NeXTstep, NeXT has improved its imaging model with the inclusion of the Adobe Type Manager, Kanji font support, a variety of performance improvements, and a more flexible printing architecture to speed printing. See **NeXT Computer, Inc**.

display recall control [ISO On a battery-powered calculator, a control for recalling a display that has been blanked out by battery-saving circuits.]

display space [ISO That portion of the device space corresponding to the area available for displaying images.]

display surface [ISO In a display device, that medium on which display images may appear. *Examples:* The screen of a cathode ray tube; the paper in a plotter.]

display type In typography, a typeface used for headline and subheadline copy. Display type is usually much larger than body type. See **body type**.

distance resolution See **spatial resolution**.

distortion Unwanted changes in the waveform of a message signal as it is being transmitted, such as the impairment of tone in a radio signal. High-frequency signals lose their clarity and strength much sooner than low-frequency signals; therefore, repeaters are used at certain points across a communications network to regenerate electrical signals to their original

strength and form, so as to increase the maximum transmission distance. The weakening of a signal is sometimes called 'attenuation', and occurs when electrons (due to friction) distort the signal they are carrying. Similarly, changes in light signals (before or after they pass through a lens) cause image distortion. In photography, special equipment is used to produce distortion for special effects, and these are known as 'distortion optics'. Delay distortion refers to a condition where phase shifting occurs between frequencies and distorts the received data. It is caused by the fact that different frequencies travel through telephone lines at slightly different speeds. See **noise** and **repeater**. The word 'distortion' comes from the Latin word *torquere*, meaning 'twist'.

distributed data processing The gathering, storing, and processing of data at various remote locations of a large computer environment. This became popular in the 1970s when minicomputers were decentralized (distributed away from the central computer) and could process data independently, yet still had access to the host. Abbreviation 'DDP'. Compare **centralized data processing**. 2. [ISO Data processing in which some or all of the processing, storage, and control functions, in addition to input–output functions, are dispersed among data processing stations.]

distributed processing system A local area network (LAN) which provides each user with a full-function personal computer, as well as access to the file server for normal LAN file and peripheral sharing. One advantage of a distributed processing system is the ability of users to work independently of the LAN, even when the LAN is out of order.

distributed TP See **distributed transaction processing**.

distributed transaction processing Unlike centralized transaction processing in which all components (user interface, application, and database) run on the same computer, distributed transaction processing (DTP) is a system in which one or more components run on separate computers and communicate across a network. The simplest distributed system may involve the running of forms processing on a front-end processor, and a database and applications manager on a back-end processor. More extensive networks of DTP may be used by a corporation that has many offices and facilities in many locations across a wide geographical area, by coordinating the activities of application components running on computers at each of those locations. Users can run the same application at different locations, or they can run different applications at each location and then integrate them. DTP can provide a number of benefits in terms of performance, availability, and local control, including better response time, higher aggregate throughput, the ability to scale up incrementally, better price/performance, greater availability, and greater local control. However, a transaction processing architecture established from the beginning can ensure that a centralized application can become a distributed application without changing any source code. An architecture (such as DECdta) not only supplies the necessary components, but also allows the integration of hardware products (processors, storage,

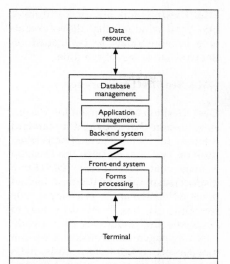

distributed transaction processing This diagram shows one of the simplest types of distributed transaction processing. It involves running forms processing on a front-end processor, and the database and application managers on a back-end processor. Typically, distributed transaction processing uses a system in which one or more components run on separate computers and communicate across a network. The main benefit of a distributed transaction processing architecture such as DECdta (from Digital) is the assurance that a centralized application can become a distributed application without changing any source code.

communications, and terminals) and software products (operating systems, programming tools, database tools, and communications software) so that: the development of components evolves through different product versions in a coordinated way; the components implemented on different operating system platforms interoperate; and many products and customer applications will be portable across different operating system platforms. See **ACID test** and **transaction processing**.

DLL Dynamic-link library; a feature of OS/2 and Windows that allows executable code modules to be loaded on demand and linked at run-time.

DMA See **direct memory access**.

DMI Desktop Management Interface; a specification that provides a standard interface for management of networked desktop systems. In 1993, the Desktop Management Task Force (DMTF), a consortium of manufacturers, delivered the specification and service-layer code for DMI. It has been designed to overcome the limitations of network-based management protocols. DMI can manage network interface cards, mass storage devices, application software, and operating systems. The charter members who developed the DMI specification were DEC, HP, IBM, Intel, Microsoft, Novell, SunConnect, and SynOptics (Bay Networks).

DML Data manipulation language; a language for changing (updating, inserting, or deleting) the contents of a database.

DMM Digital multimeter.

DMTF See **Desktop Management Task Force**.

DNA Digital Network Architecture; network architecture developed by Digital Equipment Corporation in 1976.

docking station A desktop expansion base which may consist of secondary storage and expansion ports, but lacks a central processing unit. It is used to transform a small laptop or notebook computer into a full-function desktop computer with full local area networking and file and peripheral sharing capabilities. This level of technology is replacing desktop computers which are large and not designed to be taken off-site. See **laptop computer**. ▼

doctor blade A flat blade which is part of the development unit of a laser printer. The doctor blade trims excess toner off the magnetic brush prior to contact with the photoreceptor. This ensures that the toner brush thickness remains constant. Some printers use a second doctor blade in the cleaning stage of the print cycle to scrape residual toner off the drum or belt. See **OPC cartridge**.

document comparison utility A program used to compare two documents on disk. It is especially useful when a copy of a document is given to another person to edit on disk. When the document is returned, the author is able to identify the changes made by comparing the two documents using the utility. The result is displayed on the screen, highlighting any new words or sentences. Text which was deleted is also displayed with a line through it on the screen for easy identification and comparison.

document format In word processing, a set of codes which describe the parameters of the working area, including fonts, line spacing, margins, headers, and footers.

Document Interchange Architecture A standard for file transfer. Developed by IBM to aid in file transfer among dissimilar IBM devices, Document Interchange Architecture provides logi-

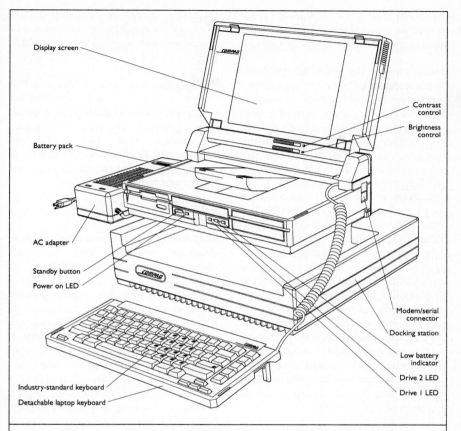

Display screen

Contrast control

Brightness control

Battery pack

AC adapter

Standby button

Power on LED

Modem/serial connector

Docking station

Low battery indicator

Drive 2 LED

Drive I LED

Industry-standard keyboard

Detachable laptop keyboard

docking station *The docking station shown above is also known as a 'desktop expansion base'. It features two full-sized slots for the installation of industry-standard expansion boards which can be used to increase system flexibility and provide the ability to customize the system for particular applications and hardware options. It also has a separate AC power supply which can power the whole system while it simultaneously charges the battery. To allow easier transition from an office to a portable environment, external devices may be connected via standard interfaces. Some docking stations can accommodate internal mass storage devices such as fixed disk drives or CD–ROM drives.*

cal addressing information. Documents which follow Document Interchange Architecture are sent via the Systems Network Architecture Distribution Services. Abbreviation 'DIA'.

document processing A complete system for creating, editing, printing, binding, and packaging a document. This may include automated indexing, table of contents, and referencing. Document processing thus goes one step further than word processing, which is limited to the automated process of creating, editing, and outputting words for letters, reports, and the like.

document reader [ISO A character reader whose input data is the text from specific areas on a given type of form.]

doduc One of the ten SPEC (Systems Performance Evaluation Cooperative) benchmarks drawn from real-world applications including scientific and engineering areas, focusing on system performance, memory, input/output, graphics, networking, multi-user, and commercial applications. A FORTRAN benchmark, doduc is a Monte Carlo simulation of the time evolution of a thermohydraulical modelization (hydrocode) for a nuclear reactor's component. It does little input/output, and has very little vectorizable code, but rather has an abundance of short branches and loops. It uses floating point numbers with 64-bit precision. Doduc has been run on a large variety of machines, and is a popular benchmark in some segments of the physics community. It emits a short sequence of outputs that can be checked, and executes code spread over many functions. It requires about 40 functions to accumulate 99% of the total central processing cycle. See **SPEC**.

domain [ISO That part of a computer network in which the data processing resources are under common control.]

dongle A hardware device required by an operating system such as Banyan Vines. It is used to prevent unauthorized duplication. Although duplication is still possible, the operating system or software it protects will not operate on another computer without the server key being attached to the hardware (usually to a serial port). Also called a 'server key'.

DOS Disk Operating System; a machine-language program developed by Microsoft Corporation for personal computers. Pronounced 'doss'. See **MS-DOS**.

dot and dot dot (. and ..) Dot (.) is the current directory of the current drive under DOS and Windows, and some other operating systems. Dot (.) is also the character that separates the two parts of a DOS file name. Dot dot (..) is the next highest (or parent) directory to the current directory.

dot EXE (.EXE) See **EXE**.

dot matrix character generator [ISO A character generator that generates character images composed of dots.]

dot matrix printer An impact printer that uses a column of pins and an inked ribbon to print a sequence of dots on paper in such a way that the dots form a pattern (matrix) of letters, numbers or other images, and graphics. Some dot matrix printers use nine pins, giving a low resolution, while others use 24 pins to enhance the output quality. For even better output, some printers offer a near-letter quality (NLQ) mode, which prints at a slower rate because the printer head passes over each line several times for greater character definition. [ISO A printer that prints characters or images represented by dots. *Note:* When a dot matrix printer is used for graphics only, it may be called a 'dot plotter'.] See **daisy-wheel** and **laser printer**. ▼

dot pitch The maximum resolution of a monitor, which is determined by the size of the smallest dot it can display. The finer the perforation in the mask, the higher the resolution. High-resolution

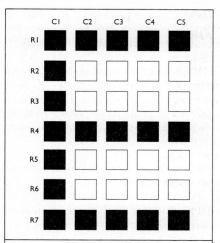

dot matrix printer A dot matrix printer head typically consists of 23 solenoids, each of which drives a stiff wire, or hammer, to impact the paper through an inked ribbon. Characters are formed by firing the solenoids to form a matrix of 'dots'. This figure shows how the character 'E' is formed using a 5 x 7 matrix. The columns are labeled C1 through C5, and rows R1 through R7. The print head moves left-to-right across the paper, so that at time T1, the head is over column C1. The character is formed by activating the proper solenoids as the print head sweeps across the character position.

monitors use a dot pitch of 0.28 milli-meter or less. See **resolution**.

dot prompt A dot (.) used as the symbol or character visible on the screen which represents a 'ready' state, asking the user for a command, as used in dBASE. In DOS, the common prompt is called a 'C' prompt. This is the letter 'C' fol-lowed by a colon, a back-slash sign, and greater-than sign (C:\>).

dots per inch See **DPI**.

double click The action of pressing a

mouse button twice in rapid succession. This usually has the effect of 'choosing' the option that happens to be under the cursor.

double density The recording technique which enables a floppy or hard disk to store twice the amount of data that a single-density medium allows. Abbre-viation 'DD'. See **diskette** and **track density**.

D

double-pulse recording [ISO Phase mod-ulation recording with unmagnetized re-gions on each side of the magnetized regions.]

double (triple) (quadruple) (N-tuple) length register [ISO Two (three) (four) (N) registers that function as a single register. *Note:* A double-length register may be used in multiplication for storing the product, in division for storing the partial quotient and the remainder, in character manipulation for shifting and for accessing character strings.]

Dow Jones Information Service An online database maintained by the pub-lisher of the *Wall Street Journal,* and made available to subscribers for up-to-date stock prices and financial informa-tion.

downlink [ISO Pertaining to data trans-mission from the head-end to a data station.]

download To transfer a file from a re-mote information service (or computer) to the local computer.

downloadable font An electronically-represented printer font which must be sent to the printer's random-access memory from a computer or the printer's own hard disk. See **bit-mapped font** and **PostScript**.

downloading utility A program used to manage the transfer of downloadable fonts from the computer's or printer's hard disk to the printer's random-access memory. Some word processing and page layout programs like Microsoft Word and PageMaker contain built-in downloading utilities. See **downloadable font**.

downsize Now a euphemism used to refer to any situation or action that 'reduces'. In computing, it refers to the reduction in computer equipment (usually from mainframes) to a smaller form such as minicomputers or PCs.

down-time [ISO The time during which a functional unit cannot be used owing to a fault. *Note:* Down-time can result from a fault within the functional unit or from an environmental fault; in the former case, the down-time equals the inoperable time.] See **unscheduled down-time**.

downward compatibility See **backward compatibility**.

DP See **data processing**.

DPCM Differential pulse code modulation. See **pulse code modulation**.

DPI Dots per inch. A common measure which counts how many dots a printer can output per linear inch. When used to refer to a monitor or display device, the horizontal measurement is given before the vertical one.

DPM 1. Data processing manager. 2. Incorrect abbreviation for decibels per milliwatt. See **decibels per milliwatt**.

DPMA Data Processing Management Association.

DPNSS Digital Private Network Signalling System; defined by British Telecom in 1983.

DPS Dots per second; a measure used for scanning devices.

DPSI Dots per square inch; a measure used for scanning devices.

DPU Data path unit.

dragging [ISO Moving one or more segments on a display surface by translating it along a path determined by a locator.]

DRAM Dynamic random-access memory; a form of memory which requires its contents to be updated at least every one thousandth of a second because the capacitors which are used to represent memory states lose their electrical charge very quickly. DRAM chips (also known as 'dynamic RAM') are very small, cheap, and relatively simple to manufacture, but they are becoming unpopular among manufacturers since the introduction of static RAM (SRAM) chips, which can retain their contents (without the need to refresh) until the power is switched off. Microprocessors operating at clock speeds above 25 megahertz need DRAM with access times faster than 80 nanoseconds (80×10^{-9} seconds). DRAM devices use one transistor and one capacitor to store each bit as a charge. The reduced logic required to store each bit makes DRAM significantly denser than SRAM, allowing more bits per chip. The silicon die and the package of DRAM is also smaller than SRAM, allowing more DRAM chips to be mounted on a single board. One disadvantage of DRAM technology is the additional overhead it requires to maintain the charge of each bit. When a memory cell is read, the charge is removed. Consequently, DRAM cells must be recharged after each read operation. During a refresh operation, each cell is read and written back into the memory cell, bringing the charge level up to that of a newly written cell. To make the refresh process more efficient, an entire row of cells is refreshed during each refresh cycle. In 1991, Fujitsu developed the first 64-megabit DRAM — a chip that can hold 8 million characters on a chip that measures only 10 x 20 millimeters. To produce Fujitsu's 64-megabit DRAM requires technology so advanced that it can produce submicron electrodes less than one-third of one one-thousandth of a millimeter wide. In comparison to a human hair, which is 30 microns in diameter, consider that a memory cell which holds one bit of information measures only 1 by 1.8 microns, meaning that approximately 30 memory cells would measure the width of a single hair. DRAM is pronounced 'dee-ram'. SRAM is pronounced 'ess-ram'. See **RAM** and **refresh cycle**.

draw program A graphics software program that produces both line art and object-oriented graphics, stored as mathematical formulas (not bits on the screen). These mathematical formulae can be manipulated for re-sizing and scaling drawings such as circles, curves, and lines — unlike paint programs which tend to cause distortion when re-sized. For the Macintosh, MacDraw is a popular entry-level draw program.

drift [ISO The unwanted change of the value of an output signal of a device over a specified period of time when the values of all input signals of the device are kept constant.]

drip-feed A technique whereby transactions are collected into groups so that they can be processed or updated as a group to save computer time or computer interruption. Sometimes this technique is called 'batch processing'.

drive duplexing A fault-tolerance feature that sets up primary and secondary partitions with identical data using separate disk drives. Drive duplexing provides protection against errors caused by a faulty controller or faulty disk. In drive duplexing and mirroring, drive verification is the process of ensuring that data on a primary partition and a secondary partition are identical. The drive that duplicates data on the primary memory is called the 'secondary partition'. This is invisible to the operating system, which sees the primary and secondary partitions as a single logical drive. Compare **drive mirroring**.

drive mirroring A fault-tolerance feature that sets up primary and secondary partitions on two disks using the same disk controller. The operating system treats these partitions as a single logical drive. Data lost from one partition can be recovered from the other. In drive mirroring and duplexing, drive verification is the process of ensuring that data on a primary partition and a secondary partition are identical. The drive that duplicates data on the primary memory is called the 'secondary partition'. This is invisible to the operating system, which sees the primary and secondary partitions as a single logical drive. Compare **drive duplexing**.

driver A file used by a particular program to execute commands to operate peripherals such as a printer or monitor.

drive synchronization For concurrency to occur on multiple data channels in a disk array, the spindles from the drives in the array are rotationally locked together. Sector 'n' passes under the drive heads of all drives at the same time.

drop cable [ISO The cable that connects a data station to a trunk coupling unit.]

drop cap Drop capital. In typography, a technique used to highlight the beginning of a paragraph or chapter. The first character is enlarged so that the top of the first character lines up with the top of the first line, and the rest of the character descends to the second or further lines. ▼

> A technique used to highlight the beginning of a paragraph or chapter. The first character is enlarged so that the top of the first character lines up with the top of the first line, and the rest of the character descends to the second or further lines.
>
> *drop cap An example of text set with a drop cap.*

drop-in [ISO An error detected by the reading of a binary character not

previously recorded, in storing or retrieving data from a magnetic storage device. *Note:* Drop-ins are usually caused by defects in, or the presence of, particles on the magnetic surface layer.]

drop-out [ISO An error caused by the failure to read a binary character, in storing or retrieving data from a magnetic storage device. *Note:* Drop-outs are usually caused by defects in, or the presence of, particles on the magnetic surface layer.]

drop shadow In typography, the shadow placed behind a symbol or character to give the illusion that a light-source is causing a shadow. ▼

drum plotter [ISO A plotter that draws a display image on a display surface mounted on a rotating drum.]

drum printer An impact printer consisting of a long cylinder with raised rows of characters on its surface. For each print position, the drum has a complete set of 64 characters (letters, numbers, and symbols) around its circumference. As the drum rotates at high speed, a hammer strikes the paper and ribbon, hitting different characters as appropriate. Print speeds may exceed 3000 lines per minute. [ISO An impact printer in which a full character set placed on a rotating drum is made available for each printing position.] See **impact printer**.

DROP SHADOW

drop shadow An example of text set with a drop shadow.

drum unit Also 'magnetic drum unit'. [ISO A device that contains a magnetic drum, the mechanism for moving it, magnetic heads, and associated controls.]

DS Dansk Standardiseringsraad; Denmark's standards body formed in 1925.

DSA Digital Storage Architecture; Digital Equipment Corporation's (DEC) solution to the twin challenges of tracking new technology while maintaining compatibility with earlier products. DSA is an extensive set of standards and specifications that is reflected in every DSA product. Besides specifying aspects of product design such as performance optimizations, error-correction code, and a unique error-detection code, DSA ensures that adding new DEC storage devices to a computer system will involve little more than plugging them in. One tool available with DSA is VAXsimPLUS software — a predictive maintenance tool that uses artificial intelligence and database information. The software alerts system managers to potential problems and suggests an appropriate course of action.

DSBSC Double sideband suppressed carrier.

DSE Data switching exchange.

DSG Distribution Symbology Group; the body which (in 1981) adopted Code 39 as one of the bar code systems. See **bar code**.

DSN Dewan Standardisasi Nasional; Indonesia's standards body formed in 1984.

DSP56001 See **Motorola DSP56001**.

DSS Decision support system.

DTE Data terminal equipment; generally devices such as terminals or computers which connect to data communications equipment.

D

DTP 1. See **desktop publishing**. 2. See **distributed transaction processing**.

DTR Data terminal ready. This signal indicates to the modem when the data terminal equipment is ready to begin communications.

DTS Digital termination systems. These are 'bypass technology' communications facilities available for local area high-speed digital communications options.

dual-cable broadband LAN [ISO A broadband LAN that uses separate cables for the forward LAN channel and the backward LAN channel.]

dual heads A technique frequently employed in large-capacity fixed disk drives with rotary positioners to improve seek times. In these drives, each access arm is T-shaped, with a slider suspension and head at each end of the T's crossbar. The two heads are separated by half the width of the recorded band on the disk. Each head thus spans half of the tracks. When a seek is performed, drive electronics select an inner or outer head as required by the target cylinder address. Dual heads on each access arm improve disk performance because the maximum distance over which the positioner must seek is halved, therefore reducing average seek time. Also, the amount of data available at the end of a seek is twice that which would normally be available with a single head per access arm. Not only do two heads per access arm improve seek performance, but they also minimize the amount of yaw at the extremes of the seek range. This improves flying height uniformity. The advantages of dual-head access arms are greatest with large-diameter disks. With smaller disks, seek ranges are inherently shorter, and the cost of two heads per surface is a more significant factor. See **yaw angle**.

dual in-line package switch See **DIP switch**.

dual operation [ISO Of a Boolean operation, another Boolean operation whose result, when it is performed on operands that are the negation of the operands of the first Boolean operation, is the negation of the result of the first Boolean operation. *Example:* Disjunction is the dual operation of conjunction.]

dumb terminal A workstation consisting of keyboard and screen, used to input data to the computer, or to receive information from the computer. Also known as 'unintelligent terminals', they were originally developed to be connected to computers running a multi-user operating system so that users could communicate directly with them. All processing is done at and by the computer, not the dumb terminal. In contrast, a smart terminal contains processing circuits which can receive data from the host computer and later carry out independent processing operations. ▼

dump 1. A hard-copy print-out (or output to secondary storage) listing the

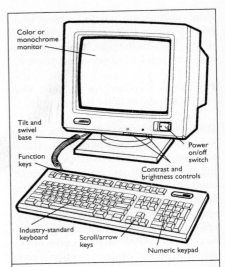

Color or monochrome monitor

Tilt and swivel base

Function keys

Power on/off switch

Contrast and brightness controls

Industry-standard keyboard

Scroll/arrow keys

Numeric keypad

dumb terminal *Terminals vary in shape and size. This 16-inch (diagonal) screen provides the ability to display 132 columns of text so that a user may view more information on the display to support terminal emulation and spreadsheet applications. Similar models are also available with the ability to display 256 colors in 1024 x 768, or 640 x 480 pixel resolutions.*

contents of primary storage available in the central processing unit. Data can be dumped in hexadecimal format or English-like code. A dump is usually requested by a programmer when an error is detected in a program or operating system. 2. [ISO Data that has been dumped.] 3. [ISO To record, at a particular instant, the contents of all or part of one storage device in another storage device. *Note:* Dumping is usually for the purpose of debugging.]

duodecillion See **exponent**.

duplex 1. A method of transmitting information over a communications channel, in which signals are sent in both directions simultaneously. Other methods of transmission include half duplex, full duplex, and simplex. Half duplex allows two-way communications, but messages can only travel in one direction at a time. Full duplex allows messages to be sent both ways along a communications line simultaneously. Simplex allows messages to be transmitted in only one direction. 2. Photographic paper that is light-sensitive on both sides. Also called 'duplex paper'. The word 'duplex' comes from Latin, where *duo* means 'two' and *plex* means 'fold'.

duplex circuit Any electronic circuit which can be used to transmit and receive data simultaneously. See **duplex**.

duplexing See **drive duplexing**.

duplex transmission [ISO Data transmission in both directions at the same time.]

duplicate [ISO To copy from a source data medium to a destination data medium that has the same physical form. *Example:* To copy a file from a magnetic tape to another magnetic tape.]

durability In transaction processing, a computer transaction is said to provide integrity of operation and data when the transaction passes the ACID (atomicity, consistency, isolation, durability) test. A transaction has 'durability' if all the changes that it makes to the database become permanent when the transaction is committed. The ACID properties and the ability to recover data (after a failure) make transaction processing a distinct style of computing for which unique

software products have been developed (such as the VAX ACMS and DECintact systems from Digital Equipment Corporation, and the CICS system from IBM). See **ACID test** and **transaction processing**.

DVI Digital Video Interface. A trademark of Intel Corporation, DVI technology (developed by RCA in 1987) is an interactive audio and video medium which enables full-motion video, video still images, stereo sound, computer graphics, and text to be completely integrated into a personal computer. The user can control high-fidelity, interactive applications, turning a personal computer into a multimedia system which can create and modify video images or computer graphics in real-time compression at 30 frames per second (FPS). Because the DVI allows direct video camera input, the expense of flat bed or drum-type image digitizers (scanners) can be avoided. DVI has been replaced on the software side with Indeo video technology, on the retail side with Smart Video Recorded, and on the hardware side with i750 processors.

Dvorak A keyboard layout introduced as an alternative to the current QWERTY standard. Studies have shown that a typist using a Dvorak keyboard makes 70% of the keystrokes on the second row (home row) compared to approximately 30% for QWERTY. August Dvorak, of the University of Washington, invented this improved keyboard in 1930. He placed all vowels and punctuation marks on the left side of the keyboard, while common consonants were placed on the right. In 1983, impressed by the Dvorak keyboard, ANSI (American National Standards Institute) adopted it as an official alternative to QWERTY. With the possibility of a very high retraining bill, users have not adopted Dvorak as fast as was expected. Changing such a standard should not be so difficult, especially when compared to other standards which were implemented overnight — such as the overnight switch in Sweden from driving on the left-hand side to the right-hand side of the road; or the switch from imperial to metric, as was the case in France, Great Britain, and Australia. Pronounced 'div-or-ack'. Compare **QWERTY**.

DX See **Intel 80386**.

dyadic (N-adic) Boolean operation [ISO A Boolean operation on two and only two (on N and only N) operands.] ▼

dyadic (N-adic) operation [ISO An operation on two and only two (on N and only N) operands. *Note:* The term 'binary operation' is deprecated to avoid confusion with 'binary arithmetic operation' and 'Boolean operation'.]

dynamic [ISO Pertaining to properties that can only be established during the

Operation number	Complementary operation	Result for: $P=0$ $Q=0$	Result for: $P=0$ $Q=1$	Result for: $P=1$ $Q=0$	Result for: $P=1$ $Q=1$	Entry	Meaning	Examples for representation — Symbolic representation	Examples for representation — Representation using Venn diagram
0	15	0	0	0	0	Zero constant	Zero constant	0	
1	14	0	0	0	1	Conjunction	P and Q		
2	13	0	0	1	0	Exclusion	P excluding Q		
3	12	0	0	1	1	(First) Variable	P		
4	11	0	1	0	0	Exclusion	Q excluding P		
5	10	0	1	0	1	(Second) Variable	Q		
6	9	0	1	1	0	Non-equivalence	Either P or Q		
7	8	0	1	1	1	Disjunction	P or Q		
8	7	1	0	0	0	Non-disjunction	Niether P nor Q		
9	6	1	0	0	1	Equivalence operation	P equivalent to Q		
10	5	1	0	1	0	Negation of second variable	Not Q		
11	4	1	0	1	1	Implication	Q implies P		
12	3	1	1	0	0	Negation of first variable	Not P		
13	2	1	1	0	1	Implication	P implies Q		
14	1	1	1	1	0	Non-conjunction	Not both P and Q		
15	0	1	1	1	1	One constant	One constant		

dyadic (N-adic) Boolean operation This is the ISO table of dyadic Boolean operations. Note that the variables P and Q are represented respectively by the right circles of this table. The defined set is represented by the shaded areas.

execution of a program. *Example:* The length of a varying length data object is dynamic.]

dynamic buffering [ISO A dynamic allocation of buffer storage.]

dynamic environment An environment in which data changes continuously, such as during an emergency situation on an aircraft where data changes by the second. Expert systems are being developed to handle such dynamic environments. Abbreviation 'DE'.

dynamic link Particularly useful in database management, a link which ensures that by using an update command, all data changed in one program is automatically changed in another program, thereby keeping the data consistent.

dynamic RAM Dynamic random-access memory. See **DRAM**.

dynamic random-access memory See **DRAM**.

dynamic relocation [ISO A process that assigns new absolute addresses to a computer program during execution so that the program may be executed from a different area of main storage.]

dynamic (resource) allocation [ISO An allocation technique in which the resources assigned for the execution of computer programs are determined by criteria applied at the moment of need.]

dynamic signature verifier A biometric security device which is used to store the dynamic characteristics of a handwritten signature so that a positive identification can be established before entry to a computer system or a room is permitted. See **biometric security devices**.

dynamic storage [ISO A storage device that does require periodic refreshment.]

E 1. Exa-. An SI unit prefix for 10^{18} expressed in decimal notation as 1 000 000 000 000 000 000, as in 'exahertz' (EHz). 2. The hexadecimal symbol for binary 1110 (which is equal to the decimal number 14). $E_{16} = 14_{10} = 16_8 = 1110_2$.

EARN European Academic Research Network; a communications network developed in 1983 by IBM France, Telic-Alcatel, and IB2 Technologies to link universities across Europe, North America, Africa, and Asia.

Earth station A special dish-shaped antenna designed to receive and transmit electromagnetic waves to and from communications satellites orbiting the atmosphere. At the base destination, Earth stations re-transmit the information using conventional equipment and devices, including microwave relay stations. See **satellite transmission**. ▼

Earth station *Available in various shapes and sizes, Earth stations are large dish antennae used to communicate with an artificial satellite in space.*

EasyCAD2 A software package published by Evolution Computing of Arizona. It is a two-dimensional CAD (computer-aided design) program written in assembly language to allow the user to pro-

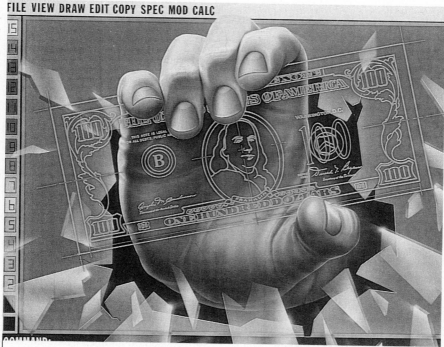

FILE VIEW DRAW EDIT COPY SPEC MOD CALC

EasyCAD2 Although CAD packages are generally used for industrial applications, this photograph shows how EasyCAD2 has been used for promotional design.

duce drawings from basic layouts to full engineering specifications for many commercial fields, including architectural, mechanical, electrical, and electronics. It uses floating point math for precise, near-infinite zoom, and includes online help, pull-down menus, a text editor for writing user-script, and macros. It also has utilities for file sharing among CAD and desktop publishing programs such as Aldus PageMaker and Ventura Publisher, and writes PostScript and HPGL files. To operate effectively, EasyCAD2 requires 640 kilobytes of random-access memory, a graphics adaptor, monitor, and a mouse or digitizing tablet. **A**

EasyFlow See **Adaptive Research Corporation**.

EAX Electronic automatic exchange.

EBCDIC Extended Binary-Coded Decimal Interchange Code. Established by IBM, EBCDIC is a coding scheme for representing 256 numbers/letters/ symbols using 8 bits for each character. EBCDIC is mainly used for IBM mainframes, while ASCII is used for personal computers. For example, the letter 'A' is represented in EBCDIC by 11000001. Pronounced 'ebb-suh-dick'. See **bit**. Compare **binary-coded decimal**. **V**

Letters	EBCDIC						
		P	11010111	3	11110011	'	01111101
		Q	11011000	4	11110100	<	01001100
A	11000001	R	11011001	5	11110101	>	01101110
B	11000010	S	11100010	6	11110110	$	01011011
C	11000011	T	11100011	7	11110111	¢	01001010
D	11000100	U	11100100	8	11111000	%	01101100
E	11000101	V	11100101	9	11111001	+	01001110
F	11000110	W	11100110			:	01111010
G	11000111	X	11100111	Symbols	EBCDIC	;	01011110
H	11001000	Y	11101000			*	01011100
I	11001001	Z	11101001	,	01101011	"	01111111
J	11010001			=	01111110	_	01101101
K	11010010	Numbers	EBCDIC	(	01001101	@	01111100
L	11010011			)	01011101	&	01010000
M	11010100	0	11110000	-	01100000	#	01111011
N	11010101	1	11110001	.	01001011	!	01011010
O	11010110	2	11110010	/	01100001	?	01101111

EBCDIC *This table shows how 8 bits are used to represent numbers, letters, and symbols. This system allows for 256 different combinations because $2^8 = 256$, allowing more than enough combinations to address 26 uppercase letters, 26 lowercase letters, the 10 decimal digits, and several special characters and symbols.*

ECC See **error correction code.**

echo 1. [ISO In computer graphics, the immediate notification of the current values provided by an input device to the user at the display console.] 2. Echo check; a method of checking the accuracy of transmission of data in which the received data is returned to the sender for comparison with the original data. In computer communications, such as modem-to-modem communications, the Echo is an on-screen display of the typed characters. This is either a return of the characters as received by the remote computer, or (where the system is considered reliable) simply what is typed (echoed locally). 3. In DOS, the term which means that activity resulting from certain processes (such as execution of the AUTOEXEC.BAT file) is displayed on the screen.

echoplex A synchronous communications protocol in which the information sent to the receiving station is echoed to the sender (transmitter) to acknowledge correct receipt of data. See **parity bit.**

echo suppressors Like equalizers, echo suppressors are used for correcting distortion. They prevent echoes from occurring when a signal is passed from a four-wire toll trunk into a two-wire circuit at the toll office. The telephone company is required to provide echo suppression on all lines where the echo would exceed 45 milliseconds. Simply stated, if there is any signal passing through an echo suppressor, the device will severely attenuate any signal in the return path of the toll trunk, thereby eliminating the return echo. Echo suppressors must be disabled if signals are to be transmitted in both directions simultaneously over a single line. This is necessary for full-duplex two-wire operation and reverse channel operation. To disable the echo suppressors, a frequency between 2010 and 2040 hertz must be transmitted for at least 400 milliseconds. This will cause the echo suppressors in both directions to drop out. They will stay disabled as long as a signal is present on one side or the other of the toll trunk. If a data signal is not present on either side for a period exceeding 100 milliseconds, both echo suppressors will become active again.

Eckert, John Presper Born in Philadelphia on 9 April 1919, Eckert, at the age of 25, was the co-inventor of the first large-scale electronic digital calculator called 'ENIAC' (Electronic Numerical Integrator And Calculator) — a project funded by the United States Department of Defense which at that time needed to find a way to quickly re-compute artillery firing tables during World War II. In 1948, Eckert and John William Mauchly formed a computer manufacturing company, and a year later, released BINAC (Binary Automatic Computer) which used magnetic tape instead of punched cards. Another of their inventions was UNIVAC 1 (Universal Automatic Computer — Model 1). Their computer company was taken over in 1950 by Remington Rand which was later known as 'Sperry Corporation' and today is called 'Unisys Corporation'. See **ENIAC** and **Mauchly, John William**.

ECMA European Computer Manufacturers' Association.

ECR Error check routine. See **parity bit**.

ECS European Communications Satellites.

EDA Electronic design automation.

EDC Error detection code.

EDI Electronic data interchange; the electronic exchange of structured business documents between an enterprise and its vendors, customers, or other trading partners. The form of these documents is based upon the use of industry, national, and international standards such as ANSI X12 and EDIFACT (EDI for administration, commerce, and trade). EDI services on a computer system should include gateways for sending, receiving, and logging of EDI data or documents, translation modules for data conversions, and applications interface modules that handle the transfer and routing between applications and the translation module. Different computer vendors are creating their own EDI services. Digital, for example, offers VAX/EDI which was first available in the United Kingdom. Pronounced 'ee-dee-eye'.

EDIFACT Electronic data interchange for administration, commerce, and trade. See **EDI**.

edit 1. [ISO To prepare data for a later operation. *Note:* Editing may include the rearrangement, addition or modification of data, the deletion of unwanted data, format control, code conversion, and the application of standard processes such as zero suppression.] 2. To alter a text file. 3. A DOS command which invokes a simple text editor for editing batch files and the like.

editing 1. [ISO In programming, transforming values to the representations specified by a given format.] 2. Altering a file.

EDP Electronic data processing; the writing and manipulating of information within a computer system. A specific field of data processing is 'word processing' which deals specifically with text being made ready for output. Compare **document processing**.

EDP Auditors' Foundation An organization whose members specialize in auditing computer systems (electronic data processing).

EDTV Extended definition television.

edutainment Refers to software that falls in the categories of entertainment and education. Edutainment software is usually written for multimedia applications, and is sold on CD–ROM. See **multimedia**.

EDVAC Electronic Discrete Variable Automatic Computer; developed by Dr John Von Neumann, a Hungarian-born mathematician who was commissioned by the United States Army to build a computer more powerful than the ENIAC. He was assisted by John Mauchly and John Presper Eckert. Pronounced 'ed-vack'. See **ENIAC**.

EEMS Enhanced Expanded Memory Specification. Most personal computers running under DOS have a random-access memory limitation of 640 kilobytes. To expand on this memory limitation, EEMS was introduced by Ashton-Tate (Borland), AST, and Quadram to enhance an earlier version of expanded memory called 'Lotus–Intel–Microsoft Expanded Memory Specification' (LIM EMS). Since the release of LIM EMS Version 4.0, enhancement issues have been solved, making it the dominant standard.

EEPROM Electrically erasable (user) programmable read-only memory. A ROM technology advancement occurred in 1980 with the introduction of Intel's 2816 — a 16-kilobit ROM that was user-programmable and electrically erasable

(hence called 'E^{2}PROM' or 'EEPROM'). Thus, instead of being removed from its host system and placed under ultraviolet light to erase its program, the 2816 could be re-programmed in its socket (single bits could be erased in one operation instead of erasing the entire chip). EEPROMs opened up new applications. In point-of-sale terminals, for example, each terminal connects to a central computer but each can also handle moderate amounts of local processing. Using an EEPROM, a terminal can store discount information to be automatically calculated during a sales transaction. Should the discount change, the central computer can update each terminal via telephone lines (or cable) by re-programming the portion of the EEPROM. EEPROMs contain floating-gate tunnel-oxide (flotox) cell structures. Based upon electron tunneling through a thin (less than 200 Ångstroms) layer of silicon dioxide, these cells permit writing and erasing with 21-volt pulses. (During read operations, the chips use conventional +5-volt power.) See **ROM**.

effective data transfer rate [ISO The average number of bits, characters, or blocks, per unit time transferred from a data source to a data sink and accepted as valid. *Note:* The rate is expressed in bits, characters, or blocks, per second, minute, or hour.]

EFT Electronic funds transfer; financial transactions made via computers, typically automatic telling machines (ATM).

EFTPOS Electronic funds transfer at point-of-sale. This is an acronym, pronounced 'eft-poss'.

EGA Enhanced Graphics Adapter; a

display adapter developed by IBM in 1984 as an improvement on the earlier version called 'Color Graphics Adapter' (CGA). EGA is capable of displaying 16 colors (from a possible 64) simultaneously with a horizontal resolution of 640 pixels (picture elements), and a vertical resolution of 350 pixels. Each character is formed in an 8 x 14 pixel matrix. This standard was superseded by Video Graphics Array (VGA). See **video adapter**.

EIA Electronic Industries Association; a United States national trade association of the American National Standards Institute. EIA-recommended standards are designated by numbers with an RS prefix. For example, EIA has developed standards used in the majority of interfaces between data processing equipment and communications equipment. These are known as the 'RS-232-C' interfaces, which are similar to the CCITT V.24 interfaces.

E/IDE Enhanced integral drive electronics. See **IDE**.

802.3 CSMA/CD See **CSMA/CD**.

8086 See **Intel 8086**.

8088 See **Intel 8088**.

8207 See **Intel 80286**.

80386DX See **Intel 80386**.

EIS Executive information system.

EISA Extended Industry Standard Architecture. To protect its investment after several companies started to manufacture clones of the IBM Personal Computer, IBM re-launched its personal computer range in 1986 with a closed-architecture series called 'PS/2' (Personal System 2). The PS/2 was designed using a new bus architecture called 'Micro Channel Architecture' (MCA) which meant that existing industry software and peripherals could not function on PS/2. Compaq Computer Corporation and eight other manufacturers (dubbed the 'Gang of Nine') joined forces to maintain the industry-standard architecture (ISA), and further developed it to take advantage of the 32-bit bus structure of the Intel 80386 and 80486 microprocessors. Extended ISA became known as 'EISA'. Today, the term 'IBM-compatible' is confusing, and it has become common to refer to such computers as 'industry-standard computers'. Pronounced 'ee-sah'. See **Gang of Nine**.

ELD Electroluminescent display; a method by which light is emitted by the stimulation of luminescent material between a pair of charged electrodes.

electrically erasable (user) programmable read-only memory See **EEPROM**.

electronic data interchange See **EDI**.

Electronic Discrete Variable Automatic Computer See **EDVAC**.

Electronic Industries Association A United States national trade association of the American National Standards Institute. Standards recommended by the Electronic Industries Association (EIA) are designated by numbers with an RS prefix. For example, EIA has developed standards used in the majority of interfaces between data processing

E

equipment and communications equipment. These are known as the 'RS-232-C' interfaces, which are similar to the CCITT V.24 interfaces.

electronic mail The wide use of communications and local area networks has made sending and receiving electronic messages possible. These messages can be sent locally within the computer network, or via telephone networks to remote sites. Recipients can read the message at their convenience, then perform one of many options such as printing the message, forwarding it, answering it, or deleting it. This is a fast and efficient way to communicate, because text and graphics files can also be attached to the message. Microsoft's electronic mail software is called 'cc:Mail'. Electronic mail is also called 'electronic text transfer'. Abbreviation 'e-mail'.

Electronic Numerical Integrator and Calculator See **ENIAC**.

electronic text transfer See **electronic mail**.

Electronic Storage Element See **ESE20**.

electron theory Since electricity cannot be seen, theories have been developed to explain the phenomenon of electricity. The basic theory, and one that is accepted as fact, is that electricity is the movement of electrons. The electron theory assumes that all electrical effects are due to the movement of electrons from place to place, and that this movement is caused by an excess or deficiency of electrons in a particular place. Within material, atoms and their electrons are in constant motion. However, this is a random motion of free electrons moving from atom to atom in no particular direction. This movement of electrons is not 'electron flow'. To have electron flow, there must be a continuous movement where most of the free electrons move in the same direction. If a path is provided that will allow electrons to move from a negatively-

---

NEWSFLASH

L AN-based and UNIX-based electronic mail packages are expected to drive worldwide revenues to US$1500 million by 1997, from US$659.2 million in 1992. US revenue will grow from US$347.1 million in 1992 to US$709.6 million in 1997.

The momentum of LAN-based and UNIX-based electronic mail adoption will boost the number of worldwide user mailboxes to nearly 100 million by 1997. Almost 57% of these will be in the United States.

Worldwide electronic mail, all segments (000s)

	1993	1994	1995	1996	1997
Shipments	350.6	471.3	606.9	797.8	831.5
Revenue US$000	703.6	839.6	1 010.8	1 258.7	1 456.6
Installed base	1 247.4	1 643.6	2 161.7	2 847.5	3 544.1
Mailboxes	34 947.0	44 772.7	58 170.3	75 336.9	95 999.8

charged material to a positively-charged material, electrons will flow. This flow of electrons is an electrical current and will continue until the current path is broken or until the electrical charge is equal at both points. To provide a measurable electrical current requires the movement of millions of electrons. Current (the flow of electrons) is measured in units called 'amperes'. To sustain current flow, some form of energy is required to produce a continuous supply of electrons. Some of the basic sources from which the energy can come are: friction — the rubbing together of certain material; chemical action — as used in a battery; heat; pressure — as applied to certain types of crystals; light; and magnetism — the movement of a wire through a magnetic field will cause electrons to move toward one end of the wire. Many turns of wire rotating in a magnetic field make an electric generator.

electrophotography The printing process used in laser printers and photocopiers. See **developer** and **laser printer**.

electrostatic latent image In laser printer technology, the electrostatic pattern of dots on the surface of the photoreceptor created by the turning off and on of the laser during the scanning process, corresponding to the pattern of dots to be printed on the page. See **laser printer** and **photoreceptor**.

electrostatic plotter [ISO A raster plotter that uses a row of electrodes to fix the inks electrostatically on the paper.]

electrostatic printer A low-impact printer which uses electrically-charged dot matrix pins to strike specially treated paper. The paper must later pass

through a chemical solution (toner) containing ink particles with the opposite charge. The ink particles are attracted to special areas on the paper to produce a visible image. Print speeds may exceed 5000 lines per minute. [ISO A non-impact printer that creates an electrostatic latent image, which is then made visible by a toner and transferred and fixed on paper. *Note:* An electrostatic printer may be used in some instances as a plotter.] See **impact printer**.

electrostatic storage [ISO A storage device that uses electrically-charged areas on a dielectric surface layer.]

electrothermal printer A non-impact printer in which imaging results from a chemical reaction when heat-sensitive paper comes into contact with the printing head. The paper darkens when heat is applied. Print speeds may exceed 5000 characters per minute. See **impact printer**. ▼

elite In typography, any fixed-space typeface pitched at 12 characters per inch.

EMA Enterprise Management Architecture; DEC's own network management plan for use with DECnet (Phase V). EMA provides a framework to integrate all network, systems, information, and applications management, treating all components as managed objects. EMA provides a methodical approach to design, installation, growth, and ongoing management of systems from multiple vendors. It supports the management of all devices, applications, and data on the network through open 'published' interfaces.

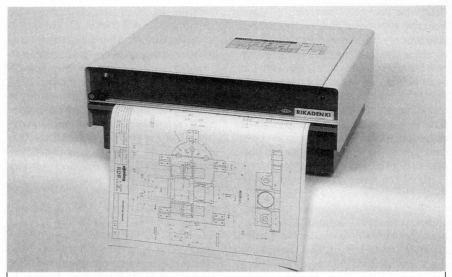

electrothermal printer *This A2/A3 thermal printer operates at high speed, using a roll of heat-sensitive paper, similar to that used in some facsimile machines.*

e-mail See **electronic mail**.

EMB Enhanced master burst.

embedded interface One of the four commonly-used device interfaces. For modern high-speed personal computers (PCs) to work efficiently with mass storage devices, there must be an effective means of transferring data between the device and the PC. The format and speed of this data transfer is determined by the type of 'device interface' built into the electronics on the drive and its controller board. The four commonly-used device interfaces are Enhanced Small Device Interface (ESDI), the Small Computer Systems Interface (SCSI), the embedded interface, and the ST-506 interface. Device manufacturers are starting to incorporate (embed) the controller and its circuits onto the physical drive so

that connection to the PC system bus is possible directly via a connector.

embedded servo control The process used in disk and tape drives to regulate positioning and seeking. Servo control relies on feedback of 'positioning data' from the media surface to generate correction signals to the positioner. Servo control may rely on a disk surface entirely dedicated to recording servo information, or servo information may be embedded among data blocks on all disk surfaces. See **access arm** and **head switching**.

embedded SQL SQL statements embedded within a source program and prepared before the program is executed.

emergent behavior See **artificial life**.

EMF Electro-motive force; the force that causes electrons to flow. It is measured in units called 'volts'. See **volt**.

EMMS Electronic mail and message system. See **electronic mail**.

emoticons Emotional icons. Character-based faces originally used to personalize electronic mail messages. Sometimes referred to as 'smiley faces', emoticons look best on-screen because they do not work well when printed using stylized or proportional fonts. ▼

empty medium [ISO A data medium that contains only marks of reference but no user data.]

empty time slot A method of using a ring network when one or more empty packets circulate around the ring. A terminal wanting to transmit must wait for the arrival of such an empty packet. See **token passing**.

EMS Expanded Memory Specification.

emulate [ISO To imitate one system with another, primarily by software, so that the imitating system accepts the same data, executes the same computer programs, and achieves the same results as the imitated system.] ▼

emulation [ISO The imitation of all or part of one system by another, primarily by software, so that the imitating system accepts the same data, executes the same programs, and achieves the same results as the imitated system.]

enabling signal [ISO A signal that permits the occurrence of an event.]

encapsulated type [ISO A module representing an abstract data type. *Example:* A stack processing module. *Note:* An encapsulated type hides the representation of its values but permits operations on the values by other modules.]

encapsulation 1. In object-oriented programming (OOP), encapsulation defines a data structure of attributes and a

:-)	Hello. This is funny. Smile.	:^(	I'm offended. My nose is out of joint.
:-(	I'm unhappy about this.	-)	This is boring. I'm asleep.
:-	Blank expression. I'm confused.	:-D	I'm ecstatic.
;-(	This makes me very sad.	:-o	I'm shocked.
[:	]	Just listen like a robot.	:-#	My lips are sealed.
:-(*)	This makes me vomit.	:-9	Licking my lips. This is great.
%-)	Cross-eyed. This makes me dizzy.	:-&	I'm tongue-tied.
P-)	Wink. I understand.	: :-))	That person is two-faced.

emoticons This list shows some of the many possible emoticons that can be constructed using simple monospaced fonts. Notice that the image should be viewed in landscape format.

emulate This instrument is called an 'emulator'. It is used to check the software that operates the circuit board. If a compatibility problem is detected in any of the microprocessors on the circuit board, with the help of the emulator, the software can be corrected and re-checked for proper operation.

group of member functions as a single unit called an 'object'. Object attributes in C++, for example, are stored in data structures that resemble ordinary C structures. Object behaviors are implemented as functions called 'member functions' in C++. This affords the programmer great flexibility in controlling access to an object's member data and member functions. For example, member data and member functions declared to be private cannot be accessed from outside the object, except by functions declared to be friends of the object.

Member data and member functions declared to be public can be accessed by an outside object, while those declared to be protected can only be accessed by certain other objects. This OOP feature is called 'information hiding', and it limits the 'visibility' of data, allowing it to be manipulated only via public member functions. Data hiding enhances reliability and modifiability of software by reducing the interdependencies between objects. If public member functions are specified correctly, the private data structures and member functions of an object may be changed without affecting the way other objects are implemented. This hiding of data can be likened to real objects in the real world, where there is often no way of knowing (and usually no need to know) how the internals on an object, such as a telephone, work. See **object-oriented programming**. 2. In networking, the process of enclosing packets of one type of protocol within another. For example, Banyan Vines can encapsulate TCP/IP packets. These packets travel through the network as Vines packets until the destination is reached. Then the packet is separated, and the TCP/IP packet is delivered to the destination system.

encode [ISO To convert data by the use of a code in such a manner that reconversion to the original form is possible.]

encoder [ISO A functional unit that has a number of input lines (such that not more than one at a time may carry a signal) and a number of output lines (such that any number may carry signals), and such that the combination of output signals serves as a code to indicate which input line carries the signal.]

Encore Computer Corporation Head-quartered in Fort Lauderdale, Florida, Encore designs, manufactures, distributes, and supports open computing solutions with mainframe performance for complex real-time online transaction processing applications. Founded in 1983 by Kenneth G. Fisher, Encore's strong presence in DARPA (the US Government Defense Advanced Research Projects Agency) began in 1986. Today it employs over 1000 staff members across 40 countries to service the real-time marketplace with processing power for commercial flight simulation, military simulation, and nuclear power plants — with an installed base of more than 25 000 computer systems worldwide. Its flagship product is the Infinity 90 Series — a scalable and high-throughput data center that offers linear scaling of processing power, I/O capacity, and I/O throughput in an open systems and standards-based computing environment. See **Fisher, Kenneth G.**

encryption Encoding of data for security purposes; especially used when transmitting confidential information. Due to the fact that data can be intercepted during transmission, an encryption of either the software or the hardware is used to counteract any abuse. A common method involves the scrambling of bit patterns. A special password or coding format must be known before a file can be decoded (decrypted).

end-around borrow [ISO The action of transferring a borrow digit from the most significant digit place to the least significant digit place.]

end-around carry [ISO The action of transferring a carry digit from the most significant digit place to the least significant digit place. *Example:* An end-around carry may be necessary when adding two negative numbers that are represented by their diminished radix complements.]

end-around shift [ISO A logical shift in which the characters moved out of one end of a computer word or register are re-entered into the other end.]

endnote In word processing, a notation made at the very end of a document, unlike a footer which is made at the end of a page.

end-of-file label [ISO An internal label that indicates the end of a file and that may contain data for use in the file control. *Note:* An end-of-file label may include control totals for comparison with counts accumulated during processing.]

end-of-tape marker [ISO A marker on a magnetic tape used to indicate the end of the permissible recording area. *Examples:* A photo-reflective strip; a transparent section of tape.]

end-of-volume label [ISO An internal label that indicates the end of the data contained in a volume.]

endpoint node [ISO A node that is at the end of only one branch.]

end user [ISO A person, device, program, or computer system that utilizes a computer network for the purpose of data processing and information exchange.]

engine In printer technology, the term

is often used to describe the main working assembly (engine) which forms the heart of laser and similar page printers.

Enhanced Graphics Adapter See **EGA**.

enhanced IDE See **IDE**.

Enhanced Small Device Interface See **ESDI**.

ENIAC Electronic Numerical Integrator and Calculator. The first large-scale electronic digital computer. It was funded by the United States Department of Defense when it needed to find a way to quickly re-compute artillery firing tables during World War II. The only tools available at that time were hand-operated calculators, punched-card accounting machines, and slow computers called 'differential analyzers'. ENIAC was completed in 1946 by John Presper Eckert and John William Mauchly at the Moore School of Engineering at the University of Pennsylvania. Its electronic calculations reached speeds more than 1000 times faster than the previous electro-mechanical calculating devices. It was estimated that because the average life span of a vacuum tube was 3000 hours, ENIAC would malfunction every 15 minutes. Critics suggested that since it would take 15 minutes to locate the faulty tube, no work could ever be performed on ENIAC. Despite this, it calculated in two hours what would have taken 100 engineers one year to complete. Although US$400 000 was approved for ENIAC, it was not built in time to contribute to the war. Once completed, ENIAC was a massive machine 100 foot (30 meters) long,

10 foot (3 meters) high, and weighing 30 tons. It used more than 18 000 vacuum tubes and 500 000 hand-soldered connections, and drew over 100 000 watts. The air conditioning system needed to keep ENIAC cool was as powerful as that needed for a modern 20-story office building. Pronounced 'any-yak'. See **Eckert, John Presper** and **EDVAC**.

Enterprise Management Architecture DEC's own network management plan for use with DECnet (Phase V). Enterprise Management Architecture (EMA) provides a framework to integrate all network, systems, information, and applications management, treating all components as managed objects. EMA provides a methodical approach to design, installation, growth, and on-going management of systems from multiple vendors. It supports the management of all devices, applications, and data on the network through open 'published' interfaces.

entry [ISO A language construct within a procedure, designating the start of an execution sequence of the procedure. *Note:* A procedure may have more than one entry; each entry usually includes an identifier, called the 'entry name', and possibly formal parameters.]

environmental condition [ISO A physical condition required for the protection and proper operation of a functional unit. *Examples:* Temperature, humidity, vibration, dust, and radiation. Notes: (a) An environmental condition is usually specified as a nominal value and a tolerance range. (b) For a device, there may be more than one set of environmental conditions; for example, one set for transport, another for storage, and another for operation.]

environmental description [ISO A language construct for the description of features that are not part of a program but are relevant to its execution. *Example:* Machine characteristics, special properties of files, interfaces with other programs.]

EOS Egyptian Organization for Standardization and Quality Control; Egypt's standards body formed in 1957.

EPA Environmental Protection Agency.

epitaxy The growth of one type of crystal onto the surface of another crystal without changing the orientation of the underlying crystal (substrate). See **molecular beam epitaxy**.

EPROM Erasable (user) programmable read-only memory. The first ROMs contained cell arrays in which the sequence of ones and zeros was established by a metalization interconnection mask step during fabrication. Thus, users had to supply a ROM vendor with an interconnect program, so that the vendor could complete the mask and build the ROMs. Set-up charges were quite high. To avoid this high set-up charge, manufacturers developed a user-programmable ROM (PROM). The first PROMs used fusible links that could be melted or 'burned' with a special programmer system. Once burned, a PROM was just like a ROM. As one alternative to fusible-link programming, Intel Corporation pioneered (in 1973) an erasable (metal-oxide semiconductor technology) PROM (an EPROM) that used charge-storage programming. It came in a standard

ceramic DIP (dual in-line package) but had a window that exposed it to light. When the chip was exposed to ultraviolet light, light energy photons could collide with the EPROM's electrons and scatter them at random, thus erasing the memory. Originally, EPROMs were not intended for use in read/write applications, but they proved very useful in research and development for prototypes, where the need to alter the program several times was quite common. As the fabrication process became mature and volumes increased, EPROM's lower prices made them attractive even for medium-volume production-system applications. Another ROM technology advance occurred in 1980 with the introduction of Intel's 2816 — a 16-kilobit ROM that was user-programmable and electrically erasable (hence called 'E²PROM' or 'EEPROM'). Thus, instead of being removed from its host system and placed under ultraviolet light to erase its program, the 2816 could be reprogrammed in its socket (single bits could be erased in one operation instead of erasing the entire chip). See **EEPROM** and **ROM**.

E²PROM Electrically erasable (user) programmable read-only memory. See **EEPROM**.

eqntott One of the ten SPEC (Systems Performance Evaluation Cooperative) benchmarks drawn from real-world applications including scientific and engineering areas, focusing on system performance, memory, input/output, graphics, networking, multi-user, and commercial applications. Eqntott is an integer-intensive benchmark written in C. The primary kind of computation performed is sorting. The benchmark translates a logical representation of a Boolean equation to a truth table. The source is from the Industrial Liaison Program of the University of California at Berkeley. The benchmark produces a truth table as output. Eqntott dynamically allocates about 1.8 megabytes of memory in 450 calls to the library routine called 'malloc( )' when run with the int_pri_3.enq input file. In addition, the benchmark spends nearly 95% of its time in the library routine called 'qsoty( )'. See **SPEC**.

equalizer Refers to the circuits in a communications device that compensates for the frequency-sensitive attenuation characteristics of a communications line. There are two types of equalizers: delay equalizers and amplitude equalizers. Delay equalizers are used to correct delay distortion. These devices delay the frequency that is traveling the fastest so as to maintain a correct phase relationship between both frequencies. Amplitude equalizers are used to correct attenuation distortion. These devices reduce the amplitude of the stronger frequency until it matches the amplitude of the weaker frequency. Both frequencies are then fed through an amplifier before continuing through the network.

equals function [ISO The function that allows the completion of a series of operations and the provision of the result.]

equivalence operation [ISO The dyadic Boolean operation whose result has the Boolean value 1 if and only if the operands have the same Boolean value.]

equivocation [ISO The conditional entropy of the occurrence of specific messages at the message source given the occurrence of specific messages at a message sink connected to the message source by a specific channel. *Notes:* (a) If x_i is the input message at the message source and y_j the output message at the message sink, the equivocation is noted as the conditional entropy $H(x|y)$. (b) The equivocation is the mean additional information content that must be supplied per message at the message sink to correct the received messages affected by a noisy channel.]

erasable optical disk While CD–ROM (compact disk–read-only memory) and WORM (write once, read many times) optical technologies are complementary to magnetic recording and will probably result in the development of new applications, erasable optical recording is a direct functional equivalent of magnetic disk recording. CD–ROM promises to foster the development of new applications for the small-system user by providing low-cost random access to very large amounts of text, audio, or graphical information. WORM technology makes high-capacity, tamper-proof online archives available at low media cost. Erasable optical recording, on the other hand, provides random read/write access to individual blocks of data — exactly equivalent to magnetic disk functionality. The difference between erasable optical and magnetic recording technology lies in cost, performance, and removability, rather than function or application. Several different media technologies for erasable optical recording include magneto-optic, phase transition, photochromic, and photodichroic recordings. In magneto-optic recording, a laser is used to raise the local media temperatures so that magnetic recording can occur. Data is read from magneto-optic media by observing variations in its reflection of polarized light. In phase transition recording, the laser is used to alter the state of localized areas on the media between amorphous and crystalline, changing its reflectivity. Phase transition recording has the advantage of being read-compatible with WORM media. Its disadvantage is that media lifetime expressed in 'number of overwrites' may be limited. In photochromic and photodichroic recordings, the laser is used to change the media color and polarization response properties respectively. These media are sensitive to ambient light, and must therefore be stored in the dark.

erasable storage [ISO A storage device in which different data can be written successively at the same storage location.]

erase [ISO To remove data from a data medium. *Note:* Erasing is usually accomplished by overwriting the data or deleting the references to them.]

erase head [ISO A magnetic head capable of only erasing data on a magnetic data medium.]

error [ISO A discrepancy between a computed, observed, or measured value or condition and the true, specified, or theoretically correct value or condition.]

error condition (In calculators.) [ISO The condition that exists when the operator attempts to make the calculator carry out a function that it cannot perform.]

error control [ISO That part of a proto-

col controlling the detection, and possibly the correction, of errors.]

error control software [ISO Software that monitors a computer system to detect, record, and possibly to correct errors.]

error correction [ISO A method used to correct erroneous data produced during data transmission, transfer, or storage.]

error-correction code A code used by most memory controllers, including those in VAX systems, to detect memory errors. Error correction code (ECC) detects errors in a manner similar to parity checking, but ECC goes one step further by correcting many of the errors it detects. The most common ECC logic is called 'single-error correction, double-error detecting' (SEC-DED). This means that the ECC will correct single-bit errors and detect double-bit errors. ECC dramatically decreases the number of system failures caused by memory errors, because most memory errors involve only a single bit. ECC generates a number of check bits for each unit of data and appends these check bits to the data before it is written to memory. If a SECDED implementation of ECC is used, a 32-bit-long word will have seven check bits appended to it. [ISO An error-detecting code designed to allow for the automatic correction of certain types of errors.] See **check bit**. ▼

error-detecting code [ISO A code in which each coded representation conforms to specific rules of construction so that their violation indicates the presence of errors.]

error detection [ISO A method of determining whether data has been transmitted or transferred incorrectly.]

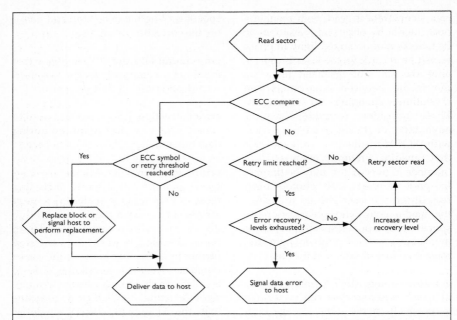

error-correction code *Some standard disk interconnections protocols use error-correction codes (ECC) like the one illustrated in the algorithm above. The ECC threshold is a drive-dependent number representing the acceptable number of error bursts in a single sector. If the controller must correct more than this number of bursts in a block read from the drive, the block should be replaced.*

error indication [ISO A visual indication that the operator has attempted to carry out a function that the calculator cannot perform.]

error range [ISO The set of values that an error may take.]

error rate [ISO The ratio of the total number of errors detected to the total amount of data transmitted or transferred.]

error recovery [ISO The process of correcting or bypassing the effects of a fault to restore a computer system to a prescribed condition.]

error span [ISO The difference between the highest and the lowest error values.]

ESA Enterprise System Architecture.

Esc See **escape key**.

escape key A key which takes on different functions depending upon the application being used, but is often used to cancel an operation or retreat from an operation. Abbreviation 'Esc'.

ESDI Enhanced Small Device Interface. For modern high-speed personal computers (PCs) to work efficiently with mass storage devices, there must be an effective means of transferring data between the device and the PC. The format and speed of this data transfer is determined by the type of 'device interface' built into the electronics on the drive and its controller board. There are four commonly-used device interfaces: Enhanced Small Device Interface (ESDI); the Small Computer Systems Interface (SCSI); the embedded interface; and the ST-506 interface. ESDI is an industry-standard interface that dramatically increases the data transfer rate of hard-disk drives. The multipurpose ESDI controller board contains a buffer that reads data requests by the central processing unit and, anticipating future requests, continues to read successive data until the buffer is filled. As a result, the amount of time the central processing unit spends accessing the fixed disk drive is significantly reduced. ESDI transfers data at 10 megabits per second — twice the speed possible from the earlier interface standard (ST-506). ESDI drives are especially useful when using Intel 80386 or 80486 microprocessors. ESDI defines the electrical and physical connection between the controller and the storage device, which could be a magnetic disk, an optical disk, or even a tape drive. Multiple devices can be driven from a single ESDI controller board. A separate 20-pin data cable runs from the controller to each drive, and a single 34-pin cable is daisy-chained from drive to drive. The maximum cable length is 9.84 foot (3 meters). In contrast to ESDI, SCSI is not concerned with the device-to-controller interface, but rather with the controller-to-system interface. SCSI defines a special bus cable dedicated to data transfer between the PC and up to eight peripheral devices, each with their own controller. In addition to the electrical and physical characteristics of the bus, SCSI defines a series of commands through which devices on the bus communicate with each other. Pronounced 'ez-dee'. See **1:1 interleave**.

ESE20 Electronic Storage Element Model 20. A nonvolatile storage device developed by Digital Equipment Corporation to offer a speed of 1 megabit DRAM (dynamic random-access memory) technology, combined with the availability advantages of magnetic disk storage. The ESE20 is capable of servicing up to 300 input/output requests, with average access times of 1.6 milliseconds. This first model could store 120 Mb and was available in a 60-inch-high storage array cabinet designed to hold two disks, with a total of 240 Mb. In the event of a power loss, all data in the ESE20's memory arrays is safely transferred onto an internal Winchester disk in a matter of minutes, using an internal power supply.

espresso One of the ten SPEC (Systems Performance Evaluation Cooperative) benchmarks drawn from real-world applications including scientific and engineering areas, focusing on system performance, memory, input/output, graphics, networking, multi-user, and commercial applications. Espresso is one of a collection of tools for the generation and optimization of programmable logic arrays (PLAs). Specifically, it is an application that performs heuristic Boolean function minimization. Espresso does not involve any floating point operations; it is categorized as an integer-intensive application bound to the central processing unit. Since it is integer-intensive, it also provides insight as to how logic simulation and routing

E

algorithms can be expected to perform an exponential back-off algorithm, which specifies a random waiting time before a station can attempt re-transmission. The random time is chosen from a window whose size is a binary multiple of the round-trip propagation delay time of the network, called the 'slot time'. The window size increases by a power of two after each collision until the tenth collision, after which it remains the same. Each transmission attempt is allowed a maximum 16 collisions before the higher layers are signaled that the message is undeliverable. The Ethernet frame is made up of seven fields. The first field is a 56-bit preamble used for hardware synchronization. This field is followed by an 8-bit start-of-frame delimiter field, two 6-byte address fields for destination and source addresses, and a 2-byte length field indicating the actual length of the data. Next comes the data or information field, which must be a minimum 46 bytes and a maximum 1500 bytes. The last field is a 32-bit frame check sequence, which contains the cyclic redundancy check (CRC) for the frame.

Ethernet access method A local area network using an Ethernet access method allows nodes to initiate transmission any time a clear channel is sensed. Since a bus topology is used, all transmissions are simultaneously sent to all nodes. Addressing information allows each node to recognize and receive individual messages. In this type of free-for-all environment, multiple nodes will occasionally transmit at the same time and message collision will occur, causing data errors. To overcome this problem, a sophisticated collision detection scheme is used. If a collision is detected, trans-

mission is halted and then re-tried after a random wait. The Ethernet access method can use twisted-pair, coaxial cable (baseband or broadband), or fiber optic media. In contrast, a token-ring local area network operates by continually passing a special data packet (or token) serially between devices electrically connected in a ring. Network stations which have data to send capture the free token and append the data along with addressing information. The entire data packet then continues to be passed around this ring until it reaches the destination node. During this process, the transmitting station is said to be in possession of the token, and no other station can talk. Once the data transfer is complete and verified, the token continues circulating, waiting for another transfer.

Ethernet/802.3 A modified version of the original Ethernet specification which was approved by IEEE standard 802.3. Ethernet/802.3 (also called 'Ethernet/IEEE') employs baseband signaling and Manchester phase encoding at a 10-megabits per second data rate using a broadcast bus topology. The medium is defined as a 0.4-inch, heavily shielded, 50-ohm cable which extends in segments of up to 1640 foot (500 meters) with passive termination at either end. These characteristics are the basis for the version name, type 10base5 (10-mega- bits per second, baseband, 500 meters). Each coaxial cable (coax) segment may have up to 100 stations attached, and networks as a whole may have up to 1024 stations. Coax segments are joined together with repeater sets and may also have between them a fiber optic link segment of up to 0.621 of a mile (1 kilometer), to which no stations may be connected. The maximum path length between any two stations on the network is three coax segments and two link segments. Stations are connected to the segment with a cable tap, a transceiver, and a shielded, twisted-pair transceiver cable which can extend up to 164 foot (50 meters). The transceiver is isolated from the main cable by use of AC/DC converters and pulse transformers or optoisolators. Three signals are carried between the transceiver and the station (transmit, receive, and collision presence).

Ethernet/IEEE See **Ethernet/802.3**.

e-time Execution time; the time it takes the arithmetic/logic unit to execute (perform) the instructions after the central processor executes a computer program. This is part of the machine cycle. See **machine cycle**. Compare **i-time**.

etiquette See **computer etiquette**.

ETSI European Telecommunications Standard Institute.

ETT Electronic text transfer. See **electronic mail**.

ETV Educational television.

evaluation report [ISO A system follow-up report that describes how the system objectives have been met, identifies the remaining problems, and is intended to assist future development.]

even header See **header**.

even parity An error-checking technique used in synchronous communications in which the number of '1' bits must add up to an even number. A parity bit is used to signal to the computer that the bits in a byte have been transmitted correctly. To do this, an extra bit (check bit) is added to the byte. For example, the EBCDIC letter 'A' is represented by 11000001. This has three ones, and is therefore an odd number. The parity (check) bit would have to be a 1 so that it becomes an even number (110000011). Should the byte be received at the other end showing an odd number of ones (for example, 110100011), then the computer knows that the information was corrupted during transmission. Errors could still occur if the incorrectly transmitted byte contains two reversing errors which coincidentally and erroneously resulted in an even number of ones, but the probability of this occurring is very low. Compare **odd parity**.

Evolution Computing A United States CAD (computer-aided design) software publisher founded by Michael Riddle in 1979. In 1978, using a US$500 000 minicomputer, Riddle set out to develop an affordable CAD system with a total target cost of under US$20 000. His first program evolved into today's leading CAD system. When EasyCAD was released in 1985, it was the first of its kind to cost less than US$500. A year later, FastCAD was launched, written entirely in assembly language. FastCAD 3D was released in 1990, and offered hidden surface removal, on-screen animation, and an automatic third-dimension without the user having to type the elevation. RenderMan was included to provide surface appearances such as grass, carpet, wood, marble, plastic, and metal.

ex. Excluding, as in 'ex. sales tax'.

exa- An SI unit prefix for 10^{18} expressed in decimal notation as 1 000 000 000 000 000 000, as in 'exahertz' (EHz). SI symbol 'E'.

ExCA Exchangeable Card Architecture; introduced by Intel in 1991 as an extension of PCMCIA 2.0 for computers using Intel's x86 chips. The ExCA standard is available free to all computer manufacturers and software developers. The architecture specifies a standard socket that is used to interface between mobile computer software and any PCMCIA-compliant enhancement device, including memory, communications, faxmodem, and networking cards.

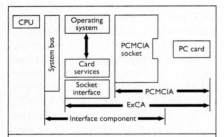

ExCA The ExCA standard defines a minimum set of the system socket hardware for the adapter card. The standard provides the implementation details for the multilayered software interface. This software allows PC cards to be accessed by multiple PCMCIA-aware devices, configuration utilities, and applications. The components of the software interface are Socket Services, Card Services, and Clients. Socket Services provide a software interface to manipulate socket adapter hardware in a way that is independent of the hardware implementation. The core software of the ExCA standard, the Card Services layer, provides a standard protocol for PC card device drivers and utility programs. ExCA Clients are the device drivers, configuration utilities, and applications that provide a link between ExCA software and application software.

The ExCA standard is intended to provide cross-platform compatibility, ease of installation, and hot insertion. In February 1992, Intel submitted the Card Services portion of the ExCA specification to the PCMCIA as a possible addition to the standard. It was approved in September 1992 as an addition to PCMCIA 2.0. Pronounced 'e-ex-sea-ay'. See **PCMCIA.** ⚠

Excel A spreadsheet program developed by Microsoft Corporation offering presentation graphics with a selection of typefaces, colors, and area shading.

exception (In programming.) [ISO A special situation which may arise during execution, which is considered abnormal, which may cause a deviation from the normal execution sequence, and for which facilities exist in the programming language to define, raise, recognize, ignore, and handle it. *Examples:* (ON-) condition in PL/1; exception in Ada.]

exception reports Computer-generated reports which highlight an unusual situation as used, for example, by management to identify unusual stock levels, or expense-to-revenue ratios.

excess-three code [ISO The binary-coded decimal notation in which a decimal digit n is represented by the binary numeral that represents in the binary numeration system the number $(n + 3)$.]

Exchangeable Card Architecture See **ExCA**.

exclusion [ISO The dyadic Boolean operation whose result has the Boolean value 1 if and only if the first operand has the Boolean value 1 and the second has the Boolean value 0.]

EXCLUSIVE-OR gate [ISO A gate that performs the Boolean operation of non-equivalence.]

EXE (.EXE) An executable file extension under DOS, Windows, and OS/2. For example, if the file is called MAX.EXE', then entering MAX at the command line will run (or execute) the file.

execute [ISO To perform the execution of an instruction or of a computer program.]

execution [ISO The process of carrying out an instruction or the instructions of a computer program by a computer.]

execution profile [ISO A representation of the absolute or relative execution frequencies or execution times of the instructions of a computer program.]

execution sequence [ISO The order of the execution of statements and parts of statements of a program.]

execution time 1. The time taken by the arithmetic/logic unit to execute (perform) an instruction. This is part of the machine cycle. Abbreviation 'e-time'. 2. [ISO The amount of time needed for the execution of a particular computer program.] 3. [ISO Any instant at which the execution of a particular computer program takes place.]

exit [ISO To execute an instruction within a portion of a computer program in order to terminate the execution of that portion. *Note:* Such portions of computer programs include loops, sub-

routines, and modules.] The word 'exit' comes from the Latin word *exitus*, meaning 'going out'.

expand [ISO To return compressed data to its original form.]

expanded memory Personal computers using DOS have a random-access memory (RAM) limitation of 640 kilobytes (kb) — a level inadequate for current applications such as spreadsheets and multiple program loading. To overcome this, a technique was developed to expand the memory by reserving a special peephole of 64 kb of memory to be used when the computer requests certain data not immediately available from RAM. The requested data is paged into the 64-kb peephole at very fast intervals, making it seem that the computer has more than 640 kb of RAM. A popular expanded memory standard is the Lotus–Intel–Microsoft Expanded Memory Specification (LIM EMS). Compare **extended memory**.

expanded type In typography, the electronic manipulation of a typeface so that it increases in width while maintaining the same height (x height). This is the opposite of condensed type.

expansion board A card (circuit board) which may be added onto the personal computer chassis (if slots are available) to improve its capabilities. These may include a memory expansion card which provides additional random-access memory; a color card which allows the connection of a color monitor; or a graphics card which improves the resolution of the monitor. ▼

expansion slot One of a number of slots

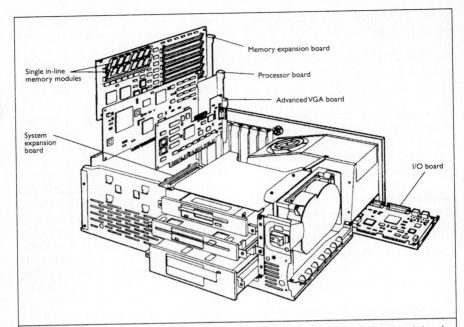

Single in-line
memory modules

Memory expansion board

Processor board

Advanced VGA board

System
expansion
board

I/O board

expansion board Although upgradable personal computers have been available for years, it is only recently that sophisticated modular systems have become available. This means that components are being separated from each other as much as possible so that components become smaller, less expensive, easier to access, and cheaper to service. For example, the traditional system board on this Compaq 'Modular' computer has been separated into five boards — the bus board, the input/output board, the processor board, the video board, and the memory board which can accommodate up to 60 megabytes of random-access memory.

in most personal computers which are connected to the motherboard and offer the ability to connect expansion cards (circuit boards) to improve the computer's capabilities. Each board must be placed in the expansion slot. The number of expansion devices which may be connected is only limited to the number of expansion slots available. To overcome slot limitations, multifunction boards were designed to maximize on the capability of each slot by providing more than one function per board. ▼

expert systems Computer systems that

rely upon artificial intelligence to assist both professionals (experts) and non-professionals in such fields as medicine, science, and exploration through the analysis of a strict database of facts, knowledge, and rules. Expert systems are useful in diagnosing, monitoring, interpreting, controlling, predicting, selecting, designing, training, planning, testing, and despatching. Using backward and forward chaining, an expert system asks users a set of questions in a dialogue fashion. The answers are compared to the knowledge base, enabling the computer to draw firm conclusions,

expansion slot Typically available within desktop computers, workstations, and servers, expansion slots may be used to enhance a computer's capabilities by allowing the user to upgrade devices such as the video boards, sound cards, and peripheral connection cards. This desktop computer has eight expansion slots, of which slots 1 and 6 are still unused.

or mere speculations or guesses about the possible answer. Using thousands of IF ... THEN rules, expert systems are particularly useful in situations when an expert is not available to assess a situation, such as the market value of a motor vehicle, the eligibility of an applicant for life insurance, or the viable deductions for an income tax return. Expert systems are sometimes known as 'knowledge-base systems' or 'intelligent assistants'. Abbreviation 'ES'. See **artificial intelligence**, **backward chaining**, **expert system software**, and **forward chaining**.

expert system software Software especially written for expert systems. Unlike conventional software which uses repetitive processes, expert system software uses inferential processes. For example, when a conventional computer adds 3 and 7, it always arrives at the answer 10. If a computer using expert system software is asked to add 3 lions to 7 lambs, the answer may be 3 animals (provided it has been told about the eat-

ing habits of lions). See **expert systems** and **knowledge acquisition**.

expiration check [ISO A comparison of a given date with an expiration date. *Example:* An expiration check for a record or a file.]

Explorer LX Produced by Texas Instruments, the Explorer LX was the first computer system to incorporate both a numeric processor (a conventional computer) and a symbolic processor (an artificial intelligence computer). See **Texas Instruments**.

exponent [ISO In a floating point representation, the numeral that denotes the power to which the implicit floating point base is raised before being multiplied by the mantissa to determine the real number represented.] ▼

export To create a new file in a format that is different to that normally used by the software package at hand. For example, in word processing software, Microsoft Word has the capability to save a particular file in a format that makes the file perfectly usable with a WordPerfect program.

exposure The second step in the electrophotography process used in laser printers. When the laser beam is turned on, the light causes specific areas of the photoreceptor to become conductive. Therefore, the potential is discharged to ground. A pattern of charges corresponding to the final image is left on the photoreceptor. See **laser printer** and **photoreceptor**.

expression [ISO A language construct for computing a value from one or more

NAME	AMERICAN SYSTEM Powers of:	Lots of '000' after the first 1 000	BRITISH SYSTEM Powers of:	1 000 000 to the power of:
million	10^6	1	10^6	1
milliard	-	-	10^9	-
billion	10^9	2	10^{12}	2
trillion	10^{12}	3	10^{18}	3
quadrillion	10^{15}	4	10^{24}	4
quintillion	10^{18}	5	10^{30}	5
sextillion	10^{21}	6	10^{36}	6
septillion	10^{24}	7	10^{42}	7
octillion	10^{27}	8	10^{48}	8
nontillion	10^{30}	9	10^{54}	9
decillion	10^{33}	10	10^{60}	10
undecillion	10^{36}	11	10^{66}	11
duodecillion	10^{39}	12	10^{72}	12
tredecillion	10^{42}	13	10^{78}	13
quattuordecillion	10^{45}	14	10^{84}	14
quindecillion	10^{48}	15	10^{90}	15
sexdecillion	10^{51}	16	10^{96}	16
septendecillion	10^{54}	17	10^{102}	17
octodecillion	10^{57}	18	10^{108}	18
novemdecillion	10^{60}	19	10^{114}	19
vigintillion	10^{63}	20	10^{120}	20
centillion	10^{303}	100	10^{600}	100

exponent *For numbers over 1 million, the American system was originally modeled on the French system of numeration. However, the French Government changed its system so that it would correspond to the German and British systems. Although the current American system is the most logical to use, it does not meet official international standards.*

In the American system, each denomination above 1000 million (being the American billion — 1 000 000 000) is 1000 times the preceding denomination, so that 1 trillion equals 1000 billion; 1 quadrillion equals 1000 trillion, and so on.

In the British system (and the one used by the Système International d'Unités), the first denomination above 1000 million (being the British milliard) is 1000 times the preceding one, but for each denomination above the 1000 milliard (the British billion = 1 000 000 000 000) it is 1 000 000 times the preceding one, so that 1 trillion equals 1 000 000 billion; 1 quadrillion equals 1 000 000 trillion, and so on.

The fundamental difference in the two systems is the interpretation of the meaning and application of the word 'bi'. In both systems, 'bi' is taken to mean 'two' (as used in bicycle and biannual), but the inconsistency occurs from the application of this meaning.

In the American system, 'bi' is taken to mean 'two lots of 000 (three zeros) after the first 1000' so that a 'bi'llion is the number 1000 with two lots of thousand after it (1 000 000 000 = 10^9). Similarly, the word 'tri' (as used in tricycle and triangle) is taken to mean three lots of '000' after the billion. So that a trillion is equal to 1000 with three lots of '000' (being 1 000 000 000 000 = 10^{12}).

In contrast, the British system calculates not from the 1000 but from the million, so that 1 000 000 to the power of 'bi' is expressed as 1 000 000^2, which equals 1 000 000 000 000. Similarly, 1 trillion is the number 1 000 000 to the third power (1 000 000^3, which equals 1 000 000 000 000 000 000. In the British system, 1 trillion is better expressed as 10^{18}).

operands. *Note:* Operands may be literals, identifiers, array references, function calls, etc.]

Extended Binary-Coded Decimal Interchange Code See **EBCDIC**.

extended character set Personal computers using ASCII have a set of 128 characters. To expand on this so that a collection of technical symbols and foreign language characters can be used, a ROM-based character set can be used to extend the original 128 to 256 characters. See **ASCII**.

Extended Industry Standard Architecture See **EISA**.

Extended ISA See **EISA**.

extended memory In an industry-standard personal computer, any amount of memory above the base configuration supplied by the manufacturer. Extended memory is especially useful with OS/2, an operating system capable of taking full advantage of the benefits of extended memory. When using DOS, a memory manager must be used to break through the 640-kilobyte barrier. Compare **expanded memory**.

extended result output function [ISO The function that allows the facility for displaying or printing the result of a calculation in successive operations where the number of digits in the result exceeds the output capacity of the calculator.]

external [ISO Pertaining to a language object that has a scope that extends beyond one module. *Example:* The entry names of a module are external.] The

word 'external' comes from the Latin word *exterus*, meaning 'outside'.

external buffer A temporary data storage area outside the computer, usually built into a peripheral device such as a printer. See **buffer**.

E

external hard disk A hard disk equipped with its own power supply, casing, and cables used primarily as a portable unit. Since the introduction of 'removable' hard disk cartridges capable of storing up to 44 megabytes of data, external hard disks have been losing their popularity. An internal hard disk is one housed inside a computer, operating on the computer's own power supply. See **Bernoulli box** and **hard disk**.

external label [ISO A label, usually not machine-readable, attached to a data medium container. *Example:* A paper sticker attached to the outside of a magnetic storage device.]

external loss time [ISO Down-time due to a fault outside the functional unit.]

external modem A modem equipped with its own power supply, casing, and cables which plugs into a computer's serial port. Many modern personal computers, especially notebook and laptop models, are being manufactured with internal modems. See **modem**.

external reports Computer-generated reports produced for people outside the immediate organization, such as customers and shareholders.

external storage [ISO Storage that is accessible to a processor only through input/output channels. *Note:* An external storage device may sometimes be considered as peripheral equipment.]

extract [ISO To select and remove from a group of items those which meet specific criteria.]

extra-pulse [ISO An inadmissible additional pulse that occurs during recording or reading.]

f Femto-. An SI unit prefix for 10^{-15} expressed in decimal notation as 0.000 000 000 000 001, as in 'femtosecond' (fs).

F The hexadecimal symbol for binary 1111 (which is equal to the decimal number 15). This is the highest hexadecimal symbol. $F_{16} = 15_{10} = 17_8 = 1111_2$.

FACOM M-190 The world's first fourth-generation large-scale computer system based on large-scale integration (LSI) semiconductor technology introduced by Fujitsu in 1974. This system featured ECL (emitter-coupled logic)-LSI with 100-gates-per-chip integration and 700-picosecond-per-gate propagation delay time. In 1977, Fujitsu introduced a medium-scale computer system TTL (transistor-transistor logic)-LSI device with an integration of 600 gates per chip. Today, all FACOM M-series models are designed to be used as the host computers in an advanced network architecture — Fujitsu Network Architecture (FNA) — that anticipates future online data processing requirements. FNA is structured to allow for the sharing of terminals, communication lines, applications, and databases. FNA distinctively separates the data communication function from the data processing function. The virtual storage system frees the user of application programs and terminals from the restrictions of data communication functions such as network structure, transmission lines, and transmission control. Furthermore, a variety of host processors, communication controllers, sub-hosts, clusters, and terminals provide flexibility of network configuration. See **Fujitsu Limited**.

facsimile An exact and detailed copy of an image composed through scanning. The dark and light shades are noted and converted into digital code then transmitted to a receiving device which decodes that data and reproduces the detailed copy — usually on paper to act

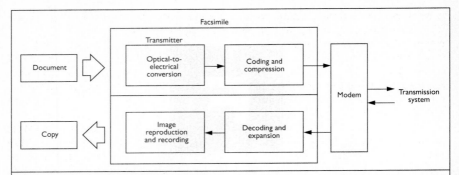

facsimile This figure illustrates the principle of facsimile transmission. At the transmitter, documents are scanned and their images converted into electrical signals, which are then sent to the receiver via a modem and transmission lines. In high-speed machines, the electrical signals are converted into digital form, then compressed to remove redundancy, shortening the transmission period. At the receiver, the signals are processed to reproduce the original images and print them on paper.

as a copy of a document. Facsimile card adapters are available for computers. Equipped with a modem, facsimile transmissions may be made via the computer. The concept of facsimile was dreamed up in 1843 by a Scottish natural philosopher and psychologist, Alexander Bain, some 35 years before the invention of the telephone. Over the past few years, much progress has been made with facsimile techniques. Modern facsimile machines are compact, reasonably priced, and easy to operate, featuring fast transmission and high resolution. In response to these developments, the CCITT set recommendations to standardize transmission so that machines made by different manufacturers can communicate with each other. To perform their electronic scanning, most facsimile machines have high-density image sensors using MOSs (metal-oxide semiconductors) or charge-coupled devices (CCDs). New developments include scanning without lens systems by using amorphous silicon imaging sensors, which actually come into contact with the document they scan. The most widely used recording methods are electrostatic and thermal, both of which are suited to electronic scanning. A disadvantage is that these methods require coated paper. Since large areas of a typical document are merely background (blank areas), coding these areas in the same way as important areas wastes time. Various data compression techniques have been developed to eliminate this waste. So that facsimile transceivers made by different manufacturers will be able to communicate with each other, the CCITT recommends the modified Huffman (MH) method for one-dimensional compression and the modified READ (MR) method for two-dimensional compression. Some facsimile machines are formed into facsimile networks in which various transmission modes are used. Microprocessors are effective in adapting facsimiles to these various modes. Microprocessors can also be used to monitor communications and perform automatic analysis of malfunctions. The word 'facsimile' is from the Latin words *facere*, meaning 'to make', and *simile*, meaning 'similar'. Pronounced 'fak-sim-il-ee'. Abbreviation 'fax'. **A**

factorial [ISO The product of the natural numbers 1,2,3, ... up to and including a given integer.]

factorial function [ISO The function that is used to compute factorials.]

failover time See **hardware-intensive fault tolerance**.

failsafe operation [ISO The operation of a computer system such that in case of failure of a component, the probabilities of loss of equipment, damage to equipment, and harm to personnel are kept low.]

failsoft [ISO Pertaining to a computer system continuing to function because of its fault tolerance.]

failure [ISO The termination of the ability of a functional unit to perform its required function.]

fake code An English-like language used instead of flowcharting when designing a computer program. This is sometimes known as 'pseudocode'. See **flowchart**.

fallback The ability of a modem to use a lower speed communications standard if connection is not possible with the standard being used.

FAM Fast-access memory.

fanfold paper [ISO Continuous forms previously folded as a fan and usually fed by means of feed holes on each side.]

FAST Federation Against Software Theft. See **software theft**.

FastCAD A software package published by Evolution Computing of Arizona. It is a powerful CAD (computer-aided design) program with advanced drawing and editing features such as associative dimensioning. FastCAD uses floating point numbers to represent entities (such as circles, lines, squares, and polygons), thus enabling the largest entity in a drawing to be over a million times larger than the smallest. **▼**

fast page-mode RAM See **page-mode RAM**.

fast SCSI A set of restrictions on the SCSI specifications, particularly with respect to termination, which permit the negotiation of faster transfer speeds than the original specification permitted: 10 megahertz versus 5 megahertz, giving a byte rate of 10 megabytes per second as opposed to 5 megabytes per second.

fast select [ISO An option of a virtual call facility that allows the inclusion of data in call-set-up and call-clearing packets.]

FAT See **file allocation table**.

fatal error [ISO An error that causes further execution, if any, to produce meaningless results.]

fault [ISO An accidental condition that causes a functional unit to fail to perform its required function.]

fault monitoring A fault-tolerance feature that detects disk errors, logs them, and alerts administrators when errors occur.

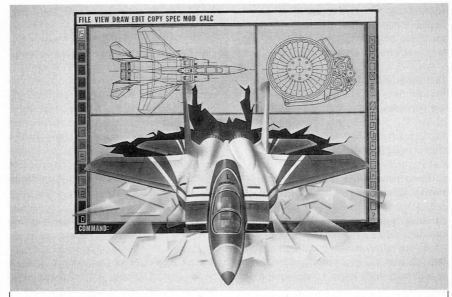

FastCAD Creating drawings on the computer screen cannot be compared to a flat airbrush and/or artist's impression because the purpose of CAD is to take a three-dimensional form which can be manipulated, scaled, re-shaped, and sliced.

fault-rate threshold [ISO A fault threshold expressed in terms of the number of faults in a prescribed period of time.]

fault threshold [ISO A prescribed limit to the number of faults in a specified category which, if exceeded, requires appropriate action. *Note:* Such actions may include notifying the operators, running diagnostic programs, or reconfiguration to exclude a fault unit.]

fault tolerance The ability of a computer system to function despite having faulty components. System failure can occur in any element of the computer system, including hardware, software, people, and environment. A fault is an event in which a system operates contrary to its specifications, although this may not always be visible to users of the system. Despite best efforts, systems can fail. For this reason, fault tolerance is one of the most important techniques used to achieve high availability in computer systems. A system is said to be 'tolerant' of a given type of fault if it can detect, isolate, and bypass the fault without any of the following: human intervention, significant delay in service, significant reduction in performance, loss of work that has been submitted by users, and loss of data integrity. [ISO The ability of a computer system to continue to operate correctly even though one or more of its component parts are malfunctioning.] See **computer system**, **hardware-intensive fault tolerance**, **software-intensive fault tolerance**, **system availability**, and **unscheduled down-time**.

fault trace [ISO A record of faults, obtained by a monitor, that reflects the sequence of states that immediately preceded the occurrence of the faults.]

fax See **facsimile**.

faxmodem A telecommunications device used with a personal computer to connect the user to other modem-equipped computers, databanks, or facsimile machines. Faxmodems, though also used to send data, offer greater flexibility than older data-only modems. They may be external peripheral devices that can connect to a computer, or internal boards that are affixed inside the computer, or PCMCIA-type cards that slot into the side of a computer. Faxmodems come with software that includes time-delayed faxing, broadcast faxing, and

other capabilities. Modern devices allow users to fax files from general applications. Faxmodems that allow the user to transmit text and graphics files directly from an application (without having to alter the file) have a WYPIWYF (what you print is what you fax) capability — a term coined by Intel. ▼

F

FCC Federal Communications Commission of the United States. A standards body created by the United States Communications Act of 1934. FCC is responsible for regulating interstate radio, television, telegraph, and telephone communications, as well as foreign-related communications.

FDC Floppy disk controller.

FDD Fixed disk drive. See **hard disk**.

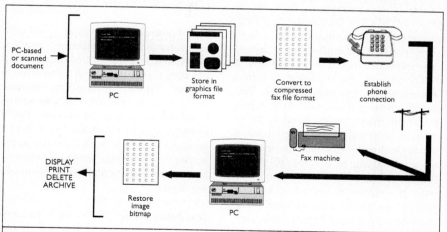

faxmodem Sending a fax involves translating and compressing a file into the international fax image format. A receiving faxmodem accepts the incoming image stream and eventually stores it as a bit-mapped image in a graphics format such as TIFF or PCX. Older telephone networks that were designed for transmitting voice can introduce errors in data and fax communication, due to the background noise or static on the phone line. Noise is a particular problem during high-speed transmissions because each period of noise can damage large amounts of data. Faxmodems can use sophisticated methods to ensure accurate transmissions of both data and faxes, including the methods specified by international standards.

FDDI Fiber Distributed Data Interface; a local area network (LAN) specification from the ANSI (American National Standards Institute) X3T9.5 committee on computer input/output interface standards. FDDI uses fiber optic cables with token-passing access in a ring topology. It transmits at 100 megabits per second (MBps) across a cable length of up to 62 miles (100 kilometers), with up to 1.25 miles (2 kilometers) between nodes. These parameters are set by the default values assigned to recovery timers, so the station count could be increased over shorter distances. For class 'A' stations, which connect both rings using two duplex cables, the effective throughput can be as much as 200 MBps. FDDI also defines a less costly class 'B' station which connects to only one of the rings through a wiring concentrator and a single duplex cable. In the event of a link failure, the dual rings automatically re-configure into a single ring, isolating the failure and maintaining operation for class 'A' stations. A FDDI station management interface automatically re-configures the ring within a few milliseconds. After repair, a station management handshake sequence allows the ring to go back to its original state. If a fault develops in the cable going to a class 'B' station, the concentrator activates a node bypass. If a station is turned off or loses power, an electrically-operated relay provides an optical bypass. The combination of these mechanisms affords FDDI a high degree of fault tolerance. FDDI-II was the second version introduced to transmit at 200 MBps. This is fast enough for real-time voice and video transmission. FDDI-II has the ability to handle circuit-switched data by allocating bandwidth in multiples of

approximately 6 MBps as synchronous channels. Each channel is split into either three 2.048-MBps or four 1.536-MBps full duplex data highways, consistent with European and North American tele–phone systems. The necessary timing is imposed by the 'cycle master' station, which emits frame slots at an 8-kilohertz rate.

FDDI II See **FDDI**.

FDM Frequency-division multiplexer. In broadband transmission and local area networking, several frequencies on a single channel may be used to send different messages simultaneously. This is done through the use of multiplexers. See **bandwidth**, **broadband**, and **multiplexer**.

FDX See **full duplex**.

FEA Finite element analysis. Used with computer-aided engineering applications, FEA is a method of determining the structural integrity of a mechanical design. Typical applications include stress analysis, vibration analysis, acoustics, and structural interaction. Finite elements are the small subdivisions of a structure's surface, usually drawn on the screen with a wire mesh of squares, highlighting particular stress points in the design.

feasibility study [ISO A study to identify and analyze a problem and its potential solutions in order to determine their viability, costs, and benefits.]

feature adapter A socket found on most modern PC graphics cards which enables the user to connect add-on cards and adapters.

Federal Communications Commission
See **FCC**.

feed hole [ISO A hole punched in a data medium to enable it to be positioned.]

feed pitch [ISO The distance between corresponding points of adjacent feed holes along the feed track.]

feed track [ISO A track in a data medium that contains feed holes.]

FEM Finite element modeling. Used with computer-aided engineering applications, FEM is the creation and rendering (drawing) of finite elements (the small subdivisions of a structure's surface, usually drawn on the screen with a wire mesh of squares, highlighting particular stress points in the design).

female connector A device wherein the connections are in the form of a receptacle.

femto- See **f**.

FEP Front-end processor; usually a minicomputer that is connected to a larger host computer so as to handle all the communications requirements quite independently, thereby leaving the host computer free to concentrate on internal data processing.

ferrite Any of several compounds of iron, oxygen, and another metal, with magnetic properties that are useful in certain microwave applications and in computer memories. Orthoferrites are various oxides of iron and either yttrium or another rare earth. The molecular structure is simpler than that of garnet.

Orthoferrites were the first materials used for the thin magnetic film in experimental bubble memories, but these have been replaced with garnets, which have more-desirable properties, such as ease of preparation as thin films with the necessary magnetic capabilities. The word 'ferrite' comes from the Latin word *ferrum*, meaning 'iron'.

ferrite head See **read/write head**.

ferrite particles One of the three components that make up the toner which is used in a laser printer. The ferrite particles allow the pigment and resin to be evenly transferred to the latent image by the magnetic brush assembly within the laser printer. See **laser printer**.

FF Also 'ff'. See **form feed**.

Fiber Distributed Data Interface See **FDDI**.

fiber optics The transmission of information at very high frequencies, requiring an infrared or even visible light as the carrier (usually from a laser). The light beam is an electromagnetic signal with a frequency in the range of 10^{14} to 10^{15} hertz. The medium is plastic or glass fiber (made from silicon dioxide) no thicker than a human hair. Although this is less susceptible to external noise than other transmission media, and is cheaper to make than copper wire, it is more difficult to connect, yet fiber optics are difficult to tamper with, making them more secure for the user. The light beams do not escape from the medium because the material used provides total internal reflection. AT&T Bell Laboratories in the United States managed to send information at a rate of 420

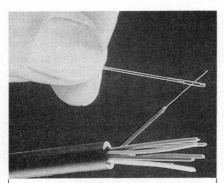

fiber optics The use of these strands has revolutionized telecommunications. The individual and delicate fibers are small enough to freely fit through the eye of a needle.

megabits per second, over 100 miles (161.5 kilometers) through a fiber optic cable. In Japan, 445.8 megabits per second was achieved over a shorter distance. At this rate, the entire text of the *Encyclopædia Britannica* could be transmitted in only one second. Currently, AT&T is working on a worldwide network to support high-volume data transmission, international computer networking, electronic mail, and voice communications (a single fiber can transmit 200 million telephone conversations simultaneously). Fiber optics is also called 'photonics'. Abbreviation 'FO'. See **optic fiber technology**. ⋀

Fibonacci search [ISO A dichotomizing search in which the number of data elements in the set is equal to a Fibonacci number or is assumed to be equal to the next higher Fibonacci number, and then at each step in the search the set of elements is partitioned in accordance with the Fibonacci series. *Notes:* (a) The series 0,1,1,2,3,5,8, ... in which each element is the sum of the two preceding terms, is a Fibonacci series. (b) A Fibonacci search

has an advantage over a binary search in slightly reducing average movement of a sequentially-accessed data medium such as a magnetic tape.]

field 1. In a file, a related group of letters, numbers, or special symbols form a 'field'. See **file**. 2. [ISO On a data medium or in storage, a specified area used for a particular class of data elements. *Example:* A group of character positions used to enter or display wage rates on a screen.]

Fifth-Generation Project The collaboration of the Japanese computer industry with its Government to research and create computers based upon artificial intelligence. The commitment to the Fifth-Generation Project was made in October 1981. Its charter was to develop 'intelligent' computers for the 1990s. See **artificial intelligence**.

file A collection of records each stored on a secondary storage medium such as a diskette or hard disk. Generally, a computer file contains either a program or data. Program files contain instructions (or commands) which are to be executed by the computer. Data files which contain only ASCII (American Standard Code for Information Interchange) characters are called 'text files', while files which contain binary data (data other than ASCII characters) are called 'binary files'. Data belonging to a file is stored on one or more sectors (a sector usually contains 512 bytes of data). Before DOS stores data on a disk, it usually breaks up the data into smaller sections of data, then writes them at various places on the disk. The location of each section is recorded in a file allocation table (FAT) which keeps control of all the clusters recorded on different sectors. Commands must be translated to binary numbers before they are executed by the computer. Commands in binary form are called 'machine language' instructions. The computer's operating system, which coordinates all the computer's activities, knows the difference between program files and data files. Different rules are used to process each type of file. Word processing files should not be confused with standard ASCII text files. Standard ASCII files include only the ASCII printable characters and four of the special control codes: cr (carriage return), lf (line feed), ff (form feed), and ht (horizontal tab). In contrast, most word processing programs create files which are mostly text but which also contain some 8-bit binary codes and many ASCII control codes which are used for text formatting purposes, such as to indicate a special typestyle. Word processing files must therefore be treated as binary files. A common mistake is to send a word processing file to a mainframe as if it were a standard transferred file. If a word processing file is sent as a transferred file, the 8-bit control codes will not be received correctly. These codes will remain embedded in the text and will no longer perform the text formatting expected. In addition, the codes are often not printable characters, which means extensive editing will have to be done to restore the file to its original condition. See **file allocation table**. [ISO A named set of records stored or processed as a unit.]

file allocation table   A table used by DOS to locate the blocks in which it writes data to a disk. When DOS stores data on a disk, it usually breaks the data into smaller sections of data ('clusters') and writes them to various places on the disk. The location of each section is recorded in a file allocation table which keeps control of all the clusters recorded on different sectors. File storage is actually allocated on the disk (by the file system) in fixed-sized areas called 'blocks'. Normally, a block is the same size as a disk sector. Files are created by finding and reserving enough unused blocks to contain the data in the file. Two file allocation methods are currently in widespread use. The first method allocates blocks (for a file) from a sequential pool of unused blocks. Thus, a file is always contained in a set of sequential blocks on the disk. As files are created, updated, and deleted, these free-block pools become fragmented (separated from one another). When this fragmentation occurs, it often becomes impossible for the file system to create a file even though there is a sufficient number of free blocks on the disk. At this point, special programs must be run to 'squeeze' or compact the files in order to re-create a single contiguous free-block pool. The second file allocation method uses a more flexible technique in which individual data blocks may be located anywhere on the disk (with no restrictions). With this technique, a file directory entry contains the disk address of a file pointer block rather than the disk address of the first data block of the file. This file pointer block contains pointers (disk addresses) for each data block in the file. For example, the first pointer in the file pointer block contains the track and sector address of the first data block in the file, the second pointer contains the disk address of the second data block, and so on. In practice, pointer blocks are usually the same size as data blocks. Therefore, some files will require multiple pointer blocks. To accommodate this requirement without loss of flexibility, pointer blocks are linked together — that is, each pointer block contains the disk address of the following pointer block. Acronym 'FAT'.

file clean-up [ISO The removal of superfluous or obsolete data from a file.]

file compression utility A program used to compress or decompress files. See **compression**.

file conversion utility A utility used to read files created by one program, and to convert them so that they can be read by another program.

file defragmentation The re-writing of all the parts of a file on contiguous sectors (one after the other). When files on a hard disk are being updated, the information tends to be written all over the disk. This fragmentation causes delays in file retrieval. Defragmentation is the reversal of this process. Special defragmentation programs like DiskExpress and DOS Rx perform automatic defragmentation, providing up to 75% improvement in the speed of disk access and retrieval. Compare **file fragmentation**.

file extension In DOS, the second part of a file name. The extension is normally used to identify a file type, such as TXT for text files, DOC for formatted document, and BAT for batch files.

file fragmentation The storage of a file in noncontiguous sections, called 'clusters'. Even though DOS stores the locations of these clusters in the file allocation table (FAT), fragmentation leads to extra movement of the read/write head and degradation in disk performance. A greater disk reading and writing efficiency (up to 75%) can be realized by using a defragmentation utility which re-writes the files on a disk so that they are placed in contiguous clusters. See **file allocation table**. Compare **file defragmentation**.

file locking 1. In local area networking, a file may be set so that only one user can access it at a time. 2. In word processing and similar applications, a file may be locked through the use of a password so that access is only available to those who know the password. See **password**.

file maintenance [ISO The activity of updating or re-organizing a file.]

file name A unique name or series of characters assigned to a file so that the operating system can find the file. In DOS, each file label has two parts: the first is called the 'file name', consisting of not more than eight characters; and the second is called the 'extension'. Up to three characters only can be assigned for the extension. The two are separated by a full stop (.). Consistency in the use of the extension, such as .DOC for all document files and .TXT for all text-only files, is advised because this method of filing makes archiving and file management much easier. Macintosh environments allow up to 32 characters for file names including spaces, but excluding the colon (:).

file protection ring See **magnetic tape unit**.

file server In local area networking, usually a powerful personal computer which is allocated the task of servicing users with data, application software, mass storage, and other utilities. File servers are frequently found in personal computer (PC) networks where individual PCs have limited online file capacity. They are also found in local area networks that are used to support database applications and transaction-based systems. The file server function allows multiple access from users to individual records on a shared basis. The individual file accessibilities are managed by the file server software. The software that provides these functions must incorporate multitasking and multi-user features. Some personal computer servers use software that is an extension of DOS. Since UNIX already has multitasking capabilities, few additional features need to be added when using UNIX-based software, but this software must provide DOS emulation to respond properly to DOS requests from other personal computers. The 'workstation' computers which the server supports also require special networking software that is loaded into random-access memory at log-on. Generally, this software is transparent to the user. The file server is also referred to as 'the server'. See **LAN**.

file sharing A set of services which allow easy storage, retrieval, and sharing of files in a distributed environment from multiple desktops. They extend the user desktop device by providing both virtual filing and 'local area disks' that take advantage of larger mass storage available elsewhere on the network. They also reduce the burden on the user for dealing with file backup and recovery,

and support workgroups through access to common file 'cabinets'. File sharing is provided today through a number of different products, including the All-in-1 file cabinet, VMS Services for PCs, and the VMS/ULTRIX Connection which enables VMS operating systems to act as file servers for ULTRIX and other UNIX operating environments.

filespec In DOS, a filespec carries all the information about a file's location including the drive where the file is stored, the path name, file name, and extension (if available). For example, 'C:\wp51\wrkfiles\memo.doc'.

file transfer utility A program used to transfer files between different computers. For example, MacLink Plus is used to transfer files from the Macintosh to the IBM Personal Computer. Brooklyn Bridge is another popular program used to link laptops to desktop computers.

file updating [ISO The activity of adding, deleting, or changing data in a file.]

file virus See **direct-action file virus** and **indirect-action file virus**.

fill [ISO In a token-ring network, a specified bit pattern that a transmitting data station sends before or after frames, tokens, or abort sequences to avoid what would otherwise be interpreted as an inactive or indeterminate transmitter state.]

filtering A process used in both analog and digital image processing to reduce bandwidth. Filters can be designed to remove information content such as high or low frequencies.

filters These are used extensively throughout the telephone network to help eliminate unwanted frequencies. These devices allow frequencies within the bandwidth of a voice-grade line to pass through the network while eliminating any frequencies outside this bandwidth. The voice-grade bandwidth includes frequencies of 200 to 3200 hertz. Equalizers are another corrective device commonly used by telephone companies. There are two types of equalizers: delay equalizers and amplitude equalizers. Delay equalizers are used to correct delay distortion. These devices delay the frequency that is traveling the fastest so as to maintain a correct phase relationship between both frequencies. Amplitude equalizers are used to correct attenuation distortion. These devices reduce the amplitude of the stronger frequency (which is normally the 1200 hertz signal) until it matches the amplitude of the weaker frequency (which is normally the 2200-hertz signal). Both frequencies are then fed through an amplifier before continuing through the network.

FIMS Form Interface Management System. See **video form**.

Finder The Apple Macintosh operating system's shell for file and memory management, and user interaction. The Finder can only handle one program at a time. See **MultiFinder**.

fine-grain parallel processing See **parallel processing**.

fingerprint sensor A biometric security device which is used to allow access (to a computer file or a room) to a person whose fingerprints match a predetermined data pattern. The fingerprint, being unique and unchangeable, remains the most reliable means of identification. Such identification systems must operate in real-time and use an algorithm that quickly compares an input with previously registered fingerprints. Such systems must also produce distortion-free fingerprint images unaffected by latent (those left behind) fingerprint images. Most conventional sensors use a prism into which a beam is introduced through one of the prism's angled surfaces. This method has two major problems: (a) trapezoidal distortion caused by unequal optical paths between each point of the fingerprint and the image focusing lens; and (b) light noise caused by latent fingerprints (those left behind by someone else). To solve these problems, Fujitsu introduced a holographic fingerprint sensor in the late 1980s. The transparent flat glass plate used in the holographic sensor has a hologram at one end and a fingerprint input port at the other. The laser beam is directed to the fingerprint input port from the back of the glass plate. The finger is simply pressed against the glass plate. The sensor produces contrast by using the differences in the scattered light reflected in the glass from the fingerprint's grooves and ridges. Because of the thin layer of air between fingerprint grooves and the glass, the reflected light enters the glass from the air layer and then exits the other side from the angle of incidence. This reflected light enters the glass at different angles depending upon how the fingerprint ridges touch the glass. Light entering at an angle of incidence below the critical angle is reflected repeatedly within the glass (total internal reflection) and propagates through the glass plate. Other light exits the glass in the same way as light scattered from a grooved surface. The repeatedly-reflected light carrying the image of the fingerprint ridges exits the glass at the hologram. The external image-forming optical system then forms an image of the ridges. See **biometric security devices**. ▼

fingerscan Any biometric access control network system which uses positive fingerprint identity verification to provide facility-wide security monitoring and control. See **biometric security devices**.

finite element analysis See **FEA**.

finite element modeling See **FEM**.

firmware Software which may be semi-permanently stored on a computer chip. Firmware may be special codes such as parts of an operating system, or computer language program translators. For example, machine-language programs are stored on a read-only memory (ROM) computer chip so that they are always available to the central processing unit. Firmware is stored on ROM chips because they are nonvolatile, meaning they retain their information after the power is switched off. See **BIOS** and **ROM**.

first generation Refers to the vacuum-tube computer technology employed extensively and commercially from 1951 to 1958. The first-generation era started with the commercial introduction of UNIVAC I, which was originally built for the United States Bureau of the Census for tabulating the 1950 census. Its inventors, John Presper Eckert and John Mauchly, started their own company which was later taken over by Remington-Rand (later known as 'Sperry Corporation', and today called

F

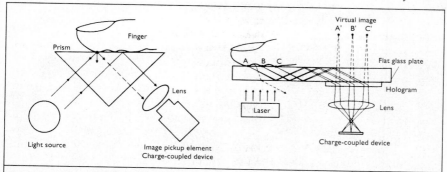

fingerprint sensor Conventional fingerprint sensors use a prism into which a beam is introduced through one of the prism's angled surfaces. When a finger is placed on the prism, total internal reflection no longer occurs at the point of contact. On the other hand, the transparent flat glass plate sensor produces contrast by using the differences in the scattered light reflected in the glass from the fingerprint's grooves and ridges.

'Unisys Corporation'). They produced general-purpose electronic computers for businesses that needed to automate their payroll processing and other labor-intensive transaction processing applications. The input/output medium for the first generation was the punched-card — a very slow medium used to process data since the 1800s. The flow of electric current was controlled by vacuum tubes which were an improvement over slower electromechanical parts such as those used for the Mark I, but they were prone to frequent failures and generated a lot of heat, thereby demanding large air conditioning systems. Internal memory was stored on rotating magnetic drums. Originally, first-generation computers were programmed using machine language — a set of instructions consisting of binary digits, being a string of zeros (0) and ones (1). In 1952, Dr Grace Hopper developed 'assembly language' at the University of Pennsylvania. Although very monotonous by today's standards, assembly language was much easier to use because it allowed programmers to write code in a form of shorthand. By 1959, the transistor was being used to pioneer the second generation. Compare **second generation**. ▼

first read rate The mode of operation of a bar code scanner which translates codes on the first pass. The scanner is known as a 'first read rate' scanner. Abbreviation 'FRR'. See **bar code**.

Fisher, Kenneth G. Chairman and Chief Executive Officer of Encore Computer Corporation, a company he founded in 1983. He was formerly President, Chief Executive Officer, and Director of Prime Computer, Inc., having resigned that position in July 1981. Fisher joined Prime in 1975, and by 1981 he had brought the company from US$7 million in sales and 150 employees, to US$365 million in sales and 4500 employees. Before joining Prime, Fisher was associated with Honeywell Information Systems from 1970 to 1975, where he served as Vice President of Central Operations. Prior to that, he was associ-

first generation In 1944, Harvard's Dr Howard Aiken and IBM completed five years' work on the Mark I, the largest electromechanical calculator ever built. It had 3300 relays and weighed 5 tons. It could multiply two 23-digit numbers in six seconds.

ated with General Electric's computer operations for ten years, where he held several marketing positions. Fisher holds a bachelor of science degree in business administration from the University of Nebraska, and an MBA from the University of Chicago. In 1989, he was awarded an Honorary Doctor of Engineering Degree from Worcester Polytechnic Institute in Massachusetts. See **Encore Computer Corporation**.

586 The logical, though incorrect, reference to Intel's fifth generation of microprocessors. The correct name is Intel Pentium processor. See **Pentium processor**.

56001 See **Motorola DSP56001**.

5¼-inch diskette A flexible disk that uses a recording surface made of plastic coated with iron oxide. As the diskette is rotated in the drive, a movable read/write head is used to read or write digital information magnetically. The data is recorded on the diskette in a series of concentric circles called 'tracks'. Each track is in turn divided into a certain number of sectors. The exact number of tracks and sectors varies depending upon the type of disk drive and the formatting used. Flexible diskettes and drives have undergone many improvements since business computers were introduced. The earliest industry-compatible computers used 'single-sided' diskettes that were 5¼-inches in diameter. These diskettes used drives with only one read/write head that only recorded on one surface of the disk. The single-sided format quickly evolved into a 'double-sided/double-density' recording standard that is still in wide use. This standard still uses 5¼-

inch diskettes, but two read/write heads are used to record on both sides of the diskette. The diskettes are formatted with 40 tracks per side and 9 sectors per track. Total storage capacity is 360 kilobytes. As flexible disk technology evolved, a new format for 5¼-inch diskettes was introduced in 1984. Called 'high capacity', this format uses 80 tracks per side with 15 sectors per track. Total storage capacity is 1.2 megabytes. The higher-quality diskettes required for this format are normally labeled 'high capacity' or 'high density' or 'high coercivity'. A special diskette drive is also required. All 5¼-inch diskettes have a flexible jacket that holds and protects the circular recording surface. The diskette has two holes in it. The large hole is the hub (center) where the drive grabs the diskette. The smaller hole provides a reference point that defines the beginning of a track. A large oval slot in the

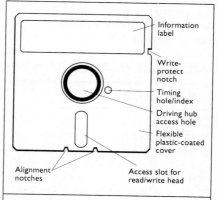

5¼-inch diskette This diskette is capable of storing 1.2 megabytes, using both sides to store 512 bytes per sector (15 sectors per track, 80 tracks per side). Older models, still available, are capable of storing 360 kilobytes, using both sides of the disk to store 512 bytes per sector (9 sectors on each of the 40 tracks per side).

jacket allows the drive's read/write head to approach the recording surface. There is also a write-protect notch on the edge of the jacket. If this notch is covered, a user cannot write to the diskette. See **diskette**. ▲

fixed decimal mode [ISO A mode in which the number of decimal places to be shown in the result of a calculation is preselected.]

fixed disk Hard disk drives can store vast amounts of data, but unlike floppy-diskette drives, their recording media is not removable. For this reason, a hard disk is often referred to as a 'fixed disk'. The use of a fixed disk can significantly increase working efficiency, because they have a much greater capacity, so the user does not have to shuffle floppy diskettes every time a program is loaded or a file is saved. A fixed disk is also able to save and retrieve data much faster than a floppy-diskette drive. In fact, more than any other input/output device, the disk storage system determines the responsiveness of the personal computer. With many applications, the speed of the hard

disk has a greater impact on system throughput than the type of central processing unit used or the clock speed. Early personal computers used full-height 5¼-inch drives with a capacity of 10 megabytes. Many modern computers use half-height drives (mostly 3½ inches in diameter) with storage capacities nearing 1 gigabyte. Prices, too, have improved, from over US$100 per megabyte to under US$3. Inside a fixed disk drive is a stack of rigid aluminum platters, each covered with iron oxide to allow magnetic storage. The platters rapidly rotate as a unit on a spindle. The only other moving part is the head system. Each side of each platter has a read/write head associated with it. The heads are linked together to form a single moving unit. The head assembly is moved across the disks by using a special solenoid. Because of the high rotational speeds and close tolerances involved, the heads and platters are contained in a sealed chamber that protects against dust and other contamination. As with diskette drives, hard drives record data within a format of tracks broken down into sectors. Typically, there are between 312 and 1024 tracks per platter, with 17 sectors per track. Since the head assembly moves as a unit, each head on each surface traces the same track at the same time. This vertical stack of common track numbers is called a 'cylinder'. See **hard disk**. ▼

fixed function generator [ISO A function generator in which the function it generates is set by construction and cannot be altered by the user.]

fixed-point register [ISO A register used to manipulate data in a fixed-point representation system.]

FUN FACT

The 5¼-inch diskette was designed by Jim Adkisson of Shugart who received a complaint over lunch from a customer who suggested that 8-inch diskettes were too large for personal computers. Adkisson asked how large it should be, and the customer pointed to a cocktail napkin and said, 'About that size'. Adkisson picked up the napkin, took it back to the laboratory, and proceeded to design the 5¼-inch diskette drive.

fixed disk Miniaturization has made it possible to manufacture fixed disks which have a 1:1 interleave factor, and an average access time of less than 19 milliseconds. Suitable for battery-operated notebook computers, this fixed disk comes in various capacities, and consumes very little power. It is only 0.75 inches (1.9 centimeters) high and 2.5 inches (6.35 centimeters) in length, and is capable of transferring 12 megabits per second. The disk contains 823 cylinders, 39 sectors per track, and can store 512 bytes per sector. It also houses four read/write heads.

fixed-point representation system [ISO A radix numeration system in which the radix point is implicitly fixed in the series of digit places by some convention upon which agreement has been reached.]

fixed radix (numeration) system [ISO A radix numeration system in which all the digit places, except perhaps the one with the highest weight, have the same radix. *Notes:* (a) The weights of successive digit places are successive integral powers of a single radix, each multiplied by the same factor. Negative integral powers of the radix are used in the representation of fractions. (b) A fixed radix

numeration system is a particular case of a mixed radix numeration system.]

flag [ISO A variable indicating that a certain condition holds.]

flag register [ISO A special-purpose register in which bits are set according to specified conditions that may occur during the execution of instructions.]

F

flash memory A type of EEPROM that can be re-programmed by the computer or peripheral to which it is connected. Flash memory may also refer to a non-volatile memory system.

flatbed plotter [ISO A plotter that draws a display image on a display surface mounted on a flat surface.]

FLC Ferroelectric liquid crystals, as used in optical neurocomputers. Optical images are captured, stored, and read by optically addressable spatial light modulators (SLM) which use ferroelectric liquid crystals. FLC–SLM can operate at 50 microseconds, with a spatial resolution of 40 line-pairs per millimeter. These enable a 1 cm^2 device to function at 3.2 giga operations (3.2 x 10^9) per second. See **optical neurocomputer**.

FLC–SLM Ferroelectric liquid crystals–spatial light modulators. See **FLC** and **optical neurocomputer**.

flicker [ISO An undesirable pulsation of a display image on a cathode-ray tube. *Note:* Flicker occurs when the regeneration rate is too low with respect of the phosphor characteristics.]

floating decimal mode [ISO A mode in which the decimal marker is automatically positioned in the result of a calculation irrespective of the mode in which the input data is entered.]

floating head [ISO A magnetic head floating on a layer of air away from the recording surface.]

floating point arithmetic In computing, the size of the numbers a central processing unit can handle is limited by that computer's word length. A computer using an 8-bit word, for example, cannot process numbers larger than 255 which is $(2^8 - 1)$. To get around this problem, computers change large numbers into fractions multiplied by a power of ten. This system is also used by scientists and mathematicians, and is called 'scientific notation'. For example, the number 173 000 000 000 can be represented by using floating point notation, and would be expressed as 1.73×10^{11}. As an alternative, prefixes have been used for the expression of floating point arithmetic. These include 'kilo' and 'milli'. See **floating point notation**.

floating point base [ISO In a floating point representation system, the implicit fixed positive integer base, greater than unity, that is raised to the power explicitly denoted by the exponent or represented by the characteristic and then multiplied by the mantissa to determine the real number represented.

floating point calculation The calculation of numbers whose decimal point is not fixed, but moves (floats) as required so that each number can be fully expressed, thereby providing greater calculation accuracy. See **floating point arithmetic**.

floating point notation The expression

of a number multiplied by its base number raised to a power. For example, the decimal number 452 can be written as 4.52×10^2, or 0.452×10^3. The range of values that may be accommodated by 16-bit operands is –32 768 to +32 767 for single precision. The range of values that may be accommodated by 32-bit operands is –2 147 483 648 to +2 147 483 647 for double precision. Floating point binary values are represented in a format that permits arithmetic to be performed in a fashion analogous to operations with decimal values expressed in scientific notation: $(5.83 \times 10^2)(8.6 \times 10^1) = (5.0138 \times 10^4)$. In the decimal system, data may be expressed as values between 0 and 10, times 10 raised to a power that effectively shifts the implied decimal point right or left the number of places necessary to express the result in conventional form (such as 50138). The value-portion of the data is called the 'mantissa'. The exponent may be either negative or positive. The concept of floating point notation has both advantages and disadvantages associated with it. The advantage is the ability to represent the significant digits of data with values spanning a large dynamic range limited only by the capacity of the exponent field. For example, in decimal notation, if the exponent field is two digits wide, and the mantissa is five digits, a range of values (positive or negative) from 1.0000×10^{-99} to $9.9999 \times 10^{+99}$ can be accommodated. The disadvantage is that only the significant digits of the value can be represented. Thus there is no distinction in this representation between the values 123451 and 123452, for example, since each would be expressed as: 1.2345×10^5. The sixth digit has been rounded. In most applications where the dynamic range of values to be represented is large, the loss of significance, and hence accuracy of results, is a minor consideration. For greater precision, a fixed point format could be chosen, although with a loss of potential dynamic range. See **floating point arithmetic**.

floating point operations See **FLOP**.

floating point register [ISO A register used to manipulate data in a floating point representation system.] Abbreviation 'FPR'.

floating point representation [ISO A representation of a real number in a floating point representation system. *Example:* A floating point representation of the number 0.0001234 is: 0.1234 −3 where: 0.1234 is the mantissa, −3 is the exponent. The numerals are expressed in the variable-point decimal numeration system.]

floating point (representation) system [ISO A numeration system in which a real number is represented by a pair of distinct numerals, the real number being the product of the mantissa, one of the numerals, and a value obtained by raising the implicit floating point base to a power denoted by the exponent indicated by the second numeral. *Note:* In a floating point representation system, there are many representations of the same number obtained by moving the radix point and adjusting the exponent accordingly.]

FLOP Floating point operations; a benchmark used to rate (in seconds) the processing capacity of very large computers, including supercomputers and professional workstations. In computing, the size of the numbers that a central processing unit can handle is limited by that computer's word length. A computer using an 8-bit word, for example, cannot process numbers larger than 255, which is $(2^8 − 1)$. To get around this problem, computers change large numbers into fractions multiplied by a power of ten. This system is also used by scientists and mathematicians, and is called 'scientific notation'. For example, the number 173 674 984 574 can be represented by floating point notation as 0.173 674 984 574 x 10^{12}. Therefore, FLOP refers to the number of operations per second that can be made when the position of the decimal point of stored numbers changes during computing. The acronym remains singular. For example: 12 FLOP, not 12 FLOPS. MFLOP is used to mean mega (million) FLOP; GFLOP is used to mean 10^9 (giga) FLOP; while TFLOP is used to mean 10^{12} (tera) FLOP. See **floating point notation**.

floppy disk See **diskette**.

flowchart A set of diagrams outlining the logical flow of a computer program using a standard set of block-shapes to represent different operations. ANSI symbols have been universally accepted as the standard set of flowchart symbols. For example, a diamond represents a 'decision' and a rectangle represents a 'process'. Readily available templates are used as drawing aids. [ISO A graphical representation in which symbols are used to represent such things as operations, data, flow, and equipment, for the definition, analysis, or solution of a problem.] See **structured flowchart**. ▼

flowchart symbol [ISO A symbol used to represent operations, data, flow direction, or equipment in a flowchart.]

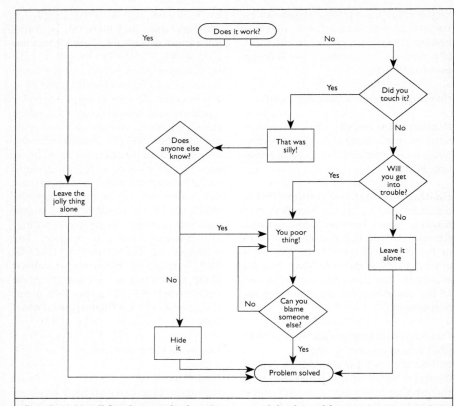

flowchart Not all flowcharts need to be serious, nor need they be used for computer programming. Shown in this problem-solving flowchart are some of the symbols that conform to the International Organization for Standardization (ISO) International Standard 1028 'Information Processing — Flowchart Symbols', and ANSI X3.5-1970 'Flowchart Symbols and Their Usage in Information Processing'.

flow control [ISO In data communication, control of the data transfer rate.]

flow direction [ISO An indication of the antecedent-to-successor relationship between the symbols in a flowchart.]

flowline [ISO A line representing a connecting path between the symbols in a flowchart to indicate a transfer of data or control.]

flush left In typography and word processing, the positioning of text on a page so that all the text is aligned with the left margin, leaving a ragged right margin. Compare **flush right**, **indent**, and **justification**. Also called 'left-justified'. ▼

flush right In typography and word processing, the positioning of text on a page so that all the text is aligned with the right margin, leaving a ragged left margin.

In the 1980s, computer professionals suffered from 'suffixation' — a compulsion to suffixion (the act of attaching suffixes to common words). They were big on hardware, software, jellyware, firmware, vaporware, freeware, shareware, shelfware, wallyware, and courseware. In the 1990s, the ailment is 'prefixation', with words like virtual reality, virtual chambers, virtual storage, virtual sound, virtual space, virtual money, virtual memory, virtual office, and virtual sex.	On the home front, most people have assimilated well to the world of 'micrology'. They own a microwave oven, use a microphone and a microcomputer, and understand the terms microcosm, microeconomics, and microsurgery. Graduates from the school of micrology may brave the invisisble world of nanology to learn about nanoconstructors, nanomachines, nanomedicine, nanaocomputers, nanotechnology, and nanosystems.
flush left An example of text set flush left. It is common to see this style of typesetting because it is believed that people have become accustomed to text that is set flush left.	*flush right An example of text set flush right. Comprehension tests on text that has been set flush right show that this form of typesetting is not easy to read.*

F

Compare **flush left**, **indent**, and **justification**. Also called 'right-justified'. ◣

flux transition Refers to the reversal of the direction of a magnetic field in a disk or tape storage media. Precisely timed flux reversals define the information content stored in the media. The word 'flux' comes from the Latin word *fluxus*, meaning 'flow'.

flying height [ISO The distance between a magnetic head and the surface of the recording medium.] See **head** and **read/write head**.

FM Frequency modulation; the modification of the frequency of a carrier wave so that it carries information. A frequency is the number of waveforms that are repeated per second, and is measured in hertz. For example, if a wave cycles at 1 000 000 waves per second, then the frequency is 1 megahertz (1 MHz). See **modulation**. Compare **amplitude modulation**.

FM encoding Frequency modulation encoding. Two standard data recording techniques are used to combine clock and data information for storage on a floppy disk. The single-density technique is referred to as 'FM encoding'. In FM encoding, a double-frequency encoding technique is used that inserts a data bit between two adjacent clock bits. (The presence of a data bit represents a binary 'one', while the absence of a data bit represents a binary 'zero'.) The adjacent clock bits are referred to as a 'bit cell', and except for unique field identifiers, all clock bits written on the disk are binary 'ones'. In single-density encoding, each data bit is written at the center of the bit cell and the clock bits are written at the leading edge of the bit cell. The encoding used for double-density recording is termed 'MFM encoding' (for modified FM). In MFM encoding, the data bits are again written at the center of the bit cell, but a clock bit is written at the leading edge of the bit cell only if no data bit was written in the previous bit cell and no data bit will be written in the present bit cell. See **FM**.

FMV Full Motion Video. See **CD–I FMV**.

FO See **fiber optics**.

font In typography, a complete set of

characters of one particular size, style, and weight, including punctuation marks, symbols, and numbers. For example, the complete character set of Helvetica 8 point constitutes one font. This term is often confused with 'typeface', which refers to a particular style of character (type family to which the font belongs) which in this example is Helvetica. This confusion has arisen as a result of the electronic manipulation of fonts. Word processing packages using Helvetica 8 point may modify this font electronically so that it appears to be a new font. See **bit-mapped font, downloadable font, outline font**, and **typeface. ▼**

font cartridge A read-only memory (ROM) module which contains font information. The font cartridge is plugged into a printer, providing immediate access to a selection of fonts. Unlike downloadable fonts, a ROM cartridge does not use random-access memory

A a	B b	C c	D d	E e
F f	G g	H h	I i	J j
K k	L l	M m	N n	O o
P p	Q q	R r	S s	T t
U u	V v	W w	X x	Y y
Z z				
1	2	3	4	5
6	7	8	9	0

~ ! @ # $ % ^ & * ( ) _ + }
{ < > ? : " | \ ¡ ™ £ ¢ ∞ §
¶ • ª º – ≠ ≤ ≥ ` □ ‹ › fi fl
‡ ° · ˜ ˘ ¿ Æ

font Shown here is the complete font for Palatino normal, set in 8 point.

which is volatile (lost when the power is switched off). See **downloadable font**.

Font/DA Mover Font/Desk Accessory Mover; a utility program for the Apple Macintosh computer that enables the user to install fonts and desk accessories in the System Folder so that they can become part of the operating environment, appearing as options in the selection menus.

Font/Desk Accessory Mover See **Font/ DA Mover**.

Fontographer A font modification program designed for the Apple Macintosh which allows users to modify and design their own outline fonts for high-resolution printing.

footer In word processing, a short message displayed at the bottom (foot) of a page for the purpose of referencing or clarifying a particular point. Automatic footers can be used to display the same message at the end of each page in the document — for instance, chapter name and page number. Compare **footnote**.

footnote In word processing, a message displayed at the end of a section. Compare **footer**.

footprint 1. The desk or floor space occupied by a computer or other office equipment such as a photocopier or facsimile machine. 2. The area of the Earth's surface covered electronically by a satellite at given times. Communications satellites are usually positioned into a geostationary orbit, meaning they remain in a fixed position above the Earth's surface usually over 22 300 miles (35 000 kilometers) above the Earth.

foreground image [ISO That part of a display image that can be changed for every transaction.]

foreground processing The processing of high-priority tasks such as those associated with real-time user interaction on a multitasking computer. In contrast, background processing is the processing of low-priority tasks such as printing — processing only occurs when the computer does not have higher priorities. Systems that are unable to perform multiple tasks (multitasking) carry out background processing during brief pauses in the system's primary (foreground) operations. See **multitasking**.

formal logic [ISO The study of the structure and forms of valid argument without regard to the meaning of the terms in the argument.]

formal parameter [ISO A language object, the identifier of which appears in an entry of a procedure, that is associated with the corresponding actual parameter specified by the procedure call for use in the execution of the procedure.]

formal specification [ISO A specification that is used to prove mathematically the validity of an implementation, or to derive mathematically the implementation.]

formal standards Clearly-defined and agreed upon conventions for specific programming interfaces developed by a standards organization such as the American National Standards Institute or the International Organization for Standardization. Proprietary standards are used only within the environment provided by a single computer vendor, and public standards are widely used across a variety of vendor equipment.

format 1. To prepare a floppy or hard disk to accept data. 'Format a:' is a user-command that instructs the computer to initialize the disk in drive 'A' by placing magnetic patterns called 'tracks' (each track is divided into nine sectors which can each store 512 bytes). Double-sided, double-density disks are formatted to contain 40 tracks, with a total of 360 sectors on each side. Formatting a disk may take up to five minutes. Some diskettes can be purchased already formatted. 2. (In word processing, graphics, spreadsheet, and database programs) the way in which data is arranged within the application, including margins, indents, fonts, and tabs. 3. Formatting [ISO The initialization of a data medium such that a particular computer system can store data in, and subsequently retrieve data from, the medium.]

format check [ISO A check to determine whether data conforms to a specified layout.]

format effector [ISO A control character used to position printed, displayed, or recorded data. *Note:* Format effectors are described in ISO 646 and ISO 6429.]

form feed 1. [ISO A paper skip used to bring an assigned part of a form to the print position.] 2. [ISO The movement of the print or display position to the predetermined first line on the next form, the next page, or the equivalent.]

form flash [ISO The display of a form overlay.]

form interface management system See **video form**.

form overlay [ISO A pattern such as a report form, grid, or map used as a background image.]

FORTRAN <u>For</u>mula <u>Trans</u>lator; the first high-level computer programming language used for scientific, technical, and graphics applications. It was first devised in 1953 by IBM and introduced in 1954 as an unstructured language. It was later upgraded with FORTRAN II in 1960. FORTRAN 77 was introduced in 1977 and offered control structures. Programs written in ANSI Standard FORTRAN 77 are portable to target platforms that have ANSI-compliant compilers available. As with other languages, degrees of portability can be lost by the use of non-standard language extension. See **portability** and **programming language**. ▼

forward chaining In an expert system, a method of collecting data before questions or inferences can be made, working through each of the rules one by one until an inference can be made, or answer found, or decision reached. The opposite to this is backward chaining, which starts with a question such as 'How much is this car worth?', and

---

Typical mathematical formula:

$$D = B^2 - 4AC$$

Equivalent FORTRAN statement:

$$D = B**2 - 4*A*C$$

FORTRAN This programming language was developed originally by IBM in 1953. It enables engineers and scientists using a computer to state a problem in familiar symbols (close to the language of mathematics) in one-fourth the time required with earlier symbolic (assembler) languages.

---

searches through the system backwards to determine which of the rules in the knowledge base must be answered before a conclusion can be reached. See **expert systems**.

forward channel [ISO A channel in which the direction of transmission is the direction in which user information is being transferred.]

forward LAN channel [ISO In a broadband LAN, the channel assigned for downlink data transmission from the head-end to the data stations.]

forward recovery [ISO The reconstruction of a newer version of a file by updating an earlier version with data recorded in a journal.]

486 See **Intel 80486**.

486 DX See **Intel 80486 DX**.

486 DX2 See **Intel 80486 DX**.

486 SL See **Intel 80486 SL**.

486 SX See **Intel 80486 SX**.

4GL See **fourth-generation language**.

fourth generation Refers to the general present-day technology used in computers. This generation was originally introduced in the 1970s and today offers, at lower cost, increased performance through solid-state circuits, miniaturized microprocessors, and advanced integrated circuits. The microcomputer revolution can be traced back to 1969 when Intel Corporation, then a small Californian company, commissioned Marcian E. Hoff to develop a general-purpose logic chip. It was called the 'Intel 4004' and dubbed the first microprocessor. It was built to enhance the capabilities of ordinary calculators. By 1971, when the fourth generation became evident, the Altair 8800 was produced to become the world's first commercially-available microprocessor. It was developed by a small group of Air Force personnel who met after work in a garage to experiment with electronics. The small group formed Micro Instrumentation and Telemetry Systems (MITS) and later hired Bill Gates, a Harvard student, to install the BASIC programming language on the 8800. Later in the 1970s, Apple Computer was born, and Stephen Wozniak and Steven Jobs offered their first computer in kit form. Later models (Apple II) were pre-assembled. VisiCalc, launched in 1978, was adopted by Apple as a business spreadsheet package which gave rise to functional business computing. In 1981, IBM introduced its microcomputer, called the 'IBM Personal Computer'. The fourth generation became characterized by microminiaturization, with silicon chips smaller than a shirt button containing over a million circuits. The use of metal oxide semiconductor (MOS) internal memory, and improvements in software, saw over 100 firms manufacture computer system units. Companies like Acer and Apple have specialized in microcomputers, while Digital Equipment Corporation and Data General have focused on minicomputers. Third-generation programming languages like BASIC and FORTRAN gave way to fourth-generation programming languages, enabling executives to access the information they needed through decision support systems (DSS), without having to rely too heavily on manage-

ment information systems personnel. Today, computing is still growing at a very fast rate. The development of very-large-scale integration (VLSI) will very soon seem inadequate when compared to ultra-large-scale integration (ULSI) offering billions of circuits. The development of the technology which can be called 'fifth generation' is well under way. Its introduction cannot be given a specific date because it is still an evolutionary technology. See **FACOM M-190**, **Fifth-Generation Project**, and **third generation**.

fourth-generation language A type of programming language which began to emerge in 1971, specifically designed to simplify both the programming task and the user operands. Some of these languages can be found in commercial software which are designed to perform specific functions. Abbreviation '4GL'. See **fourth generation** and **programming language**.

423 virus A variant of the Virus–B virus. See **Virus–B virus**.

four-wire circuit A communications channel designed for full-duplex operation. Four wires are provided at each termination, two for sending information and two for receiving information. Compare **two-wire circuit**.

fpppp One of the ten SPEC (Systems Performance Evaluation Cooperative) benchmarks drawn from real-world applications including scientific and engineering areas, focusing on system performance, memory, input/output, graphics, networking, multi-user, and commercial applications. Fpppp is a quantum chemistry benchmark that measures performance on one style of computation (two electron integral derivative) which occurs in the GaussuanXX series of programs. It is a double precision floating point FORTRAN benchmark. It is difficult to vectorize because it contains very large basic blocks and does very little input/output. The input to the program is the number of atoms. The amount of computation to be done is proportional to the fourth power of the number of atoms. Fpppp has been run on machines ranging from personal computers to supercomputers. See **SPEC**.

FPR See **floating point register**.

FPS Frames per second. In video or film recording, a frame is a single, complete picture. A video frame consists of two interlaced fields of either 525 lines (NTSC) or 625 lines (PAL/SECAM), running at 30 FPS for NTSC, or 25 FPS for PAL/SECAM.

fractals Along with raster and vector graphics, a way of defining graphics in a computer. Fractal graphics translate the natural curves of an object into mathematical formulae, from which the image can later be constructed. The term also refers to any irregular shape which is not normally described (or is impossible to describe) in geometry. Most people would be familiar with some form of fractal imagery, whether it be the irregular shapes (which eventually form a pattern) on checks or bank notes, or the colorful shapes formed inside a kaleidoscope when held up to the light. The term was coined by Benoit Mandelbrot, and it comes from the Latin *fractus*, meaning 'broken'.

fragmentation The storage of a file in noncontiguous sections, called 'clusters'. Even though DOS stores the locations of these clusters in the file allocation table (FAT), fragmentation leads to extra movement of the read/write head and degradation in disk performance. A greater disk reading and writing efficiency (up to 75%) can be realized by using a defragmentation utility which re-writes the files on a disk so that they are placed in contiguous clusters. See **file allocation table**.

frame In IEEE terminology, the unit of data transferred at the OSI data link layer. See **data link layer**.

frame grabber A device (such as a video camera) that captures (and potentially stores) one complete video frame on disk.

frames per second See **FPS**.

framing In a local area network, a data packet which 'encloses' raw data and tells the network equipment of the data's origin, its intended recipient, and other important control information. Each networking system has different protocols for framing messages. Ethernet, for example, uses a frame composed of multiple 'fields' which contain such information as the preamble (used for hardware synchronization), addressing information, message data, and a cyclic redundancy check (used to make sure the frame was correctly received). The most basic piece of information about a frame is where it begins — how one frame can be distinguished from the preceding frame or from noise on the channel. One method for making this distinction is the use of flags or delimiters. For instance, in SDLC (synchronous data link control) framing, the opening and closing flags have the binary configuration 01111110. The SDLC protocol dictates that the flag frames are the only place where this bit pattern may occur. Therefore, whenever a receiving station sees this bit pattern, it knows that a frame follows. (Should this pattern occur in the actual message, it is broken up by the hardware and then restored at the receiving end.) The opening flag is also used to allow hardware to synchronize on the new frame. Another method of creating a unique opening delimiter is used with Manchester encoding, in which the IEEE 802.5 standard for token rings specifies a starting delimiter which contains pairs of violations of the Manchester encoding rules. The ending delimiter also contains code violations, but in a different pattern so that the two delimiters can be easily distinguished. Flags and delimiters are used when frames are sent nonstop on the communications channel, so that hardware can tell when one frame is ending and another is beginning. By contrast, in an Ethernet system, the channel is unused between frames and any pattern of bits coming after this quiet period is presumed by the hardware to mark the start of a frame. See **packet-switching system**.

FRAPTL Fax receiving and passing to logistics; a term coined in June 1994 by Dion Weisler, an industry product manager, to describe sales representatives whose success comes more from the booming computer industry than from their own sales efforts. Salespeople who do very little selling and who wait around fax machines for orders to flow in are called 'FRAPTLs'. Pronounced 'fraptle'.

FreeHand An object-oriented professional illustration program from Aldus Corporation which can prepare camera-ready art. FreeHand can import files from other sources for editing.

freeware Utilities and software programs (under copyright) made available to the public free of charge. See **shareware**.

F

freeway See **data highway**.

frequency The number of times one complete incident or function occurs in a given time. In electronics, this usually refers to the number of waveforms that are repeated per second, measured in hertz. For example, if a wave cycles at 1 000 000 waves per second, then the frequency is 1 megahertz. The word 'frequency' comes from the Latin word *frequens*, meaning 'crowded'. Compare **amplitude**. ▼

frequency-division multiplexing In broadband transmission and local area networking, several frequencies on a single channel may be used to send different messages simultaneously. This is done through the use of multiplexers. See **bandwidth**, **broadband**, and **multiplexer**. Abbreviation 'FDM'.

frequency modulation See **FM**.

frequency modulation recording [ISO Non-return-to-zero recording in which there is a change in the condition of magnetization at each cell boundary, and a further change in the center of the cell to represent a one.]

frequency shift keying See **FSK**.

friction feed A printer paper-feed

ABBREVIATION	DESIGNATOR	FREQUENCY RANGE	ITU NUMBER
ELF	Extremely low frequency	less than 300 Hz	2
ULF	Ultra low frequency	300 to 3000 Hz	3
VLF	Very low frequency	3 to 30 kHz	4
LF	Low frequency	30 to 300 kHz	5
MF	Medium frequency	300 to 3000 kHz	6
HF	High frequency	3 to 30 MHz	7
VHF	Very high frequency	30 to 300 MHz	8
UHF	Ultra high frequency	300 to 3000 MHz	9
SHF	Super high frequency	3 to 30 GHz	10
EHF	Extremely high frequency	30 to 300 GHz	11
THF	Tremendously high frequency	300 to 3000 GHz	12

frequency The International Telecommunications Union (ITU) specifies a numeric value to the range of frequencies. However, it is more common to refer to frequency ranges by their two- or three-letter abbreviations.

mechanism that transports the paper by friction rollers that are usually made out of rubber.

Friday 13th virus A variant of the Jerusalem virus. See **Jerusalem virus**.

front-end processor A computer, usually a minicomputer, that is connected to a larger host computer so as to handle all the communications requirements quite independently, thereby leaving the host computer free to concentrate on internal data processing. Abbreviation 'FEP'. [ISO In a computer network, a processor that relieves a host computer of processing tasks such as line control, message handling, code conversion, and error control.]

FRR First read rate; referring to a bar code scanner which translates codes on the first pass.

FSK Frequency shift keying; a type of frequency modulation where the carrier signal frequency is shifted between two known frequencies in order to represent digital data.

FTP File Transfer Protocol; an application utility for TCP/IP that fits in the upper layer of the OSI model which permits the transfer of data between different computers. See **OSI**.

Fujitsu Limited This Japanese multinational is one of the Furukawa Group of companies — a conglomerate made up of 44 member companies. Other members of the Furukawa Group include the Daiichi Kangyo Bank Limited, The Yokohama Rubber Company Limited, Nippon Zeon Company Limited, and Fuji Electric Company Limited. Fuji Electric Company Limited began operating in 1923 in cooperation with Siemens, a large German company which still markets Fujitsu products in Europe. In fact, the name 'Fuji' is derived from Furukawa and Jimens, which is the Japanese pronunciation of 'Siemens'. In 1835, when Fuji Electric became involved in the manufacture of telecommunications equipment, a separate company was formed — Fuji Tsushinki Seizo Limited ('tsushin' — telecommunications, 'ki' — equipment, and 'seizo' — manufacture). In 1967, the name was abbreviated to 'Fujitsu'. In 1951, Fujitsu's Information Processing Division began to pioneer the manufacture of computers in Japan. As a result, the first relay-type computer in Japan (the FACOM 100) was introduced in 1954. FACOM is the product name of Fujitsu's computers and is derived from Fujitsu Automatic Computers. By 1964, the International Operations Division was established, with Fujitsu entering the international market. The company now operates worldwide, including Australia, New Zealand, Canada, Hong Kong, Italy, Malaysia, Singapore, the United Kingdom, the United States, and Germany. Today a US$17 000 million company, Fujitsu employs over 100 000 people and ranks as Japan's largest computer manufacturer. It is a world leader in the manufacture of telecommunications systems, semiconductors, and electronic components. Fujitsu independently designs, manufactures, and markets a complete line of advanced computers, from microcomputers to the largest commercial systems available in the world. In the United States, Fujitsu markets a wide range of computer peripherals including magnetic tape units, disk drives, printers, and communications equipment through Fujitsu America Incorporated. In addition, Fujitsu manufactures a wide range of equipment and components for other companies, who re-market these products under their own name. These include Siemens, Amdahl, Sun, Cray, ICL, Memorex, and Mitsui. Through its subsidiary FANUC Limited, Fujitsu is the largest supplier of industrial robots, with an estimated 60% of the world market. It also has a joint manufacturing and marketing agreement with General Motors for the supply and maintenance of industrial robots in the United States and Europe.

full duplex A method of transmitting information over an asynchronous communications channel, in which signals may be sent in both directions simultaneously. Although this technique makes the best use of line time, it substantially increases the amount of logic required in the primary and secondary stations. Full duplex operations have traditionally used four-wire circuits, with one local-loop and trunk circuit dedicated to transmitting, and a second local-loop and trunk circuit dedicated to receiving. Other methods of transmission include half duplex and simplex. Half duplex allows two-way communications, but messages can only travel in one direction at a time. Simplex allows messages to be transmitted in only one direction.

fully associative cache A cache architecture in which each item of information from main system memory is stored as a unique cache entry. For a given cache size, a fully associative cache is the highest performance cache architecture. There is no relationship between the location of the information in the data cache RAM (random-access memory) and its original location in main system memory. If there are five storage locations in the cache, for example, the cache will remember the last five main system memory locations accessed by the microprocessor. With a fully associative cache, each storage location can hold information from any location in main system memory. As a result, the cache requires complex tag entries (to map the complete main system memory space), resulting in very complex and expensive cache comparison logic. When a microprocessor makes a memory request, each tag entry in the fully associative cache is compared to the current microprocessor request to determine if the information is in the cache. To accomplish this large number of comparisons without adding wait states, fully associative caches are typically kept very small (such as 4 kilobytes or less) and are integrated devices. See **cache**. Compare **set associative cache**.

fully-connected network [ISO A network in which there is a branch between any two nodes.]

Fu Manchu virus An indirect-action file virus that adds 2086 bytes to any .COM file or .EXE file. One clue to the presence of this virus is the message that appears when the computer is soft-booted (using the Control-Alt-Delete sequence) that reads 'The world will hear from me again!' Once it becomes active, Fu Manchu loads four rude words into the keyboard's buffer and starts to search for the words 'Thatcher', 'Reagan', 'Waldheim', or 'Botha' and automatically places 'is a X' after the name, where 'X' is a random selection from one of the four rude words. Given the nature of this virus, it was popular around 1989, but has since diminished. Fu Manchu is sometimes called '2086'. See **indirect-action file virus**.

Fumble virus A direct-action file virus that infects any .COM file, adding 867 bytes to it. Fumble is a rare virus which, if it goes undetected, frustrates users to the point where they begin to question their typing competence. On even days of the week, the virus waits for the typist to enter six or more characters in under one second and then transposes two of the center characters, making the typist believe that a typographical error was made. See **direct-action file virus**.

function [ISO A function that, when executed, yields a value and the function call of which may be used as an operand in an expression. *Example:* The function SIN yields the value sin X when called with SIN(X).]

functional analysis [ISO A systematic investigation of the functions of a real or planned system.]

functional design [ISO The specification of the functions of the components of a system and of the working relationships among them.]

functional generator [ISO A functional unit whose output analog variable is equal to some function of its input analog variables.]

functional language [ISO A programming language in which computations are expressed in terms of function procedure calls. *Example:* LISP.]

functional programming [ISO A method for structuring programs mainly as sequences of possibly nested function procedure calls.]

functional unit [ISO An entity of hardware or software, or both, capable of accomplishing a specified purpose.]

function key A programmable key on a

keyboard that can execute several different tasks. Most industry-standard personal computer keyboards have 12 function keys, labeled 'F1' to 'F12'. Depending upon the application being used, function keys perform different tasks. For example, when using Word-Perfect, pressing the 'F2' key activates the forward search function; pressing 'Shift F2' activates a backward search; pressing 'Alt F2' commences a search and replace function; while pressing 'Ctrl F2' activates the spelling checker.

function preselection capability [ISO The ability to perform more than one function by a particular control or key.]

fusing The sixth step in the electro-photography process in which the toner is fused (or fixed) to the paper. Fusing typically involves two rollers; one supplies the heat to melt the toner, and the other applies the pressure. See **laser printer**.

fuzzy creativity A term used to describe the creation of facts from unrelated variables. Once an element of fuzzy creativity is crystallized, it becomes an indisputable fact that may then be used to re-calculate or re-position the surrounding elements. Fuzzy creativity may be used on its own, or it may contribute to the databank of an expert system or to the historical databank of systems that use fuzzy logic. For example, a computer may be told that all executives within a particular organization who are on a salary of $100 000, each occupy office space that is costing that organization 20 times what it costs for executives who are on $80 000. The computer may create an indisputable rule that will henceforth be applied to executives' salaries and benefit calculations. This new element (which was created as a result of fuzzy creativity) may deem that in the new building, all executives on a salary of $100 000 will only have offices that are twice as expensive as executives on $80 000. The chain of interrogation may proceed to compare office space with those earning less than $80 000. However, this may only be necessary if the computer is asked to complete an office refurbishment plan within a certain budget. The essence of fuzzy creativity is creation. Concrete elements must exist and must be able to operate within fuzzy logic. See **fuzzy logic**.

fuzzy logic A term used to describe the variables that exist between a definite 'yes' and a definite 'no'. Fuzzy logic is used in expert systems and artificial intelligence systems to give the computer human-like characteristics, and to enable it to function in an analog world where not all things are merely true or false. Computer operations and analysis produced as a result of fuzzy logic operations may be expressed as probabilities, possibilities, and potentials. Factors of truth may range from possibly true to potentially true. Such expert systems rely upon historical data, the fast processing of mathematical probabilities, plus the application of heuristics (rules of thumb). Contrary to popular belief, fuzzy logic does not tolerate illogical statements, nor paradoxical statements. Fuzzy logic relies upon facts and sound analytical data from which a computer may deduce the most likely outcome. Humans use a form of fuzzy logic in everyday life. However, humans tend to operate outside of the realm of fuzzy logic because they break funda-

F

mental rules of logic due to a lack of understanding of the strict discipline that is required to keep fuzzy logic apart from fuzzy creativity. See **fuzzy creativity** and **heuristic**.

THERE'S A BIG DIFFERENCE
BETWEEN TAKING RISKS AND GAMBLING

G Giga-. An SI unit prefix for 10^9 expressed in decimal notation as 1 000 000 000. In computing terms, giga refers to 2^{30} (which is equal to 1 073 741 824).

GaAs See **gallium arsenide**.

gain The increase in signaling power as an audio signal is boosted by an electronic device. Gain is measured in decibels.

gallium arsenide A compound used in chip technology in place of silicon for high-speed devices, because it offers less resistance to electron flow, thereby operating approximately six times as fast as conventional silicon chips. Gallium arsenide, a semiconductor, is commonly used in the making of individual transistors. Gallium arsenide field-effect transistors (GaAs FETs) are not easily damaged by temperature rise because the negative current–temperature coefficient prevents current

concentration. See **integrated circuit**. Compare **silicon**.

Gang of Nine The group of nine companies who joined forces in 1989 to maintain the industry-standard architecture (ISA), and further developed it to take advantage of the 32-bit bus structure of the Intel 80386 and 80486 microprocessors. What they developed became known as 'Extended ISA' (EISA) and was announced in September 1989, in New York. The nine companies were AST Research, Compaq Computer Corporation, Epson, Hewlett-Packard, NEC, Olivetti, Tandy, Wyse Technology, and Zenith Data Systems. See **EISA**.

garnet A naturally-occurring silicate mineral sometimes used in jewelry. Synthetic garnets with the same crystal structure can be made from oxides of iron and yttrium or another of the rare earths. Garnet is the preferred material for the thin magnetic film in a bubble memory. See **bubble memory**.

gas plasma display A display technology used with portable computers in which ionized gas, held between two transparent panels, is energized, making it glow on the screen in the form of pixels (picture elements).

gate [ISO A combinational circuit that performs an elementary logic operation. *Note:* The term 'gate' generally involves one output.]

gate array chip This is a type of computer chip made for general use, yet it can be customized to specifications by adding a final interconnecting layer at the end of its manufacturing process.

Gates, William H. Bill Gates, born 1956 in Seattle, Washington, is today considered to be one of the driving forces behind the personal computing and office automation industry. As chairman and chief executive officer of Microsoft, Gates heads a multinational company which supplies application software, operating systems, and programming language products. Gates started his career in computer software at an early age. Both Gates and Microsoft co-founder, Paul Allen, worked as consultants in the mainframe/minicomputer programming field during their high school years in Seattle. In 1974, Gates (then an undergraduate at Harvard University) worked with Allen to develop the BASIC programming language for the first commercially-available microcomputer, the MITS Altair. After successful completion of the project, the two formed Microsoft to develop and market software for the

Gates, William H. The founder of Microsoft Corporation, William (Bill) Gates, is one of the wealthiest people in the world.

emerging microcomputer marketplace. See **fourth generation** and **Microsoft Corporation**. ▲

gateway A device that operates at the transport layer (and above) of the OSI model to connect two or more dissimilar networks. Although slower than a bridge or router, a gateway has its own processor and memory to perform complex functions such as interpreting between computers that speak different 'languages' through both protocol conversion and bandwidth conversion. [ISO A functional unit that interconnects two computer networks with different network architectures.]

gather write The writing of data from discontiguous (fragmented) host computer memory addresses to consecutive logical block addresses on a disk. Gather writing is usually supported by host computer or storage subsystem mapping hardware.

Gb Gigabyte. In computing terms, giga refers to 2^{30} (which equals 1 073 741 824). Hence, a gigabyte is 1 073 741 824 bytes. See **byte**.

GB Gigabit. In computing terms, giga refers to 2^{30} (which equals 1 073 741 824). Hence, a gigabit is 1 073 741 824 bits. See **bit**.

GBP General Business Provider.

GCA Game control adapter.

GEM Graphics Environment Manager; the first operating environment to employ an easy-to-use interface between the user and the operating system through on-screen graphics (icons) which represent certain files or commands which are accessible to the user through a pointing device such as a mouse. GEM was developed by Digital Research for IBM personal computers. Such a system was later referred to as a 'WIMP' (windows, icons, mouse, and pull-down menus) interface.

gender Type of a connector. See **female connector** and **male connector**.

gender bender A double-ended connector with the same gender at both ends. It is used to convert one end of a cable to the opposite gender. This is sometimes called 'gender changer'.

general purpose register [ISO A register, usually explicitly addressable within a set of registers, that can be used for different purposes, such as an accumulator, as an index register, or as a special handler of data.]

generator [ISO A computer program that can produce other computer programs.]

generic unit [ISO A possibly parameterized model of a language construct from which, at translation time, a language construct proper is derived. *Note:* There is some analogy between generic units and macro-definitions: the language construct derived from the generic unit corresponds to the statement sequence replacing a macro call and is referred to as a 'generic instantiation'.]

genetic algorithm See **artificial life**.

genlock A device which synchronizes two video sources, such as the signal from a video recorder and from a computer.

geostationary satellite A satellite which is in such an orbit above the equator that

geostationary satellite Modern satellites are equipped with small rockets that can be used to correct their altitude should they wander off course. A satellite is launched into space using a rocket. Once released, it can be positioned above one point on the equator.

it is stationary above one point on the equator. ▲

GFLOP Giga (10^9) floating point operations per second. See **FLOP**.

GHz Gigahertz; 10^9 cycles per second. See **hertz**.

GI General intelligence; intelligence within the human framework. Compare **artificial intelligence**.

giga- See **G**.

gigabus A term used to describe the bus-based parallel processing capabilities of Elxsi's System 6400 which operates at 320 gigabytes per second. See **parallel processing**.

gigabyte In computing terms, 'giga' refers to 2^{30} (which equals 1 073 741 824); hence, a 'gigabyte' is 1 073 741 824 bytes. Abbreviation 'Gb'. See **byte**.

gigahertz 10^9 cycles per second. SI symbol 'GHz'. See **hertz** and **SI**.

giga operations A unit used to describe very-high-speed computer operations. 'Giga' refers to 10^9.

GIGO Garbage in, garbage out; a phrase used to explain that the quality of information given out by the computer cannot be expected to be better than the information first given to the computer.

gimbal The frame in which a disk slider is mounted. It permits limited roll, pitch, and vertical translation — but not yaw, longitudinal translation, nor lateral translation. The gimbal is usually fabricated from stainless steel for high strength and compliance, and rigidly attached to the access arm. See **yaw angle**.

GIS Geographic information system.

GKS Graphical Kernel System. A high-level set of services for the creation and manipulation of two-dimensional (2D) graphics in a device-independent manner.

GKS-3D A high-level set of services for the creation and manipulation of three-dimensional (3D) graphics in a device-independent manner. GKS-3D implements the ISO GKS-3D standard, and is a superset of GKS. GKS is an ANSI and ISO standard.

global backup A backup procedure for a hard disk where the entire contents of the hard disk are copied onto another secondary storage medium such as an optical disk or tape cartridge. See **backup**. Compare **differential backup**, **image backup**, and **incremental backup**.

GND Ground.

GNU C compiler gcc One of the ten SPEC (Systems Performance Evaluation Cooperative) benchmarks drawn from real-world applications including scientific and engineering areas, focusing on system performance, memory, input/output, graphics, networking, multi-user, and commercial applications. The GNU C compiler gcc is based on the GNU C compiler version 1.35 distributed by the Free Software Foundation. This benchmark measures the time it takes for the GNU C compiler to convert 19 pre-processed source files into optimized Sun-3 assembly language (.s files) output. It is derived from the GNU C compiler written principally by Richard Staltman of the Free Software Foundation. The metric used is the elapsed (real) time as output by Ibin/time. Gcc is representative of work done in a software engineering environment and can be used to predict how well a system compiles code. Gcc is mainly a central processing unit integer-intensive benchmark written in C. However, it does contain a very small amount of input/output and floating point computation. On a Sun-4/260 system, the disks are busy about 2% of the total run time of the benchmark. About 0.01% of the in-

structions on a Sun-4/260 are floating point. See **SPEC**.

Go-Screen Graphics-oriented screen technology; the projection of high-resolution computer-generated images onto wide panorama screens measuring up to 30 foot (9.2 meters) wide by 12 foot (3.7 meters) high. Go-Screens take advantage of the latest in multimedia technology by combining digital media (including CD stereo audio and digital video) onto one hardware platform that projects photo-realistic images and 3D animation directly onto the screen. This new tech-

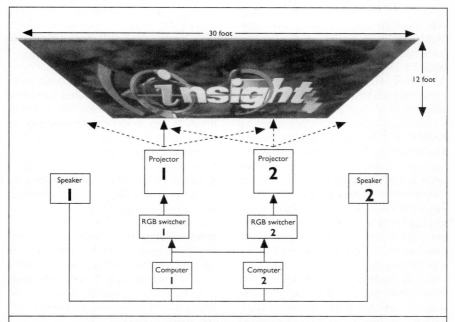

Go-Screen *The visual and audio signal flow for the Go-Screen begins at the personal computer. Audio (16-bit) is output as a stereo analog signal and is fed into a production-quality sound system. Data (visual graphics) is output from two 24-bit graphics boards into analog computer interfaces which split into RGB (red, green, blue) switchers. These are finally fed into two high-scan data projectors. The center-right and center-left halves of the projected computer images overlap each other to provide a seamless panoramic image.*

nology replaces traditional magnetic video and 35-mm slide sourceware. Using Go-Screen technology, a presentation that requires up to thirty-six slide projectors can now be replaced with two data projectors which provide a seamless panoramic presentation not possible with current video technology. The major advantage of Go-Screens is the ability to provide animation, video, and other graphics on one medium that can be manipulated much more easily than is possible with any other method. Furthermore, unlike slide platforms that would depend on a film-developing process, the Go-Screen platform allows the programmer to make last-minute changes. All files are disk-based, making presentations easy to store, duplicate, customize, and transport. Go-Screens were developed 2 January 1994 in Australia by Paul Antonievich and Randall Alexander of Go Man Go Productions — both of whom were frustrated by the inefficiencies of slide projectors. Utilizing a Macintosh Quadra with two graphics boards, they designed a unique grid to format images and provide projector line-ups for synchronized output to two or more high-scan data projectors. In the future, with increased microprocessor power, Go-Screens can be programmed to project off several data projectors to give even greater screen dimensions. Combined with surround-sound stereo, this technology transforms a simple business conference into a Hollywood-style presentation limited only by the software and the programmer's imagination. The term 'Go-Screen' was coined in October 1994 by multimedia producer, Marie Florian. ▲

GOSIP Government Open ystems Interconnection Profile; the United States Government's version of OSI. Pronounced 'gossip'. See **OSI**.

GPD See **gas plasma display**.

GPIB General-purpose interface bus.

GPR General-purpose register.

GPS Global positioning system; a satellite-based positioning system that enables users with a GPS receiver to determine their latitude, longitude, and height above sea level, anywhere in the world. This service is available day or night, and operates without the need for a license. The satellites, operated by the United States Department of Defense, orbit the Earth twice a day to give travelers and sailors their location on Earth. Such a system is accurate to within tens of meters.

grabber hand In HyperCard, paint, and graphics programs, a grabber hand is a cursor image that looks like a small hand. It can grab text or graphics to move them to a place directed by the user via a pointing device.

gradient In graphics, having an area smoothly blend from one color to another, or from black to white or vice versa.

gram An SI unit of measure (mass). One thousand grams equal 1 kilogram. A gram is one-thousandth of the weight of the platinum-iridium alloy cylinder kept in Paris by the International Bureau of Weights and Measures. SI symbol 'g'. See **metric system** and **SI**.

Graphical Kernel System See **GKS**.

Graphical Kernel System for Three Dimensions See **GKS**.

graphical user interface A collection of graphical icons, menus, clipboards, desk accessories, and alert boxes, each accessible through the use of a mouse. The graphical user interface was first featured in the Apple Lisa in 1983, and made computing much simpler (especially for novices). The Macintosh, using the Motorola 68030 microprocessor, led the way with the graphical user interface until Microsoft launched Windows and Presentation Manager for the Intel 80386 microprocessor. In contrast, a character user interface (CUI) only displays characters on the screen. Acronym 'GUI'. Pronounced 'gooey'.

graphic character [ISO A character, other than a control character, that has visual representation and is normally produced by writing, printing, or displaying.]

graphic display device [ISO A display device that provides a representation of data in any graphic form.]

graphicist The modern-day artist who uses the computer instead of traditional media to create graphics.

graphics In computing, the creation of images generated by a computer and its peripheral devices. Computer graphics can be either object-oriented or bit-mapped. Object-oriented graphics (sometimes called 'vector graphics') are produced through mathematical representation which can be re-sized or re-scaled without distortion. Typically, object-oriented graphics uses include computer-aided design, architecture, interior design, and other precision-based applications using programs like Mac-Draw. Bit-mapped graphics (sometimes called 'raster graphics') use picture elements (pixels) to form complex patterns on the screen using paint programs such as MacPaint, PC Paintbrush, and SuperPaint. Attempts to re-size these images will cause distortion.

graphics characters Printable special characters and symbols such as lines and squares used to produce graphics images, mathematical graphs, charts, and the like.

Graphics Environment Manager See **GEM**.

graphics system processor A 32-bit CMOS (complementary metal-oxide semiconductor) microprocessor designed specifically for a variety of military graphics systems applications including radar system display, satellite imaging, missile systems, air defense systems, avionics displays, image processing, weather maps, remotely-piloted vehicles, and remote targeting systems. The graphics system processor boosts system performance by off-loading the graphics processing burden from the host central processing unit, in much the same way a math coprocessor aids the central processing unit with arithmetic operations. The graphics system processor is augmented with special graphics operations already implemented in the hardware. The Texas Instruments SMJ3-4010 is an example of a graphics system processor that offers a high degree of internal parallelism, with a 256-byte, on-chip instruction cache. It is fabricated in 1.8-micron CMOS technology and characterized for operation across the military temperature range (–55 to +110°C). Abbreviation 'GSP'.

graphics tablet See **tablet**.

grave An accent which slopes upward to the left (`) to indicate pronunciation. See **accent**.

gray importing See **gray marketing**.

gray marketing The marketing and/or distribution of software and hardware imported without the permission of the copyright owner. The concept of gray marketing involves unauthorized dealing for commercial gain. Software piracy, on the other hand, is the colloquial expression used worldwide to describe the criminal act of making or distributing for financial gain an unauthorized copy (or copies) of a copyrighted software product.

gray scale In computer graphics systems using monochrome monitors, the shades of gray which are used to enhance the contrast of design elements. Gray scales are formed by varying the intensity of each picture element (pixel) on the screen. Some monitors use colors other than white, such as green or amber. The term 'gray scale' also pertains to scanners. To read images, a scanner shines a bright light onto the paper. Arrays of small components called 'charge-coupled devices' then measure the amount of light reflected from all areas of the page. The amount of image detail, or resolution, that can be scanned is dependent upon the density of the charge-coupled devices. Typical flat-bed scanners have a resolution of 300 dots per inch. To handle photographs at an acceptable level, scanners must be able to capture gray scales between black and white. Since the standard output device for these applications is a laser printer, this requirement poses a challenge because a laser can only create images using on or off

dots of uniform size. To simulate gray tones, scanner software divides the image into small cells, typically six dots by six dots each. Depending upon the average gray tone of the cell, various combinations of dots are recorded as 'on'. For example, a medium gray area would have half the dots on. From a distance, this appears as solid gray. Using the technique with '6 x 6' cells, it is possible to simulate 256 gray levels, but this technique of clustering dots does result in reduced image resolution.

greeking The use of dummy text to approximate the appearance of a finished document or publication. This is common in desktop publishing when a page layout is being designed. ▼

green technology Refers to computer equipment and peripherals that are not damaging to the environment (or are

Lorem ipsum dolor sit amet, con sectetuer adipiscing elit, sed diam nonnumy nibh euismod tempor indidunt ut labore et dolore magna ali quam erat volupat. Ut wisi enim ad minim venian, quis nostrud excerci tation ullamcorper suscipit laboris nisi ut aliquip ex ea commodo consequat. Duis autem veleum irure dolore in nenderit in vulputate velit esse consequat.

Lorem ipsum dolor sit amet, con sectetuer adipiscing elit, sed diam nonnumy nibh euismod tempor indidunt ut labore et dolore magna ali quam erat volupat. Ut wisi enim

ad minim venian, quis nostrud excerci tation ullamcorper suscipit laboris nisi ut aliquip ex ea commodo.

greeking Desktop publishers and designers often use dummy text to design a page layout. Once the page layout is approved by the client, the real text is imported into the file. Greeking may involve gray bars or a popular well-balanced Latin text sometimes referred to as 'Lorem ipsum'.

less damaging to the environment than previous models). Equipment may be deemed to be 'green' if they use recyclable or refillable products, or are capable of using recycled products. Companies are deemed to be green if they recycle their material (such as office paper) and use safe manufacturing techniques and/or biodegradable packaging material. Personal computers are deemed to be green if they comprise power-saving mechanisms. 'Light green' refers to systems that consume less than 30 watts of power. 'Super green' refers to systems that consume less than 20 watts of power. 'Ultra green' refers to systems that consume less than 5 watts of power. However, these consumption levels refer to the idle states of a computer (when the computer is not in use, and has the capability of shutting down some of the devices in order to conserve electricity). See **ultra green**. ▼

ground wave A type of radio wave capable of following the Earth's curvature for approximately 217 miles (350 kilometers). Other types are known as 'sky waves'. These are short-wave transmissions used over longer distances. They are bounced off the ionosphere — an electrically-charged layer in the atmosphere approximately 50 miles (80 kilometers) above the ground.

Group 4 An international standard for high-speed, high-resolution facsimile transmission as defined by CCITT as a switched digital 64-kilobits-per-second ISDN technology.

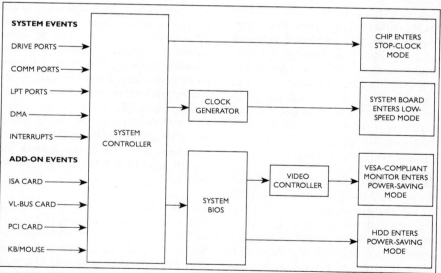

green technology *This diagram shows how a system controller on a green personal computer monitors the usage of each device and proceeds to shut down, or reduce the functionality of, those devices that are not being used by the computer. The approved period of inactivity may be pre-set by the user. In this example, the microprocessor enters a 'stop-clock' mode; the system board enters a 'low-speed' mode; while the monitor and the hard disk drive both enter a 'power-saving' mode.*

grouping isolation [ISO Electrical separation between groups of electrical circuits. *Note:* Within a group, there is an electrical connection, such as with a power supply.]

Group 3 An international standard defined by CCITT for facsimile transmission over non-digital telephone networks.

groupware A general term for software applications that are designed to streamline the collection and dissemination of information. Users operating under a groupware environment can build on the information that their co-workers generate. This is an emerging way of making groups of individuals more productive as a whole. Groupware applications may include calendars, electronic mail, conferencing, spreadsheets, databases, and word processing. In contrast to the paper-based approach for collaborating on reports, the electronic method, utilizing groupware, accomplishes the task more quickly, more efficiently, and without the drawbacks associated with paper, because information can be updated immediately, eliminating the need for users to replicate each other's efforts.

growth in depth Refers to any computer environment that is capable of expanding smoothly to support future application demands. Application growth is only possible if the system architecture is well structured, enabling the system to be divided into a small number of basic functional components. Growth in depth offers the ability to run system components on redundant hardware in order to assure a higher level of availability. This type of system is important in manufacturing operations, for example, in which an assembly line is run by a computer. Updates to one database must be coordinated with updates to a backup database, so that if one computer system goes down, the system can immediately switch control to another. Growth in depth allows the possibility of a single front-end to update two or more back-ends at the same time, using the same information, in a coordinated way. It also allows the possibility of partitioning the primary database while maintaining the backup database at a single location. For example, a manufacturing operation in which the assembly line is run by a computer can incur a large start-up cost, requiring it to run day and night. Changes to assembly line procedures modify data in a database used to operate computerized controls. Data collection front-end computers provide feedback from assembly line operations so that they can be automatically changed if necessary. By distributing the shop floor control system so that the same data collection front-end updates databases on two back-end computers at the same time, the manufacturer avoids the problem of shutting down the assembly line whenever one computer fails. Compare **growth in length**, **growth in time**, and **growth in width**. ▼

growth in length Refers to any computer environment that is capable of expanding smoothly to support future application demands. Application growth is only possible if the system architecture is well structured, enabling the system to be divided into a small number of basic functional components. Growth in length means deploying the client/server model such that the front-end, or

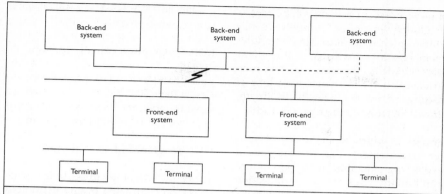

growth in depth Designed by Digital, this specific architectural approach offers the ability to run transaction processing components on redundant hardware in order to assure a higher level of availability. Transaction processing system depth is important in manufacturing operations, for example, in which an assembly line is run by a computer. Updates to one database must be coordinated with updates to a backup database, so that if one computer system fails, the user can immediately switch control to another.

G

user interface, is running on one computer system while the back-end, or database manager, is running on another system. In a transaction processing system, for example, as the utilization grows, either through an increase in the business volume or by bringing one more user to the system, off-loading the terminal processing onto a front-end can remove a significant portion of the back-end's workload, greatly improving performance and throughput. An example of growth in length is a department store point-of-sale terminal in which a sophisticated terminal has the ability to do part of the transaction, while depending on the back-end host to do the database access and updates for inventory control and in-store accounting. The terminal itself captures the stock numbers of purchased items, tallies the total sale amount including taxes and discounts, updates the cash drawer receipts, communicates with a credit card authorization center for clearance, and opens the cash drawer. Although the back-end relies on the front-end to do its job, the front-end can perform certain critical functions without the back-end, in this case supporting the point-of-sale operation. Compare **growth in depth**, **growth in time**, and **growth in width**.

growth in time Refers to any computer environment that is capable of expanding smoothly to support future application demands. Application growth is only possible if the system architecture is well structured, enabling the system to be divided into a small number of basic functional components. Growth in time allows some of the transaction processing operations to be deferred so that more efficient scheduling of computer and human resource utilization can be achieved. This is based upon the principle that all the resources necessary to complete complicated operations are not always readily available at the same time. For systems which require real-time processing, growth in time means extending the range of computers available to process a transaction by implementing software which guarantees that once initiated, a transaction always runs to completion, no matter how long it requires. Compare **growth in depth**, **growth in length**, and **growth in width**.

growth in width Refers to any computer environment that is capable of expanding smoothly to support future application demands. Application growth is only possible if the system architecture is well structured, enabling the system to be divided into a small number of basic functional components. Growth in width means partitioning the database and coordinating access to it from multiple front-end systems. Growth in width also means partitioning the front-end so that the same transaction can be executed in parallel on separate computers. Front-end and back-end systems can be at different locations. The front-end accesses the back-end that contains the data it requires. Meanwhile, another front-end may be communicating with a different back-end to access the data it needs. Compare **growth in depth**, **growth in length**, and **growth in time**.

GS Group separator.

GSM Grams per square meter. GSM (pronounced 'gee-es-<u>em</u>') is accepted usage in speech to grade weights of paper. For example, a piece of paper graded at 80 GSM is half as heavy as one graded at 160 GSM. Correct metric symbol when written: 'g/m²'.

GSP See **graphics system processor**.

guard band A band of unused frequencies, often 500 hertz wide, used to separate adjacent data bands in a frequency-division multiplexed system.

GUI See **graphical user interface**.

guide (In desktop publishing, page layout, and drawing programs) dotted lines which appear on the screen as nonprintable guides to margins, gutters, and page breaks.

guilt screen A screen that appears every time a software package is run. The screen displays the name of the owner of the licensed software, and the name of the copyright owner. It is used to make users who may have pirated the software feel guilty about using unlicensed software.

gutter The blank space which separates two facing pages of a bound document such as a book. Note that the gutter is not the blank space which separates the columns on a page.

NEWSFLASH

The installed base of all mobile PCs in 1994 was 12 million units.
In 1997, the active installed base of mobile PCs will reach 23 million units.

**IF COMPUTERS WERE HUMAN
THEY WOULD HAVE FEW FRIENDS,
SEVERAL ULCERS, AND A TWITCH TO BOOT**

h Hecto-. An SI unit prefix for 10^2 expressed as 100 in decimal notation, as in 'hectometer' (hm). See **SI**.

H 1. Height. 2. Horizontal.

hacker Initially, a serious computer user. The term now refers to a person who gains unauthorized access to a computer system (usually via remote access) and then tries to master the applications, and sometimes make modifications. Some hackers enter systems just for fun, whilst others intentionally cause damage by either committing fraud or destroying valuable data. Many countries treat hackers as criminals who can incur the same penalties as those imposed on break-and-enter criminals. See **infection** and **password**.

hacking The activity of a hacker. See **hacker**.

HAL The name of the computer which met an unfortunate end in the movie *2001*. Note that the letters H-A-L alphabetically precede the letters I-B-M. Coincidentally, the initials of the author of this book are J-C-N.

half duplex A method of transmitting information over a communications channel, in which signals may be sent in both directions, but only one way at a time. This is sometimes referred to as 'local echo'. Half duplex operations can use either a two-wire or a four-wire circuit, and either a dial-up or a dedicated line. When a half-duplex two-wire circuit is used, the transmitted and received data alternately travel through the same interoffice and toll trunks. As the direction of the data transmission changes, the transmitter and receiver circuits in each station must turn on and off. When a half duplex four-wire circuit is used, the data transfer is still in one direction at a time, but the transmitted data travels over a totally separate trunk circuit from the received data. Because of this, the turnaround time of the link can be shorter, allowing for more efficient data transfer. On a typical two-wire half duplex link, the time required for line turnaround is 200 milliseconds. In other words, after receiving a message, a secondary station must wait 200 milliseconds before it can respond to the primary station. Other methods of transmission include full duplex and simplex. Full duplex allows messages to be sent both ways along a communications line simultaneously. Simplex allows messages to be transmitted in only one direction. Abbreviation 'HDX'.

half-duplex transmission [ISO Data transmission in either direction, one direction at a time.]

half-height drive A space-saving disk drive that occupies only half the height of the original disk drive first used in the IBM Personal Computer.

halftone All photographs are continuous-tone images which are difficult to photocopy because there would be a high density of black in most areas due to the fact that photocopiers can only produce black or white, not any gray level. Therefore, before a black and white photograph can be printed, artwork must first be screened (made up of a series of evenly-spaced dots). When dark areas need to be shown, a high density of dots is used. Fewer dots are used to represent less dense areas. Prior to electronic methods, printers produced halftones by using a screened film over the photograph before it was reproduced in a brochure, magazine, or newspaper. See **gray scale**.

hand geometry verifier A biometric security device which is used to measure the length and width of fingers and their webbing, so that a positive identification can be established before entry to a computer system or a room is permitted. See **biometric security devices**.

hand-held scanner A peripheral input device used to assist in the entry of data into a computer system. In desktop publishing, a scanner may be used to digitize artwork or photographs so that they can be merged with text. See **scanner**. ▼

H&J Hyphenation and justification; the formatting of a document according to specifications.

handle In draw programs and similar object-oriented graphics programs, handles are the small black squares which appear around a selected object so that the object can be re-sized, moved, copied, or scaled by using a mouse or similar pointing device.

handshaking Before data is transmitted serially to a particular computer, certain communications conditions (protocols) must be met. Handshaking allows both the sending and receiving computers to understand the required signals (method of transmission).

hanging indent A text format in which the first line of each paragraph is flush left, while all other lines are indented to the next tab stop.

hard copy 1. Printed output, such as computer-generated reports. These are tangible and permanent records, such as printed invoices, statements, and reports.

H

hand-held scanner *Using a hand-held scanner, one can create a personal library of images from photos, drawings, logos, newspapers, magazines, brochures, or books. This ScanMan Plus scanner from Logitech uses its own optical character recognition software called 'Intelligent Character Recognition' (ICR) which enables users to scan text and use it just as if it had been typed directly into the application. It recognizes normal-contrast characters in sizes from 6 to 20 points which may have been typewritten, printed, or typeset. This includes kerned, near letter quality dot matrix, bold, italic, underlined, and foreign characters, as well as common ligatures. It can be used to scan images up to 4 inches (10 centimeters) wide by 14 inches (35 centimeters) long, offering up to 99% accuracy on all common typefaces at speeds of up to 2500 characters per minute.*

2. [ISO A document that can be read without magnification or other technical aids, and that is usually portable. *Note:* Hard copies are commonly used to reproduce the image displayed.]

hard disk A peripheral secondary mass-storage device which uses hermetically sealed rotating non-flexible disks, magnetically coated to store data and programs. The hard disk's storage capacity may vary from 5 to more than 1000 megabytes. Most modern hard disks use a system called 'Winchester' technology, a named coined by IBM in 1973 and used as a code name for the development project. Modern disks, especially those used in notebook computers, are extremely small, and revolve at 60 times per second. To ensure the disk does not encounter wear, the read/write heads are designed to float just above the magnetically coated surface. Stepper motors are no longer used to maintain alignment. Instead, voice coils control the movement of the heads. For added security and expanded disk storage capacity, removable cartridges like the Bernoulli box can be used. Abbreviation 'HD'. See **Bernoulli box, diskette**, and **Winchester**. [ISO A fixed magnetic disk.] ▼

hard error [ISO A permanent error that always recurs on successive attempts to read data.]

hard disk *This Hewlett-Packard Kittyhawk 1.3-inch hard disk is the size of a small matchbox (2 x 1.44 x 0.4 inches). Weighing less than one ounce (28 grams), it has enough storage capacity for 80 megabytes (compressed) and is suitable for integration into mobile computing devices such as peripherals, telecommunications, and consumer electronics such as digital cameras wherein it can be used to store 350 pictures. Taking only one second to power up, the Kittyhawk can withstand a shock of 150 G when operating (300 G when not operating). It operates on 5 volts, and consumes 0.015 watts when in sleep mode, and it peaks at 1.7 watts when writing to the disk.*

hard failures See **memory errors**.

hard hyphen In word processing, a command used to force proper nouns like 'Hewlett-Packard' to appear on the same line (unbroken) even when the word reaches the end of a line.

hard sectoring [ISO The physical marking of sector boundaries on a magnetic disk.]

hard space In word processing, a command used to ensure that particular combinations or words are not broken even when the first word is at the end of a line. This is particularly useful when using numbers and symbols. For example, a hard space command ensures that a long number like '400 787 870', or a measure like '20 Mb' is not broken.

hardware All electronic components of a computer system including peripherals, circuit boards, and input and output devices. [ISO Physical equipment, as opposed to programs, procedures, rules, and associated documentation.]

hardware-intensive fault tolerance The ability of a system to combine hardware and software techniques to tolerate faults. Hardware modules in these systems are redundant and run in lock step, meaning they do the same things at the same time. These modules are also self-checking. They are able to detect and isolate faults when they occur. If a fault is detected in one module, that module is taken out of service while its redundant partner continues without delay. The time needed to switch work from the failed module to its redundant partner (failover time) is usually less than one second. See **fault tolerance** and **unscheduled down-time**. Compare **software-intensive fault tolerance**.

hardware platform The standard on which a computer system is based. Some platforms include the industry-standard personal computer platform, Macintosh platform, or minicomputer or mainframe platforms.

hard wired Referring to functions built into the computer's hardware for the purpose of processing certain information (such as arithmetic) at higher speeds. Hard-wired functions improve the computer's performance for that particular function, but go against the theory of most computer scientists who prefer computers to contain logic circuits that are general in nature, relying instead on software programs for instructions. In data communications, 'hard wired' refers to a communications link (such as a remote telephone line or local cable) that permanently connects two nodes, stations, or devices.

harmonic distortion The production of unwanted frequencies that are harmonics of the fundamental (base) frequency. This distortion is produced by a non-linear circuit (an amplifier or analog signal device in which the outgoing electromagnetic wave does not match up in proportion to the incoming signal). The use of repeaters (positioned at more frequent intervals) or of equalization techniques may help to limit the effects of non-linear distortion.

hartley [ISO A unit of logarithmic measure of information equal to the decision content of a set of ten mutually exclusive events expressed as a logarithm to base 10. *Example:* The decision content of a character set of eight characters equals 0.903 hartley ($\log_{10} 8 = 0.903$).]

Harvard Graphics A presentation graphics program released by Software Publishing Corporation for industry-standard personal computers, allowing users to easily plot a variety of graphs and charts. Data can be imported from other applications, such as a Lotus 1-2-3 spreadsheet. Clip-art can be used to enhance the presentation. Output can be on-screen in the form of a slide show, or sent to a laser printer, color plotter, film recorder, or 35 mm slide-maker.

Harvard Mark I See **Mark I**.

hashing The process of applying a formula to a record key so that the records can be quickly located. Keys are used in file management on a magnetic/optical disk for quickly locating a particular file. For example, a social security number may serve as the record key, so that when records are being quickly searched, the key can be used. Hence, not all the data on the tape/disk is read unnecessarily. One formula for hashing is to divide the key number by a prime number, and use the remainder of the division as the address. For example, if the key number 1269 is divided by the prime number 17, then the answer would be 74, with 11 remaining. The remaining number (11) is therefore the track location. Some numbers can yield the same remainder, such as dividing 7 by 3 and dividing 10 by 3, both giving a remainder of 1. Records with such duplicate track addresses are called 'synonyms', and are separated by the next available location. [ISO A method of transforming a search key into an address for the purpose of storing and retrieving items of data. *Note:* The method is often designed to minimize the search time.]

hash table search [ISO A search in which the storage location of a desired data element is derived from a hash table, and an appropriate procedure is followed in case of an address collision.]

hash total [ISO The result obtained by applying an algorithm to a set of heterogeneous data for checking purposes. *Example:* A summation obtained by treating items of data as numbers.]

Hayes AT See **Hayes command set**.

Hayes command set A set of modem commands originally defined by Hayes Microcomputer Products to control the operation of intelligent modems. High-speed modems are now being used with personal computers, operating at 14 000 bits per second and higher, over standard dial-up telephone lines. To handle the high number of data errors that can occur at these speeds, most modems have some type of built-in error detection and correction circuits. Some also have the ability to automatically reduce transmission speeds if the telephone line quality is poor. Some vendors of high-speed modems are using proprietary signaling technologies. This means identical modems must be used at each end on a link. The majority of modern modems incorporate 'smart' features, such as automatic dialing, re-dialing, and answering. Controlling these features requires that commands be sent from the communications software running in the personal computer, hence the use of the Hayes command set as a de facto standard. Also referred to as 'Hayes AT' command set.

HBA Host bus adapter.

HD 1. See **hard disk**. 2. See **high density**.

HDTV High definition television. Germany and Japan have begun to play leading roles in the introduction of technological innovations in TV broadcasting. In 1978, Japan led the world in the development of multiplex TV sound broadcasts that made possible stereo TV and dual-language broadcasts. Dramatic developments are also taking place in the fields of direct satellite broadcasting, high-definition TV, and cable television. When HDTV becomes more commercially available, it will bring with it a new era in broadcasting as revolutionary as the switch from black-and-white to color TV in the 1960s. TV screens will

soon be measured in feet (not inches) and videotape will increasingly displace 35 millimeter film in the making and exhibition of motion pictures. HDTV will offer quality that is twice as sharp and 25% wider than conventional TV. The key difference between conventional TV receivers and HDTV sets is the number of scanning lines. For conventional TV broadcasting, Japan employs the US-developed NTSC system based on 525 lines. Nihon Hoso Kyokai (NHK), Japan's semi-governmental broadcasting corporation, broadcasts using 1125 lines — this being a compromise between the current 525 lines of the NTSC system used by the United States, Japan, and Canada, and the 625-line PAL and SECAM systems used in Europe and parts of Asia. The aspect ratio of the HDTV screen is the same as a movie screen (16:9), whereas conventional TV sets use a 4:3 ratio. HDTV can carry five times the amount of information as the conventional broadcasting system, but it requires a much wider frequency. To get around this problem, NHK introduced a new transmission system in 1984 called 'MUSE', which compresses the radio frequency band, allowing the broadcast of HDTV via a single satellite channel. The MUSE system transmits each frame in four separate layers that are then put back together by a decoder before projection onto the receiver screen. Apart from improved picture and sound quality, HDTV can be used for the production of high-resolution color posters from videotape frames. HDTV still pictures can be printed electronically with a high reproduction quality.

HDW See **Hong Dong Wah**.

HDX See **half duplex**.

head A component in magnetic tape units and disk drives that reads the magnetized areas on the tape/disk, and converts them into electrical pulses which are sent to the computer for processing. A head can read, write, or erase data on a tape or disk. Magnetic disks with high bit density offer very small head gaps and very low flying heights. In modern disk drives, heads typically fly at 10 to 20 millionths of an inch above the media surface. A slider three-tenths of an inch long, flying at 20 millionths of an inch above the media, is comparable to a jumbo jet flying at less than one inch above the ground. However, unlike the jumbo jet, disk heads are frequently moved abruptly to the side when a seek is performed. While undergoing sharp lateral acceleration due to seeking, the head must remain at a constant flying height to avoid surface contact. Flying heads at these heights with extreme lateral accelerations require not only very flat media surfaces, but also a very stiff air bearing for slider stability. See **read/write head**.

head/arm Digital data recorded on magnetic disks is organized in a fairly consistent way throughout the industry. The fundamental unit of data organization is the track, whose position remains fixed for an entire revolution. The data stream on a track is 1 bit wide. The head is mounted on an access arm attached to a positioner that is capable of moving the head/arm assembly across the disk surface very quickly while maintaining constant flying height and orientations to within millionths of an inch. Disk drives typically have multiple heads that span multiple media surfaces. Multiple head/arm assemblies are ganged to a positioner so that they move

in unison. When one head is positioned over a given track, all others are positioned over corresponding tracks on their respective surfaces. The collection of all tracks at a given positioner location is called a 'cylinder'. The minimum increment by which the positioner can move its head/arm assembly is one track. Thus, the data stored on a disk drive is organized into cylinders. To write data in a desired location, the drive must first seek, or move the head/arm assembly to the correct cylinder, and then select the head corresponding to the desired surface for data transfer. Finally, each track is usually organized into blocks, or sectors of fixed length. A sector of data (usually 512 bytes) is preceded by a header and followed by an error-correction code. See **read/write head**.

head crash Malfunction of a magnetic disk drive (hard or floppy) in which the head touches the rapidly spinning disk, causing permanent damage and loss of data. This sometimes occurs due to excess heat, moisture, or sudden drop in pressure. [ISO An accidental contact of a magnetic head with the surface of a rotating data medium.]

head/disk assembly [ISO In a magnetic disk unit, an assembly which includes magnetic disks, magnetic heads, and an access mechanism all enclosed in a container.]

headend [ISO In a broadband LAN, a device that receives signals from each data station and re-transmits them to all data stations. *Note:* The retransmission may require a shift of carrier frequencies.]

header 1. In word processing, the automatic placement of text at the top of each page to serve as a short title, document description, or page number. Some advanced word processing programs such as WordPerfect and Microsoft Word allow the use of odd and even headers — especially used for double-sided printing or when a mirror image of the header is required on facing pages. For example, page numbering may be better placed on the left corner of the left page, and the right corner of the right page. 2. An information field in a disk block or tape record that precedes the user data and serves to identify and characterize the block or record.

header label See **magnetic tape**.

head loading zone [ISO A peripheral area on each magnetic disk surface where heads are positioned to the proper flying height for reading and writing data.]

head switching The process of de-selecting one disk head and selecting another for data transfer during a single input/output operation. Head switching occurs whenever a data transfer command specifies blocks which reside on different tracks. For disk drives which use dedicated servo control, head switching is performed electronically, and occurs in negligible time. For drives which use embedded servo control, the newly selected head must first read several servo information bursts to center itself on track. [ISO The use of another magnetic head to read from, or write on, a magnetic data medium.] See **access arm**, **head**, and **servo control**.

Hebrew University virus A variant of the Jerusalem virus. See **Jerusalem virus**.

hecto- An SI unit prefix for 10^2 expressed as 100 in decimal notation, as in 'hectometer' (hm). SI symbol 'h'. See **SI**.

helical-scan Traditional computer tape technologies record parallel tracks of data by rapidly accelerating and moving the tape across a multitrack, stationary recording head. Helical-scan devices record data to relatively slow-moving tape from read/write heads that are mounted on a rapidly spinning drum. The combination of the helical wrap of the tape around the head drum assembly, the rotational motion of the drum mounted at a five-degree angle from vertical, and the slow linear motion of the tape causes the heads to trace an oblique path (or track) across the tape of nearly three inches (7.6 centimeters) in length. The head drum assembly contains read, write, and servo heads rotating at over 1800 revolutions per minutes. The tape moves around the drum assembly at less than one-half inch per second. The net result is an effective head-to-tape velocity of approximately 150 inches per second. This tape speed and gentle tape handling eliminates the need for high-torque reel motors and cooling fans. An additional advantage of helical-scan is that it writes data at very high track densities (approximately 1600 tracks per inch) enabling high data storage capacities and rapid transfer rates.

Helvetica A widely used sans serif typeface designed in 1957 by Max Miedinger of the Swiss Haas type foundry. It is believed that Helvetica was inspired by the work and teachings of German architect Walter Bauhaus who founded a typographic and design school in 1919. Helvetica offers clean lines for display type, making it one of

A a	B b	C c	D d	E e
F f	G g	H h	I i	J j
K k	L l	M m	N n	O o
P p	Q q	R r	S s	T t
U u	W w	X x	Y y	Z z
1	2	3	4	5
6	7	8	9	0

Helvetica *Some of the characters that form Helvetica normal.*

the most commonly-used typefaces, but it is not particularly suitable for body copy. Many laser printers offer Helvetica as a built-in font. The word 'Helvetica' comes from the Latin word *Helvetia*, meaning 'Switzerland'. See **font**. Compare **Times**. ⚑

HEMT High electron mobility transistor; a process invented by Fujitsu in 1980 whereby gallium arsenide and aluminum gallium arsenide are layered to produce transistors. HEMTs are already used in such applications as receivers for satellite television broadcasts, where they have shown low noise performance at microwave frequencies. The HEMT has often been proposed for use in other kinds of high-speed VLSI (very-large-scale integration), but difficulties in fabrication have blocked their use in higher integrations. Recently, Fujitsu announced the use of HEMT devices in both logic and memory chips — in a 45-kilobyte (kb) gate array and a 64-kb SRAM (static random-access memory). The 45-kb gate array achieved the same level of integration found in the bipolar silicon circuits currently used in mainframe computers. In contrast with conventional silicon arrays where the

power dissipation per gate is 2 milliwatts, the power dissipation using HEMTs is only 0.24 milliwatts. The time needed to operate a silicon gate is 85 picoseconds. The overall result is performance which is ten times better than some silicon circuits. The HEMT SRAM chips can hold only 8000 characters of information, but their access time is faster than silicon memories. With an access time of 1.2 nanoseconds, the latest HEMT chips are five to ten times faster than their silicon equivalent, making them practical for applications like high-speed memory used in large-scale central processing units. The introduction of both logic chips and memories opens the way for

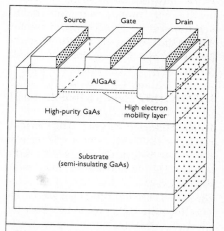

HEMT *Shown here is the basic structure of HEMT. Comprising a heterojunction crystal of high-purity gallium arsenide (GaAs) and silicon (Si) doped n-type aluminum-gallium arsenide (AlGaAs) layer, the HEMT structure is configured to generate free electrons at the interface of the heterojunction. Source and drain electrodes are arranged as shown in the figure. Applying a positive voltage to the drain electrode causes free electrons to travel from the source to the drain electrode along the heterojunction interface, setting up current flow from source to drain.*

the use of high-speed HEMT chips in computers. Mass production may lead to expanded use in supercomputers and workstations, particularly for graphics processing. ⋀

Hercules Monochrome Adapter See **HMA**.

hertz The SI unit of frequency named in honor of German physicist Heinrich Rudolf Hertz. One hertz is defined as one complete cycle per second. In this context, a cycle may, for example, relate to light, heat, or radio waves, or other vibrations. The tuning fork for the musical note 'A' may vibrate at 440 hertz — far too fast to be seen, yet easily heard. The human ear can detect vibrations up to 20 000 hertz. SI symbol 'Hz'. When using high numbers, the following symbols can be used: kHz (kilohertz — 10^3 Hz), MHz (megahertz — 10^6 Hz), and GHz (gigahertz — 10^9 Hz). See **Hertz, Heinrich Rudolf** and **SI**.

Hertz, Heinrich Rudolf The German physicist (1857–94) who, in 1886, was the first to broadcast and receive radio waves. He demonstrated that radio waves exist, and that they behave in similar ways to light and heat waves. He was therefore partly responsible for the invention of wireless telegraphy. The SI unit of frequency (hertz) was named in his honor. See **hertz** and **SI**.

heterogeneous Referring to environments which use computers and peripherals from several different vendors. The word 'heterogeneous' is from the Greek words *héteros*, meaning 'another', and *génos*, meaning 'kind'.

heterogeneous computer network [ISO

A computer network in which computers have dissimilar architectures but nevertheless are able to communicate.]

heterogeneous system A computer system composed of hardware and software components that are different and have unique features, but that in some important respects, behave as a single system.

heuristic A heuristic is thought of as a rule-of-thumb equation which is modified as the equation progresses — as may be used by a carpenter who agrees that (X and a little bit) + (Y and a little bit) = (Z and a little bit) because excess wood can always be sanded down to fit (but not up). On the other hand, an algorithm is a rigid mathematical relationship which has only one starting point and one finishing point — for example, X + Y = Z. An example of heuristics in action would be the scenario posed to a computer, stating that: a person entered a restaurant, ordered chicken, paid the cashier, and left the restaurant. If the computer is then asked, 'What did the man eat?', the computer would not be able to answer until it determined that the person was a male and understood what a restaurant is. Several hundred other questions would need to be answered, but when time is very limited, heuristics encourages a level of guessing so as to save time. Another example would involve the use of numbers. When a conventional computer adds 3 and 7, it always arrives at the answer 10. However, an expert system using heuristics would produce different results if asked the same question. This would depend upon the numbering system being used (decimal, binary, etc.) and what each number represents. If the equation is asking the computer to add 3 lions to 7 lambs, the answer may be 3 lions (provided the computer had been told about the eating habits of lions). The word 'heuristic' comes from the Greek word *heurisko*, meaning 'find'. See **artificial intelligence**.

heuristic method [ISO Any exploratory method of solving problems in which an evaluation is made of the progress toward an acceptable final result using a series of approximate results — for example, by a process of guided trial and error.]

Hewlett-Packard Based in Palo Alto, California, Hewlett-Packard Company manufactures personal computers and minicomputers, plotters, printers, and scientific and technical instruments. The company has offices and outlets in over 110 countries. It has more than 93 000 employees and an annual revenue exceeding US$18 000 million. Abbreviation 'HP'. See **Hewlett, William R.** and **Packard, David**.

Hewlett, William R. Director emeritus for the board of directors (since 1987) of Hewlett-Packard Company (HP). HP is an international manufacturer of measurement and computation products and systems used in industry, business, engineering, science, medicine, and education. William (Bill) Hewlett was born 20 May 1913 in Ann Arbor, Michigan. He attended Stanford University in Stanford, California, and received a bachelor of arts degree in 1934, and a bachelor of science degree in electrical engineering in 1939. He also received a master's degree in electrical engineering from the Massachusetts Institute of Technology in 1936. Hewlett met David Packard during their undergraduate days at Stanford. The two

engineering classmates became friends and formed a partnership in 1939 known as 'Hewlett-Packard Company'. HP's first product was a resistance-capacitance audio oscillator based on a

Hewlett, William R. Co-founder of Hewlett-Packard. Based on his love for the outdoors, Bill Hewlett has a wide range of interests and hobbies. He is a part-time botanist and an accomplished mountain climber, skier, and fisherman. He also maintains various ranching and cattle-raising operations with David Packard in California and Idaho. Hewlett holds the following honorary degrees from American colleges and universities: honorary doctor of law degrees from the University of California, Yale University, and Mills College; honorary doctor of science degrees from Polytechnic Institute of New York and Kenyon College; honorary doctor of engineering degrees from the University of Notre Dame, Dartmouth College, and Utah State University; an honorary doctor of humane letters degree from John Hopkins University; an honorary doctor of public policy degree from the Rand Graduate Institute; an honorary doctor of humanities degree from Santa Clara University; and an honorary doctor of electronics science degree from University of Bologna in Italy.

H

design developed by Hewlett when he was in graduate school. The company's first 'plant' was a small garage in Palo Alto, California, and the initial capital amounted to US$538. Hewlett was active in the management of the company until 1987, with the exception of the years he served as an Army officer during World War II. He was on the staff of the Army's Chief Signal Officer and then headed the electronics section of the New Development Division of the War Department Special Staff. During this latter tour of duty, he was on a special US team that inspected Japanese industry immediately after the war. In 1947, shortly after he returned to Palo Alto, Hewlett was named vice president of the company. He was elected executive vice president in 1957, president in 1964 (resigned in 1977), and was also appointed as the chief executive officer in 1969 (retired in 1978). Over the years, Hewlett contributed to the advancement of various organizations within the electronics industry. From 1950 to 1957, he was on the board of directors of the Institute of Radio Engineers (now the Institute of Electrical and Electronics Engineers) and served as president of the institute in 1954. In 1985, former US President, Ronald Reagan, awarded him the National Medal of Science, the nation's highest scientific honor. See **Packard, David**. ⋀

hexadecimal Whereas the decimal system has a base (radix) of 10 (0, 1, 2, 3, 4, 5, 6, 7, 8, and 9), hexadecimal refers to a base 16 numbering system using a combination of 16 symbols: the numbers 0 to 9, plus the letters A to F. Binary numbers requiring four places may be represented in hexadecimal using only one number. The decimal number '346' is written '15A' in hexadecimal. When different bases are being discussed, the number base is used as a subscript — such as $346_{10} = 15A_{16}$. Abbreviation 'hex'. ▼

hexadecimal (numeration) system [ISO The fixed radix numeration system that uses the 16 digits 0, 1, 2, 3, 4, 5, 6, 7, 8, 9, A, B, C, D, E, and F, where the characters A, B, C, D, E, and F correspond to the numbers 10, 11, 12, 13, 14, and 15, and the radix 16 and in which the lowest integral weight is 1. *Example:* In the hexadecimal numeration system, the numeral 3E8 represents the number 1000 — that is $(3 \times 16^2) + (14 \times 16^1) + (8 \times 16^0)$.]

hex dump A programmer's troubleshooting aid that prints out (for the purpose of analysis) the hexadecimal values of the data. See **dump**.

HFS Hierarchical File System; used by the Apple Macintosh computer for storing files within 'folders' on a hard disk so that files can be neatly arranged in a smaller number of folders. Creating too many folders within each other may result in tedious file searches because HFS does not allow for file name extensions like those available with DOS.

HGA Hercules Graphics Adapter; a standard monochrome graphics adapter. The correct term is 'Hercules Monochrome Adapter' (HMA). See **HMA**.

HGC Hercules Graphics Card; a standard monochrome graphics adapter. The correct term is 'Hercules Monochrome Adapter' (HMA). See **HMA**.

hidden codes In word processing and similar programs, formatting codes which are transparent to the user. This

Decimal	Hexa-decimal	Decimal	Hexa-decimal	Decimal	Hexa-decimal	Decimal	Hexa-decimal	Decimal	Hexa-decimal
0	0	26	1A	52	34	78	4E	104	68
1	1	27	1B	53	35	79	4F	105	69
2	2	28	1C	54	36	80	50	106	6A
3	3	29	1D	55	37	81	51	107	6B
4	4	30	1E	56	38	82	52	108	6C
5	5	31	1F	57	39	83	53	109	6D
6	6	32	20	58	3A	84	54	110	6E
7	7	33	21	59	3B	85	55	111	6F
8	8	34	22	60	3C	86	56	112	70
9	9	35	23	61	3D	87	57	113	71
10	A	36	24	62	3E	88	58	114	72
11	B	37	25	63	3F	89	59	115	73
12	C	38	26	64	40	90	5A	116	74
13	D	39	27	65	41	91	5B	117	75
14	E	40	28	66	42	92	5C	118	76
15	F	41	29	67	43	93	5D	119	77
16	10	42	2A	68	44	94	5E	120	78
17	11	43	2B	69	45	95	5F	121	79
18	12	44	2C	70	46	96	60	122	7A
19	13	45	2D	71	47	97	61	123	7B
20	14	46	2E	72	48	98	62	124	7C
21	15	47	2F	73	49	99	63	125	7D
22	16	48	30	74	4A	100	64	126	7E
23	17	49	31	75	4B	101	65	127	7F
24	18	50	32	76	4C	102	66	128	80
25	19	51	33	77	4D	103	67	129	81

hexadecimal Using '16' as its base, the hexadecimal numbering system utilizes the digits '0' to '9' and supplements them with the letters 'A' to 'F' to represent the numbers '10' to '15'. This system is mainly used by computer professionals who program in machine code and assembly language.

ensures that the working screen is not cluttered with codes and commands. Some programs like Wordstar and WordPerfect allow the user to reveal and edit the hidden codes for greater control over the document.

hidden line [ISO A line segment that represents an edge obscured from view in a two-dimensional projection of a three-dimensional object.]

hierarchical computer network [ISO A computer network in which the control functions are organized in a hierarchical manner and may be distributed among data processing stations.]

hierarchical database A database in which data blocks are organized 'above' and 'below' one another in a tree structure resembling an organization chart (with the root at the top and paths branching off downwards). To move through a hierarchical database, the database management system must travel up and down the branches. This is efficient if the user knows ahead of time what branches to place where. However, as the system grows, it can become very inefficient when branches do not interconnect, or are widely separated within the database. Unlike a flat file system, a hierarchical system (if managed properly) permits 'child' records to be logically related to the 'parent' record, ensuring that child records do not have any existence of their own; they only have meaning when associated with a parent. In this way, a database designer can ensure that it is impossible to create a child record without associating it with its parent, ensuring greater integrity for data in the database. See **DBMS**. Compare **network database** and **relational database**. ▼

Hierarchical File System The file system used by the Apple Macintosh for storing files within 'folders' on a hard disk so that files can be neatly arranged in a smaller number of folders. Creating too many folders within each other may result in tedious file searches because the Hierarchical File System does not allow for file name extensions like those available with DOS. Abbreviation 'HFS'.

hierarchical network A computer net-work (resembling a star network) which is controlled by a large host computer (usually a mainframe) with several smaller computers (perhaps minicomputers) connected to the host computer, but also acting as sub-hosts to a group of workstations or microcomputers.

high density An advanced storage technique used for floppy disks and other magnetic secondary storage media. High-density disks can store more data than double-density disks by using very fine-grained magnetic particles to store more than 1 megabyte of data. Abbreviation 'HD'. See **diskette** and **track density**.

high electron mobility transistor See **HEMT**.

High-Level Data Link Control A CCITT-specified, bit-oriented, data link control protocol. Abbreviation 'HLDLC'.

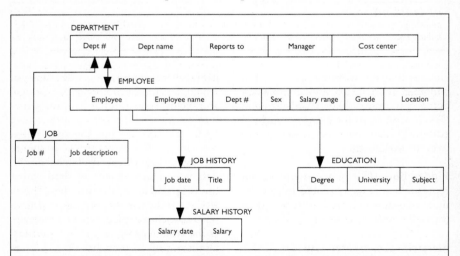

hierarchical database A hierarchical database, as the name suggests, permits records to be organized in hierarchies, with parent records at the top of the hierarchy accessed by conventional mechanisms (sequentially, relatively, or by means of one or more indices). The effect is a chart that shows an organization's genealogy.

high-level language Any programming language (such as BASIC or FORTRAN) which uses English-like codes (introduced in the mid-1950s) in which each statement corresponds to several lines of machine language instructions. A low-level language like 'machine language' is one which must be written using the binary system. Although it is much more tedious, programs written in machine language run much faster than those written in higher-level languages. Abbreviation 'HLL'. [ISO A programming language whose concepts and structures are convenient for human reasoning. *Note:* High-level languages are independent of the structures of computers and operating systems. *Example:* Pascal.] See **programming language**.

highlighting [ISO Emphasizing a display element or segment by modifying its visual attributes.]

high-speed carry [ISO In parallel addition, any procedure for speeding up the processing of carries.]

highway [ISO In a process computer system, the means for interconnection between the computer system and the process interface system. *Note:* A bus may be used as a highway.]

HIPO Hierarchy plus Input-Process-Output. Developed by IBM as a documentation tool, HIPO is a program design tool that consists of a set of diagrams that graphically describe each computer program function, giving first a general overview, then a detailed one. Pronounced 'high-poe'.

hi-res. High-resolution. See **resolution**.

HLCO chart High/low/close/open chart; a chart used in presentation graphics to simultaneously plot the highest value, the lowest value, and open/close (begin/end) or average value of events such as the weather or the movement of stock prices for a given period.

HLDLC High-Level Data Link Control; a CCITT-specified, bit-oriented, data link control protocol.

HLL See **high-level language**.

HLLAPI High-Level Language Application Programming Interface. An API that uses the 3270 data stream for the development of distributed applications between PCs and mainframes.

HMA Hercules Monochrome Adapter; a standard graphics adapter introduced in 1982 to allow a monochrome personal computer to display high-resolution graphics. It is used on industry-standard personal computers for the display of text and graphics at a resolution of 720 pixels (picture elements) horizontally by 348 pixels vertically, with characters formed in a 9 x 14 pixel matrix. See **video adapter**.

HMD Head-mounted display. A monitor (similar to data-glasses) used in virtual reality systems.

HMI 1. Human/machine interaction. 2. Horizontal motion index; in laser printer technology, the amount of space that a cursor moves in the horizontal direction in increments of 1/120th of an inch, with the minimum HMI being 0 and the maximum being 125.

HOF Head of form.

hold (input) signal [ISO A signal that causes a central processing unit to stop its activity and to relinquish control over the bus until the signal is removed.]

hold mode [ISO That operating mode of an analog computer during which integration is stopped and all variables are held at the value they had when this mode was entered.]

hole pattern [ISO An array of holes that implements on a data medium the coded representation of data. *Example:* A punching configuration that implements the representation of a single character.]

Hollerith, Herman A graduate of Columbia University, in the United States, Hollerith adopted Charles Babbage's punch card system to develop a tabulating machine to help in the analysis of the United States' 1890 census data. See **Babbage, Charles** and **IBM**. ▼

hologram scanner This is not a device that scans a hologram, but one that uses holography to input data from bar codes, or to output data to laser printers. Holography is an information recording and re-constructing technology which was invented by Professor Dennis Gabor in 1948. An English physicist, he won a Nobel Prize for his invention. The invention of the laser at the beginning of the 1960s put this technology to practical use. As far back as 1974, Fujitsu introduced hologram scanners for point-of-sale bar coding, and since 1980 IBM and NEC have developed their own. The application of hologram scanners to laser printers has been studied since the late 1970s. In conventional laser printers, composed of mirrors and lenses, an optical system with high precision is

Hollerith, Herman Perhaps one of the most important devices that laid much of the groundwork for today's computer industry was Dr Herman Hollerith's punched card tabulating machine. Developed for the United States Census of 1890, it sensed holes in cards by means of electricity. Hollerith's early census machines were limited to tallying data, but soon he incorporated separate adding machines equipped with carrying devices into his tabulating machines. A perfectionist who was often at odds with his own mechanical creations, Hollerith began an unbroken chain of development that would continue to the electronic era. In 1911, his Tabulating Machine Company became a division of the company later re-named 'IBM'.

needed. Several companies considered utilizing hologram scanners because holographic systems require less mechanical precision than previous techniques. This is achieved mainly by the use of light diffraction. In addition to Fujitsu in Japan, and Xerox and General Optics in the United States, companies which have conducted research and develop-

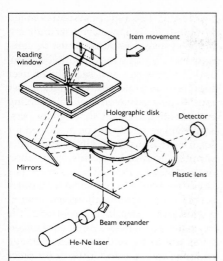

hologram scanner This figure shows the principle of a hologram scanner as used at a point-of-sale. The He–Ne laser beam is widened to an appropriate diameter by using a beam expander, and is then diffracted through a holographic disk attached to a high-speed motor. There are several hologram facets on the disk, each with its own diffraction characteristics. Each facet diffracts the laser beam differently, and by rotating the disk, a scanning pattern is created. The scanning beam is emitted from the reading window, and the bar code, back through the window. The scattered light is again diffracted through the hologram and caused to converge on a photo detector by a plastic lens.

ment of hologram scanners include NEC, Ricoh, and Tokogawa. There are two main considerations in the design of the hologram scanner. The first is the design of the holographic disk itself. This includes the construction and re-construction characteristics of the holo-gram facets, which define the laser beam direction and the focal length from the disk. It also includes the number of facets and the speed of disk rotation, which determine the number of scan lines per

unit time, and the area of each facet, which is related to the signal detection capability. The second consideration is the configuration of optical elements, specifically the size and location of each optical element in the scanner. Whilst photographic film records the amplitude (intensity) of the light reflected or scat-tered from an object, holography records a fine interference pattern formed by the light directed from the source (laser) and the light reflected or scattered from an object. This record is called a 'hologram'. The interference pattern is not usually visible to the human eye, but an incident laser light beam on a hologram repro-duces a three-dimensional image of the object.

holographic fingerprint sensor See **fin-gerprint sensor**.

home address [ISO The information writ-ten on each track of a magnetic disk, that identifies the track number on the face of the disk.]

home computer A computer designed or purchased for home use. Early versions of home computers included the 8-bit Commodore 64 and the Apple II per-sonal computers, both using the Motorola 6502 chip. Home computers were typically used for child education, entertainment, home financing, and for controlling other devices such as home security systems, heating, and lighting. The gap between home computers and business computers is narrowing be-cause home users now require the same amount of speed, memory, and storage capacity as they have become accus-tomed to at the office. Often, home computing serves as an extension of the office environment where powerful word processing and spreadsheet applications are required. See **personal computer**.

home key A programmable cursor-control key found on all industry-standard keyboards. Its functions depend upon the particular application used. In word processing, the home key (in conjunction with arrow keys) is used to move the cursor to the beginning of a line, or to the top or bottom of a page.

homogeneous computer network [ISO A computer network in which all computers have a similar (or the same) architecture.]

Hong Dong Wah The personal computer industry's words of exclamation. The term can be used in correspondence or conversation to express surprise, excitement, disappointment, disgust, or disbelief. The term has Chinese roots that allow it to be exclaimed in at least five different ways — each placing the emphasis on a different word or syllable. For example, one personal-computer company's employee may say to another, 'Did you hear that Mr Kit Connos just got fired?' To which the surprised colleague may exclaim in disbelief, 'Hong Dong Wah!' Abbreviation in correspondence 'HDW'.

host 1. Referring to a computer in a local area network which carries out all the centralized maintenance functions, and makes available to other users the programs and other application software, including storage. A host personal computer (PC) could also serve a group of non-intelligent, or dumb terminals. In this case, the terminals would share the processing power of the host computer, with each user perceiving independent

processing. This type of system is called a 'multi-user system'. Each user and each of the system's resources must be carefully monitored by the operating system, and the integrity and security of user files must be protected. Typically, a user must type a password before receiving authorization to log-on, although the password will generally not be displayed for security reasons. Both UNIX and Xenix support multi-user systems. A variation on the role of a PC as a host system is a situation where a personal computer serves as a communication controller in a wide area network. As a controller, the PC gathers data from a number of lower-level terminals and handles message routing functions under the direction of a larger mainframe computer. Another common use of a PC is as an 'intelligent terminal' in a large network connected to a mainframe. In this processing environment, the PC may use special software called 'emulation software' to simulate the operation of a dumb terminal. When not communicating with the host computer, the PC has the flexibility to perform other tasks, such as data entry and formatting, data collection, price checking, and credit look-up. The advantage of a PC in such a role is that the PC can be used for normal single-user work when it is not needed as a terminal. 2. Also called 'host computer'. [ISO In a computer network, a computer that provides end users with services such as computation and database access and that may perform network control functions.]

host-based shadowing See **shadowing**.

host node [ISO A node at which a host computer is located.]

hotfixing The ability to detect and mark

the bad sectors of a disk, then assign alternate disk sectors during routine operations. This automatically updates the original defect map.

hot inserting See **hot swapping**.

hot swapping The removing or inserting of devices such as hard disk drives or memory cards from or into a computer while the application is still running, and without having to shut down or reboot the system. For network servers using multiple hard disks, hot swapping a faulty disk is much more convenient than shutting the server down and disrupting the users. Similarly, hot swapping memory cards (such as PCMCIA cards) on a personal computer allows users to be much more productive and to use various devices interchangeably.

HP 1. See **Hewlett-Packard**. 2. High performance.

HPF High-performance FORTRAN.

HPFS High-Performance File System; an OS/2 file system that has faster input/output than the file allocation table (FAT) system. Unlike DOS, it does not restrict file naming to eight characters plus a three-character extension. It is also compatible with the FAT system. An enhanced version of HPFS (designed to work with an 80486 computer acting as a LAN Manager server) is called 'HPFS486'. This includes an enhanced disk cache for servers, and implements local security which extends LAN Manager security measures to protect the files on a server by restricting access of the users working at the server. With local security, a user must be assigned permission to access any file or directory in an HPFS486 par-

tition, whether or not the resource is shared as part of a LAN Manager resource. See **file allocation table** and **password**.

HPGL Hewlett-Packard Graphics Language. A BASIC-like language that is used to control a pen plotter.

HP LaserJet A trademark of Hewlett-Packard, assigned to its range of laser printers, first introduced in 1984 with one built-in font (Courier) offering a resolution of 300 dots per inch. See **laser printer**.

HRG High-resolution graphics.

HSB Hue saturation brightness. With the HSB model, all colors can be defined by expressing (in percentages) their levels of hue (the pigment), saturation (the amount of pigment), and brightness (the amount of white included).

HSCMOS High-speed complementary metal oxide semiconductor. See **CMOS**.

hub The central device in a star-configured local area network. See **star topology**.

hue Some graphics programs allow the user to specify color using the traditional terms: hue, saturation, and brightness. Hue is the wavelength of light, determining whether one sees red or yellow, for example. Hues include all the colors of the spectrum plus magentas and purples. See **color** and **color monitor**.

hue saturation brightness See **HSB**.

Huffman coding A file compression algorithm based on the frequency of characters in the file.

human brain The most complex of all computers. Computer scientists concentrate on the speeds and processing capabilities of computers, and they often compare computer performance to human competence. Much of the terminology associated with computer technology is derived from the human aspect. For example, the terms 'neurocomputer', 'vision systems', 'artificial intelligence', and 'memory' are often used. The human brain is used to analyze the data gathered through sight (including reading), hearing, touch, taste, and smell. This data is then organized and stored in a memory location. When an immediate response to incoming data is needed, the brain issues instantaneous orders to the body. This ability enables humans to react swiftly in order to prevent a traffic accident, or to carry on a witty conversation. Recent research has revealed that each part of the brain plays its own role in a complex division of labor. Even the part known as the 'cerebral cortex', which gathers, manages, and classifies incoming data, is subdivided, with different locations responsible for different functions. Broca's Area, located just in front of the ear, is the speech production center. If this area is damaged, the result may be a form of aphasia in which, while able to understand speech or written texts, the person affected is not able to produce speech. Wernicke's Area, to the rear of the ear, is the auditory speech center in charge of understanding what speech and written texts mean. Should anything happen to the upper part of that area, a person will not be able to read or write. The Hippocampus, which lies below the cerebral cortex, is in charge of memory formation. Damage to it does not affect older memories, but the ability to remember new material is impaired. A similar division of labor is also found in the cerebellum, diencephalon, and medulla. Different areas are responsible for different activities and transmit the information required for complex activities of which humans are capable. Their collective operation is the larger whole commonly called the 'brain'. The human cerebrum has about 14 000 million cells, formed into a distinct six-layered structure. The surface layer, a few millimeters thick, is called the 'cerebral cortex', which has approximately 15 million cells, called 'Purkinje cells', divided into three layers. Each of these millions of cells is connected to thousands of others to form a network with an enormous number of links. In this network, the cells can work in parallel. These brain cells are called 'neurons' and their junctions are called 'synapses'. Neurons exchange information using electrical impulses that travel along the brain's nerve fibers at several tens of meters per second. Upon reaching a synapse, the signal causes a chemical transmitter to be released. Branches on the other side of the synapse, called

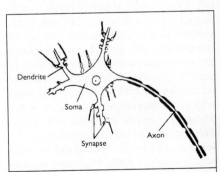

human brain *The cells in the human brain work in parallel. Neurons exchange information using electrical impulses that travel along the brain's nerve fibers at several tens of meters per second.*

'dendrites', sense this chemical transmitter and produce a corresponding electrical signal. In this way, a signal can traverse a synapse. Neurons are constantly receiving electrical impulses. If the total number of pulses exceeds a threshold value, the neuron generates an impulse which goes to the next neuron. In addition, if signals are frequently passing through a synapse, the signals are allowed through easily. This effect, called 'synaptic plasticity', is believed to be the basis of learning. See **artificial intelligence**, **neurocomputer**, and **robotics**. ⚊

hybrid computer [ISO A computer that can process both analog data and digital data.]

HyperCard Developed by Bill Atkinson at Apple Computer in 1984 and bundled with the Apple Macintosh, HyperCard is an authoring language (very-high-level programming language) used to develop such applications as computer-aided instruction (CAI) packages. It does not require the user to have any programming experience to create or customize information in the form of graphics, text, music, video, and animation. An application of HyperCard is the ability to organize information in 'stacks' — a collection of on-screen cards, each interrelated, making information easily retrievable and manageable. For example, a HyperCard application may be used to teach people a new language. Graphic representation of objects could allow the user to point and click the mouse on an object to hear what the word for that object is in another chosen language. Business applications may include sophisticated spare parts numbering, allowing the user to point to and click on

any part of a graphic image of a motor vehicle, for a complete listing of the associated parts available. Color coding and the use of video, interactive laser disks, animation, and sound can also be included through the use of a script written in HyperTalk, the software command language.

hypermedia An application mainly used for computer-aided instruction (CAI), interconnecting series of text, graphics, integrated video, interactive laser disks, animation, and sound. Hypermedia is especially useful for expert systems when diagnosing, monitoring, interpreting, controlling, designing, planning, and testing. Using a fast-access disk drive, any part of a document (or associated graphics) can be linked to another, without having to close the working document, or manually search each document. For example, a price list written using hypermedia could enable the user to select a part number and gain immediate access to the price of the product and its operating instructions, or stock analysis. Also, by selecting a particular part, the user could position the pointing device (such as a mouse) on one of a series of option boxes for a complete animated demonstration of how the part can be used, or which section may need replacing. One popular application program using hypermedia for the Apple Macintosh is called 'HyperCard'. See **HyperCard**. ▼

HyperScript The software command language used to operate Wingz, a Macintosh spreadsheet program developed by Informix, Inc. HyperScript resembles the macro commands used for Lotus 1-2-3, except that it is designed for inexperienced programmers.

hypermedia This hypermedia product allows the user to produce interactive computer-based instructional material. The application supports the use of graphics, sound, and video, and uses a linking and branching facility to help the learner proceed through simulations in a self-paced discovery fashion.

HyperTalk The software command language used to write programs for the Macintosh HyperCard application, enabling it to integrate video, interactive laser disks, animation, and sound, while fully implementing object-oriented programming standards. See **HyperCard**.

hypertext A form of nonsequential text retrieval which interconnects a series of documents so that retrieval and immediate cross-referencing is possible. Using a fast-access disk drive, any word or section of a document can be linked to another, without having to close the working document, or manually search each document. For example, a stock control system written in hypertext could enable the user to select a product number and gain immediate access to the sales history or mechanical reliability associated with that product.

hyphenation In word processing, hyphenation is used to improve the appearance of a page by breaking long words at certain points. This is especially useful for text justified in narrow columns. Hyphenation can be manual (user-defined breaks), suggested (word processor defined, but must be accepted by the user), or automated (defined automatically by the word processor). The hyphen (-) can also be used to indicate that two words should be read as one. Some word processing programs tend to break words at incorrect places, often changing the meaning of the word. For example, the word 'putting' (placing) changes its meaning if hyphenated after the second 't' (putt-ing). Similarly, the word 'therapist' would change in meaning if it were broken with a hyphen in the wrong place.

hyphen ladder Printed text which has too many hyphenations at the end of several consecutive lines. This results in bad coloring — meaning the text seems to be unevenly distributed, and displeasing or distracting.

Hz See **hertz**.

H

IA See **intelligent agent**.

IAC Interapplication communications architecture.

IAFV See **indirect-action file virus**.

IAM Intermediate access memory.

IAR Instruction address register.

IAS Immediate access store.

I-beam cursor The I-shaped cursor that is used by most GUI-based computer programs when they are in a text-editing mode.

IBG Interblock gap. Magnetic tape units spin reels at very high speeds so that, just like a motor car, the tape units need to slow down before coming to a halt. To cater for this, blanks are left between records or blocks. Once a high-speed search is completed, the magnetic reel gradually slows down. The gaps ensure that the desired data block is not accidentally passed, requiring a rewind. The gaps are called 'interblock gaps' (IBG) or 'interrecord gaps' (IRG).

IBM International Business Machines Corporation. The history of IBM goes back to 1890 when the United States Government commissioned Herman Hollerith to build a machine which would calculate the US census data. Prior to that, manual calculation of the 1880 census took seven years to complete, and it was estimated that the 1890 census would take ten years to tabulate, making the data obsolete by the time it was ready. Hollerith's electrically-powered machine, which used punched cards, completed the task in just three years. To expand on his success, he left the employ of the US Bureau of the Census and started his own company called the 'Tabulating Machine Company' in Endicott, New York. In 1911, his company merged with several others to become the Computer-Tabulating-Recording Company, whose products ranged from industrial time-recording equipment and commercial scales, to cheese slicers, punched cards, and tabulators. In 1914, Thomas J. Watson Sr (former employee of NCR) joined the company as General Manager at the age of 40, commencing a 42-year career with the company. On 14 February 1924, the company changed its name to 'International Business Machines Corporation' (IBM). In 1939, IBM contributed US$500 000 to the work of Howard Aiken of Harvard University who was working on a programmable, general-purpose computer called 'Automatic Sequence Controlled Calculator'. When completed in 1944, it was known as 'Mark I' — a machine which contained 3 million electrical connections and 500 miles (805 kilometers) of wire and was capable of performing a multiplication in six seconds and a division in 12 seconds. As soon as Mark I was built, it was technically obsolete because it faced competition from the Atanasoff-Berry Computer (ABC). Today, IBM develops, manufacturers, and sells information processing products, including computers and microelectronic technology, software, networking systems, and information technology-related services. It operates in over 110 countries through business units in the United States, Canada, Europe/Middle East/ Africa, Latin America, and Asia/Pacific. Since IBM reported a net loss of US$8900 million in 1993, it appointed a new Chairman and Chief Executive Officer, and cut its workforce from 301 000 to 256 000. Today, serving more than 740 000 shareholders, IBM has more than 210 000 full-time employees who contribute to the company's revenue

IBM *At the age of 40, Thomas J. Watson Sr joined the Computing-Tabulating-Recording Company in 1914 as General Manager. He had already made his mark at the National Cash Register Company, first as a salesman and then as General Sales Manager. As a teenager, he had driven a horse and buggy, and sold pianos and sewing machines across the countryside. During his career with the company (later known as 'IBM'), he often said 'You have to put your heart in the business, and the business in your heart'.*

which exceeds US$6500 million per annum. IBM has adopted three main microprocessor families. Most of its PCs will continue to run on Intel's 80x86 microprocessors, while its RISC work–stations, AS/400 mid-range systems, and parallel supercomputers run on PowerPC microprocessors. IBM's mainframes are powered by its range of System/390 microprocessors. Some of IBM's leading software products include the AIX and OS/2 operating systems. Each year, IBM files thousands of design patents. In 1993, it was granted 1087 patents, more than any other company in the world. See **ABC**. ▲

IBM AT See **AT**.

IBM clone See **IBM-compatible**.

IBM-compatible A term originally used to describe the compatibility of a clone computer, designed to operate software written for the IBM family of personal computers. The term 'IBM clone' usually refers to a personal computer that performs and functions in the same way an IBM personal computer would. Compaq Computer Corporation was one of the original and most successful clone manufacturers, starting out as a company which manufactured personal computers that were compatible with, and in some cases superior to, the original IBM PC model. To protect its investment after several companies started to manufacture clones of the IBM Personal Computer, IBM relaunched its personal computer range in 1986 with a closed-architecture series called 'PS/2' (Personal System 2). Compaq and eight other manufacturers (dubbed the 'Gang of Nine') joined forces to maintain the industry-standard architecture (ISA), and further developed it to take advantage of the 32-bit bus structure of the Intel 80386 and 80486 microprocessors. Extended ISA became known as 'EISA', pronounced 'ee-sah'. Today, the term 'IBM-compatible' is confusing. It has become common to refer to such computers as 'industry-standard computers'.

IBM 8514/A A video display adapter that contains its own video graphics array to produce a resolution of 1024 pixels (picture elements) horizontally by 768 pixels vertically. It is used exclusively for the IBM Personal System/2 computer. See **video adapter**.

IBM LAN Server IBM's version of Network Operating System for OS/2.

IBM PC International Business Machines' Personal Computer. First introduced in mid-1981, it offered 16 kilobytes (kb) of random-access memory (RAM) expandable to 64 kb and was based on the Intel 8088 microprocessor. It used a monochrome display adapter which was not suitable for bit-mapped graphics. It was designed with an open bus and open architecture to encourage third-party software and peripheral companies to develop products to enhance the use of the computer. Microsoft was commissioned to design the operating system which became known as 'MS-DOS' (Microsoft Disk Operating System) — based on an earlier system called 'CP/M' designed by Digital Research in the late 1970s. An improved design of the IBM PC called 'PC-2' was launched in 1983, equipped with 64 kb of RAM, expandable to 256 kb, including a Color Graphics Adapter. Later in 1983, the IBM XT was introduced, and in 1984, the AT made its mark. Since the IBM PC, many clone computers have emerged to compete with IBM. To combat this, IBM launched a new range of computers in 1986, called the 'IBM Personal System/2', operating on proprietary Micro Channel Architecture. See **clone**.

IBM PC Network A CSMA/CD network introduced by IBM in 1984 that uses a star or bus topology. It was originally a broadband network using coaxial cable, but lower-cost twisted pair wire was subsequently introduced by IBM.

IBM Personal Computer See **IBM PC**.

IBM Personal Computer AT See **AT**.

IBM Personal Computer XT See **XT**.

IBM Personal System/2 See **PS/2**.

IBM Token-Ring A baseband star-wired ring network developed by IBM. It uses the token-passing access method and runs at 4 megabits per second.

IBM XT See **XT**.

IBN Institut belge de normalisation; Belgium's standards body formed in 1946.

IBS Intelsat Business Service; an Intelsat service that offers full-time private line service at transmission rates up to 8.448 megabits per second. Over 9100 IBS channels operate to provide communications facilities including voice, data, video conferencing, facsimile, and telex. IBS can be provided through antennae as small as 11.48 foot (3.5 meters) located directly on customer premises over three ocean regions using more than 125 Earth stations.

IC 1. Information center. 2. See **integrated circuit**.

ICAI Intelligent computer-assisted instruction.

IC card See **smart card**.

Icelandic virus An indirect-action file virus that adds approximately 600 bytes to any .EXE file. Once it becomes active, Icelandic seeks to mark a bad cluster on the hard disk. It is not a stable virus because it relies on too many variables. One clue to the presence of this virus is the updating of infected files with the current computer date and time. To avoid common methods of detection, Icelandic does not infect .COM file, and does not use the DOS interrupts to get into memory. Icelandic is sometimes called 'Saratoga' or 'Disk Eater'. See **indirect-action file virus**.

ICL International Computers Limited; a computer company which manufactures and markets a wide range of information systems — from personal computers and specialist workstations, through to departmental systems and large mainframes. To drive these systems, application and operating software is provided by ICL. Around the world, ICL provides integrated solutions for the information technology needs of local, state, and federal governments, and retail, financial, and commercial markets. It also campaigns actively on behalf of open systems and international information technology standards. On 30 November 1990, Fujitsu Limited acquired 80% of the stock of ICL from the commercial group STC based in the United Kingdom. See **Fujitsu Limited**.

iCOMP Intel Comparative Microprocessor Performance; a numerical index that was introduced by Intel in 1992 to provide a simple relative measure of microprocessor performance. The iCOMP index is not a system benchmark. It is a straightforward comparison of Intel CPU (central processing unit) power introduced to supplement benchmarks by helping non-technical computer users with their computer-purchasing decision by highlighting which Intel microprocessor best meets their needs. The index is a composite of eight categories that are important to the performance of widely-used applications (and those expected to become popular in the future). An Intel microprocessor's iCOMP rating is based on the technical categories that encompass four separate aspects of both 16-bit and 32-bit CPU performance —

integer, floating-point, graphics, and video performance. Each category is weighted based upon the estimated percentage of time it enters into the processing picture. The higher the iCOMP rating, the higher the relative performance of the microprocessor. Note that although two different computers may be using the same Intel CPU with identical iCOMP ratings, that does not mean that those computers will perform the same. This is due to the fact that factors such as disk capacity, memory, bus features, and other peripheral functions can vary widely. In fact, it is possible to achieve as much as a 50% variance in system performance between two different computers using the same Intel 486 microprocessor. Because the iCOMP trademark should not be made a plural, it would be incorrect to say that a microprocessor performs at 100 iCOMPs. However, it can be said that a microprocessor performs at an iCOMP index of 100, or it has iCOMP 100 rating. Pronounced 'eye-comp'. See **Intel Corporation**. ▼

icon A graphics object displayed on the screen of a graphical user interface to

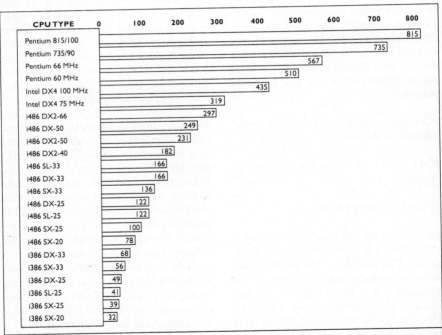

iCOMP *This graph compares the relative performance of Intel 32-bit microprocessors which are commonly used in industry-standard computers. When the iCOMP index was devised, the 25-megahertz (MHz) Intel 486 SX microprocessor was considered the entry-level member of the Intel 486 family. For this reason, it was selected as the base central processing unit (CPU) for the index and arbitrarily assigned an iCOMP rating of 100. Each of the other CPU ratings is relative to the performance of the 25-MHz Intel 486 SX microprocessor.*

represent a series of instructions or programs. The user selects the icon by pointing to it with a mouse and clicking. This automatically activates a set of commands, without having to enter complex instructions. Icons are used with the Apple Macintosh, Microsoft Windows, OS/2, and X Window. ▼

ICONTEC   Instituto Colombiano de Normas Técnicas; Columbia's standards body formed in 1963.

ID   1. Identification. 2. Input device. -

IDA   2. Integrated digital access. 2. Intelligent drive array.

IDC   International Data Corporation; an international market research, analysis, and consulting organization focusing on the computer, communications, and information technology (IT) industries.

icon Icons on a screen can take almost any shape and size. Shown here are some icons found in the Apple System Folder.

IDC is part of the International Data Group (IDG), whose subsidiary, IDG Communications, is one of the world's largest publishers of books and periodicals specific to information technology. The Group has a combined revenue in excess of US$800 million, and it employs over 5000 people in 60 countries. Its exposition management subsidiary, World Expo Corporation, runs more than 60 computer-related exhibitions and conferences in 21 countries. Since its formation in Framingham, Massachusetts, in 1964, IDC has specialized in monitoring and reporting on all aspects of the rapidly-expanding IT industry. IDC has more than 40 offices in North America, Europe, the Middle East, Africa, and the Asia/Pacific region.

IDD   International direct dialing.

IDE   Integral drive electronics; a control system used for computer storage devices where most of the control is contained on the device itself. The IDE control card provides a basic interface between the computer and the device. Enhanced IDE refers to the newer method that offers improved performance, higher capacity, and increased options. Enhanced IDE (E/IDE) allows the user to double the number of devices to four. (These may be hard disk drives.) ▼

identifier   1. In database management, a particular description code used to identify a file as being unique in some way. For example, in a library system, data on a book featuring motor vehicles may contain the identifier 'turbo'. When a search is conducted, 'turbo' can be used as a descriptor to search all titles containing information pertaining to turbo technology. 2. [ISO One or more charac-

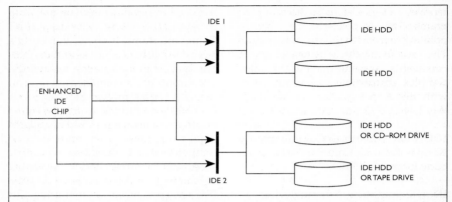

IDE *This diagram shows how enhanced IDE allows the user to double the number of devices to four. In this example, four drives are connected to the enhanced IDE chip. The first two may comprise two magnetic hard disks, each with a storage capacity of up to 8 gigabytes. The third device may be a CD-ROM drive, while the fourth may be a tape drive.*

ters used to identify or name a data element, and possibly to indicate certain properties of that data element.] 3. [ISO A lexical unit that names a language object. *Example:* The names of variables, arrays, records, labels, procedures, etc. *Note:* An identifier usually consists of a letter optionally followed by letters or digits.]

identity gate [ISO A gate that performs an identity operation.]

identity operation [ISO The Boolean operation whose result has the Boolean value 1 if and only if all the operands have the same Boolean value. *Note:* An identity operation on two operands is an equivalence operation.]

ideogram [ISO In a natural language, a graphic character that represents an object or a concept and associated sound elements. *Example:* A Chinese ideogram or a Japanese Kanji.]

idle state In data communications, a checking character or bit sent when no other messages are being sent. It provides verification that the link is still functioning and may also provide synchronization data.

idle time [ISO That part of operable time during which a functional unit is not operated.]

IDP Integrated data processing.

IDRC Improved data recording capability.

IEC International Electrotechnical Commission; the agency which writes technical standards for the world's electrical and electronic industries. IEC standards contain technical specifications and test programs for products. They help to ensure that products are compatible and reliable, and that they are able to fit or work together, no matter what their source of manufacture. IEC was formed in 1906, and today it is made up of members in 41 countries who are, in themselves, national standards bodies for the countries they represent. These countries represent over 80% of the world's population and produce more than 95% of the world's electrical energy. Recommendations and reports drawn up by IEC are usually the work of technical committees made up of standards bodies, industry representatives, government authorities, and interested professional bodies and private individuals. The standards drawn up by IEC committees have been adopted and used as a basis for national rules and standards in more than 100 countries. See **ISO**.

IEE Institute of Electrical Engineers; a professional body of electrical and electronics scientists and engineers based in the United Kingdom. IEE promotes standardization, and consults to the Brit-

ish Standards Institute on matters relating to electrical and electronic development.

IEEE Institute of Electrical and Electronics Engineers; a professional ANSI-accredited body of scientists and engineers based in the United States. IEEE promotes standardization, and consults to the American National Standards Institute on matters relating to electrical and electronic development. The IEEE 802 Standards Committee is the leading official standards organization for local area networks.▼

IEEE 802 The Institute of Electrical and Electronics Engineers' own network management standard which was developed to ensure compatibility between items of equipment made by different manufacturers. The layers within 802 are: 802.1 which is concerned with the inter-networking of local area networks

IEEE Group	Description	IEEE Group	Description
1003.2	POSIX shell and utilities document	1003.17	Directory services
1003.3	POSIX test methods	1003.18	POSIX platform environment profile
1003.4	Real-time extensions to 1003.1	1201.1	High level (toolkit) windowing project
1003.5	Ada API for IEEE 1003.1	1201.1	Windowing drivability guide
1003.6	Security extensions for POSIX	1224	X.400 application programming interface
1003.7	System administration services for POSIX	1238	Common OSI and FTAM application interface
1003.8	POSIX transparent file access	488	A common standard for real-time data collection; also known as 'HPIB'
1003.9	FORTRAN API for IEEE 1003.1 standard	802.1	Standard for how other 802.n standards relate to each other
1003.10	Supercomputer application environment profile	802.2	Standard for logical link control which specifies how data is framed and moved on the links
1003.11	Transaction processing application environment profile		
1003.12	Protocol independent interface	802.3	Standard for Ethernet LANs
1003.13	Real-time application environment profile	802.4	Standard for token bus LANs
		802.5	Standard for token ring LANs
1003.14	Multiprocessing application environment profile	802.6	Standard for MANs
		802.7	Standard for broadband transmission
1003.15	Supercomputing batch services	802.8	Standard for fiber optic transmission
1003.16	C language binding		

IEEE Some of the standards published by IEEE.

(LANs), public switched telephone networks, and other types of networks; 802.2 which is called the 'logical link control layer' (LLC) and is concerned with establishing, maintaining, and terminating a logical link between devices; the medium access control (MAC) layer which defines how a number of devices might gain access and share a single transmission medium; and the lowest layer which is the physical layer concerned with the physical and electrical aspects of the link. Three different LAN access method standards were originally developed because no single design was found to be adequate for all local networking requirements — these are 802.3 (CSMA/CD), 802.4 (token bus), and 802.5 (token ring). Fiber Distributed Data Interface (FDDI) has also been developed for fiber optic LANs.

IEEE 802.3 CSMA/CD See **CSMA/CD**.

IEEE 802.4 token bus access method See **token bus network**.

IEEE 1003.0 One of the IEEE POSIX working groups that has a charter to produce a guide that will accomplish the following: identify elements needed for a comprehensive application portability environment; explore standards that exist to address these elements; and determine whether these standards can be successfully integrated.

IEEE 1003.1-1988 The Institute of Electrical and Electronics Engineers' UniForum (formerly '/usr/group'). A group of users of UNIX derivatives in the United States established a committee with the objective of proposing a set of standards for application-level interfaces. After publishing its standard, together with a reviewer's guide, the group decided to seek IEEE status for the standard. In late 1984, the UniForum standards committee closed its activities in its own name and its members were encouraged to become involved in the IEEE group known as '1003'. The first development was the publication of IEEE Trial-Use Standard in March 1986, with the formal approval in August 1988 of the IEEE Standard 1003.2-1988, a portable operating system interface for computer environments (POSIX). IEEE 1003 is now a collection of more than ten working and special-interest groups whose mission is to extend the POSIX standard. The 1003.1-1988 POSIX standard has also been accepted as an ISO standard called 'ISO DIS9945/1 (1989)'. See **X/Open**.

IEF Information Engineering Facility; Texas Instruments' CASE tool.

IETF Internet Engineering Task Force; an organization responsible for updating and maintaining TCP/IP standards.

IF Intermediate frequency.

IF-AND-ONLY-IF gate [ISO A gate that performs the Boolean operation of equivalence.]

IFIPS International Federation of Information Processing Societies.

i486 The Intel 80486 microprocessor. See **Intel 80486**.

IFP Indexed file processing. When arranging files onto a magnetic/optical disk, it is sometimes helpful to produce a directory (index) of record keys of all files. Before searching the entire disk for the record key, the index can be consulted for the address (location) of the file. See **file allocation table**.

IFRB International Frequency Registration Board; a permanent group of the International Telecommunications Union (ITU) that regulates the allocation of radio frequencies. The other two permanent groups of ITU are the Consultative Committee on International Radio (CCIR), which deals with the coordination of long distance radio telecommunications; and the Consultative Committee on International Telegraphy and Telephony (CCITT), which is the primary group responsible for the development of standards for telephone and data communication systems among participating governments.

IF ... THEN gate [ISO A gate that performs the Boolean operation of implication.]

IGC Intelligent Graphics Controller.

IH Interrupt handler. See **interrupt**.

IIPA International Intellectual Property Alliance; an organization whose members include groups from industries which produce intellectual property such as books, motion pictures, recordings, and computer software. See **BSA**.

IKBS Intelligent knowledge-based system. See **expert systems**.

illegal character Any character not recognized by software as being a valid entry.

IMA Interactive Multimedia Association.

image backup A process by which all files on a volume are copied onto another disk. However, as they are being copied, they are sorted and reorganized so that like files are consolidated and written one after the other (become contiguous). This is a useful way to improve performance in an installation with highly volatile file structures. As files are copied during an image backup, discontiguous (fragmented) files are brought together. The backup is considered the new master file, and is copied back to the working area which then has a clean, contiguous set of files, thus decreasing average seek time for the entire volume. An image backup can be done as frequently as needed. The new volume then becomes the basis for daily or even more frequent incremental backups in installations with high data integrity requirements. See **backup**. Compare **differential backup**, **global backup**, and **incremental backup**.

image drive The primary disk drive in a mirroring scheme that stores the original data.

imagesetter A professional typesetting machine capable of recognizing PostScript (or any other page description language) commands for type and graphics output (on film or paper) exceeding 1200 dots per inch (compared to 300 dots per inch for most laser printers). Leading brands in this field include Berthold, Compugraphic, Linotronic, and Varityper. Due to the high investment cost of imagesetters, service bureaus have been set up where customers can take their diskettes for high-resolution processing, in the same way film processing labs operate.

imaging model In a graphical user interface, the method of displaying (on screen) an image of what the output will look like, very closely resembling the size, appearance, and position of the finished output. This is sometimes termed 'WYSIWYG' (what you see is what you get). In contrast, character-based programs cannot show (on the screen) any connection between the monospaced text and the proportionally-spaced output.

immediate instruction [ISO An instruction that contains the value of an operand rather than its address. *Note:* The operand is then called an 'immediate operand'.]

impact printer A printer which uses some sort of physical contact with the paper. A print-head or raised character hits the ribbon, which in turn hits the paper, leaving a mark/character. The advantage of impact printers is that carbon copies can be made. Typical impact printers are the dot matrix, daisy-wheel, and golf-ball printers/typewriters. Some printers (such as Qume and Diablo brands) are known as 'letter-quality printers', referring to the fact that they simulate the high quality produced by traditional typewriters, making them suitable for business correspondence. Daisy-wheel and similar impact printers cannot represent graphics, and for this reason they are unpopular in the modern office environment. Non-impact printers include electrostatic printers and electrothermal printers. [ISO A printer in which printing is the result of mechanically striking the printing medium.] See **dot matrix printer**. ▼

impedance In electronics, this refers to the quantity of opposition to AC (alter-

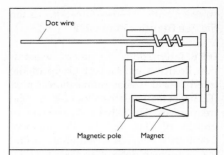

impact printer *The print-head assembly in an impact printer usually consists of a number of wires and hammers. A dot matrix printer head typically consists of 23 solenoids, each of which drives a stiff wire or hammer to impact the paper through an inked ribbon. Characters are formed by firing the solenoids to form a matrix of 'dots'.*

nating current) flow offered by a circuit or transmission line that has both resistance and reactance parameters. Resistance, capacitance, and inductance are always present in every telephone company circuit. The combined effect of all three of these factors is called 'impedance', and it is measured in ohms. At any given frequency, the impedance of a circuit can be calculated. Telephone company circuits are constructed with a known characteristic impedance. Domestic circuits are 600 ohms at 1000 hertz, and international circuits may be 600 or 900 ohms at 1000 hertz. Typical network coaxial cable has an impedance of 50 ohms. Typical TV coaxial cable has an impedance of 70 ohms. The device or modem that is used to determine the telephone circuit must match the characteristic impedance of the circuit. If the impedances do not match, part of the analog signal will be reflected back into the telephone line, causing distortion to the incoming signal.

implementation [ISO The system development phase of which the hardware, software, and procedures of the system are considered to become operational.]

implication [ISO The dyadic Boolean operation whose result has the Boolean value 0 if and only if the first operand has the Boolean value 0 and the second has the Boolean value 1.]

implicit declaration [ISO A declaration, caused by the occurrence of an identifier, and in which the attributes are determined by default.]

import To convert a file created in one program to another program so that it can be used in a different application. For example, Lotus 1-2-3 files can be imported to a Harvard Graphics program so that the information contained in Lotus can be represented in graph form by Harvard Graphics. Not all applications can import files. When importing is vital, special character and command conversion charts may be written so that the data can be manipulated in ASCII format before it can be recognized by another application. The word 'import' comes from the Latin word *portare*, meaning 'carry'.

Improv See **Lotus Improv**.

impulse noise A type of communications interference characterized by pulses of high amplitude and short duration. See **noise**.

IMS/VS Information Management System/Virtual Storage; a common IBM host operating environment, usually under the MVS operating system, oriented toward batch processing and telecommunications-based transaction processing.

in-circuit emulator A tool for use in designing systems incorporating microcontrollers. Using an in-circuit emulator, the system designer can interactively control and examine the state of the system at any chosen time. This is essential for speeding up the debugging process and enhancing the system designer's productivity. The tool is easy to use and provides not only the capabilities of the target processor, but also a set of debugging capabilities to facilitate and shorten the debugging process. This is important because it is not enough for the emulator to simply behave like the target processor; it must also provide read/write access to all signals and all data to which the microcontroller has access. This includes information which resides inside the microcontroller. Without this access, the engineer may not be able to completely control and debug the system. The many uses of the emulator can be easily visualized after examining a typical design cycle. The first use of an emulator in the design cycle is in the software-development phase. The emulator executes the program exactly as the target system would, in real time, and it provides all of the interactive debugging capabilities. Software developed using the emulator can be completely debugged, except for the hardware interface, before it is integrated with the system hardware. The second major use of an emulator in the design cycle is in the integration of the target software and the system hardware. Even when the hardware and software have each been individually debugged, new problems can surface when they are joined. The emulator is used, in this case, to solve these potential problems. After a prototype has been completely debugged, the emulator can then be used to test the system. Worst-case parametric tests can be developed and tested on the prototype. This provides the designer with valuable information about the limitations of the system. It also provides test programs which can be used in the manufacturing process. The fourth use of an emulator is in the product-manufacturing phase. The same test routines used to develop and debug the prototype, or even more comprehensive test routines, can be used to test the finished products. Any non-functioning units can be easily debugged using the emulator's full range of debugging capabilities. The fifth use of an emulator is in the field-service phase.

incremental backup A backup that only updates files which have changed since the last backup. An incremental backup can be useful with volumes that are largely static, with only a small percentage of the files on them changing from backup to backup. They offer convenience in restoring individual files, but can be a relatively awkward mechanism for restoring entire volumes if many increments to a baseline backup must be applied. For highly volatile volumes with large directory structures, incremental backups can be time-consuming because the host computer searches directories and reorganizes files for backup. See **backup**. Compare **differential backup**, **global backup**, and **image backup**.

incremental coordinate [ISO A relative coordinate where the previously-addressed point is the reference point.]

incremental vector [ISO A vector whose end point is specified as a displacement from its start point.]

increment size [ISO The distance between adjacent addressable points on the display surface.]

indent After the left and right margins have been set for a page, indentation allows further alignment of paragraphs from either the right, left, or both sides of the margin, depending upon the tab stops. A hanging indent is one which ensures the first line of each paragraph is flush left, while all other lines are indented at the left side to the next tab stop.

Indeo Intel's compression/decompression algorithm for scalable software playback video. Intel licenses Indo technology to companies (such as Microsoft) which integrate it into products such as Microsoft's Video for Windows. Indeo technology can record 8-, 16-, or 24-bit sequences, and it can store the sequence as 24-bit for scalability on higher-power personal computers. ▼

independent compilation [ISO The compilation of a source module not using the interface and context information from related source modules. *Note:* When independently compiled units are eventually combined, it may be necessary to check interface and context information for validity.]

independent software vendor A third-party software development vendor. Abbreviation 'ISV'.

index 1. In word processing programs, a list of all the important words chosen from a large document. This indexing feature automatically tracks the chosen word and assigns to it the associated page number, forming an index in al-

Indeo *Intel's Indeo provides the software component that enables video playback on Intel 486-based (or higher) personal computers without the need for additional hardware. Depending upon the microprocessor, resolutions of up to 160 x 120 at 24 frames per second can be achieved. With the addition of a video processor board based on the Intel 750 microprocessor, Indeo can play back video with 320 x 240 resolution at 30 frames per second.*

phabetical order. 2. In database management programs, a file which contains information about the location of specific records in a file so that when a search is conducted, the index is used instead of the entire document, thereby saving time. 3. [ISO A list of the contents of a file or of a document, together with keys or references for locating the contents.] 4. (In programming.) [ISO An integer that identifies the position of a data item in a sequence of data items.]

indexed address [ISO An address that is to be modified by the content of an index register.]

indexed file processing See **indexed processing**.

indexed processing The use of a directory (index) of key numbers of all files on a magnetic/optical disk. Before searching the entire disk for the record key, the index can be consulted for the address (location) of the file. See **file allocation table**.

index hole [ISO A hole punched in a floppy disk to indicate the beginning of the first sectors of the disk.]

index register [ISO A register whose contents can be used to modify an operand address during the execution of computer instructions. *Note:* An index register may also be used as a counter to control the execution of a loop, to control the use of an array, for table look-up, as a switch, or as a pointer.]

index track [ISO A track whose contents are needed to locate data on other tracks of the same data medium.]

indicator [ISO A device that gives visual or other indication of the existence of a defined state.]

indirect-action file virus Any computer virus capable of installing itself into memory and infecting executable files such as .COM or .EXE files, or a system file with any extension. An indirect-action file virus often copies its instructions from memory to any other executable file. An indirect-action file virus usually replaces DOS interrupt routines, infects the files, and proceeds with the original interrupt and function so that the user does not detect a change in the routine, although any computer running under a virus is unpredictable and may perform totally unrelated functions. Some of the better-known indirect-action file viruses are Dark Avenger, Dbase, Mix1, Vacsina, and Yankee Doodle. Abbreviation 'IAFV'. Compare **direct-action file virus**.

indirect address [ISO An address of a storage location which contains an address identifying the ultimate location. *Note:* The storage location may be the first address field of a chained list of address fields, the last of which identifies the ultimate location.]

indirect referencing [ISO A mechanism for referencing via a data object, the value of which points to the referenced language object. *Notes:* (a) This term also applies to the use of the mechanism. (b) The referencing may be done along a chain of data objects in which each data object, except the last, points to the next, the last data object pointing to the referenced language object.]

Industry-Standard Architecture See **ISA**.

infection The obvious or undetected presence of a virus or Trojan in a computer system. Infections can remain dormant for some time, then become activated to display error messages, or erase entire databases. The word 'infection' comes from the Latin words *ficere fect*, meaning 'taint'. See **logic bomb**, **Trojan**, and **virus**.

infinite loop A repetitive process, often created by accident, that causes the computer to continue to perform a given segment of a program indefinitely. It can only be stopped by re-setting the program. [ISO A loop whose execution can be terminated only by intervention from outside the computer program in which the loop is included.] See **recursion**.

infix notation [ISO A method of forming mathematical expressions, governed by rules of operator precedence and using paired delimiters such as parentheses, in which the operators are dispersed among the operands; each operator indicating the operation to be performed on the operands or the intermediate results adjacent to it. *Examples:* (a) A added to B and the sum multiplied by C is represented by the expression (A + B) x C. (b) P AND the result of Q AND R is represented by the expression P & (Q&R). *Note:* If it is desired to distinguish the case in which there are more than two operands for an operator, the phrase 'distributed infix notation' may be used.]

in-flight Referring to a transaction that has recorded a 'start transaction' command but has yet to record its 'end transaction' (or abort transaction) command.

information [ISO The meaning that is currently assigned to data by means of the conventions applied to that data.]

information analysis [ISO A systematic investigation of information and its flow in a real or planned system.]

information retrieval [ISO Actions, methods, and procedures for recovering stored data to provide information on a given subject.]

information technology A general term used to refer to all aspects of technology that encompass the creation, storage, display, exchange, and management of information for business, artistic, scientific, recreational, or personal use. Abbreviation 'IT'. Pronounced 'eye-tea'.

information theory [ISO The branch of learning concerned with the study of measures of information and their properties.]

infotainment The combination of information and entertainment. It can be said that television is an infotainment medium. However, this term is now used to refer to multimedia computer systems that inform and entertain.

infrared The electromagnetic radiation situated below the red end of the visible spectrum. This involves wavelengths longer than those of visible light. Abbreviation 'IR'.

inheritance One of the most powerful features in object-oriented programming which allows objects to acquire the at-tributes and behavior of other objects. Inheritance contributes to economical and maintainable design, because objects share attributes and behaviors without separately duplicating the program code that implements them. An analogy of this is the taxonomic scheme used by zoologists and botanists to classify living things. This scheme subdivides the plant and animal kingdoms into groups called 'phyla'. Each phylum is in turn subdivided into 'classes', 'orders', 'families', and so on. Lower-level groups inherit, or share, characteristics of higher-level groups. To say, for example, that a wolf belongs to the canine family implies several things. It says that wolves have well-developed hearing and smell, because these are characteristics of canines. Since canines are a type of carnivore, it says wolves eat meat. Since carnivores are a type of a mammal, it says that wolves have hair and regulate their body temperature. Finally, since mammals are vertebrates, it says wolves have backbones. Software objects occupy a hierarchy in much the same way. For example, we can mentally create, or subtract, a high-level 'window' object. This is done by noting that all windows on a computer screen occupy a specific X–Y position and have a specific height, width, border style, and background color. It can also be noted that a 'menu' object has all the properties of a window, but it also has several properties of its own, such as line items and perhaps a scroll bar. Also beneath the window might be an 'editor' which shares the characteristics of the window but adds the ability to accept and manipulate characters from the keyboard. Note that both menu and editor may be equally said to be windows, in that they have a width, a height and so on, but both are also distinct from one another in how they look and what they do. This hierarchy of objects can have multiple levels. For example, a further refinement of the 'editor' object might be something called a 'prompt field' which inherits all the features of an editor, but is limited to a single line of text and has a prompt string in front of it. In the object-oriented programming jargon of C++, window, menu, editor, and prompt fields are classes. Classes exist in a hierarchy that defines inheritance relationships among them. The combination of inheritance and polymorphism gives the user of object-oriented code the benefit of being able to extend that code without having the source code. See **object-oriented programming**.

inhibiting signal [ISO A signal that prevents the occurrence of an event.]

initial base font In word processing, the font to which the printer is always set unless otherwise formatted by the user.

initial condition mode [ISO That operation mode of an analog computer during which the integrators are inoperative and the initial conditions are set.]

initialization [ISO The operations required for setting a device to a starting state, before the use of a data medium, or before implementation of a process.]

initialize [ISO To give a value to a data object at the beginning of its lifetime.]

initial program load Each time a computer is switched on, it must go through a formal loading (initializing) procedure known as 'booting' or 'initial program load'. This occurs when the computer's operating system is installed. A section of this software also allows the computer to communicate with the user. Abbreviation 'IPL'. See **boot**.

inked ribbon [ISO A continuous inked ribbon used on output units.]

inking [ISO Creating a line by moving a locator over the display surface leaving a trail behind the locator in the manner of a pen drawing a line on paper.]

ink-jet printer A non-impact printer which sprays electrically-charged ink onto paper, generally at a resolution of 360 dots per inch. [ISO A non-impact printer in which the characters are formed by projecting particles or droplets of ink onto paper.] ▼

INN Instituto Nacional de Normalización; Chile's standards body formed in 1944.

inoculation The placement of the signature of a known virus onto a diskette or hard disk to trick the virus into thinking that it is already present, thereby preventing it from trying to load the virus. Inoculation of diskettes is common and safe, but inoculation of hard disks can be troublesome if the boot sector is accidentally tampered with, making it impossible to boot from it.

inoperable time [ISO That part of downtime with all environmental conditions satisfied, during which a functional unit would not yield correct results if it were operated.]

input 1. The entering of data into the computer. Input is achieved through special devices, such as keyboards, or direct cable connection. 2. (Adjective.)

ink-jet printer *This DeskJet printer from Hewlett-Packard uses plain paper and features 'true black' and color printing. 'True black' refers to the printer's capability to sense the black areas of an image, and use the black cartridge. This provides better color output at faster speeds because the printer does not have to create the black using the three colors (which also wastes the color cartridges).*

[ISO Pertaining to a device process, or channel involved in an input process, or to the associated data or states. *Note:* The word 'input' may be used in place of 'input data', 'input signal', or 'input process' when such a usage is clear in a given context.] 3. (Input data.) [ISO Data being received or to be received by any component part of a computer.]

input device Any device designed to assist in the entry of data into a computer system. Most computers support a large variety of input and output devices. In addition to the keyboard, monitor, and disk drives found on most computers, many specialized devices (such as bar code readers, optical scanners, and plotters) are also commonly used. All of these devices can be classified as serving one of three functions: to provide input; to provide output; or to provide for mass

data storage and retrieval. The keyboard (the most common input device for personal computers) typically includes a typewriter-style keyboard, a numeric keypad, cursor movement (arrow) keys, and ten or more function keys. The function keys can be programmed to perform various commands, depending upon the user application. Another very popular input device is the mouse. A mouse contains a ball that is rolled over the desktop (or by hand in newer models). Sensors inside the mouse translate the motion and move the cursor on the screen accordingly. Pressing the buttons on the mouse can activate functions such as choosing an item from a menu. (The actual functions of the buttons depend upon the program that is running.)

input/output Refers to the sending and receiving of data from the central processing unit (CPU) to other peripheral devices such as disk drives. The input/output channel carries out all the transfer of data so as to free up the CPU. The keyboard is the most common input device, and the monitor is the most common output device. Another very common output device is the printer, but as this is not part of the computer, it is considered to be an 'add-on' or peripheral device. There are sections of logic in a personal computer which manage the various input and output devices. Collectively, these sections are called the 'I/O interface', and are usually made up of a microprocessor and some supporting electronics. All of the microprocessors in the I/O interface report to the 'system microprocessor' (this being the CPU). Individually, each section of logic which is dedicated to managing one type of device is referred to as a 'controller' or an 'adapter'. For example, a disk drive will be managed by a disk controller, and a monitor by a video display adapter. Abbreviation 'I/O'. [ISO Pertaining to a device, process, or channel involved in an input process and in an output process, concurrently or not, or to their associated data or states. *Note:* The phrase 'input/output' may be used in place of 'input/output data', 'input/output signals', or 'input/output process' when such a usage is clear in a given context.]

input/output address space See **addressable memory**.

input/output channel [ISO A functional unit that handles the transfer of data between internal storage and peripheral equipment.]

input/output port A port on a computer to which input devices, such as key-

boards, barcode readers, and mice, and output devices such as printers and monitors, are connected via cables. These can use either serial or parallel paths of transmission.

input (output) (input/output) unit [ISO A device by which data can be entered into (conveyed out of) (entered into or conveyed out of) a computer.]

input primitive [ISO An item of data obtained from an input device such as a keyboard, choice device, locator, pick device, or valuator.]

input process [ISO The process that consists of the reception of data by any component part of a computer.]

input protection [ISO For analog input channels, the protection against overvoltages that may be applied between any two input connectors or between any input connector and ground.]

input subsystem [ISO That part of a process interface system that transfers data from the technical process to the process computer system.]

inquiry The extraction of data or facts stored on a database. This is usually done by asking the computer to respond with an answer. The word 'inquiry' comes from the Latin word *quaerere*, meaning 'seek'.

inquiry station [ISO A terminal primarily for the interrogation of a computer.]

Ins See **insert key**.

insert key In word processing and other text entry applications, the key which is used to either insert text by pushing all other data to the right, or overtype text by overwriting on top of existing text. Abbreviation 'Ins'.

installation program A program used to install software onto the computer. The installation program is usually packaged with the application software and used to simplify and automate the loading process of an application which may use more than ten diskettes to contain the program.

instantaneous transfer rate See **data transfer rate**.

Institute of Electrical and Electronics Engineers A professional ANSI-accredited body of scientists and engineers based in the United States. IEEE promotes standardization, and consults to the American National Standards Institute on matters relating to electrical and electronic development. The IEEE 802 Standards Committee is the leading official standards organization for local area networks. Abbreviation 'IEEE'.

Institute of Electrical Engineers A professional body of electrical and electronics scientists and engineers based in the United Kingdom. It promotes standardization, and consults to the British Standards Institute on matters relating to electrical and electronic development. Abbreviation 'IEE'.

instruction In computer programming, any statement written in (or converted to) machine language so that the computer can execute it. [ISO A language construct that specifies an operation and identifies its operands, if any.] See **programming language**.

instruction address register [ISO A special-purpose register used to hold the address of the next instruction to be executed.]

instruction format [ISO The layout of the constituent parts of an instruction.]

instruction register [ISO A register that is used to hold an instruction for interpretation.]

instruction repertoire See **instruction set**.

instruction set The list of all the words and instructions which a particular computer can recognize and perform. Most personal computers have a central processing unit based on a complex instruction set computing (CISC) chip, capable of recognizing over 100 instructions for immediate computation. A faster technology commonly used in professional workstations, and more recently in personal computers, is based on reduced instruction set computing (RISC) chips.

instruction time When the central processor executes a computer program, the control unit receives an instruction, examines it, and then gives control to the arithmetic/logic unit. The time it takes for this process to occur is called 'instruction time', and is part of the machine cycle. Abbreviation 'i-time'.

INTAP Interoperability Technology Association for Information Processing.

integer As distinguished from a fraction, an integer is a whole number, whether it be positive or negative. [ISO One of the numbers zero, plus one, minus one, plus two, minus two, ...]

Integral Drive Electronics See **IDE**.

integrated Put together in such a way that the components produced separately appear to have come from the same source. The term 'integrated application' applies to programming software applications that interact with the end user and with other software applications in a seamless manner (with overall logical consistency). The word 'integrated' comes from the Latin word *integrare*, meaning 'make whole'.

integrated accounting package An accounting software program that links all the accounting functions together, including the general ledger, accounts receivable, and accounts payable, plus other mainstream functions like payroll and inventory. The advantage is that any transaction entered in one section of the program will result in an automatic update of other related areas.

integrated application Refers to a suite of software which has been combined into one application.

integrated circuit A single chip of silicon (semiconductor after being treated) that replaced a whole network of thousands of transistors and other electrical components. Workable integrated circuits were first introduced in 1959, but their price made their common use prohibitive. The USA/USSR race to put a man on the moon spurred the race for technology, and by 1960, technology was growing at such a pace that the number of integrated circuits contained on each chip would double each year, while the unit cost declined. Integrated circuits found their way into household items by the mid-1960s. At that time, engineers

were predicting a growth pattern which estimated that by 1975, each chip could contain 65 000 integrated circuits — a number thought to be impossible. Eventually, the integrated circuit gave rise to the third-generation computer. Today, the Intel Pentium processor boasts more than 3.1 million transistors contained on a chip. The transistors are literally microscopic in size. In 1990, Fujitsu reported the development of the first integrated circuit using RHETs (resonant-tunneling hot electron transistors). An integrated circuit with only five RHETs is much smaller than conventional VLSI (very-large-scale integration) circuits, and is capable of performing with far fewer transistors, thus offering potential for supercomputer circuits with up to a tenth of the transistors currently needed. Super-lattice RHETs run at 116 gigahertz, with a processing time of 1.4 picoseconds (making them a hundred times faster than conventional silicon transistors, and 1.3 times the speed achieved by experimental gallium arsenide (GaAs) and

integrated circuit The device that would change the world looked rough by all standards. It was a 7/16-inch sliver of germanium with protruding wires, glued to a glass slide. It was first demonstrated 12 September 1958 by its inventor, Jack St Clair Kilby at Texas Instruments.

silicon bipolar chips. Also, RHET chips require half to a quarter of the power). When RHET integrated circuits and other devices using quantum mechanical effects are commercially available, super–computers delivering one teraFLOP (10^{12} floating point operations per second) and notebook computers with the power of today's supercomputers will be feasible. Abbreviation 'IC'. See **chip**, **ENIAC**, **Pentium processor**, **silicon**, **Texas Instruments**, and **third generation**. ◢

integrated circuit memory [ISO A storage device composed of transistors, diodes, and other circuit elements all fabricated on a chip of crystalline material.]

integrated network See **ISDN**.

integrated optical circuit See **IOC**.

Integrated Services Digital Network See **ISDN**.

integration test [ISO The progressive linking and testing of programs or modules in order to ensure their proper functioning in the complete system.]

integrator 1. [ISO A functional unit whose output analog variable is the integral of an input analog variable with respect to time. *Note:* For some integrators, the variable of integration may be other than time.] 2. A person or company that configures a computer, operating system, applications, and other hardware to form a complete system to solve a business need.

Intel Comparative Microprocessor Performance See **iCOMP**.

Intel Corporation Integrated Electronics.

Founded in July 1968, Intel is a technological leader in the microelectronics arena. The original 12 employees generated just under US$3000 in revenue in 1968; today Intel employs over 26 000 people in locations around the world, and generates annual revenue in excess of US$10 000 million. In its early years, the company flourished as a supplier of semiconductor memory for mainframe and minicomputer manufacturers. Today, Intel is a major supplier of microcomputer components, modules, and systems representing the largest and fastest-growing segment of the computer industry. Microprocessors based on Intel technology can be found in thousands of applications ranging from personal computers and automobiles to robots and supercomputers. The company's founders were Bob Noyce and Gordon Moore who worked together at Shockley Semiconductor Laboratory in Palo Alto, California. In 1957, Noyce and Moore co-founded Fairchild Semiconductor. In 1968, they left Fairchild to form Intel. In those days, semiconductor memory was 200 times more expensive than core memory (the standard memory at the time). Bob Noyce made many significant contributions both as a scientist and as a business leader. His co-invention of the integrated circuit won him a number of awards, including the National Medal of Science and the Draper Prize, considered the engineering world's equivalent of the Nobel Prize. Intel has sales, administration, support, design, and manufacturing facilities in the United States and in several overseas locations. Principal North American locations include Santa Clara, Livermore, and Folsom in California; Portland, Oregon; and Phoenix, Arizona. Major international sites are

Product	Intel 386 SX CPU	Intel 386 DX CPU	Intel 386 SL CPU	Intel 486 SX CPU	Intel 486 DX CPU	Intel 486 DX2 CPU	Intel 486 SL CPU	Pentium Processor
Description	Entry-level, home, and hobby standard	Home and hobby standard	Mobile 32-bit computing standard	Entry-level business computing standard	Mid-range business computing standard	Mid-range business computing standard	Professional mobile computing standard	Highest performance processor
Internal bus width	32 bits	32 bits	32 bits	32 bits	32 bits	32 bits	32 bits	32 bits
External bus width	16 bits	32 bits	16 bits	32 bits	32 bits	32 bits	32 bits	64 bits
Virtual address space	64 terabytes	64 terabytes	64 terabytes	64 terabytes	64 terabytes	64 terabytes	64 terabytes	64 terabytes
Physical address space	16 megabytes	4 gigabytes	20 megabytes	4 gigabytes	4 gigabytes	4 gigabytes	64 megabytes	4 gigabytes
Clock frequency in MHz	16, 20, or 25	16, 20, 25, or 33	20 or 25	16, 20, or 25	25, 33, or 50	50 or 66	25 or 33	60, 66, 90, 75, or 100
Math coprocessor support	Intel 387 SX	Intel 387 DX	Intel 387 SX	Intel 487 SX	Built-in	Built-in	Built-in	Built-in
First-level cache controller	80385 SX or 80395 SX	80395 SX 80396 DX	Built-in	Built-in	Built-in	Built-in	Built-in	Built-in
First-level cache location	External	External	External	8-kilobyte cache built-in	8-kilobyte cache built-in	8-kilobyte cache built-in	Built-in	Built-in
Upgrade processor support	No	No	No	Yes	Yes	Yes	No	Yes

Intel Corporation *The Intel 486 and Intel 386 computing architecture includes a 32-bit instruction set designed to run more powerful software than 16-bit 8088 or 16-bit 286-based software. This architecture has an advanced memory-management scheme capable of addressing up to 4 gigabytes of physical memory and 64 terabytes of virtual memory, which enables it to support large memory-intensive applications. Virtual memory is an area of hard disk that is treated by the processor as part of main memory. By swapping blocks of memory to and from the disk, users have an easy and inexpensive way to get extra memory capacity. The different operating modes of the Intel architecture allow it to divide the way it uses memory into different sections so that part of the processor works as a subset and can behave like an 8088 or a 286 chip. This allows the Intel 486 or Intel 386 processors to run any software that was written for either of those older Intel microprocessors, and to support multitasking. The Intel microprocessors shown in this table run most operating systems, including MS–DOS, OS/2, UNIX, Windows, and Solaris, and they support graphical user interfaces such as Windows, Presentation Manager, X Window, DESQview, OSF/Motif, and Open Desktop.*

in Paris, Munich, United Kingdom, Ireland, Japan, Hong Kong, Israel, Malaysia, Singapore, and the Philippines. Other corporate milestones include the development of the 1103 chip — the first large-scale integration dynamic random-access memory (1970); the first microprocessor/computer on a chip, called the 'Intel 4004', plus the 1702 which was the first EPROM (1971); the introduction of the 8086 microprocessor architecture (1978); the first 16-bit microprocessor (1982); the introduction of the first one-million transistor microprocessor (1989); and the introduction of the Pentium CPU (1993). By the year 2000, Intel anticipates that the microprocessor will have a die size of approximately one square inch (6.45 square centimeters), run at 250 megahertz, and will perform 2000 million instructions per second. See **integrated circuit** and **Micro 2000 Project.** ⚠

Intel 82385 For computers using the Intel 80386 and 80486 microprocessors, the 82385 acts as a cache memory controller. See **cache**.

Intel 8207 See **Intel 80286.**

Intel 8088 Used in the original IBM Personal Computer, the 8088 offered 1 megabyte of random-access memory with 16-bit internal processing, and 8-bit external processing, making it more compatible with peripherals available at the time of its introduction in 1978. It operated at a slow 4.77 megahertz (MHz), although later versions had clock speeds approaching 10 MHz. The 8086 and 8088 microprocessors consist of two process-

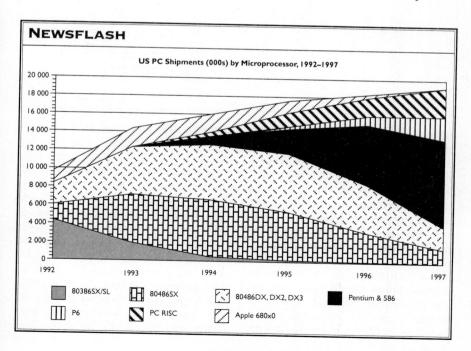

NEWSFLASH

US PC Shipments (000s) by Microprocessor, 1992–1997

Legend:
- 80386SX/SL
- 80486SX
- 80486DX, DX2, DX3
- Pentium & 586
- P6
- PC RISC
- Apple 680x0

NEWSFLASH

Waves of change in personal computing

	1990		1995		2000
Customer	Business	SOHO		Individual	
				Family	
Growth device	Notebook		Smaller notebook	Personal productivity partners	
Application focus	Connected and mobile business			Workstyle/lifestyle	
				Workgroup/collaborative	
Media type	Text/audio/graphics/video			Multimedia	
Influencers	Semiconductors				
	Distribution channels				
			Information providers		
			Intelligent networks		
			Interactive multimedia supergroups		
		OSI and GUI providers			

ing units: the execution unit (EU) which executes instructions, and the bus interface unit (BIU) which fetches instructions, reads operands, and writes results. During periods when the EU is busy executing instructions, the BIU 'looks ahead' and fetches more instructions from the next consecutive address in memory; these are stored in an internal queue. This queue is 4 bytes long for the 8088 and 6 bytes long for the 8086; under most conditions, the BIU can supply the next instruction without having to perform a memory cycle. Only when the program does not process serially does the EU have to wait for the next instruction to be fetched from memory. Otherwise, the instruction fetch time 'disappears' as it is proceeding in parallel with the execution of previously-fetched instructions. The EU then has to wait for the BIU only when it needs to read operands from memory or write results to memory. As a result, the 8086 and 8088 are less sensitive to wait states than other microprocessors which do not use an instruction queue. The BIU can fetch instructions faster than the EU can execute them, so wait states only affect performance to the extent that they make the EU wait for the transfer of operands and results.

Intel 8086 This 16-bit microprocessor introduced in 1978 was the least popular of the Intel chips because, in the same year, IBM chose the Intel 8088 microprocessor for its personal computer. The 8088 offered 16-bit internal processing and 8-bit external processing, making it more compatible with peripherals available at that time. By the time 16-bit peripherals became available, Intel had launched the 80286 microprocessor offering a maximum of 16 megabytes of random-access memory (compared to 1 megabyte in the 8086).

Intel 80486 Introduced in 1989, this central processing unit (CPU) uses a 32-bit data bus structure, with the ability to directly address up to 64 gigabytes of random-access memory. A special mode enables the 80486 to run more than one program at a time (such as a word processor plus a spreadsheet program) by separating blocks of 640 kilobytes of memory to be used by DOS as required. Mathematical processing circuits previously only available on separate math coprocessors (such as the 80387), and the cache controller, are incorporated in the Intel 80486 — a tiny chip containing 1.2 million transistors. Operating at an initial speed of 25 megahertz (MHz), the 80486 DX CPU processes up to 20 million instructions per second (MIPS), while the 50 MHz version processes up to 41 MIPS. By incorporating RISC principles in its CPU core (specifically, instruction pipelining), the 80486 DX CPU is able to execute most instructions in a single clock cycle. In 1992, Intel introduced the DX2 family that featured a technology called 'clock doubling' that

allows the processor to operate twice as fast internally as it does externally. The 80486 DX2 CPU is pin-compatible with the DX processor, and the 66 MHz version executes up to 54 MIPS. The 80486 family of processors is also referred to as the 'i486'. See **integrated circuit**. Compare **Intel 80386 SX** and **Pentium processor**. ▼

I

Intel 80486 DX The Intel 486 DX and DX2 central processing units (CPUs) integrate a RISC integer core that executes frequently-used instructions in a single clock cycle (compared to the Pentium processor's ability to execute multiple instructions in a single clock cycle).

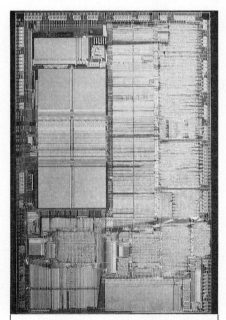

Intel 80486 Packing 1 180 235 transistors into a 0.414 x 0.649 inch die, the Intel 80486 features a high level of integration with a floating point unit, 8 kilobytes of cache, and memory management with paging.

Operating at 50 megahertz, a single Intel 486 DX or DX2 microprocessor provides sustainable performance in excess of 40 MIPS (million instructions per second). Available in several clock speeds, the Intel 486 DX CPU combines an enhanced version of the Intel 386 processor's integer unit, an optimized Intel 387 DX math coprocessor, a cache controller, and 8 kilobytes of cache memory. By integrating the math coprocessor on the chip, the CPU eliminates input/output cycles needed to pass data between the processor and an external device. The result of these functional improvements is four times more performance than an Intel 386 DX CPU with a separate Intel 387 math coprocessor. Also available in several clock speeds, the Intel 486 DX2 microprocessor is functionally identical to, and 100% binary compatible with, the Intel 486 DX CPU. The Intel 486 DX2 processor also incorporates Intel's speed-doubling technology, increasing the internal clock rate to provide a faster interface among all the high-performance subunits of the RISC-based CPU — including the integer unit, on-chip cache, and floating-point unit. The Intel 486 DX2 microprocessor can achieve up to twice the code execution speed of an Intel DX CPU at a comparable clock rate. In addition, the Intel 486 DX2 CPU is upgradable to take advantage of Pentium processor technology.

Intel 80486 SL The Intel 486 SL microprocessor combines the performance of the Intel 486 DX central processing unit (CPU) with the power-saving and space-saving advantages originally realized with the Intel 386 SL processor (Intel's first CPU designed for mobile computing, such as notebook computers).

Intel 486 SL processors deliver more than twice the integer performance of their 386 SL counterparts at the same frequency. The 486 SL CPU's on-chip enhanced math processing capabilities provide more than four times the floating-point computational performance of an Intel 386 SL CPU with an external Intel 387 math coprocessor. The Intel 486 SL microprocessor takes up to 60% less space and consumes less power than previous Intel processors. The power-saving technology extends battery life under full-on and typical intermittent usage conditions. The Intel 486 SL microprocessor's 3.3-volt implementation uses half the power of the standard 5-volt Intel 386 SL CPU, extending full-on battery life by up to one additional hour. Intel's System Management Mode (iSMM) further extends battery life. It more than doubles full-on battery life while helping to preserve data integrity. The iSMM allows designers to add more features to their notebooks, such as a brighter display, a higher-resolution screen, and additional input devices and communications options. Alternatively, notebook computer manufacturers can take advantage of the lower power consumption by using smaller, lighter batteries to reduce the overall size and weight of their notebook computers.

Intel 80486 SX The Intel 486 SX microprocessor includes on-chip cache, memory management, and the same one-clock-per-instruction RISC integer core as the Intel DX and DX2 microprocessors. The difference is that the clock rates are generally slower than those of the Intel 486 DX central processing units (CPUs), and the math coprocessor is not integrated on the chip. A 25-megahertz (MHz) Intel 486 SX CPU can execute programs up to 70% faster than a 33-MHz Intel 386 DX microprocessor. In addition, members of the Intel 486 family can be upgraded by installing OverDrive upgrade processors. Compare **Intel 80486 DX**.

Intel 80387 A special numeric coprocessor designed to accompany the Intel 80387 microprocessor. See **coprocessor**.

Intel 80386 The microprocessor which was introduced in 1986 with a 32-bit data bus structure and the ability to directly address up to 4 gigabytes of random-access memory. A special mode enables the 80386 to access more than one program at a time (such as a word processor plus a spreadsheet program) by separating blocks of 640 kilobytes of memory to be used by DOS as required. The 80386 microprocessor was first made available in the Compaq Deskpro 386. Intel designate the letters DX (80386 DX) to this chip in order to distinguish it from the 80386 SX chip. Its 32-bit architecture provides the programming resources required to directly support 'large' applications — those characterized by large integers, large data structures, large programs (or large numbers of programs), and so on. The 80386's physical address space is 64 terabytes (2^{46} bytes). The 80386's eight 32-bit general registers can be used interchangeably both as 'instruction operands' and 'addressing mode' variables. Data types include 8, 16, and 32-bit integers and ordinals, packed and unpacked decimals, pointers, and strings of bits, bytes, words, and double-words. The 80386 has a complete set of instructions for manipulating these types, as well as for controlling execution. The 80386 addressing modes support efficient access to the elements of the standard data structures: arrays, records, arrays of records, and records containing arrays. Using 1.5-micron geometry and two metal layers, the 80386 packs over 275 000 transistors into a single chip. Both 12- and 16-megahertz (MHz) versions of the 80386 run without wait states, with the 16-MHz chips achieving sustained execution rates of 3 to 4 million instructions per second. Internally, the 80386 is partitioned into six units that operate autonomously and in parallel with each other, synchronizing as necessary. All the internal buses that connect these units are 32 bits wide. By pipelining its functional units, the 80386 can overlap the execution of different stages of one instruction and process multiple instructions simultaneously — while one instruction is executed, another is decoded, and a third is fetched from memory.

Intel 80386 SX The original Intel 80386 was designed to use a 32-bit data bus structure for internal and external communications. Although this made processing much faster, users complained that 32-bit peripherals (such as disk drives) were expensive to obtain. The SX version was introduced 20 June 1988 to take advantage of 32-bit internal processing, while restricting external communications to 16 bits — making it compatible with peripherals designed to operate on the 80286 microprocessor. The SX chip (much cheaper than the 80386) is available in clock speeds of 16 or 20 megahertz (MHz), while the 80386 comes in many clock speeds including 16, 20, 25, and 33 MHz. Although the SX can be outperformed by some 80286 chips, it can access up to 4 gigabytes of random-access memory (compared to 16 megabytes in the 80286), and operate 32-

bit software. The current list of 16-bit software available for the 80286 exceeds 15 000 different packages (which include Borland's Paradox/386, Microsoft's Windows/386, and Quarterdeck's DESQview/386) compared to several hundred 32-bit programs. The SX chips have been used successfully in notebook and laptop models by over 30 manufacturers, including Acer, ALR, Compaq, Dell, Hewlett-Packard, NCR, and NEC.

Intel 80287 A special numeric coprocessor designed to accompany the Intel 80286 microprocessor. See **coprocessor**.

Intel 80286 The microprocessor which was introduced in 1984 and used for the IBM Personal Computer AT. The 80286 microprocessor is still being used, requiring 16-bit peripherals. It can address up to 16 megabytes of random-access memory (RAM), although DOS can only use 640 kilobytes. The 80286 chip is available in clock speeds of 6, 8, 10, 12, 16, or 20 megahertz (MHz), while the 80386 comes in many clock speeds including 16, 20, 25, and 33 MHz. When it was introduced, the 80286 was a high-speed microprocessor which pushed microprocessor-based systems to new performance levels. However, this high-speed bus required special design considerations to utilize that performance. Interfacing the 80286 to a dynamic random-access memory (DRAM) array required many timings to be analyzed, such as refresh cycle effects on bus timing, and minimum and maximum signal widths. The 8207 advanced DRAM controller (ADRC) was specifically designed to solve all interfacing issues for the 80286, provide complete control and timing for the dynamic RAM array, and achieve optimum system performance.

This includes the normal RAM eight warm-up cycles, various refresh cycles and frequencies, address multiplexing, and address strobe timings.

Intel Pentium See **Pentium processor**.

intellectual property In most countries, any original literary, dramatic, musical, or artistic work is regarded by law as the intellectual property of the person who created the work (the author). By law, an original computer program is also defined as a literary work and its creator is defined as the author. All such work is usually protected by copyright. Generally, when the software purchaser signs a registration card (or the software is accompanied by a license agreement), the user has the copyright owner's permission to make one backup copy only (in case the original software disk malfunctions or is destroyed). In Australia, for example, any other copy made of the original software is an unauthorized copy and is considered by law to infringe the copyright. The making, distributing, selling, or hiring of an unauthorized copy is a criminal offense in most countries. See **software piracy**.

intelligent [ISO Pertaining to a device or a functional unit that is partially or totally controlled by one or more integral processors.]

intelligent agent Software components that are task-oriented with the capability of acting intelligently to a user's requirements by utilizing historical data to predict a user's needs and act independently or collectively to improve the responsiveness of a computer or telecommunication device in the areas of elec-tronic mail, network management, workflow systems, user interfaces, information retrieval, and data simulation. Intelligent agents are an extension of object-oriented software. They are deemed to be objects that have the capacity to think. Abbreviation 'IA'.

intelligent assistants See **expert systems**.

intelligent drive An integrated storage element, such as those provided by Digital Equipment Corporation (RFx models), which has some controller functionality built into the unit itself. These are called 'intelligent' drives because they perform self-diagnosis, command queuing, seek optimization, automatic on-board error detection and correction, and bad-block replacement, all without system or host adapter intervention. Most disk drives also include ancillary mechanisms, such as power, temperature, and speed regulation.

intelligent terminal A workstation consisting of keyboard and screen, used to input data to the computer or to receive information from the computer. The intelligent terminal still relies on the remote computer, but is able to process some data (as with point-of-sale terminals at supermarkets). See **workstation**.

Intelnet Refers to a digital data service designed for use with very small aperture terminals (VSATs) operating with a larger central hub station. See **Intelsat**.

Intelsat 1. International Telecommunications Satellite Consortium; an international organization formed in 1964 by 14 countries as a cooperative effort to provide a global communications network. It was first called 'Early Bird', but later changed its name to Intelsat. Currently, it has over 110 country-members, including Australia, Canada, Italy, France, Japan, the United Kingdom, the United States, and the Vatican. Also a member is the Communications Satellite Corporation (COMSAT) — a privately owned corporation established to launch and operate communications satellites in the United States. Transponders on Intelsat satellites have been sold to many countries since the inception of the Planned Domestic Service (PDS) program in 1985. These countries include Argentina, Chad, Chile, People's Republic of China, Ethiopia, Iran, Israel, Italy, Japan, Norway, Turkey, and the United States. 2. The name of the satellites launched by the International Telecommunications Satellite Consortium. The first, called 'Intelsat 1', was launched in October 1966 from Cape Canaveral, Florida. See **satellite transmission**.

Intelsat Business Service An Intelsat service that offers full-time private line service at transmission rates up to 8448 megabits per second. Over 9100 IBS channels operate to provide communications facilities including voice, data, video conferencing, facsimile, and telex. IBS can be provided through antennae as small as 11.48 foot (3.5 meters) located directly on customer premises over three ocean regions using more than 125 Earth stations.

Intel System Management Mode See **Intel 80486 SL**.

interactive Pertaining to the exchange of information and control between a user and a computer process. Interactive also refers to time-dependent (real-time) data communications, typically one in which a user enters data and then awaits a response message from the destination before continuing.

interactive processing The immediate processing of data at the time of entry; an application in which each entry elicits a response, as in an inquiry system or an airline reservation system. An interactive system may also be conversational, implying continuous dialogue between the user and the system.

interactive video The fusion of video and computer technology where a video program and a computer program can run in tandem under the control of the user, whose actions, choices, and decisions affect the way in which the program unfolds. Abbreviation 'IV'.

interactive video disk A video disk uses read-only optical storage media to store up to 50 000 still frames, or two hours of continuous television pictures or animation. These can be designed to interact with user commands, and are used as a tool for computer-aided instruction. Information on the disk can be accessed randomly. When coupled with a touch-screen, a video disk system can also be used as a sophisticated information retrieval system. For example, medical students can search particular topics relating to surgery, and be able to view a particular operation on disk. This may also be coupled with computer-prompted questions which lead the student through a gallery of exercises and tests.

interblock gap 1. Magnetic tape units spin reels at very high speeds so that, just like a motor car, the tape units need to slow down before coming to a halt. To cater for this, blanks are left between records or blocks. Once a high-speed search is completed, the magnetic reel gradually slows down. The gaps ensure that the desired data block is not accidentally passed, requiring a rewind. The gaps are called 'interblock gaps' (IBG) or 'interrecord gaps' (IRG). 2. [ISO The space between two consecutive blocks on a data medium.]

intercoupler A low-cost substitute for a modem, used on relatively short communication circuits where the distance is too great to operate modem-less. The circuit length is usually based upon speed, but will not normally exceed 5000 foot (1525 meters).

interface Any of the electrical and logical devices that permit computers and peripherals to be interconnected. The term is synonymous with 'port'. [ISO A shared boundary between two functional units, defined by functional characteristics, common physical interconnection characteristics, signal characteristics, and other characteristics, as appropriate. *Note:* The concept involves the specification of the connection of two devices having different functions.] ▼

interlace A scheme used to display a video image by displaying alternate scan lines in two discrete fields.

interlaced monitor A monitor that uses an interlaced scan technique which paints the screen by scanning every other line — first odd lines from top to bottom, then even lines. This can cause the monitor to flicker. By contrast, non-interlaced techniques refresh the screen by painting every line down the screen

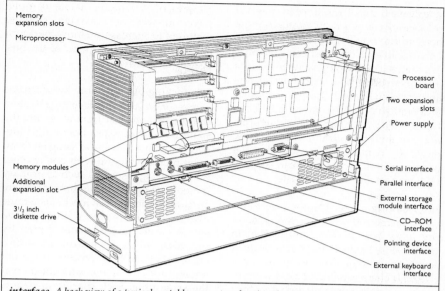

Memory
expansion slots

Microprocessor

Processor
board

Two expansion
slots

Power supply

Memory modules

Additional
expansion slot

Serial interface

Parallel interface

External storage
module interface

3¹/₂ inch
diskette drive

CD–ROM
interface

Pointing device
interface

External keyboard
interface

interface *A back view of a typical portable computer, showing the selection of interfaces.*

at up to 72 times every second. This process is determined by the video card.

interleave [ISO To arrange parts of one sequence of things or events so that they alternate with parts of one or more other sequences of the same nature, and so that each sequence retains its identity.]

interleaved memory A process of dividing the dynamic random-access memory (DRAM) chip into two separate areas of storage so that the microprocessor can alternate between storage areas, thereby speeding up the rate of data access. While one area is being read, the other is being refreshed. This process became popular because DRAM requires its contents to be updated at least every one-thousandth of a second. If this is not done, the capacitors used to represent

memory-states would very quickly lose their electrical charge. However, the introduction of static random-access memory (SRAM) eliminated the need for interleaved memory because SRAM chips can retain their contents until the power is switched off. See **RAM**.

Interleaved 2 of 5 See **Interleaved Two of Five**.

Interleaved Two of Five A numeric bar code system adopted by the American National Standards Institute in 1983, and used for industrial applications such as labeling outer shipping containers. It is also popular in the automotive and paper products industries. Two of Five means that of a five-bar code, two bars (either black or white) must be larger than the rest. Abbreviation 'ITF'. See **bar code**.

interleave factor The ratio of the number of sectors traversed by a read/write head to the number of sectors written. For example, if the interleave factor is 5:1, then the disk would write to the first available sector then skip four sectors and write on the fifth, then skip another four, and so on. Although an interleave factor of 1:1 is optimal, manufacturers may set a higher ratio in order to slow down the data flow to ensure that the computer or disk controller can keep up with the fast rate of data transfer.

interleaving A technique used to increase memory throughput. Many memory array boards store information in two or more banks. A bank is basically a set of dynamic random-access memory (DRAM) chips capable of producing or storing a single word unit each time they are accessed in tandem. One of the advantages of configuring memory into banks and array modules is that special memory optimization techniques can be used to overlap the access times to each bank and/or module. Consecutive addresses are stored in different memory array modules, and/or separate banks on the same module. For example, if two memory modules are used to store addresses A, B, C, and D, then addresses A and C will be in module 1, with B and D in module 2. When reading or writing addresses A through D, it is possible to overlap portions of the access times to one memory module with the data transfer times of the other module. Overlapping such operations results in a faster, more continuous flow of data. Interleaving between two memory modules or banks is called 'two-way interleaving', which can increase memory performance by as much as 66%. If more memory modules or banks

are present, it is often possible to implement four-way (or greater) interleaving methods to increase memory performance to the saturation point of the bus. See **sector interleaving**.

interlocking A mechanism by which one processor in a multiprocessing system can prevent another from accessing the same data. Processors operating independently in a multiprocessing environment must cooperate with one another when sharing resources such as primary memory. When multiple processors are executing a program, a mechanism must exist to control a sequence where processor 'A' waits to read data written by processor 'B'. A mechanism must also ensure that multiple processors do not attempt to write to the same location at the same time. Such sharing of data is made possible by interlocking. An interlock allows a processor to lock out other processors while accessing shared data. A processor needing to modify a portion of memory, for example, will issue an interlock instruction to gain exclusive access to primary memory, or that portion of primary memory. No other processor will be able to access the memory resources until the processor that issued the lock unlocks it.

intermediate equipment [ISO Auxiliary equipment that may be inserted between the data terminal equipment and the signal conversion equipment to perform certain additional functions before modulation or after demodulation.]

intermediate language [ISO A language into which a source program or statement is translated before it is further translated or interpreted.]

intermediate node [ISO A node that is at the ends of more than one branch.]

inter-modulation This occurs when two or more modulated signals interfere with each other on the same channel. Inter-modulation mainly occurs in wideband and audio circuits. This is also known as 'cross-modulation'. See **modulation**.

internal architecture Refers to how many bits of data can be processed (at a time) internally by the microprocessor. This has no relationship to the bus width, but rather to the size of registers.

internal hard disk A hard disk which is housed inside a computer, operating on the computer's own power supply. In contrast, an external hard disk is one equipped with its own power supply, casing, and cables — used primarily as a portable unit. Since the introduction of 'removable' hard disk cartridges capable of storing large amounts of data, external hard disks have been losing their popularity. See **Bernoulli box** and **hard disk**. Compare **external hard disk**.

internal label 1. [ISO A machine-readable label, recorded on a data medium, that provides information about data recorded on the medium.] 2. See **magnetic tape**.

internal modem A modem designed to fit inside the casing of a computer. The use of internal modems has become popular since the introduction of the notebook computer. See **modem**. ▼

internal modem *This photograph shows the relative size of a 2400-baud internal modem designed for a notebook computer. It supports standard communications protocols, standard data compression, error control, synchronous communication, pulse or tone dialing, full duplex, and automatic answering. The internal modem can communicate with other personal computers, mainframes, or outside services over telephone lines.*

internal reports Computer-generated reports produced for internal personnel only. Often these reports are of low quality, and are highly confidential.

internal storage 1. [ISO Storage that is accessible by a processor without the use of input/output channels. *Note:* Internal storage may include other kinds of storage such as cache memory and registers.] 2. See **primary storage**.

International Business Machines See **IBM**.

International Computers Limited See **ICL**.

International Electrotechnical Commission See **IEC**.

International Frequency Registration Board See **IFRB**.

International Organization for Standardization See **ISO**.

international record carriers Organizations which provide lines for transporting data communications between countries through 'gateway' facilities. The common carrier lines connect to the International Record Carrier (IRC) lines at the gateway points. In the United States, the major IRCs are International Telephone and Telegraph (ITT), Western Union International (WUI), and RCA Globecon.

international standards organization See **ISO**.

International Telecommunications Satellite Consortium See **Intelsat**.

International Telecommunications Union See **ITU**.

Internet The world's largest interconnected computer environment. It consists of millions of computers and tens of millions of users. Established in the early 1970s by the United States defense departments, Internet became popular in 1994 after the introduction of graphical user interfaces and improved content suitable for the general public.

interoperability The ability of different-vendor devices to transmit data and exchange information, while having the total capability to process and act upon such information independently. This relies heavily on international standards. See **ISO** and **OSI**.

interpolation In video technology, the process of averaging pixel information when scaling an image. When the size of an image is reduced, pixels are averaged to create a single new pixel; when an image is scaled up in size, additional pixels are created by averaging pixels of the smaller image.

interpreter 1. A programming language translator that converts source (high-level) language statements into machine code. Unlike a compiler which translates the complete program before any execution takes place, an interpreter converts then immediately executes each statement, line by line. 2. [ISO A computer program that can interpret.] 3. [ISO A device that prints on a punched card the characters corresponding to hole patterns punched in the card.] The word 'interpreter' comes from the Latin word *interpretari*, meaning 'explain'.

interrecord gap 1. Magnetic tape units spin reels at very high speeds so that, just like a motor car, the tape units need to slow down before coming to a halt. To cater for this, blanks are left between records or blocks. Once a high-speed search is completed, the magnetic reel gradually slows down. The gaps ensure that the desired data block is not accidentally passed, requiring a rewind. The gaps are called 'interrecord gaps' (IRG) or 'interblock gaps' (IBG). 2. [ISO The space between two consecutive records on a data medium.]

interrogating [ISO The process whereby a master station requests a slave station to indicate its identity or its status.]

interrupt A momentary suspension of processing caused by a deliberate instruction to the microprocessor. This is usually done so that certain input or output operations can take place. The source of an interrupt is usually external to the central processor. One of the important areas to examine when comparing bus structures is the handling of interrupt requests. These are hardware signals that are generated by an input/output device or controller to command the immediate attention of the central processing unit (CPU). For example, if a modem receives a certain character, an interrupt request is sent over the respective bus line, immediately drawing the CPU's attention. After the CPU takes care of the request, it resumes its normal work exactly where it left off. In this way the received character is processed quickly, without waiting until the end of an executing program. The original PC bus uses six interrupt request (IRQ) lines. Although the data and address lines are shared, the IRQ lines are not. Each is uniquely assigned to one device, such as a disk drive or a modem. As long as every device has its own line,

this signaling method presents no problems. However, if two boards attempt to share the same interrupt line, then errors, lost or garbled data, or system lock-up may occur. For this reason, some boards for the PC bus have switches which allow different IRQ lines to be selected. If this is not the case, and two boards are in conflict, then only one of the devices can be installed in the system at a time. The AT bus uses eleven interrupt request lines. This is five more than the PC bus, and so offers more room for add-on devices without interrupt conflicts. As with the PC bus, interrupt signals on the AT bus are edge triggered, meaning that a changing voltage level signals an interrupt. This presents a problem, in that the interrupt lines are susceptible to electrical interference in the form of noise spikes. In certain circumstances, such noise spikes can cause system lock-up. To avoid this problem, Micro Channel Architecture uses 'level sensitive' interrupt lines. This means that instead of using a changing voltage to signal an interrupt, the presence of a stable voltage is used. All devices sharing an interrupt know when it is active by examining the voltage on the line. The Extended Industry Standard Architecture (EISA) acknowledges the superiority of the level sensitive scheme while maintaining compatibility with existing expansion boards that use edge triggered interrupts. Each interrupt line in an EISA bus is individually programmable to be either edge triggered or level sensitive. During the configuration process for an expansion board, the type of interrupt signaling must be specified. [ISO A suspension of a process, such as the execution of a computer program, caused by an event external to that process, and performed in such a way that the process can be resumed.]

interrupt register [ISO A special-purpose register that holds data necessary for handling interrupts.]

interrupt vector [ISO An address held in a special-purpose register or in memory that indicates the instruction to be executed on acceptance of the associated interrupt. *Note:* The term 'interrupt vector' has also been used to describe an array of interrupt vectors that may be indexed.]

interval timer [ISO A device which, upon the lapse of a specified length of time, generates an interrupt signal.]

inverter [ISO A functional unit whose output analog variable is equal in magnitude to its input analog variable but is of opposite algebraic sign.]

I/O See **input/output**.

I/O address space See **addressable memory**.

IOC Integrated optical circuit; a circuit built on a semiconductor or transparent dielectric substrate, used for signal processing in optoelectronic devices. IOCs may consist of optical, electrical, electro-optic, or optoelectronic solid-state components. Within each circuit are logic gates, differential amplifiers, photodetectors, optical filters, memories, and thin-film optical wave-guides. IOCs should not be confused with optoelectronic integrated circuits (OEIC), which combine both optical and electronic systems, including electromagnetic systems. See **optical neurocomputer**.

I/O port Input/output port; a port on a computer to which devices such as keyboards, bar code readers, mice (input), printers, and monitors (output) are connected via cables. These can have either serial or parallel paths of transmission.

IPL Initial program load. Each time a computer is switched on, it must go through a formal loading (initializing) procedure known as 'booting' or 'initial program load'. This occurs when the computer's operating system is installed. A section of this software also allows the computer to communicate with the user. See **boot**.

IPM Manager InterProgram Messaging Manager. On the Apple Macintosh family of computers, the IPM Manager complements the System 7 interapplication communications (IAC) architecture that provides real-time program-to-program communications. IPM provides store-and-forward message delivery between applications, allowing messages to be stored for delivery whenever the recipient is ready to receive them. Messages can be exchanged between applications on one computer or across a network, regardless of whether the sender and receiver are available at the same time. In addition, one message can be sent to multiple destinations. With the addition of appropriate messaging services access modules, messages can be sent over any type of message transport, such as SMTP, MHS, cc:Mail, or X.400.

IR 1. Industry Remarketer. 2. Information retrieval. 3. Infrared; the electromagnetic radiation situated beyond the red end of the visible spectrum. This involves wavelengths longer than those of visible light.

iRAM Integrated random-access memory. A microchip that integrates a dynamic RAM (DRAM) and its control and refresh circuits on one substrate, creating a chip that has DRAM density characteristics, but looks like, and operates like, a static RAM chip. Before iRAM's introduction, users who built memory blocks smaller than 8 kilobytes typically used static RAMs, because the device's higher price was offset by the support-circuit simplicity. On the other hand, users building blocks larger than 64 kilobytes usually opted for DRAMs, because density and power considerations began to take precedence over circuit complexity issues. For the application area between these two limits, iRAMs were ideal. See **RAM**.

IRAM Instituto Argentinto de Racionalización de Materiales; Argentina's standards body formed in 1935.

IRC 1. Information retrieval center. 2. International record carrier. IRCs provide lines for transporting data communications between countries through 'gateway' facilities. The common carrier lines connect to the IRC lines at the gateway points. In the United States, the major IRCs are International Telephone and Telegraph (ITT), Western Union International (WUI), and RCA Globecon.

IRG See **interrecord gap**.

IRQ Interrupt request lines; the lines that carry hardware interrupt signals to the processor on a personal computer.

irrational number A number which is not expressible as an integer or a ratio of two integers. [ISO A real number that is not a rational number.]

IS 1. Indexed sequence. 2. Information system.

ISA Industry Standard Architecture; an architecture that evolved from the expansion bus found in the IBM PC, and first implemented in the IBM PC/AT. This bus was designed to support a system based on a single microprocessor located on the system board. All programs to be executed are executed by the system board microprocessor, and all input/output devices are controlled by the same microprocessor. Although the ISA bus was not designed to support bus masters other than the system board microprocessor, bus master expansion cards can be implemented using three of the DMA channels. The ISA bus was designed to support transactions, or bus cycles, of a relatively low frequency. The maximum limit was 8.33 megahertz. Compare **EISA**.

ISAM Indexed sequential access method. See **sequential access**.

ISDN Integrated Services Digital Network; a special kind of telecommunications network designed to handle more than just data. Using existing telephone lines and computer networks, integrated networks can handle video, text, voice, data, facsimile images, graphics, and the like. The ISDN program commenced in 1985; guided by the International Telecommunication Union, based in Geneva. It was developed by the joint efforts of multinational companies. Once completed, ISDN will allow individuals to have personal telephone numbers which will remain valid for a lifetime — no matter where they are around the world. Using sophisticated computer databases, ISDN could also be used, for example, to access the nearest Regent Hotel, simply by dialing R-E-G-E-N-T from anywhere around the world. The high-speed communications will also dramatically improve the speed (up to 200 times faster) and quality of videotext online services, providing international information at the fingertip of subscribers. ISDN is based on a set of CCITT recommendations which were aimed at providing standardized end-to-end digital communications for a wide range of services. An important aspect of the integration of services is the development of a standard set of user interfaces. Within ISDN, all signals created by a user terminal will be transmitted over a single subscriber access line in digital form. Through these interfaces, users will have a common means of selecting particular communications services ISDN channels will be labeled by 'type', where type D will offer the lowest bit rate packet-switched network at 16 kilobits per second for applications such as ISDN information signaling, and low-speed user data transmission. Type-H12 operates at a bit rate of 1.92 megabits per second for circuit-switched fast facsimile, video, and high-speed data transmission. In February of 1897, the Professor of Physics at the Central College in London, William Ayrton, made the following prediction during an address on submarine telegraphy: 'There is no doubt that the day will come, maybe when you and I are forgotten, when copper wires, gutta percha coverings, and iron sheathings will be relegated to the Museum of Antiquities. Then, when a person wants to telegraph to a friend he knows not where, he will call in an electromagnetic voice, which will be heard loud by him who has the electromagnetic ear, but will be silent to everyone else. He will

call "Where are you?" and the reply will come "I am at the bottom of the coal mine" or "Crossing the Andes" or "In the middle of the Pacific"; or perhaps no reply will come at all, and he may then conclude that his friend is dead.'

ISIRI Institute of Standards and Industrial Research of Iran; Iran's standards body formed in 1965.

ISIS Intelligent Scheduling and Information System. An expert system introduced in 1980 to help resolve common problems associated with manufacturing operations. Pronounced '<u>eye</u>-siss'.

iSMM Intel System Management Mode. See **Intel 80486 SL**.

ISO International Organization for Standardization; a worldwide federation of national standards bodies whose objective is to promote the development of standardization and related activities in over 90 countries, with a view to facilitating international exchange of goods and services. It also helps to develop co-operation in the spheres of intellectual, scientific, technological, and economic activity. ISO has published approximately 8000 international standards for industry-wide application. They are technical documents containing the basic information on the essentials of design, safety, testing, quality, and communication. The introduction of ISO dates back to 14 October 1946 when 64 delegates from 25 countries met in London to discuss the need to establish an international body. On 24 October, the first General Assembly of ISO was held in London to outline the Constitution and Rules of Procedure. ISO is made up of members who are themselves national standards bodies for the countries they represent. Annual subscription and membership fees vary for each country, depending upon their level of involvement. The detailed work of standardization for technology and science is undertaken by Technical Committees. Standards relating to electrical and electronic engineering are handled by ISO's partner organization, the International Electrotechnical Commission which was formed in 1906. Note that

ISO cannot be pronounced 'eye-ess-oh' because it is not a direct abbreviation of the full wording in any of the organization's official languages (English, French, and Russian). Coincidentially, ISO is a contraction of the Greek word *isos* which means 'equal to' or 'the same as', from which one can arrive via 'uniform' to 'standard'. Pronounced 'eye-so'. European pronunciation 'ee-zor'. See **metric system** and **SI**. ▼

Standards body	Country	Year of entry to ISO	Standards body	Country	Year of entry to ISO
ABNT	Brazil	1947	KCSA	Albania	1974
AENOR	Spain	1951	KEBS	Kenya	1976
AFNOR	France	1947	MSSB	Mongolia	1979
ANSI	USA	1947	MSZH	Hungary	1947
ASMW	Germany	1988	NC	Cuba	1962
BDS	Bulgaria	1955	NNI	Netherlands	1947
BIS	India	1947	NSAI	Ireland	1951
BPS	Philippines	1968	NSF	Norway	1947
BSI	United Kingdom	1947	ON	Austria	1947
BSTI	Bangladesh	1974	PKNMiJ	Poland	1947
COSQC	Iraq	1964	PNGS	PNG	1984
COVENIN	Venezuela	1959	PSI	Pakistan	1951
CSBS	China	1978	SAA	Australia	1947
CSK	Korea	1963	SABS	South Africa	1947
CSN	Czechoslovakia	1947	SANZ	New Zealand	1947
CYN	Cyprus	1979	SASMO	Syria	1981
DENT	Ivory Coast	1978	SASCO	Saudi Arabia	1974
DGN	Mexico	1947	SCC	Canada	1947
DIN	Germany	1951	SFS	Finland	1947
DS	Denmark	1947	SII	Israel	1947
DSN	Indonesia	1954	SIRIM	Malaysia	1969
ELOT	Greece	1955	SIS	Sweden	1947
EOS	Egypt	1957	SISIR	Singapore	1966
ESA	Ethiopia	1972	SLSI	Sri Lanka	1967
GSB	Ghana	1966	SNIMA	Morocco	1988
IBN	Belgium	1947	SNV	Switzerland	1947
ICONTEC	Colombia	1960	SON	Nigeria	1972
INAPI	Algeria	1976	SSD	Sudan	1973
INN	Chile	1947	SZS	Yugoslavia	1950
INNORPI	Tunisia	1984	TBS	Tanzania	1979
IPQ	Portugal	1949	TCVN	Vietnam	1977
IRAM	Argentina	1983	TISI	Thailand	1966
ISIRI	Iran	1960	TSE	Turkey	1956
INTINEC	Peru	1962	TTBS	Trinidad	1980
JBS	Jamaica	1974	UNI	Italy	1947
JISC	Japan	1952	ZABS	Zambia	1984
KBS	Korea	1963			

ISO *ISO member bodies listed in order of approved short name.*

isochronous transmission [ISO A data transmission process in which there is always an integral number of unit intervals between any two significant instants.]

isolated amplifier [ISO An amplifier with-out an electrical connection between the signal circuit and all other circuits, including ground.]

isolation In transaction processing, a database transaction management system is said to provide integrity of operation and data when the transaction passes the ACID (atomicity, consistency, isolation, durability) test. A transaction has 'isolation' if it is processed concurrently with other transactions and still behaves as if it were the only transaction executing in the system. Transactions must not interfere with each other's database updates. See **ACID test** and **transaction processing**.

ISONET International Organization for Standardization Network; the information network through which ISO coordinates the exchange of information on international and national standards, technical regulations, and other standards-type documents, and which links the ISO and International Electrotechnical Commission's information center in Geneva with similar centers in approximately 60 countries. See **ISO**.

ISR Information storage and retrieval.

Israeli virus A variant of the Jerusalem virus. See **Jerusalem virus**.

ISSN International Standard Serial Number.

ISV Independent software vendor.

IT Pronounced 'eye-tea'. See **information technology**.

Italian virus A boot-sector virus that infects the boot sector of any diskette which has been write-enabled, or hard disk of any computer using some of the earlier Intel microprocessors. Its presence can be detected by a dot that bounces all over the screen. When a Chkdsk (a DOS disk checking utility) is run, 1 kilobyte of sectors is shown to be bad. Italian was first reported in Turin, Italy, and it is sometimes called 'Ping Pong' or 'Bouncing Ball'. Another similar virus is called 'Big Italian'. It has a large diamond that bounces all over the screen, infecting the boot sectors of diskettes and hard disks (including those of Intel 80286 and 80386 computers). See **boot-sector virus**.

italic In typography, a typeface which slants to the right. With the introduction of sophisticated typesetters, type can be manipulated electronically so that slanting to either the left or right can be achieved with exacting controls. Technically speaking, an italic version of a typeface is not just a slanted version, because the designer of the typeface may have introduced specific characteristics to the typeface which warrant it being called 'italic'. Simply slanting any typeface electronically does not generally constitute an original italic. Designed initially in the Renaissance by Aldus Manutius, italicized typefaces were intended to appear similar to handwriting.

ITC International Typeface Corporation.

ITC Avant Garde See **Avant Garde**.

ITC Bookman See **Bookman**.

ITC Zapf Chancery See **Zapf Chancery**.

ITC Zapf Dingbats See **Zapf Dingbats**.

iteration A program technique that permits a sequence of commands to repeat several times. Iterations are sometimes called 'loops'. The word 'iteration' comes from the Latin word *iterare*, meaning 'to repeat'.

iteration control See **structured flowchart**.

iterative operation [ISO The repetition of the algorithm for the solution of a set of equations with successive combinations of initial conditions or other parameters; each successive combination is selected by a subsidiary computation based upon a predetermined set of iteration rules. *Note:* Iterative operation is usually used to permit solution of boundary value problems or for automatic optimization of system parameters.]

ITF Interleaved Two of Five. A numeric bar code system adopted by the American National Standards Institute in 1983, and used for industrial applications such as labeling outer shipping containers. It is also popular in the automotive and paper products industries. Two of Five means that of a five-bar code, two bars (either black or white) must be larger than the rest. See **bar code**.

i-time Instruction time. When the central processor executes a computer program, the control unit receives an instruction, examines it, and then gives control to the arithmetic/logic unit. Instruction time is part of the machine cycle. Compare **e-time**.

ITP Internet Transport Protocols; communications protocols underlying Xerox's proprietary network architecture.

ITU International Telecommunications Union; a United Nations agency that is headquartered in Switzerland. The ITU has three permanent groups: The International Frequency Registration Board (IFRB), which regulates the allocation of radio frequencies; the Consultative Committee on International Radio (CCIR), which deals with the coordination of long distance radio telecommunications; and the Consultative Committee on International Telegraphy and Telephony (CCITT), which is the primary group responsible for the development of standards for telephone and data communication systems among participating governments.

ITV Interactive television.

IV See **interactive video**.

IVIA Interactive Video Industry Association.

jabber A malfunction on a network involving the continuous transmission of random data. [ISO A transmission by a data station beyond the time interval allowed by the protocol.]

jabber control [ISO In a local area network, the ability of a medium attachment unit to automatically interrupt transmission in order to inhibit an abnormally-long output data stream.]

Jacquard, Joseph-Marie A Frenchman who in 1790 sought to automate the repetitious work of weavers working on looms. In 1805, after military service during the French Revolution, he had perfected an automatic looming machine which used a stiff card with a series of holes punched in it. The card blocked certain needles from lifting certain threads, making it possible to weave complex patterns with speed and accuracy. Like most new forms of automation, the Jacquard loom met with hostility from workers, who feared for their jobs. This punched-card system inspired Charles Babbage to develop the world's first digital computer, called the 'Analytical Engine'. In the weaving industry, 'jacquarding' is the term used when referring to 'woven towels' or 'woven mats'. Jacquard was born in 1752, and died in 1834. See **Babbage, Charles**.

jacquarding See **Jacquard, Joseph-Marie**.

jaggies The rough or jagged edges which undesirably appear around images on the screen when using computer-generated graphics packages. Jaggies are especially noticeable when a diagonal line is drawn, showing a stepped (staircase) appearance. The automatic reduction or removal of the jagged edges is called 'anti-aliasing'.

jam signal [ISO The signal sent by a data station to inform the other data stations that they must not transmit.

Notes: (a) In CSMA/CD networks, the jam signal indicates that a collision has occurred. (b) In CSMA/CA networks, the jam signal indicates that the sending data station intends to transmit.]

JBS Jamaica Bureau of Standards; Jamaica's standards body formed in 1968.

JCF Job control file. See **job control language**.

JCL See **job control language**.

JCS Job control statement. See **job control language**.

JEIDA Japan Electronic Industry Development Association.

Jerusalem virus An indirect-action file virus that adds approximately 1800 bytes to any .COM file or .EXE file. First activated in Jerusalem in 1988, this virus spreads without detection until the date in the computer reaches Friday 13th of any month. Once active, it deletes any program which is called and slows down the operation of the computer to approximately 25% of its normal speed. Sometimes, the Jerusalem virus is detected before it activates, because it adds approximately 1800 bytes to each .EXE file every time that file is called up. This often leads to the growth of the .EXE file to the point where it gets too large to be loaded into memory. Many viruses have been modeled around the Jerusalem virus, making it one of the most prevalent in the United States and the United Kingdom. Jerusalem is sometimes called 'Hebrew University', 'Israeli', or 'Friday 13th'. See **indirect-action file virus**.

JES Job Entry Subsystem; a control protocol and procedure for directing host processing of a task in an IBM host environment.

JISC Japanese Industrial Standards Committee; Japan's standards body formed in 1949.

job Generally, a batch of commands ready to be processed by the computer, independently of human intervention. This term is especially used in mainframe environments where the user would not have direct access to the computer, but would submit work (jobs) to be processed by the mainframe. [ISO A unit of work that is defined by a user and that is to be accomplished by a computer.]

job control file See **job control language**.

job control language A series of commands intended to control a particular job or program within a mainframe computer (typically IBM). A user-command is any instruction issued to the computer by the user, such as 'find file', 'open file', 'sort file', 'print file', and 'close file'. Each line of instruction is called a 'job control statement', and these appear in a specific order so that the computer is able to process information in batches. If such information is issued on a regular basis, the commands may be stored in a 'job control file'. Also called 'command language'. Abbreviation 'JCL'.

job control statement See **job control language**.

Job Entry Subsystem A control protocol and procedure for directing host processing of a task in an IBM host environment. Abbreviation 'JES'.

job queue A list of jobs waiting to be processed by the computer, stacked in order depending upon the priority assigned to each (job), ready for processing. During the late 1950s, a job queue was literally a queue of programmers who would line up until mainframe operators could attend to their processing needs.

Jobs, Steven P. Born 24 February 1955, Steven P. Jobs was the former employee of Atari who left to pioneer the Apple Computer with Stephen Wozniak (former employee of Hewlett-Packard) in 1976. Jobs joined Atari in 1972 to design video games. He was a member of the Homebrew Computer Club, a place where a group of electronic enthusiasts met to exchange ideas on computer hobbies and hacking. It was there that Jobs met Wozniak, an engineer and computer wizard at Hewlett-Packard. At that time, Wozniak was working on a small computer for which Jobs could see commercial potential. Together they raised US$1350 and started to produce computers in kit form for hobbyists. Jobs later met A.C. 'Mike' Markkula, a former Intel marketing manager who became involved in the Apple company, personally investing US$91 000 and securing other capital. Steve Jobs later recruited John Sculley (the former Chief Executive Officer of PepsiCo) to head Apple Computer Corporation. As Apple's Chairman, Jobs oversaw the growth of Apple into a US$2000 million company. Jobs co-designed the Apple II and later led the development of the Macintosh and the subsequent growth of the Macintosh division into a US$1000

Jobs, Steven P. At the age of 21, Steven Jobs sold his VW van, and his partner (Wozniak) sold his Hewlett-Packard programmable calculator, raising US$1350 to finance production of the Apple I boards which sold in July 1976 for US$666.66. In 1985, Jobs formed NeXT Computer Inc.

million organization. He was responsible for the LaserWriter and its implementation of PostScript, which helped to create the desktop publishing industry. His last position at Apple was that of Chairman and Executive Vice President, and General Manager of the Macintosh Division. After internal conflict in 1985, Jobs left Apple. In September of that year, he and five other colleagues founded a new computer organization, manufacturing a range of computers called 'NeXT computers'. In September 1989, the privately-held company began shipping the NeXT computer with system software through selected retail and value-added retail channels in North America, Asia, and Europe. Jobs is also a director and part-owner of Pixar, a San Rafael, California company that develops and markets technologically-advanced photo-realistic software with many graphic arts, computer-aided design, and scientific applications. In recognition of his pioneering work in technology, he was awarded the National Technology Medal by President Reagan in February 1985, and the Jefferson Award for Public Service in 1987. In 1989 he was named Entrepreneur of the Decade by *Inc.* magazine. See **NeXT Computer, Inc.** ⚑

job stream [ISO The sequence of representations of jobs, or parts of jobs, to be performed, as submitted to an operating system.]

join 1. In a relational database management program, to link several items of information to form a new data file, even though they each reside on different databases. For example, in a library book tracking program, a report can be generated to list all children's books, and another to list all children members. The two databases can be joined to report on children members who have overdue books. 2. In DOS and OS/2, a command used to connect a directory on one disk drive to a different disk drive.

Josephson junction A type of chip technology used in place of silicon because it can process binary digits up to ten times faster than current chips. Josephson junctions can operate at temperatures nearing absolute zero, diminishing the heat associated with high-speed electron flow. In the 1980s, after manufacturers in the United States abandoned research and development in this technology, the Japanese found Josephson junctions useful for the Fifth-

Generation Project because this technology offers extremely high-speed circuit switching. Josephson junctions were named in honor of Nobel Prize winner and British researcher Brian Josephson. See **silicon.**

journal [ISO A chronological record of data processing operations. *Note:* The journal may be used to reconstruct a previous or an updated version of a file.]

journaling backup A backup which records only the differences between a baseline version of a file and an updated version, unlike an incremental backup in which the volume's structure is scanned for all files created or modified since the date of the last backup (copying only those that have changed). This mode of backup (also known as a 'differential backup') is most useful in applications which make relatively small numbers of random changes to large files. See **backup.**

joystick An input device commonly used with computer games and professional applications, consisting of a small base unit to which is attached a rod that can be tilted in all directions to move a cursor or a graphics item on the screen. [ISO A lever with at least two degrees of

---

NEWSFLASH

The estimated value of the category of intelligent draw and illustration software market for the Macintosh environments in 1992 was US$80.1 million.

In 1997, the Windows and Macintosh environments will be US$121.4 million of this category alone.

freedom, that is used as an input device, normally as a locator.]

JPEG Joint Photographic Expert Group; the name of the ISO committee working on standardizing the color still image coding system to offer high-quality single-picture spatial compression. Pronounced 'jay-peg'.

JTAG Joint Test Action Group; formed in Europe in 1985 to develop economical test methodologies for systems designed around complex integrated circuits and assembled with surface-mount technologies. JTAG grew to become an international body, and its members include representatives of computer and semiconductor manufacturers, universities, and the United States Department of Defense. After JTAG conferees developed a specification for a four-wire serial scan test bus, the IEEE 1149 Test Standard Committee adopted the specifications. JTAG/IEEE 1149.1 standard is also a standard of the American National Standards Institute.

jukebox See **optical libraries**.

jump [ISO A departure from the sequential execution of instructions.]

jumper A small plastic-covered metal connector used to connect pairs of pins on computer circuit boards. This is done to alter settings such as addressing.

jump instruction [ISO An instruction that specifies a jump.]

justification In typesetting, the placing of spaces between words or characters so that each line is exactly the same length. Although this leads to a neater looking page, especially when using narrow columns (as used for this book), justified columns may be difficult to read because inter-word and inter-character spacing may vary on each line, and because of increased hyphenation at the end of lines. Compare **flush left** and **flush right**. ▼

justify [ISO To shift the contents of a register so that the character at the specified end of the data is at a particular register position.]

The term 'user-friendly', and what we expect it to mean in relation to computers, is symptomatic of our society's problems. In other words, when people expect computers to be user-friendly, they lobby technologists to move away from decisive, accurate machines in favor of wishy-washy, near enough is good enough, kind of attitude.

Odds-on that a thesis into the habits of those who dislike the rigidity of computers would reveal that they are the very folk who do not always stop at a stop sign, or who, on occasion, change lanes without indicating.

justification An example of text set justified (both left and right). This form of typesetting is typically used for newspapers and newsletters, in order to give them a neat appearance. Some tests have shown that readers prefer text that is set flush left, because justified text does not offer uniform inter-word spacing. To a greater degree, type that is too large often poses problems with inter-word spacing.

THE MORE THAT YOU KNOW,
THE MORE LIKELY IT IS
THAT OTHERS WILL IRRITATE YOU

k Kilo-. An SI unit prefix for 10^3 expressed as 1000 in decimal notation. In computing, it refers to 2^{10} (which equals 1024), expressing the capacity of storage. The prefix 'kilo' comes from the Greek word *khilioi*, meaning 'thousand'. See **metric system** and **SI**.

K Kelvin. An SI unit of thermodynamic temperature. It was agreed in 1954 at the Conférence Générale that the value 273.16 kelvin be assigned to the thermodynamic temperature at the triple point of water. See **metric system** and **SI**.

Karnaugh map [ISO A rectangular diagram of a logic function of variables drawn with overlapping sub-rectangles such that each intersection of overlapping rectangles represents a unique combination of the logic variables and such that an intersection is shown for all combinations.]

kb Kilobyte. In computing, it refers to 2^{10} bytes (which equals 1024), and is mainly used to express the capacity of storage. When used as a plural, an 's' is not added. For example, '256 kb', not '256 kbs'. See **byte**.

kB Kilobit. In computing, it refers to 2^{10} bits (which equals 1024), and is mainly used to express the speed of data transmission. See **bit**.

KB See **keyboard**.

kbps Kilobyte per second. In computing, it refers to 2^{10} bps (which equals 1024), and is mainly used to express the speed of data transmission. When used as a plural, an 's' is not added. For example, '64 kbps'. See **byte**.

kBps Kilobit per second. In computing, it refers to 2^{10} Bps (which equals 1024), and is mainly used to express the speed of data transmission. When used as a plural, an 's' is not added. For example, '64 kBps'. See **bit**.

KEBS Kenya Bureau of Standards; Kenya's standards body formed in 1973.

kelvin See **K**.

Kermit 1. A public domain communications program designed in 1981 by Columbia University, in the United States, to use an asynchronous communications protocol. 2. An asynchronous communications protocol used for the transmission of files via the public telephone network — especially with mainframe systems that use seven bits per byte.

kernel A set of essential operating routines used by the operating system (usually hidden from the user) to perform important system tasks, such as managing the system memory or controlling disk operations.

kerning In typography, the process of reducing space between certain character pairs which would normally seem badly spaced. Some page layout and word processing programs kern characters automatically. Characters typically requiring kerning are the capital pairs AW, WA, VA, and the like. The word 'kern' comes from the French word *charne*, meaning 'hinge'. ▼

key 1. A field of data stored on a magnetic tape or disk, containing a unique identifier. For example, a student number may serve as the record key for a student's record. When records are being searched, the key can be used so that not all the data on the tape/disk is read unnecessarily. 2. A common metal key

TAKE YOUR WORLD AWAY
NO KERNING

TAKE YOUR WORLD AWAY
WITH KERNING

HERE IN THE TIN
NO KERNING

HERE IN THE TIN
WITH KERNING

kerning To *kern* between characters does not necessarily mean that space is taken out. In some cases, well-kerned type has been achieved by placing extra space between characters. Sophisticated typesetting programs contain software which stores a database of 'kerning pairs'. These are combinations of pairs that often need extra attention, such as the A and W (AW) in some fonts.

used to lock the computer, preventing unauthorized access. 3. A set of symbols which form a code, as used on maps and diagrams. For example, wavy lines on a map may depict water, so the key will show a wavy line and have the word 'water' written beside it. 4. Any of the buttons on a keyboard. See **keyboard**. 5. A set of characters or a hardware device used to secure a program from unauthorized use. 6. [ISO An identifier within a set of data elements.]

keyboard An input device consisting of a set of keys in a standard layout. Symbols such as letters or numbers can be entered into a computer by placing pressure on the keys. A keyboard is usually not attached to a screen except via the computer, and signals are sent to the processing unit and echoed back in the form of a character on the screen. A keyboard can be thought of as a grid of horizontal and vertical scan lines with a keyboard switch at each intersection. The keyboard electronics constantly scans the grid to determine if a key is pressed. If a key press is detected, an interrupt is sent to the processor. Once the processor responds to the interrupt, the key-code is sent to the system board where it is decoded, stored in random-access memory, and normally displayed on the monitor. All key-code information is sent serially, one bit at a time, to the system unit. A parity bit is added to each byte, and a clock signal is carried on a separate line to ensure data integrity. There are many different types of keyboard, but alphanumeric keyboards generally consist of a matrix of eight scan lines and eight receive lines. Each set of lines connects to one port of the microcontroller. The software that controls the keyboard assigns zeros (0s) to the scan lines, and ones (1s) to the receive lines. Pressing a key connects a scan line to a receive line, thus pulling the receive line to a logic low. On some keyboards, certain keys (such as shift, control, and escape) are not part of the line matrix. These keys would connect directly to a port pin on the microcontroller, and would not cause lock-out if pressed simultaneously with a matrix key, nor generate an interrupt if pressed singly. Normally, the micro-controller would be in idle mode when a key has not been pressed and another task is not in progress. Pressing a matrix key generates an interrupt which terminates the idle. The interrupt service routine would first call a 30-millisecond (or so) delay to debounce the key, and then set about the task of identifying which key is down. Abbreviation 'KB'. See **Dvorak** and **QWERTY**.

keyboard buffer To enable an operator

K

to use the keyboard even when the processor is busy, a small area of primary storage is used to memorize the last set of keystrokes. When the processor is free again, the buffer transmits the keystrokes.

keyboard condom A plastic transparent sheet that is moulded to a keyboard and used to protect the keyboard from dust and dirt. Keyboard condoms come in two types. The rigid model is used for overnight protection and acts as a cover only. The flexible model is used to cover the keys while the keyboard is being used in an industrial area or a dirty or dusty environment.

keyboard template An overlay, usually plastic, which fits around certain keys of a keyboard (especially function keys) to provide a summary of the functions of a program.

key frame In video technology, a video frame in which all of the video information is recorded in compressed form. If the clip has a large amount of motion, better playback will occur with every frame being a key frame. If there is very little motion, a high number of delta frames will give satisfactory playback. Typically, a simple video clip could withstand every third frame being a key frame. See **delta frame**.

key matching [ISO The technique of comparing the keys of two or more records to select some of them for a particular stage of processing and to reject the other ones.]

keypunch A typewriter-like machine which punches holes in specially-designed 80- or 96-column cards. A computer can read data which is coded by the combination of holes. [ISO A keyboard-actuated punch that punches holes in a data medium.]

key status indicator A symbol (such as a flashing cursor) which appears on the screen to alert the user as to which toggle keys are activated. Some modern keyboards also incorporate a light built into the key, highlighting the fact that a particular function is in use — for example, when the 'caps lock' or 'number lock' or 'scroll lock' keys are in use.

keystone distortion In monitor technology, the screen or image where the top of the image is wider than the bottom. It is shaped like the keystone used at the top of a stone arch. Compare **barrel distortion** and **pincushion distortion**.

keystroke verification [ISO The verification of the accuracy of data entry by the re-entry of the same data through a keyboard.]

key-to-cassette See **key-to-tape**.

key-to-disk See **key-to-tape**.

key-to-diskette See **key-to-tape**.

key-to-tape A device similar in concept to a card punch, except that, instead of data being represented by punched holes in a card, a key-to-tape device places magnetized spots on magnetic tape to represent data. A variation to this was the key-to-cassette device, where data was entered directly onto a small magnetic cassette tape/cartridge. A more advanced device was the key-to-disk, where several operators shared the same system (disk). Once all the data

was keyed in, it was transferred to a magnetic tape for processing by the computer.

key variable In a spreadsheet program like Lotus 1-2-3, a variable which may be referenced from anywhere within the spreadsheet, and which is stored in a single, separate cell. The key variable might be an interest rate and is particularly useful if the interest rate changes — only the key variable needs to be updated, eliminating the need to scan through and change the figure at every affected point within the spreadsheet.

keyword [ISO A lexical unit that, in certain contexts, characterizes some language construction. *Example:* In some contexts, IF characterizes an if-statement. *Note:* A keyword normally has the form of an identifier.]

kg Kilogram; the mass of the International Prototype Kilogram — a platinum–iridium alloy cylinder kept in Paris (Sèvres) by the International Bureau of Weights and Measures (Bureau International des Poids et Mesures). One kilogram is 1000 grams. See **metric system** and **SI**.

Khornerstone benchmark A standard by which to test and compare a computer's overall performance, such as the processor, memory access, and drive access speeds. Other benchmarks include the Whetstone (speed of arithmetic operations), and the Dhrystone (microprocessor and memory performance). The Khornerstone tests were developed by Workstation Laboratories, an independent test organization that began benchmarking in 1984. The rating is a single number which represents the performance of a personal computer, technical workstation, or multi-user microcomputer under a single-user loading. In addition to central processing unit performance, the Khornerstone benchmark measures the input/output capabilities of a system. It consists of 21 programs written in C and FORTRAN. Twenty percent of the Khornerstone rating is based upon disk performance; the rest is based upon the total time required to execute the entire set of tests. Pronounced 'corner-stone'. See **benchmark**.

kHz Kilohertz. One kilohertz equals 1000 cycles per second. See **hertz** and **Hertz, Heinrich Rudolf**.

Kilby, Jack St Clair Born 8 November 1923 at Jefferson City, Missouri, Jack St Clair Kilby was a Texas Instruments (TI) engineer. In 1947, he graduated with a Bachelor of Science (Electrical Engineering) degree from the University of Illinois, and in 1950, he completed his Master of Science (Electrical Engineering) degree at the University of Wisconsin. During this period, he was designing and developing ceramic-base silk screen circuits for consumer electronic products. In 1958, he joined TI in Dallas, Texas. During the summer of that year, working with borrowed and improvised equipment, he conceived and built the first electronic circuit in which all of the components, both active and passive, were fabricated in a single piece of semiconductor material half the size of a paper clip. The successful laboratory demonstration of that first simple microchip on 12 September 1958 made history. Jack Kilby went on to pioneer military, industrial, and commercial applications of microchip technology. He headed teams that built

both the first military computer system and the first computer to incorporate integrated circuits. He later co-invented both the hand-held calculator and the thermal printer, which is used in portable data terminals. In 1970, he took leave of absence from TI to work as an independent inventor exploring, among other subjects, the use of silicon technology for generating electrical power from sunlight. From 1978 to 1984, he held the position of Distinguished Professor of Electrical Engineering at Texas A&M University. In 1970, in a White House ceremony, he received the National Medal of Science. In 1982, he was inducted into the United States National Inventors' Hall of Fame, taking his place alongside Henry Ford, Thomas Edison, and the Wright brothers in the annals of American innovation. Cur-

Kilby, Jack St Clair Inventor of the semiconductor integrated circuit in 1958 and co-inventor of the electronic hand-held calculator in 1967.

rently, Kilby holds over 60 United States patents. He is a Fellow of the Institute of Electrical and Electronics Engineers (IEEE) and a member of the National Academy of Engineering (NAE). From Jack Kilby's first simple circuit has grown a worldwide integrated circuit market whose sales exceed US$50 000 million. These components support a world electronic equipment market of US$700 000 million. On 13 November 1990, United States President, George Bush, awarded the National Medal of Technology to ten individuals and one company for their exceptional contributions to the well- being of the United States through the development or application of technology. Among those honored was Jack Kilby for his inventions while at TI. ▲

kilo- See **k**.

kilobit See **kB**.

kilobyte See **kb**.

kilogram See **kg**.

kilohertz See **kHz**.

KIPS Knowledge information process-

ing system; a computer system which uses inference capabilities in fifth-generation computers that are designed to work in conjunction with very large knowledge bases at very high processing speeds. See **artificial intelligence** and **expert systems**.

knowledge acquisition The process of gathering knowledge from experts so that a system can be devised for filing and retrieving that knowledge for expert systems. See **expert systems** and **expert system software**.

knowledge base The database portion of an expert system where the rules for assessment are stored. This contains all the information which help decide IF ... THEN questions. See **expert systems**.

knowledge-base systems See **expert systems**.

knowledge domain The field of expertise for which an artificial intelligence system is designed. Due to the complexity of system programming for artificial intelligence, knowledge domains are usually focused on specific topics and operations. See **artificial intelligence** and **expert systems**.

NEWSFLASH

W orldwide multi-user systems, comprising all large-, medium-, and small-scale systems, and all computer systems except personal computers and workstations.

	1993	1994	1995	1996	1997
Shipments	580 910	613 655	636 425	668 145	704 170
Installed base	4 578 465	4 624 935	4 709 215	4 794 160	4 991 515
Revenues US$M	73 113	71 879	70 855	70 825	70 990

knowledge engineer A professional who, in programming expert systems, has the responsibility of extracting core information from industry experts. This is done for the purpose of clearly defining, then grouping, specialist information so that it can be placed in a knowledge base and used within an expert system. See **expert systems**.

knowledge information processing system A computer system which uses inference capabilities in fifth-generation computers that are designed to work in conjunction with very large knowledge bases at very high processing speeds. Acronym 'KIPS'. See **artificial intelligence** and **expert systems**.

K

**LOSERS ASSUME THAT 'THINGS HAPPEN FOR THE BEST';
AND HEREIN LIES THE MYTHTAKE OF LIFE.
FOR IT IS THE WINNERS WHO
'MAKE THE BEST OF WHATEVER HAPPENS'.**

label 1. [ISO An identifier within or attached to a set of data elements.] 2. [ISO A language construct naming a statement and including an identifier.]

Lahore virus A variant of the Brain virus. See **Brain virus**.

LAN Local area network; a collection of computers and other devices (such as printers) connected to each other by wire (coaxial cable or fiber optics) or radio frequency devices, which usually cover a small geographical area. Computers or workstations can communicate with one another. One of the benefits of a LAN is the ability for all users to share the same software, printers, mass storage, and other devices. Where more than one computer system is available in a company, a terminal server is required. This allows users to connect to the computer of their choice. To ensure smooth communications within a network environment, industry standards (protocols) have been defined. Pronounced 'lan'. Compare **WAN**.

LAN broadcast [ISO Sending of a frame that is intended to be accepted by all other data stations on the same local area network.]

LAN broadcast address [ISO A LAN group address that identifies the set of all data stations on a local area network.]

landscape The orientation of a page so that the output is printed across the longer axis. In contrast, portrait orientation prints with text and graphics going from the left to the right of the shorter axis of a page.

LAN gateway [ISO A functional unit that connects a local area network to another network using different protocols. *Note:* The network may be another local area network, a public data network, or another network.]

LAN group address [ISO An address that identifies a group of data stations on a local area network.]

language 1. Words or symbols that the computer accepts as instructions or commands. 2. See **programming language**. The word 'language' comes from the Latin word *lingua*, meaning 'tongue'.

language processor [ISO A functional unit for translating and executing computer programs written in a specified programming language. *Example:* A LISP machine.]

LAN individual address [ISO An address that identifies a particular data station on a local area network.]

LAN multicast [ISO Sending of a frame that is intended to be accepted by a group of selected data stations on the same local area network.]

LAN multicast address [ISO A LAN group address that identifies a subset of the data station on a local area network.]

LAN server [ISO A data station that provides services to other data stations on a local area network. *Examples:* File server, print server, mail server.]

Lantastic A peer-to-peer networking system manufactured by Artisoft.

LAP Link access procedure. The data link-level protocol specified in the CCITT X.25 interface standard. The original LAP has been supplemented with LAPB (LAP-Balanced), and LAPD (a protocol designed for ISDN connections).

LAPM Link access procedure for modems. An error-control protocol specified by the CCITT V.42 standard. This provides error control between two modems that support LAPM.

laptop See **laptop computer**.

laptop computer A small, lightweight personal computer designed to be carried easily. Modern laptop computers are battery-operated, provide a thin, back-lit or side-lit liquid crystal display screen, and have either a fixed or detachable keyboard for ease of use. Early models of laptop computers are today called 'portable computers'. Earlier still, portable computers of the late 1980s are today known as 'luggable computers' because they are much heavier and bulkier than modern laptops. Advancements past laptop computers include the 'notebook computer', so named because of its size — smaller than the average textbook. Both laptop and notebook computers can become part of the office environment through the use of a docking station — a desktop expansion base (lacking a central processing unit) which may consist of secondary storage and expansion ports. A docking station is used to transform a small laptop or notebook computer into a full-function desktop computer with full local area networking, including file- and peripheral-sharing capabilities. This level of technology is doing away with desktop computers, which are large and stationary, and are not designed to be taken off-site. Laptops and notebooks may house an internal modem and car battery adapters, making them commonplace among business executives. Already, palmtop computers are being marketed. Soon, wrist-top computers may be available, and docking stations or connection

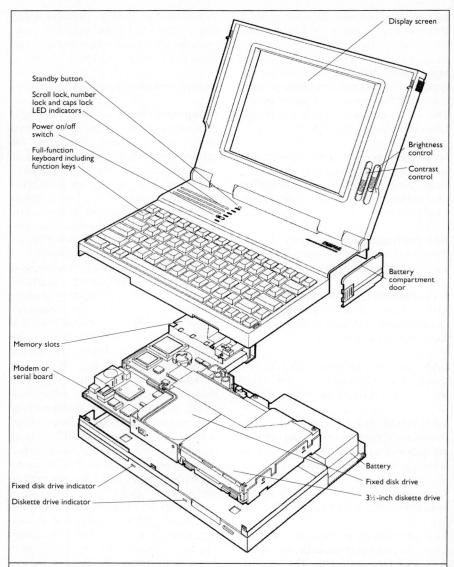

Display screen

Standby button

Scroll lock, number
lock and caps lock
LED indicators

Power on/off
switch

Full-function
keyboard including
function keys

Brightness
control

Contrast
control

Battery
compartment
door

Memory slots

Modem or
serial board

Battery

Fixed disk drive

Fixed disk drive indicator

3½-inch diskette drive

Diskette drive indicator

laptop computer With each new design, manufacturers use the latest technology to deliver an unprecedented combination of performance, portability, and functionality for users of advanced communications, project management, and other business and personal applications.

booths may become as common as public telephone booths. ▲

large-scale integration A chip technology with 500 to 20 000 logic gates per chip. The flow of electrons in chips is controlled by the transistors which form switches or logic gates. Chips are categorized by the number of logic gates available. Large-scale integration chips were first developed in the 1970s and are still widely used today. They contain over 500, but less then 20 000 logic gates on a single silicon chip approximately one centimeter square. Abbreviation 'LSI'. See **chip**, **molecular beam epitaxy**, **semiconductor**, and **silicon**.

laser Light amplification by stimulated emission of radiation. A device which transmits an extremely narrow and coherent beam of electromagnetic energy, usually light. 'Coherent' means that the separate waves are in phase with one another rather than jumbled as in normal light. Note that the radiation referred to is the light beam itself — lasers do not emit 'radioactive' radiation. The light emitted by lasers is very intense, parallel, and of a single color, which means that the frequency and phase of the light are always fixed. Unlike most light sources, lasers can generate not only visible wavelengths but also invisible wavelengths such as ultraviolet and infrared. As a result of these and other valuable qualities, the laser has been used in many fields of science and consumer products. Laser generators are classified according to the medium used to produce the light beam. This medium may be a gas, liquid, or solid. Most laser systems in printers use one of the following specific types of lasers: helium–neon, which produces a red beam; he-

lium–cadmium, which produces a blue beam; argon, which produces a blue/green beam; or a laser diode, which generates an infrared or visible beam. In most cases, the lasers in modern printers are not powerful enough to be a serious skin or fire hazard. However, if the beam is directed into the eye, it can cause damage to the retina and in some cases the cornea. The extent of possible eye injury is dependent upon the amount of light absorbed by the tissue. This in turn depends upon the wavelength of the light, the structure of the affected tissue, and the duration of exposure. Laser light which is absorbed is transformed into heat. It is this heat which may cause photochemical damage to the eye. The adverse effects of this transformation of light can best be compared to a sunburn, or to a welder's flash resulting from the accidental viewing of a welding arc without protective eye covering. Government safety regulations for exist for all lasers and laser systems. In the United States, the regulations specifically identify several classes of laser hazards. The first laser was invented in 1960 by Dr Maiman, an American physician who used a ruby to achieve successful oscillation and produce light (called a 'solid-state laser'). Subsequently, gas, liquid, and semiconductors have been used for successful laser oscillation. Since then, various laser devices have been used in many fields according to their features, such as the natural oscillation frequency and power. ▼▼

laser disk An optical-disk system that uses a laser beam as a non-contact pickup to write and/or read information such as video, audio, or computer programs, to/from a flat disk. Small elliptical convexities (called 'pits') with a width

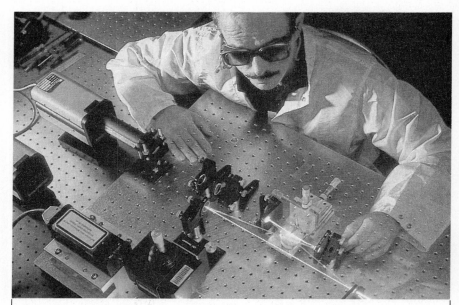

laser There are many different types of laser, and they vary in wavelength and power. A CO_2 gas laser is used when high power is required. An He–Ne gas laser is used when high accuracy is needed for measurement. Semiconductor lasers, which are used mainly with compact disk and laser disk players, are more compact, lighter, and have a longer life than solid-state or gas lasers. Other lasers are used as light sources for compact disk or laser disks, or as effective illumination in discotheques and theaters.

of 0.4 μm (micrometer) for laser disks (LD) and 0.6 μm for compact disks (CD), and a height of 0.1 μm are arranged in a continuous spiral on the surface of a laser disk at a track pitch of 1.67 μm. Each side of the disk has 30 000 million pits. If a disk that is 12 cm in diameter is compared to a baseball field, the size of each pit would be equivalent to a grain of sand. Laser disks have high recording densities for handling large volumes of information. The use of a non-contact laser pickup frees disks from wear and signal deterioration after repeated play-backs. Laser disks are easy to handle. Dust on the disk has almost no effect on signal reproduction. Another feature of laser disks is the ability to instantly access information at random. ▼

laser font See **outline font**.

LaserJet See **HP LaserJet**.

laser measuring system Vision systems (such as robot eyes) use laser measuring systems to make three-dimensional measurement possible. The system can measure (by using photosensor technology) three-dimensional profiles of objects in a wide dynamic range, from black to glistening surfaces. It also duplicates the breadth of the human eye (300 by 399 millimeters), the speed of the human eye (1 megahertz), and the resolution with which the human eye reads in three dimensions (0.1 millimeters). Laser measuring systems manufactured by Fujitsu, for example, can be used in

CLASS OF LASER

CLASS I	CLASS II	CLASS IIa	CLASS IIIa	CLASS IIIb	CLASS IV
A class I laser system is considered safe based upon medical research. This class includes all lasers or laser systems that cannot emit levels of optical radiation above the exposure limits for the eyes under any exposure conditions inherent in the design of the product. There may be a more hazardous laser inside the cabinet of a class I product, but no harmful radiation can escape the enclosure. All desktop laser printers are considered as class I during normal operations, but as class IIIa when the covers are removed.	Class II lasers and laser systems are rated as low power, but are considered to be a chronic hazard when viewed directly.	Class IIa levels of laser radiation are not considered to be hazardous if viewed continuously for any period of up to 16 minutes, but are considered to be a chronic hazard if viewed for a longer period. The laser systems used in product code scanners fall into this category.	Class IIIa lasers present a hazard if the beam is viewed directly with the unaided eye for more than an instant. If corrective optics (such as glasses) are used, even momentary viewing may be an acute hazard. Note that class IIIa lasers cannot produce hazardous diffuse reflections. In other words, reflections off a black or other non-reflective surface are not hazardous. Nor are these lasers considered a fire or serious skin hazard. Class III lasers are rated as medium power, and they may emit light of any wavelength.	Class IIIb denotes a visible or invisible laser that can produce an acute hazard if viewed directly, even momentarily. This hazard pertains not only to direct viewing of the beam but also viewing of reflections from mirrors or reflective surfaces. Except for higher power class IIIb lasers, this class does not produce hazardous diffuse reflection. In other words, reflections off a black or other non-reflective surface are not hazardous. Direct skin exposure to a class IIIb device is considered a hazard.	Class IV levels of laser radiation are considered an acute hazard to skin and eyes from direct and scattered radiation. Such lasers are rated as high power and are generally found in industrial processing applications.

laser *Government regulations for safety exist for all lasers and laser systems. In the United States, the regulations specifically identify several classes of laser hazards. Those pertaining to the computer and computer-related fields are listed above.*

L

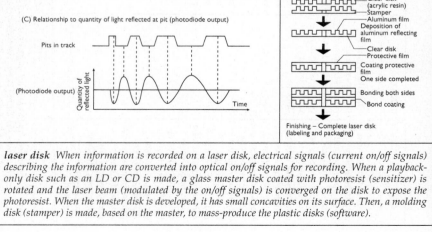

Structural enlargement of laser disk

(A) Pit strings (enlarged view) in track

(B) Pit (enlarged view)

1.67 μm

Plastic protective film
Aluminum
Transparent plastic

1.25 mm

0.4 μm

1.67 μm

Laser beam

Objective lens

0.4 μm

(C) Cross-section of a pit

Plastic protective film

1.25 mm
1.2 mm
0.4 μm

Transparent plastic

Signal pickup

(A) Laser beam irradiated on pit-less signal face (most of the beam is reflected)

(B) Laser beam irradiated on pit (most of the beam is scattered)

(C) Relationship to quantity of light reflected at pit (photodiode output)

Pits in track

(Photodiode output)

Quantity of reflected light

Time

Laser disk manufacturing processes

Pre-mastering
Recording image or audio signals

1-inch VCR edit master tape
Editing

Creating coded data (video processing)

Floppy disk

1-inch VCR release master tape (cutting master)

Mastering
Polishing glass pre-master disk

Polished glass pre-master disk

Photoresist coating

Photoresist

Photoresist pre-master disk

Laser

Laser cutting

Developing

Surface conduction process (spattering)

Glass master disk

Nickel electroforming

Separation

Nickel master disk

Stamping

Stamper

Replication
Molding clear disk (injection moulding)

Clear disk (acrylic resin)
Stamper

Aluminum film
Deposition of aluminum reflecting film

Clear disk
Protective film
Coating protective film
One side completed

Bonding both sides
Bond coating

Finishing – Complete laser disk (labeling and packaging)

laser disk When information is recorded on a laser disk, electrical signals (current on/off signals) describing the information are converted into optical on/off signals for recording. When a playback-only disk such as an LD or CD is made, a glass master disk coated with photoresist (sensitizer) is rotated and the laser beam (modulated by the on/off signals) is converged on the disk to expose the photoresist. When the master disk is developed, it has small concavities on its surface. Then, a molding disk (stamper) is made, based on the master, to mass-produce the plastic disks (software).

automating inspection procedures to the point of reading the raised letters on credit cards, and reading Braille text. See **robotics** and **vision systems**.

laser printer A non-impact high-resolution printer which uses a rotating disk to reflect laser beams onto the paper. When the beam touches the paper, it forms an electrostatic image-area which attracts electrically-charged toner (magnetized dry ink powder). The toner is then fixed (heated) onto the paper, forming an image (usually text or graphics). Gen-

erally, print resolution is 300 dots per inch (DPI), although 600 DPI for business applications is becoming popular. Laser printers using chemical photoreproduction techniques can produce resolutions of up to 2400 DPI. Print speeds may exceed 21 000 lines per minute, although most laser printers are measured by how many pages they can print per minute. If a laser printer is rated at 12 pages per minute, this figure would be true only if the printer is printing the same data on each of the 12 pages, so that the bit map is identical.

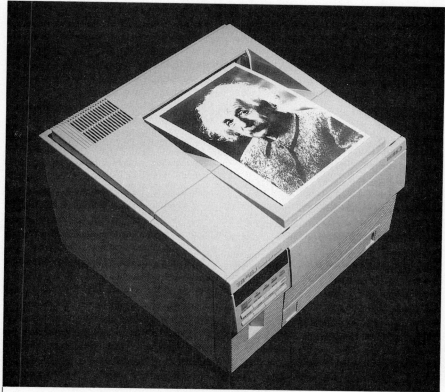

laser printer This eight-page-per-minute Canon laser printer produces output at a resolution of 600 dots per inch.

However, this speed is rarely reached if each page contains different codes, text, and graphics. Although there are dozens of retail brands of laser printers, only a few original equipment manufacturers (such as Canon, Ricoh, Toshiba, and Xerox) make the vital component called the 'print engine'. [ISO A non-impact printer that creates, by means of a laser beam directed on a photosensitive surface, a latent image which is then made visible by a toner and transferred and fixed on paper.] See **laser** and **photoreceptor**. Compare **impact printer**. ⬓

LaserWriter A trademark of Apple Computer, assigned to its range of laser printers which were first introduced in 1985, offering a built-in interpreter for the PostScript page description language primarily used with the Apple Macintosh personal computer. See **laser printer**. ▼

LATA Local Access and Transport Area. With the breakup of AT&T, the United States has been divided into over 200 LATAs in order to define areas of responsibility. A LATA typically includes all of the local exchanges and inter-office trunks, as well as the toll trunks and toll offices required to service a metropolitan area which may include several small cities and towns. Within a LATA, a local exchange common carrier provides connections, service, and a dial tone to all telephone subscribers. The local exchange carriers include the seven regional Bell Operating Companies, which range from Pacific Telesis on the west coast to Bell Atlantic on the east coast, as well as United Telephone, General Telephone, and about 1500 other smaller companies. LATAs are interconnected by toll offices and toll trunks which are installed and maintained by companies offering only long-distance services, such as AT&T MCI, GTE Sprint, and others. Telephone subscribers are free to choose a long-distance carrier, whereas there is only one local exchange carrier for a given area.

latency The time it takes for the re-

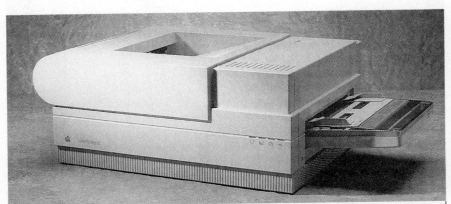

LaserWriter *The Apple LaserWriter combines high resolution with the ability to produce full-page text and graphics. The LaserWriter provides a print resolution exceeding 300 dots per inch and allows printing at up to eight pages per minute.*

quired magnetic or optical disk track or sector to rotate to the correct position under the read/write heads of a disk drive. This is one of the many factors which govern access speed. [ISO The time interval between the instant at which an instruction control unit initiates a call for data, and the instant at which the actual transfer of the data starts.] The word 'latency' comes from the Latin word *latere*, meaning 'be hidden'. See **access time**.

layer 1. In computer architectures, each part of the logical construction method which provides an interface between lower, more hardware-oriented entities, and higher, more user-oriented entities. For example, a physical layer might specify the hardware to be used, while a data link layer may exist immediately above this and pass data to the physical layer for transmission. See **OSI**. 2. [ISO In network architecture, a group of services, functions, and protocols that is complete from a conceptual point of view, that is one out of a set of hierarchically arranged groups, and that extends across all systems that conform to the network architecture.]

layered protocol The term 'protocol', as used in computer networks, refers to a set of rules governing communications between one or more devices. Network architectures are solving many incompatibility problems by isolating networking functions and establishing 'layers of protocols' to govern each set of operations. The layered approach to a network architecture leads to the isolation of functions in a system and assignment of standard rules (protocols) to govern their operations. Layered protocols accomplish three objectives: they re-

duce the complexity of a network; they accommodate peer-to-peer interaction between nodes; and they allow changes in a layer without affecting other layers. The layered approach also permits the partitioning of the design and development of many network components. This modular design makes each layer relatively self-contained. Changes to the network and isolation of problems become much simpler when the functions of each hardware and software element are clearly defined by a layer of protocol. An important characteristic of layered architectures is that the upper layers are closer to the applications functions, whereas the lower layers are concerned with the physical transport of the bit stream. See **OSI**.

layout 1. (In desktop publishing and printing); to creatively position artwork on a page, including text and graphics. 2. A rough or finished version of a page, including text and graphics positioning.

lazy write See **write-behind**.

LCD See **liquid crystal display**.

LCR Least-cost routing; the capability of a switch, typically a private branch exchange (PBX), to automatically determine an optimal route when establishing a circuit. This is also called 'automatic route selection' (ARS).

LCS Liquid crystal shutter.

LD Laser disk. The LD group comprises LD–G and LD–ROM used for multimedia. The LD–G was developed using technology in which graphics signals are recorded in the subcode area of the digital audio signal area of the LD, and the graphic images can be displayed on the video image. This technology, developed by Pioneer, was first used in Japan in 1992. With LD–G, users can enjoy a foreign feature film with superimposed film conversations in the foreign language. The first LD–G-tailored software package was *Terminator 2*. On the other hand, LD–ROM is the medium that allows 16 channels of digital audio or a large amount of digital data equivalent to a CD–ROM to be recorded in the digital audio area (the area below 2 megahertz) of an LD along with the clear images and FM audio of the LD.

LDD Laser digital disk.

LD–ROM Laser disk–read-only memory. See **LD**.

leader 1. The first few meters of mag-netic tape which is wound onto a reel. Leaders store no data, and are used for handling and loading the reel onto a magnetic tape unit. After the leader comes the load point — the place where data starts. [ISO The portion of magnetic tape that precedes the beginning-of-tape marker and that is used to thread the tape.] 2. In word processing, a row of dots or other symbols used to direct the eye across a page, such as a price list, where the item number is to the left of the page, and the price is to the right. Pronounced '<u>leed</u>-er'.

leading In word processing and typography, the distance between the baseline of one line of type and the baseline of the next line of type. Correct leading gives greater reading comfort. The term is derived from the days when type was set by hand, using lead (metal) strips

PALATINO 9 POINT WITH 11 POINT LEADING	PALATINO 9 POINT WITH 9 POINT LEADING
In word processing and typography, the distance between the baseline of one line of type and the baseline of the next line of type. Correct leading gives greater reading comfort. The term is derived from the days when type was set by hand, using lead (metal) strips between lines of type. Pronounced 'ledding'.	*In word processing and typography, the distance between the baseline of one line of type and the baseline of the next line of type. Correct leading gives greater reading comfort. The term is derived from the days when type was set by hand, using lead (metal) strips between lines of type. Pronounced 'ledding'.*
PALATINO 9 POINT WITH 10 POINT LEADING	PALATINO 9 POINT WITH 8 POINT LEADING
In word processing and typography, the distance between the baseline of one line of type and the baseline of the next line of type. Correct leading gives greater reading comfort. The term is derived from the days when type was set by hand, using lead (metal) strips between lines of type. Pronounced 'ledding'.	*In word processing and typography, the distance between the baseline of one line of type and the baseline of the next line of type. Correct leading gives greater reading comfort. The term is derived from the days when type was set by hand, using lead (metal) strips between lines of type. Pronounced 'ledding'.*

leading These lines show type set with different leading as indicated.

between lines of type. Pronounced 'ledding'. ▲

leading zero The zeros required by some programming methods in order to fill a numeric field, even when they do not seem necessary. For example, the number 76.88 may have to be written as 00076.88 in order to accommodate the program's limitations.

leaf See **nested transaction**.

leased line A telephone line that permanently connects two or more locations. It does not have any switching equipment associated with it, and runs between specific, fixed locations. Also known as a 'private line'.

leased network Private lines (also called 'dedicated' or 'leased' lines) provide a private, full-time connection that can be used for point-to-point or multipoint network configurations. They are available to any location, no matter how distant. Whereas the switched network is connected only for the duration of the call, a leased network has a dedicated line that is always connected. Therefore, no dialing is required to establish the connection. The classes of private leased lines that are available are narrow band, voice band, and wide band.

least significant digit Also called 'least significant bit'. [ISO In a positional representation system, a digit (bit) place having the smallest weight used.]

LED Pronounced 'el-ee-dee' or 'led'. See **light-emitting diode**.

left justified In typography and word processing, the positioning of text on a page so that all the text is aligned to the left margin, leaving a ragged right margin. Compare **indent** and **justification**.

legend An explanatory list defining the meaning of symbols, colors, or patterns appearing on a chart or map. This is also known as a 'key'. The word 'legend' comes from the Latin *leger*, meaning 'read'.

Lehigh virus A computer virus that, once in memory, infects (and sets a counter for) the COMMAND.COM file. Once the virus has copied itself four times (ten times in some versions), it overwrites sectors 1 to 32 with unintelligible data (retrieved at random from the computer's BIOS). This disk corruption is not so severe in hard disks because neither the file allocation table nor the root directory are deleted. Lehigh was first reported in the United States at Lehigh University.

letter [ISO A graphic character that, when appearing alone or combined with others, is primarily used to represent a sound element of a spoken language. *Note:* Diacritical marks used alone and punctuation marks are not letters.]

letter-quality printer See **impact printer**.

level 0 or 1 diagnostics See **diagnostic program**.

lexical unit [ISO A language construct that, by convention, represents an elemental unit of meaning. *Examples:* A literal such as 'G25'; a keyword such as PRINT; a separator such as a semicolon.]

Lexmark International Inc. Headquartered in Greenwich, Connecticut, Lexmark was established in March 1991 when the private investors acquired the information products business of IBM Corporation. Lexmark, employing 5000 people worldwide, specializes in the development, manufacture, distribution, and service of workstation printers, typewriters, input technologies, and related supplies.

LF Also 'lf'. See **line feed**.

library [ISO An organized collection of computer programs, or parts of computer programs, and possibly information pertaining to their use. *Note:* A program library is often called according to the characteristic of its elements — for example, a procedure library, a source program library.]

license agreement The agreement that accompanies computer software. It may be stated explicitly (in the software documentation or on the computer screen when the program is opened) or implicitly (in the purchase price of the software). In most countries, the legal purchase of software program licenses the software user to make one backup copy only, in case the original software disk malfunctions or is destroyed.

lifetime [ISO Of a language object, that portion of the execution time during which the object exists.]

ligature In typography, the joining of two or more characters or symbols to form a new symbol used to form a mark, or for the purpose of decoration. The word 'ligature' is derived from the Latin word *ligatura*, meaning to 'tie' or 'bond together'. Ligatures were printed at the beginning of news services to identify the wire service from which the news

item originated. In modern word processing, ligatures can be formed by using special function keys before two characters, so that they can be printed as one. For example in WordPerfect, joining the following pairs produces ligatures as shown: AE = Æ, ae = æ, OE = Œ, ss = ß, ox = ¤.

light amplification by stimulated emission of radiation See **laser**.

light-emitting diode Produced from semiconducting material, a diode which emits its light when an electric current flows through. Light-emitting diodes (LEDs) were widely used in peripherals as indicator lights, but their power consumption has made way to more energy-efficient liquid crystal displays. As a non-linear two-terminal device, a diode is the simplest and most fundamental semiconductor used in electronics. It acts as a one-way valve letting current flow through it in one direction, while blocking current flow in the other. ▼

light green See **green technology** and **ultra green**.

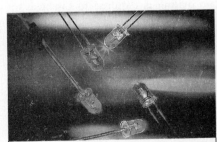

light-emitting diode A p–n junction semiconductor device that operates by injecting electrons across a junction. Under suitable operational conditions, LEDs produce incoherent radiation by spontaneous emission.

light pen An input device consisting of a small rod which resembles a writing pen. It is used to pick up or select information from the screen or tablet. Similar in concept to the touch screen, the light pen is often used in graphic design applications as well as various database applications. All light pens contain a lens and a photodetector that senses the intensity of light emitted from a given point on the monitor screen. This information is passed to the video adapter board which then determines the x and y coordinates. [ISO A light-sensitive pick device that is used by pointing it at the display surface.] Compare **touch screen**. ▼

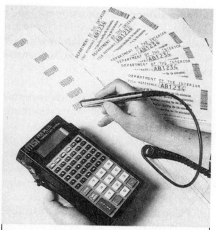

light pen The world's first hand-held computer that uses a pen instead of a keyboard for data input. It also recognizes printed handwriting, signatures, and drawings. Instead of writing information on paper, or keying information into a computer, an electronic pen is used on a flat liquid crystal display screen to print letters and numbers, draw images, or to check boxes. Applications are wide ranging, particularly in the area of form and report completion, standard reports, generation of retail sales orders, field inspection, inventory control, market research, and interview/census surveys.

light-pen detection [ISO The sensing by a light pen of light generated by a display element on a display surface.]

Li Ion Lithium ion. A type of rechargeable battery used in computer equipment such as notebook computers. Li Ion batteries are an improvement on NiCd and NiMH batteries in that they do not have a 'memory problem'. They contain no heavy metals and consist of a lithium-oxide alloy electrode, a carbon-based electrode, and an organic fluid electrolyte fluid containing lithium ions that separates the electrodes. Unlike NiMH batteries, Li Ion batteries have almost double the running time and power density, and they can be disposed of without fear of damaging the environment. Pronounced 'lion'. Compare **NiCd**.

LIM EMS Lotus–Intel–Microsoft Expanded Memory Specification. Used to combat the 640 kilobytes of random-access memory (RAM) limitations of DOS, the LIM EMS was introduced to enable computers fitted with expanded memory to work with up to 32 megabytes of RAM (LIM Version 4.0 introduced in 1987). Naturally, only specifically designed software can take advantage of extended memory. See **EEMS** and **extended memory**.

limit check [ISO A check to determine whether a value lies above or below, or has reached a stipulated limit.]

limiter (In an analog computer.) [ISO A functional unit used to prevent an analog variable from exceeding specified limits.]

line 1. In data communications, a circuit

that connects several hardware or peripheral devices. 2. In programming, a program instruction or statement. 3. [ISO The portion of a data circuit external to data-circuit-terminating equipment (DCE), that connects the DCE to a data switching exchange (DSE), that connects a DCE to one or more other DCEs, or that connects a DSE to another DSE.]

line adapter In data communications, a device used to convert signals so that transmission can take place. A modem acts as one form of line adapter between two computer devices, converting signals from digital to analog so that they may be transmitted via a telephone line for conversion at the receiving end.

linear bus See **bus topology**.

linear density Linear density (or bit density) is the measure of the number of bits which would lie along an inch of a continuously recorded track at the disk's innermost recording radius (single-bit wide). Modern disks store 15 000 to 23 000 bits per linear inch, with each sector being less than half an inch. Each sector of information is 4 kilobits (512 bytes) surrounded by a header, error correction codes, and inter-sector gaps. It is important to distinguish between linear density and unformatted capacity, or theoretical total disk capacity, because the disk's linear density is usually higher than the actual density of user data over an entire track. To improve the linear density, higher-grade or higher-technology media with lower noise characteristics is used to produce sharper output pulses so that more bits per inch can be achieved. Other improvements could include lower head flying heights for less signal loss and sharper readback pulses. To improve the transfer rate of a drive with high linear density, it is necessary to reduce the velocity of the media past the heads. This can be accomplished either by reducing the rotational velocity of the disk stack, or by reducing the disk's diameter.

linear list [ISO A linearly ordered set of data elements whose order is preserved in storage by using sequential allocation.]

linear network [ISO A network in which there are exactly two endpoint nodes, any number of intermediate nodes, and only one path between any two nodes.]

linear positioner See **positioner**.

linear search [ISO A search in which a set of data is scanned in a sequential manner.]

line art An illustration which is represented in line form only, omitting halftones.

line feed 1. A function chosen by a user to advance a printer one line at a time. 2. A programmed instruction which signals a printer to advance one line. 3. [ISO The movement of the print or display position to the corresponding position on the next line.]

line hits In telephone line distortion, any of the three interference distortion factors: dropouts, phase hits, and gain hits. These factors occur only rarely and their cause is difficult to pinpoint. Most telephone companies do not consider line hits to be a major problem. Dropouts are sudden large reductions in the signal level which may last several milliseconds. Phase hits are sudden shifts in the phase of the received signal. Gain hits are sudden increases in the amplitude of the received signal which tend to overdrive the amplifier circuits in the receiver and cause distortion.

line-of-sight Usually refers to transmission methods that require a straight line, such as microwave signals that are unable to follow the curvature of the Earth, hence, needing several relay stations over long distances. Line-of-sight is characteristic of some open-air transmission technologies where the area between a transmitter and a receiver must be relatively clear and unobstructed.

line printer An impact printer capable of printing all the characters on an entire line simultaneously. [ISO A printer that prints a line of characters as a unit.] See **impact printer**.

line spacing See **leading**.

line turnaround Reversal of the direction of transmission from sender to receiver on a half duplex data circuit. See **half duplex**.

link [ISO To interconnect items of data or portions of one or more computer programs. *Examples:* The linking of object programs by a linkage editor; the linking of data items by pointers.]

Link Access Procedure The data link-level protocol specified in the CCITT X.25 interface standard. The original LAP has been supplemented with LAPB (LAP-Balanced), and LAPD (a protocol designed for ISDN connections). Acronym 'LAP'.

linkage editor 1. [ISO A program for creating load modules from one or more object modules or load modules by resolving cross-references among the modules and, if necessary, by adjusting addresses.] 2. [ISO A program used to create one load module from one or more independently translated object modules or load modules by resolving cross-references among the object modules, and possibly by relocating elements.]

Linpack A benchmark performance test that requires a computer to solve a set of simultaneous linear algebraic equations. It is a gauge of floating point performance directly relevant to a large number of problems in technical high-performance computing such as supercomputing. Linpack was developed in 1970 by Jack Dongarra, a computer scientist at the University of Tennessee and Oak Ridge National Laboratory, as a collection of subroutines that could be run on a wide range of computers.

LIPS Logical inferences per second; a benchmark used to measure the processing speed of computers designed to handle artificial intelligence applications. See **artificial intelligence** and **benchmark**.

liquid crystal display Commonly found on digital watches, calculators, laptop computers, and testing meters, liquid crystal displays (LCDs) are usually battery-driven and low power consumers. Liquid crystal is a material that will flow like liquid but has some molecular structure. Shaped like rods, the crystals will change their orientation when confined between two (transparent) plates and energized by an electric current, producing a darkened area. To enhance their visibility and reduce eye strain, screens may be side-lit or back-lit, thereby using more battery power. An LCD consists of a backplane and any number of segments or dots that will be used to form the displayed image. Applying a voltage (4 to 5 volts) between any segment and the backplane causes the segment to darken. The only disadvantage is that the polarity of the applied voltage has to be periodically reversed, otherwise a chemical reaction takes place in the LCD that causes deterioration and eventual failure of the liquid crystal. To prevent this from happening, the backplane and all the segments are driven with an AC (alternating current) signal which is derived from a rectangular voltage waveform. If a segment is to be 'off', it is driven by the same waveform as the backplane, and it is always at backplane potential. If the segment is to be 'on', it is driven with a waveform that is the inverse of the backplane waveform — having approximately 5 volts of periodically changing polarity between it and the backplane. Some microcontrollers can perform this task with the aid of software, thereby eliminating the need for LCD drivers. In contrast, light-emitting diodes, produced from semiconducting material, actually emit light when an electric current flows through them. They were used in peripherals as indicator lights, but their power consumption has made way for more energy-efficient liquid crystal displays.

Lisa A personal computer released in 1983 by Apple Computer. Lisa was the first computer that featured a graphical user interface. See **Apple Computer Corporation** and **graphical user interface**. ▽

Lisa *The Apple Lisa was a 32-bit business computer based on the Motorola 68000. After it started shipping in 1983, it was discovered that Lisa was not as powerful as the IBM PC because its superior graphics capability was consuming most of its power. In 1985 Lisa was re-named the Macintosh XL, and by April of that year, it was dropped from Apple's product line.*

LISP A high-level programming language popular for writing programs dealing with artificial intelligence. It was first developed in 1958 by John McCarthy, and later enhanced with the assistance of his colleagues at the Massachusetts Institute of Technology in the early 1960s. Because LISP is a public domain programming language, several versions of the language have been developed over the years. In an effort to standardize LISP, Common LISP was introduced. 'LISP' is a contraction of 'list processing'. See **artificial intelligence** and **programming language**.

LISP interpreter One of the ten SPEC (Systems Performance Evaluation Cooperative) benchmarks drawn from real-world applications including scientific and engineering areas, focusing on system performance, memory, input/output, graphics, networking, multi-user, and commercial applications. Written in C, the LISP interpreter (called 'li') is

CPU (central processing unit) intensive. It measures the time 'li' takes to solve the popular eight-queen problem. The input file to the interpreter contains LIS, a code that defines the eight-queen problem. This benchmark was developed at Sun Microsystems and is based on XLISP 1.6 written by David Michael Betz. XLISP is a small implementation of LISP with object-oriented programming. The metric used is the elapsed (real) time as measured by Ibin/time. See **SPEC**.

list processing [ISO A method of processing data in the form of lists. *Note:* Chained lists are usually used so that the order of the data elements can be changed without altering their physical location.] See **LISP**.

literal [ISO A lexical unit that directly represents a value. *Examples:* 14 represents the integer fourteen; 'APRIL' represents the string of character APRIL; 3.0005E2 represents the number 300.05.]

liveline The point at which a computer program or chain of events activates. In contrast to a 'deadline' that marks the end of a series of events, a liveline marks the beginning of an event.

LiveLink A software program that allows a group of users to easily and automatically share and integrate many different types of data across different applications. An invisible link structure, in a layer beneath the data, 'connects' the local document to the remote data, enabling the user with access privileges immediate access to the most accurate, up-to-date data created by other applications that support LiveLink software.

LLC Logical link control. See **IEEE 802**.

LLL See **low-level language**.

load 1. The process of copying, from a disk to the computer's random-access memory, program instructions, or data sequences. 2. [ISO To transfer data into storage device or working registers.]

load module 1. [ISO All or part of a computer program in a form suitable for loading into main storage for execution. *Note:* A load module is usually the output of a linkage editor.] 2. [ISO A program unit that is suitable for loading into main storage for execution; it is usually the output of a linkage editor.]

Loadplan Limited This company (based in the United Kingdom) was formed in 1980 to cater for the growing requirements of software publishers to effectively duplicate and distribute software. In the late 1980s, the importance of information security was emphasized by the rapid spread of computer viruses in the personal computer industry. To continue to provide a complete service to its clients, Loadplan formed an association with S & S International Ltd, a company specializing in data recovery and antivirus technology. In 1987, an Australian subsidiary (Loadplan Australasia) commenced operation to service clients' needs in security, antivirus protection, and media duplication services.

load point [ISO The beginning of the recordable area on a magnetic tape. *Note:* Some magnetic tape drives use a beginning of tape marker to indicate the position of the load point.]

local [ISO Pertaining to the relationship between a language object and a block such that the language object has a scope contained in that block.]

Local Access and Transport Area See **LATA**.

local administration [ISO Address administration in which all LAN individual addresses are unique within the same local area network.]

local area network See **LAN**.

local bus A PC bus system that has a higher data transfer rate than the standard 8 megahertz of the ISA or AT bus. This is commonly available on two or three of the expansion slots of a personal computer.

local echo See **half duplex**.

LocalTalk A hardware device (including its cables) which enables Apple Macintosh and Apple II computers to form a local area network via Apple Computer's proprietary architecture called 'AppleTalk'. This is a baseband network with a bus topology which operates through shielded twisted pair wire at 230.4 kilobits per second using CSMA/CA.

locking A feature of a local area network preventing files from being corrupted should more than one person try to change them at the same time.

lock-out facility [ISO The facility that inhibits the entry of data when the calculator is in overflow or error condition.]

logarithmic graph A graph in which either or both of the axes is/are logarithmic. In presentation and analytical graphics, data on the y-axis (value axis) may vary dramatically. Displaying data using typical increments of ten units (or similar) all the way to the top of the chart will mean that smaller numbers will be hardly noticeable — especially if the highest number is larger than the smallest by a factor of 100 000. To balance the visual display of these increments, a logarithmic graph is used. In this example, it would not display increments in units of ten, but exponentially by powers of ten (10, 100, 1000, 10 000, and so on). The word 'logarithmic' comes from the Latin word *logarithmus,* where *log* means 'reckoning' or 'ratio' and *arithmos* (Greek) means 'number'.

logger [ISO A functional unit that records events and physical conditions, usually with respect to time.]

logical comparison [ISO The examination of two strings to discover if they are identical.]

logical interference per second A benchmark used to measure the processing speed of computers designed to handle artificial intelligence applications. Acronym 'LIPS'. See **benchmark**.

logical link control protocol [ISO In a local area network, the protocol that governs the exchange of frames between data stations, independently of how the transmission medium is shared.]

logical link control sublayer [ISO In a local area network, that part of the data link layer that supports medium-independent data link functions. *Note:* The LLC sublayer uses the services of the medium-access control sublayer to provide services to the network layer.]

logical link control type 1 [ISO An un-acknowledged connectionless-mode transmission within the logical link control sublayer.]

logical link control type 2 [ISO A connection-mode transmission within the logical link control sublayer.]

logical link control type 3 [ISO An acknowledged connectionless-mode transmission within the logical link control sublayer.]

logical operations Operations executed by the central processing unit that compare different numbers, letters, or special characters, and take alternative courses of action depending upon the outcome. Common operations include equal to (=), less than (<), and greater than (>).

logical operator In programming, a symbol or statement which specifies the relationship of two quantities by either including or excluding them from the operation or search. In query languages, three symbols include OR, AND, and NOT. Using OR widens the search, while NOT narrows the search for a set of files with a particular characteristic. For example, searching for a book on cooking OR wine will produce a much wider selection than conducting a search on cooking books which do NOT include references to wine.

logical record [ISO A set of related data elements considered to be a record from a logical viewpoint.]

logical ring [ISO The abstract representation of a token bus network, that is passing a token between data stations in a manner that simulates the passing of control in a ring network.]

logical shift [ISO A shift that equally affects all the characters of a computer word.]

logic board Usually called a 'motherboard', a logic board is one of the most important circuit boards in a computer, containing vital components including the central processing unit, microprocessor support chips, expansion slots, and some of the random-access memory.

logic bomb A program used in a form of computer crime which involves the use of an idle code which, when released, results in data destruction or other unauthorized functions. A logic bomb is a Trojan triggered by a set of conditions (such as the number of files on the disk, or a certain combination of letters being typed as determined by the programmer of the logic bomb). Famous cases involving logic bombs provide details about company personnel who programmed the corporate computer to search for their name each day, and when their name was not found (due to the employee being dismissed) the logic bomb commenced erasing and destroying vital corporate files from the computer system. By comparison, a time bomb is also a Trojan which is triggered by a particular date. See **infection, Trojan,** and **virus.**

logic design [ISO A functional design that uses formal methods of description, such as symbolic logic.]

logic device [ISO A device that performs logic operations.]

logic diagram [ISO A graphic representation of a logic design.]

logic operation 1. [ISO An operation that follows the rules of symbolic logic.] 2. [ISO An operation in which each character of the result depends only on the corresponding character of each operand.]

logic programming [ISO A method for structuring programs as sets of logical rules with predefined algorithms for the processing of input data to a program according to the rules of that program.]

logic symbol [ISO A symbol that represents an operator, a function, or a functional relationship.]

login When using local area networks, multi-user operating systems, or particular security-sensitive applications, users are required to type in their name and password before the computer will allow them access to the system, its data, or peripherals. This process is called a 'login' or a 'logon'. With users logging in, the network administrator will be in a position to monitor computer usage and provide extra support at peak periods to ensure that line traffic is kept to a minimum. See **password**. Compare **logoff**.

Logo A high-level, easy-to-learn programming language written for children in the 1970s by Seymour Paepert of Massachusetts Institute of Technology, in the United States, incorporating graphics with straight-forward English-like instructions. See **programming language**.

logoff A function which officially and properly terminates a user from a computer session, especially on local area networks. Compare **login**.

logon See **login**.

longitudinal magnetic recording [ISO A technique of magnetic recording in which magnetic polarities representing data are aligned along the length of the recording track.]

longitudinal parity check [ISO A parity check on a row of binary digits that are members of a set forming a matrix. *Example:* A parity check on the bits of a track in a block on a magnetic tape.]

longitudinal redundancy check An error-checking technique based on transmitted characters. A longitudinal redundancy check character is accumulated at both the sending and receiving stations during the transmission of a block. This accumulation is called the 'block check character' (BCC), and is transmitted as the last character in the block. The transmitted BCC is compared to the accumulated BCC at the receiving station for an equal condition. An equal comparison indicates a good transmission of the previous block. Abbreviation 'LRC'.

longword See **word**.

look-ahead carry [ISO A high-speed carry procedure in which a group of carry digits is formed in parallel from the respective input bits of the two groups that are to be added and, if it exists, from the most significant carry digit that is previous to those groups.]

look and feel The characteristics of a computer program or interface that makes a program unique. There have been many famous court battles over programs which use totally different code but, to the user, look and feel similar.

look aside cache One of the basic decisions in designing a cache is how it fits onto the bus between the microprocessor and main system DRAM (dynamic random-access memory). Caches can be designed with two basic read architectures: look through (serial) and look aside (parallel). In a look aside cache, the cache is designed to fit onto the memory bus in parallel with the microprocessor and main system memory. The cache does not interrupt memory requests from the microprocessor to main system memory. Instead, all memory requests from the microprocessor are sent simultaneously to the cache and main system memory. The microprocessor 'looks aside' at the cache when sending memory requests to main system memory. If a

cache hit occurs on a memory request, the cache returns the information to the microprocessor and sends a signal to the main system memory to abort the memory request. If a cache miss occurs, the cache does nothing. The memory request is completed by the main system memory. Since a look aside cache does not interrupt the bus between the microprocessor and main system memory, it can be removed without the need to re-design the system. This allows the designer to include or not include a cache, depending upon the system's requirements. Also, since the look aside cache does not fit serially between the microprocessor and main system memory, there is no delay (look-up penalty) from when the microprocessor requests information to when memory look-up begins. The result is that look aside caches have a faster main system memory response time than look through caches. The look aside cache is typically a simpler cache, since it needs to support only one ad-

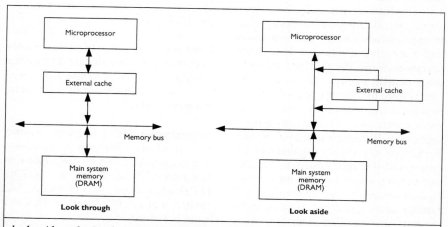

Look through

Look aside

look aside cache In a look through cache technique, the cache is designed to fit in series between the microprocessor and main memory. In a look aside cache, the cache is designed to fit into the memory bus in parallel with the microprocessor and main system memory.

dress and data bus (whereas a look through cache needs an address and data bus for both the microprocessor interface and main system memory interface). This results in easier design and cheaper packaging requirements. With a look aside cache, all memory requests from the microprocessor are sent simultaneously to the cache and main system memory. For each memory request (cache hit or cache miss), the main system memory will begin to look up the information. This results in a large number of unnecessary memory pre-charge cycles (memory location setup functions) and restricts access to main memory by other devices in the system. See **cache**. Compare **look through cache**. ▲

look through cache One of the basic decisions in designing a cache is how it fits onto the bus between the microprocessor and main system DRAM (dynamic random-access memory). Caches can be designed with two basic read architectures: look through (serial) and look aside (parallel). In a look through cache, the cache is designed to fit in series between the microprocessor and main system memory. The microprocessor 'looks through' the cache to main system memory. All memory requests from the microprocessor are first sent to the cache, then from the cache to main system memory. The main advantage of a serial cache is that it will reduce the number of memory requests to main system DRAM. This reduces the utilization of the memory bus and the amount of memory pre-charge cycles (memory location setup functions). Most memory requests are handled directly out of cache without the need to access main system memory. Only when there is a cache miss, is the memory request for-

warded to main system memory. If a dual concurrent bus structure is used, a serial cache also provides an advantage, since it can decouple the microprocessor from the rest of the system. The microprocessor can operate out of the cache while other master devices in the system utilize the memory bus. The main disadvantage of a serial cache is that it causes memory requests from the microprocessor to main system memory to be delayed. All memory requests from the microprocessor to main system memory must first serially pass through the cache. It usually takes one system clock for the cache to compare the memory request against the tag RAM to see if the information requested is in the cache. This delay is called the 'look-up penalty'. See **cache**. Compare **look aside cache**.

loop A programming technique that permits the program to repeat some operation or sequence of commands several times. Loops are sometimes called 'iterations'. [ISO A sequence of instructions that is to be executed iteratively.]

loopback The routing of a channel back to its source, so that all data transmitted is immediately received again. It is used to check the functioning of equipment, channels, and software.

loop construct [ISO A language construct that specifies an iteration in the execution sequence. *Examples:* DO loops in FORTRAN; FOR loops in ALGOL; PERFORM loops in COBOL; DO WHILE loops in PL/1; and WHILE DO loops in Pascal.]

loops invariant [ISO An assertion that holds throughout a loop construct.]

loosely-coupled multiprocessor A system that incorporates a number of processors, each with local resources that are not accessible by other processors (including memory, disk storage, and other peripherals). Processor communication is often implemented by sending and receiving messages in software with a very high degree of latency. Consequently, resource sharing and processor cooperation are limited. See **multiprocessing**.

lossless compression A form of compression where the recovered file is identical to the original. Although this is essential to text and data files, it may not be necessary for graphics files. Compression levels of between 0% and 70% are possible, depending upon the file type.

lossy compression A form of compression where detail is lost in the compression and recovery processes. Compression levels of up to 99% are possible, depending upon the acceptable level of degradation or detail 'loss'.

Lotus Improv A spreadsheet software package originally designed for NeXT computers, and now available for other platforms. This product provides a new approach to spreadsheets, allowing users to view information dynamically at the click of a mouse, use plain English formulae instead of numerical syntax, and create presentations using data, text, graphics, images, and sound. Users can further enhance presentations with clip art, logos, and photographs.

Lotus–Intel–Microsoft Expanded Memory Specification See **LIM EMS**.

Lotus Notes A shared database program

that gives people who work together a computer environment within which to create, access, and share information, using networked personal computers. Lotus Notes is used to develop and deploy such applications as customer tracking, status reporting, project management, information distribution, and electronic mail. It is useful for geographically dispersed organizations where the composition of work groups must be fluid to respond to changing business needs. Notes employs the client/server computing model.

Lotus 1-2-3 One of the first office automation program packages, combining electronic spreadsheets with graphics and database management. It was introduced in 1982 by Mitchekk D. Kapor of Lotus Development Corporation in Boston, Massachusetts, and shipped in January 1983. In the first 12 months, Lotus had a turnover of US$53 million. Ten years later, over ten million copies of Lotus software have been sold.

Lovelace, Countess of See **Byron, Ada Augusta**.

low-bit-rate encoding See **digital speech interpolation**.

PLAY ON WORDS

Lotus 1-2-3 A yoga position achieved in three easy steps.

Lotus Freelance A yoga instructor.

Optical mouse A mouse with glasses.

Spell checker Used by witches to test incantations.

---

low-level language Low-level languages are the lowest level of computer languages, such as machine or assembly language, used with first- and second-generation computers. They represent information in binary code (as ones and zeros) to correspond to the electrical states of 'on' and 'off'. They process calculations much faster than high-level programming languages which use English-like codes. Abbreviation 'LLL'. See **programming language**.

low-res. See **low resolution**.

low resolution Referring to any output (such as an image on paper or screen) which lacks definition, sharpness, and clarity. In laser printing, for example, resolution is measured in dots per inch (DPI), with 300 DPI representing acceptable business quality, while a minimum resolution of 1500 DPI is deemed essential for professional printing and publishing (2400 DPI is preferred). Contraction 'low-res.'.

LPM Lines per minute.

LPT1, LPT2, LPT3 Line printer. See **parallel port**.

LQ Letter quality. See **impact printer**.

LRC See **longitudinal redundancy check**.

LRE See **low-bit-rate encoding**.

LSI See **large-scale integration**.

luggable computer Refers to a portable personal computer designed in the mid-1980s to be carried to and from the home and office. This term is relatively new. In the mid-1980s, portable computers were much easier to carry around than heavier desktop models. However, these same portables are today out of production and they are now referred to as 'luggable computers' because, in comparison, they are much heavier and bulkier than modern laptop and notebook computers. See **laptop computer**.

LUN Logical unit number.

LUT Look-up table.

LVC Low-voltage CMOS.

LVT Low-voltage technology.

We complicate this industry's issues
by using whizz-bang titles
to describe simple concepts.
Multimedia is one of those titles in search
of a subject. Everything these days is multimedia.

m 1. Meter. From the Greek word *metron*, meaning 'measure'. An SI unit of 100 centimeters. See **meter**. 2. Milli-. An SI unit prefix for 10^{-3} expressed as 0.001 in decimal notation.

M Mega-. An SI unit prefix for 10^6 expressed in decimal notation as 1 000 000. In computing terms, when 'mega-' is used to represent storage capacity, it refers to 2^{20} (which equals 1 048 576), hence a megabyte (Mb) is a series of 1 048 576 bytes. See **byte** and **SI**.

Mac The nickname used for the Apple Macintosh. See **Macintosh**.

MAC Medium access control layer. This is a media-specific access control protocol within IEEE 802 specifications. See **IEEE 802**.

MacBinary A file conversion and transfer protocol for Apple Macintosh personal computers. MacBinary is used to ensure that data and files created on the Macintosh (but stored and used by DOS-based computers) maintain their original computer codes (including icons, graphics, creation date, and so on).

MACE Macintosh Audio Compression and Expansion.

Mace Utilities A set of powerful utilities developed by Paul Mace and distributed by Fifth Generation Systems for personal computers. The utilities include file management and file recovery programs, similar to those available through Norton Utilities (developed by Peter Norton).

machine cycle The combination of i-time and e-time (instruction time and execution time). After data and instructions are read by the input device and placed in primary storage, the control unit then: (a) fetches the instructions from primary storage; (b) decodes the instructions and makes the data available to the arithmetic/logic unit; (c) instructs the arithmetic/logic unit to perform the operation on the data; (d) places the computation into primary storage. [ISO The sequence of operations in a central processing unit that corresponds to one memory cycle, input/output (I/O) cycle, or equivalent internal operation. *Note:* An instruction may require one or more machine cycles for its execution and a machine cycle usually contains more than one clock cycle.]. See **e-time** and **i-time**.

machine function [ISO A function carried out by the calculator.]

machine language A programming language that operates using binary numbers. This is the lowest level of computer language recognized and used by the central processing unit. It represents information in binary code (as ones (1) and zeros (0)) to correspond to the electrical states of 'on' and 'off'. Early computers each had their own different machine language. Programming languages are system software development tools used by programmers to develop application systems and programs. A program is a sequence of instructions which direct the central processing unit (CPU) to perform specific tasks. When requested by the user, the operating system loads the program from disk into random-access memory. The program instructions are then analyzed and executed one at a time in the precise order specified by the programmer. When the instructions are executed, they must be in the only language the CPU can understand — binary machine language. While programmers can write programs in machine language, the machine language format is

slow and tedious, and not cost-effective for most projects. For example, the simple task of multiplying two numbers together may require more than ten instructions in machine language. To overcome the difficulties of writing in machine language, programming languages were developed. The first ones were very simple, allowing programmers to write the command in a near-English format (such as SUB for subtract). Before entering the program into memory, programmers had to translate the command into its machine language format. Programmers carried code cards so that they could correctly change near-English commands, called 'mnemonics', into the machine code. The next development was a program that could translate the mnemonic code (also known as 'assembly language') into machine code to make programming easier. See **programming language**.

Macintosh A range of personal computers manufactured by Apple Computer Corporation. The original model was one of the first personal computers to feature a graphical user interface, incorporating windows, icons, a mouse, and pull-down menus (WIMP). During the first 100 days after the Macintosh was launched in 1984, over 50 000 units were sold worldwide. The Macintosh was the first personal computer to use 3½-inch magnetic floppy disks — fully enclosed in a rigid plastic casing and used as a secondary storage medium. These 3½-inch disks were developed by Sony Corporation. The first Macintosh model offered only 128 kilobytes of random-access memory and a 400-kilobyte single diskette drive. It was also the first personal computer to offer a 32-bit microprocessor — the Motorola 68000 with a clock speed of 4.77 megahertz. More successful models were the Macintosh 512, Macintosh SE featuring a hard disk, and the Macintosh II (pronounced 'Macintosh two') which offered open architecture. The history of the Macintosh goes back to the early 1980s when Steven Jobs (co-founder of Apple Computer Corporation) was impressed with what he saw being developed at the Xerox Palo Alto Research Center and hired key scientists to help him launch a computer called 'Lisa' in 1983. Abbreviation 'Mac'. See **Apple Computer Corporation** and **Jobs, Steven P.** ▼

Macintosh II   A personal computer launched in 1987 by Apple Computer Corporation offering high-performance open-bus architecture. The Motorola 68020 microprocessor was used in the earliest model, but this was later replaced with the 68030, offering a clock speed of 15.67 megahertz (MHz). The Macintosh IIci offered 25 MHz with an 80-nanosecond dynamic random-access memory chip. A faster model is the Macintosh IIfx. It runs a 40-MHz 68030 central processing unit plus a 68882 math coprocessor. It offered 32 kilobytes of static random-access memory, and 4 megabytes of random-access memory (expandable to 128 megabytes). The Macintosh IIfx incorporated various monitors and diverse networks, sharing information with other types of computers. It was designed for corporate environments which required advanced

Macintosh *Apple's popular all-in-one Macintosh computer design has offered numerous improvements since its introduction.*

NEWSFLASH

The installed base of Macintosh systems will rise at 24% compound annual growth rate to over 25 million units by 1997.

Product	1993	1994	1995	1996	1997
Portables	1 220 000	1 853 000	2 549 000	3 267 000	3 953 000
Low-end	7 147 000	8 858 000	10 679 000	12 486 000	14 168 000
Midrange	2 929 000	3 635 000	4 370 000	5 052 000	5 685 000
High-end	418 000	817 000	1 056 000	1 410 000	1 750 000
Total	11 714 000	15 163 000	18 654 000	22 215 000	25 556 000

computer-aided design, color publishing, and image processing. Current models can also be used as file servers, and as UNIX systems (when configured with A/UX — Apple's implementation of AT&T's UNIX). See **Apple Computer Corporation** and **Macintosh**.

Macintosh Classic A new low-end entry-system personal computer from Apple, originally designed with an 8-megahertz 68000 Motorola processor. See **Macintosh**.

Macintosh SE/30 A small-footprint personal computer from Apple, incorporating a built-in monitor, diskette drive, and networking capabilities. When configured with Apple's implementation of the AT&T UNIX operating system (A/UX), the Macintosh SE/30 can also be used as a UNIX system. See **Macintosh**.

MacLink Plus A file transfer utility used to transfer files from the Macintosh to the IBM Personal Computer or IBM-compatible. It also includes a translation facility.

macro When an application requires the

user to repeat a set of commands, a macro can be written to remember those steps so that the repetitive task can be carried out automatically by the computer when the user types the name of the saved macro. Sophisticated software programs like WordPerfect, Microsoft Word, and Lotus 1-2-3 allow users to create a macro and also edit it, incorporating control structures such as DO ... WHILE loops and IF ... THEN branches.

macro call [ISO A statement, embedded in a source language, that is to be replaced by a defined statement sequence in the same source language. *Note:* The macro call will also specify the actual parameters for any formal parameters in the macrodefinition.]

macrodefinition [ISO A possibly parameterized specification for a statement sequence to replace a macro call. *Note:* A macrodefinition may be considered as a procedure to be executed by a macrogenerator yielding the statement sequence.]

macrogenerator [ISO A program for replacing macro calls with defined statement sequences according to macro-definitions. *Note:* A macrogenerator may be an independent computer program or it may be integrated as a subprogram in a compiler or assembler to generate the source program.]

magnetic bubble See **bubble memory**.

magnetic card [ISO A card with a magnetizable layer on which data can be stored.]

magnetic card storage [ISO A magnetic storage in which data is stored by magnetic recording on the surface of thin flexible cards.]

magnetic core Each magnetic core is several hundredths of a centimeter in diameter. Magnetic cores are mounted on wires and magnetized as either 'off' or 'on' when electricity passes through the wire. Magnetic cores could represent a zero or a one, and combinations of these could represent data in the form of binary digits. See **magnetic tape** and **second generation**. ▼

magnetic disk A metal plate (disk) coated with ferrous oxide, manufactured in various sizes for storing data. Disks can be stacked on top of each other in a disk pack, leaving gaps between them for the read/write arms which access data. Except for the bottom platter, most disk packs are double sided, in that data can be stored on both the top and bottom side of each disk (plate). Data is stored in the form of magnetic spots on tracks. Each track is a complete circle, unlike a vinyl record where the track is one long spiral. In

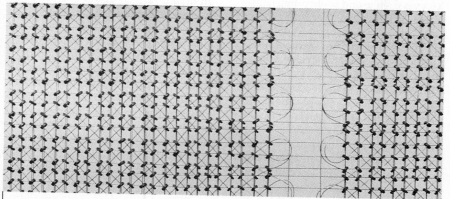

magnetic core In the 1950s, the vacuum tube vastly increased the computer's calculating speed, but it did little to improve the efficiency of two other critical aspects of the computer's configuration: storage and memory. The early vacuum tube computers stored data on punched cards or tape and drums, and they relied on cathode-ray tubes or drums for active memory. Punched cards were slow and not re-writable. Tape could be inefficient because of the time taken in reeling and unreeling. Cathode-ray tubes were expensive and unreliable. The urgent demand for faster and cheaper storage and memory devices stimulated research and development in magnetics — magnetic disks and drums for storage, magnetic cores for memory, and better material for better magnetic tapes. Current-carrying wires that pass through iron oxide cores magnetize them clockwise or counterclockwise. Cores switch from one magnetic state to the other in millionths of a second. One magnetic direction represents a 'zero', the other a 'one' in the computer's binary code.

personal computing, the term is also used to refer to industry-standard 5¼-inch and 3½-inch floppy disks. The removable nature of the medium gives convenience and security not available with a hard disk. In addition, storage space (500 megabytes to 1 gigabyte) can always be expanded simply by adding more cartridges. However, the erasable nature of both types of storage media make them vulnerable to accidental erasure, unlike WORM technology. See **diskette**. Compare **CD–ROM, compact disk**, and **magnetic tape**.

magnetic disk technology One of the most significant bulk data storage mechanisms in computing today is the magnetic disk, which offers nonvolatile storage in a wide variety of capacities, from a few million bytes (megabytes) to several thousand million bytes (gigabytes), with average access times being less than 25 milliseconds. Today, virtually every computer system employs a magnetic disk in some capacity, either as a device for loading the operating system, or as online user file storage, or for archival and backup applications. The recording and readback process for magnetic disks is similar to the process for making and using audio or video tape recordings. Recording information on the media is accomplished by changing the direction of the current in the coil, causing the magnetic field in the core to reverse its direction. A magnetic field reversal during a fixed interval of time might indicate a 1 bit, while a lack of a reversal will indicate a 0 bit. See **oxide media**. Compare **optical disk**.

magnetic drum [ISO A right circular cylinder with a magnetizable layer on which data can be stored.]

magnetic drum storage [ISO A magnetic storage in which data is stored by magnetic recording on the surface of a magnetic drum which, in use, rotates on its axis.]

magnetic head [ISO An electromagnet that can perform one or more functions of reading, writing, and erasing data on a magnetic data medium.]

magnetic ink [ISO A special ink that contains particles of magnetic material suitable for a recording of data.] See **MICR**.

magnetic ink character [ISO A character whose pattern of magnetic ink is sensed to enable automatic identification.]

magnetic ink character reader [ISO An input unit which reads characters by magnetic ink character recognition.]

magnetic ink character recognition MICR inscribers are widely used by banks to print serial numbers on the bottom of checks using magnetic ink which contains magnetized particles. A MICR reader/sorter can process checks and other documents at speeds of up to 2000 documents per minute. Abbreviation 'MICR'. Pronounced 'miker'. [ISO Character recognition of magnetic ink characters.]

magnetic media The material used in secondary storage used to store and retrieve data using magnetically-sensitive material in the form of floppy or hard disks, and tapes. The technology uses heads which emit a magnetic field over a portion of the magnetically-sensitive medium, re-orienting the magnetic particles so that they represent and correspond to bits of data. Magnetic polarities encoded on the tape can be read and decoded. See **magnetic disk**, **magnetic disk technology**, and **magnetic tape**.

magnetic recording [ISO A technique of storing data by selectively magnetizing a magnetizable material.]

magnetic storage [ISO A storage device that uses magnetic properties of certain materials.]

magnetic tape 1. [ISO A tape with a magnetizable layer on which data can be stored.] 2. Introduced in 1953, magnetic tape is a faster, more compact storage system than 'magnetic cores'. The first tape subsystem was capable of storing just over 2 megabytes on a 2400-foot (732-meter) reel. With media and recording technology improvements, today's tape subsystems can store several gigabytes on the same reel in standard formats, with even higher capacity achievable in specialized applications. Magnetic tapes are made from thin plastic tape (as used in common video cassettes), usually coated with iron oxide that can be magnetized. The oxide media coating is applied to a base whose thickness is about two-thousandths of an inch. Tape media have magnetic properties similar to those of disk media, so thinner coatings generally offer superior performance. Today, tape is available in different widths and lengths, but is still wound on reels. Data is stored on tracks as small magnetized spots, using the binary system. The presence of a spot signals an 'on', and the absence of a spot signals an 'off'. Conventional oxide media are useful at up to 20 00 bits per linear inch, but newer materials, such as chromium dioxide,

can support linear densities of up to 30 000 bits per linear inch. Internal labels are records on the tape itself and are of two types. The header label is on the area of the tape just before the first data record, giving general file name and date. The trailer label is at the end of the file and gives general information such as the number of records in the file, and completion date. Unlike disks which have one-bit wide tracks, magnetic tapes are generally recorded in eight parallel data tracks with a ninth track for byte parity or other error checking. As backup for online data and as a short-term archival storage medium, tape is popular because it can offer as much as 30:1 media cost advantage over disk packs. Tapes are much less bulky than disks, with as much as a 50:1 advantage in megabytes per cubic foot. Compare **magnetic disk** and **optical disk**. ▼

magnetic tape storage [ISO A magnetic storage in which data is stored by magnetic recording on the surface of a tape that moves longitudinally in use.]

magnetic tape unit A machine which reads from, or writes to, magnetic tape. The tape is usually wound on reels. Two reels are used at any one time. The supply reel is the main reel which has the tape with the data on it (or blank with data to be written on it), and the take-up reel which always stays with the unit. Data can only be written on the tape when the file protection (plastic) ring is attached to the center of the reel. Conversely, data cannot be written nor erased from the tape if the file protection ring is absent. See **magnetic tape**.

magnetographic printer [ISO A non-impact printer that creates, by means of

M

magnetic tape In the 1950s, new ways to store more information were in demand. The early vacuum tube computers stored data on punched cards. Later versions used tape on reels to store up to 156 megabytes of information, with current models (encased in small cartridges) storing several gigabytes of information, using special data-compression techniques. Some magnetic tapes store data in digital format, instead of analog format.

magnetic heads operating on a metallic drum, a latent image which is then made visible by a toner and transferred and fixed onto paper.]

magneto-optic recording Magnetic recording in which a laser is used to raise the local media temperatures on erasable optical disks. Data is read from magneto-optic media by observing variations in its reflection of polarized light. Because magneto-optic recording uses a low bandwidth magnetic coil (relying solely on the action of the write laser for high-frequency signal), the media must be brought to a consistent state before data is written. For this reason, overwriting a block on a magneto-optic disk is a two-stage process. During the first stage (or erase pass), the laser operates continuously at writing power to bring the media area to be overwritten to a consistent magnetic state. In the second stage (or write pass) the laser is modulated by the encoded data pattern, the sense of the magnetic coil is reversed, and data is written. All current erasable optical disk technologies require two-stage writing, which has the effect of increasing the rotational latency of optical disks, further lowering their performance relative to magnetic disks. Counterbalancing this performance disadvantage are the advantages of density and removability. Magneto-optic recording provides data densities comparable to other optical technologies on easy-to-handle, durable, removable media. A magneto-optic disk with a 5-inch diameter typically has a storage capacity of about 700 megabytes. A 12-inch magneto-optic disk might store between 1 and 2 gigabytes. See **compact disk** and **erasable optical disk**.

mailbox In a local area network using an electronic mail program, a mailbox is used to receive all incoming mail for the users associated with the network. The mail remains in the mailbox until the addressee accesses the network and retrieves the personal electronic mail. The addressees are usually alerted on their screens when mail messages have been sent to them. See **electronic mail**.

mail merge In word processing, a function which allows the user to send a personalized letter to several people without having to type the letter more than once. The addressing details (such as name and address of recipients) are left out of the main letter. Instead, the main letter contains codes in place of specific addressee details. These codes are used to automatically combine (merge) these details from a database file which only contains addressee details. The addressee file is usually called a 'secondary file'.

main control unit [ISO In a processor with more than one instruction control unit, that instruction control unit to which, for a given interval of time, the other instruction control units are subordinated. *Note:* In an operating system, an instruction control unit may be designated as the main control unit by hardware, by software, or by both.]

mainframe A large and fast central computer which offers superior data management and processing. These are usually installed in very large organizations (such as military services, aerospace corporations, and weather bureaus). The term 'mainframe' was originally used to refer to the metal framework (cabinet) which housed the computer's circuits, but today it refers to the computer itself. During the late 1950s, IBM led the way with the development of mainframe computers, setting de facto standards in both the design and the communications networks they use. Due to miniaturization, experts differentiate modern computers not by their size, but by function, and mainframes are considered to be large computers which run an organization's entire processing needs. However, this definition leaves open for debate the use of the term 'mainframe', given that some medium-sized organizations use minicomputers as their only computer. Although the boundaries between these two types of computers are narrowing, a mainframe can still be differentiated because the largest in its family, the supercomputer, is the most powerful processor, offering speeds of 800 million operations per second (MOPS). The Cray-1, developed by former CDC employee Seymour Cray, was one of the early mainframes to be called a 'supercomputer', because it was capable of executing 80 MOPS. Most mainframes are capable of processing between 14 and 20 MOPS, with computer 'word' sizes exceeding 64 bits. Prices range from a few hundred thousand dollars to US$8 million or more. Compare **supercomputer**. ▼

main storage [ISO That part of internal storage into which instructions and other data must be loaded for subsequent execution or processing. *Note:* In large computing systems, the term 'main storage' is preferred to 'main memory'.] See **primary storage**.

maintainability [ISO The ease with which maintenance of a functional unit can be performed in accordance with prescribed requirements.]

M

mainframe A typical computer room with a raised floor for easy cabling, a control desk, and an electronic communications and switching cabinet. The mainframes on the left include mass-storage units.

maintenance [ISO Any activity intended to retain a functional unit in, or to restore it to, a state in which it can perform its required function. *Note:* Maintenance includes keeping a functional unit in a specified state by performing activities such as tests, measurements, replacements, adjustments, and repairs.]

NEWSFLASH

The value of the 1992 worldwide high-performance computer market was US$3300 million, representing a 41% decline in revenue from 1991. High-performance mainframes and minicomputers accounted for the bulk of the loss, with 50.7% and 84.9% declines in revenues, respectively.

maintenance panel [ISO A part of a unit of equipment that is used for interaction between the unit of equipment and a maintenance engineer.]

majority gate [ISO A gate that performs a majority operation.]

majority operation [ISO A threshold operation in which each of the operands may take only the values 0 and 1, and that takes the value 1 if and only if the number of operands having the value 1 is greater than the number of operands that have the value 0.]

male connector A device wherein the connections are in the form of pins or protrusions.

MAN Metropolitan area network; a complete communications network set up by a local telephone company to service customers in regional locations, providing them with microwave and satellite relay stations, fiber optics, and cellular radio services with a 31-mile (50-kilometer) range (operating at speeds from 1 megabit per second to 200 megabits per second). A MAN is larger than a local area network (LAN), but smaller than a wide area network (WAN). A MAN may be made up of several LANs, using multiple-access methods operating at higher signaling rates than each individual LAN. MANs provide an integrated set of services for real-time voice, data, and image transmission. The two standards bodies that are involved with work on MANs are the IEEE 802.3 and ANSI X3T9.5.

Manchester encoding An encoding technique used for high-speed data transmission. Manchester-encoded data is self-clocking, and is used to minimize error probability. See **framing**.

man–machine interface A device which helps a computer (system software) communicate with the user in plain language. These include voice synthesizing devices as used in talking calculators. Abbreviation 'MMI'.

mantissa 1. [ISO In a floating point representation, the numeral that is multiplied by the exponentiated implicit floating point base to determine the real number represented.] 2. (Of a logarithm.) [ISO The non-negative fractional part of the representation of a logarithm.]

manual answering [ISO Answering in which a call is established only if the called user signals a readiness to receive the call by means of a manual operation.]

manual calling (In a data network.) [ISO Calling that permits the entry of selection signals from a calling data station into the line at an undefined character rate. Note: The characters may be generated at the data terminal equipment or the data circuit-terminating equipment.]

Manufacturing Automation Protocol See **MAP**.

map 1. [ISO A set of values having defined correspondence with the quantities or values of another set.] 2. [ISO To establish a set of values having a defined correspondence with the quantities or values of another set. *Example:* To evaluate a mathematical function, i.e. to establish the values of the dependent variable, for those values of the independent variable or variables that are of immediate concern.]

MAP Manufacturing Automation Protocol, developed in 1983 by General Motors to ensure all manufacturing devices were interoperable, using OSI protocols. Today, many large manufacturers (including IBM) use the MAP approach to ensure effective communication and manufacturing coordination between the manufacturing plant and its suppliers.

MAPI Massaging application programming interface.

Marconi, Guglielmo The Italian electrical engineer (1874–1937) who invented wireless telegraphy in 1895. In 1896, he migrated to England, and in 1901, he was able to send Morse Code (the letter S) across the Atlantic. He won the Nobel prize for physics in 1909. See **radar**. ▼

marginal test [ISO A technique in which certain operating conditions, such as voltage or frequency supplied, are varied about their nominal values in order to detect and locate components with incipient faults.]

Marijuana virus A variant of the Stoned virus. See **Stoned virus**.

marker [ISO A glyph with a specified appearance which is used to indicate a particular position on a display surface.]

Mark I A programmable general-purpose computing machine developed in 1944 at Harvard University, in the United States, by Howard Hathaway Aiken (1900–73) who received a grant of US$500 000 in 1939 from IBM's first chief executive officer, Thomas J. Watson.

Marconi, Guglielmo A young Marconi with some of his original wireless apparatus soon after his arrival in London in 1896. Born in April 1874, the son of an Italian country gentleman and Irish mother, Marconi pioneered and developed a new field of technology that would deliver telecommunications from its dependency on the 'wire'. After receiving the patent for the world's first wireless telegraphy, he formed The Wireless Telegraphy and Signal Company Ltd a year later in 1897.

Mark I was approximately 8.2 foot (2.5 meters) by 55.76 foot (17 meters) long, and was originally called the 'Automatic Sequence Controlled Calculator' (ASCC). Once com-pleted, it contained 3 million electrical connections and 500 miles (805 kilometers) of wire, and was capable of performing a multiplication in six seconds and a division in 12 seconds. As soon as Mark I was built, it was technically obsolete because it faced competition from the Atanasoff–Berry Computer (ABC). During his high school days in Indianapolis, Indiana, Aiken attended school by day and worked long hours by night. At the age of 23, he obtained his Bachelor of Arts degree from the University of Wisconsin, and in 1939, his doctorate from Harvard University. The term 'bug' became popular after a programmer, Grace Murray Hopper, found a moth (bug) lodged in the circuits of Mark I, causing the computer to malfunction. Hopper wrote in her log book, 'Relay #70 Panel F (moth) in relay. First actual case of bug being found.' See **ABC**.

Markkula, A.C. See **Jobs, Steven P**.

mark scanning [ISO The automatic optical sensing of marks recorded on a data medium.]

mark-sensing The detection, by an optical device, of marks on a piece of paper, commonly used to collate questionnaires or school examinations where a student, using a pencil, marks certain boxes on the examination answer sheet. Using a light beam, mark-sensing is used to detect the marks, and convert them to electrical signals which are sent to the computer for processing. Also called 'optical mark recognition'.

mask 1. The set of symbols or characters that a data field can accept. For example, in a database management program, a data field may have a numeric mask. This will allow only numeric characters to be used in that field. 2. [ISO A pattern of characters that is used to control the retention or elimination of portions of another pattern of characters.]

mass storage A form of secondary storage used to store extremely large amounts of data. Mass storage is usually measured in gigabytes. See **secondary storage**.

master clock [ISO A clock whose main function is to control other clocks.]

master station [ISO In basic mode link control, the data station that has accepted an invitation to ensure a data transfer to one or more slave stations. *Note:* At a given instant, there can be only one master station on a data link.]

math coprocessor See **coprocessor**.

mathematical induction [ISO A method of proving a statement concerning terms based on natural numbers not less than N by showing that the statement is valid for the term based on N and that, if it is valid for an arbitrary value of n that is greater than N, it is also valid for the term based on (n + 1).]

matrix A table consisting of rows and columns, in which each cell (or memory box) can be defined by its row/column number. Each cell may contain numbers or words.

matrix300 One of the ten SPEC (Systems Performance Evaluation Cooperative) benchmarks drawn from real-world applications including scientific and engineering areas, focusing on system performance, memory, input/output, graphics, networking, multi-user, and commercial applications. Matrix300 is a vectorizable FORTRAN scientific benchmark using double-precision floating point arithmetic. The code performs various matrix multiplications, including transposers using Linpack routines SGEMV, SGEMM, and SAXPY, on matrices of order 300. This program is identical to the MATRIX benchmark from Los Alamos National Laboratories, except that the problem size was increased to 300 x 300, and the number of loops around the program was reduced to 1. This benchmark measures elapsed time between two internally-defined points within the benchmark. Although this code is highly vectorizable, it is not optimized for vector computers. See **SPEC**.

MAU Media access unit; a device that both transmits and receives data, providing the electrical, and physical interface to the network cable. Also known as 'transceiver'.

Mauchly, John William In the 1930s, Mauchly was the head of the Department of Physics at Ursinus College in Pennsylvania, United States. During his work on weather analysis, he realized the need for a high-speed calculating device for complex environmental analysis. In 1941, he left the college to join the Moore School of Electrical Engineering at the University of Pennsylvania. It was there that he met John Presper Eckert with whom he engineered the first large-scale electronic digital computer, called 'ENIAC' (Electronic Numerical Integrator and Calculator). The project was funded by the United States Department of Defense which at that time needed to find a way to quickly recompute artillery firing tables during World War II. In 1948, Mauchly and Eckert formed a computer manufacturing company, and a year later released BINAC (Binary Automatic Computer), which used magnetic tape instead of punched cards. Another of their inventions was called UNIVAC 1 (Universal Automatic Computer–Model 1). Their computer company was taken over in 1950 by Remington Rand, which was later known as 'Sperry Corporation' and is today called 'Unisys Corporation'. Mauchly was born 30 August 1907 in Cincinnati, Ohio, and died in 1980. See **Eckert, John Presper** and **ENIAC**.

MAW See **Microsoft At Work**.

maxicomputer An old-fashioned name used to refer to supercomputers. See **supercomputer**.

Maxis Founded in 1987 by Jeff Braun and Will Wright, Maxis is a computer software publisher concerned with bringing sophisticated technologies to personal computer users in the form of a new generation of entertainment software such as its simulation games SimCity, SimEarth, SimAnt, and SimLife. Maxis refers to its products as 'software toys'. Unlike a traditional game, in which the players either win or lose, a software toy encourages exploration and risk taking, providing an enriching experience regardless of the outcome. Each Maxis toy allows players to create their own goals for the game, then decide for themselves whether they have won. Because these games include adaptive behaviors of their own, no two

game-playing experiences are alike. Since its release as the first Maxis product in 1989, SimCity has sold more than one million copies around the world. At the heart of SimCity is what artificial-life researchers call 'emergent behavior' in which individual components follow simple rules, yet when combined with other components, exhibit complex processes that closely mirror real life. SimCity players take control of their own city's construction and maintenance — assuming responsibility for everything from building codes and air quality, to law enforcement and nuclear waste disposal. Based upon the player's simple decisions on each factor, the city lives and grows, or decays and collapses. SimEarth gives players an even larger on-screen laboratory in which to make decisions about the atmosphere, land masses, water supply, temperature, and all geographic and physical elements of an on-screen planet. Players of SimAnt are charged with the survival of an ant colony, and must make tactical decisions about digging, expansion, foraging, and population levels in order to conquer rival ants and other enemies. SimLife is a genetic engineering game that lets players create their own ecosystem, filled with bizarre creatures and burgeoning plant life. The only limits are the natural laws governing the ecosystem. See **artificial life**. ▼

Mb Megabyte. In computing terms, mega- refers to 2^{20} (1 048 576). Hence a megabyte is a series of 1 048 576 bytes. Pronounced 'meg-a-bite'. See **byte**.

MB 1. Motherboard. 2. Megabit. In computing terms, mega- refers to 2^{20} (which is equal to 1 048 576). Hence a megabit is

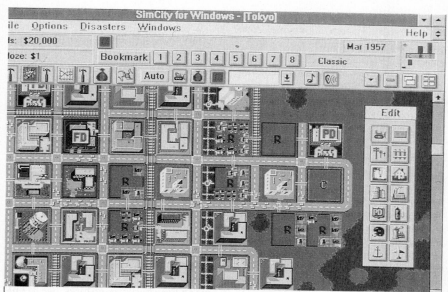

Maxis *Loaded with animation and sound effects, this computer game from Maxis (called 'SimCity') allows the player to become the mayor of an evolving, growing city. The player can start to build (simulate) a new city, or select a well-known one such as Boston, London, Tokyo, or San Francisco. The object of the 'software toy' (as it is called by Maxis) is to manage the growth and development of the city, and to take action against disasters, pollution, crime, traffic, urban decay, and similar social and financial situations. The software allows the player to select disasters at will. These include floods, earthquakes, fires, tornadoes, air crashes, or monster attacks. SimCity is written is such a way that it allows emergent behavior, meaning that although the game follows simple rules, it exhibits a complex process of evolution when it encounters certain arbitrary and evolutionary processes and decisions — thereby mirroring real life.*

a series of 1 048 576 bits. Pronounced 'meg-a-bit'. See **bit**.

MBE See **molecular beam epitaxy**.

Mbps Megabytes per second. See **byte**.

MBps Megabits per second. In computing terms, mega- refers to 2^{20} (1 048 576). Hence a megabit is a series of 1 048 576 bits. It is used for expressing the speed of data transmission. When used as a plural, an 's' is not added. For example, 1 MBps, 2000 MBps. See **bit**.

MCA 1. Media Control Architecture. System-level specification developed by Apple for addressing various media devices (such as videotape players and CD players) to its Macintosh computers. 2. See **Micro Channel Architecture**.

MCA bus See **Micro Channel Architecture**.

MCAE Mechanical computer-aided engineering.

MCGA MultiColor Graphics Array. A

video display standard used on some IBM Personal System/2 personal computers offering 64 shades of gray with a palette of 16 colors at a resolution of 640 pixels (picture elements) horizontally by 350 pixels vertically.

McNealy, Scott Co-founder of Sun Microsystems, Inc. Established in 1982, Sun is a supplier of workstations, servers, system software, printers, and networking products that use the UNIX operating system. Prior to joining Sun, McNealy was Director of Operations at Onyx Systems, and an employee of Rockwell International. McNealy was awarded a degree in economics from Harvard University, and an MBA from Stanford University. ▼

MCUPS MegaCUPS; million connection updates per second. Pronounced 'meg-a-cups'. See **neurocomputer**.

MD Minidisk.

McNealy, Scott President of Sun Microsystems Computer Corporation, and President, Chief Executive Officer, and Chairman of the Board of Sun Microsystems Inc. McNealy is on the board of directors of Iwerks Entertainment, the Stanford University Graduate School of Business Advisory Council, and the Santa Clara County Manufacturers Board. He is also a member of the Computer Systems Policy Project in the United States.

MDA See **Monochrome Display Adapter**.

MDP Market Development Partners.

MDT Mean down-time. See **system availability**.

mean access time [ISO An average access time resulting from normal operating of a device.]

mean down-time See **system availability**.

mean rate accuracy [ISO Error margin, excluding errors caused by noise at input, which should not be exceeded when a device is used under normal operating conditions.]

mean time between failures See **MTBF**.

mean time to repair The accumulation of the total amount of time it takes to repair a failed item during a period of time, divided by the number of times that item has failed. For example, if a device failed five times during a year, and repairs took 10, 20, 10, 5, and 5 hours respectively, then it can be said that the mean time to repair (MTTR) is 10 hours (50 ÷ 5 = 10). MTTR is only concerned with the time devoted to maintenance, not fault detection, fault location, nor down-time. [ISO For a stated period in the life of a functional unit, the average time required for corrective maintenance.] See **system availability**. Compare **mean time to service restoral** and **MTBF**.

mean time to service restoral The average time it takes to repair a failed item during a period of time (such as one year), divided by the number of times that item has failed. This takes into account the total down-time of the item, including the time it takes to summon a technician, the time it takes to detect and locate the fault, plus the time it takes to actually repair, test, and bring the item back to full working order. Abbreviation 'MTTSR'. See **system availability**. Compare **mean time to repair** and **MTBF**.

measure of information [ISO A suitable function of the probability of occurrence of an event or of a sequence of events from a set of possible events. *Note:* In information theory, the term 'event' is to be understood as used in the theory of probability. For instance, an event may be: (a) The presence of a given element of a set. (b) The occurrence of a specified character or of a specified word in a given position of a message.]

media The plural form of the word 'medium'. See **media technology**.

media access unit A device that both transmits and receives data, providing the electrical and physical interface to the network cable. Also known as 'transceiver'. Abbreviation 'MAU'.

Media Control Architecture See **MCA**.

media defects In disk-drive technology, the normal physical characteristics of the media which result in repetitive read errors when a functional hard disk drive is operated within specified operating conditions. At the time of manufacture, a media test system evaluates every drive and identifies each media defect location. The defect areas are identified by the head address (HD) and cylinder address (CYL). The list of manufacturer-found defects is stored on the drive in a reserved write-protected area accessible by the SCSI con-

troller. This list is known as the 'manufacturer's defect list' (MDL) or 'primary defect list' (PList). A printed list of the defects is also shipped with each drive, containing entries that can be mapped out automatically when the disk is formatted using the format control parameter bits.

M

media orientation See **oxide media**.

media technology Technology involving the development of secondary storage devices. Modern magnetic disk media must be able to assume a local magnetization state in an area of less than ten-millionths of a square inch in a few tenths of a nanosecond and retain the magnetization pattern indefinitely (representing data). The magnetization must also have sufficient field strength to cause an observable signal while it is passing a head during reading. Magnetic disk media is actually a very thin coating applied to a substrate disk that is sufficiently rigid and stable to maintain a constant flat profile while rotating at high speed, generally 3600 revolutions per minute. The most common disk medium in use today is a suspension of gamma-ferric oxide particles in a phenoxy binder. See **oxide media**.

medium 1. Any material substance that can be, or is, used for the propagation of signals, from one point to another, such as optic fiber, cable, wire, water, air, or free space. 'Medium' refers to the singular. The plural is 'media'. 2. Referring to the middle range, as in 'medium-scale integration'.

medium access control [ISO A technique used to establish the sequence of data stations that are in temporary control of the transmission medium.]

medium access control protocol [ISO In a local area network, the protocol that governs access to the transmission medium, taking into account the topological aspects of the network, in order to enable the exchange of data between data stations.]

medium access control sublayer [ISO In a local area network, the part of the data link layer that applies medium access control and supports topology-dependent functions. *Note:* The MAC sublayer uses the services of the physical layer to provide services to the logical link control sublayer.]

medium attachment unit [ISO In a data station on a local area network, a device used to couple the data terminal equipment to the transmission medium.]

medium dependent interface [ISO At a data station on a local area network, the mechanical and electrical interface between the transmission medium and a medium attachment unit.]

medium interface connector [ISO A connector on a drop cable between a data station and a trunk coupling unit at which all transmitted and received signals are specified.]

medium-scale integration A chip technology with up to 1000 logic gates per chip. The flow of electrons in microprocessor chips are controlled by the transistors which form switches or logic gates. Chips are categorized by the number of logic gates they have available. Usually associated with third-generation computers. See **third generation**.

mega- See **M**.

megabit See **MB**.

megabyte See **Mb**.

megaflop Million floating point operations per second. See **FLOP**.

megahertz Million cycles per second. SI symbol 'MHz'. See **hertz**.

MegaPixel Display See **NeXT Computer, Inc**.

membrane keyboard A pressure-sensitive two-dimensional keyboard covered with a dust-proofed and dirt-proofed plastic sheet. Although these keyboards are not designed for fast typing, they are useful in environments susceptible to dust and dirt, such as on a factory floor or in restaurants, where users may not have clean hands. Membrane keyboards are also used in hand-held input devices and in telephones because of their space-saving feature.

MEMM Microsoft Expanded Memory Manager. See **extended memory**.

memory 1. Generally refers to a computer's primary storage such as the random-access memory. The *Guinness Book of Records* noted that 'Bhandanta

---

FUN FACT

If your car is equivalent in speed to a Pentium processor, and your neighbor's car is equivalent in speed to an original Intel 4004 processor, he would not have time to start his car's engine before you had completed a 4-mile (6.4-kilometer) non-stop round-trip.

Vicitsara recited 16 000 pages of Buddhist canonical texts in Yangon (formerly known as 'Rangoon'), Myanmar (formerly Burma) in May 1974'. See **RAM**. 2. [ISO All of the addressable storage space in a processing unit and other internal storages that is used to execute instructions. *Note:* In calculators, microcomputers, and some minicomputers, the term 'main memory' is preferred to the term 'main storage'.]

memory address The exact location in primary storage where an instruction or data is temporarily stored. Address locations each have a number. As with a mailbox, the address does not change, yet the contents of each address (mailbox) may change.

memory address space See **addressable memory**.

memory board This is an expansion board used to increase a computer's memory capacity. If a board contains the maximum number of memory chips, then it is said to be 'fully populated'. Memory boards cannot permanently store information, because once electrical power is switched off, all the contents are lost. See **RAM**.

memory chips Special memory chips that are designed to hold information come in two forms: volatile and nonvolatile. Memory chips which are volatile require a constant source of electrical power so that they can hold their information. An example of this is random-access memory (RAM). Nonvolatile chips hold their information permanently, even when the power is switched off. A read-only memory (ROM) chip is an example of a nonvolatile memory

chip — sometimes referred to as 'firmware'. See **DRAM**, **RAM**, and **ROM**.

memory errors The accidental alteration of information in memory. The reliability of a system and the availability of the information stored in the memory can be enhanced through various memory design characteristics. To ensure the integrity of stored data, advanced error-handling capabilities are critical. The binary information in memory may occasionally be altered by soft errors (caused by external noise) or hard failures in the memory hardware. If a soft error occurs, there is no damage to the memory cell and the faulty bit can be re-written. On the other hand, a hard failure indicates that the memory cell has been damaged and must be isolated (or mapped out) from the memory system. In order to protect the integrity of the data, memory controllers incorporate error-handling logic to detect and, in some cases, correct the error. See **self-test**.

memory indication [ISO A visual indication that a number is being held in the memory.]

memory management program A utility program that uses a portion of a hard disk for the extension of the random-access memory (RAM) so that the size of RAM appears larger. Sometimes, sections of expanded memory and extended memory are used by this utility. See **RAM cache**.

memory management unit See **architecture**.

memory partitioning [ISO In calculators, the subdividing of a storage device into independent sections.]

memory segment [ISO A block of memory that is identified by a base address and has been allocated for a specific purpose. *Note:* In common usage, different portions of memory may be designated as, for example, data segment, stack segment.]

memory size The number of memory allocations in the computer, usually measured in multiples of kilobytes (1024) or megabytes (1 048 576).

menu An on-screen list of available functions and procedures for an operator to choose from. Selection is made by entering a code found adjacent to the option description. See **pull-down menu**.

merge [ISO To combine the items of two or more sets of data that are in the same given order into one set in that order.]

mesh network [ISO A network in which there are at least two nodes with two or more paths between them.]

Merritt virus A variant of the Yale virus. See **Yale virus**.

message (In information theory and communication theory.) [ISO An ordered series of characters intended to convey information.]

message frame See **packet-switching system**.

MessagePad See **Newton MessagePad**.

message sink [ISO That part of a communication system in which messages are considered to be received.]

message source [ISO That part of a communication system from which messages are considered to originate.]

message switching [ISO In a data network, the process of routing messages by receiving, storing, and forwarding complete messages.]

meta-data See **database definition**.

meta-language A programming language, usually nonprocedural, that is used to describe computer programs. It is also used to describe the sequence in which application programs are executed to perform a computer system transaction. The prefix 'meta-' comes from the Greek word *meta*, meaning 'with' or 'after'.

metallic media Even with orientation, oxide media have some fundamental limitations. The most important is that the nonmagnetizable binder material can take up as much as 60% to 80% of the media's volume, with the coating imposing a minimum thickness on the media. Thicker media coatings tend to result in relatively wide transitions in field direction. Wide transitions limit output signal strength at high bit-density. It would be preferable to use a much thinner material that was 100% magnetizable. The disk industry has therefore sought viable alternatives to oxide media. The best alternative is a thin metallic medium with very high coercivity and large magnetic moment. Two preferred techniques for manufacturing metallic media are plating and sputtering. Plated media are manufactured using either of two conventional plating processes in which the substrate disk is placed in a solution containing ions of the plating material. Electroplating uses the substrate disk as the cathode of an electrical circuit. Atoms of the magnetic material (usually an alloy of cobalt) are deposited on a disk when electrical current flows. In sputtering, the substrate disk is suspended in a vacuum, in the presence of a mass of the material to be deposited. This mass is bombarded with an ion stream, dislodging atoms of the coating material. These atoms are attracted to the substrate disk, resulting in a thin consistent metallic coating which is suitable for high-density recording. For the environmentally-conscious, sputtering is a dry process that may ultimately result in easier waste-disposal than chemical baths. See **oxide media**.

metal organic vapor phase epitaxy See **resonant-tunneling effect**.

metal-oxide semiconductor See **MOS**.

meter From the Greek word *metron*, meaning 'measure', the meter was first proposed by Gabriel Mouton. A meter is an SI unit of 100 centimeters (cm). When first adopted by the French in 1670, one meter was equal to one ten-millionth of the distance between the North Pole and the equator on a line running through Paris and Barcelona. In the United States, the meter was legalized by an Act of Congress in 1866. In 1872, Frenchman Jacques Babinet discovered that when the element Krypton-86 is heated (through electrical discharge) in a vacuum, 1 650 763.73 of its pulsating waves of orange–red light are exactly equal to 1 meter. This measure was later adopted by International Convention as the universal standard for measuring a 1-meter unit, because it can be easily generated, and is accurate to one part in

100 million. Using a modern laser wavelength, even higher accuracy can be achieved. SI symbol 'm'. See **metric system** and **SI**.

metric system The framework for the metric system was established as early as 1585 by the Flemish mathematician Simon Stevin. In 1670, Frenchman Gabriel Mouton further developed the idea, and his system was officially adopted by the French Government in 1795, and called the 'metric system'. During that year, US President George Washington asked Congress to investigate the introduction of a simple measuring system (such as that presented by Thomas Jefferson, which resembled the metric system), but no system was implemented. The metric system became a legal system in France in 1801, and was declared the only legal system in 1840. The gram is used as a base unit for weight. A gram is one-thousandth of the weight of a platinum–iridium alloy cylinder kept in Paris (Sèvres) by the International Bureau of Weights and Measures (Bureau International des Poids et Mesures). One thousand grams weigh one kilogram. The liter is used to measure volume, and it is agreed that one liter has the same volume as a cube that measures 10 centimeters cubed (10 cm^3) — that is, 10 cm long, 10 cm wide, and 10 cm high. Greek and Latin prefixes are used with other base units. For example, *milli-* is used with *gram* (*milligram*) to measure one-thousandth (0.001) of a gram. *Centi-* means one-hundredth (0.01); *deci-* means one-tenth (0.1); *deka-* is used with *gram* (or other unit) to increase the value of a unit by 10 (as in 'dekameter', which means '10 meters'). *Hecto-* means 100; *kilo-* means 1000; and *mega-* means 1 000 000. The use of the metric system became widely accepted; in 1793, the popularity of the metric system brought about an attempt to metricate the calendar with hopes of creating a ten-day week, but this was never adopted. Today, over 90% of countries use the metric system, albeit in varying forms. The most popular is the SI system (Système International d'Unités). Units of measure other than the metric system include the imperial units of Avoirdupois weight, Apothecaries weight, and Troy weight. See **SI**.

metropolitan area network See **MAN**.

MF Medium frequency.

MFLOP Mega (million) floating point operations per second. See **FLOP**.

MFM Modified frequency modulation. Two standard data recording techniques are used to combine clock and data information for storage on a floppy disk. The single-density technique is referred to as 'FM encoding'. In FM encoding, a double-frequency encoding technique is used that inserts a data bit between two adjacent clock bits. (The presence of a data bit represents a binary 'one', while the absence of a data bit represents a binary 'zero'.) The adjacent clock bits are referred to as a 'bit cell', and except for unique field identifiers, all clock bits written on the disk are binary 'ones'. In FM encoding, each data bit is written at the center of the bit cell and the clock bits are written at the leading edge of the bit cell. The encoding used for double-density recording is termed 'MFM encoding' (for modified FM). In MFM encoding, the data bits are again written at the center of the bit cell. However, a clock bit is written at the leading edge of

the bit cell only if no data bit was written in the previous bit cell and no data bit will be written in the present bit cell. See **frequency modulation**.

MFS Macintosh Filing System.

MHz Megahertz. Million cycles per second. See **hertz**.

MIB Management information base.

mice This term is used to refer to more than one mouse. When the mouse was first introduced to computing, some experts insisted the plural was 'mouses' but 'mice' is now universally used. See **mouse**.

mickey The smallest unit of movement of a mouse. Pronounced 'mick-ee'.

MICR Magnetic ink character recognition. MICR inscribers are widely used by banks to print serial numbers on the bottom of checks using magnetic ink which contains magnetized particles. A MICR reader/sorter can process checks and other documents at speeds of up to 2000 documents per minute. Pronounced 'miker'. [ISO Character recognition of magnetic ink characters.]

micro- An SI unit prefix for 10^{-6} expressed as 0.000 001 in decimal notation, as in 'micrometer' (μm). SI symbol 'μ'.

Micro Channel Architecture A proprietary 32-bit expansion bus architecture introduced by IBM in 1987 for its new range of personal computers called 'Personal System/2'. The Micro Channel Architecture (MCA) is not downwardly compatible with existing peripherals and adapters designed for the 16-bit AT

(Advanced Technology) expansion bus. The MCA bus increases processing speed by providing a 32-bit data bus, and further increases memory addressing capabilities by providing 32 addressing lines. The boards are about 50% smaller than their predecessors, but the standard encourages the use of surface-mounted components which can be applied to both sides of the circuit board, allowing for smaller hardware. MCA is much more complicated than any of the previous bus structures and depends more on proprietary integrated circuits. These circuits perform many functions previously supplied by adapter cards. When the MCA bus was being designed, two of the most important reasons for totally dropping the old PC standard was the need to lower electrical interference and the need to increase speed. The original PC bus was designed for very modest operating speeds, typically around 5 megahertz. On the other hand, MCA radically altered the arrangement of the connector pins and included additional ground shielding to block interference. With this design, it is estimated that the maximum operating speed of the bus may exceed 80 megahertz. See **IBM-compatible**.

Microcom Networking Protocol See **MNP**.

microcomputer Usually refers to a third-generation computer whose central processing unit is made up of a silicon chip which contains thousands of integrated microscopic electronic components housing the arithmetic and logic unit, plus the control unit. The computer would usually operate an 8- to 16-bit command bus. In the mid-1970s, Radio Shack, Commodore, and Apple intro-

duced their own microcomputers. See **third generation** and **very-large-scale integration**.

microfiche Rolls or sheets of film (sometimes called 'microfilm') on which very small images are photographed and are later read using a microfiche reader. On one 10 x 15 centimeter sheet of microfilm, 200 A4 pages can be stored, thereby saving paper and storage space.

microfilm See **microfiche**.

microinstruction [ISO An instruction for operations at a level lower than machine instructions.]

micro manager The person employed to manage the purchase, maintenance, and modification of personal computers for an organization, including the training of staff in the use of application programs. Also called 'PC manager'.

microprocessor 1. A computer chip on which thousands of programmable microscopic electronic components are assembled to form a complete central processing unit. Microprocessors con-

FUN FACT

A microprocessor has a purity rate of 10^9. In comparison, if a forest of maple trees were planted from coast to coast, border to border, at a separation of 50 foot (15 meters) across the United States (including Alaska), an impurity level of one part per 10^9 would correspond to finding approximately 25 crabapple trees in the entire maple forest.

tain the arithmetic and logic unit, plus the control unit of a computer's central processing unit. They were first developed by team leader Ted Hoff at Intel Corporation in 1969. Microprocessors can be found in watches, pocket calculators, and microcomputers using very-large-scale integration. See **third generation** and **very-large-scale integration**. 2. [ISO A processor whose elements have been miniaturized into one or a few integrated circuits.]

Microprocessor Implementation of a Reliable Architecture See **MIRA**.

microprogram [ISO A sequence of micro-instructions. *Note:* Microprograms are mainly used to implement machine instructions.]

microprogramming 1. [ISO The preparation of microprograms.] 2. [ISO The technique used in the design of hardware that is to be controlled by microprograms.]

Microsoft At Work An architecture that comprises a set of software building blocks that reside in both office machines and personal computer (PC) products, including desktop and network-connected printers; digital monochrome and color copiers; telephones and voice massaging systems; fax machines and PC fax products; hand-held systems; or a combination of the above. The purpose of this is to enable all office products to integrate and function easily together, and readily and efficiently exchange digital information. One key to achieving this cooperation between the different devices will be the storage and transmission of information in a standard digital format that each Micro-

soft At Work-based product will understand. For example, what is initially sent to one office device will be able to be transmitted to another without deterioration of information that occurs when a document is faxed or copied repeatedly. With this format, a user will be able to send the final version of a document prepared on a PC directly to the copier and avoid any loss in reproduction quality.

Microsoft Corporation A software publisher located in Bellevue, Washington. Microsoft was founded by ex-college students Bill Gates and Paul Allen in 1975. Their first product was a BASIC language interpreter. IBM later commissioned Microsoft to develop an operating system for the IBM Personal Computer. The result was MS-DOS (Microsoft Disk Operating System), now the most popular operating system for personal computers. In 1987, Microsoft released a new operating system called 'OS/2', designed to take advantage of the improved powers of Intel's 80286 and 80386 processors. Other popular application software published by Microsoft includes Microsoft Word

---

NEWSFLASH

Windows-based products will grow to represent 87% of the total spreadsheet shipments in 1997. Growth in hardware forecasts will result in a total spreadsheet market of 16.7 million units in 1997.

In 1993, the Macintosh spreadsheet market leader, Excel, earned US$100 million, capturing 91.8% of the total Macintosh revenue market. The product also earned an 89.5% shipment market share.

(word processing), Microsoft Excel (spreadsheet), plus computer language products in six computer languages. Xenix is Microsoft's version of UNIX. In June 1990, Microsoft Corporation announced record revenues and earnings, making it the first personal computer software company to exceed US$1000 million in sales in a single year. Microsoft employs more than 12 000 people worldwide. Its corporate campus comprises 23 buildings on 260 acres (105 hectares). See **Gates, William H.**

micro-to-mainframe The connection of personal computers to mainframe-based networks.

Micro 2000 Project Intel Corporation's product roadmap that plans to deliver microprocessors that can perform at up to 2000 MIPS (million instructions per second) at a 250 megahertz (MHz) clock rate by the year 2000. According to current projections, such chips could contain 100 million transistors and could incorporate multiple central processing units, special units for high-speed math, a large on-chip memory unit, and an intelligent human interface (handling such functions as full-motion video, speech and handwriting recognition, and image processing). Intel expects that such chips will be compatible with Intel 386, 486, and Pentium microprocessors. Intel is also investing in other technological innovations that complement its microprocessor architecture and accelerate the progress toward the Micro 2000 Project. See **Intel Corporation** and **Pentium Processor**.

microwaves Ultra-high to super-high frequency radio waves with very short wavelengths ranging from approximately 130 centimeters down to fractions of a millimeter. Frequencies range between 1×10^9 and 3000×10^9 hertz (3000 GHz). They are modulated and are used for data signal transmission including satellite communications and international telephone connections. Microwaves can only travel in clear straight lines of sight, so, due to the Earth's curvature, relay stations are positioned on relay towers, buildings, mountains, and other high places to continue transmission over long distances. Transmission is possible through the air and outer space via satellite relay stations which amplify electronic signals and re-transmit them to other stations. Signals may carry voice, facsimile, data, or video. Communications satellites are usually positioned in a geostationary orbit, meaning that they remain in a fixed position approximately 22 300 miles (35 000 kilometers) above the Earth's surface. From this distance, about one-third of the Earth's surface area may be reached. This area is referred to as the satellite's 'footprint'. See **satellite transmission**.

mid-grain parallel processing See **parallel processing**.

MIDI Musical Instrument Digital Interface; a standard communications protocol for the connection of a computer to a musical synthesizer. MIDI has become a standard tool for musicians, enabling them to compose complex music on a piano-style keyboard, and then capture that information using a computer which can be used to automatically write the score. The data is stored on a standard diskette, and every aspect of the music can be edited, including orchestral arrangement, tempo, pitch, and key. ▼

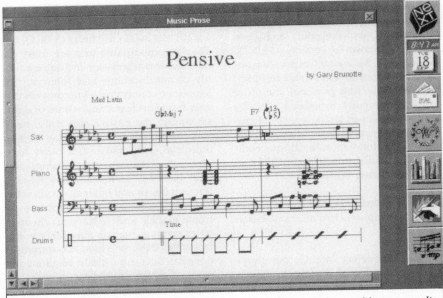

MIDI *This MIDI product is called 'Music-Prose', and is a publishing and composition program. Its more powerful features include real-time MIDI input and playback, automatic part extraction, comprehensive lyric and chord entry, and sophisticated page layout control. Included with the program are two PostScript fonts: Petrucci, the music character font, and Seville, the guitar fingerboard font. Other features include slash notation, one-line staff, music display on playback, choice of eight clefs, automatic guitar fingerboard, four voices per staff, undo/redo capability, and automatic part transposition.*

migration Taking software from one platform to another. This involves making changes to the software as necessary to make it run correctly and as expected. The term 'migration' makes no assumptions about whether or not portability was considered when the application was designed and implemented. When portability is not emphasized during the development of software, each migration of that software to a new platform will uncover different problems or areas of concern. Designing and writing portable software is not equivalent to migrating (moving) software. The phrase 'portable software' implies that the software was intended for use on a variety of platforms from its conception, and that this factor was considered throughout the design and implementation of the software. This is the only method of ensuring a high degree of portability in any software application. Compare **portability**.

milli- See **m**.

milliard See **exponent**.

million See **exponent**.

million instructions per second See **MIPS**.

millisecond A unit of measurement equal to one-thousandth of a second. Twenty-two milliseconds can be expressed as 22 x 10^{-3} seconds and written (using its SI symbol) as 22 ms. In computing, this measure is often used to specify the access time of a hard disk drive. Naturally, the higher the number, the slower the access speed.

MIMD Multiple-instruction, multiple-data. In parallel processing, over 65 000 processors may be engaged to simultaneously share a processing task. Special software manages this process by allocating equal portions of the raw data to the processors, issuing several different instructions to each of the processors. In contrast, the single-instruction, multiple-data (SIMD) method issues one 'single instruction' to all processors simultaneously only after each of the processors has received the raw data. See **parallel processing**.

MIMO Mathematics in, mathematics out. Refers to the fact that data encryption methods are not completely secure because any data protection or password creation program that uses mathematics to encrypt data can be cracked using mathematics. Pronounced 'my-mo'.

Minicom A correspondence service provided by France Telecom to all videotext users in France and in those countries interconnected to the Teletel network.

minicomposite head See **read/write head**.

minicomputer Traditionally, a medium-sized computer whose central processing unit uses a 16- or 32-bit bus, although today some microcomputers can also use a 64-bit bus. Although minicomputers are smaller and less powerful than mainframes, they can connect over 100 users for simultaneous departmental computing. The trend toward minicomputers was started by Digital Equipment Corporation and Hewlett-Packard in the early 1970s. More powerful minicomputers are called 'superminicomputers'. Accepted contraction in speech: 'mini'. Compare **mainframe**. ▼

mini-highway See **data highway**.

minisuper Deprecated abbreviation for 'minisupercomputer'. See **supercomputer**.

minisupercomputer A supercomputer capable of operating at no more than 100 million floating point operations per second. See **supercomputer**.

MIPS Million instructions per second; a measure of the speed of execution of a computer's central processing unit.

MIRA Microprocessor Implementation of a Reliable Architecture; a system which offers very high 'system availability', consisting of two MicroVAX systems which are linked together by means of an Ethernet, a watchdog timer, and

M

FUN FACT

If a person were employed to clap once every second for eight hours a day, from Monday to Friday (and if each clap were imagined to be one instruction), then a microprocessor rated at 27 MIPS can perform in one second what would take that employee four years to accomplish.

minicomputer *Digital Equipment Corporation's PDP-8/s (s for serial) was introduced in 1967 as the world's first minicomputer priced under US$10 000. It achieved its low cost (at the time) by using serial logic, which meant fewer circuits were needed. This museum display has a perspex cover so that the circuits can be seen. The 4096 (12-bit) word core memory can be seen protruding above the logic boards. This 'chunk' of memory is equivalent to a 64-kilobyte chip.*

switching modules. One MicroVAX system is normally designated as the master and the other as the standby. MIRA hardware and software gives customer applications the ability to detect the failure of the master system and to switch data communication lines to the standby system. A third-party volume-shadowing product is available with the system to provide tolerance of disk controller, disk drive, and media faults. MIRA systems are well suited to dedicated control operations rather than general-purpose data processing in a transaction processing network. See **fault tolerance** and **system availability** .

mirror drive The disk drive in a mirroring scheme that stores identical information from the original data drive. See **mirroring**.

mirroring 1. A fault-tolerance feature that sets up primary and secondary partitions on a physical drive. The drive that duplicates data on the primary memory is called the 'secondary partition'. This is invisible to the operating system, which sees the primary and secondary partitions as a single logical drive. Compare **drive mirroring**. 2. [ISO One hundred and eighty degrees of rotation of display elements about an axis in the plane of the display surface.]

MIS Management information system; a system that regularly provides management with needed business information. This system can be manual or, more commonly, uses computers to analyze data and provide information.

miscellaneous time [ISO That part of operating time that is not system production time, system test time, nor re-run time. *Note:* Miscellaneous time is typically used for demonstrations, operator training, or other such purposes.]

missing-pulse [ISO A pulse whose level cannot be read nor recorded.]

mistake [ISO A human action that produces an unintended result.]

MIT Massachusetts Institute of Technology.

mixed base (numeration) system [ISO A numeration system in which a number is represented as the sum of a series of terms, each of which consists of a mantissa and a base — the base of a given term being constant for a given application but the bases being such that there are not necessarily integral ratios between the bases of all the terms. *Example:* With bases b_3, b_2, and b_1 and mantissae 6, 5, and 4, the number represented is given by: $6b_3 + 5b_2 + 4b_1$. *Notes:* (a) A mixed radix numeration system is a particular case of a mixed base numeration system in which, when the terms are ordered so that their bases are in descending magnitudes, there is an integral ratio between the bases of adjacent terms, but not the same ratio in each case; thus if the smallest base is b, and if x and y represent integers, the numeral 654 in such a numeration system repre-

sents the number given by: $6xyb + 5xb + 4b$. (b) A fixed radix numeration system is a particular case of a mixed base numeration system in which, when the terms are ordered so that their bases are in descending magnitudes, there is the same integral ratio between the bases of all pairs of adjacent terms; thus if b is the smallest base and if x represents an integer, the numeral 654 in such a numeration system represents the number given by: $6x^2b + 5xb + 4b$.]

mixed radix (numeration) system [ISO A radix numeration system in which the digit places do not all necessarily have the same radix. *Example:* The numeration system in which three successive digits represent hours, tens of minutes, and minutes; taking one minute as the unit, the weights of the three digit places are 60, 10, and 1 respectively; the radices of the second and third digit places are 6 and 10 respectively. *Note:* A comparable numeration system that used one or more digits to represent days and two digits to represent hours would not satisfy the definition of any radix numeration system, since the ratio of the weights of the 'day' and the 'tens of hours' digit places would not be an integer.]

Mix1 virus An indirect-action file virus that infects .EXE files. The virus becomes noticeable when it displays a bouncing letter 'o' across the screen. If it hits a character along the way, it changes that character to the letter 'o'. Its other function is to confuse the data traveling along the parallel and serial ports so that data transfer across modems or printers is unintelligible. For example, the characters 'A', 'B', 'a', and 'c' are substituted with the characters 'B', 'E', 'e', and 's' respectively. See **indirect-action file virus**.

MMCD Multimedia compact disk.

MMFS Manufacturing Message Format Standard; developed in 1983 by General Motors to provide a syntax for exchanging messages in the manufacturing environment.

MMI Man–machine interface; devices which help computers understand and speak plain language. These include voice synthesizing devices as used in talking calculators.

MMP Massively Parallel Processor.

MMU Memory management unit. See **architecture**.

mnemonic A memory aid which is usually based on words. For example, the colors of the rainbow may be remembered by the name 'Roy G. Biv'.

MNP Microcom Networking Protocol; an asynchronous (packet-oriented) communications protocol which allows speed negotiation, packet re-transmission, and data compression between two different modems. MNP classes 1 to 4 are specified by CCITT V.42 as a backup error-control scheme for LAPM (link access procedure for modems). Each MNP class has all the features of the previous class plus its own. MNP class 1 (also called 'block mode') sends data in one direction at a time. MNP class 2 (also called 'stream mode') sends data in both directions at the same time. MNP class 3 asks the sending modem to strip the start and stop bits out from the data block before sending it. The receiving modem adds start and stop bits before passing the data to the receiving computer. MNP class 4 monitors the quality of the connection and streamlines the information in the headers of data blocks. If the telephone line is relatively noise-free, the modem sends larger blocks of data to increase the throughput. If the telephone line is noisy, the modem sends smaller blocks of data so that less data will have to be re-transmitted. MNP class 5 provides data compression. The sending modem detects redundant data and re-codes it to fewer bits in order to increase the effective throughput. The receiving modem decompresses the data before passing it to the receiving computer.

modem Modulator/demodulator; a peripheral device that permits a personal computer, minicomputer, or mainframe to receive and transmit data in digital format across voice communications links such as telephone lines. This is done by converting data back and forth between digital and analog signals. Modems can handle other functions such as error detection. They are also available as internal expansion devices (cards) which allow automatic dialing and transmission of data from a computer. The modem has done more to extend the utility of personal computers than many other optional peripherals by enabling users to communicate with the outside world to access online data services, transfer files, retrieve information from databases, and access electronic mail and facsimile services. Computers process information internally in the form of digital electronic signals, but because the telephone line was originally designed for sound (analog), a modem is required to convert the computer's digital electronic signals into analog electronic signals. These can then be transmitted across a public-switched telephone network (PSTN). The rate at which data characters are transferred by a modem is called 'bits per second' (Bps). Modems generally support a variety of speeds, ranging from modems with very low speeds of 300 Bps to high-speed modems (such as the NetComm's TrailBlazer) which can transfer data at speeds up to 19 200 Bps. Although the common speed is 2400 Bps, being suitable for both home and business users, 9600 Bps is becoming the popular business standard in full duplex over conventional telephone lines (this equates to approximately 1000 characters per second). High-speed modems are widely used by corporate users offering flexibility in connection, efficient large file transfers, low-cost international communications, viable connections for local area networks, and remote transfer of large and complex graphics and imaging. Any modem speed must comply with a recognized standard in order to ensure reliable connection and data transmission between different manufacturers' modems operating at the same speed. For example, V.22 defines the procedures allowing two 1200 Bps modems to communicate, while V.32 clearly defines the 9600 Bps standard worldwide. The 'V' standards are published by CCITT — a standards body based in Geneva, Switzerland, whose

standards apply to most of the Western world except the United States and Canada where the AT&T 'Bell' standard is in use, although the CCITT is dominating as the world standard. The 1200 Bps standard in the United States is referred to as the 'Bell 212A'. Any information residing in databanks or traveling through a communications network is at risk of being exposed to unauthorized personnel or hackers. For users working in security-sensitive environments such as banking and defense, modems that incorporate security features are available. They can prohibit unauthorized access when transmitting data, and facilitate password validation, encryption, and automatic dial-back for further protection. [ISO A functional unit that modulates and demodulates signals. *Note:* One of the functions of a modem is to enable digital data to be transmitted over analog transmission facilities.] See **baud rate**, **modulation**, and **S Register**. ▼

modem-less connection A back-to-back connection between two common-carrier adapters is referred to as a 'modem-less installation'. Since the RS-232-C adapter interface is not designed for connection to another adapter, a special cable is required which crosses over cer-

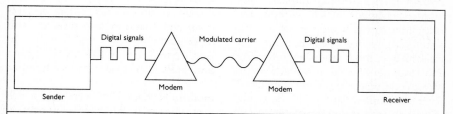

modem Using telephone lines, the first modem receives digital information and converts (modulates) the data. The receiving modem picks up the data and converts (demodulates) the analog signals to digital information, ready for processing by the computer.

NEWSFLASH

Worldwide modem shipments, revenue in US$ million

	1993	1994	1995	1996	1997
Shipments	6 323 520	7 892 000	9 665 000	11 672 400	13 690 000
Revenues US$M	1 878	1 881	2 005	2 165	2 292
Installed base	14 662 585	19 099 837	24 196 728	28 356 596	32 881 801

tain data and control terms. The maximum distance between adapters in a modemless installation is limited to 50 foot (15 meters).

modified frequency modulation recording [ISO Non-return-to-zero recording in which there is a change in the condition of magnetization in the center of a cell containing a one, and a change in the boundary between two cells each of which contains a zero.]

modulation The process of changing the amplitude, frequency, or phase of a carrier wave in a periodic or intermittent way from a digital signal to an analog signal for the purpose of transmitting information (as in the case of telephony, telegraphy, radio, television, or digital communications). The carrier wave actually carries (through imprint) low-frequency signals which, without the help of the carrier wave, cannot be radiated through space. The oldest and most basic form of modulation is the starting and stopping of a radio wave (as with Morse code, where the carrier is switched on or off). Demodulation is the decoding of a modulated analog signal after being received from a carrier wave, so that it can be converted back to digital signals. See **amplitude modulation**, **frequency modulation**, **modem**, and **phase modulation**.

modulator/demodulator See **modem** and **demodulation**.

Modula-2 A high-level programming language designed in 1980 by Niklaus Wirth, the European programmer who wrote Pascal. Modula-2 is an enhanced version of Pascal, used primarily as a teaching language at universities. Its main feature is its ability to break down the programming functions into modules, so that different programmers can each be responsible for a separate function, ensuring that each function works properly before it is added to the main program. See **Pascal** and **programming language**.

module [ISO A language construct that consists of procedures of data declarations and that can also interact with other such constructions. *Examples:* In Ada, a package; in FORTRAN, a program unit; in PL/1, an external procedure.]

modulo-N check [ISO A check in which a number is divided by a number N to generate a remainder that is compared to the remainder previously calculated.]

modulo-N counter [ISO A counter in which the number represented reverts to zero in the sequence of counting after reaching a maximum value of N–1.]

moiré distortion An optical illusion (perceived flickering) which occurs on the computer screen when high-contrast line patterns are drawn too closely together. Pronounced 'mwah-ray'.

molecular beam epitaxy The etching of growth patterns on the surface of crystals using optoelectronic laser beams. This is done so that molecules can grow on the surface. The word 'epitaxy' refers to the growth of one type of crystal on the surface of another crystal without changing the orientation of the underlying crystal (substrate). Molecular beam epitaxy (MBE) was developed by the Japanese Optoelectronics Technology Research Corporation. MBE is being used with a scanning microprobe reflection high-energy electron diffraction (RHEED) system. Using an electron beam, MBE examines the surface structure of crystals. Further research is being conducted into the possibility of using controlled epitaxy, utilizing a method of growing one atomic layer at a time. Currently, silicon epitaxy is used to make large-scale integration chips, and this technology is being explored for optoelectronic devices where MBE can be combined with a compound like gallium arsenide on a silicon substrate to be used with optical neurocomputers. See **optical neurocomputer** and **resonant-tunneling effect**.

monadic (dyadic) operator [ISO An operator that represents an operation on one and only one operand (on two and only two operands).]

monadic operation [ISO An operation on one and only one operand. *Example:* Negation.]

monitor 1. [ISO A device that observes and records selected activities within a data processing system for analysis. *Note:* Possible uses are to indicate significant departure from the normal, or to determine levels of utilization of particular functional units.] 2. A screen which can display text and graphics. The word 'monitor' comes from the Latin word *monitor*, meaning 'see'. ▼

Monochrome Display Adapter An adapter used since 1981 for personal computers to display text (not graphics) in one color only, at a resolution of 640 pixels (picture elements) horizontally by 350 pixels vertically (with each character formed by a 9 x 14 pixel matrix). Abbreviation 'MDA'. See **video adapter**.

monochrome monitor A monitor which can display text and graphics in one color only. For example, green text can be displayed against a black background, or black text against a white background.

monolithic Refers to a computer that contains several or all components in the same chassis. Monolithic construction is now typically used in notebook computers.

monolithic head technology See **read/write head**.

mono monitor See **monochrome monitor**.

monospace Refers to a typeface, such as Courier, in which all characters are equally spaced, producing type which resembles that of a typewriter.

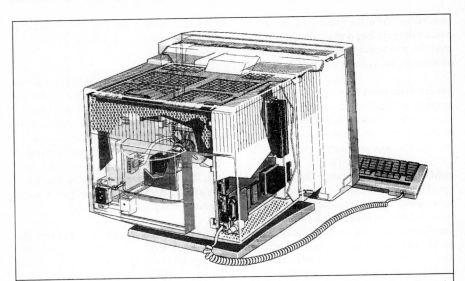

monitor *Monitors come in all shapes and sizes. Although the general trend is toward smaller and more compact monitors, users in the graphic arts industries still prefer the larger format 15-, 17-, or 19-inch color monitors. This cut-away illustration of a monitor demonstrates the need for the large housing that contains the cathode-ray tube, the cooling fan, the power supply, and other devices.*

monostable (trigger) circuit [ISO A trigger circuit that has one stable state.]

MOPS Million operations per second. Mainframes rate at 14 to 20 MOPS, while supercomputers are capable of 800 MOPS. See **mainframe**.

morphing Changing an image in shape, size, dimension, and color, into another image altogether. Although morphing has been used extensively in motion pictures to create stunning special effects, its scientific, medical, industrial, and defense applications are broad-based. The term 'morphing' was coined from contracting the word 'metamorphosis', which means to 'transform'. ▼

MOS Metal-oxide semiconductor. There are three major MOS technology families — PMOS, NMOS, and CMOS. They refer to the channel type of the

morphing *Popularized by high-budget motion pictures like* Terminator 2 *and video clips like Michael Jackson's* Black or White, *morphing uses sophisticated computer imaging equipment. The special effects for* Terminator 2 *were created by US-based Industrial Light & Magic using Silicon Graphics' computer equipment — the same systems that were used for the film* Jurassic Park.

MOS transistors made with the technology. PMOS technologies implement p-channel transistors by diffusing p-type dopants (usually boron) into an n-type silicon substrate to form the source and drain. P-channel is so named because the channel is made up of positively charged carriers. NMOS technologies are similar, but use n-type dopants (normally phosphorous or arsenic) to make n-channel transistors in p-type silicon substrates. N-channel is so named because the channel is made up of negatively charged carriers. CMOS (or complementary MOS) technologies combine both p-channel and n-channel devices on the same sili-con. Either p-type or n-type silicon substrates can be used. However, deep areas of the opposite doping type (called 'wells') must be defined to allow fabrication of the complementary transistor type. Most of the early semiconductor memory devices (like Intel's 1103 dynamic random-access memory and 1702 erasable programmable read-only memory) were made with PMOS technologies. As higher speeds and greater densities were needed, most new devices were implemented with NMOS. This was due to the inherently higher speed of n-channel charge carriers (electrons) in silicon along with improved

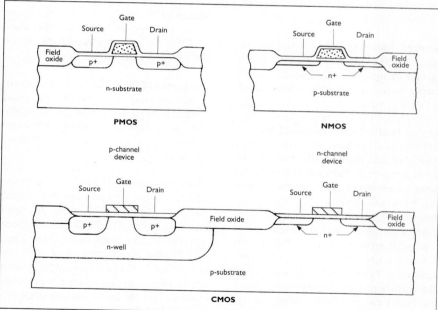

MOS *There are three major metal-oxide semiconductor (MOS) technology families. PMOS, NMOS, and CMOS. They refer to the channel type of the MOS transistors made with the technology. PMOS technologies implement p-channel transistors by defusing p-type dopants (usually boron) into an n-type silicon substrate to form the source and drain. NMOS technologies are similar, but use n-type dopants (normally phosphorus or arsenic) to make n-channel transistors in p-type silicon substrates. CMOS (or complementary MOS) technologies combine both p-channel and n-channel devices on the same silicon.*

process margins. Although many of the MOS memory devices in production today are fabricated with NMOS technologies, CMOS technology is beginning to see widespread commercial use in memory devices, which have been improved to produce higher-speed devices. See **CMOS**. ⚑

MOSFET Metal-oxide semiconductor field-effect transistor.

motherboard The most important circuit board in a computer, containing vital components including expansion slots, and containing or connecting the central processing unit, memory, and other device controllers. Abbreviation 'MB'.

motion video Video that simulates realistic motion by displaying a sequence of images (frames) rapidly enough that the eyes see the image as a continuously moving picture.

Motorola DSP56001 The Motorola Digital Signal Processor 56001 (DSP56001) provides key multimedia features for some computers. The 56001 provides the basis for on-board data communications (such as facsimile and modem) and sound syntheses (such as voice mail, voice annotated files, and high-fidelity audio). It creates compact-disk quality sound because its architecture can generate up to 144 decibels of dynamic range. Acting as a facsimile/modem processor, the 56001 can modulate incoming and outgoing data signals at rates comparable to a V.32 modem. With the 56001 in personal computers, blind people, for example, can listen to voice translations of a document on-screen; multinational companies can translate and route documents to foreign branch offices; and

advertising agencies can create on-screen audio-visual storyboards (sometimes called 'animatics'). Running at 12.5 MIPS, the 56001 handles real-time oriented applications, acting as an auxiliary processor to Motorola's 68040. See **Motorola 68040**.

Motorola 68000 A microprocessor previously used to power low-end Apple Macintosh computers, capable of addressing up to 32 gigabytes of random-access memory. The 68000 runs at 8 megahertz with a 32-bit address bus for internal communications, and a 16-bit data bus for external communications.

Motorola 68020 A full 32-bit microprocessor running at 16 megahertz, used primarily to power some of the Apple Macintosh II computers.

Motorola 68030 A full 32-bit microprocessor running at 16 megahertz, used primarily to power the high-end Apple Macintosh computers, offering advanced features including virtual memory management.

Motorola 68040 The microprocessor which was the central processor engine for NeXT computers. The 040 provided NeXT customers with a performance increase of three to ten times the original 68030-based NeXT computers while retaining 100% software compatibility with applications developed for the previous system. The 040 had a performance rating of 15 to 20 million instructions per second (MIPS) and 2 to 3.5 million floating point operations per second. It incorporated more than 1.2 million transistors, almost four times the number in the 68030. Motorola's 0.8-micron high-performance complementary metal-oxide semiconductor (HCMOS) process was incorporated into an on-chip integer unit, floating point unit, two memory management units, and data and instruction caches. See **Motorola DSP56001** and **NeXT Computer, Inc**.

mount [ISO To place a data medium in a position to operate.]

mouse An input device designed to assist in the use of a computer system. For example, in a graphical user interface environment like Macintosh or MS-Windows, an icon is displayed on the screen. The user selects the icon by moving the cursor to point to the icon with a mouse, automatically activating a set of commands without the user having to enter complex instructions. The mouse can also be used to open menus, select text for editing, move objects on the screen, and draw images or diagrams. A mechanical mouse uses a rubber-coated ball on the under-side. The movement of this ball sends electrical signals to the system unit which cause the cursor, or pointer, to move in a corresponding fashion. There are normally two buttons (one for the Macintosh) on the top of the mouse. The application program determines how the buttons function. In contrast, an optical mouse (optomechanical) uses diodes to emit light onto a metal pad, performing the same task, but usually with greater accuracy. With a mouse, the cursor can be moved very quickly to any point on the screen. This is very useful in drafting, engineering, and publishing applications where geometric figures and text must be placed in the correct position. Newer operating system environments also encourage the use of a mouse to make screen selections from graphics menus. The term 'mice' is generally used when referring to more than one mouse. The fun name for a mouse is 'rodentiometer'. [ISO A hand-held locator operated by moving it on a surface. *Note:* A mouse generally contains a control ball or pair of wheels.] Compare **tablet** and **trackball**.

Mouton, Gabriel The Frenchman who, in 1670, commenced working on the metric system of measurement which was adopted by the French Government in 1795, using the meter, gram, and liter. Around the same time, Thomas Jefferson presented a similar measuring system to President George Washington in the United States. Jefferson's proposal was rejected by Congress. See **metric system**.

MOVPE Metal organic vapor phase epitaxy. See **resonant-tunneling effect**.

MPC 1. Multimedia personal computer. A specification developed by the Multimedia Council. It defines the minimum platform capable of running multimedia software. PCs carrying the MPC logo signify that they are able to run any software that also displays the MPC logo. 2. Motorola PowerPC. See **PowerPC**.

MPEG Moving Picture Expert Group. The ISO standard on MPEG1 was drafted in 1991. MPEG1's data transfer rate is 1.5 megabytes per second for video, audio, and others — corresponding to CD–ROM, DAT, and ISDN. MPEG2 provides an image quality which is as high as existing NTSC broadcasts at a data transfer rate of 5 megabytes per second. A regular motion picture stored using the MPEG2 format would require approximately 1.5 gigabytes of disk storage. Pronounced 'em-peg'.

M

MPP Massively parallel processing.

MQWS Multiple quantum-well structures. See **optical neurocomputer**.

MRI Magnetic resonance imaging.

MRX Multiple RAID extension.

ms See **millisecond**.

MS See **Microsoft Corporation**.

MSB Most significant bit.

MSCDEX Microsoft Compact Disk Extension. A TSR program giving DOS access to CD–ROM drives.

MSD Most significant digit.

MS–DOS Microsoft Corporation–Disk Operating System; a standard operating system for personal computers, first chosen by IBM as the operating system for the IBM Personal Computer. MS–DOS was primarily a single-user operating system, until Microsoft developed version 3.1 of MS–DOS, making it suitable for use on networks. MS–DOS was based on CP/M (Control Program for Microprocessors) and was designed to ensure business software would run in the new 16-bit IBM Personal Computer environment. Historically, the first personal computers (PCs) on the market were 8-bit machines. This means that in one cycle of a computer instruction, the PC can only access 8 bits, or one data character. So, if a program command requires that 32 bits be moved from one part of RAM (random-access memory) to another, four command cycles must be completed. In the quest for faster processing, 16-bit PCs were devel-

oped which could move two data characters in a command cycle. With the advent of 16-bit PCs and the acceptance of DOS, almost overnight a separate industry dedicated to developing PC application software was born. Companies such as Borland became very successful by developing and selling thousands of copies of application packages that could run on any industry-standard PC. The birth of this separate software industry dramatically changed the relationship between PC hardware and software development. Hardware manufacturers were forced to design 'industry-compatible' machines that run certain operating systems and application programs, instead of writing software to match the hardware, as was common in the past. Although DOS has a huge installed base, it does have limitations that prevent users from taking advantage of the latest hardware advances. Microsoft addressed the limitations of DOS by releasing an operating system called 'OS/2' (Operating System number two, now an IBM product), and Windows 95. Pronounced 'em-ess-doss'. See **Microsoft Corporation** and **operating system**.

MSI Medium-scale integration. The flow of electrons in microprocessor chips is controlled by the transistors which form switches or logic gates. Chips are categorized by the number of logic gates they have available. For example, medium-scale integration chips, usually associated with third-generation computers, each contain up to 1000 logic gates. See **third generation**.

MS–Net Microsoft DOS–based networking systems software product, officially known as 'Microsoft Network'. It was announced in 1984 and first shipped in

1985. MS–Net was superseded by Microsoft LAN Manager.

MTBF Mean time between failures. When computers and peripherals are first manufactured, they are often subjected to extreme testing. One part of the test determines the average time it takes for that product to fail in any way. A statistical average is determined and is often quoted in hours of operation, kilometers, cycles, or events. Generally, computer system availability is dependent upon four areas: hardware, software, people, and environment. Availability is typically measured in terms of percentage of up-time, or in minutes of unscheduled down-time per year. The key elements in availability are reliability and recoverability. Reliability is the ability of a system to keep running correctly. Recoverability is a system's ability to be restored to full operation after a failure. Availability must be extremely high for most business applications. Ninety-nine percent availability translates into the loss of 88 processing hours a year on a 24-hours-per-day, seven-days-per-week system. If the 88 hours were lost at critical times, this level of availability might be unacceptable for many applications. [ISO For a stated period in the life of a functional unit, the mean value of the length of time between consecutive failures under stated conditions.] See **system availability**. Compare **mean time to repair** and **mean time to service restoral**.

MTSO Mobile telephone switching office.

MTTR Mean time to repair. The accumulation of the total amount of time it takes to repair a failed item during a period of time (such as one year), divided by the

number of times that item has failed. For example, if a device failed five times during a year, and each repair took 10, 20, 10, 5, and 5 hours respectively, then it can be said that the MTTR is 10 hours (50 ÷ 5 = 10). MTTR is only concerned with the time devoted to maintenance, not fault detection, fault location, nor down-time. [ISO For a stated period in the life of a functional unit, the average time required for corrective maintenance.] See **system availability**. Compare **MTTSR** and **MTBF**.

MTTSR Mean time to service restoral. The average time it takes to repair a failed item during a period of time (such as one year), divided by the number of times that the particular item has failed. This takes into account the total down-time of the item, including the time it takes to summon a technician, the time it takes to detect and locate the fault, plus the time it takes to actually repair, test, and bring the item back to full working order. See **system availability**. Compare **MTTR** and **MTBF**.

MU Multi-user.

MultiColor Graphics Array A video display standard used on some IBM Personal System/2 personal computers offering 64 shades of gray with a palette of 16 colors at a resolution of 640 pixels (picture **elements) horizontally by 350 pixels vertically.** Abbreviation 'MCGA'.

multidrop Referring to a circuit in a communications line which is a type of multipoint link where the telephone company 'drops' several sets of local-loops into various customer sites at secondary stations. This is in contrast to a standard multipoint link where there is only one set of local-loop connections at each end of the telephone network. Multipoint circuits require the use of a telephone company analog bridge. The bridge may be located in a toll trunk, or in the local loop. Analog bridges are used between modems to provide multiple analog circuits on the secondary ends of a communication link. Note that when an analog bridge is used, each secondary station must have a separate modem. An analog bridge may be owned and installed by the customer in the place of business, or may be owned and installed by the telephone company as part of the telephone network. Digital bridges are used between the modem and the secondary stations and are normally owned by the customer. Note that in this type of installation, only one modem is required for several stations. However, there is a distance limitation of approximately 50 foot (15.25 meters) between the modem and the secondaries. See **multipoint**.

MultiFinder A utility used in Apple Macintosh computers as the operating system's shell for file and memory management, and user interaction. The original version (Finder) could only handle one program at a time. However, MultiFinder was designed (with limited capabilities) to load more than one program. Although it can perform background processing such as downloading information via telecommunications, and carrying out background printing, it is not a multitasking operating system. When one program is being used, the others must cease processing. Compare **multitasking**.

multifunction board Most personal computers have only a limited number of puters have only a limited number of expansion slots to accommodate expansion boards. This issue can be addressed by using a multiple function board which capitalizes on the capability of each slot to provide more than one function per board. For example, random-access memory, a print-spooler, and other similar devices may all be resident on one board. Some boards may even offer more slots so as to increase a computer's capability and expandability.

multiloading operating system An operating system which permits the user to open more than one application program at a time. Unlike multitasking, when one program is in use the other must stop. The advantage of loading more than one program at a time is the ability to quickly switch from one to the other simply by pressing a key. Compare **multitasking**.

multimedia In computing, this term refers to the presentation of information on a computer using sound, graphics, animation, and text. Using various input and output devices, multimedia attempts, at any point in time, to combine the latest technology on the personal computer. This includes telecommunications, video technology, conferencing, sound technology, and sophisticated output devices such as audio speakers, high-resolution color monitors, color printers, and video disks. Multimedia is being spurred by advances in disk computer processing and disk capacity as it relates to education and entertainment software (also called 'edutainment software'). Compare **polymedia**.

multinode computer See **parallel processing**.

multiple-instruction, multiple-data In

parallel processing, over 65 000 processors may be engaged to simultaneously share a processing task. Special software manages this process by allocating equal portions of the raw data to the processors, issuing several different instructions to each of the processors. In contrast, the single-instruction, multiple-data (SIMD) method issues one 'single instruction' to all processors simultaneously only after each of the processors has received the raw data. Abbreviation 'MIMD'. See **parallel processing**.

multiple-precision [ISO Characterized by the use of two or more computer words to represent a number in order to enhance precision.]

multiple quantum-well See **optical neurocomputer**.

multiplexer A device which is used to transmit information more efficiently and economically across a network. A multiplexer combines a number of low-speed inputs into a smaller number of high-speed outputs. Some multiplexers temporarily store information in buffers so that it can be sent at one time when the line becomes free. Some multiplexers can use several frequencies on a single channel to send different messages simultaneously, using only that channel (broadband). This type is known as a 'frequency-division multiplexer' (FDM). The sequence which uses precisely controlled timing to send data over a single line is known as a 'time-division multiplexer' (TDM). [ISO A device that takes several input signals and combines them into a single output signal in such a manner that each of the input signals can be recovered.] Abbreviation 'MUX'. See **bandwidth** and **broadband**.

multiplexing [ISO In data transmission, a function that permits two or more data sources to share a common transmission medium such that each data source has its own channel.]

multipoint Referring to a communications controller (often a minicomputer) acting as a front-end processor which handles the requirements of a multipoint network. The term 'multipoint' refers to a circuit established between one primary station and multiple secondary stations simultaneously. This type of network groups devices together so that they can share the same communications line. Data communication links fall into one of two main categories based upon how the line is structured: either point-to-point or multipoint. The term 'point-to-point circuit' is used to describe a channel that is established between two, and only two, stations. The link may be a dedicated or a dial-up line connecting a processor and a terminal, two processors, or two terminals. Most point-to-point links which use dedicated lines are four-wire circuits where one local-loop (pair) is used for transmitted data and a second (pair) for received data. However, occasionally a two-wire dedicated line with a single local loop at each end will be encountered. In this application, four-wire dedicated lines are the rule, although it is possible to have two-wire dial-up or dedicated lines. A common example of a multipoint installation using dedicated lines can be found in the banking industry. Typically, all teller terminals within one branch office would share a common dedicated line tied to a host processor. The key element in a multipoint circuit is a hardware unit called a 'bridge', which allows the single circuit from the primary station to interface with the multiple circuits for the secondary stations. There are two types of bridges used: analog and digital. Analog bridges are used between modems to provide multiple analog circuits on the secondary ends of a communications link. Note that when an analog bridge is used, each secondary station must have a separate modem. An analog bridge may be owned and installed by the customer in the place of business, or it may be owned and installed by the telephone company as part of the telephone network. Digital bridges are used between the modem and the secondary stations and are normally owned by the customer. Note that in this type of installation, only one modem is required for several stations. However, there is a distance limitation of approximately 50 foot (15.25 meters) between the modem and the secondaries.

multipoint connection [ISO A connection established among more than two data stations for data transmission. *Note:* The connection may include switching facilities.]

multiprocessing The advent of ever higher performance microprocessors, coupled with decreasing hardware costs, has made it possible for microprocessor-based systems to compete effectively with traditional minicomputer systems. In addition, a microprocessor-based multiprocessor system offers users a smooth upgrade path that takes advantage of the same low-price/high-performance increments. By the addition of processor boards to a master chassis, the processing power of a system can increase to meet expanded user needs without having to wait for the next-generation microproces-

sor technology to become available, or force a purchase of an entirely new system. There are basically two types of multiprocessor systems: loosely coupled and tightly coupled. A loosely coupled multiprocessor system incorporates a number of processors, each with local resources that are not accessible by other processors (including memory, disk storage, and other peripherals). Processor communication is often implemented by means of sending and receiving messages in software with a very high degree of latency. Consequently, resource sharing and processor cooperation are limited. On the other hand, a tightly coupled multiprocessing system shares common memory, input/output channels, and other system resources. Because of this fundamental difference in architecture, only the tightly coupled multiprocessor can provide scalable performance and automatic load balancing to allow optimal overall system throughput. [ISO A mode of operation that provides for parallel processing by two or more processors of a multiprocessor.] ▼

multiprocessor [ISO A computer including two or more processors that have common access to a main storage.]

multiprogramming [ISO A mode of operation that provides for the interleaved execution of two or more computer programs by a single processor.]

multistar topology In a local area network, a star topology is one in which each device is connected to a central device (computer) through which all data must pass. In a multistar arrangement, several host computers are linked together, each having its own star topology network. See **star topology**.

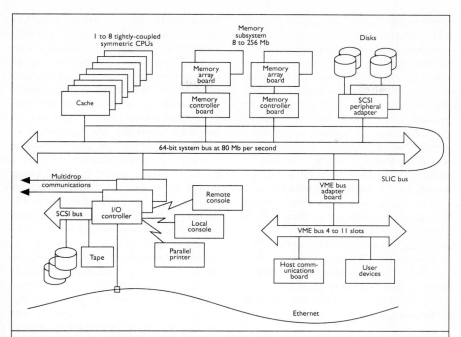

M

multiprocessing *This Wyse series 9000i system design shows an example of advanced multiprocessor architecture. All of the processors, memory boards, and input/output controllers are connected via a global 10 megahertz synchronous system bus. The system bus consists of a 64-bit data path with a 32-bit address bus, time-multiplexed on the lower 32 lines. The ability to separate requests from response cycle yields maximum bus efficiency. A separate bit-serial bus, known as the 'serial link and interrupt control' (SLIC), supports low-level message passing and interrupt handling. There is also a custom bus providing access/signaling/buffering very-large-scale integration (VLSI) on each system board. This VLSI and the SLIC free the system bus for data and address traffic, accelerating overall performance.*

multisync monitor A color display monitor designed to adjust to several frequencies so that it can receive input from various adapters. See **video adapter**.

multitasking [ISO A mode of operation that provides for the concurrent performance, or interleaved execution, of two or more tasks.] When more than one program is running at the same time in a computer, the central processing unit is said to be multitasking. Microsoft Windows and OS/2 both provide the user with the ability to load and simultaneously use more than one program. For example, a large database application could be set in motion to sort files — a task that may take ten minutes. While this is processing in the background, multitasking allows the user to remain productive and use another program such as word processing. When two functions are being processed simultaneously, they are said to be processing in parallel. The use of stand-alone single-user, multitasking workstations has become popular since the introduction of OS/2 and the adoption of UNIX as a personal computer operating system. In general terms, people multitask all the time. For example, people may be involved in three projects at work, be halfway through writing a novel, and be painting their house. In this example, each task can be picked up in turn, worked at for a while, and then put down so that something else can be done. This is called 'serial multitasking'. In serial multitasking computer environments, a user can quickly switch activities at will, working for a while at each. People can also do some tasks simultaneously, such as typing and talking. This is called 'parallel multitasking'. Both OS/2 and UNIX allow parallel multitasking, allowing many programs to run at the same time. See **OS/2** and **parallel processing**.

mutual exclusion [ISO A principle requiring that, at a given time, only one asynchronous procedure may access the same shared variable or execute members of a group of critical sections.]

MUX multiplexer; a device which is used to transmit information more efficiently and economically across a network. A multiplexer combines a number of low-speed inputs into a smaller number of high-speed outputs. Some multiplexers temporarily store information in buffers so that it can be sent at one time when the line becomes free. Some multiplexers can use several frequencies on a single channel to send different messages simultaneously, using only that channel (broadband). This type is known as a 'frequency-division multiplexer' (FDM). The sequence which uses precisely-controlled timing to send data over a single line is known as a 'time-division multiplexer' (TDM). [ISO A device that takes several input signals and combines them into a single output signal in such a manner that each of the input signals can be recovered.] Abbreviation 'MUX'. See **bandwidth** and **broadband**.

MW Medium wave.

NOTHING IS OBVIOUS!

n Nano-. An SI unit prefix for 10^{-9} expressed as 0.000 000 001 in decimal notation, as in 'nanosecond' (ns). See **SI**.

NAK Negative acknowledgment.

named pipes An application program interface for LAN Manager which allows an unlimited number of sessions on the network. Named pipes is a much higher-level interface than NetBIOS (Network Basic Input/Output System). A single named pipe function call equates to many NetBIOS calls. Through named pipes, LAN Manager handles all of the low-level details of communications, such as session establishment and user security checking, making it much easier to write sophisticated distributed applications. At the server, the application must handle all aspects of user accounts and resource access control permissions.

NAND gate [ISO A gate that performs the Boolean operation of non-conjunction.]

nano- See **n**.

nanobus Referring to the bus-based parallel processing capabilities of Encore's Multimax which operates at 100 megabytes per second. See **parallel processing**.

nanocomputer The future fourth-generation computer whose main processing chip may contain at least 100 000 000 electronic components. 'Nano-' is an SI unit prefix for 10^{-9} expressed as 0.000 000 001 in decimal notation.

nanosecond 0.000 000 001 of a second (10^{-9} seconds). A nanosecond is a unit of measure equivalent to the time it takes light to travel 30 centimeters. It is commonly used to measure the speed at which the central processing unit can execute instructions. If one nanosecond were imagined to be 1 kilometer, then one second would be equivalent to 6640 trips to the moon. A nanosecond is to a second what a second is to 30 years. SI symbol 'ns'.

narrowband The lowest-quality bandwidth, capable of transmitting between 45 and 150 bits per second, used for low-speed data terminals, or telegraph lines. See **bandwidth**.

narrowband dial-up This is a circuit-switched service for low-speed devices. Teletype and telex typically use narrowband dial-up that transmits up to 300 bits per second.

narrowband private Referring to communications lines which are leased for low-speed devices. Narrowband private lines provide a private line service for transmission from one teletype device to another, typically transmitting up to 300 bits per second.

NAS Network Application Support; a comprehensive set of software that enables application integration across a distributed, multivendor environment. It consists of well-defined programming interfaces, toolkits, and products that help developers build applications that are well-integrated and easily portable across different systems. For example, NAS can reside on VAX or DECsystem 'server' systems running VMS or ULTRIX software to transparently deliver common applications services to diverse 'client' systems across a network. Currently, NAS services support the VMS operating system, UNIX operating systems, IBM systems, and systems from other OSI vendors, MS–DOS, OS/2, Windows, and Apple Macintosh systems. NAS also supports a variety of terminals, including Digital's VT family of terminals, IBM 3270, and DECwindows terminals.

nasa7 One of the ten SPEC (Systems Performance Evaluation Cooperative) benchmarks drawn from real-world applications including scientific and engineering areas, focusing on system performance, memory, input/output, graphics, networking, multi-user, and commercial applications. Nasa7 is a collection of seven floating point intensive kernels. For each kernel, the program generates its own input data, performs the kernel, and compares the results against an expected result. The seven kernels are: (a) MXM — matrix multiply; (b) CFFT2d — complex radix 2 FFT on 2D array; (c) CHOLSKY — decomposition in parallel on a set of input matrices; (d) BTRIX — block tridiagonal matrix solution along one dimension of a four-dimensional array; (e) GMTRY — sets up arrays for a vortex method solution and performs Gaussian elimination on the resulting arrays; (f) EMIT — creates new vortices according to certain boundary conditions; and (g) VPENTA — inverts three matrix pentadiagonals in a highly parallel fashion. The nasa7 benchmark, as distributed by SPEC, uses double precision data. The benchmark does not contain code that is vectorizable, although certain kernels may be more difficult to vectorize than others. The source code contains no vectorizing compiler directives. Any floating point hardware such as vector or array processors will have a big impact on performance. See **SPEC**.

National Bureau of Standards The standards body responsible for making recommendations to the President of the United States concerning federal data processing and communications standards. Abbreviation 'NBS'.

National Communications System An

organization responsible for United States Government standards administered by the General Services Administration (GSA). Government agencies that have large telecommunications facilities belong to the National Communications System (NCS). All emergency plans for the nation's communications facilities are developed by NCS, which also works closely with EIA, ANSI, ISO, and CCITT in an effort to foster national and international standards.

natural language The languages of humans (such as English, French, Chinese, and Arabic) are called 'natural languages'. In computing, the use of natural programming languages would make programming very easy for everyone. However, this technology is not yet available. Some programs such as Lotus HAL do come close, but the programmer must follow very strict code guidelines. The development of natural languages is one of the challenges facing artificial-intelligence experts who are also concerned with developing voice input and output devices. See **programming language**.

natural language software An artificial-intelligence application designed to enable users with little or no programming skills to write English-like computer commands which will be easily recognized and converted by the computer as legitimate enquiries. See **natural language**.

natural number [ISO One of the numbers zero, one, two, etc. *Note:* Some people define natural numbers as starting at one rather than zero.]

natural unit of information content [ISO A unit of logarithmic measure of in-

formation expressed as a Napierian logarithm. *Example:* The decision content of a character set of eight characters equals $\log_e 8 = 2.079 = 3 \log_e 2$ natural units of information content.]

NBCD Natural binary-coded decimal. See **binary-coded decimal**.

N

NBFM Narrow-band frequency modulator.

n-bit byte [ISO A string that consists of n bits.]

NBS National Bureau of Standards; the standards body responsible for making recommendations to the President of the United States concerning federal data processing and communications standards.

NC 1. Network control. 2. Numerical control.

NCC 1. National Communications Committee. 2. National Computer Conference; an exhibition of computer products held annually in the United States.

NCHPC National Consortium for High-Performance Computing.

NCR 1. National Cash Registers; now owned by AT&T. 2. No-carbon-required; specially treated paper which allows impression-copies to be made without the need for individual carbon paper. NCR paper is used for multipart invoice forms, or charge-card dockets.

NCR IRX COBOL A programming language that is based on American National Standard COBOL 1974. This version of COBOL was based on the development work of CODASYL COBOL Committee through December 1971. The NCR IRX COBOL programming language was initially supported by the NCR IRX COBOL compiler associated with NCR IRX release 5 software.

NCS National Communications System. An organization responsible for United States Government standards administered by the General Services Administration (GSA). Government agencies that have large telecommunications facilities belong to NCS. All emergency plans for the nation's communications facilities are developed by NCS, which also works closely with EIA, ANSI, ISO, and CCITT in an effort to foster national and international standards.

NDIS Network Driver Interface Specifications; a network protocol and driver interface developed and published by Microsoft Corporation and 3Com Corporation. It provides a standard interface layer to which transport stacks and network adapter card drivers can be written. NDIS isolates protocol stacks from network driver dependencies. It is a standard and easy way to write low-level drivers for network adapter cards. Since transport protocols are kept independent from local area network hardware, any transport that interfaces with the NDIS layer can run on any network hardware for which an NDIS driver has been written.

near letter quality Referring to dot matrix printers capable of producing characters on paper which are almost acceptable for use in business letters. Near-letter-quality output is generally used for internal reports, price lists, and informal communications. Abbreviation 'NLQ'. See **impact printer**.

NEDO New Energy and Industrial Technology Development Organization.

negate [ISO To perform the operation of negation.] The word 'negate' comes from the Latin word *negare*, meaning 'deny'.

negation [ISO The monadic Boolean operation whose result has the Boolean value opposite to that of the operand.]

negative development Refers to the laser printer technology where the laser beam is turned on when scanning the image areas. Since the objective is to form black characters on a white background, a charge is placed on the toner which causes it to adhere to the areas exposed to the laser, which in this case is the image areas. See **developer**.

negative entry [ISO The assignment of a negative sign to a number entered in a calculator.]

negative indication [ISO A visual indication that the number shown has a negative value.]

neighbor notification [ISO In a token-ring network, the process by which each data station identifies the next active station so that all stations that are affected by a hard failure can be informed that a failure has occurred.]

nest [ISO To incorporate one or more structures of one kind into a structure of the same kind. *Examples:* To nest one loop (the nested or inner loop); to nest one subroutine within another subroutine.]

nested transaction A sequence of operations within a transaction that can be aborted without aborting the entire transaction. It is useful for the application programmer because it allows the program to have two ways of performing a transaction. If the first way fails (due to lack of resources such as storage), then it can try a different way of doing the same thing. When a nested transaction is aborted, the updates are abandoned as usual. When it is committed, its updates are not made globally visible, but simply merged with the set of updates for the higher transaction. On the other hand, its changes do become visible to other transactions nested in the same higher transaction. A nested transaction is also called a 'sub-transaction'. A transaction tree is the logical tree that results from successive sub-transaction invocations. The transaction at the root of the tree is called the 'top-level transaction'. All nested transactions on the path from the top-level transaction to a particular nested transaction are called 'ancestors'. A nested transaction created by the top-level transaction or another nested transaction is called a 'child sub-transaction'. All others that belong to the sub-tree with a common root are called 'descendants', whereas a top-level transaction or nested transaction with no descendants is called a 'leaf'. The creator of a sub-transaction is called a 'parent sub-transaction'; while the top-level transaction is called the 'parent transaction'.

NetBEUI Net**B**IOS **E**xtended **U**ser **I**nterface network device driver. The NetBEUI driver is the transport driver supplied with LAN Manager. The NetBEUI driver can bind with as many as eight media access control drivers.

NetBIOS Network Basic Input/Output System; an application program interface designed by IBM and Sytek in 1984. NetBIOS controls access to the small-scale network. Compare **named pipes**.

NetComm An Australian company that manufactures an extensive range of modems for personal computer, minicomputer, and mainframe environments. Established in 1982 by Chris Howells, NetComm has grown from a start-up operation to a profitable self-funded US$21 million company. Although it was originally founded as an export venture based on international contracts with Apple Computer Corporation, NetComm now designs and manufactures connectivity products.

netiquette See **computer etiquette**.

NetLogon A LAN Manager service that implements logon security. This service verifies the user name and password supplied by each user logging onto the local area network.

NetView IBM's network management product introduced in 1986 to operate on IBM mainframes in an SNA environment. Information from non-IBM and non-SNA equipment can be collected via NetView/PC — a PC-based network management program that funnels information back to NetView.

NetWare Novell Corporation's proprietary operating system for linking personal computers to local area networks.

network 1. A group of computers and other peripheral devices connected together so that they can communicate with each other. Sometimes, telephone connections are used, but when high-speed links are required, microwave transmissions or orbiting satellites are used. A 'centralized' network is controlled by only one large computer, while a 'decentralized' or 'distributed' network can be spread over a number of locations. Most networks only transmit data, and to do this over a telephone line, the data must be converted from digital to analog before they can be sent. This is done through the use of a modem. See **ISDN**, **LAN**, and **WAN**. 2. [ISO An arrangement of nodes and interconnecting branches. *Note:* Terms such as 'bus network' and 'star/ring network' describe more than the topological aspects of these networks.]

network administrator The person employed to maintain a local area network.

Network Applications Support See **NAS**.

network architecture The design specification of local area networks, including standards for hardware, software, and cabling. Communications networks today are no longer simple point-to-point and multipoint links. Newer networks consist of many paths for data transmission. Routing and addressing schemes are now extremely complex. A network must be able to grow as an organization grows, and with minimal difficulty. Technological advances have resulted in the declining costs of the intelligence necessary to drive these systems — thereby making distributed networking feasible. In order to accommodate these changes and avoid the unwieldy growth of communications networks, network architectures were developed to set rules, guidelines, and specifications for the design of networks, and the distribution and performance of functions within networks. Network architectures are designed not only to accommodate the changing communications environment, but also to solve some specific communications problems such as the incompatibility between different products, both hardware and software. Network architectures allow for the interconnection and interoperability of any previously incompatible devices through standardization of hardware and software interfaces. As long as the product adheres to the architectural specifications, it will be compatible with other products that conform to the same standards regardless of the vendor. Generally, this standardization can facilitate communications between different vendors' equipment, provide resource sharing, simplify applications programming, provide flexibility, and provide dynamic reconfiguration/modification. [ISO The logical structure and the operating principles of a computer network. *Note:* The operating principles of a network include those of services, functions, and protocols.]

network chart [ISO A directed graph used for describing and scheduling events, activities, and their relationships in project control.]

network database A database in which any record can be related to any other record without the restrictions inherent in a hierarchical structure. Records can be linked in relationships (called 'sets') which bring together information that may be scattered widely around the database. The network database model allows complex connections among the data with extremely high efficiency, handling a high volume of users. However, the great speed possible with the network model depends upon users identifying the database inter-record relationships ahead of time — that is, when the database is initially defined and set up with the relationships physically coded into the system. However, if the definitions and relationships do not remain stable, undefined searches slow down dramatically, with restructuring of paths requiring intervention by a trained database administrator who must make structural changes (while the database is unavailable to end users). Even if the data definitions and relationships are relatively stable, the network model can present problems if the user wants to query the database in ways that were not anticipated when the database was set up. Network databases are sometimes called 'CODASYL-compliant' after the Conference on Data Systems Languages, which has been active in developing network database specifications. See **DBMS**. Compare **hierarchical database** and **relational database**.

network design See **topology**.

Network Driver Interface Specifications See **NDIS**.

network interface card Used to connect a microcomputer directly to a local area network, the network interface card (adapter) is designed to communicate directly with the internal bus. Ethernet and ARCnet interface cards can transmit information to and from the computer and the file server much faster than serially-connected cards such as Apple-Talk. Acronym 'NIC'. See **NDIS**. ▼

network layer The third layer of the OSI

network interface card Typical Ethernet parallel tasking adapters.

(Open Systems Interconnection) model. The network layer maps out packet routing between networks or from node to node within a network, defining all possible routes that a message packet could travel to reach its destination. In so doing, this layer must account for all the transmission technologies and network types it might encounter en route. It must also segment and reassemble data units to expedite delivery and some limited error checking. See **OSI reference model**.

network operating system The system software of a local area network which connects a group of personal computer users who share common software, files, and peripherals, and manages these resources at the workgroup level. Acronym 'NOS'.

network orgy See **orgy**.

network planning [ISO A technique that uses network charts for planning, scheduling, and controlling a project.]

network topology See **topology**.

network version A version of application software written especially for concurrent access, enabling several users to access and modify information in one session. Software written for single-user applications may not be licensed for use on a local area network, and may not run efficiently.

neural network A computer which works like a human brain. Most of the computers used around the world today are little more than very-high-speed number-crunchers (calculators). Whilst their hardware is well adapted to this kind of work, they are no match for the human brain when faced with tasks such as control, pattern recognition, and knowledge-based information processing. For example, although the electrical signals of the brain are handled one million times slower than those in a semiconductor device, a human can recognize a face instantly — a task beyond even the most powerful modern computer. Also, despite not having been programmed with the equations of motion or a knowledge of how the body works, humans can perform a very wide range of movements (usually without mishap). A task as basic as walking up or down a set of stairs is one of the most difficult for a robot to negotiate. The difference lies in the fact that humans can use what they have learned to manipulate information in the most efficient way. If a computer could process information in the same way as the human brain, it could be made capable of learning, and of using what it had learned to make decisions. Such computers, now in their developmental stages, are called 'neural networks' or 'neurocomputers'. See **human brain** and **neurocomputer**.

neurocomputer Referring to a computer which is much more powerful than a supercomputer and in which the term 'neuro' implies that the computer behaves and calculates at the speed of nerve tissues of the human brain. By definition, a neurocomputer should not need to be programmed from the outside; instead it should actually learn from the work it is asked to do. In a neurocomputer, the input and desired output (the latter referred to as the 'teacher signal') are presented to the network together. In 1990, Fujitsu launched a super neurocomputer with parallel architecture which set a new record for neural network learning speed. According to a report made to the International Joint Conference on Neural Networks in January 1991, the fast-learning neural network is capable of 500 MCUPS (million connection updates per second). The architecture uses 256 DSPs (digital signal processors) as processing elements, making it 2000 times faster than an engineering workstation and 400 times faster than a conventional neurocomputer. To learn the text/vocalization software (NETtalk) takes a regular minicomputer approximately a day and a half, but the Fujitsu super neurocomputer completes the task in 30 seconds. The architecture consists of multiple trays (registers) and PEs (processing elements). Each tray acts as a container and router, and is connected to its two neighbors to form a ring (some trays have associated PEs). Possible applications include intelligent robots with real-time learning capabilities, pattern and voice recognition with real-time learning, and real-time financial forecasting. The roots of the neurocomputer can be traced back to the neuron model proposed in the United States in 1943 by doctors W. McCulloch and W. Pitts. In that model, a neuron receives signals

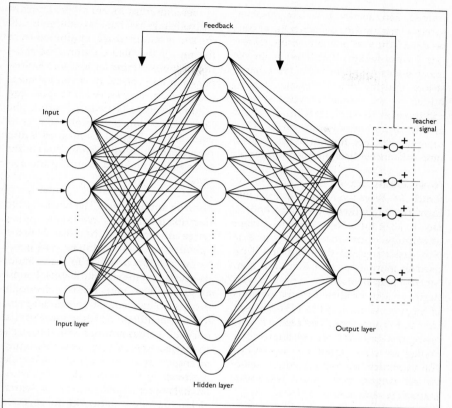

Feedback

Input

Teacher
signal

Input layer

Output layer

Hidden layer

N

neurocomputer *This figure shows the basic structure of a neurocomputer. Each circle represents a neuron model. The models are linked into a network of three layers: an input layer, a hidden layer, and an output layer. When a signal enters the input layer, the units of that layer transfer the signal to those of the hidden layer. The units of the hidden layer receive the signals, weigh and sum them, then send the result to the output layer, which then performs the same processing on the signals it receives. The neurocomputer, on the basis of what it already knows, takes the input signal and processes it to produce an output. If, after comparing the output with the teacher signal, it finds a difference, it adjusts the synaptic weightings to subsequently reduce the error. The network repeats this process to adjust to its environment. This adjustment constitutes learning and allows the network to make correct decisions regardless of how much its circumstances have changed. This is far removed from conventional computers which, being controlled by programs, are limited to performing a single given task.*

from other neurons, gives each signal a weighting called a 'synaptic weight', and then sums them. The neuron outputs a signal only when the sum exceeds a certain value (threshold). Doctor D.O. Hebb (a psychologist) later went on to propose a brain model where the synaptic weightings could be changed as a result of a 'learning' process. In 1985, D.E. Rumelhart developed a 'back propagation' method by which the synaptic weightings of each neuron can be determined. It is noted in the *Guinness Book of Records* that 'The results of experiments published in 1966 have shown that the fastest messages transmitted by the human nervous system can travel at 180 mph (288 km/h). With advancing age, impulses are carried 15% more slowly'. See **human brain**, **neural network**, and **optical neurocomputer**. ⋀

New Century Schoolbook The Century family of faces was created by Linn Boyd Benton, who cut the first Century face in 1874 for a New York magazine, attempting to produce a typeface that was easier to read than the fine type used in journals at that time. His son, Morris Fuller Benton, was a prolific type designer who produced many versions of the original face and in 1934 released Century Schoolbook. The typeface was especially designed for children's textbooks. In 1984, Linotype introduced New Century Schoolbook with a selection of weights for books, newspapers, magazines, and manuals. ▼

newspaper columns In typesetting, a page layout where two or more columns

A a	B b	C c	D d	E e
F f	G g	H h	I i	J j
K k	L l	M m	N n	O o
P p	Q q	R r	S s	T t
U u	W w	X x	Y y	Z z
1	2	3	4	5
6	7	8	9	0

New Century Schoolbook Some of the characters that form New Century Schoolbook normal.

of text and graphics are aligned next to each other. When the first column is full, the text is automatically continued from the top of the next column. The most popular positioning of text in newspaper columns is justified, where the inter-character and inter-word spaces are automatically adjusted to ensure the lines of text within the columns are of equal length. Vertical justification is also possible, making all columns start at the same height and end evenly at the bottom.

Newton Intelligence The term used to describe the intuitive nature of Apple's range of products that use Newton Architecture. Newton Intelligence refers to the product's ability to learn about its user's preferences and habits. For example, a user may receive electronic messages that request an appointment to be scheduled. Newton Intelligence, once it becomes familiar with the user's reactions, may act on new incoming messages and automatically schedule meetings in the electronic diary. Similarly, Newton Intelligence may search electronic news networks for articles that may interest the user. When it comes to scheduling meetings, Newton Intelligence may use previous meeting habits and apply these to future meetings. For example, after instructing a Newton MessagePad to 'arrange lunch with Jane', it will search its database and do some or all of the following: contact Jane and make an appointment; send a facsimile to the preferred restaurant and make the booking; and place a diary note for lunch from 12.00 noon to 2.00 pm, knowing that lunches with Jane usually take two hours. Other intelligence features include the recognition of handwriting and preferred symbols.

Apple has licensed this technology to several companies, including Matsushita, Motorola, Sharp, and Siemens. See **Newton MessagePad**.

Newton MessagePad A hand-held communications device that allows users to gather, manage, and share information via sophisticated communications procedures. First in a family of products from Apple, the MessagePad became available 2 August 1993. Known as a 'PDA' (personal digital assistant), its main attraction was its ability to learn the user's preferences and requirements using both hardware and software via a concept that Apple calls 'Newton Intelligence'. The communications capabilities in the MessagePad allow users to send, receive, and share information through communications methods such as telephone lines, wireless networks, and computer networks. When equipped with an on-board modem, the Message-Pad acts as a hand-held facsimile machine that can send and receive. Using a stylus (pen-like device), the user can

Newton MessagePad Apple's investigations into a new generation of mobile personal information devices began in 1987 with the formation of Apple's Special Projects division. Headed by Steve Sakoman and Jean-Louis Gassée, the Special Projects team defined the Newton architecture in 1990, choosing the microprocessor designed by Advanced RISC Machines Limited.

write directly onto the screen of the MessagePad. The handwriting is automatically formatted and stored or sent to an address, either via the modem, or via an in-built infrared function that beams the data to another Newton device across a 3-foot (1-meter) distance without any wiring or cabling. Beaming is useful for exchanging business cards, meeting notes, maps, or appointments. See **Advanced RISC Machines Limited** and **Newton Intelligence**.

New Wave A windowing environment compatible with MS-Windows, developed by Hewlett-Packard.

New Zealand virus A variant of the Stoned virus. See **Stoned virus**.

NeXT Computer, Inc. Founded in 1985 by Steven P. Jobs and five senior managers formerly with Apple Computer, Inc., NeXT employs 250 people and is headquartered in Redwood City, California. In September 1989, NeXT introduced the NeXT Computer and NEXTSTEP Release 1.0. The same year, Canon, Inc. invested in the company, and subsequent software releases were developed and sold on NeXT Cube. In 1990, the NeXTstation product family was introduced, and in February 1993, as the date neared for the release of NEXTSTEP for Intel processors, NeXT announced that it would cease manufacturing its own Motorola 68040-based computer hardware and would become a software company focusing on making NEXTSTEP an industry standard running on standard Intel-based computers. See **Jobs, Steven P**.

NFNT New Font Numbering Table; a font identification and numbering scheme introduced with the Apple Macintosh System 6.0.

NFS Network File System; a network service originally developed by Sun Microsystems. NFS has been ported to several operating systems.

NIC See **network interface card**.

NiCd Nickel cadmium. Refers to rechargeable batteries used in the first battery-powered laptop computers. NiCd batteries were unpopular because they seemed to 'remember' the last discharge level, and to diminish in effectiveness as a result. This was due to the fact that recharging a NiCd battery before it is fully discharged causes electrode crystallization in the charged battery cells. Crystallization prevents some of the cells from accumulating a full recharge. Since the cells in a battery discharge sequentially, the amount of charge remaining varies between the cells. The total amount of power stored after the recharge is therefore less than a total charge. Another recharge that begins before the battery is fully discharged further shortens the resulting operating period. Repeatedly recharging a partially-charged battery results in rapidly-decreasing operating time. Pronounced 'nigh-cad'.

NiMH Nickel metal hydride. A type of rechargeable battery used in portable computer equipment.

nines complement [ISO The diminished radix complement in the decimal numeration system.]

Nippon Telegraph and Telephone See NTT.

NITS The United States Government's National Institute of Standards and Technology, formerly the National Bureau of Standards.

NLM Network loadable module.

NLQ See **near letter quality**.

NLS Natural language software; an artificial-intelligence application designed to enable users with little or no programming skills to write English-like computer commands which will be easily recognized and converted by the computer to legitimate enquiries. See **natural language**.

NMP Network Management Protocol.

NMR Nuclear Magnetic Resonance; the use of a series of scanners which surround a patient's body in a magnetic field so as to generate pictures of the body (without the use of X-rays).

NNI Netherlands Normalisatie-instituut; Netherlands' standards body formed in 1959.

noc The computer industry's term used to describe a person's complete absence of computer technical skills or knowledge. It refers to one who holds a senior position in the industry, but who has no knowledge about the industry nor its technology. In contrast, the antonym is 'propeller head' — the term used to describe a person who is extremely well-versed in technical matters. The term 'noc' was coined 30 September 1994 by Dion Weisler, an industry propeller head and product manager who is well known for his intolerance toward unqualified industry practitioners. Pronounced 'knock'.

node 1. In a local area network, a computer, repeater, file server, or similar peripheral device used to create, receive, or repeat a message. 2. In general terms, a node refers to a workstation connected to a local area network. A personal computer (PC) may be used as a node (member) in a data processing network. In a network, data communication links are used to tie together various computer systems to allow the sharing of information and resources. For example, a local area network which ties together all PCs in a word processing department can enable anyone to access common template files or print on a single high-speed laser printer. A PC may also serve as a node in a metropolitan area network, where mainframes and PCs located throughout multiple buildings in a complex are tied together. As well as functioning as a node, a PC may serve as a network host. See **host**. 3. [ISO In a data network, a point where one or more functional units interconnect channels or data circuits.] 4. [ISO In a network, the point at an end of a branch.] The word 'node' comes from the Latin word *nodus*, meaning 'knot'.

noise In data transmission, any unwanted electrical signal which interferes with a communications channel. This is often a random transmission of varying frequency, amplitude, and phase. Such noise may radiate from fluorescent lights and electric motors, and can also be caused by static, changes in temperature, electric or magnetic fields, and even from the sun and the stars (galactic noise). Where a lot of noise exists, communications devices and computers have to be shielded. Impulse noise may arise from external sources such as lightning, and sparks from motor-vehicle ignition systems, causing interference to VHF radio reception such as FM radio and broad bandwidth television signals. Other sources of impulse noise include sparking contacts in refrigerator and central heating thermostatic systems, and computer systems. Impulse noise affects AM more than FM, and HF more than VHF. The most common noise found on telephone company lines is 'random' noise, or as it is frequently called, 'white' noise. White noise is made up of many different frequencies but maintains a fairly constant amplitude. Random noise 'riding' on a data signal generally does not cause a problem unless the amplitude is unusually high. Another source of distortion is 'impulse' noise. This is made up of short-duration, high-amplitude spikes generally two to three milliseconds in length. If severe enough, this type of distortion will destroy data. The major source of impulse noise is telephone company switching equipment. The *Guinness Book of Records* noted that the highest note (60 gigahertz) was generated from a laser beam 'striking a sapphire crystal at the Massachusetts Institute of Technology, USA, in September 1964'. It also recorded that the loudest noise 'in a laboratory has been 210 decibels or 400 000 acoustic watts reported by NASA from a 48-foot (14.63-meter) steel and concrete test bed for the SaturnV rocket static with 60-foot (18.3-meter) deep foundations at Marshall Space Flight Center, Huntsville, Alabama, USA, in October 1965. Holes could be bored in solid material by this means, and the audible range was in excess of 100 miles (161 kilometers)'. [ISO A disturbance that affects a signal and that may distort the information carried by the signal.] See **distortion**.

noise burst signal [ISO In a token bus network, a signal indicating that there is activity on the transmission medium that did not result in a valid frame.]

noise immunity The attribute of circuits which are protected from, or are capable of ignoring or filtering, unwanted signals caused by static or other electric fields. See **noise**.

noise record On a magnetic tape, a record that is so short that it is indistinguishable from noise on the media.

nominal transfer rate [ISO The designated or theoretical number of characters that can be transferred per unit of time.]

non-add function [ISO On a printing calculator, the function that allows the printing of characters without affecting the calculations.]

nonconjunction [ISO The dyadic Boolean operation whose result has the Boolean value 0 if and only if each operand has the Boolean value 1.]

nondestructive read [ISO Reading that does not erase the date in the source location.]

nondisjunction [ISO The dyadic Boolean operation whose result has the Boolean value 1 if and only if each operand has the Boolean value 0.]

non-equivalence operation [ISO The dyadic Boolean operation whose result has the Boolean value 1 if and only if the operands have different Boolean values.]

non-identify operation [ISO The Boolean operation whose result has the Boolean value 1 if and only if all the operands do not have the same Boolean value.]

non-impact printer Having fewer parts than impact printers (such as the common typewriter), non-impact printers are faster and quieter. Common types are electrostatic, electrothermal, laser, xerographic, and ink-jet printers. [ISO A printer in which printing is not the result of mechanically striking the printing medium.] See **laser printer**. Compare **impact printer**.

non-interlaced monitor A monitor that uses a non-interlaced scan technique that refreshes the screen by painting every line down the screen at up to 72 times every second. By contrast, interlaced screens use a technique that paints the screen by scanning every other line — first odd lines from top to bottom, then even lines. Interlaced techniques can cause the monitor to flicker. This process is determined by the video card.

non-isolated amplifier [ISO An amplifier that has an electrical connection between the signal circuit and another circuit including ground.]

nonlinear distortion Refers to an amplifier or analog signaling device in which the outgoing electromagnetic waves (signals) are not in proportion to the incoming signals. This may cause harmonic distortion or cross-modulation. Repeaters positioned at more frequent intervals, or the use of equalization techniques, may help to limit the effects of nonlinear distortion. In comparison, a linear system is one where the relationship of output signals to input signals produces a straight line when plotted on a graph. See **repeater**.

nonlinearity See **nonlinear distortion**.

nonpollable terminal A hardware device that cannot buffer or store messages and cannot recognize an identification code in a poll or select message. Such a device is also known as a 'dumb terminal'. Terminals of this type are usually restricted to point-to-point operation.

nonprint function [ISO The function that allows the disengagement of a printing mechanism on a calculator.]

nonprocedural language See **programming language**.

nonprogrammable calculator [ISO A calculator whose program cannot be changed by the operator.]

non-return-to-zero recording 1. [ISO The magnetic recording of bits such that patterns of magnetization used to represent zeros and ones occupy the whole storage cell, with no part of the cell magnetized to the reference condition.] 2. Non-return-to-zero change recording. [ISO Non-return-to-reference recording in which the zeros are represented by magnetization to a specified condition and ones by another condition; the magnetization changes only when the value to be represented changes. *Note:* The two conditions may be saturation and zero magnetization, but are more commonly saturation in opposite senses.] 3. Non-return-to-zero change-on-ones recording. [ISO Non-return-to-zero recording in which the ones are represented by a change in the condition of magnetiza-

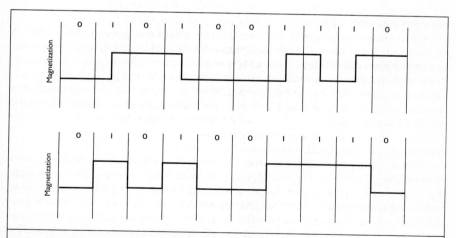

non-return-to-zero recording *The first diagram shows non-return-to-zero change-on-ones recording in which the ones are represented by a change in the condition of magnetization, and the zeros are represented by the absence of a change. Note that this method is called 'mark recording' because only the 'one' or 'mark' signals are explicitly recorded.*

The second diagram shows non-return-to-reference recording in which the zeros are represented by magnetization to a specified condition, while the ones are represented by another condition. The magnetization changes only when the value to be represented changes. Note that the two conditions may be saturation and zero magnetization, but are more commonly saturation in opposite senses.

tion, and the zeros are represented by the absence of a change. *Note:* This method is called 'mark recording' because only the one or mark signals are explicitly recorded.] 4. Non-return-to-zero change-on-zeros recording. [ISO Non-return-to-zero recording in which the zeros are represented by a change in the condition of magnetization, and the ones are represented by the absence of a change.] △

nontillion See **exponent**.

nontransactional application In a local area network, a program or file produced for a single user, meaning that it is not designed to be accessed by other users on the network. Unlike database files, word processing files are nontransactional because files are not always shared by other network users.

nonvolatile memory Memory chips (such as read-only memory) which retain their information even after the electrical power has been switched off. This contrasts with volatile chips (such as random-access memory) which lose their information when the power is switched off. Abbreviation 'NVM'.

nonvolatile storage [ISO A storage device whose contents are not lost when power is cut off.]

no operation instruction [ISO An instruction whose execution causes the computer to proceed to the next instruction to be executed, without performing an operation.]

no parity In asynchronous communications, a protocol that does not use parity checking bits. See **asynchronous transmission** and **parity bit**.

NOR gate [ISO A gate that performs the Boolean operation of nondisjunction.]

normalize (In a floating point representation system.) 1. [ISO To make an adjustment to the mantissa and the corresponding adjustment to the characteristic in a floating point representation to bring the mantissa within some prescribed range, the real number represented remaining unchanged.] 2. [ISO To make an adjustment to the fixed-point part and the corresponding adjustment to the exponent in a floating point representation to ensure that the fixed-point part lies within some prescribed range, the real number represented remaining unchanged. *Example:* In order to bring the fixed-point part into the range 1 to 9.99 . . . the floating point representation 123.45×10^2 may be normalized to 1.2345×10^4.]

normalized device coordinate [ISO A device coordinate specified in an intermediate coordinate system and normalized to some range, typically 0 to 1. *Note:* A display image expressed in a normalized device coordinate lies in the same relative position on any device space.]

normalized form (In a floating point representation system.) [ISO The form taken by a floating point representation when the mantissa lies within some prescribed standard range, so chosen that any given real number is represented by a unique pair of numerals. *Note:* The number zero must have a prescribed characteristic, often 0.]

normal mode voltage [ISO That unwanted part of the voltage, between the two input connection points of an amplifier, that is added to the voltage of the original signal.]

Norton SI Norton System Information; designed by Peter Norton to benchmark a computer's throughput. This is included in the Norton Utilities program to rate the speed of internal processing and the speed of a hard disk drive. The original IBM XT computer is used as a base reference point, with ratings referring to the comparative speed. A Norton SI rating of 40 means the tested computer performs 40 times faster than the IBM XT, which has a rating of 1.0.

Norton Utilities A personal computer management program which consists of several useful utilities such as an 'undelete' program which can be used to restore accidentally-deleted files. The program was developed by Peter Norton. ▼

NOS Network operating system; the system software of a local area network which connects a group of personal computer users who share common software, files, and peripherals, and man-

ages these resources at the workgroup level.

notation [ISO A set of symbols, and the rules for their use, for the representation of data.]

notebook computer Lightweight full-function personal computer, so named because of its size — approximately the same size as an average textbook. See **laptop computer. ▼**

NOT gate [ISO A gate that performs the Boolean operation of negation.]

NOT-IF-THEN gate [ISO A gate that performs the Boolean operation of exclusion.]

NOVA See **Data General**.

Novell An international supplier of network operating system software and services that provides the foundation for local and enterprise-wide distributed computing solutions. Established in January 1983, and headquartered in Provo, Utah, United States, Novell has a

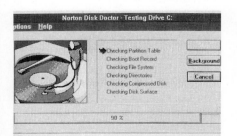

Norton Utilities The Norton Disk Doctor for Windows saves down-time by providing data recovery and continuous background protection. It tracks and verifies data integrity on the hard disk, and automatically repairs problems before they damage the data.

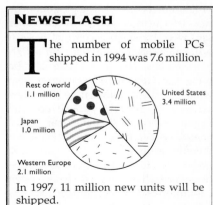

NEWSFLASH

The number of mobile PCs shipped in 1994 was 7.6 million.

Rest of world
1.1 million

United States
3.4 million

Japan
1.0 million

Western Europe
2.1 million

In 1997, 11 million new units will be shipped.

notebook computer *Laptop computers which are approximately the same size as general textbooks are called 'notebook' computers. This full-function Canon notebook can rival desktop computers, and it features a built-in bubble jet printer.*

sales turnover in excess of US$10 000 million and employs more than 3600 employees worldwide. System software products include NetWare, Novell DOS, and UnixWare. The basis for the majority of Novell's products was a piece of networking software written by four young programmers in 1981. The programmers, who later became known as 'the Superset', were hired on a contract basis to write networking software for CP/M workstations. This initial code later became the NetWare Operating System, which Novell acquired from the Superset in 1983. In 1991, Novell acquired Digital Research (a developer of advanced operating systems software) and thereby acquired DR–DOS. In 1992, Univel was formed as a partnership between Novell and AT&T's Unix System Laboratories (USL) to provide open system software solutions for distributed

enterprise-wide computing. Univel's first product was UnixWare — an operating system that provided access to UNIX on the desktop in a networked environment for use on industry-standard microprocessors that are based on Intel's microprocessors.

Novell network A local area network which uses Novell NetWare as its network operating system.

novemdecillion See **exponent**.

NRZ Non-return-to-zero. See **non-return-to-zero recording**.

ns See **nanosecond**.

NSAI National Standards Authority of Ireland; Ireland's standards body formed in 1961.

NSF National Science Foundation.

NSFNET National Science Foundation Network; designed (as a substitute to ARPANET) to perform all the civilian functions of the Defense Department's ARPANET. NSFNET was developed by the Office of Advanced Scientific Computing at the National Science Foundation to ensure that (for security reasons) ARPANET was not available for public access. Pronounced 'en-es-ef-net'.

NT New Technology. See **Windows NT**.

NTSC National Television Standards Committee. A color television broadcast standard wherein the image consists of a format that has 525 scan lines; a field frequency of 60 hertz; a broadcast bandwidth of 4 megahertz (MHz); a line frequency of 15.75 kilohertz; a frame frequency of one-thirtieth of a second; and a color subcarrier frequency of 3.58 MHz. NTSC is an arm of the Electronic Industries Association that prepared the standard of specifications approved by the Federal Communications Commission in 1953 for commercial broadcasting. NTSC is the standard for the United States, Canada, and other countries.

NTT Nippon Telegraph and Telephone; the Japanese service and research organization which is the Japanese counterpart of AT&T Bell Laboratories of the United States.

NuBus The Apple Macintosh II high-speed expansion bus.

nuclear magnetic resonance A series of scanners that surround a patient's body in a magnetic field to generate pictures of the body (without the use of X-rays). Abbreviation 'NMR'.

nucleus [ISO That part of a control program that is resident in main storage.]

null character A special character which has no value. It is used to satisfy a computer program which requires that a particular data field be completed, even when there is no data actually available for that field. The ASCII null character has the value 0 (or hexadecimal 00).

null modem cable A serial cable designed to eliminate the need for a modem when two computers are directly connected to each other.

null string [ISO A string that contains no element.]

number representation [ISO A representation of a number in a numeration system.]

numeral [ISO A discrete representation of a number. *Example:* The following are four different numerals that represent the same number, i.e. a dozen, by the methods shown: (a) twelve by a word in the English language; (b) 12 in the decimal numeration system; (c) XII by a Roman numeral; and (d) 1100 in the binary numeration system.]

numeration system [ISO Any notation for the representation of numbers.]

numeric [ISO Pertaining to data that consist of numerals.]

numerical control [ISO Automatic control of a process performed by a device that makes use of numeric data usually introduced while the operation is in progress. *Note:* The term 'numerical control' is commonly used in machine-tool applications.]

numeric characters Printable characters which represent numbers 0 to 9 in the decimal numbering system. The digits 0 and 1 are used in the binary system, while the ten decimal digits plus the alphabetical characters A to F are used in the hexadecimal numbering system. The decimal point (.), the plus (+), and minus (–) signs are also considered numeric characters.

numeric character set [ISO A character set that contains digits and may contain control characters, and special characters, but normally not letters.]

numeric coprocessor Also called 'math coprocessor'; a microprocessor chip which supports the main chip to more efficiently handle specialist mathematics-intensive applications. For computations using binary-coded decimals, and floating point calculations, a microprocessor can perform at speeds of up to 100 times faster when a numeric coprocessor is used (handling approximately 80 bits at a time). Floating point operands are large, and the useful set of operations on them is quite complex; many thousands of transistors are required to implement a standard set of floating point operations such as those defined by IEEE standard 754. Consequently, a microprocessor such as the Intel 80386 provides hardware support for the numerics in a separate numeric coprocessor chip. The numeric coprocessors are invisible to application software; they effectively extend the 80386 architecture with IEEE 754-compatible registers, data types, and

instructions. The combination of an 80386 microprocessor and an 80387 coprocessor can execute 1.8 million Whetstones per second. Intel numeric coprocessors are numbered to match the microprocessor, but end with the number '7'. For example, the coprocessor designed for the Intel 80286 microprocessor is called the 'Intel 80287'. The Intel 80486, 80486DX, and Pentium processors have an in-built numeric coprocessor. The Intel math coprocessor instruction set includes 68 numeric functions for extended precision, floating point trigonometric, logarithmic, and exponential functions. While a program is running, the central processing unit (CPU) controls overall program execution. When it encounters a floating point operation, it generates an 'escape' instruction to the math coprocessor. The math coprocessor operates independently from the time it receives the instruction to the time it is ready to pass the result back to the CPU. While the coprocessor is working, the CPU can be either waiting for the result or processing other tasks. In addition to performing many calculations considerably faster than the CPU, the Intel math coprocessor can often provide much more accurate answers than software subroutines. The Intel math coprocessor can perform arithmetic on integers with 64-bit precision in the range of ± 1018, and can process decimal numbers up to 18 digits without round-off errors.

numeric coprocessor registers See **coprocessor registers**.

numeric data [ISO Data represented by numerals.]

numeric keypad On most industry-standard keyboards, a section to the

numeric keypad *Most keyboards today have a numeric keypad built-in. This Macintosh LC keyboard also has a two-level tilt adjustment.*

right of the alphabet keys is dedicated to entering numbers. On most keyboards, the numeric keypad serves two functions — it can be used either for cursor movement or for entering numbers. The 'Num Lock' key is used to set the keypad into position so that it can only be used to enter numbers, in the same way a 'Caps Lock' key is used to enter capital letters only. Enhanced keyboards may have a small light built into the key which indicates when this function is chosen. For computers which do not have dedicated numeric keys grouped together in a cluster (such as earlier laptops), an external numeric keypad (peripheral device) may be attached. ⒜

numeric representation [ISO A discrete representation of data by numerals.]

numeric word [ISO A word that consists of digits and possibly space characters and special characters. *Example:* In the Universal Decimal Classification, the numeric word 61(03)=20 is used to identify any medical encyclopedia in English.]

Num Lock key See **numeric keypad**.

NVM See **nonvolatile memory**.

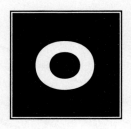

**IN THE COMPUTER BUSINESS, OPPORTUNITY,
NOT NECESSITY, IS THE MOTHER OF INVENTION**

OA Office automation; the use of effective communications techniques between computers and peripheral devices to help speed up and simplify (automate) certain business functions such as report generation, data storage and retrieval, and the use of word processors and other labor-saving and time-saving devices.

object code The program which a computer executes after translating (assembling) it from a higher-level programming language (source code). See **programming language**.

object language [ISO A target language for expressing objects programs.]

object module 1. [ISO All or part of an object program sufficiently complete for linking. *Note:* Assemblers and compilers usually produce object modules.] 2. [ISO A program unit that is the output of an assembler or a compiler and that is suitable for input to a linkage editor.]

object-oriented graphics Graphics which are produced through mathematical representation which can be re-sized or re-scaled without distortion. Typically, object-oriented graphics are used for computer-aided design, architecture, interior design, and other precision-based applications using programs like Mac-Draw. Also called 'vector graphics'. Compare **bit-mapped graphics**.

object-oriented language [ISO A programming language that reflects the concepts of object-oriented programming.]

object-oriented programming In the physical world, an object can be anything: a car, a person, or an integrated circuit. Objects have attributes, such as color or size. They also exhibit behavior, such as running or changing state in response to a set of inputs. Objects in the real world can be used repeatedly without having to be re-designed. For example, a large portion of the components used on circuit boards for electronic products are standard, inexpensive, off-the-shelf items. The availability of such items allows designers to concentrate on solving the problem at hand instead of re-inventing the tools with which to solve the problem. Programmers would like software to work in this way. In theory, the modularity achieved by 'top down' design ought to provide software components that fit well together. In practice, the fit is seldom perfect, and conventional software components nearly always require modification before they can be re-used. Object-oriented programming (OOP) changes all this by providing the programmer with built-in features for managing the great complexity of software development. The three features that help programmers take advantage of the object paradigm are encapsulation, inheritance, and polymorphism. OOP did not spring up overnight as a fully developed concept; the idea of using software 'objects' has been developed over many years of study. Research-oriented systems ably demonstrated OOP benefits such as re-usability and extensibility of code. However, as attractive as OOP was in theory, it retained a number of features that blocked its widespread acceptance. OOP systems were typically slow and ponderous and involved specialized programming languages. While suited to research laboratories, such OOP systems were not usable for the production of commercial applications. Before the current wave of interest in OOP, and particularly in C++, most work was done in specialty languages like Smalltalk and Simula. Because of their large size and slow execution speed on small systems, these tools have not read-

ily migrated to the DOS environment. OOP has now entered the mainstream for DOS programming. At a high level, the object-oriented paradigm can be viewed as a technique for managing complexity. [ISO A method for structuring programs as hierarchically organized classes describing the data and operations of objects that may interact with other objects.] See **encapsulation, inheritance,** and **polymorphism.**

object program [ISO A target program suitable for execution. *Note:* An object program may or may not require linking.]

oblique In typography, the italicized form of a typeface. Pronounced 'obleek'. See **italic.**

OC Optical computer. Optics is the branch of physics that specializes in light and vision. An optical computer combines both optics and electronics to transmit signals at high speed. The race for optical neurocomputers is led by the Japanese Ministry of International Trade and Industry (MITI), who claims that electronics has been the science of the 20th century and that optics will be the science of the 21st century. See **optical neurocomputer.**

OCR 1. Optical character recognition; software that uses a light source to read

---

NEWSFLASH

The United States produces an average of 74% of the total worldwide packaged software, but consumes only 44%. Europe consumes 37%.

and recognize the symbol of text. It reproduces characters as text, as if they had been keyed in manually. OCR can be used to read a price tag in a retail store, or to read entire documents in an office. The *Guinness Book of Records* states that 'The unaided human eye, under the best possible viewing conditions, comparing large areas of color, in good illumination, using both eyes, can distinguish 10 000 000 different color surfaces. The most accurate photoelectric spectrophotometers possess a precision probably only 40% as good as this'. 2. Optical character reader; the hardware device which can read and recognize the symbols of text. [ISO An

input unit that reads characters by optical character recognition.]

OCR–A Optical character recognition–alphabet; a standard typeface used for general optical character recognition, agreed upon by the American National Standards Institute.

octal 1. Whereas the decimal system has a base (radix) of ten (0, 1, 2, 3, 4, 5, 6, 7, 8, and 9), octal is a base-eight numbering system using a combination of eight symbols: the numbers 0 to 7. For example, the decimal number '7' is written '7' in octal, but decimal '8' is written '10' in octal. When different bases are being

Decimal	Octal	Decimal	Octal	Decimal	Octal	Decimal	Octal	Decimal	Octal	Decimal	Octal
0	0	22	26	44	54	66	102	88	130	110	156
1	1	23	27	45	55	67	103	89	131	111	157
2	2	24	30	46	56	68	104	90	132	112	160
3	3	25	31	47	57	69	105	91	133	113	161
4	4	26	32	48	60	70	106	92	134	114	162
5	5	27	33	49	61	71	107	93	135	115	163
6	6	28	34	50	62	72	110	94	136	116	164
7	7	29	35	51	63	73	111	95	137	117	165
8	10	30	36	52	64	74	112	96	140	118	166
9	11	31	37	53	65	75	113	97	141	119	167
10	12	32	40	54	66	76	114	98	142	120	170
11	13	33	41	55	67	77	115	99	143	121	171
12	14	34	42	56	70	78	116	100	144	122	172
13	15	35	43	57	71	79	117	101	145	123	173
14	16	36	44	58	72	80	120	102	146	124	174
15	17	37	45	59	73	81	121	103	147	125	175
16	20	38	46	60	74	82	122	104	150	126	176
17	21	39	47	61	75	83	123	105	151	127	177
18	22	40	50	62	76	84	124	106	152	128	200
19	23	41	51	63	77	85	125	107	153	129	201
20	24	42	52	64	100	86	126	108	154	130	202
21	25	43	53	65	101	87	127	109	155	131	203

octal Although the octal numbering system was originally used for programming mainframe computers, it was overtaken by the hexadecimal numbering system which is easier to use. In the octal system, the first column represents single units. The second column (known as the 'tens' column in the decimal system) is to a base 8. This means that the octal number '10' has one digit in the second column (therefore an 8) and zero units, making it equivalent to the decimal number '8'. The octal number '12' has one digit in the second column (therefore an 8) and two digits in the units column, making it equivalent to the decimal number '10' (8 + 2 = 10).

discussed, the number base should be used as a subscript, such as $16_{10} = 20_8$. [ISO The fixed radix numeration system that uses the digits 0, 1, 2, 3, 4, 5, 6, and 7, and the radix eight, and in which the lowest integral weight is 1. *Example:* In the octal numeration system, the numeral 1750 represents the number one thousand, that is: $(1 \times 8^3) + (7 \times 8^2) + (5 \times 8^1) + (0 \times 8^0)$.] Also called 'octal (numeration) system'. The word 'octal' comes from the Greek word *okto*, meaning 'eight'. ⚑

octillion See **exponent**.

octodecillion See **exponent**.

ODBC Open database connectivity.

odd header See **header**.

odd parity The data transmission system in which the number of '1' bits must add up to an odd number. A parity bit is used to signal the computer that the bits in a byte have been transmitted correctly. To do this, an extra bit (check bit) is added to the byte. For example, the EBCDIC letter 'A' is represented by 11000001. This has three ones and is therefore an odd number. The parity (check) bit would have to be a '0' so that it remains an odd number (110000010). Should the byte be received at the other end showing an even number of ones (for example, 110100010), then the computer knows that information was corrupted during transmission. Errors could still occur if the incorrectly transmitted byte contained two reversing errors which coincidentally and erroneously resulted in an odd number of ones, but the probability of this occurring is very low. Compare **even parity**.

ODP OverDrive processor. See **OverDrive**.

OE Optoelectronics; the combined use of optical and electronic systems (or devices), using light and electricity to transmit signals. See **optical neurocomputer**.

OEIC Optoelectronic integrated circuit; a computer chip which combines both optical and electronic systems, using light and electricity to transmit signals. See **optical neurocomputer**.

OEJRL Optoelectronics Joint Research Laboratory; set up in 1980 by a consortium of six Japanese electronics firms that focused on optoelectronic integrated circuits (OEIC). When the OEJRL project ended in 1986, more than 170 patent applications had been filed, including the development of the world's fastest semiconductor lasers, and the world's lowest-frequency visible-light semiconductor laser. OEJRL was headed by the Japanese Ministry of International Trade and Industry (MITI), who in 1986 sponsored a similar consortium called the 'Optoelectronics Technology Research Corporation' (OETRC) whose founding members were made up of 13 Japanese electronics and optics firms who were interested in joining the race to develop the optical neurocomputer. See **optical neurocomputer**.

OEM Original equipment manufacturer; a company which manufactures hardware or software which is modified, or re-configured, or re-badged by other value-added resellers (VAR) and sold under a different brand name.

OETRC Optoelectronics Technology Research Corporation. Founded in 1986 by the Japanese Ministry of International Trade and Industry (MITI) to further develop optoelectronic integrated circuits, OETRC was sponsored by 13 Japanese electronics and optics firms who were interested in joining the race to develop the optical neurocomputer. See **optical neurocomputer**.

office automation See **OA**.

off-line Refers to a peripheral device (such as a printer) which is not turned on or not connected to the computer, disabling it from receiving data from the computer. [ISO Pertaining to the operation of a functional unit when not under the direct control of the computer.]

off-screen formatting See **hidden codes**.

Ogre virus A boot-sector virus that infects any diskette or hard disk by moving the boot-sector information and replacing it with the virus. The virus becomes active when the computer is left running for 48 hours. After this period, any attempt to access the hard disk triggers the virus which clears the screen and places the message 'Disk Killer – Version 1.00 ...'. Another message is displayed warning the user to refrain from turning the computer off. Whatever the user does, the virus would have already rendered the disk inoperative. The only way to proceed would be to initialize the disk and restore from a backup disk. Although Ogre is infectious, it only activates if the hard disk is used within the first hour after the first 48 hours of the infection, although if a file is open and a regular automatic backup is set, the virus can trigger without human intervention. If no disk activity occurs within the hour after the first 48 hours of infec-

tion, then the virus waits for another 255 hours before it can trigger itself. Ogre is sometimes called 'Computer Ogre' or 'Disk Killer'. See **boot-sector virus**.

Ohio virus A variant of the Denzuk virus. See **Denzuk virus**.

ohms Resistance is measured in units called 'ohms'. Resistance refers to the opposition to electrical current flow. If resistance in a circuit increases, current flow will decrease because the opposition to current flow will be greater. Voltage, current, and resistance are directly related to each other and, in a given circuit, if the values of any two of these three factors is known, then the third factor can be calculated. This relationship of voltage, current, and resistance is expressed in Ohm's law, which states that current flowing in a circuit is equal to the voltage across the circuit divided by the resistance of the circuit. Three forms of the basic Ohm's law formula are: (1) power (current) is equal to voltage divided by resistance; (2) resistance is equal to voltage divided by power; and (3) voltage is equal to power multiplied by resistance.

Ohm's law An electrical principle which states that current flowing in a circuit is equal to the voltage across the circuit divided by the resistance of the circuit. Three forms of the basic Ohm's law formula are: (1) power (current) is equal to voltage divided by resistance; (2) resistance is equal to voltage divided by power; and (3) voltage is equal to power multiplied by resistance.

OHP Overhead projector. ▼

OIS Open Industry Standard.

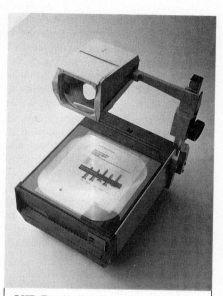

tries, plus 40 production facilities around the world. The Olivetti Group has significant holdings in over 230 companies operating in the information technology field and related sectors (such as components, tooling, service, and engineering). Beyond these, its most important acquisitions include West Germany's Triumph–Adler (typewriters, personal computers, minicomputers, and office automation equipment); Britain's Acorn (personal computers for education); and, in the United States, Bunker Ramo (banking automation). Since its formation in the early 1980s, the Olivetti Group assumed a new organizational structure in January 1989. This new structure was based on three company units, each fully dedicated to a specific product/market area and responsible for a complete cycle of operations — from design to production and sales. These units are Olivetti Office, Olivetti Systems and Networks, and Olivetti Information Services. Operating alongside these area-specific organizations is the Olivetti Technological Group. It heads the Teknecomp, Conner Peripherals Europe, and Laserdrive companies.

OHP Despite the advances in computerization, and the proliferation of computer equipment and presentation software, the overhead projector is still a popular business and education tool. Its simplicity and portability make it a well-entrenched device that is used to project printed or handwritten foils onto a large screen or a wall.

OLE Object linking and embedding. Enables documents to take advantage of objects created in other applications. For example, to access a voice-embedded object attached to a document, the user can double-click on that object which will automatically play back, even if the user's application currently in use does not have voice capabilites.

Olivetti The Olivetti Group; a leading Italian information technology group operating worldwide, active in the areas of computer office automation including workstations and minicomputers. The group employs over 56 000 people, with ten research laboratories in seven coun-

OLTP Online transaction processing. This is a key business application of database management systems. OLTP systems are used in a variety of business environments, from banking to medical record keeping. In all such environments, a database is updated as a result of a business action. For example, an inventory management system not only maintains the parts inventory level, but also triggers an automatic re-order of a part as indicated by its inventory level. A production manager makes decisions based on current information about the status of all the manufacturing elements as they exist on the shop floor. This information comes from production equipment sensors and management system databases. Another example of online transaction processing is the ability of a travel agent to book and confirm travel arrangements with the airline, hotel, and car rental company, all done while the customer is still on the telephone. See **DBMS** and **transaction processing**.

OMDD Optical memory disk drive.

OMF Object module format.

OMR Optical-mark recognition; the sensing by a device of marks on a piece of paper, commonly used to collate questionnaires or school examinations where a student, using a pencil, marks certain boxes on the examination answer sheet. Using a light beam, optical mark recognition is used to detect the marks and convert them to electrical signals which are sent to the computer for processing.

ON Österreichisches Normungsinstitut; Austria's standards body established in 1920.

ONC See **optical neurocomputer**.

1:1 interleave An interleave factor of 1:1. This requires only one disk revolution to read or write an entire track of data. The platter of a hard disk drive revolves very quickly — quicker than the head can read data from the surface and pass it on to the system. 'Interleave' refers to the process of interspersing logical sectors during write and read operations to allow time for the controlling device to process the data to and from the disk drive. For example, an ST-506 controller

employs a 3:1 interleave which requires at least three complete disk revolutions to read an entire track of data, since data is recorded on only every third track. On the other hand, a 1:1 interleave, such as that found in ESDI devices, writes to (or reads from) every sequential sector around the disk. It therefore requires only one complete disk revolution to write (or read) an entire track of data, leading to overall improved performance. See **ESDI**.

1base5 The IEEE 802.3 standard for bus topologies. 1base5 refers to 1 megabit per second, baseband, using 1640-foot (500-meter) maximum cable length (twisted pair wire). See **StarLAN**.

one-byte languages Roman languages such as English and Spanish that require only 1 byte of memory to fully represent their character set which includes A to Z and 0 to 9 as the standard characters. Arabic and Hebrew are examples of one-byte non-Roman languages. The characteristic shared by one-byte languages is that their character sets contain fewer than 256 characters. Compare **two-byte languages**.

One-in-Eight virus A variant of the Vienna virus. See **Vienna virus**.

1168 virus A variant of the Datacrime virus. See **Datacrime virus**.

ones complement [ISO The diminished radix complement in the binary numeration system.]

1702 virus A variant of the Cascade virus. See **Cascade virus**.

one-way communication [ISO Data communication such that data is transferred in one pre-assigned direction.]

online 1. Referring to a peripheral device (such as a printer) which is turned on or connected to a computer, enabling the device to receive data from the computer. [ISO Pertaining to the operation of a functional unit when under the direct control of the computer.] 2. In data processing, referring to real-time operation.

online help A utility available to the user when difficulty is encountered with a computer network or an application program. Most software applications offer on-screen help messages to guide the user through the different tasks. In some applications, like Microsoft Word, a special help command will display an index of all the help functions available, and the user is expected to nominate in which area help is required. Some programs offer context-sensitive help which immediately identifies the type of query being made, and displays help relative to where the user is at a particular point in the operation. For example, if a WordPerfect user (version 5.1 onwards) is having difficulty setting tabs, the context-sensitive nature of the program will detect this requirement and immediately display all the tab-related options. In this way, the user need not navigate through hundreds of options, and thereby minimizes keystrokes and wasted time.

online information service A large public subscription-based bulletin board which offers users up-to-date information on news, stock quotes, and other special-interest information. Users can connect to such services via telecommunications links.

online transaction processing See **OLTP**.

on-the-fly printer [ISO An impact printer in which the type band or type slugs do not stop moving during the impression time.]

OOAD Object-oriented analysis and design.

OOD Object-oriented design.

OODBMS Object-oriented database management system.

OOP See **object-oriented programming**.

OOPDE Object-oriented programming and development environment.

OOPS Object-oriented programming system. See **object-oriented programming**.

OPC Organic photosensitive compound. A photoreceptor belt or drum in a laser printer consists of two layers. The inner layer is a conductive aluminum base, and the outer layer is an organic photosensitive compound. The OPC layer acts as a photoconductor (a light-sensitive material that conducts electricity in the light and insulates against electrical conduction in the dark). See **laser printer** and **photoreceptor**.

OPC cartridge Organic photosensitive compound cartridge. In most laser printers, the photoreceptor is contained in an OPC cartridge. The construction of this cartridge varies greatly from one manufacturer to another. In some printers, the OPC cartridge contains only the photoreceptor belt. In other printers, this cartridge houses the photoreceptor drum, the charge corona, the entire development unit, the doctor blade, and the tank for collecting residual toner. See **laser printer** and **photoreceptor**.

open architecture The architecture of any computing system that uses standards which are published for public use so that compatibility is achieved between different users and manufacturers of peripheral products and software. Today, many systems are referred to as 'open', yet often they are not vendor-independent. An open computing environment must be vendor-neutral, compliant with international standards, and available to everyone for implementation, supporting enterprise-wide functions. Open architectures should permit authorized users to access applications and information anywhere on a network of systems from different vendors, providing network and system interoperability (the ability for applications on multiple vendors' systems to work together). Application portability is important so that applications can be moved to different hardware and software systems without affecting the network, data, applications, nor user access. In open computing, all networks, systems, data, and applications should be manageable as one unified computing environment. In contrast, a closed architecture is one that is compatible only with hardware and software products available from a single vendor.

Open Desktop A unified UNIX system from The Santa Cruz Operation launched in 1990. Open Desktop is an advanced, 32-bit operating environment that integrates UNIX, graphical user interface, data management, distributed networking, and other services. It provides multi-user, multitasking, security, and integrated networked windowing capabilities, and supports applications compliant with major open software standards, including POSIX 1003.1, X/Open XPG3, and SVID Issue 2. See **Advanced Computing Environment**.

open environment See **open architecture**.

Open Software Foundation See **OSF**.

open system See **open architecture**.

Open Systems Interconnection See **OSI**.

Open Systems Interconnection reference model See **OSI reference model**.

operable time [ISO The time during which a functional unit would yield correct results if it were operated.]

operand [ISO An entity on which an operation is performed.]

operating system A set of computer programs (first introduced in the 1960s) that are specifically used by the computer so that it can manage its own resources. A section of this software also allows the computer to communicate with the user (computer operator). The operating system is usually loaded (booted) each time the computer is switched on. This is generally an automatic loading procedure controlled by the read-only memory chip. During the booting process, several diagnostic tests are performed to check on the order of internal and external devices such as printers or disk drives. Operating systems can be likened to an orchestra conductor because they control the entire resources of the computer system. Operating systems coordinate the flow of data to and from the central

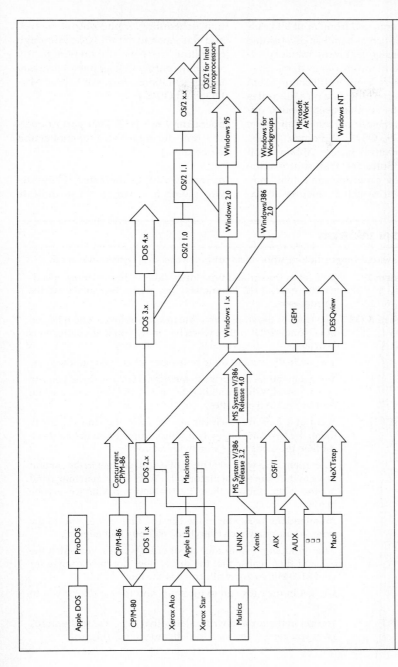

operating system *Personal computer operating systems originated in the mid-1970s along four main lines. Today, there is a multitude of personal computer operating systems and environments. Some of them show early influences from the mainframe/minicomputer world, and some are, for the most part, based on personal computers. This chart shows the chronological evolution of personal computer operating systems, and the influences and cross-influences over time.*

processing unit, and from input and output devices such as a mouse or a printer. They also assign and recall memory addresses, and in multi-user systems, they prevent users from obstructing each other, or overwriting data on a file as it is being read by another user. Popular operating systems for personal computers include DOS, OS/2, Windows, UNIX, and the Macintosh System. Abbreviation 'OS'. [ISO Software that controls the execution of programs and that may provide services such as resource alloca-tion, scheduling, input/output control, and data management. *Note:* Although operating systems are predominantly software, partial or complete hardware implementations are possible.] See **MS-DOS** and **OS/2**. ⟁

operating time [ISO That part of operable time during which a functional unit is operated.]

operating voltage indicator [ISO A device giving a visual signal to indicate

---

Play on Words

Here is what driving to the local store would be like if an operating system ran your car.

Apple System 7	You get in the car and type 'drug store'. After reaching speeds of 200 miles (322 kilometers) per hour, you arrive at the hairdressers.
Microsoft's new OS	You walk to the store with a Microsoft employee who tells you how wonderful it will be when he can fly you to the store in his Lear jet.
MS–DOS	You get in the car and try to remember where you put the keys.
MVS/VM	You get in the car and drive to the store. Halfway there, you run out of petrol. While walking the rest of the way, you are run over by children on skates.
Netware SFT III	You put a foot into each car and drive to the store. Halfway there, the two-lane highway divides, ripping you in half. Each car then proceeds to the store without you.
OS/2	After fueling up with 6000 liters of petrol, you get in the car and drive to the store with a motorcycle escort and a marching band in procession. Halfway there, the car blows up, killing everyone in town.
OS/400	An attendant locks you in the car and then drives you to the store, where you watch everybody else buy filet mignon.
UNIX	After graduating from the school of linguistics, you catch the bus and then realise that the driver does not have change for your $100 bill; so you walk home in the rain.
Windows	You get in the car to go to the store, and the car drives you to church.
Windows NT	You get in the car and write a letter that says, 'Go to the store'. Then you get out and mail the letter to your dashboard.

---

that the correct voltage is applied to a battery-powered calculator.]

operation [ISO A well-defined action that, when applied to any permissible combination of known entities, produces a new entity. *Example:* The process of addition in arithmetic; in adding five and three and obtaining eight, the numbers five and three are the operands, the number eight is the result, and the plus sign is the operator indicating that the operation performed is addition.]

operational amplifier [ISO An amplifier connected to external elements to perform specific operations or functions.]

operation code [ISO A code for representing the operation parts of the machine instructions of a computer.]

operation code trap [ISO A specific value that replaces the normal operation part of a machine instruction at a particular location to cause an interrupt when that machine instruction is executed.]

operation part [ISO The part of a machine instruction or micro-instruction that specifies the operation to be performed.]

operation table [ISO A table that defines an operation by listing all appropriate combinations of values of the operands and indicating the result for each of these combinations.]

operator (In symbols manipulation.) [ISO A symbol that represents the action to be performed in an operation.] The word 'operator' comes from the Latin word *operari*, meaning 'work'.

operator control panel [ISO A functional unit that contains switches used to control a computer (or part of it) and possibly indicators giving information about its functioning. *Note:* An operator control panel may be part of an operator console or other operator-controlled device.]

opportunity study [ISO A study to examine a problem and determine whether or not it requires being solved during the time period under consideration.]

optical character [ISO A graphic character printed or handwritten according to special rules in order to facilitate automatic identification by optical means.]

optical character reader [ISO An input unit that reads characters by optical character recognition.]

optical character recognition See **OCR**.

optical computer A computer which combines both optics and electronics to transmit signals at high speed. The race for optical neurocomputers is led by the Japanese Ministry of International Trade and Industry (MITI), who claim that electronics has been the science of the 20th century, and that optics will be the science of the 21st century. Abbreviation 'OC'. See **optical neurocomputer**.

optical disk [ISO A disk that contains digital data readable by optical techniques.] See **compact disk**. ▼

optical jukebox See **optical libraries**.

optical laser unit In a laser printer, the enclosed assembly which houses the laser, various reflective surfaces, a focus-

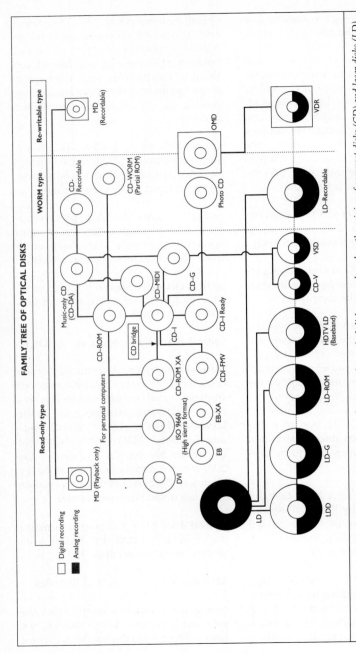

FAMILY TREE OF OPTICAL DISKS

optical disk This family tree of optical disks shows the two major optical-disk groups based on the origins of compact disks (CD) and laser disks (LD). The biggest difference between the two groups is that the LD group uses an analog recording system for images, while the CD group records all signals digitally. The CD group started as a music-only CD (CD-DA) in 1982. Music-only CDs revolutionized the audio world in the 1980s. They form the major share of optical disks in the market. Another development is the CD-ROM — optical disks that are identical to music-only CDs, but which are used mainly as computer external memory or game software packages. In the LD group, there is HDTV (high-definition television). In other groups, there are WORM (write-once, read-many times) disks, and rewritable OMDs (optical memory disks). In addition, some manufacturers have announced standards for the MD (mini disk) which uses a 64-millimeter diameter disk to record and/or reproduce audio, as well as for photo CD which displays 35-millimeter film images on a TV or computer screen, and for EB-XA which allows video reproduction for electronic publishing.

ing lens, the polygonal mirror, and the scanning motor assembly. See **laser** and **laser printer**.

optical libraries Proceeding along with the development of optical recording technology itself is the companion technology of media selectors, usually called 'optical libraries', or 'jukeboxes', because of their functional and physical resemblance to audio jukeboxes. Digital's RVxx Optical Jukebox Subsystem is based on WORM drive technology, and uses robotics to store more than 128 gigabytes of information in a single, 5 x 5 foot (1.5 x 1.5 meter) cabinet. Multiple jukeboxes can be configured in a system for even larger applications. Disk cartridges are introduced to the jukebox through a loading station, which accepts one cartridge at a time and moves it along a track to a storage slot. System commands to access data stored on disks resident in the library specify the disk using its storage slot and the drive it is in. The selector mechanism extracts the disk from its storage slot and moves it along a track to the loading station for the target drive. Optical libraries offer access in the 10–15 second range for any data record within the selector. The largest component of this time is for spin-up of the selected disk (and spin-down of the disk it replaces, if any). For data on a disk already mounted in a drive, typical access times are in the range of 100 to 400 milliseconds. Because of the high capacity and low cost of optical disk cartridges relative to magnetic disks, optical libraries offer significant potential for automated backup and archiving of very large amounts of online data. See **compact disk**.

optical-mark recognition The ability of a device to sense marks on a piece of paper. Commonly used to collate questionnaires or school examinations where a student, using a pencil, marks certain boxes on the examination answer sheet. Using a light beam, optical mark recognition is used to detect the marks and convert them to electrical signals which are sent to the computer for processing. Abbreviation 'OMR'.

optical neurocomputer A computer which combines both optical and electronic systems (or devices), using light and electricity to transmit signals. Japanese and American computer manufacturers are currently working on a new level of technology which may supersede current supercomputers and launch a new era of optical computing using optoelectronic integrated circuits (OEIC). These will be used in optical neurocomputers (ONC) with switching devices topping speeds of 1 picosecond (10^{-12} seconds), operating at 1 gigahertz (10^9). The race for ONCs is led by the Japanese Ministry of International Trade and Industry (MITI), which claims that electronics has been the science of the 20th century, and that optics will be the science of the 21st century. The development of optoelectronics has been accelerated by the invention of light-emitting diodes (LED), the semiconductor laser, optical disks, optical connectors, and the optic fiber (industries for these in Japan alone account for more than US$2500 million). In 1980, MITI established the Optoelectronics Joint Research Laboratory (OEJRL) — a consortium of six Japanese companies who focused on optoelectronic integrated circuits (OEIC). When the OEJRL project ended in 1986, more than 170 patent applications had been filed, including the development of the world's fastest semiconductor lasers, and the world's lowest-frequency visible-light semiconductor laser. Also in 1986, MITI founded the Optoelectronics Technology Research Corporation (OTRC), which was sponsored by 13 Japanese electronics and optics firms who were interested in joining the race to develop the ONC. The fast speed of ONCs is due to the use of multiple quantum-well structures (MQWS), which consist of aluminum gallium arsenide layers only several atoms thick. These are sandwiched (alternated) between wider gallium arsenide layers which are 30 atoms thick. This alternating structure is called a 'tunneling biquantum-well'. Optical images are captured, stored, and read by the use of optically-addressable spatial light modulators (SLM) which use ferroelectric liquid crystals (FLC). FLC–SLM can operate at 50 microseconds with a spatial resolution of 40 line-pairs per millimeter. These enable a 1 centimeter-square device to function at 3.2 giga operations (10^9). Competing technology developed by AT&T Bell Laboratories of the United States in 1987 includes photonic integrated circuits consisting of 2048 MQWS (on a 2 millimeter-square array). These are called 'symmetric self electro-optic effect devices' (S-SEED), and serve as the logic, the memory cell, and/or the switch that operates at clock speeds exceeding 1 gigahertz. Compare **supercomputer**.

optical recognition The ability of an electronic scanning device to read numbers, letters, special characters/symbols, bar codes, and handwritten characters. The scanning device then converts the data into electrical signals and sends the data to the computer for processing. See **OCR**.

optical scanner [ISO A scanner that uses an optical process for examining patterns. *Note:* Optical scanners are often used in pattern recognition or character recognition.]

optical storage 1. [ISO A storage device that uses optical techniques.] 2. See **compact disk**.

optic fiber See **fiber optics** and **optic fiber technology**.

optic fiber technology Like its predecessors (the telegraph, coaxial cable, radio, and satellite), optic fiber technology is revolutionizing communications. Optic fibers transmit messages from point-to-point as a succession of laser-generated light pulses through hair-thin strands of glass. Using laser light instead of electrical signals, optic fiber digital cables offer more than 30 times the capacity of the analog systems they replace, while maintaining the highest integrity in that data and offering new levels of transmission security. The material is immune to electromagnetic and radio interference, and transmissions via optic fiber will not contribute delay, crosstalk, nor echo to digital services. Optic fibers are made of silica (SiO_2) containing refractive index-controlling dopants. They consist of a core with a high refractive index, surrounded by cladding with a low refractive index to prevent light waves from escaping from the core. There are three types of fibers: step-index multi-mode, graded-index multi-mode, and single-mode. With the advance of manufacturing techniques, transmission loss of optic fibers has decreased from 20 decibels per kilometer (dB/km) in 1970 to much less than 1 dB/km. Optic fiber cables usually contain anywhere from one to over 100 fibers. Cables are usually delivered in several hundred to 1000 meter lengths and are usually joined by fusion splicing. Events that triggered the development of fiber optic systems were the invention of ruby lasers in 1960 by T.H. Maiman; the fabrication by Corning Glass Works in 1970 of optic fibers with losses of only 20 dB/km; and Bell Laboratories' success in building semiconductor (GaAs) lasers which, operating at room temperature, generated a continuous wave at the same wavelength as the low-loss optic fiber (introduced in 1980). Light waves are electromagnetic waves with frequencies 10 000 times higher than microwaves. Like conventional transmission systems, the fiber optic system consists of terminals, transmission lines, and repeaters. At the transmitting end, the electric signals to be transmitted are converted to light signals and sent through a fiber. Before too much of the light has faded, the signals are electrically intensified by a repeater consisting of optoelectronic transducers and conventional electronic circuits, and sent to the next fiber. At the receiving end, the light signals are reconverted to the original signals. The key components of fiber optic transmission systems are the optic fibers themselves, the light sources, and detectors. See **fiber optics**.

optics The branch of physics that specializes in light and vision. It deals with the properties of electromagnetic waves which have wavelengths greater than X-rays (0.001 microns), and smaller than microwaves. This range includes the ultraviolet (0.001 to 0.4 microns), visible (0.4 to 0.8 microns), and infrared (0.8 to 100 microns) fields of the optical (electromagnetic) spectrum. An optical computer combines both optics and

Wavelength limits in microns (μ)		
Electromagnetic region	Lower	Upper
Optical	0.001	100
Ultraviolet	0.001	0.4
Lightwave	0.3	3
Visible	0.4	0.8
Infrared	0.8	100
Near-infrared	0.8	3
Middle-infrared	3	30
Far-infrared	30	100

optics The optical spectrum is also referred to as the 'lightwave' region. Note that the optical spectrum lies between (the lower parts of) radio waves at 100 microns, and (the upper limits of) X-rays, at 0.001 microns.

electronics to transmit signals at high speed. The race for optical neurocomputers is led by the Japanese Ministry of International Trade and Industry (MITI), which claims that electronics has been the science of the 20th century, and that optics will be the science of the 21st century. See **optical neurocomputer**. ⚠

optoelectronic integrated circuit A computer chip which combines both optical and electronic systems, using light and electricity to transmit signals. Abbreviation 'OEIC'. See **optical neurocomputer**.

optoelectronics The combined use of optical, electromagnetic, and electronic systems (or devices) which use light and electricity to transmit signals. Optoelectronic devices can function as electrical-to-optical or optical-to-electrical transducers. Optoelectronic devices commonly used in fiber optic systems include photodiodes, light-emitting diodes, injection lasers, repeaters, and integrated optical circuits. Not to be confused with electro-optic, which relates to the effect that an electric field has on a lightwave. The prefix 'opto-' comes from the Greek word *optos*, meaning 'seen'. Abbreviation 'OE'. See **optical neurocomputer**.

optomechanical mouse See **mouse**.

Oracle A database management system developed by Oracle Systems Corporation to enable users to access data from large corporate databases. The word 'oracle' comes from the Latin word *orare*, meaning 'speak'. See **Oracle Corporation**.

Oracle Corporation One of the largest suppliers of RDBMS software, developing and marketing an integrated line of software products for database management, application development, decision support, and office automation, as well as families of financial and manufacturing applications packages. All Oracle products are available on personal computers, minicomputers, mainframes, and massively parallel supercomputers. Founded in the United States in 1977 and headquartered in Redwood Shores, California, Oracle offers its products, along with related consulting, education, and support services, in 92 countries.

orbiting satellite See **satellite transmission**.

order 1. [ISO A specified arrangement resulting from ordering. *Note:* In contrast to a sequence, an order need not be linear, for example the ordering of a hierarchy of items.] 2. [ISO To place items in an arrangement in accordance with specified rules.]

OR gate [ISO A gate that performs the Boolean operation of disjunction.]

orgy The act of exchanging erotic scenes or ideas across a telecommunications or computer network. This may take the form of electronic mail, or live discussions across a video or telecommunications network. Sophisticated orgy sessions may involve a party connected from around the world, using erotic film or still pictures which may be pre-stored images or live, using videophones through a multimedia or virtual reality system.

orientation The way a page is turned to be printed on; the direction of the long axis. In portrait orientation, the output is printed across the shorter axis. In contrast, landscape orientation would print text and graphics from left to right on the longer axis of a page.

oriented oxide recording See **oxide media**.

original equipment manufacturer A company which actually manufactures hardware and software which is modified, re-configured, or re-badged by other value-added resellers (VAR) and sold under a different brand name. Abbreviation 'OEM'.

orphan In publishing, an orphan is the first line of a paragraph which appears alone at the bottom of a page. Some page-layout programs allow the user to suppress orphans, forcing the line to join the rest of the paragraph over the page. In contrast, a 'widow' refers to the last line of a paragraph which appears alone at the top of a new page. Some page-layout programs allow the user to suppress widows, forcing the paragraph to remain intact, or to automatically move more than one line over the page.

OS See **operating system**.

OSCAR Orbital Satellite-Carrying Amateur Radio; one of the first group of satellites launched by AMSAT (The Radio Amateur Satellite Corporation). AMSAT was formed in the United States in 1969 to coordinate a range of national and international space projects.

OSF Open Software Foundation; a nonprofit organization founded by Digital Equipment Corporation and six other leading systems vendors (including IBM) to develop a set of specifications (the Application Environment Specifications, or AES) for an open software environment, and to license a source code implementation that conforms to those specifications. OSF membership and licensing is open to all hardware vendors, software vendors, users, and research and university organizations. OSF's goal is to develop a standard for proprietary versions of UNIX, independent of AT&T.

OSI Open Systems Interconnection; a set of universally-accepted standards published in 1977 by the International Organization for Standardization and the Institute of Electrical and Electronic Engineers. The OSI reference model lists seven layers which define the activities that must take place when devices communicate on a network. The seven layers are application (highest), presentation, session, transport, network, data link, and physical (lowest). The goal of OSI is to enable computerized systems in multivendor environments to share information more easily. With this as a goal, the primary purpose of OSI is to define standards for interconnecting systems of different computer manufac-

turers in order to provide the broad range of functions required for information exchange in an 'open systems environment'. OSI defines a system as a set of one or more computers and associated software, peripherals, terminals, human operators, physical processes, and information transfer means which form an autonomous 'whole' capable of performing information processing and/or information transfer. An open system is one which adheres to OSI standards in its communications with other systems. See **OSI reference model**.

OSI/NMF Open Systems Interconnection/Network Management Forum; a computer-industry group made up of leading computer companies (including AT&T, Hewlett-Packard, and Unisys) whose aim is to speed up the introduction of networking standards. See OSI.

OSI reference model Open Systems Interconnection reference model. This provides a common basis for the coordination of standards development by dividing the large problem of data communications into smaller, more manageable sub-problems — isolating them from each other in order to prevent changes and advances in one area from impacting on unrelated areas. The model defines the abstract concepts to be used throughout the definition of OSI, and provides a common terminology for the development of OSI. The OSI concept represents the relationships between a network and the services which it can support as a hierarchy of protocol layers. Each layer uses the services offered by layers lower than itself in conjunction with its own functions to create new services which are then made available to higher layers. Each of the seven OSI layers performs unique and specific tasks, has knowledge of its immediate adjacent layer, uses the services of the layer below, and performs functions and provides services to the layers above. As vendors and user groups gain experience with the OSI model, and as new technologies require additions to the existing model, all the layers will continue to grow and change. However, the existing standards are internationally accepted, and offer stability through a wide selection of compatible products. See **application layer, data link layer, network layer, physical layer, presentation layer, session layer,** and **transport layer.** ▽

OS/2 Operating System/2; announced in November 1987 by IBM and Microsoft, with the first version (1.0) released in 1988. The objective for OS/2 was to develop a personal computer operating system with the characteristics of a mainframe — a robust platform for business applications with the ability to run

multiple programs and provide protection between multiple applications. The initial release had almost 1000 people working on it, with the Presentation Manager developed in Hursley, UK, by a team comprising IBM UK and Microsoft personnel. Subsequent versions of OS/2 were developed in the United States at the IBM Boca Programming Center in Boca Raton, Florida. OS/2 version 1.1 saw the release of the first IBM personal computer graphical user interface as a standard part of an operating system, while version 2.0 contained the first object-oriented workplace shell. Following the release of versions 1.1 and 1.2, IBM decided to sever ties with Microsoft and develop version 1.3 on its own (while Microsoft concentrated on its 16-bit Windows product). The first 32-bit version of OS/2, version 2.0, was released in March 1992, with the multimedia Presentation Manager offered as an option. This facility was rolled into the release of 2.1 in May 1993, to become

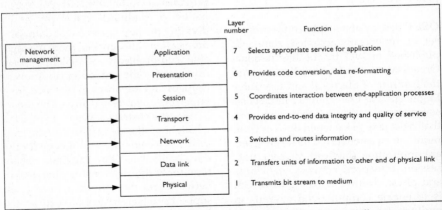

	Layer number	Function
Application	7	Selects appropriate service for application
Presentation	6	Provides code conversion, data re-formatting
Session	5	Coordinates interaction between end-application processes
Transport	4	Provides end-to-end data integrity and quality of service
Network	3	Switches and routes information
Data link	2	Transfers units of information to other end of physical link
Physical	I	Transmits bit stream to medium

Network management

OSI reference model *The International Organization for Standardization, in an effort to encourage 'open' networks whereby equipment (and/or networks) from multiple vendors can be interconnected, developed the Open Systems Interconnection (OSI) reference model to form the basis for all network development. In simple terms, it logically groups the functions and sets of rules necessary to establish and conduct communications between two or more parties, into seven layers.*

a standard feature of OS/2. OS/2 for Windows was released in November 1993, providing an option for users already running DOS and Microsoft Windows 3.1 to load OS/2 using their existing Windows code and retain any customized setting. The five-millionth copy of OS/2 was shipped in May 1994, providing pre-emptive multitasking, multithreading, and support for Windows, DOS, and native OS/2 applications. Pronounced 'owe-ess-too'. See **multitasking, operating system,** and **virtual memory.** ▼

OTS Orbital Test Satellite.

outage A state that occurs when a system denies service to at least one user for a period of time. This clearly interrupts the user's work and leads to a loss of personnel time, business, money, customer goodwill, or other valuable resources. The period of time is not precisely defined and varies based upon application requirements.

outline font A font (complete set of characters of a typeface) whose characters are generated by a mathematical formula. The outline of each character is then filled in by the printer depending upon the printer's maximum resolution. Unlike bit-mapped fonts, the size of an outline font is easily changed without distortion through a mathematical formula stored either in the printer or in the memory of the personal computer. Adobe Systems Incorporated is a leading supplier of outline fonts. See **PostScript**.

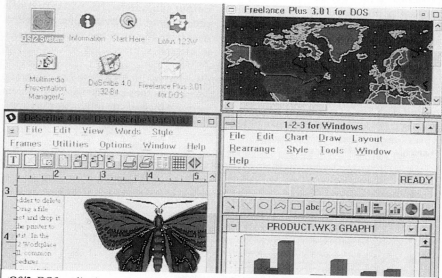

OS/2 DOS applications can emulate some of the benefits of OS/2 by using shells like DESQview and Microsoft Windows. All the operating system codes reside in a central area known as the 'kernel'. The kernel does not interact directly with peripheral devices, but must have software written that describes the device. These drivers can be customized to support specialized peripherals, or optimized to increase the performance of standard peripherals.

outline utility In extensive word processing, a mode which hides all text, and displays on-screen only the headings and subheadings available in a (lengthy) document.

out of phase The phase difference (delay measured in degrees) between two waveforms which may be of identical frequency and identical voltage amplitude. Two signals which travel together without a time delay are said to be in phase, while signals which travel at different speeds are out of phase. See **phase modulation**.

output 1. The transfer of data from a computer's internal storage unit to another device such as a monitor or printer — usually after the information has been processed. 2. [ISO Pertaining to a device, process, or channel involved in an output process, or to the associated data or states. *Note:* The word 'output' may be used in place of 'output data', 'output signal', or 'output process' when such a usage is clear in a given context.]

output data [ISO Data being produced or to be produced by any component part of a computer.]

output device Any device designed to assist in the output of data from a computer system. An output device may be a monitor, printer, disk drive, or other peripheral. In contrast, an input device is one designed to assist in the entry of data into a computer system, such as a keyboard or scanner.

output port A connection that permits information from the computer (or other device) to be passed to some other device such as a printer or monitor.

output process [ISO The process that consists of the production of data from any component part of a computer.]

output subsystem [ISO That part of a process interface system that transfers data from the process computer system to a technical process.]

OverDrive Intel's single-chip upgrade processors that can increase the system performance of an Intel 486 micropro-

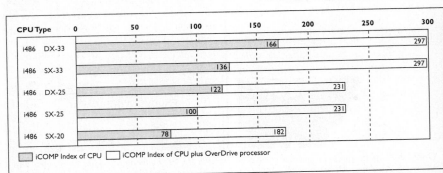

CPU Type	0	50	100	150	200	250	300
i486 DX-33				166			297
i486 SX-33			136				297
i486 DX-25			122		231		
i486 SX-25			100		231		
i486 SX-20		78		182			

☐ iCOMP Index of CPU ☐ iCOMP Index of CPU plus OverDrive processor

OverDrive This graph shows the increase in performance of standard Intel 486 microprocessors when an OverDrive processor is installed. The iCOMP index is used to measure the relative performance of Intel microprocessors.

cessor by up to 70%. Although OverDrive processors were first introduced for the Intel 486 DX and SX chips, they are now available for most Intel microprocessors. OverDrive processors can be inserted into the vacant OverDrive processor socket found on some system motherboards of computers using Intel microprocessors. See **Intel Corporation.** ⚊

overflow 1. [ISO The state in which the calculator is unable to accept or process the number of digits in the entry or result.] 2. [ISO That portion of a word expressing the result of an operation by which its word length exceeds the storage capacity of the intended storage device.]

overflow check [ISO A limit check to determine whether a representation of data exceeds a stipulated length.]

overflow indication [ISO A visual indication that the calculator is in the overflow state.]

overlay In video technology, the ability to superimpose computer graphics over live or recorded video signals, and perhaps store the resulting video image on videotape or disk. This is often used to add titles to video footage.

overlay (segment) [ISO Each of several segments of a computer program that, one at a time, occupy the same area of main storage, when executed.]

overwrite To write data to a secondary storage device (or random-access memory) so that the new data replaces the old.

oxide media Magnetic media is actually a very thin coating applied to a substrate disk that is sufficiently rigid and stable to maintain a constant flat profile while rotating at high speed, generally 3600 revolutions per minute. The most common disk medium in use today is a suspension of gamma-ferric oxide particles in a phenoxy binder. Gamma-ferric oxide is a crystalline material. For disk media applications, it is formed into tiny acircular (sharpened pencil-shaped) particles. Disks for magnetic recordings are manufactured by spin-coating the phenoxy binder with these particles. The media coating is typically between 20 and 40 millionths of an inch thick, applied to an aluminum substrate that is typically 0.075 of an inch thick. To further improve media characteristics for greater areal density, media orientation was developed during the 1970s. Oriented media use the same basic material with a refined manufacturing process. After the aluminum substrate has been spin-coated with the media solution, it is placed in the presence of a strong magnetic field while drying. This magnetic field orientates the oxide particles within the binder material so that their longest dimension tends to be tangential to the disk. Oriented particles permit higher magnetic movements and sharper transitions in field direction, and therefore produce pulses of narrower width and larger amplitude. Most high-density disk drives today use oriented oxide recording media. Densities in the range of 5 to 30 million bits per square inch have been achieved. Improved technology lies in metallic media. See **media technology** and **metallic media**.

PERFECTION HURTS

p Pico-. An SI unit prefix for 10^{-12} expressed in decimal notation as 0.000 000 000 001. A picosecond (ps) is a unit of time equal to 0.000 000 000 001 of a second. Commonly used to measure the speed at which the central processing unit can execute instructions. If one picosecond was imagined to be one second, then one second would be equivalent to 31 710 years. See **SI**.

P Peta-. An SI unit prefix for 10^{15} expressed in decimal notation as 1 000 000 000 000 000. See **SI**.

PABX Private automatic branch exchange; a telephone switching exchange privately owned by a business or organization. It provides automatic access to and from the public telephone network, and it is used to control all in-coming and out-going calls. In-house calls do not incur a charge by the telephone company, and they require minimal assistance from the switchboard operator.

pack [ISO To convert data to a compact form in a storage medium by taking advantage of known characteristics of the data and of the storage medium, in such a way that the original form of the data can be recovered. *Example:* To make use of bit or byte locations that would otherwise remain unused.]

Packard, David Chairman of the board of directors of Hewlett-Packard Company (HP). HP is an international manufacturer of measurement and computation products and systems used in industry, business, engineering, science, medicine, and education. Packard was born 7 September 1912, in Pueblo, Colorado, United States. He attended Stanford University in Stanford, California, and received a bachelor of arts degree in 1934, and a master's degree in electrical engineering in 1939. From 1936 to 1938, Packard was an engineer with the General Electric Company in Schenectady, New York. In 1938, he returned to Palo

Alto, California, and in the following year he formed a partnership known as 'Hewlett-Packard Company' with William (Bill) R. Hewlett, a friend and Stanford classmate. HP's first product was a resistance-capacitance audio oscillator based on a design developed by Hewlett when he was in graduate school. The company's first 'plant' was a small garage in Palo Alto, and the initial capital amounted to US$538. Packard served as partner in the company from its founding in 1939 until it was incorporated in 1947. He became president of the company in 1947 and held that post until 1964, when he was elected Chairman of the Board and Chief Executive Officer. Packard left the company in 1969 to become US Deputy Secretary of Defense for the first Nixon administration. He served in this capacity for almost three years and resigned his post in 1971. When he returned to California, he was re-elected Chairman of the Board of HP. Over the years, Packard has been active in a number of professional, educational, civic, and business organizations. He is a fellow of the Institute of Electrical and Electronics Engineers, a member of the National Academy of Engineering, and a lifetime member of the Instruments Society of America. He is a co-founder and past Chairman of the American Electronics Association. In 1985, Packard was appointed by former President Reagan to chair the Blue Ribbon Commission of Defense Management. He was also a member of The Trilateral Commission from 1973 to 1981. From 1975 to 1982, he was a member of the US–USSR Trade & Economic Council's committee on science and technology, and he chaired the US–Japan Advisory Commission from 1983 to 1985. He was also a member of the

Packard, David Co-founder of Hewlett-Packard. Apart from his current role as Chairman and Chief Executive Officer of HP, Packard is the Chairman of the Monterey Bay Aquarium Foundation — a US$49 million philanthropic project of the Packard family. He has been active in the Business Roundtable, and is founding Vice Chairman of the California Roundtable. He has also been a director of several business organizations, including Boeing Company, Caterpillar Tractor, Chevron Corporation, and Genentech Inc. Packard holds several honorary degrees, including doctor of science from Colorado College; doctor of law from the University of California, Catholic University, and Pepperdine University; doctor of letters from Southern Colorado State College; and doctor of engineering from University of Notre Dame. With over 50 awards to his credit, the most recent include the Pueble Hall of Fame, the Silicon Valley Engineering Hall of Fame, the Public Welfare Medal, the Presidential Medal of Freedom, the Gandhi Humanitarium Award, and the National Medal of Technology.

President's Council of Advisors on Science and Technology from 1990 to 1992. See **Hewlett, William R.**

packed decimal notation [ISO A binary-coded decimal notation in which two consecutive decimal digits, each having 4 bits, are represented by 1 byte.]

packet 1. A unit of data transmitted at the OSI network layer. 2. Any addressed segment of data transmitted on a network. See **packet switching**. 3. [ISO A sequence of binary digits, including data and control signals, that is transmitted and switched as a composite whole. *Note:* The data, control signals, and possibly error control information, are arranged in a specific format.]

packet assembler/disassembler [ISO A functional unit that enables data terminal equipment not equipped for packet switching to access a packet-switched network.]

packet assembly The conversion of a message signal into smaller packets of data, usually 8000 bits each, so that they can be transmitted independently and efficiently over a network. See **packet-switching system**.

packet disassembly The re-grouping of packets of data in their correct order after they have been successfully received, so as to make up the original full-length message. See **packet-switching system**.

packet mode terminal [ISO Data terminal equipment that can control, format, transmit, and receive packets.]

packet sequencing [ISO A process of ensuring that packets are delivered to the receiving data terminal equipment (DTE) in the same sequence as they were transmitted by the sending DTE.]

packet-switched data network In the UK, Eurpoe, Canada, Australia, and New Zealand, packet-switched data networks (PSDNs) have become a viable alternative (or supplement) to the public-switched telephone network. The majority of such networks are based on X.25. This standard was developed by the international standards body known as the 'Comité Consultatif International de Télégraphique et Téléphonique' (CCITT). In countries where it is impossible (or too costly) to obtain private leased lines for data transmission, computer networks can be established using only those public packet-switched facilities available from the telephone authority of the particular country. A PSDN allows large numbers of users to share a powerful message packaging and delivery service. It also permits the terminal equipment of a subscriber to communicate with the equipment of any other subscriber, simply by presenting data (plus certain control information) in a prescribed manner to the network. The subscriber need not be concerned with how the message arrives at its destination. In order to transmit over a PSDN, data must be broken into 'packets' of data (typically 128 bytes). The concept of handling information in packets resulted from a study by the Rand Corporation which investigated the potential for a national network supporting both voice and data communications. Once the data is broken into packets, the PSDN then routes the packets to their destination. To guarantee its safe delivery, each individual packet identifies its destination, source, and number. Packets are numbered because a message may be segmented into several packets, which must be re-assembled in the correct order when they arrive. PSDNs are cost-effective over long distances when traffic volume is low. Conversely, circuit-switched leased lines are more economical over short distances when traffic volume is high. Compare **circuit-switched network**.

packet switching A data communications technique where data is transmitted in manageable segments (packets) and sent the fastest possible way. When the packets are received at their destination, the receiving device (node) is responsible for re-grouping the data in the correct order. [ISO The process of routing and transferring data by means of addressed packets so that a channel is occupied only during the transmission of a packet; upon completion of the transmission, the channel is made available for the transfer of other packets.] See **packet assembly** and **packet-switching system**.

packet-switching system The method of breaking down a message into small uniform groups (packets) of data (usually 8000 bits) so that they can be sent across a communications network in the most efficient way. This means the collection of packets (information) which makes up the complete message may be sent independently via different routes, and arrive at the destination node at different times, and possibly in the wrong order. Addressing, error-checking, and sequencing information is also sent with each packet, making it possible for the receiving node to re-compile the packets in the correct order. The standard CCITT packet-switching protocol is called 'X.25'. It is typically used in wide and local area networks to define the structure of commands, responses, and bit-patterns associated with successful switching. Users perceive that they

are on a permanent connection but they actually share the connection with other users. The delay is not noticed because it rarely exceeds 200 milliseconds for interactive data users. Abbreviation 'PSS'. See **framing** and **X.25**.

PacRimEast See **South Pacific Network**.

PacRimWest See **South Pacific Network**.

PAD Packet assembler/disassembler. Devices that do not contain the resources necessary to implement the three levels of X.25 (a CCITT standard that defines the accessing protocol for public packet-switching networks) may still access the public data network for packet data transmission. However, they cannot transmit to a special DCE (data circuit-terminating equipment) device, nor network node. They must transmit to a special DTE (data terminal equipment) device called a 'packet assembler/disassembler'. PADs are used to provide 'dumb' (nonprogrammable) character-oriented terminals with a way of connecting to a packet network. The basic function of a PAD is to provide a buffer and is a way of establishing virtual calls. A PAD can either be provided by the network supplier, or by a third-party vendor. At the host computer, PAD support software is required in order to communicate with remote devices using PADs. See **packet-switching system** and **virtual call**.

padding [ISO Concatenating a string with one or more characters, called 'fillers', usually in order to achieve a specific length of the string.]

page (In a virtual storage system.) [ISO

447

Λ

A fixed-length block that has a virtual address and that is transferred as a unit between real storage and auxiliary storage.]

page description language A programming language (such as PostScript) that uses special commands to describe how an image will be printed on a page. Output to any printer which contains an interpreter for the same page description language can drive that printer, regardless of its make or model. This means all processing is transferred from the computer to the printer which has its own central processing unit and random-access memory for converting the mathematical representation of images. See **outline font**.

page frame [ISO In real storage, a storage location having the size of a page.]

PageMaker The first page-layout program designed for personal computers. This product was launched in 1985 by Aldus Corporation. It helped the Apple Macintosh to lead the desktop publishing race.

page-mode RAM Page-mode random-access memory; a spatial static RAM chip that carries information without having to rely on the central processing unit to refresh it several thousand times per second (as is the case with dynamic RAM). Page-mode RAM is used with very fast processors to ensure that each processor does not have to wait for information when it is needed, thereby reducing or eliminating the wait state. 'Fast page-mode RAM' refers to the column address strobe (CAS) cycle time of the dynamic memory incorporated in a personal computer. With a shorter CAS

pre-charge time, the access time to the system memory is reduced if the second or subsequent address is close to the initial memory access. As a result, the total cycle time for reading and writing back is reduced, leading to faster memory performance. See **DRAM** and **wait state**.

page orientation The orientation of a page when the output is printed across the shorter axis. In contrast, landscape orientation prints text and graphics across the longer axis of a page.

page printer [ISO A printer that prints one page as a unit. *Example:* A COM printer; a laser printer.]

pager A small electronic radio signal receiver which can be activated to alert the carrier that a message awaits. More sophisticated pagers are used as alternatives to cellular radios (mobile phones) and messages (data) can be viewed on liquid crystal display screens. Pagers are sometimes called 'beepers' because of the sound they emit when activated.

page reader [ISO A character reader whose input data is a printed text.]

paging A method of memory management which is useful for virtual memory multitasking operating systems. Unlike segmentation which modularizes programs and data into variable-length segments, paging divides programs into multiple uniform size pages. Pages bear no direct relation to the logical structure of a program. While segment selectors can be considered the logical 'name' of a program module or data structure, a page most likely corresponds to only a portion of a module or data structure. By taking advantage of the locality of reference displayed by most programs, only a small number of pages from each task need be in memory at any one moment. The Intel 80486 microprocessor, for example, uses two levels of tables to translate the linear address (from the segmentation unit) into a physical address. There are three components to the paging mechanism of the 486 microprocessor: the page directory; the page tables; and the page itself. All memory-resident elements of the 486 paging mechanism are the same size (4 kilobytes). A uniform size for all of the elements simplifies memory allocation and re-location schemes, since there is no problem with memory fragmentation. [ISO The transfer of pages between real storage and auxiliary storage.] See **virtual memory**.

paging technique [ISO A real storage allocation technique by which real storage is divided into page frames.]

paint program A software program such as MacPaint, PC Paintbrush, or Super-Paint that uses bit-mapped graphics (sometimes called 'raster' graphics) which use picture elements (pixels) to form complex, artistic patterns on the screen. Unlike object-oriented graphics which are stored as mathematical formulae to allow re-sizing and manipulation without distortion, attempts to re-size images produced on a paint program will cause distortion. The first paint program (MacPaint) was designed by Bill Atkinson of Apple Computer, and used for the Apple Macintosh, offering a resolution of 72 dots per inch. ▼

Pakistani virus A variant of the Brain virus. See **Brain virus**.

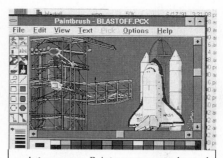

paint program Paint programs can be used to sketch diagrams or manipulate graphics files. Although they are easy to use, paint programs are only a tool for an artist. For those with little or no artistic ability, clip art files can help to build an image.

PAL 1. Programmable array logic. 2. Phase alternation line; a European color television coding system first developed by Telefunken in West Germany and later adopted in the United Kingdom, to standardize on broadcasting using 625 lines and a 50-hertz frequency. 3. See **Paradox Application Language**.

Palatino A serif typeface (as used here) derived from the traditional stone-cut design with early Renaissance traits such as the slight dip where the curve of the capital 'P' joins the stem. It is often included as a built-in font with PostScript laser printers. It was designed in 1950 for Linotype by renowned German typr designer Hermann Zapf.

PAL D Phase alternate line delay; a signal decoding sequence used in phase alternate line (PAL) color televisions, designed to reduce color errors. See **PAL**.

palette The on-screen display containing a selection of colors or patterns that can be used in a computer graphics application such as computer-aided design or animation. Derived from the Latin word *pala*, meaning 'thin oval', in which a thumb hole is made near one end to enable an artist to hold the board horizontally when mixing paint.

PAL S Phase alternate line simple. See **PAL**.

PAN Personal area network.

panning [ISO Progressively translating the display image to give the visual impression of lateral movement of the image. *Note:* Panning may be restricted to a viewport.]

paper feed [ISO On a printing calculator, the device for manually positioning the paper vertically according to the requirements of the operator.]

Paper Keyboard Software developed by Datacap Incorporated translates hand-printed characters on a piece of paper, into data. This technology is 150 to 200% faster than keyboard data entry, and it is better known as 'computer-aided data entry' (CADE). Like optical character recognition products (OCR), Paper Keyboard reads pages directly from a scanner. Instead of typed text, the software recognizes hand-printed characters on paper forms and automatically inputs names, addresses, dates, numbers, and multiple-choice check boxes. This data is then output in database or spreadsheet format.

paperless office The ideal (futuristic) office situation where paper will not be needed for communications nor record storage. Computers would be used for electronic mail, message handling, and data storage. In some cases, the legal standing of the use of electronic files for taxation or court submissions is unclear, and for this reason, hard copies of files are still being maintained. While many offices use less paper in some areas of their operation, the consumption of paper since the introduction of computers has dramatically increased, hence the irony of the claim that computers will reduce paper usage. ▼

paper sizes In the early 1920s, there was agreement on four series of sizes for paper and printed matter — the A, B, C, and D series. The D series was discontinued in 1928, and by 1934, the B series was only used for specialist purposes. The A series became the standard, while the C series was maintained especially for envelope sizes to accommodate the A series of paper. The basic paper size as defined by the International Organization for Standardization (ISO) commences with a surface area of 1 square meter (called 'A0') with sides of 0.841 meter and 1.189 meter. Folding a sheet of a given size (for example, A0) in half gives the next smaller size (A1). ISO recommends A4 for letterheads, which measures 210 x 297 millimeters (mm) (approximately 11¾ x 8¼ inches). The smallest size is A10, which measures 26 x 37 mm (approximately 1 x 1½ inches). The C series starts with C0, which measures 917 x 1297 mm (approximately 36½ x 51 inches). The smallest is C8, which measures 57 x 81 mm (approximately 2¼ x 3¼ inches). Before the introduction of ISO paper sizes, there was much confusion about the 26 different sizes of writing and drawing paper, 19 sizes of printing paper, eight sizes of brown paper, and 19 bound book sizes. They each had a name like 'Elephant' — which for writing or drawing paper measured 28 x 23 inches,

paperless office *The notion that computers will revolutionize the office may have been confirmed. However, there is no end in sight to the masses of paper that is used in offices. This set was constructed for Apple's award-winning television commercial 'Swamped with work', which promoted the Apple Macintosh as the computer that comes to the rescue.*

but for brown paper measured 34 x 24 inches. Other names just as confusing included 'The Post' and 'Pinched Post'. See **metric system**. ▼

paper skip [ISO The movement of paper through a print mechanism at a speed effectively greater than that of individual single line spacing.]

Paradox Produced by Borland International, Paradox was the first relational database (for personal computers) with multi-user and multitasking capabilities. Its QBE (query by example) system ena-

bles users to retrieve data simply by showing an example of the information needed. Since release 3.5, Paradox has incorporated VROOMM (Virtual Run-time Object-Oriented Memory Manager) technology in its Turbo Drive feature. Turbo Drive allows Paradox to make maximum use of whatever hardware it is running on. It also features improved reporting and querying capabilities, as well as transparent connectivity to SQL (Structured Query Language) data residing in minicomputers, mainframes, and database servers through Paradox SQL Link. The Paradox Engine is a C library

A SERIES	MILLIMETERS	INCHES	B3	500 x 353	19.68 x 13.90
			B4	353 x 250	13.90 x 9.84
A0	1189 x 841	46.81 x 33.11	B5	250 x 176	9.84 x 6.93
A1	841 x 594	33.11 x 23.39	B6	176 x 125	6.93 x 4.92
A2	594 x 420	23.39 x 16.54	B7	125 x 88	4.92 x 3.46
A3	420 x 297	16.54 x 11.69	B8	88 x 62	3.46 x 2.44
A4	297 x 210	11.69 x 8.27	B9	62 x 44	2.44 x 1.73
A5	210 x 148	8.27 x 5.83	B10	44 x 31	1.73 x 1.22
A6	148 x 105	5.83 x 4.13			
A7	105 x 74	4.13 x 2.91	ENVELOPES	MILLIMETERS	INCHES
A8	74 x 52	2.91 x 2.05			
A9	52 x 37	2.05 x 1.46	DL	110 x 220	4.33 x 8.66
A10	37 x 26	1.46 x 1.02	C6	114 x 162	4.49 x 6.38
			B6	125 x 176	4.92 x 6.93
B SERIES	MILLIMETERS	INCHES	C5	162 x 229	6.38 x 9.02
			B5	176 x 250	6.93 x 9.84
B0	1414 x 1000	55.57 x 39.37	C4	229 x 324	9.02 x 12.76
B1	1000 x 707	39.37 x 27.83	B4	250 x 353	9.84 x 13.90
B2	707 x 500	27.83 x 19.68	C3	324 x 458	12.76 x 18.03

paper sizes *Paper sizes commonly used around the world.*

that opens the architecture of Paradox. It supports Microsoft Windows, Turbo Pascal, and Turbo C++. See **Borland**.

Paradox Application Language A high-level programming language that serves as an extension of Paradox's script-recording capability. Paradox Application Language (PAL) is designed as a productivity tool to enable advanced Paradox users to customize Paradox to their style of working. It is also part of a complete application development environment including a built-in script editor and interactive debugger. Numerous built-in functions are available, as are third-party (non-Borland) application development tools. PAL supports procedure concepts, including the selective definition of local and global variables, and dynamic scoping of variables. There are no restrictions on the number of procedure definitions that can be active. Through PAL, Paradox queries, forms, reports, and tables can be incorporated into applications. In addition, PAL pro-

vides structured support for creating Paradox-style menus. Through the 'set-key' command, the keyboard can be completely re-mapped so that any keystroke or script is triggered by pressing the prescribed key. See **Paradox**.

parallel [ISO Pertaining to a process in which all events occur within the same interval of time, each one handled by separate but similar functional unit. *Example:* The parallel transmission of the bits of a computer word along the lines of an internal bus.]

parallel adder [ISO An adder in which addition is performed simultaneously on all corresponding digit places of the operands.]

parallel addition [ISO Addition that is performed in parallel on digits in all corresponding digit places of the operands.]

parallel card reader A card reader which reads all of the columns of a punched card at once (in parallel), starting from the top or bottom of the card. A serial reader is slower because it only reads a column (character) at a time, starting from one side to the other.

parallel computer See **parallel processing**.

parallel conversion A method of transferring to a new computer system or software program, whereby an organization chooses to use the old and new system side by side (in parallel). Once the new system proves to be stable and satisfactory, the old system is either phased out or immediately abandoned. Although this procedure is much more expensive than other methods, it is the safest. Other methods include: (1) The direct conversion method, where an organization may choose to immediately discard the old system and implement the new one. This method may create problems if the new system fails or does not meet expectations. (2) The phased conversion method, which slowly implements the new system while slowly relinquishing the old one. This process takes the longest time, but allows staff the time to train and become familiar with the new system. (3) The pilot conversion method, which involves a conversion by only one division of an organization. Once a system proves that it works satisfactorily, then all divisions convert.

parallel importing See **gray marketing**.

parallel interface See **parallel port**.

parallelism Operations occurring simultaneously. Differs from concurrency in that concurrent events occur over a period of time, whereas parallel events occur simultaneously.

parallel port An input/output port that sends and receives information synchronously in lots of eight bits at high speeds along parallel lines to peripheral devices (typically printers). Connecting printers via the parallel port is the quickest and easiest method, providing the cable does not exceed approximately 15 foot (6 meters) in length. (The longer the cable, the higher the risk of interference (crosstalk) occurring between the lines.) The parallel port also checks with the peripheral device to ensure that it is ready to receive data, otherwise the user is alerted by way of an error message. Most industry-standard personal computers may be configured with three parallel ports, called 'LPT1', 'LPT2', and 'LPT3'. LPT is an abbreviation for 'line printer'.

parallel printer A printer that can be connected to the computer via the parallel port. See **parallel port**.

parallel processing The use of several processors (nodes or computers) to simultaneously share the calculation/computation of a large task. Parallel processing is much faster than the traditional serial processing method, which uses one central processing unit to carry out several instructions one after the other. The limitation of serial processors is in the fact that circuit switching speeds ultimately reach their limits. Their components on the microprocessor, therefore, are positioned closer and closer together so as to reduce the distance electrical signals must travel, but the generated heat becomes more difficult to dissipate. Parallel computers, on the other hand, divide the processing task into a series of processors. These can range from standard microprocessors to supercomputers, forming multinode computers linked together through diverse communications schemes. The term 'coarse-grain' is used to describe systems which employ very small numbers of very powerful processors like those provided by Cray research. 'Fine-grain' configurations combine thousands of weak nodes that provide powerful processing when used in concert. Between these two extremes, the term 'mid-grain' processing is used to describe the use of tens or hundreds of processors, often based on general-purpose microprocessors like those provided by Intel, Motorola, and National Semiconductor. There are two main connection schemes which currently dominate. The first is a bus-based architecture in which all memory and input/output facilities reside on a common communications bus, typical to most general-purpose computers. Systems like the Elxsi-6400 operate at over 320 gigabytes per seconds, using optic fiber links between nodes. The company calls this bus-based design a 'Gigabus'. Encore's Multimax uses the term 'nanobus' to refer to the 100-megabyte-per-second bus architecture. The second design is called 'hypercube' (or 'n-cube'), where a set of processing nodes is connected to a certain number (n) of its neighbors, with distributed memory schemes providing each node with local memory for faster processing. Some bus-based systems, like the Cray X-MP48, peak at 1000 million floating point operations per second (1000 MFLOP) using only four very powerful processors. In contrast, parallel hypercube-based machines (first marketed by Intel) can now exceed 65 536 nodes with possible speeds exceeding

262×10^9 floating point operations per second (262 GFLOP). Such speeds are particularly useful for complex image processing, in which the calculations can be divided into hundreds or thousands of parts, for simultaneous processing by the cube's nodes. Abbreviation 'PP'. See **SIMD**. Compare **serial processing**.

parallel run [ISO Operation of two information processing systems, a given one and its intended replacement, with the same application and source data, for comparison and confidence.]

parallel transmission (In computer communications.) Transmission of data (binary digits) simultaneously (in parallel with each other) using separate lines. In contrast, serial transmission sends only one bit after the other using only one communications line. Typically, connections over very short distances (such as a computer to a peripheral device) use parallel transmission because it is much faster than the serial method. Centronics Incorporated developed a parallel standard for connecting printers to computers, while a special IEEE protocol (developed by Hewlett-Packard) is used for connecting digital networks. To illustrate parallel transmission, consider a large number of people waiting to get into a movie theater. If eight entrances are available at the same time, eight people can get into the movie at the same time. When eight lines move at the same time, the lines are said to be in parallel. Similarly, if eight (or more) data lines are available simultaneously to transmit data, the transmission is called 'parallel' and is very fast. Since a full byte is received together, the receiving computer does not have to count bits and decide when the end of a byte is reached. Because parallel transmission is faster, it is sometimes used for transmission to local printers and for high-speed links between computers. However, since each bit of datum is sent on a separate wire, the cable is expensive and considerable cost is incurred if parallel transmission is used for any significant distance. [ISO The simultaneous transmission of the signal elements of a group representing a character or other entity of data.] Compare **serial transmission**.

parameter [ISO A variable that is given a constant value for a specified application and that may denote the application.]

parameter association [ISO The association of formal parameters with the corresponding actual parameters that are specified by a procedure call.]

parent transaction See **nested transaction**.

PA–RISC Precision Architecture–RISC.

parity A scheme that computers use to check the validity of transmitted characters. This scheme adds an extra bit to each character, which the transmitting computer sets or clears based upon the type of parity the computers agree to use (odd or even). For example, if the computers use even parity, the transmitting computer sets or clears the parity so that there are an even number of bits set in each character it transmits. The receiving computer checks each character and flags a parity error if any character has an odd number of bits set. See **parity bit**.

parity bit A check bit that is added to each byte to signal to the computer that the bits in a byte have transmitted cor-

rectly. For example, the EBCDIC letter 'A' is represented by 11000001. This has three ones and is therefore an odd number. If using odd parity, the parity (check) bit would have to be a '0' so that the quantity of 'ones' remains an odd number (110000010). Should the byte be received at the other end showing an even number of ones (for example, 110100010), then the computer knows that information was corrupted during transmission (parity error). Errors could still occur if the incorrectly transmitted byte contained two reversing errors which coincidentally and erroneously resulted in an odd number of ones, but the probability of this occurring is very low. The same principles apply when the sending and receiving devices are configured to accept even parity — when the number of ones must always be even instead. [ISO A binary digit appended to a group of binary digits to make the sum of all the digits, including the appended binary digit, either odd or even as predetermined.] The word 'parity' comes from the Latin word *par*, meaning 'equal' or 'equality'. See **even parity** and **odd parity**.

parity checking A technique used to quickly check the integrity of data received after a transmission, or from memory. Parity checking can apply to bytes, words, longwords, and other units of information. [ISO A redundancy check by which a re-calculated parity bit is compared to the predetermined parity bit.] See **parity bit**.

parity error See **parity bit**.

park To move the read/write heads of a hard disk to a stationary position in a designated landing zone to guard against possible damage during the movement or transportation of a personal computer.

partial carry [ISO In parallel addition, a procedure in which some or all of the carries are temporarily stored instead of being immediately transferred.]

partition Before a hard disk can be used for the first time, it must be partitioned and then formatted. Partitioning is a software function that involves dividing the storage space into usable sections, with each section assigned a letter as though it were a separate drive. This process conceivably allows each partition to be assigned to a different operating system. However, even if the entire disk is to belong to the same operating system, partitioning must still be performed. The DOS command 'FDISK' is used for hard disk partitioning. The size of each partition is variable, and must be specified. The 'FDISK' command also specifies the partition from which the operating system is to boot (this is called the 'active partition'), and specifies the drive letter assignments. Normally the command automatically assigns letters starting with 'C'. However, other letters may be assigned if there are multiple hard disks. After a hard disk is partitioned, each partition must be formatted by the operating system to which it is dedicated. Under DOS, the 'format' command lays out the DOS structure on the disk and establishes how and where files can be stored. Note that the DOS 'format' command works differently on a diskette drive as opposed to a hard disk drive. On a diskette drive, the command performs both low-level and high-level formatting. Low-level formatting involves the creation of sectors complete

with their address markings (this process is called 'initializing'). High-level formatting lays out the operating system structure on the disk and establishes how and where files are stored. A new hard disk normally comes with low-level formatting already done. Consequently, the 'format' command on a hard disk only performs high-level formatting. Utility programs (such as MultiDisk) are available to help manage partitioned disks.

partitioned database A database whose contents are divided physically among multiple input/output subsystems, and governed by multiple operating systems.

partition-sector virus Any computer virus capable of replacing the original code of the partition sector found on a hard disk (diskettes do not have a partition sector). The hard disk's partition sector contains important information about the disk, such as the number of sectors that can be found in each partition, and where the DOS partition can be found. When a personal computer is turned on, it first turns to drive A to read the boot sector. If a diskette is not present in drive A, it turns to the hard disk (usually drive C) and looks to the partition sector for information about where the DOS partition starts. The computer loads what it finds into memory and proceeds to run the program. Although a partition-sector virus is similar to a boot-sector virus, it is much harder to find because many antivirus programs are unable to access the partition sector. Some of the better-known partition-sector viruses are EDV, Stoned, The Swedish Disaster, and Zapper. Abbreviation 'PSV'. See **virus**. Compare **boot-sector virus**.

Pascal A high-level structured programming language developed in 1971 by the Swiss computer scientist Niklaus Wirth who named his new language after the French mathematician, Blaise Pascal. Although rivaled by the C programming language, Pascal is widely used both as a teaching and as an application development language. Its procedural structure is similar to BASIC and FORTRAN, but offers the ability to program an application in modular structures, so that mini-programs can be written and tested independently before they are joined together to form one large program. Pascal is available in several versions. For personal computing, Borland International produced a high-performance compiler called 'Turbo Pascal'. To improve on Pascal, its inventor developed a new language called 'Modula-2' and launched it in 1980. Programs written in ANSI Standard Pascal are portable to target platforms that have ANSI-compliant compilers available. As with other languages, degrees of portability can be lost by the use of non-standard language extensions. See **Modula-2**, **portability**, and **programming language**.

Pascal, Blaise The French mathematician who, in 1642, developed the first adding machine (called the 'Pascaline'), using gears and wheels. See **Pascaline**.

Pascaline A desktop mechanical adding machine developed by Blaise Pascal in 1642. A set of interlocking cogs and wheels turned the appropriate amount when people dialed the numbers they wished to add. The result was displayed in the windows. Only 50 Pascalines were built because clerks and accountants objected to them, fearing the machines

might do away with their jobs. Several years later, the German philosopher and mathematician Gottfried von Leibniz further developed the idea of the Pascaline and invented a similar machine which could divide and multiply, as well as add and subtract.

passive station [ISO On a multipoint connection or a point-to-point connection using basic mode link control, any tributary station waiting to be polled or selected.]

password Originally a secret word, phrase, or formula used to gain access beyond a barrier or guard, or a sign of recognition among members of a secret society. In computing, a password is used as a security tool to identify users of a computer application, file, or network. A password or personal identification number may take the form of an alphanumeric word or phrase. Passwords are used to prevent unauthorized entry into confidential files. Monitoring systems can record and report on the network activities of a user by monitoring the use of the password. Varying levels of access can be assigned to different users. For example, the manager of a division may have a password which permits access to a file for both reading and writing of files, whereas an assistant's password may only be used to read but not alter data. Some application software such as WordPerfect enables each user to set a password to protect nominated files, so that only those who know the password can access the file. Using the 26 letters of the English alphabet, plus the 10 decimal numbers (from 0 to 9), gives a total of 36 alphanumeric characters which can be used to create a random password.

When a password consists of only one character, then it is obvious that a total of 36 possible combinations can be achieved. Assuming that it takes a hacker (an unauthorized person) a few seconds to test each of the 36 combinations, then it would take approximately six minutes to discover the correct password (assuming that the correct password is only discovered at the very end of each test). A two-digit password has 1300 possible combinations, and may take four hours to discover. A four-digit password offers 1 700 000 combinations, and may take six months to discover. Although it is much harder to remember longer passwords, they are much harder to discover. A ten-digit password offers 3 700 000 000 000 000 different combinations. Even if a hacker used a computer to try all these possibilities, it would still take approximately 1 200 000 000 years of non-stop testing to discover the password. Using common words (such as 'summer' or 'motorcar') as passwords may be much easier to discover, given that a 60 000-word computer-dictionary can be used to automatically search for combinations. It is likely that the computer dictionary can find the password within seven days of processing. More random usage of less meaningful characters (such as the first line of a song (silentnightholynight) will give the hacker 10^{27} possibilities, taking approximately 3×10^{21} years to discover. Naturally, passwords combined with personal physical characteristics (such as thumb prints or voice patterns) are even more secure. [ISO A character string that enables a user to have full or limited access to a system or to a set of data.] See **biometric security devices**.

paste To position text or graphics in a location, after it has been copied or removed from another location.

PAT Public access terminal; a computer terminal accessible to anyone. These may be positioned in a public library or in the foyer of a building. In years to come, public access terminals will be as common as public telephones.

patch [ISO To modify an object module, a load module, or a loaded computer program. *Note:* The modification is usually a temporary or expedient one.]

path [ISO In a network, any route between any two nodes. *Note:* A path may include more than one branch.]

path control layer Each of the layers of IBM's Systems Network Architecture (SNA) has its own set of rules for communicating with its peer layer in the other node. The layers communicate with each other by adding header information to user data. The path control layer (third layer) is responsible for the routing of messages and defines the class of services offered. See **SNA layers**.

pattern recognition [ISO The identification of shapes, forms, or configurations by automatic means.]

PBX Private branch exchange. A telecommunications switching network privately owned and operated by an organization on its premises.

PC See **personal computer**.

PCB Printed circuit board. See **circuit board**.

PC board A sheet of non-conducting

PC board *This Ariel QuintProcessor features five 27-megahertz digital signal processors that enhanced the speed and versatility of a computer's music kit and array processing library. With the added benefits of interprocessor communication, DRAM, and private mass storage, this board makes possible a sophisticated signal-processing and array-processing system previously unattainable on any commercial computer platform.*

fiberglass or plastic that serves to support and interconnect a collection of chips and other devices which may be used in a computer. They are covered with copper which is etched with acid or ferric chloride, leaving conducting pathways for microprocessors or other chips to be affixed. ▲

PC bus See **bus**.

PC–DOS IBM's version of MS–DOS. See **MS–DOS**.

PCI Peripheral component interconnect. A local bus architecture designed to put peripherals on an electrical pathway closer to the central processing unit in order to improve the performance of graphics and up to ten peripherals. The architecture of a computer built around the PCI local bus is fundamentally different from other personal computers. As in a workstation, the PCI architecture puts the graphics chip, the LAN I/O, SCSI, and base I/O components onto the PCI local bus rather than on an ISA, EISA, or Micro Channel Architecture bus. When first introduced in 1993, the PCI local bus spanned 32 bits wide and operated at 33 megahertz (MHz). ISA, in contrast, is only 16 bits and runs at 8 MHz; EISA and Micro Channel Architecture are both 32 bits wide, but run at 8 and 10 MHz, respectively. With a peak bandwidth of 133 megabytes per second, the PCI local bus breaks the input/output bottleneck between the central processing unit and conventional peripheral expansion buses. PCI licenses are free to systems and peripheral manufacturers, software houses, BIOS suppliers, and other interested parties. Pronounced 'pea-sea-eye'. ▼

PC LAN An operating system designed by IBM in 1986 for its token-ring network to provide electronic mail facilities, shared access to data and file programs, and network printers.

PCM 1. Plug-compatible manufacturer; a peripheral equipment manufacturer (PEM) that makes compatible 'plug-in' devices which can be used interchangeably between different computers. 2. See **pulse code modulation**.

PCMCIA Personal Computer Memory Card International Association; a joint effort between the Japanese Electronic Industry Development Association, PCMCIA, and special interest groups to develop a standard for memory cards that can be used in personal computers.

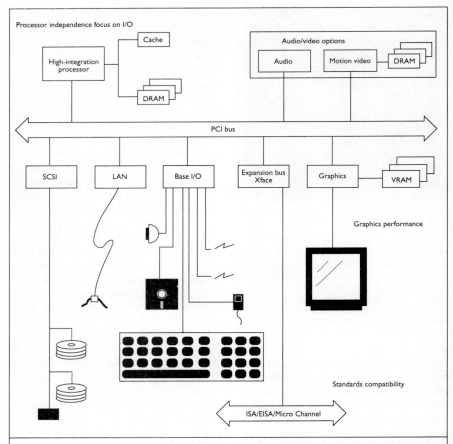

PCI *The PCI specification, originally developed as a high-performance local bus for advanced workstation applications, is being used for business workstations and desktop personal computers, enabling them to run advanced graphics, multimedia, and network applications.*

PCMCIA was established in 1989 and comprises more than 300 member companies. The first release of the card was in November 1990, and in September 1991, PCMCIA version 2.0 added input/output (I/O) capabilities. There are several types of cards, each varying in thickness, though they are the same in length and width (85.6 x 54 millimeters (mm)) and have the same thickness at the connector end and along the rails. They include a 68-pin connector socket. Type 1 is the thinnest card at 3.3 mm thick. It is typically used for memory enhancements including EEPROM, SRAM, and RAM. Type 2 is 5 mm thick, mainly used for I/O features such as LANs, host communications, and modems. Type 3 is 10.5 mm thick, mainly used for rotating media (hard disk) devices and wireless communications devices. Type 4 is 13.5 mm thick and is used for I/O and communications devices that require miniaturized hardware integration. PCMCIA cards include Ethernet connectors, fax - modems, token ring, SCSI, and sound cards. PCMCIA offers users the ability to improve their computer's memory capacity, or to connect the computer to external networks and services such as global positioning systems. Cards are available for storage, encryption, multimedia, and video capture. High-capacity hard disk drives are available in Type 3 cards, offering over 100 megabytes of magnetic disk storage which uses less than 0.5 watts in idle mode. The drives are shock-proof to 500 G, meaning that they can be dropped without causing damage to the drive. PCMCIA cards will become useful in electronic devices other than computers. These may include video cameras, telephones, and consumer electronic devices. See **ExCA**. ▼

PCSA Personal Computing System Architecture; an extension to Digital Network Architecture introduced by Digital Equipment Corporation in 1986.

PCMCIA This modem card from New Media Corporation is suitable for data and fax transmission. Before it can be used, the PCMCIA must be fully inserted inside the slot until only the plug on the right is showing.

NEWSFLASH

By 1997, PCMCIA modems will make up almost 50% of the data/fax modem market.

PCSA allows MS–DOS computers to participate in a DECnet network.

PC Tools A file management utility program developed by Central Point Software for personal computers.

PDA Personal digital assistant; a term coined in 1992 by John Sculley (then Apple's Chairman) to describe handheld electronic computerized products that can be used to assist users with telecommunications and messaging. Apple's first PDA was the Newton MessagePad. The term 'PDA' is now used to refer to any device capable of assisting its user to become better organized in terms of administrative and telecommunications tasks. See **Newton MessagePad**.

PDL See **page description language**.

PEAN Pan European ATM Network; where ATM is the abbreviation for 'asynchronous transfer mode'.

peer-to-peer Referring to communication in which two systems communicate as equal partners sharing the processing and control of the exchange, as opposed to host-terminal communication in which the host does most of the processing and controls the exchange. The term 'peer computer' is used to refer to a mainframe, minicomputer, or personal computer that communicates with another computer as an equal partner. The word 'peer' is from the Latin word *par*, meaning 'equal'.

peer-to-peer file transfer In a local area network, the ability for every user to access every other user's files. If a file is confidential, then restrictions can be placed on it to prohibit certain users from accessing it.

pel An abbreviation sometimes used to refer to picture elements. The term 'pixel' is preferred. See **pixel**.

PEM Peripheral equipment manufacturer.

Pentium processor Intel Corporation's microprocessor released 22 March 1993. Incorporating more than 3.1 million transistors (compared to 2.1 million in the Intel 486), the 32-bit (internal) Pentium processor is a highly integrated semiconductor device that has an external bus width of 64 bits. The first release featured clock speeds of 60 and 66 megahertz (MHz), achieving a performance of over 100 MIPS (million instructions per second), being almost twice as fast as the Intel 486 DX2 microprocessor (although in some applications it can be up to five times more powerful). This performance is largely due to the Pentium processor's superscalar architecture, and its dual-execution pipeline implementation which utilizes advanced design techniques that enable it to transparently execute multiple instructions per clock cycle. The term 'superscalar' refers to a microprocessor architecture that contains more than one execution unit. These executing units (or pipelines) are where the chip processes the data and where instructions are fed to it by the rest of the system. By comparison, the Intel 486 processor was only

able to execute instructions in one clock cycle, while previous generations of Intel microprocessors required multiple clock cycles to execute a single instruction. Complementing the Pentium processor's

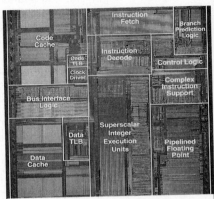

Pentium processor *The heart of the Pentium processor is its superscalar design (built around two instruction pipelines) each capable of performing independently. These allow the Pentium processor to execute two integer instructions in a single clock cycle, nearly doubling the chip's performance, relative to an Intel 486 chip at equal frequency. In many instances, the Pentium processor can execute two instructions at once, one to each of the pipelines, in a process known as 'instruction paring'. Each pipeline has its own ALU (arithmetic logic unit), as well as address generation circuitry, and they interface to the data cache. The 'data cache' has two interfaces, one to each of the pipelines, which allows it to provide data for two separate operations in a single clock cycle. When data is removed from the data cache, it is written into main memory — a technique known as 'write-back caching' in which the processor writes data to the cache and main memory at the same time. For situations where data integrity is crucial, the Pentium processor supports functional redundancy checking (FRC). This requires the use of two Pentium chips, one acting as the master while the other acts as the checker. The two chips run in tandem, and the checker compares its output with that of the master processor.*

superscalar design are the separate 8-kilobyte (kb) code and 8-kb data cache. These increase performance by doubling the available cache bandwidth and reducing cache conflicts. Larger page sizes (8 kb or 4 Mb compared to the Intel 486, which had a maximum of 4 kb) reduce the amount of page swapping required to execute tasks. This is of benefit when running compute-intensive applications such as graphics, where data files tend to be large and comparatively unwieldy. The Pentium processor's enhanced 64-bit data bus carries information between the processor and the memory subsystem at 528 Mb per second at 66 MHz, compared to 160 Mb per second at 50 MHz for the Intel 486 DX microprocessor. The Pentium processor is 100% code compatible with previous members of the x86 family, and is fully compatible with existing software (more than 50 000 applications) written for the Intel architecture. Other features of the Pentium processor include branch prediction; floating-point unit; 64-bit data bus; multiprocessing support; memory page size option; error detection and functional redundancy; OverDrive processor upgradability; and performance monitoring. Performance monitoring is a feature of the Pentium processor that enables system designers and application developers to optimize their hardware and software products by identifying potential code bottlenecks. Designers can observe and count clocks for internal processor events that affect the performance of data reads and writes, cache hits and misses, interrupts, and bus utilization. Although it would have been logical to call this new processor 'Intel 586', Intel decided that it was better able to secure its product through a trademark of a unique name. This decision resulted from a court ruling which stipulated that companies cannot register general numbers as part of the trade mark. The name 'Pentium' was conceived by an Intel staff member who entered a competition that asked the members of staff to forward their suggestions. The name was inspired by the Greek word *penta* which means 'five'. See **Intel Corporation.** ⚠

percentage function [ISO The function that automatically multiplies two entered numbers, one of which is understood to be a percentage, and divides the result by 100.]

percent character (%) A pointer used in DOS batch files. It is used by DOS to pass arguments from programs, or from the keyboard to programs. For example, if a batch file called 'TEST.BAT' has the single line 'PROCESS %1 %2', and the batch file is executed with the command 'TEST 1.TXT 2.TXT', then the batch file will substitute the two strings '1.TXT' and '2.TXT' for %1 and %2 as the file is run.

periodic reports Computer reports generated automatically and periodically by the computer for such uses as payroll, sales, and accounts analysis.

peripheral Any optional input or output device that connects to a computer's central processing unit. Mass-storage devices, printers, and modems are typical peripherals for personal computers.

peripheral component interconnect See **PCI**.

peripheral equipment [ISO With respect

to a particular processing unit, any equipment that provides the processing unit with outside communication. *Examples:* Input/output units; auxiliary storage.] The word 'peripheral' comes from the Greek word *periphereia*, where *peri* means 'around' and *phereia* means 'to bear'.

permanent storage [ISO A storage device that is non-erasable.]

permanent virtual circuit A public packet-switching network is implemented over leased channels and over conventional facilities. Data is transferred between data terminal equipment (DTE) through 'virtual' connections. This is called a 'virtual circuit' because no single physical connection is established between the sending and receiving stations. Instead, the network establishes the route of least delay for each packet. A connection between two subscribers can be established by either a virtual call, or permanent virtual circuit. A permanent virtual circuit is established by prior arrangement between the network subscribers and the network provider. The permanent virtual circuit provides for a fixed logical connection between two subscribers by reserving buffer space in the switching nodes (computers). On a permanent virtual circuit, the network is aware of the fixed association between two stations, and for this reason, permanent logical channel numbers are assigned exclusively to the permanent circuit, and devices do not require permission to transmit to each other. Since the transmit and receive addresses of the logical channels assigned to a permanent virtual circuit are known to the network, there is no need to initiate 'call request'

or call accepted sequences which are necessary for virtual calls. Compare **virtual call facility**.

perpendicular magnetic recording [ISO A technique of magnetic recording in which magnetic polarities representing data are aligned perpendicularly to the plane of the recording surface.]

personal computer Any independent (stand-alone) computer fully equipped with its own central processing unit, memory, software, storage, and other utilities which make it useful for an individual to successfully accomplish tasks. The term 'personal computer' became popular in 1981 after IBM announced a computer whose model name was 'IBM Personal Computer'. The term is now used generically, and very loosely. Apart from personal computers, there are computers called 'neurocomputers' (the most powerful of computers), 'supercomputers', 'mainframes', 'superminicomputers', 'minicomputers', and 'microcomputers'. Within each type are several divisions. For example, within the microcomputer range are personal computers which can be further divided into personal computer systems, desktop computers, portable computers, laptops, and now notebook computers. Personal computers are complete business tools. They were introduced to help users break away from the mainframe and minicomputer applications which did not give users any autonomy. Local area networking has brought back the cohesion, but still allows users independence and flexibility when choosing applications. Abbreviation 'PC'. ▼

personal digital assistant See **PDA**.

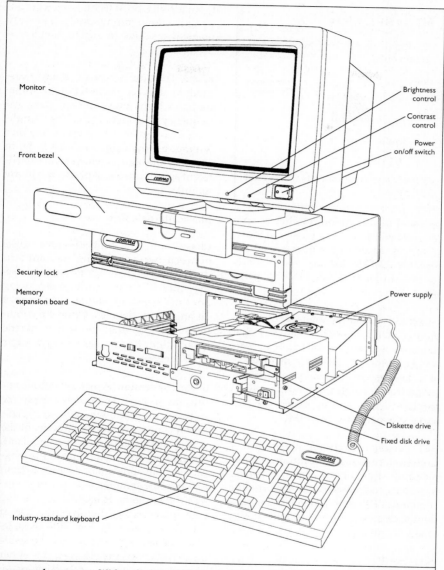

P

Monitor

Brightness control

Contrast control

Power on/off switch

Front bezel

Security lock

Memory expansion board

Power supply

Diskette drive

Fixed disk drive

Industry-standard keyboard

personal computer *With each new model, personal computers (PCs) are becoming smaller, more powerful, and more affordable. Although the trend is moving toward laptop and notebook PCs, this basic design is still being used. PCs offer full compatibility with industry-standard software, expandable random-access memory, graphics accelerators to optimize performance in Windows environments, and include integrated serial, parallel, and pointing device interfaces.*

NEWSFLASH

PC shipments for 1994 numbered 41 million units.

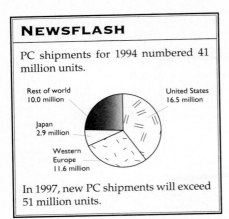

Rest of world
10.0 million

United States
16.5 million

Japan
2.9 million

Western
Europe
11.6 million

In 1997, new PC shipments will exceed 51 million units.

personal identification number A special code which acts as a password into a computer system or automatic telling machine (ATM) for electronic funds transfer (EFT). Acronym 'PIN'. See **password**.

personal information manager A program (such as Lotus Organizer) that manages a person's collection of personal information. Similar in many ways to a database management program, it keeps track of notes, memos, appointments, events, and a telephone and address book. Acronym 'PIM'.

PET Personal Electronic Transactor; a Commodore personal computer manufactured by Commodore Business Machines, a Pennsylvanian calculator company. PET offered 8 kilobytes of random-access memory and 14 kilobytes of read-only memory.

peta- See **P**.

PETT III Positron Emission Transaxial Tomography version three; a computerized brain scanner which allows researchers to see a color-coded 'map' of

brain activity. Such technology (computer-aided tomography) can help identify manic-depressive or schizophrenic patients.

phase The time difference (delay measured in degrees) between two waveforms which may be of identical frequency and identical voltage amplitude. Two signals which travel together without a time delay are said to be in phase, while signals which travel at different speeds are out of phase. See **phase modulation**.

phase alternate line See **PAL**.

phase angle The time difference (lag) between two waveforms, measured in degrees. When two signals are in phase, they travel together without any delay nor time difference and are said to have an angle of 0 degrees. Opposite conditions such as the expression of the binary digits 0 and 1 have a phase angle of 180 degrees.

phase conversion A method of transferring to a new computer system or software program, whereby an organization chooses to slowly implement the new system while it slowly relinquishes the old one. This method takes the longest time, but allows staff the time to train and become familiar with the new system. Other methods include: (1) Parallel conversion, which involves the use of the old and new system side by side. Once the new system proves to be stable and satisfactory, the old system is either phased out, or immediately abandoned. Although this procedure is much more expensive than other methods, it is the safest. (2) An organization may choose to immediately discard the old system and implement the new one. This method is called 'direct conversion' and may create problems if the new system fails or does not meet expectations. (3) The pilot conversion method, which involves a conversion by only one division of an organization. Once a system proves it works satisfactorily, then all divisions convert.

phase distortion Distortion caused by the unwanted difference between the phase of the current and voltage of a waveform when reactive components are present in the path of an electrical current. See **phase**.

phase inverter Any circuit capable of changing the phase of a signal by 180 degrees. Normally, when two signals are in phase, they travel together without any delay nor time difference and are said to have a phase angle of 0 degrees. Opposite conditions such as the expression of the binary digits 0 and 1 have a phase angle of 180 degrees.

phase modulation The time difference between two identical waveforms which are delayed (phased) to represent the binary digits 0 and 1. Normally, when two signals are in phase, they travel together without any delay or time difference

and are said to have a phase angle of 0 degrees. However, they are said to be out of phase by a certain angle when one signal is delayed. In binary notation, the digits 0 and 1 are expressed as opposites; therefore, they are 180 degrees out of phase. The process of changing the phase of a carrier wave in a periodic or intermittent way from a digital signal to an analog signal is done for the purpose of transmitting information (as in the case of telephony, telegraphy, radio, television, or digital communications). Abbreviation 'PM'. See **modulation**.

phase modulation recording [ISO A magnetic recording in which each storage cell is divided into two regions which are magnetized in opposite senses; the sequence of these senses indicates whether the binary digit represented is zero or one.] ▼

phase transition recording See **erasable optical disk**.

PHIGS Programmer's Hierarchical Interactive Graphics System; a sophisticated, three-dimensional graphics and modeling support system that controls the definition, modification, and display of hierarchical graphics data. PHIGS includes extensions to the ISO standard to

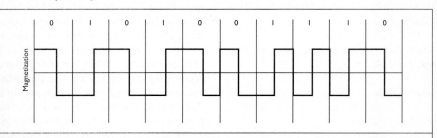

phase modulation recording Each of the two regions in a storage cell is magnetized in the opposite sense.

provide capabilities for hidden-surface removal, shading, and depth cueing.

phoneme Any of the 45 different sounds that English-speakers use. Computers can be programmed to 'speak' using phonemes. This is common in children's toys that teach them how to read and spell. The word 'phoneme' comes from the Greek word *phonema*, meaning 'sound' or 'speech'. Pronounced 'foeneem'.

phono plug A type of plug mainly found at the back of audio devices, and in computers. The ports are used to connect composite monitors and audio output. The word 'phono' comes from the Greek word *phone*, meaning 'voice' or 'sound'. Also called 'RCA plug'.

phosphor The electrofluorescent coating on the inside of cathode-ray tubes that makes them glow when activated by a beam of electrons. The glow only lasts for a fraction of a second and must be constantly refreshed.

photochromic recording See **erasable optical disk**.

photoconductor A light-sensitive material that conducts electricity in the light and insulates against electrical conduction in the dark.

photodichroic recording See **erasable optical disk**.

photodiode A sensor that senses light and its intensity, and converts it to an electrical signal.

photoelectric reader A machine that translates the meaning of the holes found on punched cards into electrical pulses which in turn are fed into the computer as data for processing. A photoelectric reader sends beams of light at the card. Light passing through the holes causes electronic signals (representing data) to be transmitted to the computer as data.

photoelectric scanner A laser scanner commonly used in supermarkets to read bar codes. The scanner recognizes the marks, and converts them to electrical signals which are then sent to the computer for processing.

photonics See **fiber optics**.

photoreceptor In a laser printer, the bit map is binary information which describes a pattern of dots that makes a character or graphic image. To convert the bit map information into an image, laser printers use a scanning technique much like that used in a television set. Although the laser itself remains stationary, the beam scans across a special drum or belt by reflecting off a rotating multifaceted polygon mirror. Other stationary mirrors also play a role in directing the beam. As the laser beam scans a line, the bit map information is sent to the laser in a serial fashion. As each binary bit is received, the laser beam turns on or off as required to form an image. The special drum or belt on which the scan occurs is called a 'photoreceptor'. When printing, the photoreceptor rotates so that the print lines are scanned one under another. The photoreceptor has electrostatic properties that cause the electrical charge on its surface to change when exposed to light. The turning on and off of the laser creates an electrostatic pattern of dots on the surface of the photoreceptor, corresponding to the pattern of dots to be printed on the page. This dot pattern is called the 'electrostatic latent image', since the charges on the drum are invisible to the human eye. After the image is scanned, the photoreceptor is brushed with a dry ink (called 'toner') which clings to the pattern of the electrostatic charges. This is the stage where the latent image is developed, or made visible on the photoreceptor. A sheet of paper is next pulled from the paper tray. The paper is given a charge and then brought into contact with the surface of the rotating photoreceptor. The electrostatic charge causes the toner on the drum or the belt to be transferred to the paper. The paper, now carrying the imaged dot patterns, is separated from the photoreceptor and passed through a heat fusing mechanism that permanently fuses the image onto the paper. See **laser printer**.

physical access control See **biometric security devices**.

physical control layer Each of the layers of IBM's Systems Network Architecture (SNA) has its own set of rules for communicating with its peer layer in the other node. The layers communicate with each other by adding header information to user data. The physical control layer (first layer) defines the physical, electrical, mechanical, and functional procedures used to connect the equipment. This is where RS-232-C (or the equivalent CCITT interface) is located. See **SNA layers**.

physical layer The first (and lowest) layer of the OSI (Open Systems Interconnection) reference model. The physical layer defines the mechanical, electrical, and signaling characteristics of the physical medium, such as coaxial cable or twisted-pair wire. It also outlines the type of connectors to be used, data rates, signal levels, synchronous or asynchronous transmission, and how connections are activated and deactivated. See **OSI reference model**.

physical medium attachment sublayer [ISO In a local area network, that portion of the physical layer implemented by the functional circuits of the medium attachment unit.]

physical record [ISO A record considered with respect to its physical position on a data medium or in storage.]

physical recording density [ISO The number of flux transitions recorded on a track per unit of length or of angle. *Note:* Usually, the units used are flux transitions per millimeter (ftpmm) for length, and flux transitions per radian (ftprad) for angles.] See **track density**.

physical signaling sublayer [ISO In a local area network, that portion of the physical layer that interfaces with the medium access control sublayer and performs bit symbol encoding and transmission, bit symbol reception and decoding, and optional isolation functions.]

PICD Personal information and communication device.

Pick An open operating system that has developed into an applications-based database management system. The system was designed by Dick Pick and Don Nelson, and was first released in 1973. In 1984, Pick Systems released a PC version

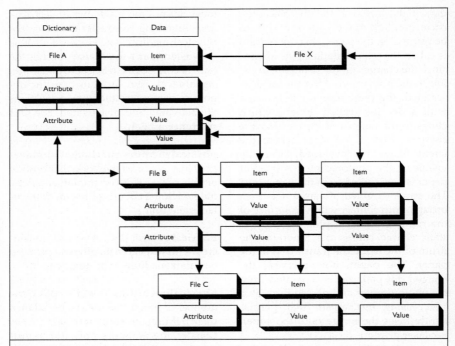

Pick *The Pick data model allows multidimensional relationships between data. Pick is dictionary-driven, so any given file is comprised 'items' which may contain 'values'. Both of these have 'attributes' which are located in a file dictionary. Users can retrieve data based on any relationship that makes sense to them. They can also navigate through their data and information, and write any kind of ad hoc report. For a software developer, this data model means that any application requires only one repository for data, meaning one database where data is entered, modified, and updated in real-time, with automatic data updates for the entire organization — without requiring intervention on the part of a programmer.*

to provide a low-end offering in the microcomputer marketplace for multiuser business solutions. Today, Pick can run as many as 33 users from a common Intel microprocessor in native mode, and up to 128 users with SCO UNIX multiprocessor systems. ⚠

pick device [ISO An input device used to specify a particular display element or segment. *Example:* A light pen.]

pico- An SI unit prefix for 10^{-12} ex-

pressed as 0.000 000 000 001 in decimal notation. SI symbol 'p'. A picosecond (ps) is a unit of time equal to 0.000 000 000 001 of a second and is commonly used to measure the speed at which the central processing unit can execute instructions. If one picosecond was imagined to be one second, then one second would be equivalent to 31 710 years. See **SI**.

picocomputer The future fifth-generation computer whose main processing chip may contain at least 100 000 000 000 electronic components. From an analogy with 'microcomputer'. See **optical neuro-computer** and **pico-**.

PICT The standard graphics file format for the Apple Macintosh that uses the QuickDraw toolbox stored in the computer's read-only memory.

picture (In programming languages.) [ISO A language construct that describes a data type by means of a model character string literal.]

picture element See **pixel**.

PID Personal identification.

PIE Personal Interactive Electronics division of Apple Computer Corporation. PIE was set up to lead Apple's research, development, and marketing efforts of PDA (personal digital assistant) products such as the Newton MessagePad. It includes Apple Online Services, the Telecommunications Group, publishing activities, and ScriptX-based multimedia PDA development.

PIF Program information file.

PILOT Programmed Inquiry Learning or Teaching. An authoring language developed in 1968 by John Starkweather for computer-aided instruction. Although PILOT is now being overtaken by new authoring languages (such as Hyper-Talk), it was popular because of its ease of use when developing on-screen instructional material.

pilot conversion A method of transferring to a new computer system or software program, whereby an organization chooses to convert only one division of an organization. Once a system proves to work satisfactorily, then all divisions convert. Other methods include: (1) Parallel conversion, which involves the use of the old and new system side by side. Once the new system proves to be stable and satisfactory, the old system is either phased out, or immediately abandoned. Although this procedure is much more expensive than other methods, it is the safest. (2) An organization may choose to immediately discard the old system and implement the new one. This method is called 'direct conversion' and may create problems if the new system fails or does not meet expectations. (3) A phased conversion slowly implements the new system while it slowly relinquishes the old one. This process takes the longest time, but allows staff the time to train and become familiar with the new system.

pilot project [ISO A project designed to test a preliminary version of an information processing system under actual but limited operating conditions, and which will then be used to test the definitive version of the system.]

PIM See **personal information manager**.

PIN Personal identification number; a

special code which acts as a password into a computer system or automatic telling machine (ATM) for electronic funds transfer (EFT). See **password**.

pincushion distortion In monitor technology, the screen or image distortion where the sides bow inwards like a pincushion. Compare **barrel distortion** and **keystone distortion**.

Ping Pong virus A variant of the Italian virus. See **Italian virus**.

pipeline processor [ISO A processor in which instruction execution takes place in a series of units, arranged so that several units can be simultaneously processing the appropriate parts of several instructions.]

PIPO Parallel input/parallel output.

piracy See **software piracy**.

PISO Parallel input/serial output.

pixel Picture element; the smallest possible addressable 'dot' displayed on a monitor. It is generated by the electron beam activating the phosphor in the monitor. For example, 1280 x 960 means 1280 horizontal pixels by 960 vertical rows of pixels; this equals 1 228 800 picture elements. The higher the number of pixels, the higher the resolution. Pronounced 'picks-el'. See **resolution**. [ISO The smallest element of a display surface that can be independently assigned color or intensity.]

plasma display A display technology used with laptop and portable computers in which ionized gas, held between two transparent panels, is energized,

making it glow on the screen in the form of pixels (picture elements).

plasma panel [ISO A part of a display device that consists of a grid of electrodes in a flat, gas-filled panel. *Note:* The image can persist for a long period of time without refresh.]

plated media See **metallic media**.

PL/C See **PL/1**.

PL/1 Programming Language One; a high-level structured programming language sponsored by IBM, and introduced in 1964. PL/1 was developed to overcome the inadequate file handling capabilities of FORTRAN, and the inadequate scientific calculation capabilities of COBOL. PL/C is the name given to the version created at Cornell. See **programming language**.

plotter An output device which uses colored ink pens to draw maps, charts, schematic diagrams, and other drawings on paper or other material. A flatbed plotter looks like a drafting table with mechanical pens suspended over it. It is commonly used for engineering and drafting applications. A drum plotter works in the same way except the paper is rolled around a drum. Both the pens and the drum may move at the same time. [ISO An output unit that directly produces a hard copy record of data on a removable medium, in the form of a two-dimensional graphic representation.] ▼

plotter step size [ISO The increment size on a plotter.]

plug and play A term used to describe a device that will easily connect to an-

P

plotter *The Ioline Signature plotter was the first plotter to use interactive operating menus, on-board logic and memory, and open architecture design. This plotter handles A–E (A4–A0) formats, and features user-installable options which include a pen-changer rail that holds 1 to 25 pens, roll feed system, add-on memory modules, vinyl cutter, and a file server. It operates at speeds of up to 36 inches (91 centimeters) per second with microcalibrated accuracy to 0.0002 inches (0.005 millimeters).*

other and immediately work, without the need for lengthy installation procedures nor complex configuration. A formal plug and play (PnP) specification was drawn up by Compaq, Intel, Microsoft, and Phoenix Technologies in the hope that other component and peripheral manufacturers will adopt the standard. Those dubious about the promises made by computer manufacturers in relation to ease-of-use and interoperability prefer to call this 'plug and pray'. Recently, with the advent of data highways such as Internet, it is called 'plug and pay'.

PLV Production level video; an asymmetric compression algorithm that runs on Intel i750 processors. Source video is sent to a digital compression facility, where a supercomputer processes it frame by frame to provide superior image color and quality. PLV was designed by Intel.

PM 1. See **phase modulation**. 2. Product manager.

p–n junction Positive–negative junction. As a non-linear two-terminal device, a diode is the simplest and most fundamental semiconductor used in electronics. It acts as a one-way valve letting current flow through it in one direction, while blocking current flow in the other. In the manufacture of a diode, two or more materials are joined together (such as the doping of silicon). The point where they join is called the 'junction'. Since one part of the diode is p-type material (positive), and the other n-type material (negative), the junction is called a 'p–n junction'. At the p–n junction, a neutral zone is formed when n-type material joins with p-type material to share electrons. The atoms at this junction are stable because they neither want to give up nor attract electrons. The junction forms a barrier that will resist current flow through the diode. When a voltage is placed across the diode, the number of atoms that share electrons will increase or decrease, depending upon the polarity of the voltage. This either increases the resistance of the barrier or decreases the resistance of the barrier. A diode will not conduct when it is reversed biased (when the atoms are moving away from each other). The p-type material (called the 'anode') is connected to a negative potential and the n-type material (called the 'cathode') is connected to a positive potential. With the diode biased in this manner, charges are attracted away from the p–n junction, thus reducing the number of atoms that can share electrons. This increases the internal resistance of the junction, which in turn blocks current flow through the diode. In a forward-biased diode, charges are forced toward the p–n junction, causing many atoms to share electrons. ▼

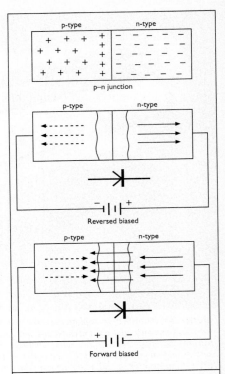

p–n junction *At the p–n junction, a neutral zone is formed when the negative-type material joins with positive-type material to share electrons. The second diagram shows a reversed-biased diode and will not conduct. The positive-type material (called the 'anode') is connected to a negative potential and the negative-type material (called the 'cathode') is connected to a positive potential. The third diagram shows a forward-biased diode. In this situation, charges are forced toward the p–n junction, causing many atoms to share electrons.*

PnP See **plug and play**.

pocket [ISO A card stacker in a card sorter.]

pocket calculator [ISO A calculator, capable of operating independently of electric power mains, that is sufficiently light in weight and small in size to be operated in the hand or carried in a pocket.]

point In typography, a universal unit of measure (height) in which 72 points equal 1 inch.

pointer [ISO A data element that indicates the location of another data element.]

point-to-point Data communication links fall into one of two main categories based upon how the line is structured: either point-to-point or multipoint. The term 'point-to-point' is used to describe a channel that is established between two, and only two, stations. The link may be a dedicated or a dial-up line connecting a processor and a terminal, two processors, or two terminals. Most point-to-point links which use dedicated lines are four-wire circuits where one local-loop (pair) is used for transmitted data and a second (pair) for received data. However, occasionally a two-wire dedicated line with a single local loop at each end will be encountered. The term 'multipoint' refers to a circuit established between one primary station and multiple secondary stations simultaneously. In this application, four-wire dedicated lines are the rule, although it is possible to have two-wire dial-up or dedicated lines. A common example of a multipoint installation using dedicated lines can be found in the banking industry. Typically, all teller terminals within one branch office would share a common dedicated line tied to a host processor.

point-to-point connection [ISO A connection established between two data stations for data transmission. *Note:* The connection may include switching facilities.]

polarized return-to-zero recording [ISO Return-to-zero recording in which the zeros are represented by magnetization in one sense and the ones are represented by magnetization in the opposite sense.] ▽

polling The process in which a computer periodically asks each terminal or device on a local area network if it has a message to send, and then allows each to send data in turn. The network manager can control the sequence and frequency of polling to allow some users longer transmission time. [ISO On a multipoint connection or a point-to-point connection, the process whereby data stations are invited one at a time to transmit.]

polygon mirror A mirror assembly with multiple flat sides of equal dimensions. A scanning motor rotates the polygon mirror at a fixed rate. As the mirror rotates, it reflects a laser beam and causes side-to-side scanning across the photoreceptor. See **laser printer**.

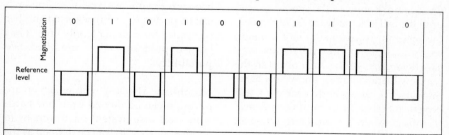

polarized return-to-zero recording *Return-to-zero recording in which the zeros are represented by magnetization in one sense, while the ones are represented by magnetization in the opposite sense.*

polymedia In computing, this term refers to a more advanced and highly sophisticated multimedia system used in defense, industrial, or medical fields. Polymedia computer systems use supercomputers to format data to provide the user with immediate calculations for real-time animation or simulation. Unlike virtual reality systems, polymedia workstations are more concerned with providing accurate simulations including true-to-life colors and representative smells. Compare **multimedia** and **virtual reality**.

polymorphism Polymorphism, encapsulation, and inheritance are the three major features that help make object-oriented programming a powerful methodology. Polymorphism (in conjunction with 'late binding') is a very powerful and complex idea. The terms 'early binding' and 'late binding' refer to the time at which a procedure call is paired with a procedure address. Early binding occurs when the addresses of all functions and procedures are known when the program is compiled and lined. This allows every procedure call to be assigned an appropriate address. Most traditional languages, including C and Pascal, use only early binding. By contrast, in late binding the procedure address is not bound to the procedure call until the call is actually made, at the time the program is executed. Since a menu, for example, is not drawn the same way as a field or an editor, each object in the window hierarchy must know how to re-draw itself. Consequently, each class will have a member function that re-draws the object on the screen. Thus, when an object must be re-drawn, the program does not have to figure out what type of window must be re-drawn (as is the case

in early binding programs); it simply calls the object's re-draw member function. The object then executes its own member function and correctly re-draws itself on the screen. If there are seven kinds of windows in an application, there will be seven different re-drawing methods, each with the same name (called 're-draw'). The behavior is the same (re-drawing a window) but it happens to each object in a way appropriate to its needs. This multiplicity of forms for a single method name is called 'polymorphism', meaning 'many shapes'. Polymorphism is an extremely powerful technique for generalizing a single behavior across many different kinds of objects. It allows for a higher level of abstraction in the design of software, since the programmer worries only about specifying actions and not how to implement those actions. Late binding makes polymorphism possible. See **object-oriented programming**.

pop-up menu Unlike pull-down menus which always appear in the same place, pop-up menus may appear on the screen at any location, usually for user instructions, help, or warnings.

port 1. A connector on the computer or peripheral device used to send and receive data. 2. When an application has been written on one type of computer, it can be ported (moved) across to another computer environment, only after it has been re-programmed or modified. See **portability**.

portability The ease with which an application can be moved from one hardware/software system environment to another. Portability can be defined as the ability to compile and run unaltered source programs on any platform and execution environment with identical behavior. True portability is extremely difficult to achieve, and when one speaks of portability, it would be a more accurate measure if one could estimate the degree of compatibility, and the degree of change required when one program is ported (moved) from one environment (computer system) to another. There are various forms of portability. One measure of portability might be the amount of code that can be shared between platforms. Another measure can be the amount of effort required to modify a program to run on a new platform or environment. Naturally, due to various coding schemes and coding requirements, it is much easier to port software that was designed and written to be portable than it is to port existing code that was not written in adherence to portability guidelines. Higher-level programming languages like Ada, C, FORTRAN, Common LISP, and Pascal provide the greatest degree of portability. The word 'portability' comes from the Latin word *portare*, meaning 'carry'. See **Ada**. Compare **migration**.

portable computer A personal computer designed to be carried by the user for the purpose of transporting it from one location to another (such as from the office to the home). The keyboard on a portable computer is usually designed so that it can be folded away, and the monitor is usually fixed into the system. Early portable models (such as the Osborne I and Compaq portable computer) were not battery operated, and most were quite heavy. Modern technology has made laptop and notebook computers more practical for transportation. Today, early portable models are called 'luggables'. See **laptop computer**. ▼

NEWSFLASH

The value of the mobile PCs sold in 1994 was US$15 800 million.

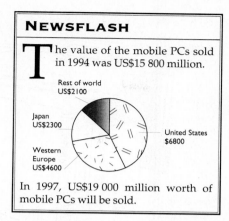

Rest of world US$2100
Japan US$2300
Western Europe US$4600
United States $6800

In 1997, US$19 000 million worth of mobile PCs will be sold.

portrait Refers to the orientation of a page when the output is printed across the shorter axis. In contrast, landscape orientation would print text and graphics across the longer axis of a page.

POS Point-of-sale; the place where a sale is made, such as a retail department store. POS terminals (such as cash registers) may also input inventory data to the central computer when a sale is made.

position [ISO Any location in a string that may be occupied by an element and that is identified by a serial number.]

positional representation [ISO A representation of a number in a positional representation system.]

positional representation system [ISO Any numeration system in which a number is represented by an ordered set of characters in such a way that the value contributed by a character depends upon its position as well as upon its value.]

positioner In disk drive technology, the assembly consisting of one or more

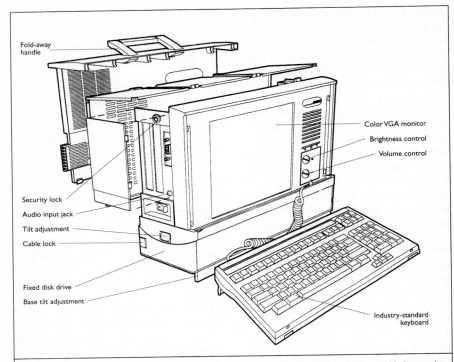

Fold-away handle

Color VGA monitor

Brightness control

Volume control

Security lock

Audio input jack

Tilt adjustment

Cable lock

Fixed disk drive

Base tilt adjustment

Industry-standard keyboard

portable computer This was a high-end full-function portable computer that provided superior quality color display at less than a 50-millisecond screen response for animation. It can display up to 256 colors out of a palette of 4096 colors in 640 x 480 graphics resolution and 256 colors out of a palette of 256 000 colors in 320 x 200 graphics resolution. The monitor incorporates six transistors for each pixel on the screen, giving a total of 1.8 million transistors for superior color selection and fast response time.

access arms with slider suspensions attached (or 'ganged') to a positioner motor. Voice coil positioners, so called because of their functional resemblance to loudspeaker voice coils, are a frequently-used mechanism. Positioners may be linear (moving access arms along a radius), or rotary (swinging access arms in an arc across the disk). An important facet of positioner design is determining the precise timing and degree of current applications to minimize the seek time between any two positions. The solution to this problem for a particular positioner

is called the 'positioner's (electrical) current profile'. The profile of current applied during seeking determines the positioner's velocity profile. A velocity profile is a graph of seek velocity expressed as a function of the number of tracks between the current and desired head positions. Another common configuration is the rotary positioner used in most fixed-media magnetic drives such as those manufactured by Digital Equipment Corporation. The rotary positioner offers a mechanical advantage over the linear voice coil — more head motion for a given combination of flux density in the permanent magnet and applied (electric) current in the coil. Because the access arms of a rotary positioner sweep an arc as they traverse the disk surface, the heads have a different yaw angle depending upon which track they are following. See **yaw angle**.

positive development The laser printer technology in which the laser beam is turned on when scanning the background (non-image areas). The toner is then attracted to the unexposed areas which correspond to the image. See **developer**.

POSIX Portable Operating System Interface for Computing Systems; a set of 'operating system' interface standards developed by the working groups 1003.0 to 1003.9 of the Institute of Electrical and Electronics Engineers (IEEE). POSIX has become the standard for operating system interfaces. POSIX.1 (1003.1–1988) defines the interface between portable application programs and the operating system, based on historical UNIX system models. The first version of the standard consisted entirely of the C language interface to the system. Subsequent versions of POSIX.1 were re-written as language-independent service specifications with a C language binding provided as a separate section. POSIX.2 specifies a shell command language based on the System V shell. It provides approximately 70 utilities to be called from shell scripts or from the applications directly.

POST Power-on self test. See **diagnostic program**.

postamble [ISO A sequence of bits re-

corded at the end of each block on a magnetic medium, for the purpose of synchronization when reading backward.]

postcondition [ISO An assertion that pertains to a joint immediately following, in the execution sequence, a specified portion of a program.]

postfix notation [ISO A method of forming mathematical expressions in which each operator is preceded by its operands and indicates the operation to be performed on the operands or the intermediate results that precede it. *Examples:* (a) A added to B and the sum multiplied by C is represented by the expression AB + Cx. (b) P AND the result of Q AND R is represented by the expression PQR&&.]

postmortem dump [ISO A dump produced immediately after an abnormal termination of a run.]

PostScript A page description (programming) language that uses special commands to describe how an image will be printed on a page. Output to any printer which contains a PostScript interpreter can drive that printer, regardless of its make or model. This means that all processing is transferred from the computer to the printer, which has its own central processing unit and random-access memory for converting the mathematical representation of images. Although the PostScript language had its beginnings in 1976 at the Evans & Sutherland Computer Corporation, it was finally developed by John Warnock and Chuck Geschke (founders of Adobe Systems, Incorporated). PostScript output can take advantage of a printer's maximum resolution, ranging from 300 dots per inch to 2400 dots per inch on some professional typesetters. Abbreviation 'PS'. See **downloadable font** and **outline font**.

PostScript laser printer A laser printer capable of interpreting printing instructions written in PostScript — a page description language widely used in desktop publishing. See **PostScript**.

potentiometer set mode [ISO That set-up mode of an analog computer during which the coefficients of the problem are set.]

power line filter When using electricity from a wall socket, voltage may fluctuate, sometimes causing an appliance (such as a computer system) to lose power, thereby creating errors and causing computer failures. A filter removes a certain amount of hash and spikes from the mains voltage. In some cases, it is combined with a surge protector that will absorb large spikes such as lightening-induced voltages. A power conditioner is able to make up for some voltage changes.

PowerPC The RISC-based processor jointly designed by Apple, IBM, and Motorola at Austin, Texas, and launched in 1993. The first chip, MPC 601, was fabricated on a 0.6-micron CMOS process, packing 2.8 million transistors into an 11-square-millimeter die.

PP See **parallel processing**.

PPM Pages per minute. See **laser printer**.

PQFP Plastic quad flat pack.

preamble [ISO A sequence of bits recorded at the beginning of each block on a magnetic medium for the purpose of synchronization.]

precedence [ISO An order relation defining the sequence of the application of operators within an expression.] Also called 'operator precedence'.

pre-charge lamp In the cleaning stage of the electrophotography cycle of a laser printer, not only must the residual toner be removed, but the residual charges on the drum or belt must also be neutralized. On some units this is accomplished by a fluorescent light called a 'pre-charge lamp'. See **laser printer**.

precision [ISO A measure of the ability to distinguish between nearly equal values. *Example:* Four-place numerals are less precise than six-place numerals; nevertheless a properly computed four-place numeral may be more accurate than an improperly computed six-place numeral.]

precondition [ISO An assertion that pertains to a point immediately preceding, in the execution sequence, a specified portion of a program.]

prefix notation [ISO A method of forming mathematical expressions in which each operator precedes its operands and indicated the operation to be performed on the operands or the intermediate results that follow it. *Examples:* (a) A added to B and the sum multiplied by C is represented by the expression x + ABC. (b) P AND the result of Q AND R is represented by the expression &P&QR.]

preprocessor [ISO A functional unit that

effects preparatory processing of computer programs. *Example:* A macrogenerator may function as a preprocessor of a translator.]

pre-read head [ISO A read head adjacent to another read head and used to read data before the same data is read by the other read head.]

prerecorded (data) medium [ISO A data medium on which certain preliminary items of data are present, the remaining items of data being entered during subsequent operations.]

presentation graphics Any form of graphics used to aid a person when making a presentation. These could be pie graphs, column graphs, text chart in the form of slides, overhead transparencies, animation, computer slide show, or video. Presentation graphics programs such as Harvard Graphics and Power-Point are designed to assist the user to easily create charts and graphs.

presentation layer The sixth layer of the OSI (Open Systems Interconnection) model. The presentation layer ensures that the receiving station understands what was sent by the transmitting station. The communicating parties negotiate how the data will be sent (for instance, ASCII-coded characters instead of binary) and which end will do the

NEWSFLASH

The value of the presentation graphics software market for the Macintosh environment in 1992 was US$26 million (153 500 units). In 1997, it is estimated that it will be US$55.6 million (418 000 units).

translation, if necessary. This layer also allows the application to interpret the information to be transferred (such as code conversion, file formats, and character sets). See **OSI reference model**.

Presentation Manager A graphical user interface and application and programming interface for OS/2, developed by IBM and Microsoft Corporation. Presentation Manager was designed to rival the on-screen performance of the Apple Macintosh environment (such as pull-down menus, multiple on-screen typefaces, desktop accessories, and multiple on-screen windows). See **Microsoft Corporation**.

presentation services layer Each of the layers of IBM's Systems Network Architecture (SNA) has its own set of rules for communicating with its peer layer in the other node. The layers communicate with each other by adding header information to user data. The presentation services layer (sixth layer) formats data for different presentation media and coordinates the sharing of resources. See **SNA layers**.

Prestel One of the largest videotext databases in the world. It was introduced by British Telecom in the mid-1980s. See **videotex**.

preventive maintenance [ISO Maintenance performed specifically to prevent faults from occurring.]

primary station [ISO In high-level data link control (HDLC), the part of the data station that supports the primary control functions of the data link, generates commands for transmission, and interprets received responses. *Note:* Specific responsibilities assigned to the primary station include initialization of control signal interchange, organization of data flow, and actions regarding error control and error recovery functions.]

primary storage The part of the computer that holds data and instructions for processing. Primary storage is used only temporarily by the control unit (inside the central processing unit). After being processed, the data is held once again in primary storage until it is sent to the output unit or secondary storage (such as a hard disk). At the top of the storage hierarchy is primary storage, followed by secondary storage, then tertiary storage. Primary storage products include random-access memory, which is usually sold in the form of modules that can be plugged into the backplane of a computer system and contain numbers of dynamic random-access memory chips. This form of memory is termed 'primary' because on most computing systems, it is the medium through which data must pass before being used by the system's processors. Depending upon their size and use, some computer systems can be configured with primary memory ranging from 1 megabyte to 2 gigabytes, with access measured in nanoseconds. See **storage hierarchy**. Compare **RAM**.

print drum [ISO A rotating cylinder that presents characters at each of the possible print positions.]

printed circuit board See **circuit board**.

printer 1. A machine that produces images on paper or film. Printers may be known by the technique they employ to do this. [ISO An output unit that produces a hard copy record of data mainly

NEWSFLASH

Worldwide printer market share for 1992.

Vendor	Units sold	Market share %
HP	4 181 322	20
Epson	2 927 904	14
Panasonic	2 003 707	9
Star	1 510 645	7
Apple	1 207 429	6
Canon	940 410	4
Okidata	865 533	4
Citizen	755 371	4
Lexmark	666 521	3
Others	6 132 393	29
Total	21 191 235	100

Of these, 10 178 215 units were dot matrix; ink-jet prepresented 4 057 356 units; and 4 606 254 units were laser printers.

Shipments of laser printers are expected to grow at fairly even rates across the world at slightly more than 13% compound annual growth rate to 1997.

in the form of a sequence of discrete graphic characters belonging to one or more predetermined character sets. *Note:* In many instances, printers may be used as plotters.] See **daisy-wheel**, **dot matrix printer**, **impact printer**, **ink-jet printer**, and **laser printer**.

print server In local area networking, a personal computer which is used to share printers between users. They generally include substantial file storage capacity to support a spooling system. All authorized devices attached to the network are allowed to queue print requests to the printers attached to the print server. Print requests are first copied as files to the disk storage attached to the print servers. Later, these files are printed either under the control of the network or in a sequence determined by the print server operator, who may have to mount special stationery in the designated printer before each request is completed.

print through [ISO An undesired transfer of a recorded signal from one part of a magnetic medium to another part when these parts are brought into proximity.]

print wheel [ISO A rotating disk that presents any of the characters of the set at a single print position. *Note:* A daisy-wheel is a type of print wheel.] See **wheel printer**.

privacy protection [ISO The implementation of appropriate administrative, technical, and physical safeguards to ensure the security and confidentiality of data records, and to protect both security and confidentiality against any threat or hazard that could result in substantial harm, embarrassment, inconvenience, or unfairness to any individual about whom such information is maintained.]

private branch exchange See PBX.

private line See **leased line**.

private network Private lines (also called 'dedicated' or 'leased lines') provide a private, full-time connection that can be used for point-to-point or multipoint network configurations. They are available to any location, no matter how distant. Whereas the switched network is connected only for the duration of the

call, a dedicated line is always connected — therefore, no dialing is required to establish the connection. The classes of private leased lines that are available are narrow band, voice band, and wide band.

privileged instruction [ISO An instruction that can be executed only in a specific mode. *Note:* This mode is called the 'privileged mode' and is usually reserved for the operating system.]

PRML Partial-response maximum-likelihood.

problem definition [ISO A statement of a problem, which may include a description of the data, the method, the procedures, and algorithms used to solve it.]

problem-oriented language [ISO A programming language that reflects the concepts of a particular application area. *Examples:* SQL for database applications; COBOL for business applications.]

procedural language 1. [ISO A programming language in which computations are expressed in terms of statement sequences. *Example:* Pascal.] 2. See **programming language**.

procedure [ISO A block, with or without formal parameters, the execution of which is invoked by means of a procedure call.]

procedure call [ISO A language construct for invoking the execution of a procedure. *Note:* A procedure call usually includes an entry name and possible actual parameters.]

process 1. [ISO To perform operations on data in a process.] 2. [ISO A course of events defined by its purpose or by its effect, achieved under given conditions.] 3. [ISO A course of events occurring according to an intended purpose or effect.]

process computer system [ISO A computer system with a process interface system, that monitors or controls a technical process.]

process control [ISO The control of a process in which a computer system is used to regulate usually continuous operations or processes.]

process control equipment [ISO Equipment that measures the variables of a technical process, directs the process according to control signals from the process computer systems, and provides appropriate signal transformation. *Examples:* Sensors; transducers; actuators.]

processing unit [ISO A functional unit that consists of one or more processors and their internal storages. *Note:* In English, the term 'processor' is often used synonymously with 'processing unit'.]

process interface system [ISO A functional unit that adapts process control equipment to the computer system in a process computer system.]

process interrupt signal [ISO A signal that originates from a technical process and that causes an interrupt in the process computer system.]

processor [ISO In a computer, a functional unit that interprets and executes instructions. *Note:* A processor consists of at least an instruction control unit and an arithmetic and logic unit.]

Prodigy An online information service developed by IBM and Sears to offer personal computer users (via modem) home shopping convenience plus other benefits such as up-to-date news, stock quotes, and community information.

producer [ISO An asynchronous procedure that provides data to be used by other asynchronous procedures.]

production level video See **PLV**.

professional workstation See **workstation**.

program 1. A set of instructions that is used to tell the computer (and other peripheral or mechanical devices) how to perform a specific task. 2. In the United States, a definite list of pre-arranged activities, such as a program of events scheduled for a concert or play. [ISO A sequence of instructions suitable for processing. *Notes:* (a) Processing may include the use of an assembler, a compiler, an interpreter, or another translator to prepare the program for execution as well as the execution of the program. (b) The sequence of instructions may include statements and necessary declarations.] Compare **programme**. 3. [ISO To design, write, and test programs.] 4. (In programming languages.) [ISO A logical assembly of one or more interrelated modules.]

program counter [ISO A special-purpose register used to hold the address of the next instruction to be executed.]

programmable calculator [ISO A calculator whose program can be changed by the operator.]

programmable read-only memory See **PROM**.

program maintenance manual [ISO A document that provides the information necessary to maintain a program.]

programme In the United Kingdom, Australia, and New Zealand, a definite list of pre-arranged activities, such as a program of events scheduled for the concert or play. These three countries also use 'program' when referring to a set of code used to tell the computer (and other peripheral or mechanical devices) how to perform a specific task. Compare **program**.

Programmed Inquiry Learning or Teaching An authoring language developed in 1968 by John Starkweather for computer-aided instruction. Although it is now being overtaken by new authoring languages (such as HyperTalk), it was popular because of its ease-of-use when developing on-screen instructional material. Acronym 'PILOT'.

programmer A person capable of designing, writing, testing, and implementing computer programs (software). A programmer must first define the problem, then identify the opportunity, plan the solution, code the program, test it, and document it.

Programmer's Hierarchical Interactive Graphics System A sophisticated, three-dimensional graphics and modeling support system that controls the definition, modification, and display of hierarchical graphics data. It includes extensions to the ISO standard to provide capabilities for hidden-surface removal, shading, and depth cueing. Acronym 'PHIGS'.

programming [ISO The designing, writing, and testing of programs.]

programming environment [ISO An integrated collection of software and hardware to support the development of computer programs.]

Programming in Logic See **Prolog**.

P

programming language A strict set of codes and rules that enable the computer to operate in a desired way. There are over 180 programming languages currently in use. Popular business languages include FORTRAN, COBOL, and Pascal, although other languages were written for specialized purposes. Some were designed for children, beginners, scientists, and engineers, while others were tailored for very small or very large computers — optimized to take advantage of a computer's speed. During the first generation of computing (1951–58), machine language was the only language used to program a computer. Also called a 'low-level language', machine language required programmers to write code in strings of '0' and '1' bits, depending upon the computer's own machine language, where each code corresponded to a single action or calculation by the computer. The second generation (1959–64) of computers saw the introduction of assemblers, compilers, and interpreters which represented machine language in codes a little easier for programmers to recognize and understand. From 1965 to 1970, the third generation of computers saw the introduction of many high-level programming languages such as BASIC, FORTRAN, COBOL, Pascal, PL/1, and APL, which use English-like codes. These traditional programming languages require less coding because their translators convert the high-level codes and assign values to specific storage locations and registers in the central processing unit. Since 1971, the fourth generation of computers has started using very-high-level programming languages known as '4GL' (4th-generation languages). Programmers using 4GL need not specify every step a computer should take when making a calculation. Instead, the programmer needs only to identify the desired end-result. This can be likened to asking a colleague to perform a task such as 'make a photocopy of a piece of paper'. An inexperienced colleague (likened to a high-level language) would need detailed instructions on how to get to the photocopier; how to place the paper in the correct position; how to select the options of the photocopier; and which button to press in order to make a copy. Programming languages which require this amount of detail are sometimes called 'procedural languages'. An experienced colleague (likened to a very-high-level language) would only need to be told to make a photocopy. Very few instructions would be needed. 4GLs which require very little detail are sometimes called 'nonprocedural languages'. [ISO An artificial language designed to generate or to express programs.] See **assembly language** and **structured language**.

programming system [ISO In a programming environment, the software required for the development and use of computer programs.]

program production time [ISO That part of system production time during which a user's computer program is successfully executed.]

program-sensitive fault [ISO A fault that is revealed as a result of the execution of some particular sequence of instructions.]

program specification [ISO A document that describes the structure and functions of a program in sufficient detail to permit programming and to facilitate maintenance.]

program test time [ISO That part of system production time during which a user's computer program is tested.]

program verification [ISO Proving that a program behaves according to its program specification.]

project [ISO An undertaking with pre-specified objectives, magnitudes, and duration.]

project control [ISO The activities concerned with monitoring the progress of a project, its direction, quality, and resource utilization, as compared to project plans.]

project management [ISO The activities concerned with project planning and project control.]

project planning [ISO The activities concerned with the specification of the components, timing, resources, and procedures of a project.]

project specification [ISO A specification of the objectives, requirements, scope of a project, and its relations to other projects.]

Prolog Programming in Logic; a high-level nonprocedural programming language developed in the early 1970s by French computer scientist Alain Colmerauer and logician Philippe Roussel for use in artificial intelligence research and applications such as expert systems. LISP, a similar language developed in the 1960s, rivals Prolog, but the decision by Japanese fifth-generation computer designers to work with Prolog has given Prolog a temporary lead in the industry. See **programming language**. Compare **LISP**.

PROM Programmable read-only memory, also referred to as 'firmware'; used to store permanent instructions for the computer's general housekeeping operations. Unlike ROM, the contents of PROM can be altered prior to being assembled within the computer system. PROM is stored on a nonvolatile memory chip, meaning the information is retained even after the power is switched off. Avalanche-induced migration (AIM) is a permanent process of short-circuiting a diffused junction in a PROM. This is based on aluminum migration through silicon. The first ROMs contained cell arrays in which the sequence of ones and zeros was established by a metalization interconnection mask step during fabrication. Thus, users had to supply a ROM vendor with an interconnect program so that the vendor could complete the mask and build the ROMs. Set-up charges were quite high. To offset this high set-up charge, manufacturers developed a super-programmable ROM. The first PROMs used fusible links that could be melted or 'burned' with a special programmer system. Once burned, a PROM was just like a ROM. As one alternative to fusible-link programming, Intel Corporation pioneered an erasable (metal-oxide semiconductor technology) PROM (termed an 'EPROM') that used charge-storage programming. [ISO A storage device that, after being written on once, becomes a ROM.] See **EPROM** and **ROM**.

promiseware Software that, while long promised by the manufacturer, is not yet delivered.

propagation delay In satellite communications, the transmission time between the satellite and the Earth station, which could take a quarter of a second. This delay is also known as 'dead time' or 'satellite delay'. These unusually long delays require special equipment to ensure that the channel is not interrupted or broken, because the receiving device may assume a termination of the link.

proprietary Referring to a set of unique standards owned and controlled by a single company, and rarely licensed or published freely for others to use.

proprietary standards Clearly defined and agreed-upon conventions for specific programming interfaces. Proprietary standards are used only within the environment provided by a single computer vendor. On the other hand, public standards are widely used across a variety of vendor equipment, and formal standards are those developed by a standards organization such as the American National Standards Institute or the International Organization for Standardization.

protection [ISO An arrangement for restricting access to (or use of all or part of) a computer system.]

protocol A strict set of rules that govern the exchange of information between computer devices. To communicate successfully, the communicating computers must use the same protocol. [ISO A set of semantic and syntactic rules that determines the behavior of functional units in achieving communication.]

P

protocol converter A communications control unit which can convert information from one coding system to one recognized by the computer or communications device. For example, a protocol converter can, if necessary, convert code from ASCII to EBCDIC format so that it can be processed.

prototype [ISO A model or preliminary implementation suitable for evaluation of system design, performance, and production potential; or for better understanding or determination of the requirements.]

PS See **PostScript**.

PSDN Packet-switched data network. In Europe, the United Kingdom, Canada, Australia, and New Zealand, packet-switched data networks (PSDNs) have become a viable alternative (or supplement) to the public-switched telephone network. The majority of such networks are based on X.25. This standard was developed by the international standards body known as the 'Comité Consultatif International de Télégraphique et Téléphonique' (CCITT). In countries where it is impossible (or too costly) to obtain private leased lines for data transmission, computer networks can be established using only those public packet-switched facilities available from the telephone authority of the particular country. A PSDN allows large numbers of users to share a powerful message packaging and delivery service. It also permits the terminal equipment of a subscriber to communicate with the equipment of any other subscriber, simply by presenting data (plus certain control information) in a prescribed manner to the network. The subscriber need not be

concerned with how the message arrives at its destination. In order to transmit over a PSDN, data must be broken into 'packets' of data (typically 128 bytes). The concept of handling information in packets resulted from a study by the Rand Corporation that investigated the potential for a national network supporting both voice and data communications. Once the data is broken into packets, the PSDN then routes the packets to their destination. To guarantee its safe delivery, each individual packet identifies its destination, source, and number. Packets are numbered because a message may be segmented into several packets, which must be re-assembled in the correct order when they arrive. PSDNs are cost-effective over long distances when traffic volume is low. Conversely, circuit-switched leased lines are more economical over short distances when traffic volume is high. Compare **circuit-switched network**.

PSE Packet-switching exchange; any node in a packet-switching network which is capable of switching packets, managing transmission lines, and performing packet assembly and disassembly functions. See **packet-switching system**.

pseudocode An English-like language used instead of flowcharting when designing a computer program. This is sometimes known as 'fake code'. See **flowchart**.

pseudo-random number sequence [ISO A sequence of numbers that has been determined by some defined arithmetic process but is effectively a random number sequence for the purpose for which it is required.]

PSI Pakistan Standards Institution; Pakistan's standards body formed in 1951.

PSK Phase-shift keying.

PSN Packet-switching network. See **packet-switching system**.

PSS 1. See **packet-switching system**. 2. Packet-Switched Service; the network commissioned in the United Kingdom in 1980. 3. Packet-switched stream.

PS/2 IBM Personal System/2; a line of personal computers developed by IBM in 1986. They use Intel microprocessors, operating on IBM's proprietary Micro Channel Architecture.

PSV See **partition-sector virus**.

PTN Public telephone network. These are typically voice networks which are also known as 'switched' networks. They allow typical home telephones to be connected (switched) to any other telephone on the network. Examples of PTNs are provided by British Telecom, Telecom Australia (Telstra), and AT&T. On the other hand, private telephone networks, usually owned by a business, go under such names as private branch exchange (PBX), private automatic branch exchange (PABX), and computerized branch exchange (CBX).

public access terminal A computer terminal accessible by anyone. These may be positioned in a public library or in a foyer of a building. In years to come, public access terminals will be as common as public telephones. Acronym 'PAT'.

public domain software Software available for use free of charge because it is not protected under copyright. This arrangement differs from shareware which makes available protected software on a trial basis, on the condition that if the program is adopted, the user will forward payment to the author. Shareware and public domain software are often distributed via mail order, or copied from public bulletin boards.

public standards Clearly defined and agreed-upon conventions for specific programming interfaces, widely used across a variety of vendor equipment. On the other hand, formal standards are those developed by a standards organization such as the American National Standards Institute or the International Organization for Standardization, while proprietary standards are used only within the environment provided by a single computer vendor.

public telephone network See **PTN**.

pull-down menu Unlike pop-up menus, which may appear on the screen at any location, pull-down menus are accessed from the menu-bar, and used to access application commands easily and quickly. When the cursor or pointer from a mouse is positioned at the menu-bar, a list of options is automatically displayed. The command or option highlighted by the cursor is the one that will be activated.

pulse [ISO A variation in the value of a magnitude, short in relation to the time schedule of interest, the final value being the same as the initial value.]

pulse code modulation In telephone and voice communications, pulse code modulation (PCM) systems use a minimum bit rate of 64 000 bits per second. The PCM samples speech signals at a sampling rate of say, 8 kilohertz (kHz), in order to transmit frequency components of up to say, 4 kHz. Because most voice signal energy is below 1 kHz, amplitude does not vary at a fast rate. Consequently, when the difference in amplitude between a sample and the preceding sample is encoded, fewer bits are required per sample than for PCM systems that encode the amplitudes of samples. The method of encoding the differences in amplitude between a present sample and the preceding one is called 'differential pulse code modulation' (DPCM). Another waveform coding technique, called 'adaptive differential

PCM' (ADPCM), lowers bit rates even further. This system predicts the amplitude at a sampling point by using the amplitudes of samples preceding it, then encodes the difference between the actual sample value and the predicted value. The rules for predicting and encoding dynamically change to adapt to the current state of signals. See **digital speech interpolation**.

pulse train [ISO A series of pulses having similar characteristics.]

punch [ISO A device for making holes in a data media.]

punched card A card punched with holes in certain places so that a computer can

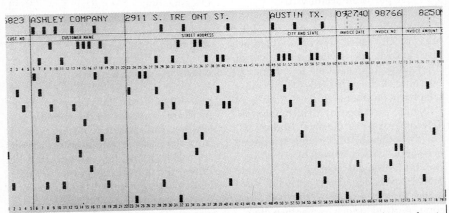

punched card Between 1890 and 1946, electromechanical machines to punch, tabulate, and sort cards at high speed were the heart of information processing. Originally developed by Dr Herman Hollerith for the 1890 United States Census, punched card machines were later put to use by government, railroads, and insurance companies. Progressively faster machines came into use in business, science, and government. Nonetheless, even the fastest punched card machines were bypassed by technological change, as vacuum tubes began to replace the electromechanical wheels and levers in the late 1940s. Information is stored in cards by holes punched in columns on the card. Numbers are represented by single holes, while letters of the alphabet are represented by two holes. The machine 'reads' the holes electrically as the card is moved across sensors. When asked how he came to invent such a system, Hollerith said the idea occurred to him when he saw a railroad conductor use a ticket punch. In 1896, Hollerith founded the Tabulating Machine Company, one of three firms that later merged to become IBM Corporation.

read data coded from the combination of holes. Punched cards were first used in the 1800s by the French weaver Joseph Jacquard who sought to automate his weaving factory. Later developed for computing by Herman Hollerith, 80-column cards were used in the 1950s, and 96-column cards were introduced in 1969. Sturdy paper cards were also programmed to control communications devices (telex) and some musical instruments such as the player piano (Pianola). A more advanced system was the key-to-tape device which used magnetized dots on magnetic tape to represent data. Also called 'punch card'. [ISO A card punched with hole patterns.] ∆

punched tape reader [ISO An input unit that reads or senses the hole patterns in a punched tape, transforming the data from hole patterns to electric signals.]

punch path [ISO In a punch, a card path that has a punch station.]

punch position [ISO A defined location on a data medium on which a hole may be punched to record data.]

punch station [ISO The location in a punch where a data medium is punched.]

punch tape [ISO A tape in which hole patterns can be punched.]

punctuation capability [ISO The ability to divide displayed or printed numbers into groups of three digits to the left of the decimal marker.]

P

pushdown list [ISO A list that is constructed and maintained so that the next data element to be retrieved is the most recently stored. *Note:* This method is characterized as 'last in, first out' (LIFO).]

pushdown storage [ISO A storage device in which data is ordered in such a way that the next data element to be retrieved is the most recently stored. *Note:* This method is characterized as 'last in, first out' (LIFO).]

pushup storage [ISO A storage device in which data is ordered in such a way that the next data element to be retrieved is the one stored first. *Note:* This method is characterized as 'first in, first out' (FIFO).]

PX64 A video compression process similar to MPEG, but adapted to slower bit rates. PX64 is typically used for video conferencing over ISDN telephone lines.

**THE ILL-DESIGNED LAYOUT OF THE QWERTY KEYBOARD
SITS ON EVERY DESK AS A TESTIMONY TO INEFFICIENCY,
AND A SLAP IN THE FACE OF STANDARDIZATION**

QAM Quadrature amplitude modulation; a method of modulation that uses a combination of amplitude and phase modulation to increase data throughput.

QBE Query by example; a query technique used in database management programs to help novice users specify the type of information that should be searched. See **query language**.

QEMM Quarterdeck Expanded Memory Manager. See **expanded memory**.

QIC Quarter-Inch Cartridge Drive Standards; an international trade association incorporated in November 1987 to encourage and promote the widespread use of quarter-inch data cartridge tape drives and media, as used for computer data backup, secondary storage, and software distribution. The primary purpose of QIC is to provide a forum for technical discussions that lead to the generation of industry standards, pro-

viding compatibility among various manufacturers' tape cartridges, drives, and systems. Membership of QIC is open to all manufacturers of quarter-inch data cartridge drives and media, and any interested party. A quarter-inch cartridge system consists of a drive unit and one or more removable, portable tape cartridges which contain integral tape motion and guidance mechanisms, and are loaded with up to 1000 foot (305 meters) of quarter-inch magnetic-coated tape. The single-capstan drive units (which contain magnetic read/write heads, electronics for read/write, motion control, and system interface functions) are available in 2½-inch, 5.35-inch, or 8-inch form factors for installation within computer system hardware or as stand-alone, plug-compatible units. Data is recorded on up to 32 tracks along the tape, usually in a serial fashion. Data storage capacities, which earlier ranged from 10 megabytes to 150 megabytes, increased to 1 gigabyte in 1990. The industry has now extended quarter-inch cartridge tape technology to achieve capacities in excess of 2.7 gigabytes. Quarter-Inch Cartridge Drive Standards are supported by system manufacturers such as Apple, AT&T, Compaq, Data General, Hewlett-Packard, IBM, ICL, NCR, NEC, and Olivetti.

QL See **query language**.

quadrature amplitude modulation See **QAM**.

quadrillion See **exponent**.

quadword See **word**.

qualification [ISO A mechanism for referencing a component of a language object by means of a reference to the object and an identifier declared for the component. *Examples:* Used for referencing record components (B OF A in COBOL); members of a library; language objects in a module.]

quality assurance [ISO The planned systematic activities necessary to ensure that a component or system conforms to established technical requirements.]

quantize [ISO To divide the range of a variable into a finite number of non-overlapping intervals that are not necessarily of equal width, and to designate each interval by an assigned value within the interval. *Example:* A person's age is for many purposes quantized with a quantum (interval) of one year.]

quantum A discrete quantity of electromagnetic energy (photon) which can be released when an electron is activated, or when a radioactive chemical element drops from a higher to a lower energy level. The quantum is the smallest possible amount of energy at a given frequency. The lowest electromagnetic energy is located at the extreme end of the far infrared region of the optical spectrum. It has the longest wavelength (100 microns) with a frequency of 3 THz (terahertz, or 3×10^{12} hertz). The highest electromagnetic energy has a wavelength of 0.001 microns, with a frequency of 0.3 EHz (exahertz, or 0.3×10^{18} hertz). The energy of a photon with a wavelength of 1 micron is approximately equal to 1.2 eV (electron-volts). The significance of quanta lies in the study of quantum mechanics, a field which has led to the development of high-speed optical neurocomputers which can use multiple quantum-well structures (MQWS) which consist of aluminum gallium arsenide layers only several atoms thick. These are sandwiched (alternated) between wider gallium arsenide layers which are 30 atoms thick. This alternating structure is called a 'tunneling biquantum-well'. Optical images are captured, stored, and read by the use of optically-addressable spatial light modulators (SLM) which use ferroelectric liquid crystals (FLC). FLC–SLM can operate at 50 microseconds, with a spatial

---

NEWSFLASH

The shipment value in the total worldwide multi-user systems market will be down between 1992 and 1997, shrinking from US$75 300 million in 1992 to US$71 000 million in 1997. However, it is expected that the PC-based server market for the same period will grow from US$3600 million in 1992 to US$6600 million in 1997.

resolution of 40 line-pairs per millimeter. These enable a 1-square-centimeter device to function at 3.2 giga operations (10^9). The word 'quantum' comes from the Latin word *quantus*, meaning 'how much'. See **optical neurocomputer**.

Quark XPress A professional page layout program originally developed for the Apple Macintosh environment (competing with Aldus PageMaker) that provides word processing functions with advanced typographic features plus color separation, graphics, scaling, and cropping.

Quarter-Inch Cartridge Drive Standards See **QIC**.

quarter-squares multiplier [ISO An analog multiplier whose operation is based on the identity $xy = [(x+y)^2 - (x-y)^2]/4$, incorporating inverters, summers, and square-law function generators.]

Quattro Pro A three-dimensional spreadsheet program (now owned by Novell) designed by Borland International for use on personal computers using DOS.

quattuordecillion See **exponent**.

query by example See **QBE**.

query language A very-high-level programming language introduced to assist programmers to access data from a computer. It is considered the highest-level language because it uses simple English commands which resemble a conversation. Database management systems (DBMS) each have their own query language to enable users to quickly search through a set of information in order to access particular data, which

may be grouped in a variety of ways. For example, in a financial system, one query might ask for a particular customer's investment status, while another query might list all customers who meet a certain set of criteria (such as those who purchased more than a certain number of shares of a particular stock on a specific day). Abbreviation 'QL'.

question mark (?) The wild card that represents just one character. See **wildcard character**.

queue A data structure in which items are removed in a first in, first out (FIFO) manner. In contrast, a stack removes items in a last in, first out (LIFO) manner. [ISO A list that is constructed and maintained so that the next data element to be retrieved is the one stored first. *Note:* This method is characterized as 'first in, first out' (FIFO).] The word 'queue' comes from the Latin word *cauda*, meaning 'tail'.

quindecillion See **exponent**.

quintillion See **exponent**.

QWERTY Refers to the style of (common) keyboard which has the letters Q,W,E,R,T,Y on the first six keys of the top row of letters. This configuration was chosen in 1867 after Christopher Sholes, a leading typewriter manufacturer, received many complaints that the keys on the typewriter he manufactured were constantly jamming together when the operator typed at high speeds. The management of Sholes & Co. asked its engineers to remedy this problem, and the engineers decided that instead of making the typewriter work faster, they would do something to slow down the typist. They analyzed keys and re-arranged them to place the most frequently-used letters of the English alphabet away from the home row (meaning on either the top or bottom rows which were less accessible). For example, it was discovered that the letters 'O' and 'I' were the third and sixth most popular letters in the English alphabet.

This change saw the introduction of the QWERTY keyboard — purposely designed to be inefficient, yet living on as the standard even when no typist today can type fast enough to jam a word processor. Pronounced 'kwertee'. Compare **AZERTY** and **Dvorak**. ▼

Q

QWERTY The QWERTY keyboard has been in use since 1867. It is considered to be an inefficient layout, yet it is well entrenched as a standard.

I DON'T MIND REBELLION
SO LONG AS IT'S DONE IN AN ORDERLY FASHION

radar Radio detecting and ranging; a radio device used for locating an object. This is done by emitting an ultrahigh-frequency radio signal, usually in the form of pulses which are reflected back (echoed) from the distant target object and received by the original transmitting device. Radar is used to determine the range, speed, bearing, and other characteristics of the target object. This technology dates back to 1922 when the pioneer of radio, Guglielmo Marconi, tried to find a way of detecting ships in bad weather by bouncing radio waves off them. By 1936, French ships were using on-board radar to detect icebergs, while the British were finding ways to detect enemy aircraft at distances of 8 miles (13 kilometers). During World War II in 1939, radar was successful in detecting aircraft at ranges beyond 100 miles (161 kilometers). The same type of technology is being used by the American Ballistic Missile Early Warning System with a range of up to 2000 miles (3220 kilometers). After World War II, radar was used to detect radio noise associated with violent activity on the sun's surface. This saw the introduction of the radio telescope. See **noise** and **radio telescope**.

radio frequency interference Any unwanted human-made or natural electrical signal which interferes with radio transmission. This is often a random transmission of varying frequency, amplitude, and phase. Natural noise may be caused by radiation from the movement of ions in the ionosphere and upper atmosphere, and even from lightning, the sun, and the stars. Human-made noise may arise from external sources such as sparks generated in refrigerator and central heating thermostatic systems, and computer systems. Noise may radiate from other transmitters, fluorescent lights, electric motors, car ignition systems, and static — causing interference to radio reception. This is usually regulated to avoid excessive interference with radio and television signals. Abbreviation 'RFI'.

radio telescope A device that brought with it the science of radio astronomy. Scientists and astronomers use clusters of radio telescopes to detect such things as the remains of distant stars (called 'pulsars'). The world's largest dish radio telescope is the ionospheric assembly built in 1963 at Arecibo, Puerto Rico, at a cost of US$9 million. The dish has 1000-foot (304.8-meter) diameter and covers 18.5 acres (7.48 hectares). See **radar**.

radio wave See **carrier wave**.

radio wave propagation When radio waves are radiated, there are usually two components: the 'ground' wave, which is propagated direct from the transmitting aerial to the receiving aerial in a straight line; and the 'sky' wave, which is propagated upward over a wide range of angles until it meets an ionized layer high above the Earth's surface. On reaching the reflecting layer ('F' layer) approximately 143 miles (230 kilometers (km)) above the Earth, the 'sky' waves are bent back again over a wide area toward the Earth. In daylight hours there is an intervening ionized layer ('D' layer) approximately 62 miles (100 km) above the Earth. This layer absorbs radio waves on frequencies below 5 megahertz (MHz). Hence, signals on these frequencies do not pass to the higher layer for reflection back to Earth. Radio signals on frequencies above 5 MHz are successfully propagated as 'sky' waves during daylight. They pass through the 'D' layer and are reflected back to Earth by the higher 'F' layer. At night, the 'D' layer disappears, and

signals on lower frequencies are reflected from the 'F' layer. Thus they can be heard over very long distances at night.

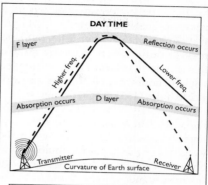

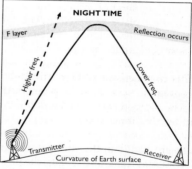

radio wave propagation Radio signals on frequencies above 5 megahertz (MHz) are successfully propagated as 'sky' waves during daylight. They pass through the 'D' layer and are reflected back to Earth by the higher 'F' layer. At night, the 'D' layer disappears, and signals on lower frequencies are reflected from the 'F' layer. Thus they can be heard over very long distances at night. The 'ground' wave component also has its difficulties, whether at night or by day. As a straight-line transmission, the 'ground' wave is attenuated (reduced) by the type of terrain over which it passes. Signals propagated by 'ground' waves over water suffer little, but land masses cause severe attenuation. For this reason, signals on 2 MHz during the daylight hours may be heard as far away as 248 miles (400 km) over water.

The 'ground' wave component also has its difficulties, whether at night or by day. As a straight-line transmission, the 'ground' wave is attenuated (reduced) by the type of terrain over which it passes. Signals propagated by 'ground' waves over water suffer little, but land masses cause severe attenuation. For this reason, signals on 2 MHz during the daylight hours may be heard as far away as 248 miles (400 km) over water. ▲

radix [ISO In a radix numeration system, the positive integer by which the weight of any digit place is multiplied to obtain the weight of the digit place with the next higher weight. *Example:* In the decimal numeration system, the radix of each digit place is 10. *Note:* The term 'base' is deprecated in this sense because of its mathematical use.]

radix complement [ISO In a fixed radix numeration system, a complement that can be derived from a given number by subtracting it from a specified power of the radix. *Example:* 830 is the radix complement of 170 in the decimal numeration system using three digits, the power of the radix being 1000. *Note:* The radix complement may be obtained by first deriving the diminished radix complement, then adding one to the least significant digit of the result and executing any carries required.]

radix numeration system [ISO A positional representation system in which the ratio of the weight of any one digit place to the weight of the digit place with the next lower weight is a positive integer. *Note:* The permissible values of the character in any digit place range from zero to one less than the radix of that digit place.]

radix point [ISO In a representation of a number expressed in a radix numeration system, the location of the separation of the characters associated with the integral part from those associated with the fractional part.]

RAFT Running away from things; referring to a severe bout of procrastination that befalls a person who is affected by the fast pace of the computer industry. When RAFTing, a person undertakes new projects, thereby exacerbating the problem.

ragged left In typography and word processing, the positioning of text on a page so that all the text is aligned to the right margin, leaving a ragged left margin. Also called 'right justified'. Compare **flush left**, **indent**, **justification**, and **ragged right**. ▼

ragged right In typography and word processing, the positioning of text on a

Doubtless, design and style beg individual consideration. However, only when one reaches a certain level of appreciation for design will one agree that there is no such thing as a 'fine line' between typographic beauty and vulgarity.

ragged left

Doubtless, design and style beg individual consideration. However, only when one reaches a certain level of appreciation for design will one agree that there is no such thing as a 'fine line' between typographic beauty and vulgarity.

ragged right

page so that all the text is aligned to the left margin, leaving a ragged right margin. Also called 'left justified'. Compare **flush left**, **indent**, **justification**, and **ragged left**. ⋀

RAID Redundant arrays of inexpensive disks; a term coined in 1988 at the University of California at Berkeley in a paper that outlined the fact that hard disk drives are susceptible to failure due to head crashes, temperature variances, motor failures, controller failures, and similar mechanical and electrical problems, and the increasing reliance on shared hard disks. To address this, RAID was developed to offer a range of benefits such as fault-tolerance, increased reliability, and higher performance. RAID was designed to replace a single large-capacity disk drive with several smaller-capacity disk drives. Using an array of disk drives, a computer system can stripe data across the drives as if it were writing to only one drive. This allows multiple heads to operate simultaneously, thereby providing high input/output (I/O) and data transfer rates. The downside to introducing additional devices into a computer system is the increased probability that device failures may occur. To address this, several levels of RAID can be used to suit certain applications. RAID 0, a very old technique, transfers data across an array of disks in parallel, thereby spreading the data across several drives in order to allow simultaneous read and write operations for increased performance in data access and transfer. Although RAID 0 provides higher transaction rates, a drive failure is unrecoverable. RAID 1, also known as 'mirroring', 'dual-copy', or 'shadowing', has been used in mainframe and mini-computer environments. RAID 1 copies all the contents of one disk to another, giving the user immediate access to data in the event of one disk failing. Although this level of RAID is the most expensive to operate, due to the fact that it requires twice the disk space, it is popular in mission-critical applications. RAID 2, although not used for transaction-processing systems due to its inefficiency, is used in supercomputer environments that require single and double error-detection. RAID 3 is suitable for applications like CAD or CAM that require the fast transfer of large amounts of information. RAID 3 uses an even number of drives, plus an additional parity drive. Any drive, including the parity drive, can fail without causing the whole disk subsystem to shut down. The advantages of RAID 3 include higher bandwidth for large data throughput. However, it has poor performance in transaction environments because the drives cannot operate independently. RAID 4 also has a dedicated parity drive, but it allows the array controller to write data one sector at a time, enabling reads and writes to occur on independent drives, thereby speeding up the I/O rates. One disadvantage with RAID 4 is the weaker write performance, due to the need for it to constantly update, with each write, the parity information of each drive. RAID 5 is increasing in popularity because it reads and writes data to separate disks independently while allowing simultaneous read and write operations to take place. RAID 5 stores the parity information on all drives, thereby increasing the I/O rates sometimes decreased when using only one parity drive. However, RAID 5 has a major drawback in write-intensive applications because RAID 5 must update data by reading the old data, reading the old parity, writing

R

the new data, and writing the new parity. Future technology may overcome this write penalty by using techniques such as write-caching. 'RAID N' refers to levels above RAID 5 which will eliminate the write penalty associated with RAID 5, and offer increased levels of data protection. It is important to note that it cannot be assumed that increased performance is offered according to the increase on the RAID levels. Each level has its own set of advantages and disadvantages, each depending upon the environment. Pronounced 'raid'.

RAM Random-access memory; used as the computer's primary storage area to write, store, and retrieve information and program instructions so that they can be used by the central processing unit. RAM allows any portion of memory to be read or written as quickly as any other. In the early days of computers, RAM storage consisted of metal wire woven through iron rings. This was known as 'core memory' and was very expensive, bulky, slow, and required a great deal of power to operate. Primary memory is now made up of arrays of inexpensive semiconductor-based storage devices called 'dynamic random-access memory' (DRAM) chips that provide fast access to information and use very little power. Unlike read-only memory (ROM), the contents of RAM are not permanent. RAM contains the program and data that is in use, and is said to be volatile, meaning it requires a continuous flow of electricity to keep its contents. If power is lost or turned off, the contents of RAM are also lost. PC memories have had to keep pace with growing demands placed upon them by more powerful central processing units, and more sophisticated software. While early PCs came with 16 to 64 kilobytes of RAM, newer PCs come standard with one to hundreds of megabytes. Pronounced 'ram'. [ISO A storage device in which data can be written and read. *Note:* RAM is the abbreviation of 'random-access memory', and it is deprecated in the sense of direct access storage device.] See **byte**, **DRAM**, **interleaved memory**, **memory chips**, **memory management program**, **page-mode RAM**, and **RAM cache**. Compare **ROM**.

RAM cache An area on a random-access memory chip reserved for use when the central processing unit (CPU) is using the disk drives. RAM cache is used to improve the performance of a computer by temporarily acting as the hard disk, because RAM can transfer data and program instructions to the CPU hundreds of times faster than a disk drive. The RAM cache chip continues to carry data that is most frequently required by the CPU so that waiting time is minimized. This technique is also used when writing to a disk drive, because RAM cache can accept data much faster than a disk drive. Pronounced 'ram-cash'. See **cache** and **disk cache**.

RAM disk An area in random-access memory configured by a software program to emulate a disk drive. See **RAM cache**.

R&D Research and development.

random access A storage and retrieval technique in which the information required by the computer can be immediately accessed, without having to go through all the data in every location. Random access (sometimes called 'direct access') differs from sequential access in that the computer knows exactly where to locate particular information, and is able to do so, depending upon the storage medium used. For example, data being read from magnetic tape cannot be accessed randomly (directly) because the tape must first wind to the desired location, and if the information is at the end of the tape, this could take some time. Data stored on a disk can be accessed much more quickly because the access arm can move the read/write heads to the exact location within milliseconds. See **RAM**. Compare **sequential access**.

random-access memory See **RAM**.

random number [ISO A number selected from a known set of numbers in such a way that each number in the set has the same probability of occurrence.]

random number sequence [ISO A sequence of numbers each of which cannot be predicted only from a knowledge of its predecessors.]

range check [ISO A combination of two limit checks, one of which applies to an upper limit, and the other to a lower limit.]

RAP Remote access point.

raster display device [ISO A display device in which display images are generated by raster graphics.] The word 'raster' comes from the Greek word *rastus*, meaning 'screen'.

raster graphics [ISO Computer graphics in which a display image is composed of an array of pixels arranged in rows and columns.] See **bit-mapped graphics**.

raster image processor The device that

interprets the instructions of a page description language (such as PostScript) and composes the image on the photosensitive drum of a laser printer. Abbreviation 'RIP'. See **laser printer** and **PostScript**.

raster plotter [ISO A plotter that generates a display image on a display surface using a line-by-line scanning technique.]

raster scan The raster scan display gets its name from the fact that the image displayed on the cathode-ray tube (CRT) is built up by generating a series of lines (raster) across the face of the CRT. Usually, the beam starts in the upper left-hand corner of the display and simultaneously moves left to right and top to bottom to put a series of zigzag lines on the screen. Two simultaneously operating independent circuits control the vertical and horizontal movement of the beam. As the electron beam moves across the face of the CRT, a third circuit controls the current flowing in the beam. By varying the current in the electron beam, the image on the CRT can be made as bright or as dark as the user desires. This allows any desired pattern to be displayed. When the beam reaches the end of a line, it is brought back to the beginning of the next line at a rate much faster than was used to generate the line. This action is referred to as 're-trace'. During the re-trace period, the electron beam is usually shut off so that it does not appear on the screen. As the electron beam is moving across the screen horizontally, it is also moving downward, and because of this, each successive line starts slightly below the previous line. When the beam finally reaches the bottom right-hand corner of the screen, it re-traces vertically back to the top left-hand corner. The time it takes for the beam to move from the top of the screen to the bottom and back again to the top is usually referred to as a 'frame'. In the United States, commercial television broad-casts use 15 750 hertz (Hz) as the horizontal sweep frequency (63.5 microseconds per horizontal line) and 60 Hz as the vertical sweep frequency of the 'frame' (16.67 milliseconds per vertical frame). As the horizontal frequency increases, the number of horizontal lines per frame increases (hence the resolution on the vertical axis increases). Increased resolution is needed on high-density graphics displays and on special text-editing terminals. Although many CRTs operate at non-standard horizontal frequencies, very few operate at vertical frequencies other than 60 Hz. If a vertical frequency other than 60 Hz is chosen, any external or internal magnetic or electrical variations at 60 Hz will modulate the electron beam, and the image on the screen will be unstable. Since, in the United States, the power line frequency happens to be 60 Hz, there is a good chance that 60 Hz interference will exist. Transformers can cause 60 Hz magnetic fields, and a power supply ripple can cause 60 Hz electrical variations. To overcome this, special shielding and power supply regulations must be employed.

raster unit [ISO The unit of measure equal to the distance between adjacent pixels. *Note:* This term has been used in the past to denote increment size.]

rational number [ISO A real number that is the quotient of an integer divided by an integer other than zero.]

raw data A collection of unanalyzed facts.

RBOC Regional Bell Operating Company. See **Bell Operating Company**.

RBW RISC-based workstation. See **RISC**.

RCA plug See **phono plug**.

RDBMS Relational database management system; a program in which several items of information may be joined together to form a new data file, even though each resides on a different database. For example, in a library-book tracking program, a report can be generated to list all children's books, and another to list all children members. The two databases can be joined to report on children members who have overdue books. Edgar Codd proposed the relational database model in 1970 using a mathematical theory which treats all data as tables (using rows and columns), and the result of all queries as new tables. Two organizations started work on developing the first RDBMS in the mid-1970s. One was IBM, with a project known as 'System R', and the other was undertaken at the University of California, Berkeley — a project called 'INGRES'. It was from this project that the company 'Ingres' was formed in 1980, when three professors recognized the commercial viability of the project and decided to turn it into an enterprise. The first commercial implementation of an RDBMS was by Oracle in 1978. Ingres the company launched its RDBMS in 1981.

read [ISO To obtain data from a storage device, from a data medium, or from another source.]

read-ahead An advanced disk-caching technique used, for example, in Microsoft's LAN Manager. Disk caching reserves a portion of the server's memory to store frequently-used data so that they are available for instant access. This cache memory, in turn, enables LAN Manager to improve performance by automatically implementing sophisticated file-handling techniques. In a read-ahead operation, the server uses file input/output heuristic methods to analyze read requests, trying to anticipate which data will be requested next. If a pattern of sequential reads is detected, the server begins to read ahead in the file, storing the data in cache memory instead of reading directly from the slower mechanical hard disk.

read and write head See **read/write head**.

read (write) cycle time [ISO The minimum time interval between the starts of successive read (write) cycles of a storage device that has separate reading and writing cycles.]

read head [ISO A magnetic head capable of reading only.] Compare **read/write head**.

read only A DOS file attribute that prevents the system from overwriting or changing a file.

read-only memory See **ROM**.

read/write head The part of a disk drive which reads and writes data, consisting of a core, usually made of ferrite or permalloy, around which is wrapped a coil of wire. The coil is used to induce a magnetic field (for writing data), or to sense change in magnetic flux direction (for reading data). Topologically, the core is a toroid, or ring-shaped solid, with a split, or gap in it. The gap is filled with a non-magnetic material, usually glass or aluminum oxide, so that a leakage field is forced across it when data is written. The core is mounted on a slider that has carefully shaped surfaces to provide aerodynamic lift and stability. One conventional head technology uses a slider and core made from the same monolithic block of ferrite material; hence its name 'monolithic head technology'. Another common technology uses a composite structure in which the magnetic core is bonded to a non-magnetic slider. A monolithic head is built up of layers of ferrite. The resulting structure is machined to the precise track width and slider profile required by the drive. Ferrite is a relatively brittle material that fractures easily during machining. For this reason, monolithic ferrite heads have been supplanted by composite heads which also use ferrite as the magnetic path, but instead of a ferrite slider, the head is bonded to a very hard ceramic slider for greater strength. Glass is used in the bonding process to lend durability and thermal stability to the very thin ferrite head structure. Although many high-performance disk drives today use composite or minicomposite heads, the industry is rapidly switching to thin film head technology because it offers greater advantages. The magnetic head in a disk storage device flies over the rotating disk on a cushion of air. By balancing the aerodynamic pressure against a spring force, the head is controlled automatically to fly at a pre-determined height of less than 1 micrometer. Under such conditions, even a small particle of dust or foreign matter between the head and disk may damage both components (causing a head crash). In order to appreciate the size of the elements which affect this technology, consider that if the rotating magnetic disk were as large as a baseball field, then the magnetic head that flies over it to read and write data would be approximately the size of a single bed. Even at this scale, the height at which the head would fly over this 'rotating baseball field' would be less than the thickness of a sheet of paper. Any defect on the disk, like a sesame seed on a baseball field, would be likely to induce a data error. [ISO A magnetic head capable of reading and writing.] See **thin film head**.

read/write register [ISO Register that is used to hold data received from, or to be transmitted to, the bus.]

read/write slot [ISO An opening in the jacket of a diskette to allow access to the tracks by the read/write heads.]

ready signal [ISO Signal from a device to indicate to another device: (a) that it is ready to send or receive data; or (b) that the data transfer has been completed.]

real address [ISO The address of a storage location in real storage.]

real number [ISO A number that may be represented by a finite or infinite numeral in a fixed radix numeration system.]

real storage [ISO The main storage in a virtual storage system. *Note:* Physically, real storage and main storage are identical. However, conceptually, real storage represents only parts of the range of addresses available to the user of a virtual storage system. Traditionally, the total range of addresses available to the user was provided by the main storage.]

real-time Referring to transactions being made by the computer fast enough that records are activated or updated immediately — as external events occur. Real-time systems must be able to provide quick and precisely-predictable response times, and to communicate with the external sensors and actuators required by the application. Real-time applications provide the intelligence for robots, scientific and medical devices, flight simulators, automated factories, and many other devices that perform data acquisition and analysis. In contrast, batch processing is a technique in which transactions are collected into groups so that they can be processed or updated as a single job. Where large databases are involved, batch processing saves on computer time and avoids unnecessary computer interruption. Sometimes, batch processing is called 'dripfeed'. [ISO Pertaining to the processing of data by a computer in connection with another process outside the computer according to time requirements imposed by the outside process. *Note:* The term 'real time' is also used to describe systems operating in conversational mode, and processes that can be influenced by human intervention while they are in progress.]

real-time operation (In analog computing.) [ISO Operation in the compute mode, during which the time scale factor is 1.]

reasonableness check [ISO A check to determine whether a value conforms to specified criteria.]

reboot See **boot**.

recognition time [ISO The time elapsed

between the change of the value of a digital input signal and its recognition by a digital input device.]

reconstruction (Of data.) [ISO The restoration of data to a previously known or specified state.]

record A collection of related fields. For example, a doctor may keep electronic data about a client. The total information about that client is usually shown on screen simultaneously, and is referred to as a 'record'. [ISO A set of data elements treated as a unit.] 2. (In programming languages.) [ISO An aggregate that consists of data objects, with possibly different attributes, which usually have identifiers attached to them.] The word 'record' comes from the Latin word *recordari*, meaning 'remember'.

recording media See **media technology**.

record length [ISO The number of bytes, or any other appropriate unit, in a record.]

recover [ISO After an execution failure, to establish a previous or new status from which execution can be resumed.]

recovery [ISO A process in which a specified data station resolves conflicting or erroneous conditions arising during the transfer of data.]

recovery function [ISO The capability of a functional unit to resume normal operation after a failure.]

recovery time [ISO When sending or receiving pulses, the time required between the end of a pulse and the beginning of the next pulse. *Note:* The term usually applies to the equipment that sends or receives pulses.]

recto In printing and desktop publishing, 'recto' refers to a right-hand page (always odd-numbered). In contrast, 'verso' refers to a left-hand page (always even-numbered).

recursion See **recursion**.

recursively defined sequence [ISO A sequence of terms in which each term after the first is determined by an operation in which the operands include some or all of the preceding terms. *Note:* In a recursively defined sequence, there may exist a finite number of non-defined terms, possibly greater than one.]

recursive subroutine [ISO A subroutine that may invoke itself. *Note:* A recursive subroutine normally contains a call that invokes this subroutine directly or indirectly.]

red, green, blue See **RGB**.

reduced instruction set computing See **RISC**.

redundancy Duplication of information or components in an effort to increase system availability and reliability.

redundancy check [ISO A check that uses one or several extra digits or characters associated to data for the detection of errors.]

redundant arrays of inexpensive disks See **RAID**.

reel [ISO A cylinder with flanges on which tape may be wound.]

re-entrant program [ISO A computer program that may be entered at any time before any prior execution of the program has been completed.]

reference [ISO A language construct designating a declared language object. *Example:* An identifier.]

reference edge [ISO That edge of a data medium used to establish specifications or measurements in or on the medium.]

reference model See **OSI reference model**.

refresh [ISO The process of repeatedly producing a display image on a display surface so that the image remains visible.]

refresh cycle The cycle unique to dynamic random-access memory (DRAM) in which each bit-cell is recharged in order to retain data. DRAMs achieve their high density and low cost mostly because of the very simple bit-storage cell they use, which consists only of one transistor and a capacitor. The capacitor stores one bit as the presence (or absence) of a charge. This capacitor is selectively accessed for reading and writing by enabling its associated transistor. If left unrefreshed, the charge will leak out and the data will be lost. To prevent this, each bit-cell must be periodically read, the charge on the capacitor amplified, and the capacitor recharged to its initial state. The circuits which perform this amplification of charge are called a 'sense amp'. This must be done for every bit-cell every two milliseconds or less to prevent loss of data. Each column in DRAM has its own sense amp, so a refresh can be performed on an entire row at a time. Because RAMs cannot engage in a read or write cycle and a refresh cycle at the same time, some form of arbitration must be provided to determine when refresh cycles will be performed. Arbitration may be done by the microprocessor or by the DRAM controller. A counter, running from the microprocessor's clock, is used to time the period between refresh cycles. At terminal count, the arbitration logic asserts the bus request signal to prevent the microprocessor from performing any more memory cycles. When the microprocessor responds with a bus grant, the arbitration logic generates a refresh cycle. After a refresh is complete, the arbitration logic releases the bus. This method has several disadvantages. First, time is wasted in exchanging bus control, which would not be required if the RAM controller was responsible for arbitration. Second, while refresh is being performed, all bus activity is stopped; for instance, even if the microprocessor is executing out of read-only memory (ROM) at the time, it must stop until refresh is over. Third, bursts of direct memory access (DMA) transfers must be kept very short, since refresh cannot be performed while DMA is in progress. It is preferable to have arbitration performed by the DRAM controller itself. This method avoids all the problems described above, but introduces a complication. If the microprocessor issues a read or write command while the DRAM is in the middle of a refresh cycle, the RAM controller must make the microprocessor wait until it is finished with the refresh before it can complete the read or write cycle. See **DRAM**.

refresh rate [ISO The number of times per second at which a display image is produced for refresh.]

regeneration [ISO The sequence of events needed to generate a display image from its representation in storage.]

register A temporary hardware storage area that assists with the speedy transfer of arithmetic/logical operations within the central processing unit. There are several types of registers, two of which are located in the arithmetic/logic unit. The first is called the 'accumulator' because it holds all accumulated data, and the second is called the 'storage register' because it holds all the data that is to be sent to (or has been taken from) the primary storage. Two others are located in the controller. The first is the 'instruction register' which is used to decode instructions, and the second is called the 'address register' because it holds the address of a location which contains the data required by an instruction. Other general registers are also used to increase the speed of the computer, especially for arithmetic and addressing operations. Register-resident data can be accessed without running bus cycles, thereby improving instruction execution time and leaving more bus bandwidth for other processors, such as direct memory access controllers. The Intel 80386 microprocessor, for example, provides programmers and compilers with eight general registers; an additional eight registers can be supplied by an optional 80387 numeric coprocessor. Two other 80386 registers, which are oriented toward processor control and status rather than data storage, are also important to programmers; these are 'flag' registers and 'instruction pointers'. [ISO A part of internal storage having a specified storage capacity and usually intended for a specific purpose.]

register insertion See **time slot**.

register length [ISO The storage capacity of a register.]

rejection Common mode rejection. [ISO The capability of a differential amplifier to suppress the effects of the common mode voltage.]

relational database Like the network database, the relational database can define multiple and complex relations among different data. However, whereas the network database model predefines those relationships in a way that is efficient for the computer to process but difficult for the user to change, the relational database model pre-defines the relationships in a very flexible way, using tables. A table (also called a 'relation') is a collection of rows and columns. At each row–column intersection, a user can store a single data item (such as a specific customer's surname — Smith, for example). Each table typically contains many individual data records (for example, one record for each customer). In the relational model, relationships among data items are not physically stored. Instead, data is stored in tables, and relationships between two or more records are established by matching the values of fields common to those tables. The relational structure provides more flexibility than either hierarchical or network structures because data relationships are not pre-defined. To increase the complexity of the relationships that can be drawn among data in the database, it is relatively easy to change existing tables. Therefore, the relational database permits quick and easy maintenance of any database that is volatile — for example, one that is

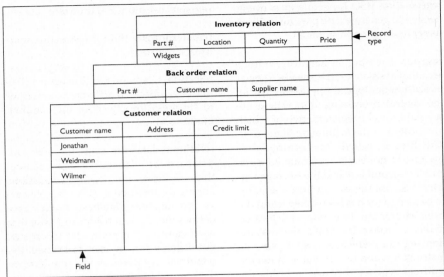

relational database This diagram shows that any relation may be connected to any other by a common field such as part number or customer name. A common 'ad hoc' query might be: 'List all customers alphabetically who have back-orders and who are over their credit limit.'

affected by tax laws or government regulations which are constantly changing. Relations can be re-defined dynamically to add, modify, or delete fields, because fields have an identity of their own. In most relational databases this can even be done while the database is in use, and the modifications are immediately reflected in applications that use it. The major relational database access language is called 'Structured Query Language' (SQL). This language is now an ANSI standard supported by all the leading database vendors. See **DBMS**, **hierarchical database**, and **network database**. ⚠

relational database management system See **RDBMS**.

relative address [ISO A direct address

that identifies a location by means of its displacement from a base address.] Compare **direct address**.

relative command [ISO A display command using relative coordinates.]

relative coordinate [ISO One of the coordinates that identify the position of an addressable point with respect to another addressable point.]

relative error [ISO The ratio of an absolute error to the true, specified, or theoretically correct value of the quantity that is in error.]

reliability [ISO The ability of a functional unit to perform a required function under stated conditions for a stated period of time.]

relocatable program [ISO An object program that is in such a form that it may be relocated.]

relocate [ISO To move all or part of an object program in an address space and to make the necessary adjustment of addresses so that the object program can be executed in the new location.]

remote-access data processing [ISO Data processing in which some input/output functions are performed by devices that are connected to a computer system by data communication means.]

remote batch entry [ISO Submission of batches of data through an input unit that has access to a computer through a data link.]

remote batch processing [ISO Batch processing in which input/output units have access to a computer through a data link.]

remote job entry [ISO Submission of a job through an input unit that has access to a computer through a data link.]

remote terminal A hardware device used to collect data at the source, and transmit the data to the computer (located elsewhere) for processing.

repeater 1. A device used at certain points across a communications network to regenerate electrical signals to their original strength and form, in order to increase the maximum transmission distance. Repeaters are required because signals lose their clarity and strength as they are being transmitted. This weakening (decay) is called 'attenuation'. The type of transmission medium used de-termines the maximum distance between repeaters. For example, copper wire would require more repeaters than fiber optic systems. Microwave signals are regenerated automatically at each station. Repeaters are used to link local area networks (LAN) at the physical level of the OSI model. They relay the physical layer data and control signals, thus extending the connecting channel segments directly or across point-to-point links. This interconnection requires that the segments are not only networks of the same type, but with identical protocols and speeds. For example, a repeater might interconnect two IEEE 802.3 CSMA/CD LAN segments, each of which supports such characteristics as 'Manchester encoding' (a data rate of 10 megabits per second, and a 50-ohm impedance coaxial cable as a transmission medium). 2. [ISO At a node of a local area network, a device that regenerates signals in order to extend the range of transmission between data stations or to interconnect two branches.]

repetitive operation [ISO The automatic repetition of the solution of a set of equations with fixed combinations of initial conditions and other parameters. *Note:* Repetitive operation is often used to permit the display of an apparently steady solution; it is also used to permit manual adjustment or optimization of one or more parameters.]

Report Program Generator A computer programming language introduced by IBM in 1964, intended primarily for small computer systems generating complex business reports. A more powerful version, RPG II, was introduced in 1970, and later, RPG III provided a very-high-level, nonprocedural language.

Abbreviation 'RPG'. See **programming language**.

requirement [ISO An essential condition that a system has to satisfy.]

requirements analysis [ISO A systematic investigation of user requirements to arrive at a definition of a system.]

re-run time [ISO That part of operating time used for re-runs due to faults or mistakes in operating.]

res. See **resolution**.

research network Since the early 1970s, several kinds of wide area networks (WAN) have evolved, including research networks (like ARPANET), company networks (such as EASYNET, VNET, and SWIFT), cooperative WANs (such as NSFNET and RARE), and value-added networks (like TYMNET and TELENET). Research networks were originally developed to foster research in computer networks, but many of them now support researchers in many disciplines. Research networks are usually financed and administered by government agencies. The following are well-known research networks: (1) ARPANET is used to support the interconnection of over 2000 hosts. Work began on ARPANET in 1969, and it was split in 1983 to form a military network called 'MILNET', which uses a layered protocol suite which is known as 'TCP/IP'. (2) MFENET connects over 120 hosts in the United States. It is used by those interested in magnetic fusion energy. (3) SPAN connects over 100 hosts and is used mainly by researchers in solar, terrestrial, and interplanetary physics. (4) JANET connects nearly 1000 computer centers throughout the United Kingdom. (5) COSAC supports over 27 hosts throughout France.

reserved word [ISO A keyword that may not be used as an identifier. *Example:* In Ada, all keywords are reserved words; FORTRAN has no reserved words.]

reset [ISO To cause a counter to take the state corresponding to a specified initial number.]

resident [ISO Pertaining to computer programs or data while they remain on a particular storage device.]

resistance Opposition to electrical current flow, without which there would be nothing to control or regulate the flow of current in a circuit. If resistance in a circuit increases, current flow will decrease because the opposition to current flow will be greater. Resistance is measured in units called 'ohms'. It has been found that voltage, current, and resistance are directly related to each other and that in a given circuit, if the values of any two of these three factors are known, then the third factor can be calculated. The word 'resistance' comes from the Latin word *sistere*, meaning 'stop'. See **Ohm's law**.

resolution The detail of an image (produced on a monitor or output from a printer onto paper or film). It is usually expressed in dots per linear inch (DPI). In monitors, the resolution depends upon the number of picture elements (pixels) that can be displayed on the screen. The higher the number of pixels, the sharper the image, and therefore the higher the resolution. In laser printing, 300 DPI represents acceptable business quality, and a minimum resolution of 1200 DPI is deemed essential for professional printing and publishing, and 2400 DPI is preferred. The *Guinness Book of Records* notes that 'Birds of prey have the keenest eyesight in the avian world, and large species with eyes similar in size to those of a man have visual acuity at least two times stronger than human vision. It has also been calculated that a large eagle can detect a target object at a distance 3–8 times greater than achieved by man. Thus the Golden Eagle (*Aquila chrysaetos*) can detect an 18-inch (46 centimeters) long hare at a range of 2 miles (3.2 kilometers) in good light and against a contrasting background, and a Peregrine falcon (*Falco peregrinus*) can spot a pigeon at a range of over 5 miles (8 kilometers).' Contraction 'res.'. See **dot pitch**.

resolver [ISO A functional unit whose input analog variables are the polar coordinates of a point, and whose output analog variables are the cartesian coordinates of the same point, or vice versa. *Note:* A resolver can be qualified as PR (Polar–Rectangular/Cartesian) or RP (Rectangular/Cartesian–Polar).]

resonant transducer See **transducer**.

resonant-tunneling effect A quantum effect used in high-speed transistors. The very first transistor, created by William Shockley and his colleagues in 1847, was made from gold-covered plastic and germanium. Today, manufacturers use advanced technology to create microscopic structures such as the superlattice which consists of many layers, each only a few nanometers thick. The crystal growth technologies used to form them include molecular beam

epitaxy (MBE) and metal organic vapor phase epitaxy (MOVPE). Of the superlattice's many properties, researchers are focusing on the resonant-tunneling effect. The effect causes the tunneling of electrons of a specific energy to increase resonantly when a quantum well is sandwiched between energy barriers. When a conventional semiconductor structure includes a barrier, only particles with energies greater than that of the barrier can pass through. When a quantum well is sandwiched between two barriers, such that the thickness of the quantum well, and the barriers are equal to the electron wavelength, then the quantum mechanical tunneling effect lets only electrons with a specific wavelength (equal to twice the well width) pass through resonantly. This occurs even when the electrons have a lower energy than the barrier. Proposed in the mid-1970s by doctors R. Tsu and L. Esaki, resonant-tunneling has been studied by major research institutes including Bell Laboratories and the Massachusetts Institute of Technology. Fujitsu has developed two transistors that use the resonant tunneling effect: a resonant-tunneling hot electron transistor (RHET) in 1985; and a resonant-tunneling bipolar transistor (RBT) in 1986. Both are ideal for use in computers as high-speed circuit elements. See **integrated circuit, molecular beam epitaxy**, and **RHET**. ▼

resonant-tunneling hot electron transistor See **RHET**.

resource allocation [ISO The assignment of the facilities of a computer system for the accomplishment of jobs. *Example:* The assignment of main storage, input/output units, files.]

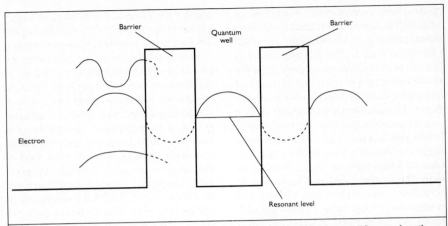

resonant-tunneling effect *In resonant tunneling, only electrons with a specific wavelength or energy can pass through the barriers. If the energy of an electron is too high or too low, the electron cannot pass through the barriers. Using this effect, a transistor can be given a negative voltage-current characteristic, and high-speed electrons can be injected into the base.*

Resource Interactive File Format. See **RIFF**.

response time The time taken between sending an instruction to a computer and receiving a reply. For example, in terminal-initiated transactions, 'response time' usually refers to the time that elapses from the last character of input to the first character of output. Acceptable response times vary according to the application. For example, a 15-second response time per transaction may not seem like a long period, but if this was the response time for seat reservation, at a busy airport or rail station, customers may complain about having to wait. [ISO The elapsed time between the end of an inquiry or demand on a computer system and the beginning of the response. *Example:* The length of time between an indication of the end of an inquiry and the display of the first character of the response at a user terminal.]

response time window [ISO In a token-bus network, a controlled interval of time, equal to one slot time, during which a data station, having transmitted a medium-access control frame, pauses and listens for a response.]

restart [ISO To resume the execution of a computer program using the data recorded at a checkpoint.]

result [ISO An entity produced by the performance of an operation.]

retention period [ISO The length of time for which data on a data medium is to be preserved.]

retinal scan verifier A biometric security device which is used to measure the eye's blood vessel pattern so that a positive identification can be established before entry to a computer system or a room is permitted. See **biometric security devices**.

return 1. See **carriage return**. 2. [ISO A language construct within a procedure designating an end of an execution sequence in the procedure. *Note:* Usually the execution sequence continues from the point of the procedure call.]

return-to-reference recording [ISO The magnetic recording of bits such that the patterns of magnetization used to represent zeros and ones occupy only part of the storage cell; the remainder of the cell is magnetized to a reference condition.]

return-to-zero recording [ISO Return-to-reference recording in which the reference condition is the absence of magnetization.]

reverse channel On some asynchronous modems, referring to the transmission of a 'circuit assurance' signal over a two-wire dial-up line in a direction opposite to that of the data flow. The feature gives the secondary receiving station notification of any error conditions as they arise. Generally, use of this technique is limited to remote stations that do not have the ability to communicate error status by line protocol. An example of this application would be a remote printer which uses the reverse channel signal to indicate that the printer's buffer is about to overflow or a paper-out condition exists. With reverse channel operation, two channels (primary and secondary) may be in use simultaneously. The primary channel carries the data, while the secondary channel carries the assurance signal. These reverse channel modems normally transmit data over the primary channel at 1200 bits per second and use a standard 1200-hertz signal for a mark and a 220-hertz signal for a space. The second channel used for signaling error

conditions uses a 387-hertz frequency, which is far below the mark and space frequencies. This signal cannot exceed five baud, meaning that it cannot be turned on and off more than five times per second. Reverse channel modems must also incorporate a feature which allows them to disable the echo suppressors that may be present on toll trunks. The telephone company echo suppressors are designed to drop out if a frequency between 2010 and 2240 hertz is transmitted for 400 milliseconds. Reverse channel modems will transmit a 2025-hertz signal for 3.5 seconds.

rewind [ISO To bring a magnetic tape or punched tape back to its starting position.]

RFI Radio frequency interference. Computer equipment and computer peripherals can cause interference with other signals in the radio frequency spectrum due to the electromagnetic radiation typically caused by all electronic devices. RFI is usually regulated to avoid excessive interference with radio and television signals.

RGB Red, green, blue; usually refers to digital color monitors which accept separate video inputs for the red, green, and blue display guns for sharper on-screen images. See **color monitor**.

RHEED Reflection high-energy electron diffraction. See **molecular beam epitaxy**.

RHET Resonant-tunneling hot electron transistor. A logic circuit developed by Fujitsu, an RHET is a superlattice device utilizing hot electrons emitted from superlattice crystals. The resonant-tunneling effect gives the RHET a distinctive characteristic, enabling a current to run in it only when a signal of a certain voltage is applied. This characteristic makes the RHET multifunctional, and reduces the number of transistors needed in logic circuits. A triple-input, majority logic circuit, of a type usually used for generating the carry signal in full adders, was also fabricated. Use of the RHET permits an extremely simple circuit design. In the design, the negative differential resistance of RHET-1 is used to discriminate whether the number of 'high' inputs is more than one or less. RHET-2 acts as an amplifier, while RHET-3 is a buffer that drives the next stage. Continued research in this field will enable Fujitsu to build significantly smaller and faster integrated circuits with less power drain. Pronounced 'are-het'. See **integrated circuit** and **resonant-tunneling effect**.

RIFF Resource Interactive File Format; a platform-independent multimedia specification published in 1990 by Microsoft and others. It allows audio, image, animation, and other multimedia elements to be stored in a common format.

rightsizing The re-scaling of an organization's information technology system to fit precise needs. Downsizing refers to the move away from mainframe and minicomputer environments to smaller platforms such as departmental servers and personal computers. Downsizing does not necessarily make mainframe computing obsolete. It re-assigns them to compute-sensitive functions to which they are best suited. Upsizing has become prevalent as organizations replace their earlier generation desktop systems with modern higher-performance, lower-cost hardware platforms. Upsizing is

taking place both on the users' desktops and at departmental or group computing levels, because users are moving beyond personal productivity applications to information sharing between multiple applications which may reside on systems anywhere in the enterprise. These new applications, which allow users to share information, are referred to as 'groupware'.

ring latency [ISO In a token-ring network, the time, measured in bit times at the data transmission rate, required for a signal to propagate once around the ring. *Note:* The ring latency includes the signal propagation delay through the ring medium, including drop cables, plus the sum of propagation delays through each data station connected to the token-ring network.]

ring network [ISO A network in which every node has exactly two branches connected to it and in which there are exactly two paths between any two nodes. *Note:* The nodes are all on the closed line.] See **ring topology**.

ring topology In a local area network, a ring topology is one in which each device is connected in a series to form a closed loop — usually via telephone lines. Because a host computer is not required, ring topologies perform distributed data processing, meaning each device performs its own processing. Typically, minicomputers share data, programs, and processing loads. When one device requests information from a computer in the network, data cannot be sent directly to the requesting device, but must travel in a loop around the ring in a serial bit stream along a unidirectional path until it reaches its destination. Not all ring networks are configured with the same brand of computer, and for this reason communication errors may occur due to incompatibilities. However, a break in the cable is easily detected. Ring topology is particularly suited to fiber optics, and is easily expandable. Messages circulate on the ring in only one direction and are regenerated as they pass through each station. In some ring designs, the destination station removes the message frame, while in others it is removed by the transmitting station after being copied by the destination station. Signal clocking can be passed from station to station from a central source or generated at each station. Rings have a number of advantages as a network architecture, but have not been popular until recently because of the added complexity and cost of the station electronics and the ring architecture. Among the architecture's benefits are high data transfer rates, large connectivity (number of stations), large physical extent (network size), reliability (ease of fault isolation), performance stability under load, and the uncomplicated use of a fiber optic medium. While a simple ring is subject to the same failure modes as a bus topology, the monitoring functions performed by each ring station can immediately pinpoint a fault for repair. However, the network must still be brought down to effect repairs. On the other hand, a star-wired ring using bypass switches, concentrators, and a dual counter-rotating ring arrangement circumvents the failed node during both detection and repair. Bypasses in the wiring concentrators permit a wraparound function, cross-linking the redundant ring to the primary ring on both sides of the fault. This function

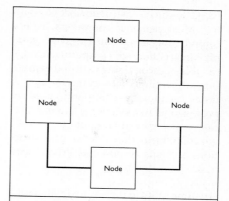

ring topology A ring topology forms a continuous, closed path composed of a series of point-to-point links in which each station is connected to exactly two other stations. Messages circulate on a ring in only one direction and are regenerated as they pass through each station. Among some of the benefits of a ring topology are high data transmission rates, large connectivity (station number), large physical extent (network size), reliability (ease of fault isolation), performance stability under load, and the uncomplicated use of a fiber optic medium.

isolates the cable fault between concentrators while still serving every station on the newly-configured ring. During repair, the network can continue to operate. See **topology**. Compare **bus topology** and **star topology**. ⚠

RIP Raster image processor; the device that interprets the instructions of a page description language (such as Post-Script) and composes the image to the photo-sensitive drum of a laser printer. See **laser printer** and **PostScript**.

ripple carry [ISO In parallel addition, a carry which is produced in one digit place as a result of addition for that digit place and which is propagated to the next high-order digit place.]

RISC Reduced instruction set computing. Most personal computers have a central processing unit based on complex instruction set computing (CISC), capable of recognizing over 100 instructions for immediate computation. A faster technology commonly used in professional workstations, and more recently in personal computers, is RISC, which reduces the number of instructions as much as possible. Pronounced 'risk'. ▼

rise time [ISO In the approximation of a step function, the time required for a signal to change from a specified low value to a specified high value. *Note:* Usually these values are 10% and 90% of the step height.]

RJ connectors US standard connectors used with telephone systems. They are also called 'modular connectors'.

RJE Remote job entry.

RLE Run length encoding; a method of data compression. For example, Micro-

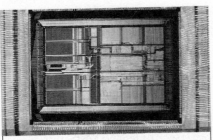

RISC The MIPS R4400 RISC processor delivers immense computing power. A RISC chip is cheaper to produce and debug, and is designed to run up to 75% faster than a CISC chip. RISC technology incorporates more than a million transistors into the microprocessor chip and processes data 64 bits at a time.

soft's video compression algorithm for base-level multimedia PCs uses RLE by compressing 8-bit sequences. Playback is also in 8 bit and is not scalable for higher-performance personal computers.

robot 1. See **robotics**. 2. Robot eye. See **vision systems**.

robotics The technological study of the design, construction, and use of robots. Any programmable and multifunctional machine which is operated by electronic integrated circuits can be called a 'robot'. Robotics is commonly used in motor vehicle manufacturing plants, or in harsh working environments (such as coal mines and radioactive zones). As an artificial intelligence application, robotics plays an important role in computer-aided manufacturing. Robots equipped with vision systems can 'see' or assess distances and shapes by scanning the immediate environment. Applications for robots extend beyond the factory floor to medicine, where scientists are working to develop miniature robots which can be implanted into the human bloodstream to unblock arteries and clean lungs. The ultimate robot would be one indistinguishable from a human in terms of looks, behavior, and/or thinking patterns and judgment. In 1990, Fujitsu released new software based on an artificial neural network model of the cerebellum in order to enable robots to 'learn' faster. The multilayered network includes golgi cells modeled on those that exist in the granule cell layer of the cerebellum. Golgi cells are responsible for pattern separation, and have been observed to monitor the activities of both mossy and parallel fibers. In the artificial network, a golgi cell is excited

R

robotics Science fiction stories describe robots as human-like in shape and movement, but some of the most successful robots used in manufacturing look like normal machinery. Any programmable and multifunctional machine which is operated by electronic integrated circuits can be called a 'robot'. This photograph shows a robot arm in a Texas Instruments' manufacturing process.

by both the first-layer and second-layer neurons. It also inhibits the granule cells and regulates activity in the second-layer neuron. The word 'robotics' comes from 'robot' + '-ics', where 'robot' comes from Czech *robotnik*, meaning 'slave labor' (coined by Capek in the play *R.U.R.*). See **artificial intelligence, human brain**, and **vision systems**. ⚠

roll 1. (Roll in.) [ISO To restore to main storage the sets of data that were previously rolled out.] 2. (Roll out.) [ISO To transfer sets of data, such as files or computer programs of various sizes, from main storage to auxiliary storage for the purpose of freeing main storage for another use.]

rollback The act of removing the updates of a transaction. Rollback (or 'backout') is usually performed when a transaction has aborted.

rolling [ISO Scrolling restricted to an upward or downward direction.]

ROM 1. Read-only memory. Hardware used to store permanent instructions for the computer's general housekeeping operations. A user can read and use the data stored in ROM, but cannot change them. ROM is stored on a nonvolatile memory chip, enabling the information to be retained, even after the power has been switched off. When a computer is turned on, ROM supplies a series of instructions to the central processing unit (CPU) which in turn performs a series of tests. As one of the first tests, all random-access memory (RAM) locations are checked to verify their ability to store data. Several other electronic components are tested, including the keyboard, the timer circuit, and the CPU itself. Pronounced 'rom'. Compare **RAM**. 2. [ISO A storage device in which data, under normal conditions, can only be read.]

rotary positioner See **positioner**.

rotation (In computer graphics.) [ISO Turning display elements about a fixed axis.]

rotational latency In magnetic disk technology, the time elapsed between the completion of a seek and the beginning of a data transfer. It occurs because at seek completion, the target starting sector is generally not directly at the head. At the end of the seek, the target data may be the next to pass the selected head. Alternatively, it may have just passed, and not be available again for a full revolution. If the rotational latency of a large number of random input/output commands is averaged, the result is half the drive's revolution time. While various mechanisms can improve seek performance, rotational latency is much more difficult to optimize for a single drive. See **average seek time**.

rotational position sensing [ISO A technique for continuously monitoring a disk position to indicate the position currently available for reading and writing. *Note:* This technique uses continuous comparison of the read/write head position with appropriate synchronization signals.]

round [ISO To delete or omit one or more of the least significant digits in a positional representation and to adjust the part retained in accordance with some specified rule. *Notes:* (a) The purpose of rounding is usually to limit the precision of the numeral or to reduce the number of characters in the numeral, or to do both these things. (b) The most common arithmetic forms of rounding are rounding down, rounding up, and rounding off.]

round down [ISO To round, making no adjustment to the part of the numeral that is retained. *Example:* The numerals 12.6375 and 15.0625, when rounded down to two decimal places, become 12.63 and 15.06, respectively. *Notes:* (a) If a numeral is rounded down, its absolute value is not increased. (b) Rounding down is a form of truncation.]

round down function [ISO The function that allows the elimination in the result of the calculation of all digits beyond the least significant digit.]

round off 1. [ISO To round, adjusting the part of the numeral retained by adding one to the least significant of its digits and executing any necessary carries, if and only if the most significant of the digits deleted was equal to or greater than half the radix of its digit place. *Example:* The numerals 12.6375 and

15.0625, when rounded off to two decimal places, become 12.64 and 15.06, respectively.] 2. [ISO To round, adjusting the part of the numeral retained by adding one to the least significant of its digits and executing any necessary carries if: (a) The most significant of the digits deleted was greater than half the radix of that digit place. (b) The most significant of the digits deleted was equal to half the radix, and one or more of the following digits were greater than zero. (c) The most significant of the digits deleted was equal to half the radix, all the following digits were equal to zero, and the least significant of digits retained was odd. *Example:* The numerals 12.6375 and 15.0625, when rounded off to three decimal places, become 12.638 and 15.063, respectively.]

round-off function [ISO The function that allows the adding of one to the least significant digit in the result of a calculation together with the necessary carries, where the subsequent digit in the result is 5 or above; where the subsequent digit is 4 or below, the least significant digit remains unchanged.]

round-trip propagation time [ISO Twice the time required for a bit to travel between the two most distant data stations in a bus network. *Note:* In a network using carrier sense, each frame must be long enough so that a collision or jam signal may be detected by the transmitting station while this frame is being transmitted. Its minimum length is therefore determined by the round-trip propagation time.]

round up [ISO To round, adjusting the part of the numeral that is retained by adding one to the least significant of its

digits and executing any necessary carries, if and only if one or more non-zero digits have been deleted. Example: The numerals 12.6375 and 15.0625, when rounded up to two decimal places, become 12.64 and 15.06, respectively. Note: If a numeral is rounded up, its absolute value is not decreased.]

round-up function [ISO The function that allows the adding of one to the least significant digit in the result of a calculation together with the necessary carries, if any, of the highest decimal places dropped off has a value of more than zero.]

router In local area networks (LANs), routers are used to transfer data packets from a particular station on a LAN to a remote station that is attached to another LAN. LANs connected by routers do not have to operate at the same speed. The transmitting or 'local' station must know that the destination station is not on the same LAN. The transmitting station sends the message to the router, which acts as a store-and-forward message relay system. Routers must use an inter-

router An intermediary device used in local area networks (LANs) to ensure that messages are delivered to the right place via the fastest or most efficient route. Routers may also be used to link several LANs together, and to send and receive messages from each LAN.

network protocol that is recognized by the attached LANs. The router approach allows for the interconnection of two or more physically-distinct networks through the implementation of OSI layer 3 protocol. The constituent networks are not contained at the physical layer and data link layer. The router contains one common network address that is known to all attached networks. The local station only sends specific messages to the router for onward transmission, based upon control information that the transmitting local station first includes in the message. The router uses this control information and its own control and 'routing tables' to pass the message onto the appropriate LAN. The message may pass through more than one router. Because the router acts as a store-and-forward system, considerable delays may be added to the time taken to transmit messages when routers are used. An example of the router approach is the selection of the ISO packet level protocol (PLP), which is equivalent to CCITT X.25, as a layer 3 protocol to enable the interconnection of distant IEEE 802.3 CSMA/CD and IEEE 802.4 token-passing bus LANs. ◮

routine [ISO A program, called by another program, that may have some general or frequent use.]

ROW Rest of world.

row pitch [ISO The distance between adjacent tape rows measured along a track on a recorded data medium.]

RPC Remote procedure call.

RPG Report Program Generator; a computer programming language introduced

by IBM in 1964, intended primarily for small computer systems generating complex business reports. A more powerful version, RPG II, was introduced in 1970, and later, RPG III provided a very-high-level, nonprocedural language. See **programming language**.

RPM Revolutions per minute.

RRP Recommended retail price.

RS 1. Record separator. 2. The prefix for all standards recommended by the Electronic Industries Association (EIA). For example, the EIA has developed a standard used in the majority of interfaces between data processing equipment and communications equipment, known as the 'RS-232-C interface' which is similar to the CCITT V.24 interface.

RS-423 A communications interface with greater sensitivity for a distance of up to 1000 foot (305 meters), longer than an RS-232 which caters for up to 50 foot (15.25 meters). By design, the RS-423 interface is compatible with most RS-232 hookups. RS-423 is the standard interface for DEC (Digital Equipment Corporation) type serial communications, and it is becoming increasingly popular with newer serial communicating products.

RS-422 A high-speed serial interface used to connect data communications equipment (such as the Apple Macintosh). RS-422 governs the asynchronous transmission of computer data at speeds of up to 920 000 bits per second. The RS-422 standard is defined by the Electronic Industries Association.

RS-232 A standard which defines the physical and electrical interface used to connect data communications equipment and data terminal equipment. This is the most commonly-used interface, especially between modems and computers.

RS-232-C A low-speed serial interface used to connect data communications equipment (like modems and terminals) defined as a standard by the Electronic Industries Association. All standards recommended by the Electronic Industries Association are designated by numbers with an RS prefix. RS-232-C is very similar to the CCITT V.24 standard.

RSI Repetitive strain injury. Computer operators who perform repetitive tasks under stress may suffer from RSI and feel wrist aches, and sharp pains in the hands, shoulders, and neck.

RS170 The Electronic Industries Association's standard for the combination of signals required to form NTSC monochrome video. The color standard is RS170A.

RTC Remote terminal controllers.

RTL Request translation layer.

RTS Request to send.

RTV Real-time video.

rubber-banding [ISO Moving the common ends of a set of straight lines while the other ends remain fixed.]

run 1. Also 'job run'. [ISO A performance of one or more jobs.] 2. Also 'program run'. [ISO A performance of one or more programs.]

run length encoding See **RLE**.

running head See **header**.

R

s Second; an SI unit of time. It is the duration of 9 192 631 770 periods of radiation corresponding to the transition between the two hyperfine levels of the ground state of the atom of cesium-133. See **metric system** and **SI**.

SAA 1. Systems Application Architecture; announced by IBM in 1987, SAA provides a common programming interface, common user access, and a common communications support for IBM operating systems. SAA was created to help developers standardize applications so that software can function in different operating environments with minimal program modification and re-training of users. 2. Standards Association of Australia; formed in 1929.

SABS South African Bureau of Standards; South Africa's standards body formed in 1945.

SAGE Software Action Group for Europe.

salami shaving A form of computer crime which involves the unauthorized transfer of money from a group of bank accounts so that it can be deposited into the criminal's account. The amounts taken out individually are too small to be noticed, and could even be as small as the rounding off of decimal points in excess of two, yet they add up in total to substantial sums of money. Such transactions are usually the work of a bank official, and are often conducted automatically on a regular basis. Such crime is rarely noticed because most customers do not usually calculate their own interest.

SAM Security accounts manager.

sample [ISO To obtain the values of a function for regularly- or irregularly-spaced distinct values from its domain. *Note:* Other meanings of this term may be used in particular fields — for example, in statistics.]

sample-and-hold device [ISO A device that senses and stores the instantaneous value of an analog signal.]

Sanyo Icon Founded in 1984, Sanyo Icon is a subsidiary of Sanyo Electric. It designs, develops, manufactures, and markets high-performance mass storage disk subsystems used in local area networks, and a range of multi-user computers specifically designed for the Pick, UNIX, and MS–DOS markets. Headquartered in Anaheim, California, the company has an annual revenue in excess of US$3000 million.

SANZ Standards Association of New Zealand; New Zealand's standards body formed in 1965.

Saratoga virus A variant of the Icelandic virus. See **Icelandic virus**.

SASMO Syrian Arab Organization for Standardization and Metrology; Syria's standards body formed in 1969.

SASO Saudi Arabian Standards Organization; Saudi Arabia's standards body formed in 1972.

SATCOM In partnership with the French communications company MATRA, British Aerospace Space Systems has formed a joint-venture company called 'SATCOM International', and developed a medium-sized satellite communications platform called 'Eurostar', a mass-efficient satellite providing up to 2.5 times the power of the European Communications Satellites. SATCOM is the prime contractor for the four satellites required by INMARSAT. The French telecommunications company has also selected a variant of Eurostar for its

second-generation Telecom series. Two Eurostar satellites with payloads specially tailored for business communications were designed and manufactured for the American company Orion Network Systems, Incorporated. The spacecraft, launched in 1992, provides Ku band communications capacity for international very-small-aperture terminal networks and other applications. Studies are being carried out into inter-satellite links to avoid the need to 'double hop' for signals traveling to destinations outside the coverage zone of one satellite. New designs of antenna feed systems and selective shaping of carbon fiber reinforced plastic reflectors developed by the company optimize coverage areas, making the ground segment smaller, cheaper, and more efficient in operation.

satellite See **satellite transmission**.

satellite delay In satellite communications, the transmission time between the satellite and the Earth station, which could take a quarter of a second. This delay is also known as 'dead time' or 'propagation delay'. These unusually long delays require special equipment to ensure that the channel is not interrupted nor broken, because the receiving device may assume a termination of the link. See **satellite transmission**.

satellite transmission Data transmission via satellite relay stations which amplify electronic signals and retransmit them to other stations. Signals may carry voice, facsimile, data, or video. Communications satellites are usually positioned in a geostationary orbit, meaning they remain in a fixed position, usually 22 300 miles (35 000 kilometers) above the Earth's surface. From that distance, about one-third of the Earth's surface area may be reached. This area is called the satellite's 'footprint'. With three satellites in geostationary orbit, the entire Earth's surface can be covered. The first artificial satellite (Sputnik I) was launched into orbit by the USSR in 1957. Although it was not a communications satellite, it did pioneer future communications units like the United States' communications satellite, SCORE (Signal Communication by Orbiting Relay), which was launched in December 1958, carrying a pre-recorded Christmas greeting from President Eisenhower. The United States Army launched the first communications satellite capable of amplifying signals (called 'Courier 1B', it was launched 4 October 1960, weighing almost a quarter of a ton and powered by more than 19 000 solar cells). The first television signals were transmitted by Telstar, a satellite built by AT&T. Telstar could transmit either one television channel or 60 telephone calls. In 1963, Syncom was the first to reach a geostationary (geosynchronous) orbit, meaning it was at a height where the inward force of gravity balanced against the outward centrifugal force which kept it at a speed where Syncom would take exactly 24 hours to complete one revolution around the Earth — appearing to be stationary. A global communications system called 'Intelsat' (today formed by a consortium of over 110 countries) was launched in October 1966. The current system can carry well in excess of 12 000 telephone conversations plus several television channels. The average life-span of a satellite is approximately seven years. Once a satellite is launched into space, it cannot be returned because once it reaches the Earth's atmosphere, it disintegrates.

Modern satellites are fitted with small rockets used to correct their altitude should they wander off course. The *Guinness Book of Records* notes that 'The first artificial satellite was successfully put into orbit at an altitude of 142 miles (228.5 kilometers) and a velocity of more than 17 750 miles (28 565 kilometers) per hour from the Baikonur Cosmodrome at Tyuratam, 170 miles (275 kilometers) east of the Aral Sea and 155.34 miles (250 kilometers) south of the town of Baikonur, on the night of 4 October 1957. This spherical satellite 'Sputnik' (Fellow Traveler) 1, officially designated "Satellite 1957 Alpha 2", weighed 184.3 pounds (83.6 kilograms), with a diameter of 22.8

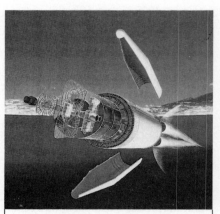

satellite transmission *There are hundreds of artificial satellites orbiting the Earth, many of which are out of order. In this illustration, a rocket is shown to deploy a telecommunications satellite 22 300 miles (35 000 kilometers) above the Earth's surface. It is interesting to note that the first dog into space was carried aboard a satellite called 'Sputnik II' (USSR). The dog, called 'Laika', made the journey 3 November 1957, but it never returned. The first American Earth satellite, called 'Explorer I' was launched 17 March 1958. The first moon satellite was launched 31 March 1966.*

inches (58 centimeters), and its lifetime is believed to have been 92 days, ending on 4 January 1958.' ⚠

saturation Some graphics programs allow the user to specify color using the traditional terms: hue, saturation, and brightness. 'Saturation' refers to vividness, or the absence of white in a color. It is the difference between pink and red, or between lavender and purple. The word 'saturation' comes from the Latin word *saturatus*, meaning 'full'. See **color** and **color monitor**.

scalar [ISO A quantity characterized by a single value.]

scalar processor A supercomputer which processes collections (scalars) of data simultaneously at speeds of 100 MFLOP. The common computer is known as a 'vector processor' because it can handle only single-dimensional items of data at any one time. The word 'scalar' comes from the Latin word *scalaris*, meaning 'ladder'. See **FLOP** and **supercomputer**.

scale [ISO To change the representation of a quantity, expressing it in other units, so that its range is brought within a specified range.]

scale factor [ISO A number used as a multiplier in scaling. *Example:* A scale factor of 1/1000 would be suitable to scale the values 856, 432, –95, and –182 to lie in the range –1 to +1 inclusive.]

scaling (In computer graphics.) [ISO Enlarging or diminishing all or part of a display image. *Note:* Scaling does not have to be carried out with the same factor in all directions.]

SCAM SCSI Configuration Auto Magically.

scanner 1. A peripheral input device used to assist in the entry of data into a computer system. In desktop publishing, a scanner may be used to digitize artwork or photographs so that they can be merged with text. One technique is called 'dithering'. This process separates the dots which form the image so that extra white space can be seen between the dots to simulate halftone images used by professional printers. A superior method which uses 16 shades of gray uses a technique called 'Tagged Image File Format' (TIFF). Photoelectric scanners are commonly used in supermarkets to read bar codes. They recognize the marks, and convert them to electrical signals which are then sent to the computer for processing. PETT (Positron Emission Transaxial Tomography) is a computerized brain scanner which allows researchers to see a color-coded 'map' of brain activity. Such technology can help identify manic-depressive or schizophrenic patients. Hand-held scanners are becoming popular for general desktop publishing. Although they are cheaper and smaller, their input quality is not yet suitable for professional publishing. 2. [ISO A device that examines a special pattern, one part after another, and generates analog or digital signals corresponding to the pattern.] ▼

scanning [ISO The systematic examination of data.]

scatter read The reading of logically-contiguous blocks of data from a disk, and storing them at discontiguous host computer memory addresses. Scatter

scanner *Using a scanner, photographs, line art, and other images can be digitized for desktop publishing and other applications. This flatbed scanner is being used for desktop publishing. Once the image has been scanned, it can be re-touched, re-sized, or manipulated as required by the user.*

reading is necessary in virtual memory systems. It is usually supported by a storage subsystem or host computer mapping hardware.

scavenging 1. A form of computer crime which involves the collection of information, usually from trash sites and garbage bins in and around high-security areas, in the search for clues to passwords and access codes to a computer system. 2. Reconstruction of the contents of a file after it has been deleted. This is done by examining the disk space it occupied.

SCC Standards Council of Canada; Canada's standards body formed in 1970.

schedule [ISO To select jobs or tasks that are to be dispatched. *Note:* In some

operating systems, other units of work such as input/output operations may also be scheduled.] The word 'schedule' comes from the Latin word *schedula*, meaning 'slip of paper'.

scheduled maintenance [ISO Maintenance carried out in accordance with an established time schedule.]

Schoolbook See **New Century Schoolbook**.

Schottky noise Unwanted electrical signals caused by the emission of electrons from vacuum tubes and similar devices, sometimes referred to as 'shot noise'. See **noise**.

scientific notation See **floating point notation**.

SCO The Santa Cruz Operation. Pronounced 'sko' or 'es-sea-owe'.

scope [ISO That portion of a program within which the declaration applies. *Notes:* (a) 'The scope of an identifier' is used as a synonym for 'the scope of its declaration'. (b) A language object may not be referable throughout its scope since it may be hidden by the declaration of the same identifier in an inner block.] The word 'scope' comes from the Greek word *skopos*, meaning 'target'.

SCRAM Static-column random-access memory.

screen capture Copying all or part of what appears on a computer screen to a program, and then usually saving the image as a graphics file.

screen saver A program which, upon detecting a period of inactivity, blanks the screen or displays a changing screen to prevent an image from 'burning' into the screen. Some screen savers can be set to request a password when a user wants to resume operation. Other screen savers

screen saver Now becoming common, screen savers are available in animated format. This one simulates a fish tank, and provides relaxing sound effects with random surprises, including run-away fish, fighting fish, and big fish eating little fish.

are used for cosmetic purposes so that a pleasant image appears on the screen after a period of inactivity. Screen savers may also be used in an office to discretly hide a person's work from passersby when a user is not working at the computer.

scrolling 1. The vertical movement of data that occupies more lines than can be shown on the screen at once, so that the rest of the data can be seen on the screen. The word 'scrolling' comes from the Anglo-French word *escrowe*, meaning 'to roll'. 2. [ISO Moving a window vertically or horizontally in such a manner that new data appear within the viewport, as old data disappear.]

SCSI Small computer system interface; an interface standard for connecting peripheral devices (such as hard disks and printers) to a computer system. For modern high-speed personal computers (PCs) to work efficiently with mass storage devices, there must be an effective means of transferring data between the device and the PC. The format and speed of this data transfer is determined by the type of 'device interface' built into the electronics on the drive and its controller board. There are four commonly-used device interfaces: Enhanced Small Device Interface (ESDI); the Small Computer Systems Interface (SCSI); the embedded interface; and the ST-506 interface. In contrast to ESDI, SCSI is not concerned with the device-to-controller interface, but rather with the controller-to-system interface. SCSI defines a special bus cable dedicated to data transfer between the PC and up to eight peripheral devices, each with their own controller. In addition to the electrical and physical characteristics of the bus, SCSI defines a series of commands through which devices on the bus communicate with each other. The system circuits for a SCSI interface are normally contained on a single board which plugs into one expansion slot. A special connector extends through the back of the PC, allowing for a 50-pin cable connection. This single cable, which functions as a data and control bus, can daisy-chain up to eight peripheral devices together (where the maximum total cable length is 80 foot (25 meters)). The SCSI specification is intended primarily for external storage devices. Theoretically, any device that supports the standard can quickly be connected to a PC with a SCSI port, thus allowing for the interchangeability of peripherals. However, each external device must have its own controller, power supply, and casing. Pronounced 'skuzzy'.

SCSI initiator Typically, a device which requests or initiates a command sequence on a SCSI bus (channel).

SCSI target Typically, a device (such as a disk drive) which receives and responds to commands from the disk controller.

SCSI-2 A revision on SCSI which provides some additional commands and some new options. Typically, devices supporting SCSI-2 are faster than those which do not, but this is a result of product evolution rather than any specific merits of SCSI-2 itself.

SD Single Density. Early magnetic storage disks used a digital storage technique called 'frequency modulation' (FM) that managed low-density capacities such as 90 kilobytes per disk (using large-grained magnetic particles). Sin-

gle-density disks have been superseded by double-density and high-density disks, which use much finer magnetic particles. See **diskette**.

SDLC 1. Synchronous Data Link Control; a communications standard controlled by the American National Standards Institute. See **framing**. 2. System development lifecycle; the many activities a systems analyst must perform when developing a system. These include five phases: preliminary investigation; systems analysis; design; acquisition; and implementation.

sealed data module A sealed data module is a unit wherein the access arm and the magnetic data disk are enclosed in one unit (a fixed disk). This is referred to as 'Winchester' technology. See **hard disk** and **Winchester**.

search [ISO The examination of one or more data elements of a set to find those elements that have a given property.]

search cycle [ISO The sequence of events of a search that is repeated for each data element.]

search key [ISO A key used for data retrieval.]

search time [ISO The time required for the read/write head of a direct access storage device to locate a particular record on a track corresponding to a given address or key.]

Search virus A variant of the Denzuk virus. See **Denzuk virus**.

SECAM <u>Se</u>quential <u>C</u>ouleur <u>a</u> <u>M</u>émoire; the television broadcast standard used in France, Eastern Europe, and some other countries. Its format is 625 lines of resolution at 25 frames per second.

SECDED Single-error correcting, double-error detecting. See **error-correction code**.

second 1. See **s**. 2. Referring to the next instance after the first.

secondary station [ISO In high-level data link control (HDLC), the part of a data station that executes data link control functions as instructed by the primary station and that interprets received commands and generates responses for transmission.]

secondary storage Units such as disks or tapes which hold permanent or semi-permanent data, sometimes referred to as 'auxiliary storage'. In contrast, primary storage is used only temporarily by the control unit (located inside the central processing unit, or CPU). Breakthroughs in CPU technology have always grabbed more technology press headlines than comparable achievements in storage, but storage systems have evolved just as dramatically over the past 20 years. Not long ago, users kept their data on punched cards and paper tapes, or on large, noisy magnetic disks. Today, those devices have been replaced by technologies such as thin-film media and read/write heads, optical products, and solid state disks. In general, these products enable users to store and retrieve data in less time. They use less floor space and power. They support more users, as well as the development of larger applications to solve bigger problems. They are more reliable and require less maintenance, and on a dollars-per-megabyte basis, they are

considerably more cost-effective. Also evolving are the devices that enable CPUs to access this new class of storage devices. Technologies such as cross-bar switches and intelligent input/output controllers have brought storage devices logically much closer to the CPU, allowing access times and transfer rates never considered possible. Information stored on secondary storage devices such as disks must first be read into primary memory before it can be accessed by the processor. See **compact disk**, **diskette**, **storage hierarchy**, and **thin film head**. Compare **primary storage**. ▼

second generation Referring to the transistor technology primarily employed between 1959 and 1964. A small electrical device, the transistor was developed by three Bell Laboratories' scientists who later received the Nobel prize for their invention. Compared to vacuum tubes, transistors do not need warming up, they consume less electricity, generate less heat, and are faster and more

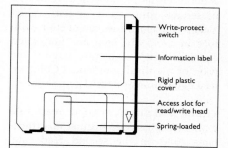

secondary storage This 3½-inch disk is a common secondary storage device. It is capable of storing 1.44 megabytes using both sides of the disk to store 512 bytes per sector (18 sectors per track, 80 tracks per side). Older models, still available, are capable of storing 720 kilobytes (per side) to store 512 bytes per sector (9 sectors on each of the 80 tracks per side).

reliable than vacuum tubes. Unlike first-generation computers which used rotating magnetic drums, second-generation computers used magnetic tape and disk storage for faster input/output, packing more data into less space. Having no moving parts, magnetic-core internal memory was used. Repairing second-generation computers was made faster and easier by using modular hardware components such as portable electronic boards. Related components were placed on different boards, so that the entire board could be replaced when a failure occurred. High-level programming languages such as FORTRAN and COBOL started to replace assembly languages, making programming a much simpler process. Elementary words and mathematical expressions such as 'A + B = C' eliminated the need for programmers to write endless strings of binary digits using zeros and ones. High-level business and scientific applications were being used. For example, American Airlines took advantage of second-generation computing and developed a passenger reservation system called 'Sabre' (developed in conjunction with IBM in 1962). By 1965, the integrated circuit began to emerge, paving the way for the third generation. Compare **first generation** and **third generation**.

second read rate A second read rate scanner is a bar code scanner that translates code on the second read rate, should the first read rate be unsuccessful. Abbreviation 'SRR'. See **bar code** and **programming language**.

sector A section of a disk in which stored information is located. Most industry-standard personal computers use sectors which can store 128 or 256 or 512 or 1024 bytes of information. The sector size is specified when the track is initially formatted by the controller. Each sector within a track is composed of the following four fields: (1) Sector ID field. This field, consisting of 7 bytes, is written only when the track is formatted. The ID field provides the sector identification that is used by the controller when a sector must be read or written. The first byte of the field is the ID address mark, a unique coding that specifies the beginning of the ID field. The second, third, and fourth bytes are the cylinder, head, and sector addresses, respectively, and the fifth byte is the sector length code. The last 2 bytes are the 16-bit cyclic redundancy check (CRC) characters for the ID field. During formatting, the controller supplies the address mark. The cylinder, head, sector addresses, and the sector length code are supplied to the controller by the processor software. The CRC character is derived by the controller from the data in the first 5 bytes. (2) Post ID field gap. This is written initially when the track is formatted. During subsequent write operations, the drive's write circuits are enabled within the gap, and the trailing bytes of the gap are re-written each time the sector is updated (written). During subsequent read operations, the trailing bytes of the gap are used to synchronize the data separator logic with the upcoming data field. (3) Data field. The length (number of data bytes) of the data field is determined by software when the track is formatted. The first byte of the data field is the data address mark, a unique coding that specifies the beginning of the data field. When a sector is to be deleted (such as when a hard error occurs on a disk), a deleted data address mark is written in place of the data address mark. The CRC character occupies the last 2 bytes of the data field. (4) Post data field gap. The field gap is written when the track is formatted and separates the preceding data field from the next physical ID field on the track. Note that a post data field gap is not written following the last physical sector on a track. The gap itself contains a program-selectable number of bytes. Following a sector update (write) operation, the drive's write logic is disabled during the gap. The actual size of gap 3 is determined by the maximum number of data bits that can be recorded on a track, the number of sectors per track, and the total sector size (data plus overhead information). The gap size must be adjusted so that it is large enough to contain the discontinuity generated on the floppy disk when the write current is turned on or off (at the state or completion of a disk write operation) and to contain a synchronization field for the upcoming ID field (of the next sector). [ISO A predetermined angular part of a track or a band on a magnetic drum or a magnetic disk, that can be addressed.]

sector interleave factor The ratio of the number of sectors traversed by a read/write head to the number of sectors written. For example, if the interleave factor is 5:1, then the disk would write to the first available sector then skip four sectors and write on the fifth, then skip another four, and so on. Although an interleave factor of 1:1 is optimal, manufacturers may set a higher ratio in order to slow down the data flow to ensure the computer can keep up with the fast rate of data transfer. See **sector interleaving**.

sector interleaving The initial formatting of a floppy disk determines where sectors are located within a track. It is not necessary to allocate sectors sequentially around the track. It is often advantageous to place the sectors on the track in a nonsequential order. Sequential sector ordering optimizes sector access times during multisector transfers (such as when a program is loading) by permitting the number of sectors specified (up to an entire track) to be transferred within a single revolution of the disk. A technique known as 'sector interleaving' optimizes access times when, although sectors are accessed sequentially, a small amount of processing must be performed between sector reads/writes. For example, an editing program performing a text search reads sectors sequentially, and after each sector is read, performs a software search. If a match is not found, the software issues a read request for the next sector. Since the floppy disk continues to rotate during the time that the software executes, the next physical sector is already passing under the read/write head when the read request is issued, and the processor must wait for another complete revolution of the disk (approximately 166 milliseconds) before the data may actually be input. With interleaving, the sectors are not stored sequentially on a track; rather, each sector is physically removed from the previous sector by some number (known as the 'interleave factor') of physical sectors. This method of sector allocation provides the processor with additional execution time between sectors on the disk. For example, with a 26-sector/track format, an interleave factor of two provides 6.4 milliseconds of processing time between sequential 128-byte sector accesses. To calculate the correct interleave factor, the maximum processor time between sector opera-

S

tions must be divided by the time required for a complete sector to pass under the disk read/write head. After determining the interleave factor, the correct sector numbers are passed to the disk controller (in the exact order that they are to physically appear on the track) during the execution of a format operation. ▼

security levels See **C2**.

seek time The time it takes the read/ write heads to get into position over a particular track of a magnetic/optical disk. This is one of the many factors which govern the access speed. [ISO The time required for the access arm of a direct access storage device to be positioned on the appropriate track.] See **access time**.

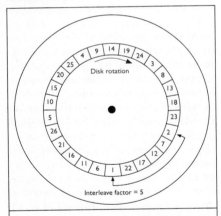

sector interleaving To calculate the correct interleave factor, the maximum processor time between sector operations must be divided by the time required for a complete sector to pass under the disk read/write head. After determining the interleave factor, the correct sector numbers are passed to the disk controller (in the exact order that they are physically to appear on the track) during the execution of a format operation.

segment 1. An operating system can organize the logical address space (of a microprocessor such as the Intel 80486) as a collection of variable-length segments. An operating system can define many segments or just a few, as appropriate to its view of logical memory; the 80386 does not dictate the use of segments, but rather allows them to be used as they support application needs. The extent to which an application program actively uses segments depends upon the framework established by the operating system. Segments are logical units that map well to programming structures, which are inherently variable in length. For example, a 1516-byte procedure fits exactly into a 1516-byte segment, as an 8-megabyte array (such as a 1028 x 1028 x 8 display buffer) fits exactly into a segment of the same size. By providing architectural support for segments, the 80486 improves the performance of systems that choose segments as a structuring mechanism. For example, segments can be individually protected, and can be shared selectively between tasks. An Intel 80486 segment can be any size from 1 byte to 4 gigabytes. For every segment, the operating system maintains an architecture-defined descriptor that specifies the attributes of the segment. These attributes include a 32-bit base address and limit (length), and protection information that can guard a segment against incorrect use. Application programs deal only indirectly with descriptors, referring to segments by means of logical addresses. 2. [ISO A portion of a computer program that may be executed without the entire computer program being resident in main storage.] 3. (In computer graphics.) [ISO A collection of display elements that can be manipulated as a unit. *Note:* A segment may consist of several and separate dots, line segments, or other display elements.] The word 'segment' comes from the Latin word *secare*, meaning 'cut'.

segmentation See **virtual memory**.

selection signal [ISO In a switched network, the sequence of characters that indicates all the information required to establish a call.]

self-test The series of testing operations performed by the memory controller when a computer is powered up to ensure that the memory modules are operating properly. The self-test reads and writes every dynamic random-access memory (DRAM) location several times. Any detected hard failures are logged in the control status register (CSR) and reported to the operating system. The operating system isolates the areas in which any hard failures have occurred by marking them as bad blocks. Bad blocks are then mapped out by the memory controller, allowing the system to operate normally, ignoring the faulty memory cells.

semaphore [ISO A variable that is used to enforce mutual exclusion.]

semiconductor An element or compound whose normal conductivity is between an insulator and a conductor, but whose resistance to an electrical current can vary depending upon its level of impurities. Examples of semiconducting elements are germanium, selenium, and silicon. Semiconducting compounds include antimony trisulphide, cadmium sulphide, and gallium arsenide. See **semiconductor storage** and **silicon**. Compare **conductor**.

semiconductor storage Data storage which uses very small silicon chips on which thousands of circuits are etched. The chip can be in one of two states — either conducting a current or not (on or off). This form of large-scale integration is reliable, compact, fast, and a cheap form of storage which uses very little power. It is also volatile, meaning that it will lose the data should the electrical current be interrupted. See **large-scale integration**.

separation corona When a high AC (alternating current) voltage is applied in a laser printer, the separation corona generates a field that neutralizes the electrostatic forces on the paper and photoreceptor, thus allowing the paper to be separated (or 'detacked'). A separation corona is sometimes called a 'detack corona'. See **laser printer** and **photoreceptor**.

septendecillion See **exponent**.

septillion See **exponent**.

sequence 1. [ISO To place items in an arrangement in accordance with the order of the natural numbers. *Note:* Methods or procedures may be specified for mapping other natural linear orders onto the natural numbers; then, by extension, sequencing may be, for example, alphabetic or chronological.] 2. [ISO A series of items that have been sequenced.] The word 'sequence' comes from the Latin word *sequi*, meaning 'to follow'.

sequence check [ISO A check to determine whether items follow one another in a prescribed manner.]

sequence control See **structured flowchart**.

sequential [ISO Pertaining to a process in which all events occur one after the other, without any time lapse between them.]

sequential access A storage and retrieval technique in which the computer must read through a sequence of data (or files) until the desired item is found. For example, data being read from magnetic tape cannot be accessed randomly (directly) because the tape must first wind to the desired location; if the information is at the end of the tape, this could take some time. This process is much slower than random access, which can immediately access data without having to go through all the files in every location. Random access (sometimes called 'direct access') differs from sequential access in that the computer knows exactly where to locate particular information; the time taken to do so would depend upon the storage medium used. The word 'sequential' comes from the Latin word *sequi*, meaning 'follow'. [ISO The capability to enter data into a storage device or a data medium in the same sequence as the data is ordered, or to obtain data in the same order as it has been entered.] Compare **random access**.

sequential circuit [ISO A logic device whose output values, at a given instant, depend upon its input values and the internal state at that instant, and whose internal state depends upon the immediately-preceding input values and the preceding internal state. *Note:* A sequential circuit can assume a finite number of internal states and may therefore be regarded, from an abstract point of view, as a finite automation.]

sequential file If files in secondary storage are arranged in a particular order (sequence), they can be accessed by going directly to the required file without having to read every file preceding (as is the case with magnetic tape reels). Sequential files each contain a unique identifier. For example, a social security number may serve as the record key, so that when records are being quickly searched, the key can be used to prevent all the data on the tape/disk from being read unnecessarily.

serial [ISO Pertaining to a process in which all events occur one after the other. *Example:* The serial transmission of the bits of a character according to the V.24 CCITT protocol.]

serial adder [ISO An adder in which addition is performed by adding, digit place after digit place in sequence, the corresponding digits of the operands.]

serial addition [ISO Addition that is performed by adding, digit place after digit place, the corresponding digits of the operands.]

serial card reader A card reader which reads punched cards from one side to the other, a column (character) at a time. A parallel reader is faster because it starts at the top or bottom of the card and reads all the columns at once (in parallel).

serial computer See **serial processing**.

serializer [ISO A functional unit that converts a set of simultaneous signals into a corresponding time sequence of signals.]

serial mouse A mouse (input device)

designed to be connected directly to the computer's serial port for transmitting data asynchronously (one bit at a time). See **mouse**.

serial number [ISO An integer denoting the position of an item in a sequence.]

serial port A connector on a computer (or peripheral device) that can send and receive data one bit at a time. On early personal computers (PCs), the serial port adapter was offered as an optional plug-in board. On modern PCs, these circuits come as standard, often combined on a board with other functions. When the PC transmits data, the adapter converts the data from a parallel format into bit-serial format required for transmission over a single telephone line. When receiving data, the adapter performs just the opposite conversion, from serial to parallel. The adapter circuits are also responsible for controlling the modem and performing some data formatting and error-checking functions. The serial port adapter is sometimes called an 'asynchronous communication adapter'. The word 'asynchronous' refers to the lack of a regular time interval between transmitted characters. In other words, characters can be transmitted one at a time. This is in contrast to synchronous transmission, in which data characters must be transmitted sequentially with no time gap between characters. Synchronous transmission adapters are also available for PCs. Serial data and control information is passed between the adapter and the modem over a standard connection called an 'RS-232 interface'. In addition to allowing a connection to a modem, a PC's serial port may be used for connection to a printer or for a direct connection to another PC's serial port.

These applications all require different cables that may not be interchangeable.

serial printer A printer (output device) designed to be connected directly to the computer's serial port for transmission of data asynchronously (one bit at a time).

serial processing Traditional serial processing methods use one central processing unit to carry out several instructions one after the other. The limitation of serial processors is that circuit switching speeds ultimately reach their limits. Their components on the microprocessor, therefore, are positioned closer and closer together so as to reduce the distance that electrical signals must travel. However, the generated heat becomes more difficult to dissipate. Parallel computers, on the other hand, distribute the processing task to a series of processors (nodes or computers) to simultaneously share the processing of a large task.

serial transmission Transmission in which data (binary digits) can be transmitted only 1 bit at a time using only one communications line. In contrast, parallel transmission sends each byte (a series of bits) simultaneously using separate lines. Typically, connections exceeding 3.28 foot (1 meter) in distance use serial transmission. A significant advantage of serial transmission compared to parallel transmission is reduced cost of wiring, since only one wire is needed. [ISO The sequential transmission of the signal elements of a group representing a character or other entity of data.] Compare **parallel transmission**.

server See **file server**.

server key A hardware device required

by software or an operating system such as Banyan Vines. It is used to prevent unauthorized duplication. Although duplication is still possible, the operating system or software it protects will not operate on another computer without the server key being attached to the hardware (usually to a serial port). Also called a 'dongle'.

server management The monitoring, analysis, and control of all aspects of server operation. Monitoring is the acquisition of data, analysis is the process of making sense of the acquired data, and control is the resulting commands. For example, a network manager can be alerted that a server on the network is down, access the server to run diagnostics, and determine that a memory error has occurred. The network manager, or the server, is then able to automatically remap the memory (to bypass the bad memory location) and re-boot the server.

service [ISO In network architecture, the capabilities that a layer provides to the adjacent layer closer to the end user. *Note:* The service in a given layer may depend upon services in layers closer to the physical media.]

servo control The process used in disk and tape drives to regulate positioning and seeking. Servo control relies on feedback of 'positioning data' from the media surface to generate correction signals to the positioner. Servo control may rely on a disk surface entirely dedicated to recording servo information, or servo information may be embedded among data blocks on all disk surfaces. See **access arm** and **head switching**.

session [ISO In network architecture,

for the purpose of data communication between functional units, all the activities which take place during the establishment, maintenance, and release of the connection.]

session layer The fifth layer of the OSI (Open Systems Interconnection) reference model. The session layer is responsible for establishing, managing, and terminating conversations between stations, and for mapping logical names onto physical addresses. Logging on and off a network is an example of a session layer operation. Dialogue may proceed in either full duplex or half duplex mode. See **OSI reference model**.

set associative cache These are less complex and are of lower performance than fully associative caches. However, because they are less complex, large set associative caches are possible. Set associative caches are useful because they can tolerate software that frequently crosses page boundaries of main system memory. Set associative cache organizations divide the data cache RAM into banks of memory, or 'ways'. A two-way set associative cache divides the data cache RAM in two ways. It sees system memory as logically broken up into pages. Each page is equal in size to the size of a way. Each location in a memory page can map only to the same location in a cache way. When the microprocessor makes a memory request, the set associative cache will compare the memory request with the tag entry at that page location in each of its ways to determine if the information is in the cache (a hit). This means that the cache has to do only one comparison for each way, for a total number of comparisons equal to the number of ways. While the tag and comparison logic of a set associative cache is much simpler than a fully associative cache, it is still complex. To handle the complexity, set associative caches are almost always integrated devices. While there have been discrete designs of two-way set associative caches, they are very rare and limited to lower microprocessor speeds. See **cache**. Compare **fully associative cache**.

settle time The time taken by the read/write heads to stabilize (settle) once they are correctly positioned over a particular track of a magnetic/optical disk. This is one of the many factors which govern the access speed. See **access time**.

settling time [ISO Following the initiation of a specified input signal to a system, the time required for the output signal to enter and remain within a specified narrow range centered on its steady-state value. *Note:* The input may be a step, impulse, ramp, parabola, or sinusoid. For a step or impulse, the range is often specified as +2% of the final steady-state value.]

SEX Systems engineers' expo.

sexdecillion See **exponent**.

sextillion See **exponent**.

SFT System fault tolerance. Novell's term for software which enables a network operating system to survive failures.

SGML Standard Generalized Markup Language. An application-, system-, and device-independent language for marking structural content of text. SGML is an ISO 8879 standard.

shadowing A mechanism for achieving fault tolerance, shadowing involves some duplication of processing. For disk operations, it means the duplication of updates to another disk volume or volumes. Shadowing implies some synchronization between a primary and a duplicated entity. The term 'shadowing' is often used to refer to duplication at the level of physical volume and is mediated by the input/output subsystem; as opposed to 'replicated database', which refers to duplication at the level of the database, mediated by the application program or the database management system. The term 'host-based shadowing' is used for file or volume shadowing which is controlled from the input/output supervisor component of the operating system.

shadow memory Shadow memory is sometimes used with 32-bit microprocessors which use only a 16-bit bus architecture for their read-only memory (ROM) routines. Shadow memory is an area of the random-access memory (RAM) which is set aside to temporarily store some ROM routines, thereby doubling such processing speeds because the RAM chip operates with the full 32-bit bus architecture.

shadow ROM Shadow read-only memory may be installed in some personal computers to boost overall system speed by copying the system BIOS (basic input/output system) and VGA (Video Graphics Array) BIOS directly into system RAM (random-access memory) at the time the system is booted. RAM typically runs two to three times faster than the ROM that holds the BIOS. As a result, the system's response to all BIOS calls is much quicker.

shannon [ISO A unit of logarithmic measure of information equal to the decision content of a set of two mutually exclusive events expressed as a logarithm to base two. *Example:* The decision content of a character set of eight characters equals 3 shannons ($\log_2 8 = 3$).]

shared variable [ISO A variable that can be accessed by two or more asynchronous procedures or concurrently executed computer programs.]

shareware Software which is protected under copyright and made available to users on a trial basis, on the condition that if the program is adopted, the user will forward payment to the author. Shareware is often distributed via mail order or copied from public bulletin boards. This differs from public domain software, which is available for use free of charge because it is not protected under copyright. Freeware refers to utilities and software programs (under copyright) that are made available to the public free of charge.

sheep-dip The testing of a file or diskette on a special isolated computer for any known viruses, or for any unusual patterns that may point to the existence of a virus. Some companies insist that all new files and diskettes be sheep-dipped using a virus-checking program for additional protection against viruses. See **virus**.

shelfware Software which is destined to do little more than adorn the shelf of the owner.

shielding [ISO Suppression of all the display elements that lie within a given boundary.]

shift [ISO The movement of some or all of the characters of a word each by the same number of character places in the direction of a specified end of the word.]

shift register [ISO A register in which shifts are performed.]

Shih, Stan Co-founder, Chairman, and Chief Executive Officer of Acer Group; Chairman of the Brand International Promotion Association; one of the five members on the Republic of China Space Program Steering Committee; a member of the International Advisory Board of the Multi-Function Polis in Australia; and an advisor to the IEC Eurasia Institute in France. Shih started his career at Unitron Industrial Corpora-

Shih, Stan Born in 1944, Shih is a graduate of the National Chiao Tung University in Taiwan. As co-founder, Chairman, and Chief Executive Officer of Acer Group, Shih was presented with the Engineering Medal in 1988 by the Chinese Institute of Engineers. He received the Hall of Fame award from the Greater Los Angeles World Trade Center Association in recognition of his individual and corporate contributions to world trade and commerce. In 1993, he was named The Most Outstanding MIT (made in Taiwan) Public Spokesperson for his efforts in raising Taiwan's image on the world stage.

tion in 1972, during which time he designed, developed, and commercialized the first desktop calculator in Taiwan. Later in 1972, he helped to set up Qualitron Industrial Corporation, where he led in the design of the world's first pen watch. In June 1976, together with four partners, Shih co-founded Multitech International Corporation which later became known as 'Acer' — an international computer company with sales in excess of US$4200 million. See **Acer Group**. ⚠

Shockley, William The inventor who started work on the first miniature energy-efficient transistor at Bell Telephone Laboratories in 1948.

shot noise Unwanted electrical signals caused by the emission of electrons from vacuum tubes and similar devices. Sometimes referred to as 'Schottky noise'. See **noise**.

SHPC Scalable high-performance computer system.

SI Système International d'Unités (International System of Units); an internationally-agreed metric system first approved in France in 1960 by the Conférence Générale des Poids et Mesures (General Conference of Weights and Measures). It is one of the most comprehensive published standards which is an extension and refinement of the traditional metric system. It uses only one unit for each physical quantity. Although there are numerous SI units, the seven basic units are: meter (length); kilogram (mass); second (time); ampere (electric current); kelvin (thermodynamic temperature); candela (luminous intensity); and the mole (amount of substance).

Any two (or more) SI units combined together form a 'derived unit' (such as a hertz used for energy; watt for power; and volt for electrical potential difference). In computing, it has become traditional to merge nonmetric, obscurely-derived words such as byte (binary digit eight) with SI prefixes to form commonly used measures such as kilobyte, megabyte, and gigabyte. Further complicating the issue is the fact that the metric system uses decimals (based on units of 10), whereas the computer uses binary numbers based on units of 2. This difference interferes with the use of the term 'kilobyte' because the metric meaning of 'kilo' is one thousand (10^3), but in computing, it refers to 1024 (being 2^{10}). Similarly, 'mega' means 1 million (10^6), but in computing a 'megabyte' refers to 1 048 576 (2^{20}) bytes. Another situation which compounds the problem is the inconsistency in usage and meaning of quantitative measures such as 'billion'. Many people are not aware that the part-Latin word *billion* in an American dictionary means 10^9 (1 000 000 000), while in a British or French dictionary it means 10^{12} (1 000 000 000 000), so terms such as 'gigabyte' (10^9) should not be referred to as a 'billion bytes'. Increased speed and storage capacity in computing may some day see the usage of the term 'centillion' (10^{600}) which, if not used in accordance with the international standard, could cause excessive errors and miscommunication because some dictionaries claim a centillion to be 10^{303}. This type of problem resulted from years of disagreement. Mathematicians and historians could not agree on the meaning of the Latin prefix *bi* as used in 'billion'. One school of thought supports the view that 'bi' means two, and a billion is the number 1000 with two lots of thousands after it

Symbol	Prefix	Multiplication Factor	Decimal Value
E	exa	10^{18}	1 000 000 000 000 000 000
P	peta	10^{15}	1 000 000 000 000 000
T	tera	10^{12}	1 000 000 000 000
G	giga	10^{9}	1 000 000 000
M	mega	10^{6}	1 000 000
k	kilo	10^{3}	1 000
h	hecto	10^{2}	100
da	deka	10^{1}	10
d	deci	10^{-1}	0.1
c	centi	10^{-2}	0.01
m	milli	10^{-3}	0.001
μ	micro	10^{-6}	0.000 001
n	nano	10^{-9}	0.000 000 001
p	pico	10^{-12}	0.000 000 000 001
f	femto	10^{-15}	0.000 000 000 000 001

SI *The prefixes shown here are used for 'derived units' such as 'kilometer' and 'microsecond'. These are used in addition to the base SI units.*

(1 000 000 000), while others suggest that 'bi' relates to the number 1 000 000 raised to the power of two (1 000 000^2), which results in 1 000 000 000 000. More than ever, the use of international standards is vital. The leading standards organization is the International Organization for Standardization (ISO) based in Geneva, Switzerland. Members of ISO include the American National Standards Institute, the French standards body AFNOR, and the Standards Association of Australia. See **metric system**. ⚠

side effect [ISO Any external effect caused by the execution of a function procedure other than that of yielding the result value.]

SIG Special interest group; a group of users who share an interest in a particular topic. Pronounced 'sig'.

SIGCHI Special Interest Group on Computer–Human Interaction.

SIGGRAPH Special interest group for computer graphics; supported by the Association for Computing Machinery. Pronounced 'sig-raph'.

sigma memory [ISO A storage device in calculators used to accumulate the results of a series of calculations.]

signal [ISO A variation of a physical quantity used to convey data.]

signal regeneration [ISO Signal transformation that restores a signal so that it conforms to its original characteristics.]

signal transformation [ISO The action of modifying one or more characteristics of a signal, such as its maximum value, shape, or timing.]

signature verifier A biometric security device which is used to store the dynamic characteristics of a handwritten signature so that a positive identification can be established before entry to a computer system or a room is permitted. See **biometric security devices**.

sign bit (sign character) (sign digit) [ISO A bit (character) (digit) that occupies a sign position and indicates the algebraic sign of the number represented by the numeral with which it is associated.]

sign change function [ISO The function that allows a reversal of the sign of the number held in a calculator.]

significant digit [ISO In a numeral, a digit that is needed to preserve a given accuracy or a given precision.]

significant digit arithmetic [ISO A method of making calculations using a modified form of a floating point representation system in which the number of significant digits in each operand is indicated, and in which the number of significant digits in the result is determined with reference to the number of significant digits in the operands, to the operation performed, and to the degree of precision available.]

sign position [ISO A position, normally located at one end of a numeral, that contains an indicator denoting the algebraic sign of the number represented by the numeral.]

SIGSMALL Special interest group for small computers; supported by the Association for Computing Machinery.

SII Standards Institute of Israel; Israel's standards body formed in 1948.

silicon A dark-gray, hard, nonmetallic, crystalline element found in common beach sand, rocks, and clay. After oxygen, it is the most abundant element in the Earth's crust. Silicon is not naturally found in its pure state, but as a compound with other elements, as with oxygen in silica. Silicon was first identified in 1823 by the Swedish chemist Jöns Jacob Berzelius. After silicon is 'doped' with chemical impurities, it becomes a semiconductor. A cylinder of silicon is sliced into wafers, and later up to ten layers are etched with a pattern of electrical circuits to form a 'silicon chip'. Unlike old vacuum tubes which had a high failure rate, silicon chips are reliable for over 33 million hours of operation. Common alternatives to silicon include biochips, gallium arsenide, and Josephson junctions. The word 'silicon' comes from the Latin word *silex*, meaning 'flint'. See **biochips** and **integrated circuit**. Compare **gallium arsenide**. ▼

silicon chip See **silicon**.

Silicon Valley In 1965, Santa Clara Valley, approximately 31 miles (50 kilometers) south of San Francisco, was dubbed Silicon Valley because it was the principal site of the electronics industry. See **silicon**.

SIM Society for Information Management.

SimAnt See **Maxis**.

SimCity See **Maxis**.

SIMD Single-instruction, multiple-data processing. In parallel processing, over 65 000 processors may be engaged to simultaneously share a processing task. Certain software manages this process by allocating equal portions of the raw

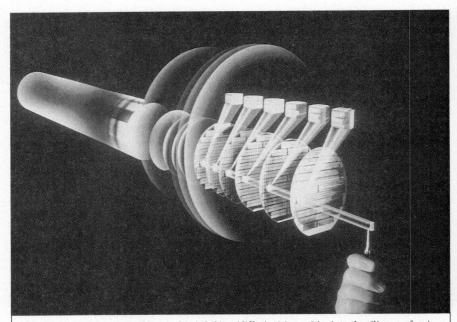

silicon *An early step in building a chip is baking (diffusing) impurities into the silicon wafers in a diffusion furnace. The impurities alter the electrical characteristics of the silicon, creating separate regions with excess negative or positive charges. To determine the flow of these charges in any circuit, the impurities are diffused along a pattern defined by previous photolithography and etching processing. The example shown in this drawing is the beginning (slice a) of a high-density memory chip. In this operation, the wafer moves to a plasma reactor where electrically-excited gases etch the surface into the pattern defined by the photolithography process. In this manner (slice b), trenches about three microns deep are etched into a wafer. The trenches conserve valuable surface area and allow the manufacturer to place a million capacitors and a million transistors on a single chip. Repeating this basic cycle (laying down materials, patterning, and etching) builds up the layers of the circuit (slices c, d, e). One of the final steps is to lay down an aluminum interconnect pattern that joins (integrates) the circuit components. The finished chips (there can be hundreds on each wafer) are tested, separated from each other, mounted in a frame, and wired to fit product specifications. The mounted chips are then sealed in packages of either ceramic or plastic to prevent damage and contamination, and to facilitate handling. Reliability is assured through a series of stress tests simulating operating environments and a final electrical test.*

data to the processors. Once this is done, it issues one 'single instruction' to all processors simultaneously. An even more common method used with parallel processing is multiple-instruction, multiple-data (MIMD) processing — a method of issuing several instructions attached to groups of data. See **parallel processing**.

SimEarth See **Maxis**.

SimLife See **Maxis**.

SIMM Single in-line memory module. SIMM technology involves soldering or surface-mounting individual random-access memory chips onto tiny circuit boards called 'carrier modules', creating a component module that can be plugged into sockets on a personal computer's system board. The key advantage of this approach is that the modules are simple to install (require no soldering) and occupy minimal space.

simple buffering [ISO A technique for assigning buffer storage for the duration of the execution of a computer program.]

simple variable A unit of data such as a number or a character string, which is not intended to be subdivided. It can often be manipulated as an operand of a machine instruction, and is often represented by a single storage extent.

simplex A method of transmitting information over a communications channel, in which signals may be sent in only one direction. In the simplex mode, the receiver has no means of responding to the transmitted signal. Simplex circuits would normally use a single two-wire circuit. Although not commonly used, simplex circuits are occasionally employed when a processor has a need to output data to a remote printer. See **full duplex** and **half duplex**. Abbreviation 'SPX'.

simplex transmission [ISO Data transmission in one pre-assigned direction only.]

simulation [ISO The use of a data processing system to represent selected behavioral characteristics of a physical or abstract system. *Example:* The representation of air streams around airfoils at various velocities, temperatures, and air pressures.] The word 'simulation' comes from the Latin word *similis*, meaning 'like'. ▼

simultaneous [ISO In a process, pertaining to two or more events that occur within the same interval of time, each event handled by a separate functional unit. *Example:* In the execution of one or more programs, several input/output operations handled by input/output channels, input/output controllers, and associated peripheral equipment may be simultaneous with one another, and with other operations handled directly by the processing unit.] The word 'simultaneous' comes from the Latin word *simul*, meaning 'at the same time'.

single-cable broadband LAN [ISO A broadband LAN that uses one cable for both the forward LAN channel and the backward LAN channel.]

single-cylinder seek time The time required to seek from one cylinder to the next. In the distance between two adjacent cylinders (typically one-thousandth of an inch or less), seek time is determined by positioner acceleration and settling time, or the time required for centering on the target track. Average seek time, on the other hand, depends primarily upon maximum positioner acceleration, with settling time being a minor factor. Single-cylinder seek time is a stronger indicator of relative disk drive performance than average seek time in applications which use sequential processing of large files, or high-speed data acquisition. DEC's RAxx drive, with an average seek time of 19 milliseconds and a single-cylinder seek time of 5 milliseconds, is representative of modern large-system disk drives. Generally, products currently available in the industry have average seek times of between 15 to 30 milliseconds for large-system disk drives, and 4 to 6 milliseconds for single-

simulation Graphic simulation is the emerging technology that was once the domain of military superpowers. The wizardry that went into the construction of flight simulators that cost tens of millions of dollars is now available on high-end desktop computers and minicomputers. The technology behind flight simulators is being used to simulate weather conditions, volcanic activity, and tidal movements. This is a photograph of a sophisticated flight simulator that offers unlimited flying scenarios.

cylinder seek times. Compare **average seek time**.

single density Early magnetic storage disks used a digital storage technique called 'frequency modulation' (FM) that managed low-density capacities such as 90 kilobytes per disk (using large-grained magnetic particles). Single-density disks have been superseded by double-density and high-density disks which use much finer magnetic particles. Abbreviation 'SD'. See **diskette**.

single-error correcting, double-error detecting See **error correction code**.

single in-line memory module See **SIMM**.

single-instruction, multiple-data See **SIMD**.

single- (double-) (triple-) precision [ISO Characterized by the use of one computer word (of two computer words) (of three computer words) to represent a number in accordance with the required precision.]

single-sided disk Early magnetic storage disk which could only record information on one side, offering half the storage capacities of those which can use both sides of the disk for read/write operations. Abbreviation 'SS'. See **diskette**.

single step operation [ISO A mode of

operation of a computer in which a single computer instruction, or part of a computer instruction, is executed in response to an external signal.]

SIO Serial input/output.

SIPO Serial input/parallel output.

SIRIM Standards and Industrial Research Institute of Malaysia; Malaysia's standards body formed in 1975.

SIS 1. Staff information system; a system that regularly provides staff with needed business information. This system can be manual or, more commonly, uses computers to analyze data and provide information. 2. Standardiseringskommissionen i Sverige; Sweden's standards body formed in 1922.

SISD Single instruction/single data.

SISIR Singapore Institute of Standards and Industrial Research; Singapore's standards body formed in 1969.

SISO Serial input/serial output.

site license A license from a software publisher which permits an organization to make a (limited) large number of copies of the software in order to equip multiple network users with rights to use the program. This is generally far cheaper than purchasing multiple copies of the package.

68040 See **Motorola 68040**.

648 virus A variant of the Vienna virus. See **Vienna virus**.

SKD Software development kit.

skew [ISO The angular or longitudinal deviation of a tape row from a specified reference.]

sky wave A type of radio wave capable of reaching long distances. To do this, short-waves must bounce off the ionosphere — an electrically charged layer in the atmosphere approximately 50 miles (80 kilometers) above the ground. Another type of radio wave is known as a 'ground wave'.

slash See **backslash**.

slave station [ISO In basic mode link control, the data station that is selected by a master station to receive data.]

SLED Single large expensive disks.

slider A rigid block of material upon which a disk head is mounted. The slider provides aerodynamic lift and stability. It also provides mechanical strength to the assembly. See **read/write head**.

sliding window protocol When used in reference to error-correction protocols, a protocol which allows several blocks of data to be transmitted before acknowledgment is required from the receiver. If very few errors are detected on a communications path, the size of the window may increase so that data throughput is increased. If a significant number of errors occur, the size of the data window may decrease to ensure data integrity and maintain throughput.

SLM Spatial light modulators, used in optical neurocomputers. Optical images are captured, stored, and read by the use of optically-addressable spatial light modulators which use ferroelectric liquid crystals (FLC). FLC–SLM can operate at 50 microseconds, with a spatial resolution of 40 line-pairs per millimeter. These enable a 1-cm^2 device to function at 3.2 giga operations (10^9) per second. See **optical neurocomputer**.

slosh See **backslash**.

slot 1. See **time slot**. 2. See **expansion slot**.

slotted-ring network [ISO A ring network that allows unidirectional data transmission between data stations by transferring data in pre-defined slots in the transmission stream over one transmission medium such that the data returns to the originating station. *Note:* In a slotted-ring network, a slot is a kind of frame.]

slot time 1. (In a CSMA/CD network.) [ISO An implementation-dependent unit of time which, in case of collision, is used to determine the delay after which data stations may attempt to re-transmit.] 2. (In a token-bus network.) [ISO The maximum time any data station must wait for a response from another station.]

SLSI 1. Sri Lanka Standards Institute; Sri Lanka's standards body formed in 1984. 2. Super-large-scale integration. The flow of electrons in chips is controlled by the transistors, which form switches or logic gates. Chips are categorized by the number of logic gates available. Super-large-scale integration chips exceed several hundred thousand logic circuits. See **chip**.

small computer system interface See **SCSI**.

small-scale integration The flow of electrons in chips is controlled by the transistors, which form switches or logic gates. Chips are categorized by the number of logic gates they have available. Small-scale integration chips, usually associated with second-generation computers, were the first to replace vacuum tubes, each containing up to four logic gates. Abbreviation 'SSI'. See **chip** and **second generation**.

Smalltalk A high-level nonprocedural object-oriented programming language (and environment) developed at Xerox Corporation's Palo Alto Research Center by a team led by Alan Kay. Smalltalk enables a word processing user to open a file by pointing to the icon or file (object) on the screen. This form of graphical user interface is now very popular. See **graphical user interface** and **programming language**.

smart card A plastic card (the size of a normal credit card) with an embedded microprocessor and memory chip, used for identification and storage of medical records and other personal information. The most advanced smart cards (sometimes called 'IC cards') have a small liquid-crystal display which, in the future, will be able to digitize versions of their owners' signatures, retina prints, or fingerprints. For this reason, smart cards may in future be used as high-security keys, allowing access to telephone networks, corporate data banks, and restricted buildings. The least sophisticated cards consist of little more than a simple processor and a small amount of memory. With a storage capacity 100 times that of magnetic stripe cards and the ability to manipulate information, smart cards are versatile, with the potential for many new applications because they are far more secure than magnetic stripe credit and cash cards which are vulnerable to fraud and abuse. Smart cards were invented in France in the mid-1970s. Unlike conventional credit cards, which are entirely passive, some smart cards contain a single chip which combines logic and memory, while others contain two or more separate chips connected by wire circuits. The logic portion performs 'intelligent' tasks, while the memory (originally 64 kilobits) stores information. Vital data, including cardholder account numbers, secret passwords, and financial information such as account balances are stored in nonvolatile memory. Most manufacturers are using either erasable programmable read-only memory (EPROM) chips or electrically erasable programmable read-only memory (EEPROM) chips, whose memory can be erased selectively and re-used. The International Organization for Standardization (ISO) recognized as early as 1981 that the smart card required international standardization if it were to be used in worldwide credit card applications. The TC 97 (information processing) and TC 68 (banking) technical committees have been working toward standardization. See **biometric security devices**.

smart machine Any device which uses a microprocessor to evaluate the input and make decisions about which path to take. For example, a smart car headlight can be designed to automatically monitor the level of external light. When it becomes sufficiently dark outside, the microprocessor switches on the driving lights, and continues to monitor the environment in order to switch the light off when the sun rises (conditional on the ignition system being turned on).

smart terminal Unlike a dumb terminal which consists of a keyboard and screen only, a smart terminal contains processing circuits which can receive data from the host computer and later carry out independent processing operations.

SMDR Station message detail recording. A feature of private branch exchanges where each telephone call is logged, typically by time, number dialed, and charges. The details are then retrievable by the network operator for cost charging by department. SMDR is sometimes called 'CDR' (call-detail recording).

SMFA Specific Management Functional Area; OSI standards which define network accounting, performance, and security management services.

SMI Structure of Management Information; an ISO standard which defines the basic identification and format of the network management data.

SMILE Shared Memory Interconnect for Local Environments.

smiley faces See **emoticons**.

SMM Intel System Management Mode. See **Intel 80486 SL**.

SMP Symmetric multiprocessing. The processors found in symmetric systems are functionally identical. Any processor is capable of executing any task and servicing interrupts. Operating systems designed to operate with symmetric processors divide the workload into tasks and assign the next task to the next available processor. Each processor typically incorporates a large local cache, enabling it to create its own copy of the task assigned to it by the operating system. Having copied the task/s into its local cache, the processor can minimize its need for access to the system bus. This reduces the overall load on the system bus, freeing it up to be utilized by other processors.

SMPTE Society of Motion Picture and Television Engineers.

SMPTE time code See **time code**.

SMT Surface mounting technology; before the introduction of surface mounting technology, all circuit boards were assembled using the dual in-line package (DIP) method. In the DIP method, the pins of a chip are inserted through holes in the circuit board and soldered on the other side using a wave solder machine. In surface mounting, the pins of chips, instead of being soldered into holes, are bent in 'J' or gull-wing shapes

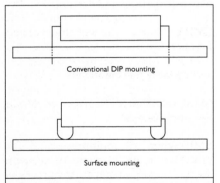

Conventional DIP mounting

Surface mounting

SMT Surface mounting technology not only applies to the physical mounting of chips onto circuit boards, but also refers to the research and development and the scientific and technical projects which are aimed at improving the applications and placement of the difference between securing chips via the conventional system and the surface mounting method.

and placed in position over pads of solder. The board is then baked to melt the solder and complete the electrical connections. Surface mounting allows a greater density of chips on a module because SMT chips require only half the surface area of the same capacity DIP chips. Also, the pins of the chips do not go through the boards, thus allowing chips to be mounted on both sides of the boards. Overall, approximately four times as many SMT chips as DIP chips of the same capacity can be mounted on a circuit board. ◢

SMTP Simple Mail Transfer Protocol; a TCP/IP application utility.

SNA Systems Network Architecture; a proprietary network that links IBM and non-IBM devices together. Introduced in 1974, before the OSI reference model was defined, it was originally a mainframe-centered hierarchical network architecture. SNA is an architecture or 'design specification' which defines the data communications facilities, functions, and procedures that are distributed throughout the network. It also defines the formats and protocols used to support communication between programs, device operators, storage media, and workstations which may be located anywhere in the network. Prior to SNA there were no formalized architecture standards nor guidelines for computer-based online data processing systems. See **SNA layers**.

SNADS Systems Network Architecture Distribution Services; an architecture developed by IBM to aid in file transfer among dissimilar IBM devices. Documents which follow Document Content Architecture and Document Interchange Architecture are sent via the SNADS.

SNA layers Systems Network Architecture layers. SNA is a proprietary network that links IBM and non-IBM devices together. Introduced in 1974, before the OSI reference model was defined, SNA was originally a mainframe-centered hierarchical network architecture. Each SNA node has six layers plus a physical link layer which defines the connection between nodes. Each of the layers of SNA has its own set of rules for communicating with its peer layer in the other node. The layers communicate with each other by adding header information to user data. The transaction services layer (seventh layer) is SNA's highest. It was formalized by IBM in 1968 to provide users with a single-system image into the network services through common command language formats. It provides the application services such as distributed database access and document interchange. The presentation services layer (sixth layer) formats data for different presentation media and coordinates the sharing of resources. The data flow control layer (fifth layer) synchronizes the data flow between end points of a session, correlates exchange of data, and groups related data into units. The transmission control layer (fourth layer) is responsible for session set-up and disconnection, and the overall end-to-end connectivity. It paces data exchanges to match the processing capacity at the end points of a session. This layer will also code data for security if needed. The path control layer (third layer) is responsible for the routing of messages and defines the class of services offered. The data link control layer (second layer) governs the transmission of data on a single link. This is where the synchronous data link control (SDLC) protocol resides. It initializes and disconnects logical links between adjacent nodes and it controls the transfer of data over the logical links. The physical control layer (first layer) defines the physical, electrical, mechanical, and functional procedures used to connect the equipment. This is where RS-232-C (or the equivalent CCITT interface) is located. See **SNA**.

SNAK Serial number activation key; an identification number or password that enables a user to access specific features or additional software stored on a high-capacity storage medium such as a CD–ROM disk. SNAKS are used in cases where a software manufacturer sends a demonstration diskette to a potential buyer and authorizes that person to use the software a limited number of times. After the initial trial period, the software becomes inaccessible until the user purchases the SNAK (password) that will unlock the disk. SNAKs are also used in cases where a software vendor bundles several software products onto one CD–ROM disk. The user would purchase the relevant SNAKs to unlock the other software programs available on the disk. This method of software distribution is convenient and cost-effective. However, hackers have already found a way to abuse the system and to access the software without having to pay the license fees.

SNMP Simple Network Management Protocol; used with TCP/IP.

SNOBOL String-Oriented Symbolic Language; a high-level programming language developed in 1962 at AT&T's Bell Laboratories for text-processing applications. It was created by Ralph Griswold, David Farber, and Ivan Polonsky. The version used for personal computers is called 'SNOBOL4'. Pronounced 'snow-bol'.

SNV Swiss Association for Standardization; Switzerland's standards body formed in 1919.

Society of Mind A special general intelligence study conducted by Marvin Minsky, one of the founding fathers of artificial intelligence. His concept is to connect several thousand expert systems together in an attempt to construct a general intelligence computer. Abbreviation 'SOM'. See **expert systems**.

soft copy [ISO A nonpermanent display image. *Example:* A cathode-ray tube display.]

soft error 1. [ISO An error that occurs sporadically and that may not appear on successive attempts to read data.] 2. See **memory errors**.

soft sectoring [ISO The identification of sector boundaries on a magnetic disk by using recorded data.]

software 1. A computer program; a set of instructions written in a specific language that commands the computer to perform various operations on data contained in the program or supplied by the user. 2. [ISO Intellectual creation comprising the programs, procedures, rules and any associated documentation per-

---

taining to the operation of a data processing system. *Note:* Software is independent of the carrier used for transport.]

Software Engine Borland's software product which allows applications to access common data. An engine is designed to be incorporated into a variety of different applications. For example, the Paradox Engine is built into Paradox, Quattro Pro, and Sidekick for Presentation Manager. It allows Borland products and programs written in C, C++, and object Pascal to access data kept in Paradox tables.

software flow control See **XON/XOFF**.

software house A business established to provide systems analysis and custom-designed or prepackaged (off-the-shelf) software.

software-intensive fault tolerance A fault is an event in which a system operates contrary to its specifications, although this may not always be visible to users of the system. Systems with software-intensive fault tolerance use hardware redundancy, meaning if a fault is detected in one module, that module is taken out of service while its partner continues without delay. However, unlike hardware-intensive fault tolerance, the hardware does not run modules in lock step (performing the same task at the same time). Instead, software-intensive systems run two or more processors that are loosely coupled with each other through checkpoints or shared data. The processors share disk and communication controllers. If one processor fails, then another can take over after a failover time of a few seconds.

NEWSFLASH

In 1993, sales of worldwide packaged software reached US$71 700 million.

In 1997, this figure will climb to US$116 000 million.

The checkpoints or shared data enable the other system to catch up quickly with the state of the failed system. See **fault tolerance** and **unscheduled downtime**. Compare **hardware-intensive fault tolerance**.

software package [ISO A complete and documented set of programs supplied to several users for a generic application or function. *Note:* Some software packages are alterable for a specific application.]

software piracy The criminal act of making or distributing for financial gain, an unauthorized copy (or copies) of a copyrighted software product. In most countries, the law prohibits such actions, but as with fashion accessories and books, criminal activity in the form of software piracy accounts for millions of dollars each year. Many computer manufacturers resorted to setting stringent protection codes in their software programs which limited the number of times a program could be copied, but this was phased out due to complaints from legitimate users who were disadvantaged by this. In the past, some computer viruses spread as a result of manufacturers placing logic bombs into their software programs. When unauthorized copies were made, a virus would be released onto the copied file. However, this method can also backfire. In most countries, it is illegal: (1) to copy or distribute software or its accompanying documentation including programs, applications, data, codes, and manuals, without permission or license from the copyright owner; (2) to run purchased software covered by copyright on two or more computers simultaneously unless the license agreement specifically allows it; (3) for organizations to consciously or

unconsciously encourage, allow, compel, or pressure employees to make or distribute illegal software copies sourced from within the organization or within employee's homes or from any other location, on the organization's behalf; (4) to infringe the laws against unauthorized software copying because a superior, colleague, or friend compels it; (5) to fail to disclose to law enforcement agencies knowledge that the law against unauthorized software copying has been breached, is being breached, or will be broken; and (6) to loan software in order that a copy be made or to copy software while it is on loan — including an individual loan to a friend or colleague. In Australia, for example, if an individual is found to have copied more than one article of software to which an offense relates (multiple copying of software), that individual can be fined for each copy made, up to a maximum penalty of A$50 000. For the same offense, a company may be fined a maximum penalty of A$250 000. In both cases, the figures quoted relate to criminal prosecutions. Civil damages are unlimited, meaning that in addition to any penalty which may be exacted for criminal offenses, the owner of an infringed copyright can sue the offender and also obtain an injunction. Some countries do not impose any upper limit to the amount for which the complainant can sue for damages in relation to intellectual property. See **BSAA**, **gray marketing**, **intellectual property**, and **virus**.

software theft A term used to describe illegal copying of software by a person or organization for their own use or for use by others. Organizations which consciously encourage or otherwise pressure or compel employees to make unauthorized software copies are committing software theft. Most software theft represents white collar crime and typically involves conspiracy and secrecy within an organization or company. Surveys recently conducted by the Business Software Association of Australia found that at least 50% of all business software products in use in Australia have been obtained in an unauthorized way, through unauthorized copying of existing software products, the importation or local production and sale of pirated versions of property software, or illegal gray marketing of proprietary software. See **software piracy**.

SOHO Small office, home office; refers to a market segment of the personal computer industry which uses computers in a small office situation, either at home or at the place of work.

solar noise See **radio frequency interference**.

solid state disk A secondary storage peripheral that uses semiconductor memory as its storage medium (rather than a magnetic disk) providing performance 10 to 30 times better than that of a magnetic disk. Solid state disks (SSD) provide a significant performance boost in environments where shared files cause a throughput bottleneck. SSDs are also useful in reducing bottlenecks in situations where the input/output system is constantly required to provide access to small amounts of data, such as application and system software control files.

sonar Sound navigation ranging. A device used to detect the presence and location of a submerged object (such as a submarine or underwater mine). Sonic and ultrasonic waves are used to hit the distant object, and bounce back (echo) to the transmitter for analysis. The development of the sonar dates back to 1916 when the British developed a hydrophone to locate German underwater boats by detecting the turbulence caused by the propellers. This technique became so sophisticated that through acoustic detection, almost every type of engine or propeller could be identified by its sound 'signature'. The early hydrophones could not detect silent objects, but in the 1920s, the British Admiralty developed 'active' equipment capable of detecting motionless submarines. It was called 'ASDIC' (Allied Submarine Detection Investigation Committee). ASDIC was later known as 'sonar', named after a similar American development. Because sonar signals were distorted by differing water temperatures, salt content, and ocean currents, nuclear submarines sought shelter beneath such layers. However, the development of the variable-depth sonar (VDS) has solved that problem.

SONET Synchronous Optical Network; a CCITT/ITU standard for digital telephony services over fiber.

sort To arrange data into a particular sequence. When sorting information in ascending (increasing) order, items are arranged from the smallest to the largest (1,2,3,4) or from the first to the last (a,b,c,d). Depending upon the software program, other characters, including punctuation marks and symbols, may alter the expected order, causing words like 'A/D converter' to be placed before 'abacus'. When sorting information in descending (decreasing) order, items are arranged from the largest to the smallest (4,3,2,1) or from the last to the first (d,c,b,a). Depending upon the software program, other characters, including punctuation marks and symbols, may alter the expected order, causing words like 'A/UX' to be placed before 'abacus'. When sorting data in ASCII (American Standard Code for Information Interchange), all capitalized letters or words are placed after lowercase letters or words. 2. [ISO To segregate items into groups according to specified criteria without necessarily ordering the items within each group.]

SOS Silicon on sapphire. See **silicon**.

Sound Blaster A common personal-computer sound card.

source code The set of instructions written in a high-level language which is yet to be translated (assembled) into machine language (object code). See **programming language**.

source data automation The use of special equipment (such as a bar code reader) to collect data at the point where a transaction takes place (source), and to send it to a computer for processing. This ensures speedy, accurate, and automatic data input.

source language [ISO The programming language for expressing source programs that a particular translator can accept.]

source module [ISO All or part of a source program sufficiently complete for compilation.]

source program [ISO A program that a particular translator can accept.]

South Pacific Network Designed to provide high-quality optic fiber connection for the South Pacific region, the South Pacific Network has the capability to transmit voice, data, text, and video to virtually anywhere in the world. Planning to finance the network began in the early 1980s by AT&T (USA), KDD (Japan), OTC (Australia), and TNI (New Zealand). A further 32 telecommunications carrier administrators from Europe, North America, and Asia joined the initial party on 5 December 1990 to finance the systems. The South Pacific Network combines with systems in the North Pacific to form a telecommunications loop. The network extends more than 10 250 miles (16 500 kilometers) across the floor of the Pacific Ocean at depths of up to 5.3 miles (8.5 kilometers). The system gives countries in the South Pacific access to the worldwide optic fiber network. It consists of three submarine optic fiber cables (PacRimEast, PacRimWest, and TASMAN 2). PacRimEast links New Zealand to Hawaii, with connections to North America and Europe. PacRimWest links Australia to Guam, with connections to Japan and Asia. The TASMAN 2 cable provides a high-quality digital telecommunications link between Australia and New Zealand, connecting PacRimEast to PacRimWest. Using a second-generation 560 megabits-per-second optic fiber cable (using 1550 nanometer technology), PacRimEast and PacRimWest provides 7560 digital channels (more than 30 000 voice circuits) each, and TASMAN 2 provides 15 120 digital channels (more than 60 000 voice circuits). This configuration allows for future service applications such as video conferencing, video phones, broadband ISDN, broadcast video, interlink for fast packet-switching nodes and other forms of high-speed information transfer. Each of the PacRim sectors has two fiber pairs (one for service and one for protection), while TASMAN 2 has three fiber pairs (two for service and one for protection). See **optic fiber technology**.

SP Symbolic processor; an artificial intelligence computer which represents and manipulates knowledge instead of data. A conventional computer is known as a 'numeric processor'. See **artificial intelligence**.

space character [ISO A character that causes the print or display position to advance one position along the line without producing any graphic character. *Note:* The space character is described in ISO 646, ISO 4873, and ISO 6937-1.]

space graphics As developed by NASA (National Aeronautics and Space Administration), a picture taken by a camera on a space vehicle or satellite which is converted into a group of dots, each of which has a certain color and density. The dots are converted into numbers which are transmitted to Earth via radio waves. The numbers are then re-assembled and interpreted by a computer to show a color picture of matter in space.

span [ISO The difference between the highest and the lowest values that a quantity or function may take.]

spatial locality The tendency of programs to reference information that is located in the vicinity of recently-accessed information. Data retrieved from primary memory is written to the cache, where it is then read by the processor. Any data modified by the processor is also written to the cache. The cache has very limited storage, so a replacement strategy is used to determine what existing data to replace from the cache when new data is read from primary memory. Cache memory design takes advantage of a principle known as 'locality'. Programs tend to exhibit temporal locality and spatial locality. Some caches pre-fetch data when a cache miss occurs. The process of pre-fetching cache data takes advantage of spatial locality. For example, if the program accesses location 'x', it will probably access location 'x + 1' in the near future. When a cache miss occurs, the cache pre-fetches fill blocks consisting of several word units. Pre-fetching increases the probability that future cache misses will be avoided by already having the data in the cache. The word 'spatial' comes from the Latin word *spatium*, meaning 'space'. See **cache**. Compare **temporal locality**.

spatial resolution A measure of how close together two events, pulses, waves, or faults can be distinguished as separate events. In optical neurocomputers which use optoelectronic integrated circuits (OEIC), optical images are captured, stored, and read by the use of optically-addressable spatial light modulators (SLM) which use ferro-electric liquid crystals (FLC). FLC–SLM can operate at 50 microseconds, with a spatial resolution of 40 line-pairs per millimeter. The word 'spatial' comes from the Latin word *spatium*, meaning 'space'. Also called 'distance resolution'.

SPEC Systems Performance Evaluation Cooperative; an international group of manufacturers of workstations, servers, and other computer systems who have resolved to work together to provide performance summaries based on results from a suite of standardized programs run under specified conditions. The benchmark (SPECmark) results are released quarterly by Waterside Associates of Fremont, California. SPEC was founded in November 1988 by Apollo Computer, Hewlett-Packard, MIPS Computer Systems, and Sun Microsystems. The current membership of over 21 vendors includes these companies plus AT&T, Bull S.A., Compaq, Control Data Corporation, Data General, Digital Equipment Corporation, DuPont, Fujitsu, Intel, Integraph, IBM, Motorola Microcomputer Division, NCR Corporation, Prime Computer, Siemens AG, Silicon Graphics, Solbourne, Stardent, and Unisys. The ten programs used in arriving at the SPECmark figures are described in this book under their alphabetical listing: doduc, eqntott, espresso, fpppp, GNU C compiler gcc, LISP interpreter, matrix300, nasa7, spice 2g6, tomcatv. See **benchmark** and **SPEC Rating**.

special carrier In competition with the public telephone companies, special carriers offer high-capacity data transmission lines. These may use fiber optics, coaxial cables, or microwaves before they finally connect to the standard telephone lines. Compare **common carrier**.

special characters 1. These are printable symbols often used with numeric characters. They include the dollar sign ($), comma (,), and percent sign (%). 2. [ISO A graphic character that is not a letter, digit, nor blank character, and usually not an ideogram. *Examples:* A punctuation mark, a currency symbol, a percent sign, a mathematical symbol.]

special interest group See **SIG**.

specification [ISO A detailed formulation, in document form, which provides a definitive description of a system for the purpose of developing or validating the system.]

SPECmark See **SPEC**.

SPEC Rating The Systems Performance Evaluation Cooperative (SPEC) is a nonprofit organization formed in November 1988 by a group of vendors (which included Data General, DEC, and Fujitsu) to develop a standard suite of benchmark programs that effectively measures the performance of computing systems in actual application environments. The SPEC benchmark suite (release 1.0) is a collection of ten central processing unit intensive programs that were developed and endorsed by SPEC, four of which are integer benchmarks and six of which are floating point benchmarks. While the floating point benchmarks can be used to predict system performance under a technical workload, the integer programs represent a more appropriate instruction mix for commercial applications. The instruction mix and the functions performed by the integer programs of the SPEC are closer to those used in commercial application programs than are the floating point benchmarks. The SPEC suite integer programs do not contain any business applications but they can be used to roughly forecast 32-bit business performance. The performance of the system under test is measured by comparing the execution times of individual programs to those of a VAX 11/780. A SPEC ratio is the ratio of the elapsed time on a VAX 11/780 to the elapsed time on a specific platform for a specific benchmark. The integer

SPEC ratio represents the overall performance of the system under test when running the four integer programs and is calculated as the geometric mean of the individual benchmarks. Pronounced 'speck'. See **SPEC**.

speech recognizer Since the 1940s, many scientists and engineers have researched speech recognition methods and systems. A speech recognizer is a device which imitates the function of the human ear and brain electronically. Instead of an eardrum, it has a microphone and instead of the cochlea of the inner ear, it has a bank of electronic band-pass filters to analyze sound waves. Each band-pass filter has a characteristic band of frequencies. When the microphone picks up a sound wave and converts it to an electrical signal, each band-pass filter outputs a voltage in proportion to the strength of the electrical signal in its characteristic band of frequencies. Even sounds of the same frequency generate different frequency components. For example, a 300 hertz 'ee' sound includes a high-frequency component of higher magnitude than an 'ah' sound of the same fundamental frequency. They are the same frequency, but their tones are different. If the sound is high-pitch-toned, the high-frequency filters output relatively large voltages and the low-frequency filters output relatively low voltages. A low-pitch-toned sound reverses these outputs. If the sound has both low- and high-frequency components, outputs of both the low- and high-frequency filters are large. Breaking down a wide range of frequencies into many smaller bands and measuring the signal strength of each is called 'spectrum analysis'. Since a voice is a continuously varying sound, the voice spectrum must be analyzed every five milliseconds or so to obtain a reasonable correspondence to the spoken sound. Just as the telephone functions as a person-to-person communications instrument, scientists may soon offer person-to-computer speech recognizers capable of recognizing thousands of common words, with varying tolerances to the changes in tone and pitch. Speech-recognition techniques could be used in typewriters, automatic teller machines, and order entry systems. In the same way, programmers could soon be in a position to write computer code simply by speaking at the machine. Speech-dependent systems have a dictionary memory in which characteristics of words spoken by a particular operator are stored in advance. The characteristics of input speech are compared to the contents of the dictionary memory, and the closest match is selected. ▼

speed matching Adjustment between different characteristic data transfer rates

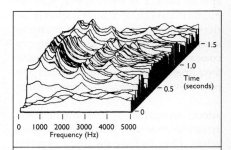

speech recognizer There is a considerable variation in the way different people pronounce the same word, so a speaker-dependent system cannot usually recognize words spoken by a person who has not 'trained' the system. A speaker-independent system, which can recognize words spoken by an operator who has not trained the system, must have samples of many operators' voices.

at two ends of a data transmission; usually achieved by inserting a buffer in the transmission path, and filling it at the transmitter's characteristic transfer rate then emptying it at the receiver's characteristic rate.

spelling checker A program or utility within another program which checks the spelling of words and suggests the correct spelling.

spherical aberration The failure of a lens (or reflective object) to bring to focus the rays of light (image) due to defects in the optical system. Spherical aberration is the distortion of an image (straight lines seen curved), while chromatic aberration causes an image to be seen with a colored fringe (typical when a television picture is distorted due to incorrect adjustment or a bad signal).

spice 2gc One of the ten SPEC (Systems Performance Evaluation Cooperative) benchmarks drawn from real-world applications including scientific and engineering areas, focusing on system performance, memory, input/output, graphics, networking, multi-user, and commercial applications. Spice is an analog circuit simulation and analysis application. It is a general-purpose circuit simulation program for nonlinear direct current, nonlinear transient, and linear alternating current analyzers. Circuits may contain resistors, capacitors, inductors, mutual inductors, independent voltage and current sources, four types of dependent sources, transmission lines, and the four most common semiconductor devices: diodes; base junction transistors; junction field-effect transistors; and metal-oxide semiconductor field-effect transistors. Spice is

primarily a floating point application bound by the central processing unit. Since spice is a real application (versus a synthetic benchmark), it is a very good predictor for this general type of processing. As such, spice is commonly used as a system benchmarking tool. Spice 2g6 was developed by the University of California at Berkeley's CAD Group. Spice 3a7 was developed as the C version. Spice performs most of its operations in double-precision floating point and makes some use of complex floating point data. The operations performed appear to be heavily weighted toward addition, subtraction, multiplication, division, exponentiation, and logarithms. The FORTRAN version consists of approximately 16 800 source code lines that compile into 223 kilobytes of instructions and 1.5 megabytes of static data on an Apollo DN3000. It is large enough to stress a small instruction/data cache. Spice runs on a very wide range of operating systems and processors, including UNIX and VMS. Many commercial versions of spice are based on the Berkeley source. See **SPEC**.

spice 3a7 See **spice 2gc**.

spike A momentary, sharp surge in voltage, usually on the mains.

SPL Sound pressure level.

spool Simultaneous peripheral operation online. When several programs are running in the same operating system and files need to be printed, or when different users are attached to the same printer, files are spooled to ensure that they are printed quickly and correctly. To 'spool' the files, they are sent to the printer-buffer (memory) and queued until they can be printed. One advantage of spooling is that the relatively slow printer does not hold up the computer because files can be sent down to the buffer very quickly. Processing then occurs between the buffer and the printer, thereby freeing the computer to proceed with its normal tasks.

spooling [ISO The use of auxiliary storage as a buffer storage to reduce processing delays when transferring data between peripheral equipment and the processor of a computer.]

spot beam In satellite communications, a narrow and focused down-link transmission, typical of newer satellite designs. A spot beam covers a much smaller geographic area (footprint) than older satellite down-link transmissions, thereby raising the effective power. See **satellite transmission**.

spot punch [ISO A device for punching one hole at a time in a data medium.]

SPP Scalable parallel processing.

spreadsheet A large work area in a computer software program (like Lotus 1-2-3) consisting of an array of cells in which data and formulae can be entered for speedy calculations. Financial managers use spreadsheets to generate financial/business reports. Income statements, balance sheets, loss statements, and payroll summaries have always been created on large journal pages or 'spreadsheets'. Spreadsheet programs take this difficult, time-consuming task, traditionally done with pencil and paper, and put it on a personal computer. The user can create columns and rows of numbers, along with headers, and have the computer perform calculations on the numbers. The calculations are performed according to formulae specified by the user. Presentation-style graphs and charts can also be created to depict the data on the spreadsheets. And, as with a word processor, all the work is done on the computer before printing out a 'hard copy'. ▼

sputtering A technique used to produce metallic media. The substrate disk is suspended in a vacuum, in the presence

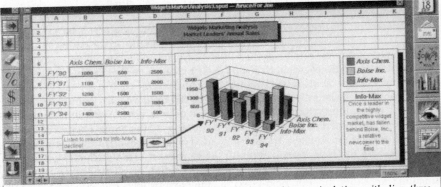

spreadsheet This spreadsheet package offers real-time graphic manipulation with live three-dimensional chart rotation, voice annotation, and a publishing feature for high-quality reporting.

NEWSFLASH

The total installed base for industry-standard PC-based spreadsheet products reached 31.1 million units in 1993.

In the Windows-based spreadsheet market for 1993, Excel for Windows held the largest installed base with approximately 7 million units.

of a mass of the material to be deposited. This mass is bombarded with an ion stream, dislodging atoms of the coating material. These atoms are attracted to the substrate disk, resulting in a thin consistent metallic coating suitable for high-density recording. For the environmentally-conscious, sputtering is a dry process that may ultimately result in easier waste-disposal than chemical baths. See **metallic media** and **oxide media**.

sputtering media See **metallic media**.

SPX Simplex.

SQL Structured Query Language; an ISO data definition and data manipulation language for relational databases. Variations of SQL are offered by most major vendors for their relational database products. For example, Digital's VAX SQL provides an interface to VAX Rdb/VMS. SQL is an application programming and database administration interface to relational databases and is not generally intended for the user as a language for ad hoc query. SQL grew out of the research on relational database models conducted by IBM in the 1970s, and is supported by IBM's database product called 'DB2', and 'SQL/DS' — IBM's mainframe database prod-

ucts. SQL is consistent with IBM's Systems Application Architecture (SAA), and it has been standardized by the American National Standards Institute (ANSI). At the personal computer level, powerful database servers from IBM, Microsoft, and Oracle have adopted dialects of the SQL language as their exclusive data query and manipulation language. Borland's Paradox SQL Link uses these different SQL dialects for easy, transparent operations with each of these database servers.

SQL Server Microsoft's SQL (Structured Query Language) Server is a high-performance, multi-user relational database management system (RDBMS) designed to support high-volume transaction processing (like online order entry) as well as less demanding decision-support applications (like sales analysis) on personal computer-based local area networks. Transaction processing ensures that SQL Server databases are consistent and can be recovered in case of system failure — whatever the cause. Built-in data integrity logic provides a mechanism that enforces complex business policies within the database itself. The key to transaction processing is the write-ahead transaction log that SQL Server maintains. This log ensures that an SQL Server database can always be recovered in case of hardware or media breakdown, system software failure, application program problems, or transaction cancellation requests. Whenever a request to modify the database is received, a copy of both old and new states of the database's affected portions is recorded in the transaction log. These changes are always recorded in the log before they are made to the database itself. See **SQL**.

SQL/Services Developed by Digital Equipment Corporation, SQL (Structured Query Language)/Services is a client/server product that allows desktop application programs to access Rdb/VMS databases via a standard Application Program Interface. It includes application programming interfaces for the VMS, ULTRIX, and MS–DOS operating systems. Users of popular desktop application programs can gain transparent access from their applications to Rdb/VMS databases for decision support and other end-user tasks.

square function [ISO The function that multiplies a number by itself directly.]

square root function [ISO The function that directly provides a number that, when multiplied by itself, produces the original number.]

SRAM Static random-access memory. See **DRAM**.

S Register Any of the registers of a modem which allow the user to tailor the modem to particular applications. The information is retained by the modem in its own nonvolatile memory. For example, S Register 0 contains a decimal value (from 0 to 255) equivalent to the number of rings the modem will wait before answering an incoming call. Thus, if S Register 0 contains a value of five, the modem will go online immediately after the fifth ring of an incoming call. If this register contains a zero value, the automatic answering operation will be disabled. However, allowable values depend upon the local environment. Telecom New Zealand, for example, requires that S Register 0 must be set to a value of three or greater. Any setting un-

der three will not enable the modem to answer automatically. Some of the many other S registers include: S Register two which contains the ASCII value of the three characters which form the escape sequence; S Register three which contains the ASCII value of the character recognized by the modem as the carriage return character; and S Register 39, whose seventh bit determines whether the modem will generate V.25 calling tones through the phone when operating in original mode. V.25 calling tones are generated as a measure of courtesy if the telephone number being dialed is answered by a person rather than a modem or other electronic device. The tones are used to indicate to the person who answers the telephone that the originator of the call is an electronic calling device (such as a modem). See **modem**.

SRP Suggested retail price.

SRPI Service requestor programming interface. An interface used by IBM Enhanced Connectivity Facilities.

SRR Second read rate; refers to a bar code scanner which translates code on the 'second read rate' should the 'first read rate' be unsuccessful. See **bar code** and **programming language**.

SS Single-sided; referring to an early magnetic storage disk which could only record information on one side, offering half the storage capacities of those which can use both sides of the disk for read/write operations. See **diskette**.

SSB Single sideband. Refers to a modulation technique used in radio communications.

SSBSC Single sideband suppressed carrier.

SSD 1. See **solid state disk**. 2. Sudanese Standards Department; Sudan's standards body formed in 1967.

S-SEED Symmetric self electro-optic effect devices. These were developed by AT&T Bell Laboratories of the United States in 1987. They are photonic integrated circuits consisting of 2048 multiple quantum-well structures (MQWS) placed on a 2-square-millimeter array. They serve as the logic, the memory cell, and/or the switch that operates at clock speeds exceeding 1 gigahertz. Prior to this technology, NEC had developed a 1-kilobit high-speed optical memory integrated circuit that integrates 1024 vertical-to-surface transmission electron-photonic (VSTEP) MQWS which were capable of amplifying optical signals. See **optical neurocomputer**.

SSI Small-scale integration; the flow of electrons in chips is controlled by the transistors which form switches or logic gates. Chips are categorized by the number of logic gates they have available. Small-scale integration chips, usually associated with second-generation computers, were the first to replace vacuum tubes, each containing up to four logic gates. See **chip** and **second generation**.

SS/TDMA Satellite-switched time division multiple access.

stable state [ISO In a trigger circuit, a state in which the circuit remains until the application of a suitable pulse.]

stack A collection of jobs waiting in a queue for processing. Each job in the

stack will be treated by the computer according to its assigned priority. In a stack, items are removed in a last in, first out (LIFO) manner. In contrast, a queue removes items in a first in, first out (FIFO) manner.

stack pointer [ISO The address of the storage location that contains the item of data most recently stored in a pushdown storage.]

Standard Generalized Markup Language An application-, system-, and device-independent language for marking structural content of text. This is an ISO standard. Abbreviation 'SGML'.

standardization In networking and communications, the exchange of data between different vendors' equipment (using facilities supplied by different common carriers) in different countries requires agreement between the vendors and common carriers on the methods of presentation and expression (character sets and languages). For efficient widespread exchange of data, a set of universal standards is required. International and national standards have developed over the years in response to changing technology and the increased demand placed on communications systems. These standards have had a major impact in the area of computer networking. One large United States' standards organization, the American National Standards Institute (ANSI), is composed of representatives from industrial firms, technical societies, consumer organizations, and government agencies. ANSI does not develop standards, but controls their development. A standards committee called 'X3' deals with computers and information processing. Subcommittees of 'X3' specialize in data communications. ANSI identifies what standards are needed and assigns the development of a standard to a competent organization or group. ANSI represents the United States in the International Organization for Standardization (ISO). See **ISO**.

standards Clearly defined and agreed-upon conventions for specific programming interfaces. Standards may be proprietary (used only within the environment provided by a single computer vendor), public (widely used across a variety of vendor equipment) or formal (developed by a standards organization such as the American National Standards Institute or the International Organization for Standardization).

Standard Tape Interconnect The Digital Storage Architecture standard for connecting tape formatters and controllers. Abbreviation 'STI'.

standing-on-nines carry [ISO In the parallel addition of numbers represented by decimal numerals, a procedure in which a carry to a given digit place is bypassed to the next digit place if the current sum in the given digit place is 9, and the 9 is changed to 0.]

StarLAN A star topology local area network using baseband CSMA/CD, running on twisted pair cable (1 megabit per second) where the maximum cable distance between a device and the central controller is 1640 foot (500 meters). StarLAN was developed by AT&T to meet the criteria for low-cost personal computer environments. Subsequently, this system has been included under IEEE 802.3 as type 1base5. As with Ethernet and Cheapernet, StarLAN op-

erates with baseband signaling and Manchester phase encoding, but at a 1-megabit-per-second data rate over a rooted-tree or star topology. StarLAN's greatest attraction is its use of a building's 'structured wiring', most often the unused pairs of unshielded twisted-pair wiring which already exist in most office buildings. Costs are also lowered because StarLAN, rather than requiring a special transceiver or cable taps like Ethernet, uses low-cost, standard RS-422 or RS-485 drivers/receivers, and standard modular telephone jacks. With StarLAN, each desk connects point-to-point in a star fashion through two unshielded twisted pairs with a local wiring closet which serves as a hub. Intermediate hubs (IHUBs) are wired together as a rooted-tree, with as many as five levels of hubs. There is no limit on the number of nodes or hubs at any given level, except at the trunk or base. The single hub at the tree base is called the 'header hub' (HHUB), which would normally be found in a building's equipment room. The maximum distance between a node and its adjacent hub or between two adjacent hubs is 800 foot (about 244 meters) for 24-gauge wire and 600 foot (183 meters) for 26-gauge wire. Thus the maximum node-to-node distance with one hub is 1600 foot (488 meters). See **1base5**.

StarLAN 10 A higher-performance version of StarLAN, transmitting at 10 megabits per second, developed by AT&T.

Starnet AUSSAT's Starnet service is an all-digital data communications system that directly links geographically disperse sites into an integrated network which can also support a broadcast video service. The customer's equipment at each branch site is connected to a small Earth station. The equipment, such as data terminals or controllers (operating within a variety of protocols), group 4 facsimile, or microcomputers, is linked via satellite to the customer's central site. The connection between the Starnet system and the customer's central computer is via either terrestrial means or satellite to an AUSSAT Major City Earth Station (MCES), which forms the hub of the Starnet data network. The very small Earth station at each branch site is known as a 'very small aperture terminal' (VSAT). The Starnet system, designed to support 'star' networks associated with mainframe and minicomputer systems, replaces terrestrial multidrop leased lines with VSATs at each branch site. The hub of the Starnet network is usually based upon an existing MCES. The hub is the system interface point for the customer's central computer, and is responsible for data transfer to and from each branch VSAT. The optional broadcast video service is also relayed to each VSAT from the customer's central office by the hub.

star network [ISO A tree network in which there is exactly one intermediate node.] 2. See **star topology**.

star/ring network [ISO A ring network with unidirectional transmission laid out in such a manner that several data stations are grouped and interconnected to the network by means of trunk coupling unit. *Note:* This configuration allows attaching and removal of data stations without disrupting network operation.]

star topology In a local area network, a topology in which each device is con-

nected to a central device (computer) through which all data pass. All users are usually connected to a central host computer. Star networks use time-sharing systems which allocate a certain amount of time for each user. The allocated time is called a 'time slice', and length can be varied depending upon the individual's needs. However, well-configured networks operate so quickly that users are not aware of their time slice. Star networks are especially useful when very remote locations need to connect for a few hours a day for processing. This setup minimizes the hardware costs, but could result in high telephone bills due to long-distance connections. Star networks are easily controlled, and are well suited to both voice and data transmission. Any defective nodes can be quickly isolated, with the exception of the controlling node which will usually render the whole network inoperative unless provisions have been made for fault-tolerant components. Star networks do not follow an

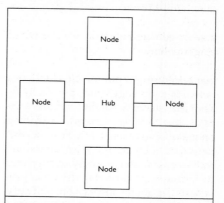

star topology In a network using a star topology, all communications must first pass to the central unit called the 'hub' or 'controller'. A cable fault in a station-to-hub affects only that station.

IEEE standard. See **topology**. Compare **bus topology** and **ring topology**. ⚑

start signal [ISO In start–stop transmission, a signal at the beginning of a character that prepares the receiving device for the reception of the code elements. *Note:* A start signal is limited to one signal element generally having the duration of a unit interval.]

start–stop transmission [ISO Asynchronous transmission such that each group of signals representing a character is preceded by a start signal and is followed by a stop signal.] See **asynchronous transmission**.

start-up diagnostics See **diagnostic program**.

starvation [ISO A situation in which an activation of an asynchronous procedure is incapable of proceeding within any predictable period of time because other concurrent activations permanently retain required resources.]

star wired ring network See **star wired ring topology**.

star wired ring topology In a local area network, a topology which physically resembles a star network, but operates logically like a ring network providing operational advantages which allow easy detection of breaks in cables, simplified traffic control, and coverage over greater distances. Star wired ring networks provide the flexibility and sustainability of a star network by easily identifying and isolating defective nodes, allowing easy modifications to provide for changes.

statement [ISO A language construct

that represents a step in a sequence of actions or a set of declarations.]

static [ISO Pertaining to properties that can be established before the execution of a program. *Example:* The length of a fixed-length variable is static.]

staticizer [ISO A functional unit that converts a time sequence of signals into a corresponding set of simultaneous signals.]

static RAM Static random-access memory. See **DRAM**.

static storage [ISO A storage device that does not require periodic refreshment.]

static test mode [ISO That setup mode of an analog computer during which special initial conditions are set in order to check the patching and, consequently, the proper operation of all computer devices except integrators.]

station A device connected to a network.

stationary message source [ISO A message source from which each message has a probability of occurrence independent of the time of its occurrence.]

station message detail recording A feature of private branch exchanges whereby each telephone call is logged, typically by time, number dialed, and charges. The details are then retrievable by the network operator for cost charging by department. Station message detail recording is sometimes called 'CDR' (call-detail recording). Abbreviation 'SMDR'.

status (Of a central processing unit.) [ISO One or more data bits showing which one of a class of operations is being performed, has been completed, or is recognized by the central processing unit.]

status register [ISO A register containing one or more status bits.]

STD Subscriber trunk dialing.

stepwise refinement [ISO A method for constructing programs in successive steps such that at each step an action is expressed in terms of more primitive actions.]

ST-506 disk interface The original interface between a hard disk and its controller, named after the model number of an early drive from Seagate Technology. For modern high-speed personal computers (PCs) to work efficiently with mass storage devices, there must be an effective means of transferring data between the device and the PC. The format and speed of this data transfer is determined by the type of 'device interface' built into the electronics on the drive and its controller board. There are four commonly-used device interfaces: Enhanced Small Device Interface (ESDI); the Small Computer Systems Interface (SCSI); the embedded interface; and the ST-506 interface. For older PCs, the ST-506 interface was adequate because the ST-506 standard could transfer data much faster than the Intel 8088-based PCs could handle, forcing designers to reduce the data transfer rate by formatting the hard disk with an interleave factor of six. For high-speed 32-bit personal computers, the ST-506 interface is not suitable, since it would create a serious data flow bottleneck between the hard drives and the computer. Most high-end computer systems use either ESDI or SCSI. Although these two standards differ greatly in scope, they both transfer data at approximately twice the speed of the ST-506.

ST-506 Winchester drive Promoted by Seagate Technology, the ST-506 Winchester disk contains from one to eight hard disks (or platters) which are made from aluminum (hence the term 'hard disk') and are coated with some type of recording media. The recording medium is typically magnetic-oxide, which is similar to the material used on diskettes and cassette tapes. Each side of a hard disk is coated with recording media and each side can store data. Each surface of a disk has its own read/write head. Hard disk drives are sealed units because the read/write heads actually 'fly' above the disk surface at about 8 to 20 microinches. A piece of dust or dirt, which appears as a boulder to the gap between the heads and the disk surface, may cause permanent damage to both the read/write heads and the disk. The read/write heads are mechanically connected together and move as a single unit across the surface of the disk. There are two basic methods for positioning the heads. The first is with stepper motors, which is the most common method and is also used on most diskette drives. These positioners are used mainly because of their low cost. The second method of positioning the heads is to use a voice-coil mechanism. These units do not move in steps but swing across the disk. These mechanisms generally permit greater track density than steppers, but also require complex feedback electronics, which increases the cost of the drive. Generally, voice-coil head positioners use closed-loop servo positioning, as compared to the open-loop positioning used with stepper motors. See **Winchester**.

STI See **Standard Tape Interconnect**.

Stoned virus A partition-sector virus that infects the partition sector of a hard disk and the boot sector of a diskette. Its presence can be detected by the message 'Your PC is now Stoned' every eighth time that an infected computer is turned on (booted). Within the partition sector is the message 'Legalise Marijuana', although variants of this virus have replaced this message with other random bytes. Stoned is sometimes called 'New Zealand', 'Marijuana', or 'Australian'. See **partition-sector virus**.

stop signal [ISO In start–stop transmission, a signal at the end of a character that prepares the receiving device for the reception of a subsequent character. *Note:* A stop signal is usually limited to one signal element having any duration equal to or greater than a specified minimum value.]

storage 1. Computer systems use two kinds of storage — main and secondary. Main storage is where programs and data required for their execution are stored. Access to main storage must be fast, and in the case of large-scale systems it is often measured in nanoseconds — a nanosecond being the time it takes light to travel 30 centimeters. Semiconductor memory devices are used for main storage. Secondary storage, also called 'mass storage', is for data and programs that do not necessarily have to be accessed immediately. Secondary storage has two classifications: online and off-line. Online storage acts as an extension to

main storage, and provides access speeds in milliseconds. Direct access storage devices (DASDs) are used for online storage and consist mainly of magnetic disk systems. Off-line storage provides backup, or archiving storage, and the media is usually magnetic tape. Semiconductor memories are much faster than magnetic storage but disk storage has ten times greater packaging density at only 1/100th of the cost per bit. See **compact disk**, **diskette**, **primary storage**, **secondary storage**, **storage hierarchy**, and **thin film head**. 2. [ISO The retention of data in a storage device.]

storage capacity [ISO The amount of data that can be contained in a storage device, measured in units of data. *Notes:* (a) A unit of data can be a binary character, a byte, a word, etc. (b) For registers, the term 'register length' is used with the same meaning.]

storage cell [ISO The smallest unit that can be addressed in storage.]

storage density See **areal density**.

storage device [ISO A functional unit into which data can be placed, in which they can be retained, and from which they can be retrieved.]

storage hierarchy Storage device 'function' and logical 'proximity' to the central processor and operating system software dictates where it fits in the storage hierarchy. At the top of the hierarchy is primary storage, followed by secondary storage, then tertiary storage. Primary storage products include random-access memory, which is usually sold in the form of modules that can be plugged into the backplane of a computer system and contain numbers of dynamic random-access memory chips. This form of memory is termed 'primary' because on most computing systems, it is the medium through which data must pass before being used by the system's processors. Depending upon their size and use, some computer systems can be configured with primary memory ranging from 1 megabyte to 2 gigabytes, with access measured in nanoseconds. Secondary storage products include magnetic disk devices (sometimes known as 'Winchester drives'). Magnetic disk secondary storage devices provide a relatively inexpensive source of potentially hundreds of gigabytes of data with an access time in the area of 15 to 30 milliseconds. Tertiary storage products are generally used for archival purposes; that is, as a backup for secondary storage. They include a variety of open-reel and cartridge magnetic tape drives as well as optical products such as CD–

ROM and WORM devices. Generally, tertiary products provide access to vast amounts of data in a small space but at slower access speeds than those used for secondary storage. ▲

storage image [ISO The representation of a computer program and its related data as they exist at the time they reside in main storage.]

storage location [ISO A position in a storage device that is uniquely specified by means of an address.]

storage protection [ISO Limitation of access to a storage device, or to one or more storage locations, by preventing writing or reading or both.]

storage register A type of 'register' which holds information taken from (or sent to) primary storage.

STP Shielded twisted pair.

streaming A magnetic tape motion control technique which sacrifices start–stop performance to achieve high reliability at low product cost by eliminating tape buffers. Streaming tape drives are optimized for applications in which a steady supply of data is available from, or demanded by, the host computer.

streaming tape drive [ISO A magnetic tape unit especially designed to make a non-stop dump or restore of magnetic disks without stopping at interblock gaps.]

STREAMS The network communications framework for UNIX V.3.

string [ISO A sequence of elements of

storage hierarchy This diagram shows the relationship between different storage/memory devices and their capacity/performance. The faster the access speed, the lower the storage capacity. Cache and flash memory offer lightning-fast access, but low storage capacity. By comparison, an optical disk system can hold vast amounts of memory (several gigabytes), but cannot be accessed very quickly.

the same nature, such as characters, considered as a whole.]

String-Oriented Symbolic Language A high-level programming language developed in 1962 at AT&T's Bell Laboratories for text-processing applications. It was created by Ralph Griswold, David Farber, and Ivan Polonsky. The version used for personal computers is called 'SNOBOL4'. Abbreviation 'SNOBOL', pronounced 'snow-bol'.

stripping [ISO An action taken by an originating data station to remove its frames from the network after a successful revolution on the ring.]

stroke character generator [ISO A character generator that generates character images composed of line segments.]

stroke device [ISO An input device that provides a set of coordinates that record the path of the device. *Example:* A locator that is sampled at a uniform rate.]

structured flowchart A flowcharting technique which uses control structures to minimize the complexity of the programs, thereby reducing error rates. It is related to structured programming — a method of breaking a program into logical sections, using universal programming standards. These sections, sometimes managed by different programmers, make it easier to write, check, and maintain a complex program. The three basic control structures are: (1) Sequence, where each flowchart statement simply follows another in sequence. (2) Selection (condition), where a flowchart requests certain actions be made (selected) only if certain criteria are met.

(3) Iteration, where a flowchart requests that certain action be repeated (iterated) until further instruction. This is also called a 'loop'. See **flowchart**.

structured language A technique which uses control structures in a language to minimize the complexity of the programs, thereby reducing error rates. It is related to structured programming — a method of breaking a program into logical sections, using universal programming standards. These sections, sometimes managed by different programmers, make it easier to write, check, and maintain a complex program. The three basic control structures are: (1) Sequence, where each statement simply follows another in sequence. (2) Selection (condition), where certain actions are requested (selected) only if certain criteria are met. (3) Iteration, where requests are made for certain action to be repeated (iterated) until further instruction. This is also called a 'loop'. See **programming language**.

structured programming [ISO A method for constructing programs using only hierarchically nested constructs each having a single entry and a single exit point. *Note:* Three types of control flow are used in structured programming: sequential; conditional; and iterative.] See **structured language**.

structured query language See **SQL**.

structured walkthrough A procedure in which a group of programmers, each working on a different segment of the same program, meet to inspect each others' work in the hope of minimizing the error rate. Although this is a formal meeting, its aim is to improve the program, not criticize a programmer's performance. [ISO A systematic examination of the requirements, design, or implementation of a system, or any part of it, by qualified personnel.] See **structured flowchart**.

StuffIt A shareware program (created by Raymond Lau) specifically for the Apple Macintosh, designed to compress data before it is archived. A similar program called 'PKZIP' was designed specifically for archiving data from DOS-based personal computers.

subcode area The area of a compact disk where control signals other than images or audio signals are recorded. CDs have an 8-bit capacity. Two bits are used for recording the title number and recording time. The information recorded in this area is used to permit random access, which is one key feature of CDs.

submarine cable The first submarine cable system with active repeaters was put into operation at the end of the 1940s. In 1956, the first long-distance submarine cable system, called 'TAT-1', was successful in carrying 36 telephone channels across the Atlantic Ocean. In the 1960s, with the advent of space technology, satellite communications systems using geostationary satellites were rapidly developed, and many Earth stations were constructed throughout the world. At that time, industry professionals speculated that submarine cable systems would be replaced by satellite communications as the major international telecommunications network media, but this has not been the case. From both technical and economic standpoints, the submarine cable system has proved to be a useful and important telecommuni-

cations system, and usage of both systems is expected to continue to grow. There are many design requirements unique to submarine cable systems. For example, once the cable with active repeaters is laid, the equipment under water (approximately 5.3 miles (8.5 kilometers)) is usually inaccessible for maintenance and repair. For this reason, all equipment, especially the repeaters which contain high-precision electronic components, must be of extraordinarily high reliability, and the system must have a long operation life (usually more than 20 years). A long cable in one piece with active repeaters connected at appropriate intervals (usually from 20 to 80 miles (35 to 140 kilometers)) is launched from a cable ship. The cable and repeaters must be rugged enough to absorb a strong shock and to withstand high water pressure. To meet strength requirements, the cable is given sufficient tensile strength by including high-tensile steel wire within the inner conductor for deep-water applications. In the case of shallow-water applications, the cable is strengthened by armoring it with steel wires for protection against damage from trawlnets. Sometimes shallow-water cables are buried up to 3.28 foot (1 meter) deep for added safety. See **South Pacific Network**.

subnet A network (linked via bridges, routers, or gateways) that is part of a larger extended network.

subroutine [ISO A sequence of instructions whose execution is invoked by a call.]

sub-sampling A compression process that uses a bandwidth reduction technique. For example, in video technology, it reduces the amount of digital data that is used to represent an image.

subscripting [ISO A mechanism for referencing an array element by means of an array reference and one or more expressions that, when evaluated, denote the position of the element. *Note:* This term also applies to the use of the mechanism.]

substrate The underlying disk or tape material upon which media is layered for magnetic or optical recording. Substrates give the resulting disk or tape its desired mechanical properties, such as rigidity or flexibility. The word 'substrate' comes from the Latin word *substratum*, meaning 'strewn beneath'.

subtotal function [ISO The function that allows the display or printing of an interim result of a calculation.]

subtracter [ISO A functional unit whose output data is a representation of the difference between the numbers represented by its input data.]

subtransaction See **nested transaction**.

summary punch [ISO A card punch used to record data that was calculated or summarized by another device.]

summation check [ISO A comparison of checksums, computed on the same data on different occasions, or on different representations of the data, to verify data integrity.]

summer [ISO A functional unit whose output analog variable is equal to the sum, or a weighted sum, of the input analog variables.]

summing integrator [ISO A functional unit whose output analog variable is the integral of a weighted sum of the input analog variables with respect to time or with respect to another input analog variable.]

Sun Sun Microsystems Incorporated; a hardware manufacturer.

supercomputer One of the largest, fastest, and most powerful class of computer. The name was first coined to refer to the Cray- 1 computer. Supercomputers can cost over US$30 million. Until recently, Japanese manufacturers boasted supercomputer speeds up to 1000 times faster than American efforts. Another popular supercomputer was Control Data Corporation's CYBER 205, capable of processing over 800 million operations per second, and primarily used for weather forecasting, weapons research, and specialist applications such as high-quality animation and scientific research demanding massive calculations within a short period of time. Other leading supercomputer manufacturers include Fujitsu, NCUBE, MasPar Computer Corporation, Intel, Silicon Graphics, and Network Systems Corporation. The exact definition of a supercomputer is the concern of the United States Commerce Department and the supercomputer industry alike, because trade restrictions govern which computers can and cannot be sold to Communist countries, or to countries which re-export to members of the former Warsaw Pact. United States' trade regulations state that supercomputers can only be sold to 23 allies who are members of the Coordinating Committee (CoCom) for Multilateral Export Controls. Since Congress asked for a definition in 1988, finding one has been a difficult task. Early in 1991, the Commerce Department's third attempt at a definition proposed that super-computers should be classified into three categories: (1) Machines capable of oper-ating in excess of 300 million floating point operations (MFLOP) per second. (2) Those capable of 150 or more MFLOP. (3) Those capable of 100 or more MFLOP. Anything less than 100 MFLOP

is called a 'minisupercomputer'. It was recommended that the highest category be sold only to CoCom countries (with restriction), while other supercomputers could be sold to other countries under special conditions. Under the new Supercomputer Safeguard Plan (SSP), all computer sales will have to meet special (auditable) guidelines relating to the agreed usage of such machines. Manu-

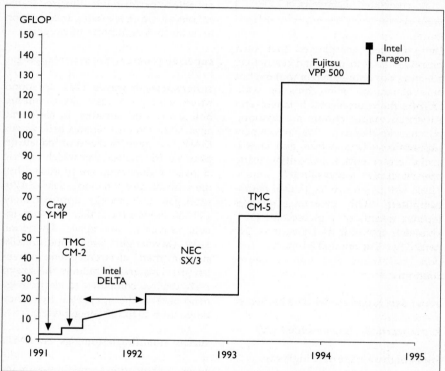

supercomputer *This graph shows the rate of growth in speed (GFLOP) of supercomputers since 1991 using the Linpack benchmark that requires a computer to solve a set of simultaneous linear algebraic equations. A Linpack record was set in May 1994 by the Intel Paragon XP/S supercomputer at 143.4 double-precision GFLOP. It had 1840 compute nodes, 64 nodes for disk input/output, and nine server nodes. 512 nodes had 32 megabytes (Mb) of memory, and the remaining nodes had 16 Mb. The 1840 nodes were connected in a 16 x 115 mesh (2D), with individual links each capable of a transfer rate of 175 Mb per second. The system ran the SUNMOS operating system kernel as well as the native Paragon operating system. The previous record of 124.5 GFLOP was set in August 1993 by Fujitsu's Numerical Wind Tunnel, a unique system owned by the Japanese National Aerospace Laboratory.*

NEWSFLASH

Supercomputers experienced an 8.8% loss, and minisupercomputers and massively parallel processor computers posted gains of 1.1% and 12.9% respectively.

For the period 1992–97, the overall high-performance multi-user market is expected to decline in revenues at a rate, compounded annually, of 1.2%.

facturers have complained that such proposals are too wide and restrictive, affecting not only supercomputers, but new generation microchips as well. Despite these problems, Japanese and American manufacturers are working on a new level of technology which may supersede such machines, and launch a new era of optical computing using optoelectronic integrated circuits. These will be known as 'optical neurocomputers' with switching devices topping speeds of 1 picosecond (10^{-12} seconds), operating at 1 gigahertz (10^9 hertz). See **CoCom** and **Linpack**. Compare **mainframe** and **optical neurocomputer**. ⚑

super data highway See **data highway**.

super green See **green technology**.

super highway See **data highway**.

super-large-scale integration The flow of electrons in chips is controlled by the transistors, which form switches or logic gates. Chips are categorized by the number of logic gates available. For example, super-large-scale integration chips exceed several hundred thousand logic circuits. Abbreviation 'SLSI'. See **chip**.

super neurocomputer See **neurocomputer**.

superzapping Computer crime which involves the use of a computer's 'superzap program' — a master control program used by computer maintenance professionals in disaster recovery, or when a computer cannot be started in the normal way after it crashes. Criminals with access to the superzap codes are able to perform unauthorized transactions very quickly, being in a position to escape before they can be caught.

superzap program See **superzapping**.

surface acoustic waves These are sound waves which propagate along (and are bound to) solid surfaces. In electronic applications, the surface acoustic waves (SAWs) are generated and propagate on piezoelectric material, in which electric signals produce (and are produced by) mechanical deformation. The SAWs propagate at velocities approximately 100 000 times slower than electromagnetic waves in free space. Therefore, SAW wavelengths are proportionally shorter than electromagnetic wavelengths. This greatly reduces the size of SAW devices compared to electromagnetic ones in the applicable frequency range from 10 to 1000 megahertz.

surface mounting technology See **SMT**.

surge A short-term to medium-term increase in voltage, usually on the mains.

surge resistance [ISO The capability of a device to remain functionally intact after exposure to overvoltages.]

Suriv virus An indirect-action file virus that has three popular versions. Version

FUN FACT

What a supercomputer could calculate in one second could take 3000 years to perform on a calculator (assuming that one calculation were performed every second, 24 hours a day, for 3000 years).

1.01 infects .COM files and, on 1 April each year, displays the message 'APRIL 1ST HA HA HA YOU HAVE A VIRUS' and then it proceeds to cause a system failure. Version 2.01 does a similar thing, except that it only infects .EXE files. Version 3 of Suriv infects both .COM and .EXE files and proceeds to delete any program that is run. See **indirect-action file virus**.

SVID System V (5) Interface Definition; an AT&T standard devised to support application migration between various derivatives of UNIX.

SW Short wave.

swapping [ISO A process that interchanges the contents of an area of main storage with the contents of an area of auxiliary storage.]

switch [ISO A choice of one jump from a selection of jumps, controlled by a flag.]

switched lines Telecommunications lines available through a telephone exchange (switch). These are available for general data transmission.

switching function [ISO A function that has only a finite number of possible values and whose independent variables each have only a finite number of possible values.]

switching variable [ISO A variable that may take only a finite number of possible values or states. *Example:* An unspecified character of a character set.]

symbolic address [ISO An identifier that represents an address.]

symbolic language Also called 'assembly language'; the use of abbreviations for instructions rather than numbers. For example, 'L' is used to mean 'load', and 'R' is used to mean 'run'. Symbolic language was mainly used between 1959 and 1964. See **programming language**.

symbolic logic [ISO The discipline in which valid arguments and operations are dealt with using an artificial language designated to avoid the ambiguities and logical inadequacies of natural languages.]

symbolic processor An artificial-intelligence computer which represents and manipulates knowledge instead of data. A conventional computer is known as a 'numeric processor'. See **artificial intelligence**.

symmetrical compression A compression system that requires an equal processing capability for compression and decompression of an image. This form of compression is used in applications where both compression and decompression will be utilized frequently — for example, in still-image databases, still-image transmission (color fax), video production, video mail, videophones, and video conferencing.

symmetrical list [ISO A chained list in which each data element also contains information for locating the preceding one.]

symmetrical multiprocessing See **SMP**.

symmetric binary channel [ISO A channel that is designed to convey messages consisting of binary characters and that has the property that the conditional probabilities of changing any one character to the other character are equal.]

symmetric self electro-optic effect devices See **S-SEED**.

synchronization [ISO The action of forcing certain points in the execution sequences of two or more asynchronous procedures to coincide in time.]

synchronous [ISO Pertaining to two or more processes that depend upon the occurrence of a specific event such as a common timing signal.] The word 'synchronous' comes from the Greek words *sun*, meaning 'with', and *khronos* meaning 'time'.

synchronous transmission In computer communications, data (binary digits) can be transmitted in synchronous mode or asynchronous mode. When sending in synchronous mode, it is mandatory that both the sending and receiving devices be precisely timed with each other. This ensures that data can be sent speedily, with control signals used only when there is a major break in transmission (unlike asynchronous transmissions which require a special 'start bit' to be sent ahead of each character, and a 'stop bit' at the end of each character). This process continues until the final character is sent. In EBCDIC, where 8 bits form a character (byte), a total of 10 bits must be sent for each character (making transmission relatively slow). The difference between asynchronous and synchronous communications can be compared to the difference between motor car traffic on a freeway and a train. Asynchronous data is like the cars, all going in the same direction and at about the same speed but with different distances between. Each car must be driven on its own. On the other hand, the train (synchronous data) has one engine and all carriages are closely coupled, all traveling at the same speed, precisely and closely synchronized. Asynchronous is a little more error-prone and less efficient but it uses a simpler technology. It was the first form of data communication and was originally designed for the telex service. Synchronous communications is more sophisticated, more accurate, and more efficient. It is more complex and is mainly used when connecting mainframe computers. Other types of transmission are half duplex and full duplex. To continue the car/train analogy, half duplex describes a one-way street (or train track) where the traffic can only 'turn around' if the way is clear. Full duplex is a two-way lane system where data can flow freely in both directions at the same time. Half duplex is used only in specialized mainframe applications (such as point-of-sale and electronic funds transfer terminals). Full duplex links can support higher traffic throughput, where the sender and receiver can be processing different applications. Some modems can switch from asynchronous to synchronous communications as required. [ISO Data transmission in which the time of occurrence of each signal representing a bit is related to a fixed time base.] See **parity bit**.

synonym See **hashing**.

SynOptics Communications, Inc. A network products and network management systems supplier founded in 1985. Headquartered in Santa Clara, California, the company has more than 1400 employees in more than 50 offices worldwide. The company merged with Wellfleet Communications 20 October 1994 to form Bay Networks, Inc.

syntax error An error, other than a logical error, in a computer program caused by, for example, spelling, or grammatical mistakes. The word 'syntax' comes from the Greek word *syntaxis*, meaning 'arrangement'.

sysop System operator. Pronounced 'siss-op'.

system See **computer system**.

system analysis [ISO A systematic investigation of a real or planned system to determine the information requirements and processes of the system and how these relate to each other and to any other system.]

system availability A computer system is said to be 'available' if it delivers correct service to its users when service is required. Despite strong efforts, not all systems can be available 100% of the

---

PLAY ON WORDS

Peer-to-peer networking When sales and marketing staff finally kiss and make up.

Syntax A new government revenue generator for adult bulletin boards.

Yuppies Those who understand the complexity of a computer. Usually under the age of ten.

---

time because unexpected faults may occur and lead to its failure, or partial failure. The availability of a system depends upon both its operational system reliability and its recoverability. Operational system reliability is the ability of a system as a whole to continue running and to perform correctly when it is running. This reliability is typically measured in terms of the mean time between failures (MTBF) of the system as a whole. Recoverability is the ability of a system to be restored to full operation after a failure. The recoverability rate depends upon how quickly the operating system is re-booted, the database is recovered to a consistent state, the application is restarted, and in some cases, how quickly failed hardware or software is repaired. The recoverability is typically measured in terms of mean down-time (MDT). See **computer system**, **fault tolerance**, **MTBF**, and **unscheduled down-time**.

system description [ISO Documentation that results from system design defining the organization, essential characteristics, and the hardware and software requirements of the system.]

system design [ISO A process of defining the hardware and software architecture, components, modules, interfaces, and data for a system to satisfy specified requirements.]

system development [ISO A process that usually includes requirements analysis, system design, implementation, documentation, and quality assurance.]

system documentation [ISO The collection of documents that describe the requirements, capabilities, limitations, design, operation, and maintenance of an information processing system.]

Système International d'Unités International System of Units; the internationally-agreed metric system. See **SI**.

system follow-up [ISO The study of the effects of a system after it has reached a stabilized state of operational use.]

system generation [ISO The process of selecting optional parts of an operating system and of creating a particular operating system tailored to the requirements of a data processing installation.]

system integration [ISO The progressive assembling of system components into the whole system.]

system lifecycle [ISO The course of developmental changes through which a system passes from its conception to the termination of its use.]

system maintenance [ISO The modification of a system to correct faults, to improve performance, or to adapt the system to a changed environment or changed requirements.]

system recovery The processing that must be performed after operating-system initialization, but before normal use can resume; it restores the system to a consistent and valid state following a system failure. System recovery may require restoring in-memory structures from nonvolatile media, and performing backout for transactions that were in-flight at the time of failure.

systems analysis See **system analysis** and **systems analyst**.

systems analyst A professional whose task it is to determine (analyze) why a particular set of procedures is required, and how best to design a computer program which will improve the method of operation (system). For example, when an airline needs to ensure that travelers are not overbooked on flights, a systems analyst first needs to understand every step in the process, suggest improvements to this process, then design a computer program (if deemed necessary) to accommodate the process.

systems design See **system design** and **systems analyst**.

Systems Network Architecture See **SNA**.

Systems Network Architecture Distribution Services An architecture developed by IBM to aid in file transfer among dissimilar IBM devices. Documents which follow Document Content Architecture and Document Interchange Architecture are sent via the Systems Network Architecture Distribution Services. Abbreviation 'SNADS'.

system software [ISO Application independent software that supports the running of application software.]

Systems Performance Evaluation Cooperative An international group of manufacturers of workstations, servers, and other computer systems who have resolved to work together to provide performance summaries based on results from a suite of standardized programs run under specified conditions. The benchmark (SPECmark) results are released quarterly by Waterside Associates of Fremont, California. SPEC was founded in November 1988 by Apollo Computer, Hewlett-Packard, MIPS Computer Systems, and Sun Microsystems. The current membership of over 21 vendors includes these companies plus AT&T, Bull S.A., Compaq, Control Data Corporation, Data General, Digital Equipment Corporation, DuPont, Fujitsu, Intel, Integraph, IBM, Motorola Microcomputer Division, NCR Corporation, Prime Computer, Siemens AG, Silicon Graphics, Solbourne, Stardent, and Unisys. The ten programs used in arriving at the SPECmark figures are described in this book under their alphabetical listing: doduc, eqntott, espresso, fpppp, GNU C compiler gcc, LISP interpreter, matrix300, nasa7, spice 2g6, tomcatv. Abbreviation 'SPEC'. See **benchmark** and **SPEC Rating**.

system support [ISO The continued provision of services and material necessary for the use and improvement of an implemented system.]

system test time [ISO That part of operating time during which the functional unit is tested for proper operation. *Note:* Since a functional unit may consist of a computer and its operating system, system test time in some cases includes the time for testing computer programs belonging to the operating system.]

System/360 IBM's family of computers which cost US$5000 million to develop. The System/360 was the world's largest family of computers, incorporating five different processors with a total of 19 different configurations using Solid Logic Technology. See **third generation**.

System V Interface Definition See **SVID**.

S

**WHEN IT COMES TO COMPUTER INNOVATION,
THOSE WHO FAIL TO BELIEVE THE UNBELIEVABLE
WILL BE IN FOR A SURPRISE**

T Tera-. An SI unit prefix for 10^{12} expressed in decimal notation as 1 000 000 000 000.

table [ISO An arrangement of data each item of which may be identified by means of arguments or keys.]

tablet A sensitized drawing area used in conjunction with a mouse or stylus to input/manipulate data on the screen. A graphics tablet is a popular input device that consists of a flat drawing surface, and some type of pointing device similar to a pen that translates the motion into digital data. The majority of graphics tablets are dedicated to computer-aided design and computer graphics applications. Most graphics tablets are small enough to fit on a desktop, but some are as large as a standard drafting table. The tablet normally connects to a computer's standard serial or parallel port. A stylus or hand-held cursor controller is used for drawing. The stylus is simply a blunt point shaped like a pen that does not deposit ink. The hand-held cursor controller resembles a mouse in shape, but has a window in the center or at one end with fine cross-hairs. Drawings can be traced by guiding the cross-hairs over the lines. The most common digitizing method is the antenna-transmitter technique. The tablet itself, which is the antenna, has a fine grid of wires just under its surface. The pen or stylus transmits a signal which is picked up by the x and y grid wires. The control circuits in the tablet convert the signals into x and y coordinates which are sent to the computer. [ISO A special flat surface with a mechanism for indicating positions thereon, normally used as a locator.] Compare **mouse**.

tabulator [ISO A device that reads data from a data medium such as punched cards or punched tape and produces lists, tables, or totals.]

tandem data circuit [ISO A data circuit

that contains more than two data circuit-terminating equipment in series.]

tape drive A mass-storage magnetic device used to store large amounts of data on a tape cartridge for the purpose of archiving important files. The magnetic tape is available in many sizes, and resembles the tape found in video cassettes. The data on an entire hard disk can be copied onto one or two tapes in a matter of minutes. To protect against a media failure in the hard drive, this procedure would typically be performed on a daily basis, with the tape being continually re-used. Unlike other mass-storage devices, a tape drive is not intended for use with an executing application program because random data cannot be accessed quickly. Since any 2 bytes of data may be separated by hundreds of feet of tape, it can take several minutes to locate a required file record. Conse-

quently, a tape unit on a personal computer serves no purpose other than backup. The tape itself is coated with an oxide material similar to that used on audio tape. The surface of the tape is divided into a number of tracks, often nine, although standards vary. Data is recorded magnetically in a serpentine fashion. In other words, rather than rewind the tape at the end of each track, the drive motors reverse direction, the read/write head shifts position, and recording continues on the adjacent track. Most tape drives can function in either an 'image' mode or a 'file-by-file' mode. In image mode, the hard disk heads read each cylinder only once, starting at the outer edge of the disk and working in. On tape, this creates an exact copy of the surface of the disk without regard to the distribution of files. This method is fast, but there is not an easy way to backup or restore a single file without copying

tape drive Unattended high-capacity backups are possible using industry-standard magnetic tape media like the one shown in this photograph. Over 11 megabytes (Mb) of data can be backed-up and verified every minute. Similarly, restoring data from the tape can be done at 11 Mb per minute. The high-capacity tape shown here can store 525 Mb. The magnetic tape is a quarter of an inch (6.35 millimeters) wide and 1020 foot (330 meters) in length, capable of transferring data at 1920 kilobits per second. The tape drive can read or write data while the tape is winding at 120 inches (3 meters) per second. New technology using digital audio tape drives provides as much as 4 gigabytes of data on a single tape using advanced hardware for data compression features.

every sector on the disk. The file-by-file mode is more flexible. Whole files are recorded, one after another. This method is significantly slower, due to increased disk head movement. However, any one file or group of files can be reclaimed without altering other data on the disk. [ISO A device for moving magnetic tape and controlling its movement.] ∆

tape punch [ISO A punch that automatically produces on a punch tape, a record of data in the form of hole patterns.]

tape reproducer [ISO A device that prepares one tape from another tape by copying all or part of the data from the tape that is read.]

tape row [ISO A group of binary characters recorded or sensed in parallel on a line perpendicular to the reference edge of a magnetic tape.]

tape spool [ISO A cylinder without flanges on which tape may be wound.]

tape unit [ISO A device containing a magnetic tape drive, magnetic heads, and associated controls.]

target language [ISO The output language of a translator.]

tariff A list of services and rates charged by a common carrier (bureau) offering communications services.

TASI Time-assignment speech interpolation. See **digital speech interpolation**.

task [ISO In a multiprogramming or multiprocessing environment, one or more sequences of instructions treated by a control program as an element of work to be accomplished by a computer.]

task switching A very important attribute of any multitasking/multi-user operating system is its ability to rapidly switch between tasks or processes. The Intel Pentium microprocessor directly supports task switching by providing a task switch instruction in hardware. The microprocessor task switch operation saves the entire state of the machine (all of the registers, address space, and a link to the previous task), loads a new execution state, performs protection checks, and commences execution in the new task, in approximately 17 microseconds.

TASMAN 2 See **South Pacific Network**.

TAT Turnaround time.

TBQWS Tunneling biquantum-well structures. See **optical neurocomputer**.

TBS Tanzania Bureau of Standards; Tanzania's standards body formed in 1975.

T-carrier services A time division multiplexed digital transmission facility which handles very-high-speed transmission rates and accepts information from multiple data, voice, or video channels. It consists of a variety of 'T' services (such as T1) which operates at 1.544 megabits (MB) per second nationally, and up to 2.048 MB internationally. (1.544 megabits per second is equivalent to 24 voice-frequency channels.) With advanced compression technology, T1 circuits can deliver up to 48 or 96 voice-grade channels. The T3 service is a private fiber optics channel that operates at 44.736 MB (the equivalent of 28 T1 channels).

TCM Thermal control module.

TCP/IP Transmission Control Protocol/ Internet Protocol; transport layer and network layer protocols for a protocol suite originally for wide area networks. Developed in the 1970s to link the research center of the United States Government's Defense Advanced Research Projects Agency. The US government has now adopted OSI in place of TCP/IP through GOSIP. See **OSI reference model**.

TDM Time-division multiplexer. See **multiplexer**.

TDMA Time division multiple access; an integrated services digital network (ISDN) used primarily for international public-switched telephony traffic of very large volume. It is offered on a bearer channel basis.

TDS Transaction-driven system.

technical process [ISO A set of operations performed by equipment in which physical variables are monitored or controlled. *Example:* Distillation and condensation in a refinery; autopiloting and automatic landing in an aircraft.]

technophobia See **computerphobia**.

telco Telephone company; a name used in 1984 to refer to any of the seven independent regional telephone companies which formed part of AT&T in the United States. Each telco functions as a holding company which controls a number of smaller telephone companies.

telecommuting See **telecomputing**.

telecomputing A word coined by Jack

Nilles of the University of Southern California to describe the actions of a modern worker who is no longer required to travel to the office to be productive. Researchers, accountants, writers, and secretaries can work from home or at a nearby productivity center. Also called 'telecommuting'. ▼

teleconferencing Meetings held by people in various locations, communicating with each other via telephone, radio, satellite, or computer terminals. All parties can hear each other or see each other via video monitors, thereby avoiding lengthy and expensive travel. Video teleconferencing is usually a real-time, two-way transmission of digitized video images between two or more locations. See **video conferencing**.

teledildonics The use of computers, body suits, data glasses, and other stimulators (psychological and physical) to

telecomputing Professionals around the world are using the convenience of the computer to produce part, or all, of their work away from the office. Telecomputing does not necessarily do away with offices altogether, but it does make it easier for people to work from home, or to spend more time in the field or at client sites. Most hotels are now equipped with telecommunications and computer devices, including fax machines, personal computers, mobile phones, modems, and associated peripherals.

engage in sexual activity or erotic pursuits. This may be through the use of virtual-reality systems, or via multimedia systems, either singularly, or with other remote partners who may be connected via a network or telephone line.

Telenet A public packet-switching network. See **packet-switching system**.

telepresence A form of virtual reality where people are separated from the world that they are in, then re-mapped into a computer program that enables them to believe that they are elsewhere. By wearing a datasuit and dataglasses, one can connect to a computer to make things happen at one's command. For example, an astronaut inside a spaceship can manipulate a robotic arm outside the spaceship. Wearing a datasuit, the astronaut's movements will be mimicked by the robot, enabling the astronaut to repair the spaceship through telepresence. Another very useful form of telepresence might be the ability to enter a computer program and virtually travel to another country (using video and satellite technology). Sophisticated telepresence applications in the airforce may soon see the pilot of a fighter aircraft stationed at headquarters, and not inside the aircraft, thereby ensuring the pilot's safety should the aircraft be shot down by the enemy. The pilots still have total control of the aircraft, and can still see, using dataglasses, exactly what they would see if they were in the aircraft. See **virtual reality**.

teleprocessing system A method of centralizing a computer system through the use (sharing) of communication lines such as common telephone lines. This method became popular in the 1960s.

teletext A non-interactive information system that was the predecessor to videotex. Teletext terminals consist of a specially-modified television set and keypad to provide 24 lines of 40-column color text and graphics. Connection is made to teletext systems by specially-assigned television broadcast channels, hence the need to use a television set. Compare **videotex**.

Telnet An application utility that provides terminal emulation.

temporal locality Locality in time; the tendency of data and subroutines that have been used recently to be used again in the near future. Data retrieved from primary memory is written to cache memory, where it is then read by the processor. Any data modified by the processor is also written to the cache. The cache has very limited storage, so a replacement strategy is used to determine which existing data to replace from the cache when new data is read from primary memory. Cache memory design takes advantage of a principle known as 'locality'. Programs tend to exhibit temporal locality and spatial locality. An example of temporal locality is the loops in software that tend to get executed many times, meaning the instructions are re-used over and over. The amount of temporal locality that a processor cache can take advantage of is related to the size of the cache, its organization, and its replacement strategy. See **cache**. Compare **spatial locality**.

10base2 The IEEE 802.3 standard for bus topologies. 10base2 refers to 10 megabits per second, baseband, using 656-foot (200-meter) maximum cable length (thin coaxial). See **Cheapernet**.

10base5 The IEEE 802.3 standard for bus topologies. 10base5 refers to 10 megabits per second, baseband, using 1640-foot (500-meter) maximum cable length (thick coaxial). See **Ethernet/802**.3.

10broad36 The IEEE 802.3 standard for bus topologies. 10broad36 refers to 10 megabits per second, broadband, using a 2.24-mile (3.6-kilometer) maximum cable length (coaxial).

tens complement [ISO The radix complement in the decimal numeration system.]

TEP Terminal emulation program; a program which enables a personal computer to surrender its processing powers to allow it to act like a dumb terminal so that it can communicate with a mainframe or minicomputer.

ter Third version. See **V.xter**.

tera- See **T**.

teraFLOP Tera (10^{12}) floating point operations per second. See **FLOP**.

terminal A keyboard (for input) and a screen/monitor or printer (for output) that connect to a computer and serve as its input/output system.

FUN FACT

How fast is a teraFLOP? If every person on Earth had a calculator and each performed nonstop calculations for one minute, then by comparison, a computer operating at one teraFLOP could perform the same amount of work in only one second.

---

terminal emulation program A program which enables a personal computer to act like a dumb terminal so that it can communicate with a mainframe or minicomputer. Abbreviation 'TEP'.

terminal server In local area networking (LAN), terminal servers can be used to allow terminals, microcomputers, printers, and modems access to the devices attached to the LAN via RS-232-C ports. Users can establish multiple sessions on several hosts that are attached to the LAN. Only one session is active at any one time, but the user may access different sessions without having to log in each time. When more than one node offers the same service, the terminal server will assign the terminal user to the node that would best balance the overall load on the network. If a host fails, those terminals that are logically connected to it are allowed to access other hosts on the LAN. The terminal server performs many of the input/output (I/O) and terminal handling functions that would otherwise have to be performed by the host. This considerably reduces the central processing unit's overhead caused by terminal I/O. Modern terminal servers perform multiple levels of security checking and are designed to prevent unauthorized access to any of the hosts attached to the LAN.

terminate and stay resident See **TSR**.

tertiary storage Storage which is generally used for archival purposes — that is, as a backup for secondary storage. Tertiary storage products include a variety of open-reel and cartridge magnetic tape drives, as well as optical products such as CD–ROM and WORM devices. Generally, tertiary products provide access to vast amounts of data in a small space, but at slower access speeds than magnetic disks.

test [ISO The operation of a functional unit and comparison of its achieved result with the defined result to establish acceptability. *Example:* A device test or a program test.]

test data [ISO The data used for a check problem.]

test plan [ISO A plan that establishes detailed requirements, criteria, general methodology, responsibilities, and general planning for test and evaluation of a system.]

tester A member of a programming team who prepares challenging data used to exhaustively test the new program.

Texas Instruments As one of the leading high-technology companies in the United States, Texas Instruments (TI) engages in worldwide development, manufacture

---

NEWSFLASH

Of the five major terminals (IBM 3270, 5250, ASCII, ANSI, and X Windows), X Windows is projected to be the fastest growing in each segment worldwide. At the end of 1992, X Windows terminals represented 4.6% of total worldwide unit terminal shipments and occupied last or fifth place among various terminal segments. X Windows' market share is expected to increase each year. In 1997, it should represent 36.2% of the worldwide unit shipments and the second position.

---

and sale of semiconductors, defense electronics systems, computer systems, industrial control systems, electrical controls, metallurgical materials, and consumer electronic products. Based in Dallas, Texas, TI has manufacturing operations in more than 50 facilities in 17 countries, and sales offices and service centers throughout the world. The company was founded in 1930 as Geophysical Services to provide geophysical exploration services to the petroleum industry using new technology designed for the United States Navy. In 1946 it formally added electronic systems manufacturing to its operations, thereby entering a new era of dynamic growth. In 1951 the company adopted its current name, Texas Instruments Incorporated, and in the following year, TI entered the semiconductor business. TI's position as a world leader in electronics is founded on a long tradition of transforming technological ideas into useful products and services. A pioneer in the development and application of microelectronics, TI's 'firsts' include the development of the commercial pocket radio, which proved the practicality of using transistors in a mass-produced commercial product (1954); the commercial silicon transistor, which made it possible to use transistors in military products (1954); the integrated circuit, which laid the foundation for the electronics revolution (1958); the terrain-following airborne radar, which enhanced the survivability of military aircraft penetrating enemy air defense systems (1958); the forward-looking infrared (FLIR) system, which used thermal energy radiating from a scene to provide the military with a television-like display of the setting in total darkness or through smoke screens (1964); the hand-held calculator, which changed the way mathematics and science are taught around the world (1967); the single-chip microcomputer, the 'miracle chip' that placed all the logic circuits and memory cells of a computer on a single, small piece of silicon (1970); and the LISP (list processing) chip, the first 32-bit microcomputer developed specifically for artificial intelligence (AI) applications (1987). Today, semiconductors are TI's principal business, making it one of the world's largest suppliers of integrated circuits, TI is also a leading United States producer of dynamic random-access memory (DRAM) chips, focusing on application-specific integrated circuits (ASICs), very-large-scale integration (VLSI) logic circuits, applications processors, advanced linear circuits, and military semiconductors. See **Kilby, Jack St Clair.**

TFLOP Tera (10^{12}) floating point operations per second. See **FLOP.**

TFTP Trivial file transfer protocol.

thermal agitation See **thermal noise.**

thermal noise Noise is any unwanted electrical signal which interferes with a communications channel. This is often a random transmission of varying frequency, amplitude, and phase, and is externally generated. See **noise.**

thermal plotter A non-impact printer. See **electrothermal printer.**

thermal printer [ISO A non-impact printer in which the characters are produced by applying hot elements to heat-sensitive paper directly or by melting ink from a ribbon onto plain paper.]

thin film head Some read/write head manufacturing techniques require the head/slider assemblies to be machined separately, with the coils wound by hand or machine, thereby limiting the head width, and therefore limiting track density. To overcome this problem, a technology called 'thin film head technology' has emerged. It allows narrower tracks for greater track (radial) density. Thin film heads are actually an application of integrated circuit technology. Instead of a ferrite toroid with a bonded glass gap and wire coil, functionally-equivalent elements are layered onto a durable substrate of alumina titanium carbide using a photolithographic technique similar to that used to manufacture integrated circuits. Hundreds of such structures are built up on a wafer of substrate material, which is then cut into individual head assemblies. Thin film heads actually help to improve both dimensions of areal density. In addition to reducing track widths, they help increase bit density because their gaps have more consistent size and shape than can be achieved with other technologies. See **read/write head** and **track density.** ▼

Thinnet See **Cheapernet.**

Thinwire ENET See **Cheapernet.**

third generation The integrated circuit technology used in computers from 1965 to 1970. The transistor was replaced by the integrated circuits which were first introduced in 1959, but their price made their common usage prohibitive until IBM launched the System/360 family of computers which cost IBM US$5000 million. The System/360 was the world's largest family of computers. It incorporated five different processors with a

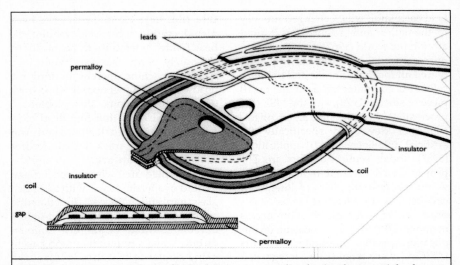

thin film head *Structure of a thin film head. To increase recording density, the magnetic heads must be made smaller, and to increase storage capacity, data must be transferred faster. Thin film head technology resolves both problems. It has a magnetic circuit which is formed by photolithography and thin film techniques. This figure illustrates the structure of the head. The head has several applications: (a) as a multiturn, narrow-track head for high recording density; (b) as a multitrack head for magnetic tape and fixed-head disk drives; and (c) as a magnetoresistive head for perpendicular recording.*

total of 19 different configurations using Solid Logic Technology. The third generation introduced the concept of 'operating systems'. Previous-generation computers were known as 'serial processors' because they could only process one job at a time. Because they did not use operating systems, trained operators had to individually monitor programs, and manually coordinate communications between the central processing unit and other devices such as printers. The IBM Operating System/360 was developed by hundreds of programmers using over 3 million program instructions. Upward compatibility within the family range was possible — a feature which made third generation computing much easier to use and upgrade. This period saw over 80 manufacturers launch some 200 new products for business and scientific applications. Software improvements included the introduction of BASIC for beginner programmers, and RPG (Report Program Generator) which made report generation an easy task for information systems managers. In 1969, IBM bowed to public and government pressure to relinquish its monopoly on proprietary software for its new systems, opening the way for hundreds of manufacturers to publish cheaper software. During the third generation, minicomputers became accepted as small, robust, and inexpensive computers that did not need the attention of senior computer professionals to maintain, replacing some of IBM's large mainframes. Around that time in an old brick wool mill in Massachusetts,

Digital Equipment Corporation (DEC) was founded by Kenneth Olsen and his brother. Their first minicomputer (the PDP-8) sold for US$18 000. Fierce competition saw the emergence of Data General, whose first minicomputer (called 'Nova') was launched in 1969 for US$8000. By 1971, the fourth generation saw the introduction of the microprocessor, opening the way for very-large-scale integration technology. See **integrated circuit**. Compare **fourth generation** and **second generation**.

3+ A network operating system from 3Com Corporation.

385 See **Intel 82385**.

386 See **Intel 80386**.

386 Smart Cache A cache chip produced by Intel Corporation to integrate the entire cache subsystem onto a single chip: control logic, 16-kilobyte data SRAM (static random-access memory), a four double-word write buffer, and a four double-word line buffer. The 80486 central processing unit's on-chip cache architecture is utilized by the 386 Smart Cache, allowing it to achieve equal or greater performance than previous 64- and 128-kilobyte caches. See **cache**.

386SX See **Intel 80386 SX**.

387 See **Intel 80387**.

3D Three-dimensional or three dimensions.

3M Trademark of Minnesota Mining and Manufacturing.

3rd generation See **third generation**.

3½-inch disk A magnetic flexible disk fully enclosed in a rigid plastic casing and used as a secondary storage medium for personal computers. This 3½-inch disk was developed by Sony Corporation and introduced by Apple Computer Corporation in their Apple Macintosh range. IBM, Compaq, and other leading computer manufacturers followed suit. As yet, the 3½-inch disk has not entirely replaced the 5¼-inch disk, but it does offer several advantages. For example, the 5¼-inch disk has an exposed section which can be easily damaged by dust, fingerprints, and other particles, whereas each 3½-inch disk employs an automatic aluminum gate which only opens after the disk has been inserted into the disk drive. Another advantage of the smaller disk is the ease of write-protecting. This is simply done by moving a plastic device located at the back — unlike the 5¼-inch disk which requires a piece of adhesive tape to cover the notch on the side. When a double-density 3½-inch disk is formatted for Macintosh computers, it has a storage capacity of 800 kilobytes, while a high-density disk has 1.44 megabytes. When formatting for DOS, OS/2, and Intel-based UNIX products, a double-density 3½-inch disk offers a storage capacity of 720 kilobytes, while a high-density disk offers 1.44 megabytes. See **diskette**.

3066 virus A variant of the Traceback virus. See **Traceback virus**.

threshold function [ISO A two-valued switching function of one or more not necessarily Boolean arguments that takes the value one if a specified mathematical function of the arguments exceeds a given threshold value, and zero otherwise.]

threshold gate [ISO An operation that evaluates the threshold function of its operands.]

throughput [ISO A measure of the amount of work performed by a computer system over a given period of time. Example: Number of jobs per day.]

thumb wheel [ISO A wheel, rotatable about its axis, that provides a scalar value. *Note:* A pair of thumb wheels can be used as a locator.]

TI Pronounced 'tea-eye'. See **Texas Instruments**.

TIFF Tagged Image File Format; a graphics file format for scanned images which can be stored at up to 300 dots per inch.

tightly-coupled multiprocessing A system that shares common memory, input/output channels, and other system resources. Because of its fundamental

architectural difference to loosely-coupled systems, only the tightly-coupled multiprocessor can provide scalable performance and automatic load balancing to allow optimal overall system throughput. See **multiprocessing**. ▼

tilde An accent which is shaped like a wave (~) to indicate pronunciation. See **accent**.

time bomb Computer crime which involves the use of an idle code which, when released, could result in data destruction or other unauthorized functions. A 'time bomb' is a Trojan triggered by the recognition of a particular date code (as determined by the programmer of the time bomb). In comparison, a 'logic bomb' is also a Trojan which is triggered by a set of conditions (such as the number of files on the disk, or a certain combination of letters being typed as determined by the programmer of the logic bomb). See **infection**, **Trojan**, and **virus**.

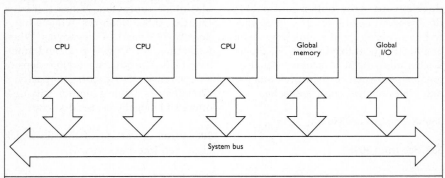

tightly-coupled multiprocessing There are two basic types of multiprocessor system in the marketplace today: loosely-coupled and tightly-coupled. A loosely-coupled multiprocessor system incorporates a number of processors, each with local resources that are not accessible by other processors. On the other hand, a tightly-coupled multiprocessing system shares common memory, input/output channels, and other system resources. Some systems, such as those from Wyse Technology, have exploited the tightly-coupled architecture to create a fully-symmetric system supporting up to eight Intel processor boards, along with 256 megabytes of shared main memory.

time code In video technology, a frame-by-frame address reference recorded on the spare track of a videotape or inserted in the vertical blanking interval. It is an eight-digit number; encoding time in hours, minutes, seconds, and video frames. For example, 04:17:29:30.

time division multiple access See **TDMA**.

time out [ISO An event that occurs at the end of a pre-determined period of time that began at the occurrence of another specified event. *Note:* The time out can be prevented by an appropriate signal.]

timer [ISO A register whose contents are changed at regular intervals in such a manner as to measure time.]

Times A built-in font offered by many laser printers and considered the most successful typeface ever designed. Times was the creation of Stanley Morison who in 1932 was commissioned by the London *Times* newspaper to design a typeface which was legible and offered economy of space. Morison produced a face with a large x-height, short descenders and ascenders, and slightly condensed characters. Its distinguishing characteristics include the low thickening of the lowercase 'c' and 'e'. From the original 10 point masters, Linotype offers the Times family which includes roman, italic, bold, and bold italic.

time scale factor [ISO A number used as a multiplier to transform the real time of the problem into computer time.]

time sharing A system in which two or more users can, through individual terminals, share the processing power of the central computer. Usually, processing is quick and the user does not notice that the computer is dedicating part of its time to other users. Time slices are usually measured in milliseconds. [ISO An operating technique of a computer system that provides for the interleaving in time of two or more processes in one processor.]

time slicing [ISO A mode of operation in which two or more processes are assigned quanta of time in the same processor.]

time slot In a local area network (LAN), whenever a single resource is to be used by multiple entities, some control method is required to regulate the use of the resources. There are several ways by which each station can gain access to the LAN when it needs to send a message. The three main categories of LAN access methods are: token passing; contention access; and time slot. One of the earliest access methods was developed for telephone systems and involves time division multiplexing (TDM), in which fixed-length data 'slots' circulate in the system. This control method is most commonly associated with ring topologies and is then called 'slotted-ring access'. For bus systems, the free slots are usually pre-assigned to specific stations, while in ring networks the slots are claimed 'on the fly'. The most prominent example is the 'Cambridge ring', designed at Cambridge University in England. In a slotted ring, a station can place a data packet in the first available empty slot. As the packet circles the ring, the station or stations to which it was sent copy it as it passes, setting a control bit to indicate that the frame was received. The transmitting station eventually receives its own packet and must remove it to free the slot. Because access can be made available on a regular, repeatable basis, slotted rings are well suited for carrying voice transmissions. A version of the Cambridge ring exists as an international standard under ISO. A 50-megabit per second, fiber-optic-based, slotted-ring proposal (carrying data, voice, and video) is used as the basis for the IEEE 802.6 metropolitan area network (MAN) standard. Another scheme, called 'register insertion', also utilizes the ring topology. This approach uses shift registers which are switched in and out of the ring for data transmission and reception. The shift register length fixes the frame size. To transmit, a station waits for idle characters on the channel, removes its shift register from the ring, loads a message frame into the register, inserts the register back into the ring, and shifts the contents out. Received messages feed into the shift register temporarily while addressing is checked and then shift back onto the ring. Frames can be removed by either the sending or the receiving station. On a large network, where frames are removed by the destination station, more than one message could be on the network at one time. Compare **contention access** and **token passing**.

TISI Thai Industrial Standards Institute; Thailand's standards body formed in 1969.

TLB Translation lookaside buffer. See **virtual memory support**.

TLI Transport Level Interface; an Application Program Interface developed by AT&T.

TM 1. Transmission media; the means

by which data can be transferred, such as wire, light, and radio. 2. Trademark.

token [ISO In a local area network, the symbol of authority passed successively from one data station to another to indicate the station temporarily in control of the transmission medium. *Note:* Each data station has an opportunity to acquire and use the token to control the medium.]

token bus network A local area network using a bus topology which uses the token-passing access method. The IEEE 802.4 token bus access method is deterministic. This means that each station is assigned a logical position and therefore each station is allowed the right to use the channel in a pre-determined order. A station must first have a 'free token' before it can transmit. A station that receives a free token may change the token's status to 'busy', add a data message to the token, and place it back on the cable with the address of the destination device. Three options are provided in the IEEE 802.4 for the physical layer. All three use broadband coaxial cable, modems, and analog signaling. The simplest option uses a form of frequency shift keying (FSK) and is referred to as 'single channel broadband' which operates at 1 megabit per second (MBps). The second option also uses a single channel approach and FSK. It operates at speeds of 5 and 10 MBps. The third option supports full broadband facilities which can support more than one data channel and operates at 1, 5, and 10 MBps. [ISO A bus network in which a token passing procedure is used.]

token passing In a local area network (LAN) using baseband communication links, the passing of a signal (token) to each device in turn. If the device has data to send, it seizes the token to ensure exclusive control over the link. When transmission is completed, the device then releases the token to the next device on a network because only the device which has the token may transmit. When the device which has the token does not want to transmit, it passes the token on once again to another device. As the token circulates, a station wishing to transmit examines the received token to see whether it is free or busy. If the token is busy, the station checks the addressing of the attached message, and either copies it first or just passes it on. If the token is free, the station attaches its own message behind the token, re-issues it as a busy token and puts it on the network. The message completes a full circuit around the ring and is removed by the transmitting station, which then re-issues a free token and passes it on. A station must release the token after each transmission and is not allowed to transmit beyond a set time limit on each token possession. All other nodes on the LAN will have an opportunity to capture the token before that station can capture the token again. This routing introduces some access delay, which is called 'token latency time' or 'ring latency time'. This latency, based on the physical length of the cable and the number of stations attached, is completely predictable. In some token schemes, token capture is based on multiple levels of priority depending upon the class of service required for a particular message. For example, network recovery messages and synchronous (real-time voice) transmissions could be assigned higher priority access to the channel. The token passing protocol re-

quires that one of the network stations be an active monitor to generate the initial token and to check for a lost token or a continuously-circulating message (stuck token). The remaining stations act as passive monitors and must be capable of assuming the active monitor function should the active monitor fail. Compare **contention access.** ▼

token passing procedure [ISO In a local area network using a token, the set of

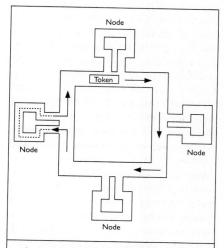

token passing This diagram illustrates how, in a token ring topology, a message is sent around a network using a token. Unlike a token bus, a token ring has no address field, circulating freely until it is claimed by a station wishing to transmit. It is then chained to a 'busy' token with an attached message, which makes one round trip. This busy token is then removed by the transmitting station. When the transmitting station has finished its data transfer or a pre-set time limit has expired, a new 'free' token is issued. Token operation is maintained by an active monitor station which is selected by arbitration at network initialization. The monitor checks for a lost token or persistently busy (stuck) token situation, and also generates the network master clock.

rules that governs how a data station acquires, uses, and transfers the token.]

token ring network A local area network (LAN) using a ring topology which uses the token-passing access method. The IEEE 802.5 token ring access method is deterministic, meaning that each station is assigned a logical position and therefore each station is allowed the right to use the channel in a pre-determined order. On a token ring network, token passing operates by allowing each node the chance to transmit on a 'round robin' basis. It can use twisted pair, co-axial cable, or fiber optic cable (called 'FDDI'). The token ring can operate at data rates from 1 to 16 megabits per second. Although all personal computers in a token ring LAN are electrically connected in a ring, the physical connection of cables resembles a star topology. At the center of the star is a device called a 'multistation access unit'. This unit contains an electrical ring circuit. The single cable from each computer actually contains two pairs of wires — one pair for receiving and the other for sending. This design makes it easy to add or remove network nodes. [ISO A ring network that allows unidirectional data transmission between data stations, by a token passing procedure, such that the transmitted data return to the transmitting station.]

tomcatv One of the ten SPEC (Systems Performance Evaluation Cooperative) benchmarks drawn from real-world applications including scientific and engineering areas, focusing on system performance, memory, input/output, graphics, networking, multi-user, and commercial applications. Tomcatv is a highly vectorizable double-precision floating point FORTRAN benchmark. It is a vectorized mesh generation program. On most systems, the sum of system time and user time should be very close to the elapsed time because this benchmark does little input/output. The original intent of the benchmark was to measure only the time for the computation, omitting set-up code. Substantial speed-ups have been observed on several shared-memory multiprocessor systems. In most cases, the executable file has been well under 1 megabyte. The uninitialized arrays in the program total about 3.7 megabytes. See **SPEC**.

T1 Developed by AT&T, a digital communications network that transmits at 1.544 megabits per second. See **T-carrier services**.

toolsmith A programmer who designs/prepares special program utilities (tools) which may be used by the entire programming team of a particular project.

TOP Technical and Office Protocols. Using OSI protocols, TOP specifies a document exchange format and a method for exchanging computer graphics.

top-down [ISO Pertaining to a method or procedure that starts at the highest level of abstraction and proceeds toward the lowest level.]

top-level transaction See **nested transaction**.

topology The way in which local area networks are designed, wired, and arranged, and how the devices connected to the network are able to communicate and to share and exchange information and resources. There are two types of network topology: centralized and decentralized. A star topology is an example of a centralized network where one central file server controls access to the network. Bus and ring topologies are examples of decentralized networks where each workstation can independently access the network. The word 'topology' comes from the Greek word *topos*, meaning 'place'. See **bus topology**, **ring topology**, and **star topology**.

total function [ISO The function that allows the provision of the result of a calculation that may be displayed or printed and that cannot be re-used without manual re-entry.]

touch screen Like most supplements to the keyboard, a touch screen is an input device that functions primarily as a pointing device. When a user's finger touches the monitor screen, the cursor moves, or a software command is issued. Touch screens are most commonly used in point-of-information displays, such as those that appear in many shopping centers, hotels, and airports. Many training courses and simulators also use touch screens. Touch screens involve some type of hardware that fits over or around the face of the video monitor. Some implementations use a touch-sensitive membrane. When pressure is applied, a circuit is closed at the point of touch and x/y coordinate information is made available to the application software. Other touch screens use light-emitting diodes to generate a grid of light beams over the face of the monitor. When a finger approaches the screen's surface, the beams of light are broken. The touch screen's electronics send the coordinates of the broken beams to the computer. [ISO A display device that allows the

user to interact with a data processing system by touching an area on its screen.] Compare **tablet**.

TP 1. Teleprocessing. 2. See **transaction processing**.

TP designer Transaction processing designer; the person with the overall responsibility for translating a set of business requirements into a computing system. Also called 'application designer'.

TP4 OSI's connection-oriented transport-layer protocol.

TP monitor Transaction processing monitor; a software product that provides, in a single bundled package, all the elements of an environment in which transaction processing application programs can be designed and run efficiently. Its essential purpose is to optimize the use of system resources for the specialized way transaction processing applications tend to use a computer. Hence, it is usually a layered software package, used in conjunction with a particular base operating system, and may provide a standard interface between the application program and such facilities as the terminal and the database.

TPNS Teleprocessing Network Simulator; an IBM program that simulates holding a conversation with a computer.

TP1 benchmark Transaction processing benchmark. The TP1 benchmark is based on a set of specifications originally introduced in 1985. This set of specifications simulates a simple user withdrawal or deposit to an account in a retail banking environment. The processing power of a system is measured in transactions per second (TPS). The TP1 benchmark measures the performance of a system under multi-user commercially-oriented workloads. It is considered one of the more complete benchmarks, because it depend heavily upon input/output architecture, memory subsystem, and software efficiency as well as the central processing unit. TP1 performance may vary when run with different database management systems, so the results quoted by various vendors depend upon implementation details such as choice of database management software and the actual scenario. For these reasons, the results are not entirely comparable to competitive TP1 benchmarks on other platforms. Nevertheless, TP1 is widely used to measure the ability of a system to support large numbers of online transactions. These transactions include such activities as withdrawing money from an account (banking), purchasing shares of stock (securities trading), or reserving a seat on a flight (airline reservation). See **benchmark**.

TPS Transactions per second.

TQFP Thin quad flat package. Usually a flat plastic unit approximately 1.4 millimeters thick, used to house a microprocessor for use in small devices such as personal digital assistants.

Traceback virus An indirect-action file virus (capable of operating as a direct-action file virus) which adds 3066 bytes to any .COM file or .EXE file. Once it becomes active, Traceback acts in a similar, though less entertaining, way to the Cascade virus. All of the letters on the screen drop, one at a time, to the bottom of the screen, and on occasion, are made

to rise up again. However, unlike Cascade, there are no sound-effects. Traceback is sometimes called '3066'. See **direct-action file virus** and **indirect-action file virus**. Compare **Cascade virus**.

trace program [ISO A diagnostic program that can monitor the execution of some or all of the instructions of a computer program and record the effects of each step.]

track 1. On a disk, the band described by the field of coverage of a single head as the disk rotates past it. The data in a track is recorded serially in a stream that is 1 bit wide. Tracks on magnetic/optical disks each form complete circles, unlike a music album where the track is one long spiral. Although the outer tracks are longer (because of the larger circumference) and travel faster, each track on the disk stores the same amount of data. The read/write arm takes the same amount of time to read data on the outer track as on the inner. The outermost track is labelled with the lowest number (usually 0, 00, or 000). Each track consists of five fields: (1) Pre-index gap — the fifth gap, which is only written when the track is formatted. (2) Index address mark — a unique code that indicates the beginning of a data track. One index mark is written on each track when the track is formatted. (3) Post index gap — the first gap, which is used during disk read and write operations to synchronize the data separator logic with the data to be read from the ID field (of the first sector). The post index gap is written only when the disk is formatted. (4) Sector — the sector information is repeated once for each sector on the track. (5) Final gap — the fourth gap, which is written when the track is formatted and extends from the last physical data field on the track to the physical index mark. The length of this gap is dependent upon the number of bytes per sector specified, the length of the program-selectable gaps specified, and the drive speed. See **diskette** and **track density**. 2. On a tape, a 1-bit-wide band running in the longitudinal direction. See **head/arm**. 3. [ISO On a data medium, a path associated with a single read/write head as the data medium moves past it.] ▼

track and hold unit [ISO A functional unit whose output analog variable is equal to either the input analog variable or a sample of this variable selected by the action of an external Boolean signal. *Note:* When tracking, the functional unit

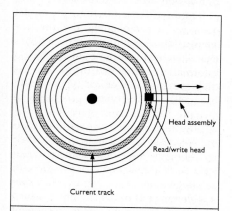

track *The surface of a disk is divided logically into concentric circles. Each concentric circle is called a 'track'. The group of same tracks on all cylinders is collectively called a 'cylinder'. The number of tracks on a surface (which affects storage density) is determined by the head positioners. Typically, stepper head positioners have fewer tracks than drivers that use a voice-coil positioner. Once the surface is divided into cylinders, it is further divided radially. The area between the radial spokes is referred to as a 'sector'.*

follows the input analog variable; when holding, it holds the value of the input analog variable at the instant of switching.]

trackball A variation on the mouse (input device), looking like a mouse turned on its back. Instead of moving a ball over a table, cursor movement is achieved by moving a ball in a stationary housing. Like a mouse, a trackball has application anywhere that rapid and accurate cursor movement is required. An advantage of the trackball is that it does not require a large amount of desk space. Trackballs work using the same technology as mice, either mechanical or optomechanical, sensing both x and y coordinate movements. Trackballs are now a standard device on most notebook computers. See **mouse**. Compare **tablet**.

track density Track density is measured along a radius of the disk by counting the number of tracks in an inch of recorded surface. Track density is primarily determined by track width, which is limited by head width. If a narrow core with adequate signal level and signal-to-noise ratio can be manufactured, then track width can be reduced, and track density increased accordingly. (Note that tracks are separated from each other by an isolation zone to avoid overwriting data on adjacent tracks when a track is written on.) In addition to core width, positioning accuracy also limits track density. A modern disk drive positioner must be capable of bringing a head to the center of a track less than a thousandth of an inch wide for signal recovery. For an average disk drive, this means moving a 3½-inch-long access arm to within less than three-thousandths of an inch of the target position in an average time of 17 milliseconds, and maintaining this position indefinitely. Scaled up, this is roughly equivalent to a man holding a 4-foot-long (1.2-meter) pointer with his arm extended, swinging it as fast as possible, and stopping suddenly with the tip pointing directly at a point of a needle. Techniques developed within the last few years, notably embedded servo (the embedding of servo positioning signals on data tracks), make very high positioning accuracy possible. To enhance seeking performance, more powerful positioner mechanisms have been combined with such optimization techniques as controller-based seek ordering. Average seek times can be reduced by mounting multiple heads on each access arm. Projections of much higher areal densities in the future imply correspondingly higher track densities without penalty in average seek time. Positioning with this speed and accuracy, as well as manufacturing heads with much narrower core widths than is possible today, are the key engineering challenges that must be met to achieve higher track densities in the future. [ISO The number of tracks per unit of length, measured in a direction perpendicular to the tracks. *Note:* The track density is inversely related to the track pitch.]

tracking (In computer graphics.) [ISO The action of moving a tracking symbol.]

tracking symbol [ISO A symbol on the display surface that indicates the position corresponding to the coordinate data produced by a locator.]

track pitch [ISO The distance between adjacent tracks, measured in a direction

perpendicular to the tracks. *Note:* The track pitch is inversely related to the track density.]

trailer [ISO The portion of magnetic tape that follows the end-of-tape marker.]

Trailer Boss IBM's internal code name used to describe the project and the product that was introduced to replace the 3990 disk controller.

trailer label See **magnetic tape**.

transaction processing Transactions fall into either business transactions or computer transactions. It is important to distinguish between these two types of transactions, because a single business transaction often requires several computer transactions, providing the mechanism for accomplishing the business transaction. A computer transaction is characterized by the amount and type of information exchanged in the terminal dialogue, the number and types of database calls, and the type of processing required. Transaction processing (TP) applications process pre-defined types of business transactions interactively, modeling the state of a business in real-time. Such applications are mission-critical, large-scale, and complex. They span a wide range of industries and business functions, including order fulfillment, general ledger, payroll, distribution, work-order processing, shop-floor data collection, securities clearing, and financial trading. Historically, most TP applications have been developed to run in a single system. The application programs written to perform computer transactions usually involve updating a database to reflect changes to data. They are also written to notify the user that the change has taken place as intended. TP flows through all aspects of the business and can provide, in real-time, the information necessary to make informed business decisions on the spot. TP minimizes costs by reducing the number of times that data must be handled and by providing timely updates to the information databases. When transactions are processed in real-time, the database always reflects the most current information. For example, an inventory management system not only maintains the parts inventory level, but also triggers an automatic reorder of a part as indicated by its inventory level. TP embodies the concept of a user-defined transaction that has a start point and an end point. A transaction is both atomic (either all of the operations take effect or none of them do) and recoverable (after a failure, the system recovers the effect of all completed transactions). For example, in a money transfer transaction, one account is debited while another is credited with the same amount. Should a failure occur between the debit and the credit, the transaction processing system aborts the transaction and does not update the database. The system can then automatically re-submit the transaction for processing at a later stage. Today, there is a significant trend toward distributed TP in which the application runs on a set of cooperating systems linked together in a network. Distributed TP can provide a number of benefits in terms of performance, availability, and local control, including better response time, higher aggregate throughput, the ability to scale up incrementally, better price/performance, better availability, and greater local control. See **ACID test, distributed transaction processing**, and **OLTP. ▼**

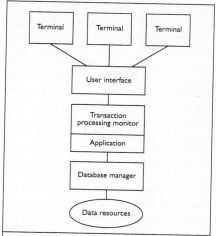

transaction processing This diagram shows the user interface (being a forms handling capability) as the data input element in the transaction processing system. The user interface provides screen designs and validation of input data, and includes such presentation services as the windowing environment and the forms management subsystem. The transaction processing monitor provides a standard interface between the application programs and input devices such as terminals, and between the application programs and the database manager. The term 'application' refers to the entire set of programs that collectively implement a specific business process. Individual programs that implement part of this business process are 'application programs'. The database manager is a database management system that implements and manages a database. The database is a collection of data items that represent business information.

transaction processing benchmark See **TP1 benchmark**.

transaction processing designer Also called 'application designer'; the person with the overall responsibility for translating a set of business requirements into a computing system. Abbreviation 'TP designer'. See **transaction processing**.

transaction processing monitor A software product that provides, in a single bundled package, all the elements of an environment in which transaction processing application programs can be designed and run efficiently. Its essential purpose is to optimize the use of system resources for the specialized way transaction processing applications tend to use a computer. Hence, it is usually a layered software package, used in conjunction with a particular base operating system, and may provide a standard interface between the application program and such facilities as the terminal and the database. Abbreviation 'TP monitor'.

transaction services layer Each of the layers of IBM's Systems Network Architecture (SNA) has its own set of rules for communicating with its peer layer in the other node. The layers communicate with each other by adding header information to user data. The transaction services layer (seventh layer) is SNA's highest. It was formalized by IBM in 1968 to provide users with a single-system image into the network services through common command language formats. It provides the application services such as distributed database access and document interchange. See **SNA layers**.

transceiver Transmitter and receiver; a device that both transmits and receives data, providing the electrical and physical interface to a network cable. Also known as a 'media access unit' (MAU).

transcribe [ISO To copy data from one data medium to another, converting them as necessary for acceptance by the receiving medium.]

transducer Analog transducers are often used to convert the value of a physical property, such as temperature and pressure, to an analog voltage. These kinds of transducers then require an analog-to-digital converter to put the measurement into a form that is compatible with a digital control system. Another kind of transducer is now available that encodes the value of the physical property into a signal that can be directly read by a digital control system. These devices, called 'resonant transducers', are oscillators whose frequency depends upon the physical property being measured. They output a train of rectangular pulses whose repetition rate encodes the value of the quantity being measured. The word 'transducer' comes from the Latin word *transducere,* where *trans* means 'across' and *ducere* means 'lead'.

transfer [ISO To send data from one storage location to another.]

transfer interpreter [ISO A device that prints on a punched card the characters corresponding to hole patterns punched in another card.]

transfer time [ISO The time interval between the instant at which a transfer of data starts and the instant at which it is completed.]

transform [ISO To change the form of data according to specified rules, without fundamentally changing the meaning of the data.]

transistor A digital solid-state miniaturized replacement for the vacuum tube; used to modulate or control the flow of an electric current. ▼

translate (In programming languages.)

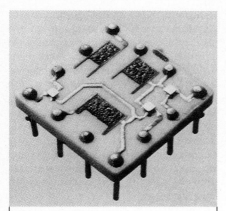

transistor The invention of the transistor at Bell Laboratories in 1947 foreshadowed the time, a decade later, when the device would give birth to a new 'generation' of computer technology. As a replacement for the vacuum tube, the tiny transistor shortened the time needed for electrical pulses to complete a circuit. It generated less heat, was much more reliable, and lowered production costs. Ways were found to incorporate the new transistor technology into computers and to automate the manufacture and testing of transistors by the millions. Only 1/200th the size of an early vacuum tube and using less than 1/100th the power, the transistor came into general use in computer systems in about 1960. The transistor's basic function in a computer is that of an electrical switch to perform logical operations. To form circuits, transistors were combined with capacitors, resistors, and other electrical elements on circuit cards.

[ISO To transform all or part of a program expressed in one programming language, into another programming language or into a machine language suitable for execution.]

translating [ISO Applying the same displacement to the position of one or more display elements.]

translation lookaside buffer See **virtual memory support**.

translation (compilation) (assembly) time 1. [ISO Any instant at which translation (compilation) (assembly) takes place.] 2. [ISO The amount of time needed to translate (compile) (assemble) a program.]

translator A computer program that translates a high-level language (like FORTRAN) into machine language. Particular language translators are called 'compilers' — for example, FORTRAN compiler, or COBOL compiler. [ISO A computer program that can translate.]

transliterate [ISO To convert data character by character.]

transmission control character [ISO A control character used to control or facilitate transmission of data between data terminal equipment. *Note:* Transmission control characters are described in ISO 646 and ISO 6429.]

transmission control layer Each of the layers of IBM's Systems Network Architecture (SNA) has its own set of rules for communicating with its peer layer in the other node. The layers communicate with each other by adding header information to user data. The transmission control layer (fourth layer) is responsible for session set-up and disconnection, and the overall end-to-end connectivity. It paces data exchanges to match the processing capacity at the end points of a session. This layer will also code data for security if needed. See **SNA layers**.

transmission medium In a telecommunications system, the type of media used for the transmission of data (message signals), voice, and images. The choice of the transmission medium will depend upon the distance involved, the desired transmission speed, and the associated costs. Common media include twisted pair wires, coaxial cable, microwaves, and fiber optics. All of these are known as 'bounded media', while radio is said to be an 'unbounded medium'. Each transmission medium, operating in a defined bandwidth, is susceptible to different noise (impairment) problems. The word 'transmission' comes from the Latin word *transmissio*, where *trans* means 'across' and *missio* means 'send'. [ISO The physical medium that conveys signals between data stations. Example: Twisted pair, optic fiber, coaxial cable.] See **noise**.

transmission path delay [ISO The time required for a bit to travel between the two most distant data stations in a bus network.]

transponder An electronic communications device (built into a communications satellite) designed to receive a weakened signal from an Earth station. The signal is then strengthened and re-broadcast. Each satellite may contain a large number of transponders, thereby increasing the transmission capacity. See **satellite transmission**.

transport layer The fourth layer of the OSI (Open Systems Interconnection) reference model. The transport layer maintains end-to-end reliability through data flow control and error recovery methods. It is responsible for breaking the message up into properly-sized packets and re-assembling them in the proper order at their destination. It also provides reception acknowledgment and initiates re-transmission when necessary. Another transport layer duty is to determine the most cost-effective means of data transport based upon the quality-of-service (QOS) requirements imposed by the session layer. The session layer requests a class of service, and the transport layer matches it with the services available in the network layer. See **OSI reference model**.

transverse parity check [ISO A parity check on a column of binary digits that are members of a set forming a matrix. *Example:* A parity check on the set of bits on a tape row.]

trapdoor 1. When developing complex computer programs, trapdoors are sections of code used by programmers as diagnostic tools which enable them to gain access to certain parts of a program. Before the programs are sold, the trapdoors should be removed for security purposes. 2. A term used to identify computer crime which involves the use of trapdoors (accidentally or intentionally left behind by programmers) to gain unauthorized access to certain parts of programs which may contain valuable confidential or proprietary information.

tredecillion See **exponent**.

tree network [ISO A network in which there is exactly one path between any two nodes.]

tree search [ISO In a tree structure, a search in which it is possible to decide, at each step, which part of the tree may be rejected without a further search.]

tributary station [ISO On a multipoint connection or a point-to-point connection, using basic mode link control, any data station other than the control station.]

trichromatic The technical name for the RGB representation of color to create all the colors in the spectrum. See **RGB**.

trigger circuit [ISO A circuit that has a number of stable states or unstable states, at least one being stable, and is designed so that a desired transition can be initiated by the application of a suitable pulse.]

trillion See **exponent**.

TRL Transistor–resistor logic.

Trojan The name given to any computer program in which is purposefully hidden special code written to intentionally cause damage to information (computer files). Unlike viruses, which can cause the same types of problems, Trojan horses cannot replicate themselves within a system. The term comes from the gigantic hollow wooden horse filled with Greek soldiers and used to gain entry and conquer the city of Troy during the Trojan war. Trojans are usually an act of espionage and sabotage designed to undermine established institutions. On occasions, newspaper headlines detail elaborate schemes which have caused widespread damage to large organizations. See **infection**. Compare **salami shaving** and **virus**.

truncated binary exponential backoff [ISO In a CSMA/CD network, the algorithm used to schedule re-transmission after a collision such that the re-transmission is delayed by an amount of time derived from the slot time and the number of attempts to re-transmit.] The word 'truncate' comes from the Latin word *truncare*, meaning 'maim'.

truncation 1. (Of a computation process.)

[ISO The termination of a computation process, before its final conclusion or natural termination, if any, in accordance with specified rules.] 2. (Of a string.) [ISO The deletion or omission of a leading or of a trailing portion of a string in accordance with specified criteria.]

truncation error [ISO An error due to truncation.]

trunk cable [ISO A cable connecting trunk coupling units for the purpose of allowing communication among data stations.]

trunk coupling unit [ISO A physical device that connects a data station to a trunk cable by means of a drop cable. *Note:* The trunk coupling unit contains the means for inserting the station into the network or bypassing it.]

truth table [ISO An operation table for a logic operation.]

TSE Türk Standardlari Enstitüsü; Turkey's standards body formed in 1954.

TSO Time-sharing option; a system introduced by IBM in which two or more users can, through individual terminals, share the processing power of the central computer. Usually, processing is quick and the user does not notice that the computer is dedicating part of its time to other users. Time slices are usually measured in milliseconds.

TSR Terminate and stay resident; normally, when programs finish executing, they relinquish the random-access memory (RAM) to the next program that is to be loaded. However, TSR utilities do not give up their memory space.

They terminate but stay resident in RAM, sharing the memory with application software so that they can be accessed with a unique combination of keystrokes. One popular TSR program developed by Borland is called 'Turbo Lightning'. By pressing a combination of keys, this utility will check the spelling of all text being displayed on the monitor by the current application program. TSR utilities offer many other services such as calendars, key re-programming, notepads, and calculators. When using large TSR utilities, it may be necessary for the user to increase the amount of RAM available on the computer so that the TSR utility and other application packages can be used simultaneously.

TSW Telesoftware.

TTBS Trinidad and Tobago Bureau of Standards; Trinidad's standards body formed in 1974.

TTC Telecommunications Technical Committee.

TTC&M Tracking, telemetry, control, and monitoring.

T3 Developed by AT&T, a digital communications network that transmits at 44.736 megabits per second. See **T-carrier services**.

TTL Transistor–transistor logic. Pronounced 'tee-tee-el'.

TTY Teletypewriter.

tumbling [ISO Dynamic display of the rotation of display elements about an axis the orientation of which is continuously changing in space.]

tunneling biquantum-well See **optical neurocomputer**.

turnaround time [ISO The elapsed time between submission of a job and the return of the complete output.]

turn-on stabilizing time [ISO The time interval between the instant power is applied to a device and the instant at which the device performs according to its operating specifications.]

twisted pair Wire such as that commonly used to connect telephones to wall jacks. Insulated, color-coded twisted pairs of copper wire help reduce the leakage of a signal from one wire to another. When bundled, they can have up to 25 pairs of wires. To protect the wire from external electronic noise, it can be shielded (enclosed in a metallic braid or sheathing), although common telephone wire is unshielded. Because attenuation and crosstalk may be severe at higher frequencies, twisted pairs are limited to broadband multiplexed channels using analog signals. Carefully positioned repeaters allow twisted pair wires to transmit at frequencies exceeding 500 kilohertz. When used to transmit computer data, the line speed of the wire is rated by the number of bits per second (Bps) it can successfully transmit. Generally, 9600 Bps is the optimum line speed over telephone lines. However, twisted pair wires used across short distances in local area networks can successfully transfer data at millions of bits per second. Although twisted pair wires generally operate between 12 and 24 multiplexed (voice-grade) channels, they can handle bandwidths exceeding 1 megahertz when special amplifying devices are used. If used only for baseband transmission, up to 1.5 megabits per second can be carried.

two-byte languages Languages that require 2 bytes to fully represent each character in their set (which may consist of up to 65 536 characters). Two-byte languages are also characterized by multiple character sets. For example, the Japanese language uses two different types of Roman text (1-byte and 2-byte), two unique phonetic character sets (Kana) with more than 160 unique characters in each, and an autographic character set (Kanji) with more than 7000 characters. A phonetic character set describes pronunciation, while in an autographic character set, each character has a specific meaning. For example, a single Chinese character represents the word 'sun'.

286 See **Intel 80286**.

287 See **Intel 80287**.

two-out-of-five code [ISO A binary-coded decimal notation in which each decimal digit is represented by a binary numeral consisting of five bits out of which two are of one kind, conventionally ones, and three are of the other kind, conventionally zeros. *Note:* The usual weights are 6-3-2-1-0 except for the representation of zero, which is then 00110.]

2PC See **two-phase commit**.

two-phase commit A protocol used to synchronize the 'commit' actions of multiple independent resource managers. Either all resource managers commit the transaction or all roll it back because the transaction cannot be committed by some participants. Without such synchroniza-

tion, a transaction cannot make updates involving more than one resource manager without putting its atomic properties at risk — if the transaction succeeds, all updates must be made visible automatically, whereas if a failure occurs, all updates must be backed out. The protocol has a 'prepare phase' in which each resource manager must indicate its willingness to commit. The protocol requires a coordinator to manage transactions. Abbreviation '2PC'. See **ACID test**.

twos complement [ISO The radix complement in the binary numeration system.]

two-way alternate communication [ISO Data communication such that data is transferred in both directions, one direction at a time.]

two-way interleaving See **interleaving**.

two-way simultaneous communication [ISO Data communication such that data is transferred in both directions at the same time.]

two-wire circuit A circuit that provides one pair of wires which are used alternately for transmission in each direction. It is also a communications channel designed for simplex or half-duplex operation. Two wires are provided at each termination and, with the exception of reverse channel circuits, information is usually transmitted in only one direction at a time. See **half duplex** and **simplex**. Compare **four-wire circuit**.

2086 virus A variant of the Fu Manchu virus. See **Fu Manchu virus**.

type (Of data.) [ISO A set of values together with a set of permitted operations.]

type bar [ISO A bar, mounted on an impact printer, that holds type slugs.]

typeface In typography, a particular style of character (type family to which a font belongs) including condensed, bold, or italics. Compare **font**. ▼

Typo virus A boot-sector virus that infects the boot sector of any diskette or hard disk operating with some Intel microprocessors. The virus is erratic and can affect the functions of the printer and even make the hard disk inaccessible. Its main purpose is to create typographical errors throughout a document. A pre-defined set of characters are programmed to be substituted. For example, the characters 'M', 'G', 'O', and '3' are substituted with the characters 'N', 'J', 'U', and '6' respectively. See **boot-sector virus**.

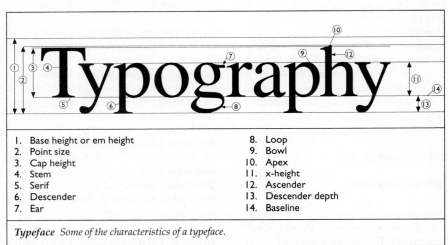

1. Base height or em height
2. Point size
3. Cap height
4. Stem
5. Serif
6. Descender
7. Ear
8. Loop
9. Bowl
10. Apex
11. x-height
12. Ascender
13. Descender depth
14. Baseline

Typeface Some of the characteristics of a typeface.

UA Unnumbered acknowledgment.

UACC Universal access authority.

UARS Upper Atmospheric Research Satellite.

UART Universal asynchronous receiver-transmitter. Pronounced 'you-art'.

UBASIC Sperry Univac's version of Beginners' All-purpose Symbolic Instruction Code. See **BASIC**.

UCF Utility control facility.

UCS Universal character set.

UDP User datagram protocol.

UDS Utility definition specification.

UECB User exit control block.

UFP Utility facilities program.

UHF Ultra-high frequency.

UI 1. See **UNIX International**. 2. User interface.

UID User identification. See **password** and **biometric security devices**.

UL Underwriters Laboratories. The US authority charged with approving electrical devices.

ULA Uncommitted logic array.

Ultimedia IBM's multimedia product that supports Ultimotion and Indeo video technology.

Ultimotion IBM's video compression algorithm.

ultra green The ability of a computer to move into different power management modes depending upon the level of usage, and ultimately shutting down to use less than 4 watts of power. The computer would progress through the power management stages, starting with light green, which refers to operation under 30 watts of power. Super green refers to systems that can shutdown to less than 20 watts of power, and ultra green machines can suspend operation to use less than 4 watts of power. See **green technology**. ▼

ULTRIX A BSD-based version of UNIX that runs on DEC VAXs and MicroVAXs. This is an enhanced operating system derived from AT&T's UNIX System V and Berkeley's 4/3 implementation. ULTRIX is a powerful and portable operating system that is compliant to

POSIX 1003.1 standards as well as specifications from X/Open and OSF. See **operating system**. Compare **UNIX**.

unavailable time [ISO From the point of view of a user, the time during which a functional unit cannot be used.]

unbuffered Referring to a device that transmits data characters as they are entered on the keyboard, or prints/displays the data characters as they are received, without storing the characters in memory.

unconditional jump instruction [ISO A jump instruction that specifies a mandatory jump.]

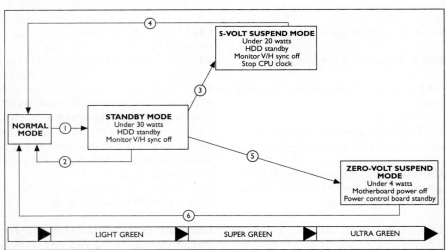

ultra green This diagram shows how a computer can be programmed to move into different power management modes, depending upon the level of usage. (1) When the computer detects that the input/output (I/O) is idle in accordance with the user's pre-set number of minutes (from 1 to 150 minutes), it goes into standby mode. (2) To get out of standby mode, the computer must detect I/O activity. The recovery time is three seconds. (3) If the I/O is idle and the suspend button is pushed, the computer enters suspend mode. (4) To resume normal operation, the resume button must be pushed. The recovery time may take up to ten seconds. (5) If while in suspend mode a second level of power management features is activated, the computer will go into zero-volt suspend mode (called 'ultra green'). (6) To resume normal operation, the resume button must be pushed or the faxmodem must be activated (due to an incoming call). The recovery time is up to 15 seconds.

unconditional statement [ISO A statement that specifies only one possible execution sequence.]

undecillion See **exponent**.

underflow 1. [ISO In an arithmetic operation, a result whose absolute value is too small to be represented within the range of the numeration system in use. *Examples:* (a) The condition existing, particularly when a floating point representation system is used, when the result is smaller than the smallest non-zero quantity that can be represented. (b) The result may underflow because of the generation of a negative exponent that is outside the permissible range.] 2. [ISO The state in which the calculator shows a zero result for the most significant part of a number, while the least significant part of the number is dropped. *Example:* If the calculator output capacity is four digits, the number .0000432 will be shown as .0000.]

underflow indication [ISO A visual indication that the calculator is in the underflow state.]

UNI 1. Ente Nazionale Italiano di Unificazione; Italy's standards body formed in 1921. 2. User network interface.

Uniform Product Code Council The body that adopted the Interleaved Two of Five bar code system in 1981. Abbreviation 'UPCC'. See **bar code**.

uniform referencing [ISO A property of a programming language such that two or more language constructs for referencing are of the same form. *Examples:* Language constructs for name qualification and indirect references; language constructs for subscripting and actual parameters.]

United States of America Standards Institute Former name of the American National Standards Institute. See **ANSI**.

unit string [ISO A string that contains one element.]

unit test [ISO A test of individual programs or modules in order to ensure that there are no analysis or programming errors.]

UNIVAC Universal Automatic Computer; a first-generation computer (using vacuum tubes) which processed both numerical and alphabetical calculations with ease. It was developed for the United States Bureau of the Census for tabulating the 1950 census. It was built by John Presper Eckert and John William Mauchly — the inventors who built the first large-scale electronic digital calculator, called 'ENIAC' (Electronic Numerical Integrator and Calculator). See **ENIAC** and **Mauchly, John William**.

universal administration [ISO Address administration in which all LAN individual addresses are unique within the same or other local area networks.]

Universal Automatic Computer See **UNIVAC**.

Universal Product Code See **UPC**.

UNIX The uniprogrammed version of Multics. The name was coined by Brian Kernighan, a colleague of Kenneth Thompson and Dennis Ritchie (two of the original group of scientists who met in the mid-1960s at the Massachusetts

Institute of Technology to build the new operating system which they called 'Multics'). UNIX was developed in 1971 at AT&T Bell Laboratories as a simple multitasking, multi-user operating system mostly written in C. UNIX can be ported to Intel, Motorola, Sun Sparc, and both RISC and proprietary microprocessors. It offers record and file locking through sophisticated system administration and security features. UNIX has become very popular, especially for 32-bit microprocessors, and there are many organizations trying to develop a standard for UNIX because it can be used on everything from personal computers to mainframes. Interestingly, when AT&T launched its own personal computer in 1984, it used MS–DOS and PC–DOS instead of UNIX. Like MS–DOS, UNIX was derived as a general-purpose operating system. Its flexibility ultimately led to many different variations of UNIX that were targeted at specific market segments. The major derivatives (Xenix from Microsoft, Sun OS from Sun Microsystems, and BSD from the University of California at Berkeley) are now being reconsolidated by AT&T into a single version of UNIX. This version is called 'System V' (the initial release being '4.0'). Like many mainframe operating systems, UNIX timeshares the host central processing unit (CPU) to be able to run multiple tasks (or jobs) and to support multiple users. UNIX polls individual users to determine whether any system CPU intervention is needed. It also provides features for managing access to data by multiple users. These include the ability to lock a record or file in order to prevent unauthorized or simultaneous access, a file system capable of handling simultaneous access to multiple records, password security clearance to access user accounts, and system administration features for maintenance. UNIX has gained popularity with many

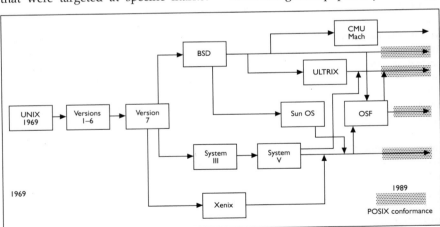

UNIX *Although the UNIX operating system is now widely accepted, it currently has multiple, incompatible versions. Standards efforts, for example POSIX, are being used in attempts to reconcile these various versions. The Open Software Foundation was founded to advance open system technology. X/Open is similarly focused on advancing open systems. This figure illustrates the evolution of the UNIX operating system.*

technical users because of its flexibility and large feature set. It has found wide support in the engineering, scientific, and manufacturing markets. It has also been gaining popularity in the business arena. Industry organizations such as the Open Software Foundation (OSF), UNIX International, and X/Open are all advancing standards for UNIX (although sometimes these standards conflict). Pronounced 'you-nicks'. See **operating system**. ⋏

UNIX International A non-profit organization founded in December 1988 to direct the evolution of the open systems environment based on the UNIX System V operating system. The organization was established to ensure that future enhancements and releases of System V contain the features demanded by a changing marketplace, while conforming to the specifications formulated by industry standards organizations such as X/Open. International membership exceeds 250 users, independent software vendors, computer manufacturers, systems integrators, value-added resellers, industry standards bodies, academic and research institutions, and government agencies worldwide. Annual membership fees range from US$500 to US$500 000 depending upon the class of membership which includes educational institutions, nonprofit associations, prin-

cipal members, and general members. Abbreviation 'UI'.

UNMA Unified Network Management Architecture; AT&T's network architecture announced in 1987 primarily for wide area networks and voice transmission, using Network Management Protocol.

unpack [ISO To recover the original form of the data from packed data.]

unpacked decimal notation [ISO A binary-coded decimal notation in which each decimal digit is represented by one byte.]

unrecoverable error [ISO An error for which recovery is impossible without the use of recovery techniques external to the computer program.]

unscheduled down-time A computer system is said to be 'available' if it delivers correct service to its users when service is required. Despite strong efforts, not all systems can be available 100% of the time, because unexpected faults may occur and lead to their failure or partial failure. Availability requirements for different systems vary greatly. Achieving less down-time may in some instances be far too costly. For example, based upon a system (say, in a bank) which is scheduled to service 24 hours a day, 365 days per year, a 99% level of availability translates to 88 hours of unscheduled down-time per year. This figure may be far too high for most transaction processing environments, especially considering that 88 hours can translate (multiply) to a much higher cost if each of the (bank) branches experiences the same down-time. On the other hand, a

NEWSFLASH

By 1997, 81.9% of revenue in the UNIX small-scale market is expected to be from commercial systems (business, accounting, or inventory control), and 18.1% is expected to be from technical systems (scientific, engineering, or design use).

99.999% level of availability translates to 5.25 minutes of unscheduled down-time per year, which may be far too costly in price/performance terms to achieve. See **MTBF** and **system availability**. ▼

unstable state [ISO In a trigger circuit, a state in which the circuit remains for a finite period of time at the end of which it returns to a stable state without the application of a pulse.]

UPC Universal Product Code; the familiar striped bar code as commonly used on products in retail outlets. Both narrow and wide bars, and narrow and wide spaces, form unique ten-digit numbers which indicate the manufacturer and other product information. See **bar code**. ▼

UPCC Uniform Product Code Council; the body that adopted the Interleaved

Two of Five bar code system in 1981. See **bar code**.

update To add new information to a record, ensuring that it remains current and accurate.

uplink [ISO Pertaining to data transmission from a data station to the headend.]

UPS Uninterruptible power supply; a device connected between a power source (usually the mains) and a device such as a computer. When the power fails, the UPS provides the necessary power. It uses a battery and power circuits to produce the required voltages. Depending upon the battery size and the load, a UPS may last from several minutes to several hours. Pronounced 'you-pea-<u>ess</u>'.

URC Unit reference code.

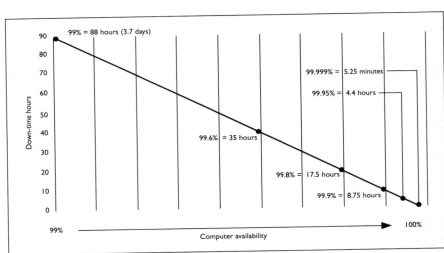

unscheduled down-time This chart puts availability requirements into perspective. A 99% level of computer availability translates to 88 hours of unscheduled down-time per year. On the other hand, 99.999% translates to 5.25 minutes of unscheduled down-time per year.

UPC A bar code symbol shows numerals, letters, or symbols by means of stripes which have a different reflective index from that of the background. Bar code symbols were invented to be read by machines, and it is difficult for humans to read them. This type of symbol was adopted for the first time in the United States in 1973 and was named UPC (Universal Product Code). After that, bar coding was adopted in Western Europe in 1974 (EAN: European Article Number) and then in Japan in 1978 (JAN: Japanese Article Number). The most typical bar code symbol has 13 digits, although there are other kinds which have six or eight digits. The first two of the 13 digits (4 and 9 in this figure) are the nation code. The next five digits (01904) are the maker code. The next five digits (51029) are the product code. The last digit (8) is the check digit, which is used to confirm that the code was read without errors. The merchandise is recognized by reading these 13 digits with the bar code reader/scanner.

US Unit separator.

usability test [ISO A test to determine whether an implemented system fulfills its functional purpose as determined by its users.]

USASI United States of America Standards Institute; its new name is the American National Standards Institute. See **ANSI**.

user class of service [ISO A category of

a data transmission service provided by a data network in which the data signaling rate, the data terminal equipment operating mode, and the code structure (if any) are standardized.]

user coordinate [ISO A coordinate specified by a user and expressed in a coordinate system that is device independent.]

U

user facility [ISO A set of functions available on demand to a user, and provided as part of a data network transmission service. *Note:* Some facilities may be available on a per-call basis, and others may be assigned for an agreed period of time at the request of the user. On certain assigned facilities, per-call options may also be available.]

user-friendly Refers to software which prompts the user in non-technical terms so that the novice user may easily operate the software. This term may also refer to easy-to-operate hardware devices such as modern telephones or printers, or to manuals and the like.

user interface The way a user interacts with a specific computing system or application using a specific device.

user manual [ISO A document that describes how to use a functional unit, and that may include description of the rights and responsibilities of the user, the owner, and the supplier of the unit.]

user terminal [ISO An input/output unit by which a user communicates with a computer.]

U.S. Robotics U.S. Robotics, Incorporated; a worldwide designer, manufacturer, and marketer of modems. Founded in 1976 and based in Illinois, the company evolved from a primarily low-speed, private-label manufacturer to a major brand manufacturer. With the 1982 introduction of the 'Password' modem, U.S. Robotics brought to market the industry's first 1200 bits per second auto-dial modem to use standard, off-the-shelf microprocessors. In 1983, the company signed the industry's first large-scale private-label manufacturing agreement with Apple Computer, and later supplied private-label modems to Commodore, Zenith, Grid, Kaypro, and Televideo. In 1988, U.S. Robotics introduced the Courier HST Dual Standard — the first industry-standard CCITT V.32 modem. With over 300 employees and revenue exceeding US$190 million, the company distributes its products through national, regional, and industrial computer products distributors, who in turn sell to computer dealers and value-added resellers. In 1990, the company acquired Communications Research Group, a software developer and maker of BLAST communications products.

USS Unformatted system services.

utility program A program which relieves the programmer from having to write a repetitive function (such as file handling). Although many utility functions are provided with a computer's operating system, a user may require additional utilities. These may be purchased or even downloaded via modem from electronic bulletin boards. One commercial package which is very popular with PC users is The Norton Utilities. This collection includes many specialized routines such as a program which can recover a disk file if it is accidentally deleted. In recent years, the distinction between application software and utility routines has also become unclear; many application packages either include built-in utility functions or come packaged with additional freestanding utilities. For example, dBASE includes internal functions for copying and deleting files. One popular word-processing package, Microsoft Word, comes with a freestanding utility which can convert text documents created with other word processors into Word format. Another category of utility software is called 'terminate and stay resident' (TSR). When most programs finish executing, they relinquish the random-access memory (RAM) to the next program that is to be loaded. However, TSR utilities do not give up their memory space. They terminate but stay resident in RAM, sharing the memory with application software so that they are always available. One popular TSR program developed by Borland is called 'Turbo Lightning'. By pressing a combination of keys, this utility will check the spelling of all text displayed on the monitor by the current application program. TSR utilities offer many other services, such as calendars, key reprogramming, notepads, and calculators. When using large TSR utilities, it may be necessary for the user to increase the amount of RAM available on the computer so that the TSR utility and other application packages can be used simultaneously.

utility routine (program) [ISO A routine (a computer program) that provides general, frequently-needed services for computer users and service personnel. *Examples:* An input routine; a diagnostic program; a trace program; a sort program.]

UTP Unshielded twisted pair.

UTS Unbound task set.

UUCP UNIX-to-UNIX copy program.

UV Ultraviolet. Electromagnetic radiation situated above the violet end of the visible spectrum. The wavelength is shorter than that of visible light (0.4 to 0.8 microns) but longer than that of X-rays. The UV region extends from approximately 1 nanometer (where the optical spectrum starts) to approximately 400 nanometers (the beginning of the visible region). See **optics**.

U

IT IS UNLIKELY THAT HUMANS WILL EVER COEXIST WITH FULLY SELF-AWARE COMPUTER SYSTEMS BECAUSE, UNDOUBTEDLY, ONE WILL SILENCE THE OTHER

V 1. Vertical. 2. Volt; the SI unit of electrical potential. One volt is defined as the difference in potential between two points of a conducting wire carrying a constant current of 1 ampere, when the power dissipated between these points is equal to 1 watt. See **ampere**, **metric system**, **SI**, and **volt**.

V.x A series of CCITT standards that define modem operations and error correction/data compression, as well as diagnostic tests for modems. Since the public telephone lines are designed to carry analog voice information, the serial digital data from the adapter must be converted into analog audio tones. This is the function of the modem. When receiving data, the modem performs just the opposite function: it converts data from analog to digital. Many modems used with personal computers are classified as 'medium speed', meaning they can send and receive data at either 1200 or 2400 bits per second (Bps). For 2400

Bps operation, all manufacturers follow a standard signaling scheme. This means that different modems can function together. However, at 1200 Bps, there are several different signaling standards, causing potential compatibility problems. Most United States computer vendors market 1200-Bps units that are 'Bell 212-A' compatible, but for international communications, a popular signaling scheme conforms to the 'V.22' standard. Some 1200-Bps modems support both standards. High-speed modems are being used with personal computers, operating at 9600 Bps and higher, over standard dial-up telephones lines. To handle the high number of data errors that can occur at these speeds, most modems have some type of built-in error detection and correction circuits. Some also have the ability to automatically reduce transmission speeds if the telephone line quality is poor. Most vendors of high-speed modems are using proprietary signaling technologies, which

CCITT V SERIES STANDARD	DESCRIPTION
V.21	300 Bps duplex modems used with dial-up lines
V.22	1200 Bps duplex modems used with dial-up and leased lines
V.22bis	2400 Bps duplex modems used with dial-up and leased lines
V.23	600/1200 Bps half-duplex synchronous or asynchronous modems used with dial-up and leased lines
V.24	List of definitions for interchange circuits between data terminal equipment and data circuit-terminating equipment
V.25	Automatic answering equipment and/or parallel automatic calling equipment standard including procedures for disabling of echo control devices for calls established manually or automatically
V.25bis	Same as V.25, but using the 100-Series interchange circuits
V.26	2400 Bps duplex modems used with four-wire leased telephone-type circuits
V.26bis	2400/1200 Bps duplex modems used with dial-up lines
V.26ter	2400 Bps duplex modems using the echo cancellation technique (general switched phone networks) and point-to-point two-wire leased telephone-type circuits
V.27	4800 Bps duplex modems used with a manual equalizer on leased telephone-type circuits
V.27bis	2400/4800 Bps duplex modems used with an automatic equalizer on leased telephone-type circuits
V.27ter	2400/4800 Bps duplex modems used with dial-up lines
V.28	Electrical characteristics for unbalanced double-current interchange circuits
V.29	9600 Bps duplex or half-duplex modems for use on point-to-point four-wire leased telephone-type circuits
V.32	9600 Bps duplex modems with echo canceling for general and leased lines circuits
V.32bis	Two-wire duplex modems operating at data signaling rates of up to 14 400 Bps for general and leased line circuits
V.42	Error-correction scheme (called 'LAPM') with MNP-4 fall-back
V.42bis	Data compression techniques superior to that of MNP-5
V.54	Loop test devices/methods for modems
V.fast	Working name for the proposed high-speed modem communications standard to exceed 14 000 Bps

V.x Common CCITT standards.

means that identical modems must be used at each end of a link. ▲

V.xbis Refers to a second version of a particular standard from the series of CCITT standards. See **V.x**.

V.xter Refers to a third version of a particular standard from the series of CCITT standards. See **V.x**.

VAC Value-added carrier. A corporation that sells the services of a value-added network. Such a network is built using the communications offerings of traditional common carriers connected to computers which permit new types of telecommunications tariffs to be offered. The network may be a packet switching or a message switching network. Services offered include transmission of facsimile documents.

vaccine A computer program written to search for unusual disk activity, and report to the user on any presence of a disk infection such as a virus. Known viruses can be detected quickly, but authors of computer viruses are constantly designing new viruses with which to cause malicious and widespread computer damage. See **virus**.

vacuum column [ISO In a magnetic tape drive, a cavity in which a lower air pressure is maintained so as to attract a tape loop between the spool and the driving mechanism.]

vacuum tube A small electronic device which resembles a light bulb, used in early first-generation computer equipment to control the flow of electrical current, and also used in radios and television sets. Although they were a vast improvement over previous electromechanical parts, vacuum tubes had high failure rates, and they generated a lot of heat, thereby demanding large air conditioning systems. The first large-scale electronic digital calculator was the ENIAC (Electronic Numerical Integrator and Calculator). It used over 18 000 vacuum tubes. Also called 'valve'. See **ENIAC**. ▼

VAD Value-added dealer.

validation [ISO A process used to deter-

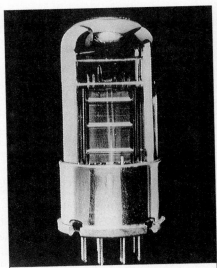

vacuum tube The electronic computer was born of the vacuum tube. Developed for the radio industry, the vacuum tube permitted machines to calculate several thousand times faster than did earlier mechanical relays. Among the first calculators and computers to use vacuum tubes, built in the years 1946 to 1952, were 'ENIAC' at the University of Pennsylvania, and 'UNIVAC I' built by Eckert and Mauchly. The vacuum tube was used basically to switch electrical signals to perform operations such as adding, multiplying, storing, and comparing. In 1946, vacuum tube computers, such as those built in New York by IBM, could multiply two ten-digit numbers in 1/40th of a second; by 1953, in 1/2000th of a second.

mine if data is inaccurate, incomplete, or unreasonable. *Note:* Data validation may include format checks, completeness checks, check key tests, reasonableness checks, and limit checks.]

validation test [ISO A test to determine whether an implemented system fulfills its specified requirements.]

value-added network See **VAN**.

VAM Value-added marketer.

VAN Value-added network; a service provided by a third-party company which leases communications lines from a public telephone company and then enhances the service by attaching special equipment such as modems, filters, and multiplexers, providing error detection and faster response times. These services are then sold to customers for a profit. VANs utilize a 'store-and-forward' method in their network whereby messages are stored until the trading partner's system is available to receive information. The store-and-forward process is often referred to as a 'mailbox service'.

V&V Verification and validation.

vaporware Software which is promised by the manufacturer but is not available to consumers or not yet published in mass production.

VAR 1. Value-added reseller. 2. Vision-aided robot.

variable [ISO A language object that may take different values, one at a time. *Note:* The values of a variable are usually restricted to a certain data type.]

variable function generator [ISO A function generator in which the function it

---

---

generates may be set by the user before or during computation.]

variable-length 1. Referring to a computer which moves data a character at a time, because each record may have a different length. 2. Referring to records in a file which may contain varying numbers of characters.

variable-point representation system [ISO A radix numeration system in which the radix point is explicitly indicated by a special character at that position.]

variant part of a record [ISO A part of a record the data objects of which are defined in alternative ways. *Note:* Both the number and composition of data objects can vary.]

VASI Value-added systems integrator.

VAX Virtual Access Extension; Digital Equipment Corporation's range of computers supported by the VMS operating system. ▼

VAX DBMS A 'network' database model developed by Digital Equipment Corporation. It is a CODASYL-compliant database management system that lets many users simultaneously retrieve and update data stored in the same database files. Typically, stable production applications using VAX DBMS involve complex relationships among data items which require high volume retrieval and update. See **network database**.

VAX FMS See **video form**.

VAX Notes An electronic conferencing software that allows people to create

VAX The VAX 11/750 was introduced in 1980 as the second member of the VAX family. About the size of a washing machine, it provided a central processor with power much higher than the original VAX-780. It could contain up to 4 megabytes of memory and typically serviced 20 to 30 users. Software was initially loaded via a small cassette tape drive located on the front panel.

VAX Rdb/VMS This is a full-function relational database management system designed for VMS and MicroVMS operating systems. It is intended for general-purpose, multi-user, centralized, or distributed applications offering high data capacity (up to 50 gigabytes) and throughput for general-purpose, multi-user, centralized, or distributed applications. VAX Rdb/VMS supports a complete set of utilities (including an SQL interface) and pre-compilers that enable users to maintain and manipulate databases. It also contains an optimizer, a mechanism that uses a combination of algorithms to evaluate a query and then choose the most efficient method to retrieve data in the database. With significant performance improvements, VAX Rdb/VMS is appropriate across a broad range of applications in enterprise-wide environments. See **DBMS**.

VAXsimPLUS See **DSA**.

VAX TDMS See **video form**.

VCR Video cassette recorder.

VDC Volts direct current.

VDD Virtual device driver.

VDI Video device interface.

VDISK A device driver that is included with the Wyse Enhanced Operating System that permits the creation of virtual drives in memory for MS–DOS-based applications. Its key advantage is that operations occurring in the random-access memory disk take place at the much higher speed of system memory and not the slower access and transfer rates of hard-disk drives. This 'drive'

and access online conferences or meetings. Through the network, users can exchange ideas to resolve specific issues, or maintain an ongoing 'discussion' on a particular subject. People in different geographic locations and time zones can join in conferences from their desks, at their convenience. VAX Notes users keep a personal 'notebook' of the conferences they wish to track. Conferences have a topic-and-reply format, and they can be searched using a variety of criteria, such as name of participant, subject, or keyword.

appears to the system as a hard-disk drive, and is accessed in the same manner, but the data is stored in volatile memory and will be lost when the system is turned off or re-set.

VDRV Variable Data Rate Video.

VDS Variable-depth sonar. See **sonar**.

VDT Video display terminal.

VDU Video display unit.

vector A list of numbers or words. [ISO A quantity usually characterized by an ordered set of scalars.]

vector generator [ISO A functional unit that generates directed line segments.]

vector graphics Originally, a term that refers to images created by sets of straight lines, defined by the locations of the end point. However, vector graphics images are manipulated using their pixels rather than their lines.

vector processor The common computer which can only handle one single-dimensional item of data at any one time. These are unlike array processors which are purpose-built computers for high-speed mathematical calculations.

VEIB Virtual external interrupt block.

Veitch diagram [ISO A means of representing Boolean functions in which the number of variables determines the number of squares in the diagram: the number of squares needed is the number of possible states — that is, two, raised to a power determined by the number of variables.]

vendor network See **VAN**.

Venezuelan virus A variant of the Denzuk virus. See **Denzuk virus**.

Venn diagram [ISO A diagram in which sets are represented by regions drawn on a surface.]

verification (test) [ISO A test of a system to prove that it meets all its specified requirements at a particular stage of its development.]

verifier A machine used to check the accuracy of punched cards. Unlike a card punch, the verifier does not actually punch holes in the cards, but confirms (verifies) that the holes that are there are correct.

verifying punch A card punch machine which both punches holes in cards (punched cards) and later verifies the accuracy of the holes automatically. Inaccurate cards are discarded and new ones re-punched by the verifying punch.

verso In printing and desktop publishing, verso refers to a left-hand page (always even-numbered). In contrast, recto refers to a right-hand page (always odd-numbered). The word 'verso' comes from the Latin word *verso*, meaning 'turned leaf'.

vertical application Application software generally consists of a suite of programs working together to accomplish a needed goal, so it is often referred to as an 'application system' or 'application package'. Application systems can be written to satisfy the needs of many users, regardless of their business. Word processing systems or spreadsheet systems are two examples of this. They can be used successfully by many different organizations. This type of application system is called a 'general application'. Other application systems are much more specific to the needs of a single business. For example, a trucking company would be interested in an application that helps schedule its drivers over a period of time. A hospital, meanwhile, would be more interested in a patient accounting and billing system. Such specialized applications are called 'vertical applications'.

vertical mode index In laser printer technology, the amount of space that a cursor moves in the vertical direction in increments of 1/48th of an inch, with the minimum vertical mode index being 0 and the maximum being 125. Abbreviation 'VMI'.

vertical-to-surface transmission electronphotonic See **S-SEED**.

very-high-level language Since 1971, the fourth generation of computers started using very-high-level programming languages known as '4GL' (4th-generation languages). Programmers using 4GL need not specify every step that a computer should take when making a calculation. Instead, the programmer need only identify the desired end result. This can be likened to asking a colleague to perform a task such as 'make a photocopy of a piece of paper'. An inexperienced colleague (likened to a high-level language) would need detailed instructions on how to get to the photocopier; how to place the paper in the correct position; how to select the options of the photocopier; and which button to press in order to make a copy.

Programming languages which require this amount of detail are sometimes called 'procedural languages'. An experienced colleague (likened to a very-high-level language) would only need to be told to make a photocopy. 4GLs which require very little detail are sometimes called 'nonprocedural languages'. Abbreviation 'VHLL'. See **programming language**.

very-large-scale integration A chip technology with 20 000 to 900 000 logic gates per chip. The flow of electrons in chips is controlled by the transistors which form switches or logic gates. Chips are categorized by the number of logic gates available — for example, very-large-scale integration chips first produced in 1975 and still used today. Miniaturization has reduced the memory required to store 1 million characters of information from 141 cubic meters (in 1953) to 0.01 cubic meters today. Abbreviation 'VLSI'. See **chip**.

VESA Video Electronic Standards Association. An organization, comprising hardware and software manufacturers, dedicated to improving graphics standards. The VL-bus (VESA local bus) is designed to improve the performance of graphics and other peripherals connected to notebooks, desktops, and servers. The VL-bus bypasses the system bus to put up to four peripherals on an electrical pathway closer to the central processing unit. It is a 32-bit local bus standard that is compatible with both ISA and EISA cards.

VF Voice frequency. In a communications system (such as a telephone), speech can be recognized by the human ear between the frequencies 300 and 3400 hertz (Hz). The human ear has an audio frequency (AF) range which extends from 20 to 20 000 Hz.

VFU Vertical format unit.

VGA See **Video Graphics Array**.

V/H Vertical/horizontal.

VHLL See **very-high-level language**.

VIA VAX Information Architecture; the rules for describing, organizing, and accessing data used in Digital Equipment Corporation's VAX computer systems. VIA provides data forms and descriptions which are compatible across a wide variety of programming languages and data manipulation software products.

VID See **voice-input device**.

video adapter Also called 'video display board'; a circuit board placed in a computer for the purpose of manipulating display information before it is made visible. The memory is made up of random-access memory (RAM) chips which store the image to be displayed. Under software control, the central processor places data in the display memory. Circuits on the adapter look at this data and convert it into the video signals which are sent to the monitor. To provide flexibility, most video adapters are capable of operating in a variety of display modes. The major division is between text mode and graphics mode. In text mode, the screen is divided into character cells, usually 80 columns by 25 lines. Each cell is made up of many pixels (picture elements). Within each cell, any one character from a pre-defined character set can be dis-

played. However, the pixels which make up the character cells cannot be individually controlled. In graphics mode, the individual dots on the screen can be controlled, allowing detailed engineering drawings or graphic designs to be displayed. Since a high-resolution graphic mode screen may involve over one million individual pixels, a large display memory is required, especially if color information must also be stored. To quickly display and update high-resolution graphic screens, considerable processing power is also required. To allow even further flexibility, most adapters support multiple graphic modes. Working with a given amount of display RAM, these modes typically offer trade-offs between screen colors and effective resolution. In other words, one mode may support 256 on-screen colors, but sacrifice resolution. Another mode may offer very high resolution, but only in two colors. There are seven main specifications for video adapters, which include: the Monochrome Display Adapter (MDA); Color Graphics Adapter (CGA); the Hercules Monochrome Adapter (HMA); the Color/Graphics/Monochrome Adapter (CGMA); the Enhanced Graphics Adapter (EGA); the Video Graphics Array (VGA); and Super VGA. The introduction of the VGA standard led to the significant shift from digital to analog video technology. All previous graphic standards used digital monitors that received on/off digital video signals from the adapter. This limited the number of colors that could be displayed. On the other hand, with analog technology each signal can vary in intensity. With only three variable signals representing red, green, and blue, an analog monitor can potentially produce any shade of any color, allowing for realistic images and greater flexibility. The word 'video' comes from Latin, meaning 'I see'.

video conferencing A real-time, two-way transmission of digitized video images between two or more locations for the purpose of conducting meetings between two or more remote locations, thereby avoiding lengthy and expensive travel. This requires a wideband transmission facility for which satellite communications have become a popular choice. Transmitted images may be slow scan (where a television screen is repainted every few seconds) or full motion. The bandwidth requirements for two-way video conferencing range from 56 kilobits per second for slow scan to 1.544 megabits per second for full motion. Also called 'teleconferencing'. ▼

video digitization The process of transforming analog video signals into digital information.

video conferencing No longer a complex operation, video conferencing has become a simple task that requires a powerful desktop or notebook computer, a small camera, and a microphone. Through the use of a telephone line, colleagues can contact each other and communicate via multimedia-based applications that might also allow them to exchange documents while they speak.

video display board An electronic circuit board that resides in the computer as part of its hardware to generate the images (text and/or graphics) on the monitor. Using a special section of the computer's memory, the video display board also controls the resolution and colors on the monitor. See **video adapter**.

Video Electronic Standards Association See **VESA**.

video form Most forms (such as tax forms and insurance forms) contain two types of information. One type is information that is already printed on the forms: titles, headings, description of items, and instructions. The second type of information is to be filled in by the user of the form. Resembling paper forms, video forms are displayed on a terminal screen and contain information that never changes, such as titles and headings. The areas that can be changed by the user are called 'fields'. One major difference between paper forms and video forms is the ability of a video form to be validated as soon as it is entered to ensure that the user does not, for instance, type a letter instead of a number or leave important fields blank. Also, most video forms display error messages on the terminal screen to notify the users of their mistake, allowing users to display 'help' information by pressing a special key. In transaction processing, video forms help to automate a company's business in areas such as order entry, ensuring that data entered by users immediately becomes part of the database of information that is centrally stored and can be used by all users of the transaction processing system. During the developmental stages of video forms, manufacturers designed one of two methods of communicating with the terminal: block mode and character mode. IBM chose block mode, in which a whole screenful of information is collected before it is validated and sent to the application program. DEC chose character mode, because users have immediate feedback because each character is validated as the user enters it. Forms packages that DEC developed were VAX FMS and VAX TDMS. These have both been successful in their time, but like many other screen-handling packages from other manufacturers, they cannot easily take advantage of newer devices such as bit-map workstations. Also, neither contains all of the features that designers seek in a standard user interface management system. A new industry-standard interface between an application and the user is called the 'Forms Interface Management System' (FIMS) proposed by CODASYL and supported by ANSI and ISO.

Video Graphics Array A graphics display standard introduced in 1987 by IBM for its PS/2 line of personal computers. Video Graphics Array (VGA) offers improved graphics and text resolution and an expanded number of available colors for both text and graphics while maintaining software compatibility with most CGA and EGA applications. It has a maximum screen resolution of 640 by 480, or 720 by 400 pixels (picture elements) where each character is formed in a 9 by 16 pixel matrix. A maximum of 256 colors can be displayed at once, from an overall selection of 256 000 colors. Many manufacturers other than IBM produce extended VGA boards that offer additional features such as improved resolutions (up to 1024 by 768 pixels). Although VGA is an all-purpose display

standard for specialized graphics processing and computer-aided design, still greater resolution and processing speed is required. There are specialized adapter boards and monitors that can handle these requirements. With pixel resolution of 1280 by 960 and even higher, the adapters use several features to boost image processing speed. The most common is VRAM, a new type of memory chip that is approximately three times as fast as a standard dynamic random-access memory chip. Many also use a dedicated graphics microprocessor chip to relieve the central processing unit from tasks such as plotting the slope of a curve. See **video adapter**.

videotex An interactive information system which is also known as 'videotext' or 'viewdata'. The system can be used for public access, or broadcast to a select user/subscriber base, making large volumes of information available to an authorized audience — for example, corporate policies and procedures, corporate services information, and competitive news and stock updates can be broadcast to members only. Videotex systems usually operate over switched telephone lines and allow 40 columns by 24 lines of color text and graphics to be displayed on the screen. Information is arranged in pages, each page having a unique page number. Well-known videotex systems include Viatel (Australia), Prestel (Britain), and Minitel (France). The logical extension to videotex is the electronic circulation of newspapers and magazines. This will offer speed, and reduce paper consumption. The *Guinness Book of Records* notes that 'The United States had 1642 English-language daily newspapers at 1 Feb 1989, with a combined net paid circulation of 62.7 million copies per day. The peak year for US newspapers was 1910, when there were 2202.'

videotext See **videotex**.

Vienna virus A direct-action file virus that infects (and corrupts) one in every eight files. When, by chance, it infects the COMMAND.COM file (which is accessed every time the computer is turned on), the computer goes into a continual re-boot loop. In some versions of Vienna, the computer fails, and will usually not respond to a re-boot from the hard disk. Vienna is sometimes called '648' (because it always adds 648 bytes to every file it infects), 'One-in-Eight', or 'Austrian' (because it is very common in Austria). See **direct-action file virus**.

viewdata See **videotex**.

viewport [ISO A pre-defined part of a display space.]

vigintillion See **exponent**.

Vines Virtual Networking System; a network operating system from Banyan Systems Incorporated. It is based on UNIX, and allows file and print services, among others, for DOS, Windows, OS/2, and Apple workstations.

VIO Virtual input/output.

virtual address [ISO The address of a storage location in virtual storage.]

virtual call A public packet-switching network is implemented over leased channels and over conventional facilities. Data is transferred between data terminal equipment (DTE) through 'vir-tual' connections. This is called a 'virtual circuit' because no single physical connection is established between the sending and receiving stations. Instead, the network establishes the route of least delay for each packet. A connection between two subscribers can be established by either a virtual call or a permanent virtual circuit. A virtual call is established when a subscriber sends a special message called a 'call request' packet into the network. When a logical path through the network has been established, the subscriber will be notified by receiving a 'call connected' packet. A relationship between sender and receiver is maintained for the length of the virtual call. As each packet is physically transmitted, a temporary physical link is established through the network to the receiving station. At the conclusion of the virtual call, the subscriber issues a 'clear request' packet, thus terminating the virtual call. Compare **permanent virtual circuit**.

virtual call facility [ISO A user facility in which a call-setup procedure and a call-clearing procedure determine a period of communication between two data terminal equipment (DTEs) in which users' data is transferred in the network, in the packet mode of operation. All the users' data is delivered from the network in the same order in which they are received by the network. *Notes:* (a) This facility requires end-to-end transfer control of packets within the network. (b) Data may be delivered to the network before the call set-up has been completed, but they are not delivered to the destination address if the call set-up attempts are unsuccessful. (c) Multi-access DTEs may have several virtual calls in operation at the same time.]

Virtual 86 A capability of the Intel 80386 chip to establish an 8086 environment. Two generations of the Intel 86 family processors have preceded the Intel 80386 microprocessor. These are the 80286 and the 8086. The 80386 is compatible at the binary level with both of them. This compatibility preserves software investments, allows rapid market entry, and can provide access to the vast library of software written for computers based on the 86 family. The 80386 can run 8086 programs; it can also run 80286 and 80386 programs concurrently. But the 80386's most innovative compatibility feature is Virtual 86 capability, which establishes a protected 8086 environment within the 80386 multitasking framework. Complementing the Virtual 86 facility, 80386 paging can be used to give each Virtual 86 task a 1-megabyte address space anywhere in the 80386 physical address space. Moreover, if the 80386 operating system supports virtual memory, Virtual 86 tasks can be swapped like other tasks without special attention.

virtual memory A technique whereby a computer offloads some of the data/program from its primary memory onto disk, thereby giving the impression that primary memory can continue to accept/store almost (virtually) unlimited amounts of data. This is done through segmentation — a process of dividing a program into manageable blocks and placing them in the most convenient locations on a disk. Paging is also used in the same way as segmentation. However, paging is always of a fixed block size, typically measured in kilobytes. 'Thrashing' (inefficient use of virtual memory) occurs when pages are constantly sent back and forth (thrashed)

between disk and memory. Virtual memory originated as a means of gaining more addressable memory by representing the limited physical address space provided by the primary memory hardware as a much larger virtual address space to the software. However, as the physical memory in computer systems has grown, virtual memory is used primarily to provide software with a simple and consistent interface to the memory hardware. Every time a processor references memory, it translates (maps) the virtual address used by the software into a physical address in primary memory. However, if a virtual address does not have a corresponding physical address in memory, a page fault occurs and a 512-byte page containing the target address is read from the disk into memory. In order to make room for a new page from the disk, one or more existing pages in memory may have to be written to the disk. This operation is referred to as 'paging', which is handled by the memory management portion of the operating system. Abbreviation 'VM'. See **OS/2**.

virtual memory support Virtual memory enables the maximum size of a program, or a mix of programs, to be governed by available disk space rather than by the size of physical memory (random-access memory), which is approximately seven times more expensive. The resulting flexibility benefits manufacturers (who can supply multiple performance levels of a product that differ only in memory configurations), programmers (who can leave storage management to the operating system, rather than writing overlays), and end users (who can run more and larger applications without being concerned about running out of memory). Virtual memory is implemented by an operating system with support from the hardware. Some of Intel's central processing units (CPUs) support virtual memory systems based on segments or pages. Segment-based virtual memory is appropriate for smaller 16-bit systems whose segments are 64 kilobytes (kb) in length. However, some support segments as large as 4 gigabytes; therefore most large-scale systems will base their virtual memory systems on the CPU's demand paging facilities. For each page, the CPU supplies the 'present', 'dirty', and 'accessed' bits required to efficiently implement demand-paged virtual memory. Some CPUs automatically trap to the operating system when an instruction refers to a not-present page. When the operating system has swapped the missing page in from the disk, the CPU automatically re-executes the instruction. To ensure high virtual memory performance, the CPU provides an associative on-chip cache for paging information. The cache (called a 'translation lookaside buffer', or TLB) contains the mapping information for the 32 most-recently used pages. For example, in the Intel 80386, each page is 4 kb long. By mapping 128 kb of memory at once, the TLB enables the 80386 to translate most addresses on-chip without consulting a memory-based page table. In typical systems, 98–99% of address references will 'hit' a TLB entry.

Virtual Memory System Digital Equipment Corporation's general-purpose operating environment for development and execution of a wide range of applications that run across the entire line of the VAX family of processors. Abbreviation 'VMS'. See **virtual memory**.

Virtual Networking System A network operating system from Banyan Systems Incorporated. It is based on the UNIX System V, but can also work on DOS-based applications. Abbreviation 'vines'.

virtual push button [ISO Display elements used to simulate a function key by means of a pick device.]

virtual reality The word 'virtual' refers to something being so in function and effectiveness, though not actually of the kind it is purported to be. In computing, the term 'virtual reality' refers to a computer program, coupled with other tools and devices, that enable a person to perform tasks 'virtually' with all the function and effectiveness of a real situation, but not within a real situation. For example, pilots being trained in a flight simulator can be made to feel that they are flying over a city, when in fact, they are stationary on the ground. Virtual representation of houses on a computer screen can help architects understand what the rooms look like on the inside of the building. Wearing special data-glasses, architects can see computer representation of the inside of the building. Turning knobs on the computer, architects are also able to look up, down, left, or right and see a faithful representation of each room on their dataglasses (these are small liquid crystal color monitors attached to the computer). Virtual reality is not only for browsing. Interior designers can visit each room in virtual reality and move around, manipulate objects, and interact with other visitors whom they invite in to look at the building. Given a very powerful computer system, a designer in New York could telephone colleagues in London and ask them to connect into their computer sys-

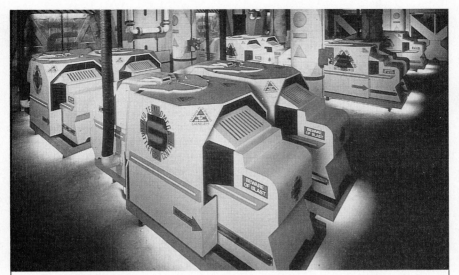

virtual reality *Virtual World Entertainment's BattleTech Center was the first location-based virtual reality entertainment center in the world when it opened in Chicago in July 1990. The cockpit contains more than 100 input and output devices. Set in the year 3025, BattleTech games can be linked on a worldwide network so that players can challenge other groups around the world.*

tem via modem so that they could both browse within the building and discuss the decor while in a state of telepresence. Furthermore, they could both dial up a special furniture store in Paris and, using virtual reality, walk through the showroom to select the furniture. They could take a datapicture of a particular lounge suite and re-map it into their building to see what it would look like. If they like it, they could purchase the lounge suite using their American Express card. Using such systems may require the person to not only wear powerful dataglasses, but perhaps wear a special sound helmet, computerized clothing, datagloves, and lightwave body sensors. To illustrate how powerful such systems can be, consider that the human visual system is the most dominant

sense in the human body. For example, amusement parks often have a room which makes people entering it feel dizzy and unbalanced. People feel that the floor or plank they are standing on is moving vigorously, when in fact they are perfectly stationary. This is a perfect example of virtual reality, because each person reacts to something that is not happening. In this example, only the walls and ceiling are rocking to trick the person's visual system. Abbreviation 'VR'. See **telepresence**. ⚠

Virtual Runtime Object-Oriented Memory Manager See **VROOMM**.

virtual sex See **teledildonics**.

virtual space (In computer graphics.)

[ISO A space in which the coordinates of the display elements are expressed in a device-independent manner.]

virtual storage 1. [ISO The storage space that may be regarded as addressable main storage by the user of a computer system in which virtual addresses are mapped into real addresses. *Note:* The size of virtual storage is limited by the addressing scheme of the computer system and by the amount of auxiliary storage available, and not by the actual number of main storage locations.] 2. See **virtual memory**.

Virtual Telecommunications Access Method A set of IBM mainframe programs that control communications between application programs and terminals by providing SNA services such as managing communication sessions and API (Application Program Interface) — a programming language interface that allows a user-written application program to access the functions of a hardware or software system. Abbreviation 'VTAM'.

Virtual Terminal An OSI application utility that provides remote terminal emulation.

virus A set of purposefully-hidden computer codes written to intentionally cause damage. A virus is a form of infection which can remain dormant within a computer system, a hard disk, or software program for some time. The virus then becomes activated to display error messages, or to erase an entire database or hard disk. Viruses can be transmitted from one computer to another by using an infected diskette, or by downloading information from another contaminated

system (or via modem connections). A 'Trojan' is the name given to any computer program which purposefully carries special codes written to intentionally cause damage. Viruses are potentially the most damaging form of infection because they replicate, and spread quickly. The first instances of viruses in the personal computer environment were recorded in 1986. The number of known viruses grew from six in 1988, to over 5000 viruses in 1995. Detection is generally difficult because the virus may be inactive for some time, then unexpectedly cause widespread damage. However, virus detection programs (such as 'Scan' from McAfee Associates) are readily available and simple to use. Computer users can suspect the presence of a virus if their system behavior changes, or if their system response time is dramatically reduced. Some viruses reverse bytes of information over a long period of time, so that a database and any backup files are scrambled. Other symptoms include unusual error messages, illegible output, sudden decreases in memory or disk capacity, or unusual sound effects or musical tones, plus irregular or obscene on-screen messages. These are as a result of virus authors using increasingly sophisticated programming techniques to enable their programs to avoid detection and disassembly by antivirus researchers such as Loadplan Limited of the United Kingdom. A virus can remain inactive until triggered by particular events such as a particular date or number of keystrokes. Programs which do not replicate themselves are known as 'Trojans'. The *Guinness Book of Records* notes that 'The smallest known viruses are the nucleoprotein plant viruses such as the satellite of tobacco "Necrosis virus" with spherical particles 17 nanometers in diameter'. See **infection**, **Trojan**, and **vaccine**.

Virus-B virus A direct-action file virus that infects .COM files (except for the COMMAND.COM file) and adds 1399 or 976 or 423 bytes to the file (depending upon the version of the virus). This virus does not survive for long because it alerts the user to its presence by flashing a warning the moment that an infected application is executed. Virus-B is some-

times called '423' or 'Friday 13th' because it is activated only on Friday 13th. See **direct-action file virus**.

Virus virus A direct-action file virus that immediately renders program files (.COM files in DOS) inoperative. This instant damage means that its presence is noticed, causing users to take action to irradicate the virus. For this reason, the Virus virus is not common. See **direct-action file virus**.

V

PLAY ON WORDS

Adam and Eve virus	Takes a couple of bytes out of your Apple.
Airline virus	You're in Dallas, but your data is in Singapore.
Bureaucrat virus	Divides your hard disk into hundreds of little units, each of which do practically nothing, but all of which claim to be the most important part of the computer.
Elvis virus	Your computer gets fat, slow, and lazy, and then self-destructs, only to re-surface at shopping malls and service stations across rural America.
Euthanasia virus	Helps your computer to shut down whenever it wants to.
Gallup virus	Sixty percent of the PCs infected will lose 38% of their data 14% of the time (plus or minus a 3.5% margin of error).
Government economist	Nothing works, but all your diagnostic software says that everything is fine.
Healthcare virus virus	After keeping you waiting for six weeks, it tests your system for a day, finds nothing wrong, and sends you a bill for $5000.
New World Order virus	Probably harmless, but it makes a lot of people really mad just thinking about it.
Nike virus	Just does it.
Oedipus virus	Your computer becomes obsessed with marrying its own motherboard.
Police virus	It claims that it feels threatened by other files on your PC and erases them in 'self-defence'.
Politically-correct virus	Never calls itself a 'virus', but instead refers to itself as an 'electronic microorganism'.
President's virus	It starts by boldly stating 'Read my text, no new files', then proceeds to fill up all the free space on your hard disk with new files, and then blames it on the Congressional virus.
Texas virus	Makes sure that it's bigger than any other file.

VisiCalc Visible Calculator; an early spreadsheet software program.

vision systems A branch of artificial intelligence which enables computer-controlled devices to 'see' through the use of scanners and sensors. For example, a robot on a manufacturing line may be equipped with a sensor to detect solid objects in front of it in order to avoid a collision. Other vision systems may be used to scan an object, convert the image into data, and compare the data with a template stored in memory to check the quality of products being manufactured on a production line. Vision systems can also be used for security screening — a camera can digitize the image of a person's face or fingerprints in order to decide if a person may be granted entry to a high-security area, or if a person is a wanted criminal. In 1990, Fujitsu Laboratories created the world's first intelligent robot eye capable of detecting high-speed motion, following a procedure similar to that occurring in the human brain. The intelligent robot eye, consisting of a fuzzy-logic processor, a television camera, and a motor control interface, was the first to offer the possibility of intelligent robots which could, for instance, perform the complex actions entailed in driving a car. The fuzzy-logic-based system goes beyond the reception of visual images to process incoming images and base its actions upon them, as a human observer does when traveling among moving objects. To simulate the human ability to predict the movements of multiple objects and act in response, Fujitsu Laboratories developed two approaches. One enables the robot eye to sample the individual movements of a number of objects, by calculating an average value for the amount of movement of the objects from changes in its visual field (a television camera frame) at 1/30th of a second intervals. That value indicates the speed and direction of the movement. The other approach predicts conjunctions between moving objects. The observer can then avoid collision or else speed up to reach an object. Since the way objects are seen varies with their location, a prediction system was also developed that can infer the three-dimensional structure from the two-dimensional image. The *Guinness Book of Records* notes that 'The human eye is capable of judging relative position with remarkable accuracy, reaching limits of between 3 and 5 seconds of arc. In April 1984 Dr Dennis M. Levi of the College of Optometry, University of Houston, Texas, USA, repeatedly identified the position of a thin white line within 0.85 seconds of arc. This is equivalent to a displacement of some 0.25 in (6 millimeters) at a distance of 1 mile (1.6 kilometers).' Abbreviation 'VS'. See **artificial intelligence**, **laser measuring system**, and **robotics**.

Vista This communications service was developed to meet the needs of Intelsat users with low-density traffic streams, particularly in isolated and remote communities. In June 1989, Intelsat approved for use with Vista, digital modulation techniques, such as SCPC/QPSK (single channel per carrier/quadraphase shift keying) with voice activation. Previously, the service had been restricted to the analog SCPC/CFM (companded frequency modulation) technique.

VIT Video intelligent terminal.

VL-bus VESA local bus. See **VESA**.

VLIC Vertical licensed internal code.

VLSI See **very-large-scale integration**.

VLT Video lookup table.

VM See **virtual memory**.

v-mail See **voice mail**.

VMI Vertical mode index; in laser printer technology, the amount of space that a cursor moves in the vertical direction in increments of 1/48th of an inch, with the minimum VMI being 0 and the maximum being 125.

VMS Virtual Memory System; Digital Equipment Corporation's general-purpose operating environment for development and execution of a wide range of applications that run across the entire line of the VAX family of processors. See **virtual memory**.

VM/SP Virtual machine/system product.

VMTP Versatile message transfer protocol.

VM/XA Virtual machine/extended architecture.

VOD See **voice-output device**.

voice band private Private leased lines most commonly used for data communications. The lines can be conditioned, thereby providing transmission rates above 4800 bits per second. Conditioned voice grade lines can generally provide up to 14 400 bits per second. Line conditioning refers to circuits in the telephone company's equipment that improve the quality (transmission characteristics) of the communications channel. Conditioning allows higher transmission speeds with fewer errors.

voice coil positioner See **positioner**.

voice grade bandwidth A standard voice grade bandwidth used for telephone lines, capable of transmitting 1800 bits per second. Higher-quality, special-purpose data lines (such as facsimile lines) can be used for 9600 bits per second. See **bandwidth**.

voice grade channel A communications channel that can be operated in the frequency range of 300 to 3200 hertz.

voice-input device A device, such as a microphone, which can input human speech into a computer. A voice-recognition device (VRD) then converts the voice signal into digital codes that can be recognized and processed as data by the computer. These are commonly used by physically disabled computer users, pilots in airplane cockpits, and workers on assembly lines. Abbreviation 'VID'.

voice mail A home telephone answering machine is the most basic form of voice mail. More sophisticated systems are commonplace at offices. Through the PABX, each staff member is able to send a spoken message to any or all other staff members. Messages are stored digitally in security-coded memory chips or a disk storage device which can only be accessed by the addressee from any touch-tone telephone. Abbreviation 'v-mail'.

voice-output device Any computer programmed to convert data to pre-recorded vocalized sounds which are understandable to humans. Voice-output devices are commonly used in computerized telephone exchanges and children's learning aids. Speech-impaired people sometimes use voice-output devices (VODs) to communicate with others. For English-speaking audiences, VODs are programmed with phonemes — the 45 basic sound elements used to make up words. Some travelers use pocket-sized VODs to translate foreign words and phrases. Abbreviation 'VOD'. ▼

voice-output device The electronic message of Texas Instruments' 'talking ad' came from an integrated circuit no larger than an infant's fingernail. The message is delivered by a speaker module which is the size of a credit card. Three pill-sized batteries provide the power — enough for some 650 plays through the 1-inch piezoelectric speaker in the module. Believed to be the world's first 'talking' magazine advertisement, the four-page advertisement appeared in Business Week, 20 October 1989, circulating to over 140 000 readers in the eastern United States. One month later, it was inserted in the international edition of the magazine for distribution in Europe and Asia/Pacific.

voice-recognition See **voice-input device**.

volatile Referring to memory chips such as random-access memory which lose their information when electrical power is switched off. This contrasts with non-volatile chips such as read-only memory chips which retain their information even after the power has been switched off. The word 'volatile' comes from the Latin word *volare*, meaning 'fly'.

volatile storage 1. A storage area which requires continuous electrical current to represent data. If the current is interrupted, the data is lost. 2. [ISO A storage device whose contents are lost when power is cut off.]

volt The SI unit of electrical potential. One volt is defined as the difference in potential between two points of a conducting wire carrying a constant current of 1 ampere when the power dissipated between these points is equal to 1 watt. When a material is charged, it is said to have an 'electrical potential'. The difference in electrical potential between two materials is the force that causes electrons to flow when a current path is provided between them. This force is called an 'electromotive force' (EMF) and is measured in units called 'volts'. Voltage, current, and resistance are directly related to each other; in a given circuit, if the values of any two of these three factors is known, then the third factor can be calculated. This relationship of voltage, power (current), and resistance is defined in Ohm's law, which states that current flowing in a circuit is equal to the voltage across the circuit divided by the resistance of the circuit. In a circuit where resistance remains constant and there is an increase in voltage, there will be an increase in current. (If there is a decrease in voltage, there will be a decrease in current.) The opposite is also true. Keeping resistance constant, a change in current will cause the voltage across the resistance to change. That is, an increase in current will cause an increase in voltage. If voltage is constant and resistance changes, current will change in the opposite direction. That is, an increase in resistance will result in a decrease in current. Likewise, a decrease in resistance will cause an increase in current. Abbreviation 'V'. See **ampere**, **metric system**, and **SI**.

VR 1. See **virtual reality**. 2. Virtual route.

VRAM Video random-access memory.

VRC Vertical redundancy checking.

VRD Voice-recognition device. See **voice-input device**.

VRID Virtual route identifier.

VROOMM Virtual Runtime Object-Oriented Memory Manager. This object-oriented technology was developed by Borland International, Incorporated. It allows Borland's software to make the most efficient use of personal computer memory. By swapping small code objects in and out of memory on an 'as-needed' basis, software incorporating VROOMM technology makes the trade-off between program code and application data residing in memory.

VRPRS Virtual route pacing response.

VRT Voice recognition terminal; a computer terminal which accepts selected

voice commands. This is useful for the blind, or professionals who need to keep their hands free for other tasks. See **voice-input device**.

VRU Voice response unit.

VS 1. Virtual storage. See **virtual memory**. 2. See **vision systems**.

VSAM Virtual storage access method.

VSAT Very-small-aperture terminal.

VSD Video single disk.

VSE Virtual storage extended.

VSM Virtual storage management.

VSS Vector symbol set.

VSTEP Vertical-to-surface transmission electronphotonic. See **S-SEED**.

VTAM Virtual Telecommunications Access Method; a set of IBM mainframe programs that controls communications between application programs and terminals by providing SNA services such as managing communication sessions and API (Application Program Interface — a programming language interface that allows a user-written application program to access the functions of a hardware or software system).

VTM Virtual terminal manager.

VTM/FM Virtual terminal manager/function manager.

VTR Video tape recorder.

VU Voice unit.

wafer A small piece of silicon, from which smaller pieces are cut and called 'chips' after they have been photographically etched with up to ten layers of electrical circuits, and baked in an oxygen furnace. A wafer consists of two types of silicon — n-type (negative) and p-type (positive). See **silicon**.

wafer-scale integration The name given to the manufacturing process which uses thin sheets of silicon (wafers) to produce several chips at a time. Different areas (zones) of the wafer are allocated a different type of chip, such as RAM or ROM. Often, each wafer contains more chips than is actually required, and these can be used as spares should some chips be faulty. Abbreviation 'WSI'. See **silicon**.

wait signal [ISO A signal indicating that the device addressed by the central processing unit has not yet completed its data transfer.]

wait state A processing cycle programmed into the computer system which does nothing but occupy time for the purpose of waiting for other components such as the dynamic random-access memory (DRAM) chip to refresh its contents and catch up to the central processing unit (CPU). Although wait states force a very fast processor (cycling at over 25 megahertz) to waste time, they are necessary to ensure that errors do not occur as a result of one component processing too fast for others to catch up. Static random-access memory (SRAM) chips and page-mode RAM chips are becoming popular because they store information without the need for the CPU to refresh them several thousand times per second, thereby reducing or eliminating the wait state. A computer which can process information at its optimal speed without having to wait for other components is said to have a 'zero wait state' (ZWS). For most microprocessors, the effect of one wait state, for example, is easily calculated. If a bus cycle is normally three clocks long, adding a wait state to every bus cycle will make all bus cycles four clocks long, decreasing performance by 33%. See **zero wait state**.

wallyware Software collected by a user for the sole purpose of boasting about having it, though it may never be used. Wallyware is usually pirated software.

WAN Wide area network; a communications network (similar in operation to a local area network) that covers hundreds or thousands of miles, using microwaves or telephone lines (private or public). The largest and most familiar example of a WAN is the public telephone system. A WAN usually consists of data terminal equipment owned or controlled by the user, together with data communication equipment provided by a common carrier. A WAN may be made up of private or public facilities or a combination of both. Private networks use leased dedicated lines which offer higher transmission speeds than those available through the Public Switched Telephone Network (PSTN). Public networks, on the other hand, are operated by common carriers that support the inter-networking of equipment from different suppliers. These suppliers comply with internationally-agreed standards, known as the 'X' Series Recommendation. Public WANs are also used to enable several private networks to communicate with each other. A WAN may be configured in various ways such as: star, where one central node is linked to a number of outlying nodes; ring, where each node is connected to adjacent nodes by a continuous line that forms a closed ring; bus, where all the nodes occur in a linear sequence from one end of the line to another; mesh, where different nodes are interconnected by direct lines; satellite and radio, where no physical connection exists but each node can communicate with any other node; and compound, which is obtained by joining together one or more of the basic structures described above. Compare **LAN**.

wand A hand-held optical input device, usually an optical character reader as used in department stores to automatically input information from a price tag.

warm boot See **warm start**.

warm start If computer processing is interrupted in a minor way, a 'warm start' (function reset) is sufficient to resume from where an operator left off. A 'cold start' (total system reset) would be required if all the power was switched off, or if a system crashed during processing and required re-booting. Also called 'warm boot'.

Waterfall virus A variant of the Cascade virus. See **Cascade virus**.

WATS Wide area telephone service.

wavelength The distance between the peak of one electromagnetic wave, and the peak of the next. Most electromagnetic waves travel through space at 940 000 000 foot (300 000 000 meters) per second. The wavelength of such a wave is obtained by dividing the speed by the frequency in cycles per second (hertz), so a signal of 1 000 000 cycles per second (1 MHz) has a wavelength of 984 foot (300 meters). The higher the frequency, the shorter the wavelength.

WBFM Wideband frequency modulation.

WCC Write control character.

WEB Work element block.

weight [ISO In a positional representation system, the factor by which the value represented by a character in a digit place is multiplied to obtain its additive contribution in the representation of a number.]

Weitek 3167 coprocessor Many early-model personal computers provided a separate socket on the memory cache controller board for the high-powered Weitek 3167 coprocessor. An accelerator typically used in minicomputers, the Weitek coprocessor was a powerful tool for speeding up performance when running one of the many floating point-intensive applications that were designed to take advantage of this capability. The ideal applications for the Weitek options are CAD/CAE, scientific/engineering, and solids modeling.

WG Workgroup; a small unit of approximately ten users on a local area network who, in a group situation, share peripherals and information.

WGA Workgroup application.

WHD Width, height, depth.

wheel printer An impact printer that uses several print wheels, each containing 48 characters (letters, numbers, and symbols). Several wheels are stacked side-by-side (as used in calculators) and each rotates to the appropriate character until the word or line is ready for the hammer to strike the paper from behind, thereby printing the line. The print speed may exceed 150 lines per minute.

Whetstone benchmark A standard by which to test and compare a computer's performance when processing arithmetic operations. It was developed during the late 1960s at the National Physical Laboratory in Whetstone, England, by Curnow and Wichman. Being a small benchmark which can fit in the cache memory of most systems and workstations, the Whetstone is a synthetic mix of transcendental functions, floating-point array computations, floating point and integer arithmetic, and floating-point subroutine calls. Other benchmarks include the 'Khornerstone' (overall system performance, including the processor, memory access, and disk drive access speeds), and the 'Dhrystone' (microprocessor and memory performance). Pronounced 'wet-stone'. See **benchmark**.

wide area network See **WAN**.

wideband For direct data transfer from one computer to another, a wideband channel is used to transmit thousands of bits per second. When transmitting computer data via a communications channel, the information can be sent across either the entire bandwidth, or only a portion of that bandwidth. Naturally, more information can be transmitted when the entire bandwidth is used — this is called 'baseband transmission'. See **bandwidth**.

wideband dial-up This is a circuit-switched service that combines voice band channels to provide wider bandwidth for very-high-speed data transmission on a dial-up, or switched basis. Wideband channels provide data transmission rates above 9600 bits per second.

widow In word processing and desktop publishing, a widow is the last line of a paragraph which appears alone at the top of a new page. Some page-layout programs allow the user to suppress widows, forcing the paragraph to remain intact, or to automatically move more than one line over the page. In contrast, an orphan refers to the first line of a paragraph which appears alone at the bottom of a page. Some page-layout programs allow the user to suppress orphans, forcing the line to join the rest of the paragraph at the next column or over the page.

wildcard character A character which represents one or several unknown characters. Wildcard characters are especially used in databases when searches are being made. For example, the asterisk (*) can be used as a wildcard when performing a spelling search on a word where only the first four characters are known — skip* will search all words beginning with 'skip', therefore giving: skip, skipped, skipper, skipping, and skips. Another typical wildcard is the question mark (?). It functions like the asterisk, but only represents one character at a time — s?ip will search for all possible combinations, giving: ship, skip, slip, and snip.

WIMP Windows, icons, mouse, and pull-down menus; an acronym used generically to refer to any system designed to offer an easy-to-use interface between the user and the operating system through the use of on-screen graphics (icons) which represent certain files or commands, which are accessible to the user through a pointing device such as a mouse. The first such operating environment was the 'Graphics Environment Manager' (GEM) developed by Digital Research for IBM personal computers. ▼

Winchester A fixed disk drive technology in which a sealed data module houses the access arms and the magnetic data disk. Most modern hard disks use 'Winchester technology', a named coined by IBM in 1973 and used as a code name for the development project. For Winchester technology, where the read/write heads fly at heights of 15 millionths of an inch or less, media must be extremely flat in order to avoid surface contact. In addition, in fixed-media drives (drives from which the disks cannot be removed), heads actually land on the media when power is removed and the disk stack spins to a halt. Media for non-removable drives, therefore, are usually either lubricated or coated with a carbon wear surface to avoid damage when the head and media surface make contact. A lubricant prevents direct head–media contact. A wear surface provides durability in the event of such contact. Because thousands of landings may occur during the life of a disk drive, these compounds must be very durable. Lubricants are typically molecular monolayers, and do not significantly change the distance between the flying head and the media. Carbon wear surfaces are about one millionth of an inch thick. See **hard disk** and **ST-506 Winchester drive**. ▼

window [ISO A pre-defined part of a virtual space.]

windowing The ability to have several individual 'screens' on one display. Microsoft's Windows, Digital Research's

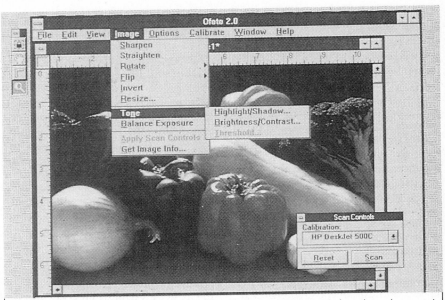

WIMP *This screen shot shows three of the four characteristics of WIMP; windows, icons, (mouse not shown though used), and pull-down menus.*

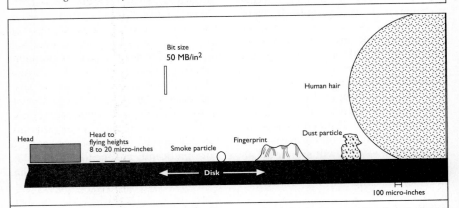

Winchester *Housing the head/disk assembly in a sealed compartment makes it possible to keep the disk's operating environment entirely free of dust, allowing higher-density recording. A manufacturer's expertise in magnetic recording techniques can be measured by the level it has achieved in Winchester technology. This figure illustrates how important it is to keep the disk operating environment clean. Compare the thickness of a human hair with that of 1 bit (binary digit — the smallest unit of information) at a recording density of 50 megabits per square inch. Even a microscopic dust particle is larger than the bit. To achieve higher and higher recording density, it is necessary to fly the recording head much closer to the disk surface. With the head floating on a cushion of air only 8 to 20 micro-inches thick, even a fingerprint can cause damage as the disk spins at over 4000 revolutions per minute.*

Gem Desktop, Quarterdeck's DESQview, and IBM's Topview and OS/2, are all windowing environments which offer 'alternative' operating environments. These systems move away from using text-based commands. Instead, they interface with their operating systems through a menu-oriented 'desktop' for selecting and running computer applications. Windowing is particularly useful for multitasking environments where a user can switch between two or more programs so that they seem to be running at the same time. Windowing programs offered by Microsoft and DESQview both use a built-in memory management scheme that can swap programs between memory and disk.

Windows NT Microsoft's Windows New Technology. A portable 32-bit preemptive multitasking member of the Microsoft Windows operating system family that operates on Intel and RISC systems, and symmetric multiprocessing systems. Windows NT is compatible with Banyan VINES and Novell Net-

Ware, and supports MS–DOS, Windows, and 32-bit Windows-based applications, as well as OS/2-character-based and POSIX-compliant applications. It can access 4 gigabytes of random-access memory, and multiple terabytes of storage using 64-bit addressing. Windows NT is implemented in the C language and offers Level C2 security. The Windows NT design team was assembled in 1988 by Dave Cutler, who was then better known as the developer of the VMS operating system and MicroVAX while he was employed by Digital Equipment Corporation. **A**

W

window/viewport transformation [ISO A mapping of the boundary and contents of a window into the boundary and interior of a viewport.]

WIPO World Intellectual Property Organization.

wire frame representation [ISO A mode of display showing all edges of a three-dimensional object without distinguishing hidden lines.]

wiretapping Computer crime which involves the use of tapping devices which 'listen in' to confidential data transmissions whether they be via cable or radio waves.

Three-layer Windows NT Micro-Kernel Architecture

Win-32 applications	Win-16 applications	DOS applications	POSIX applications
Win-32 Subsystem	Win-16 Subsystem (translation layer)	DOS Subsystem/ virtual machine	POSIX Subsystem
Windows NT Micro-Kernel			
Hardware			

Windows NT This 32-bit operating system offers multithreaded processes, synchronization, security, and input/output and object management with no internal system constraints on resources. Windows NT offers compatibility with Windows, MS–DOS, OS/2, and POSIX applications.

NEWSFLASH

By 1997, Microsoft's Windows NT is expected to own the power desktop market. The traditional workstation market will remain 91% UNIX, while the personal workstation market will be dominated in market share by Windows NT.

word 1. The term 'word' typically refers to a 2-byte unit of information, although it can also be defined as the number of bits that constitute a common unit of information in a particular computer system. Microcomputers commonly use 8-bit and 16-bit words; minicomputers commonly use 16-bit words; mainframes commonly use 32-bit words; and super-computers commonly use 64-bit words. As technology develops, these figures will change. For example, some personal computer systems now process 32-bit words. In both IBM and VAX systems, the basic unit of information is an 8-bit byte, which represents a single character, a number, or a proportion of a number. In primary memory, bytes are logically grouped into storage registers. The width of the storage register may be 2 bytes (known as a 'word'), or 4 bytes (longword), or 8 bytes (quadword), depending upon the system. Most VAX systems store instructions and data as 4-byte longwords, while the VAX 600 series stores information as 8-byte quad-words. In recording the longest word, the *Guinness Book of Records* notes that 'Lengthy concatenations and some compound or agglutinative words or nonce words are or have been written in the closed-up style of a single word e.g. the 182-letter fricassee of 17 sweet and sour ingredients in Aristophanes' comedy "The Ecclesiazusae" in the 4th century BC. A compound "word" of 195 Sanskrit characters (which transliterates into 428 letters in the Roman alphabet) describing the region near Kanci, Tamil Nadu, India, appears in a 16th-century work by Tirumalamba, Queen of Vijayanagara.' 2. [ISO A character string considered as a unit for a given purpose.]

Word for Word A file conversion utility used to read files created by one word processing program and to convert them so that they can be read by another word processing program.

word-organized storage [ISO A storage device into which data can be stored or from which data can be retrieved in units of a computer word, or, with the same duration, in parts of a computer word.]

word processing The use of a software program to write, change, edit, and print letters, manuscripts, or reports. For languages like English where there are fewer than 100 characters, word-based processing does not present any difficulties. However, in a language like Japanese, not only are there two phonetic systems, *hiragana* and *katakana*, totaling nearly 100 characters themselves, but a system of 10 000 complicated characters called 'kanji' is also used. To appreciate this, it must be understood that the 'meaning' of words is derived from the *kanji*, many of which were originally pictures of objects they stood for. The two *kana* (*hiragana* and *katakana*) systems work well together, but make reading and understanding difficult when they stand alone because they lack all visual clues to their meaning. Another problem is the vast number of homonyms in Japanese. A purely phonetic system presents a much higher probability for misunderstanding than one in which each character has a unique meaning. Until recently, computer operators in Japan used a character set made up of alphanumeric characters, special symbols, and *katakana*, thus restricting the use of computers mainly to calculating applications. In computer systems, everything is expressed in combinations of bits (binary digits). By lining up 7 bits, a code can be devised to express 128 characters, numerals, and symbols. However, to handle 10 000 characters, at least 14 bits are necessary. Thus, with the alphanumeric characters and the *kana* character set, a group of 7 bits is satisfactory. However, for *kanji*, a 16-bit coding system is required. In printing or displaying characters, computer systems select from a pool of characters located either in the hardware as print elements and the like, or in the software as patterns in memory. Approximately 900 dots (30 x 30 dots) are required to print each *kanji*, and when this is multiplied by 10 000, more than 9 million bits (approximately 1.1 megabytes) of memory is required. In addition, a special keyboard is required. Several computer companies are beginning to dedicate resources to develop better Japanese word processors because, of the world's population of approximately 5500 million, nearly 1400 million use the Chinese writing system (these include people from China, Japan, North and South Korea, Taiwan, Hong Kong, and Mongolia). As early as 1979, Fujitsu announced the 'Japanese Processing Extended Feature' (JEF) for total character processing. JEF also features *kanji* dictionaries which contain dot patterns for *kanji* characters and *kanji* attributes.

word size [ISO The number of characters in a word.]

workgroup A small unit of approximately ten users on a local area network who, in a group situation, share peripherals and information. Abbreviation 'WG'.

work(ing) space [ISO A portion of stor-

W

age used by a computer program to hold data temporarily.]

workstation 1. A personal computer from which a user communicates to a file server or central computer. 2. A technical or engineering computer capable of 3 MIPS (millions of instructions per second) or more using a 32-bit processor, high-resolution graphics, digitizer, network connection, multitasking operating system, and having access to at least 8 megabytes of random-access memory, with built-in software. Traditionally, workstations were bundled with special software and were designed by the manufacturer to run specialized graphics applications such as computer-aided design. The difference between traditional workstations and powerful personal computers is narrowing because all of these features can be available on personal computers, such as those running Xenix, UNIX, Windows NT, and OS/2 operating systems, with Intel high-powered microprocessors.

world coordinate [ISO A device-independent cartesian coordinate used by the application program for specifying graphical input and output.]

WorldScript A set of integrated software technologies released by Apple in 1992 as part of System 7.1, designed to simplify global software development by providing a unified platform on which developers can create applications for world-wide markets. With WorldScript, the same system-level support that is available for Roman languages such as English, French, German, and Spanish is provided for non-Roman languages such as Japanese, Chinese, Arabic, and Thai. Language support needs, such as contextual formatting, 2-byte support, and multidirectional text capabilities, are provided via WorldScript in a single systems software version to determine the keyboard layout, character encoding, fonts, input methods, sorting, currency, date/time/number formats, and script-specific access routines. With World-Script, all script-specific behavior is defined by tables in system resources, and all processing is done by common routines in the corresponding World-Script extension. Note that WorldScript technology is not a translation technology because it cannot take input in one language and translate it into another language.

worm 1. A form of electronic chain-letter that can be sent to a user to trigger another message which in turn can be sent to another user, and so on. In a short period of time, thousands of messages can be propagated throughout the network. A worm is not a virus, but a chain of events that can be human-assisted or triggered autonomously. Although they are harmless, worms can spread at a rate that slows the entire computer network, occupying most of its bandwidth. A popular worm spread on IBM's corporate network in December 1987 when one staff member sent an electronic message to another asking that person to type the word 'christmas'.

The worm activated a pretty screen that showed a graphic of a Christmas tree. Unbeknown to the user, the worm was working in the background to attach and send itself to all of that person's electronic mail addresses, asking several more people to do the same. Compare **virus**. 2. WORM. Write once, read many times. Unlike CD–ROM, this technology gives the user the ability to record data, but only one time. In other words, once data has been recorded, that portion of the disk cannot be over-written. The disks used with WORM drives are coated with a very thin metal film. To record, the laser essentially burns a series of pits in the film. Information can be recorded on both sides of the disk, but the disk cartridges must be removed and flipped over. A WORM drive can store 200 to 700 megabytes of information on a 5¼-inch disk. Also available are 12-inch disks which can store 2 to 3 gigabytes. The typical data access time is 0.23 seconds. See **compact disk**.

WOSA Windows Open Services Architecture.

Wozniak, Stephen A self-taught engineer and computer wizard, Woz (as he was better known) worked for Hewlett-Packard and was a member of the Homebrew Computer Club — a place where a group of electronic enthusiasts met to exchange ideas on computer hobbies and hacking. It was there that Wozniak met Steve Jobs. At that time, Wozniak was working on a small computer for which Jobs could see commercial potential. Together they raised US$1350 and started to produce computers in kit form for hobbyists. Jobs later met A.C. Markkula, a former Intel marketing manager who became involved in their project. They

Wozniak, Stephen *Co-founder of the Apple Computer Corporation. In an interview with John Sculley (for his book* Odyssey), *Wozniak said; 'If I'd had enough money, I would have bought a computer. I could not afford to buy one so I built my own ... I got turned down for personal computers at Hewlett-Packard three times. But I was so into it that that was going to be the next part of my life ... We were driving along the freeway once and started talking about maybe starting a company and he (Jobs) said, how about this: Apple Computer. We started tossing names back and forth ... It was clear nothing would beat Apple Computer for sounding so good.'*

formed Apple Computer Corporation, with Markkula personally investing US$91 000 and securing other capital. See **Apple Computer Corporation**. ⚠

WP 1. See **word processing**. 2. WordPerfect.

WPM Words per minute.

wraparound [ISO Making that part of an image which lies outside an edge of the display space to be displayed at the opposite edge of that space.]

WRE Waiting request element.

write [ISO To make a permanent or transient recording of data in a storage device or on a data medium. *Note:* The phrases 'to read to' and 'to read from' are often distinguished from the phrases 'to write to' and 'to write from' only by the viewpoint of the description. For example, the transfer of a block of data from internal storage to external storage may be called 'writing to the external storage' or 'reading from the internal storage', or both.]

write-back caching See **write-through caching**.

write-behind Referring to a disk-caching technique used by Microsoft's LAN Manager. The large memory support inherited from the OS/2 system enables LAN Manager to use advanced disk-caching techniques. Disk caching reserves a portion of the server's memory to store frequently-used data so that the data is available for instant access. This cache memory, in turn, enables LAN Manager to improve performance by implementing file-handling techniques. In a write-behind operation, data arriving at the server from a workstation is quickly transferred to cache memory, allowing the server to rapidly return to processing other requests. Later, when network input/output activity is light, the data is written to disk in a single operation. This is also known as a 'lazy write'.

write-enable ring [ISO A removable plastic or metal ring, the presence (or sometimes absence) of which on a magnetic tape reel prevents writing on the magnetic tape and, thereby, the accidental erasure of a file.]

write head [ISO A magnetic head capable of writing only.]

write protection label [ISO A label, the presence (or sometimes absence) of which on a floppy disk prevents writing on that floppy disk.]

write-through caching Primary memory must be kept up to date (coherent) with any new data written to the cache. Two basic strategies are used for coordinating writes to the cache with primary memory: write-through caching and write-back caching. Most processors use a write-through cache, meaning that the processor writes the modified word unit to both the cache and primary memory to ensure that both memories always have updated copies of the word unit. In contrast, a write-back cache keeps track of which word units in the cache have been modified by the processor. This is done by marking modified word units with a dirty bit. When displaced from the cache, the word units containing dirty bits are then written to primary memory. See **cache**.

WSI Wafer-scale integration; the manufacturing process which uses thin sheets of silicon (wafers) to produce several chips at a time. Different areas (zones) of the wafer are allocated a different type of chip, such as RAM or ROM. Often, each wafer contains more chips than is actually required, and these can be used as spares should some chips be faulty. See **silicon**.

WSU Workstation utility.

WTO Write to operator.

WUS Word underscore character.

WYPIWYF What you print is what you fax. Referring to a faxmodem device that will allow the user to fax a document directly from the computer file, without having to print the document first. However, a WYPIWYF faxmodem will ensure that the document sent looks as it would have, had it been printed, meaning that all the page formatting codes and fonts are applied. Pronounced 'whippy-whiff'.

WYPIWYFIWYCIWYS What you print, is what you fax, is what you copy, is what you see. A term coined in 1993 by Microsoft's Karen Hargrove to describe the advantages of the Microsoft At Work architecture. Pronounced 'wippy-wiffy-wicky-wizz'. See Microsoft At Work.

Wyse Technology, Inc. A company founded in 1981 by the husband and wife team Bernie Tse and Grace Yang. By 1984, Wyse had become a leading manufacturer of terminal products that are both market-specific and general-purpose. The company also manufactures personal computers and graphics stations, plus mid-range multi-user systems incorporating fully symmetric multiprocessing architecture, supporting the extended industry standard architecture (EISA). The systems are designed around Intel microprocessors and use a common operating system. Headquartered in San Jose, California, Wyse is now privately owned by a group of Taiwan-based investors who employ 2000 people in the United States, Canada, Australia, Hong Kong, and Western Europe. Tse and Yang had intended to call their company 'Wise Technology' to reflect the fact that they were the first to manufacture 'intelligent' terminals (as opposed to dumb terminals). However, that name was already registered, so they changed the spelling to 'Wyse'.

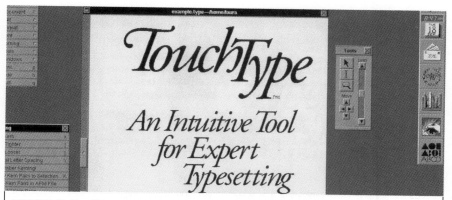

WYSIWYG *TouchType is a WYSIWYG package that allows users to easily adjust tracking, pair kerning, leading, and layout. Instead of using a command, users can manipulate type directly with the mouse by clicking on a character to select it and then moving it as required. The user can see exactly what the output would look like.*

WYSIWYG What you see is what you get; in a graphical user interface, the method of displaying (on screen) an image of what the output will look like, very closely resembling the size, appearance, and position of the finished output. In contrast, character-based programs cannot show (on the screen) any connection between the monospaced text, and the proportionally-spaced output. Pronounced 'wizzy-wig'. ⋀

WYSIWYGMOL What you see is what you get — more or less. Pronounced 'wizzy-wig-mol'. See **imaging model** and **WYSIWYG**.

WYSIWYM What you say is what you mean. Referring to jargon-free statements that require little (or no) interpretation by the receiver of the message. Pronounced 'wizzy-wim'.

XA Extended architecture.

XCA External communication adapter.

X.11 See **X Window System**.

XGA Extended graphics adapter. An IBM graphics standard that includes video graphics array and supports resolutions of up to 1024 pixels by 768 lines interlaced.

XID Exchange identification.

XMIT Transmit.

XPT External page table.

XRF External recovery facility.

X2.23-1968 See **CODASYL**.

X.25 A CCITT standard that defines the accessing protocol for public packet-switching networks. X.25 is a dynamic standard with many variations in the United States and abroad. The X.25 'recommendation' specifies a three-level structure for the transmission of data between data terminal equipment (DTE) and data circuit equipment. X.25 outlines three levels of operation: the physical level; the link level; and the packet level. These layers parallel the bottom three layers of the Open Systems Interconnection (OSI) reference model. The significance for X.25 is that the highest level of protocol it defines, level three (packet level), provides all OSI network (level three) functions and some transport (level four) functions. The OSI protocols at level four and above are concerned with the controlling processes on the hosts themselves. Therefore, X.25 alone does not guarantee that the data arriving from remote locations will be meaningful for the local host system. It is the user's responsibility to define and implement the protocols and functions above level three of X.25. See **OSI**

reference model and **packet-switching system**.

X.25 level 1 One of three levels of the CCITT standard that defines the accessing protocol for public packet-switching networks. The physical level specifies the physical and electrical characteristics of the data terminal equipment (DTE) and data circuit equipment. The CCITT X.25 'recommendation' specifies that a duplex synchronous link should be used to provide a physical transmission path between the DTE and the network. The CCITT also specifies the use of X.21 and X.21 'bis' as the standard interface to digital and analog networks. The X.21bis recommendation was issued to comply with existing standards for this type of interface — the RS-232-C in the United States, and the V.24/V.28 in Europe.

X.25 level 2 One of three levels of the CCITT standard that defines the accessing protocol for public packet-switching networks. The link level provides the packet layer with a reliable error-free facility to move packets across the physical link. The link level has no knowledge of the logical channel or virtual circuit which is used to transmit a packet.

X.25 level 3 One of three levels of the CCITT standard that defines the accessing protocol for public packet-switching networks. The packet level defines procedures for constructing and controlling a data packet. The packet level describes the formats of packets passed between data terminal equipment and data circuit equipment. These formats are used to set up and clear virtual calls. The need to develop such a standard was motivated by the need for a standard interface between the packet-switching networks already in use or planned by many nations, and by the requirements to provide connectivity for a wide variety of terminal equipment.

X3 See **ANSI**.

X.400 A standard for electronic mail developed by CCITT.

X.75/X.121 The CCITT X.75 'recommendation' defines the procedures for the interconnection of separate packet-switched networks (such as those between France and Germany). Networks that are interconnected by X.75 subscribe to yet another CCITT standard, called 'X.121'. This describes the international numbering plan for public data networks. Similar to the numbering system used in making an international telephone call, X.121 defines a network addressing plan using codes for country, network within a country, and network nodes. Once the virtual circuit is established, the DTEs (data terminal equipment) can exchange packets and may be unaware of the distance or number of packet-switched data networks between them.

Xenix A version of UNIX (System V) developed by IBM and Microsoft for personal computers based on Intel's 80x86 microprocessors.

xerographic printer A non-impact printer which operates in the same way as a common photocopier. The image is electronically transferred onto a photoconductive surface (usually a drum) to which toner (magnetized dry ink) is applied. Electrically-charged paper then passes over the photoconductive surface and attracts the toner. The toner is then fixed (heated) onto the paper, forming an image, usually text or graphics. Print speeds may exceed 21 000 lines per minute. The word 'xerographic' comes from the Greek word *xeros*, meaning 'dry'. See **laser printer**.

Xmark A composite benchmark created and released 8 June 1993 by the X Performance Characteristics Group as a project of the Graphics Performance Characterization Committee of the National Computer Graphics Association. Companies including Apple, Hewlett-Packard, IBM, Intel, and Sun Microsystems are supporting Xmark as the benchmark of choice for real-world application performance for the X Window environment, challenging Xstones — an older composite of over 40 tests that focuses on how fast a processor can handle requests. Xmark comprises more than 440 tests that are normalized against the Sun SPARCstation 1 system. Xmark includes network performance tests and tests that address graphics primitives, text primitives, multiple drawing modes, window functions, and X-specific functions.

XModem A communications protocol developed in the late 1970s by Ward Christensen to perform error checking on data sent between two data transmission devices. XModem protocol adds a check-sum to each block of data at transmission. This sum is re-calculated when the block is received, and the new number is compared to the received checksum. If there is a difference, this reflects an error. As a result, the last block of data is re-transmitted. XModem is sometimes known as the 'Christensen Protocol' after its designer. Compare **YModem** and **ZModem**.

XNS Xerox Network Systems; Xerox's proprietary network architecture and protocols. Although not based on the OSI reference model, XNS is consistent with the model.

XON/XOFF Transmission on, transmission off. A method of controlling the flow of data between a modem and its host computer, or between two modems. If the modem receiving the data needs time to process the data or perform some other task, it sends an XOFF signal to the host computer (or sending modem), requesting that the host computer (or sending modem) waits until it received an XON signal before sending more data. This is also known as 'software flow control'.

X/Open Founded in 1984, X/Open is a worldwide, independent, open systems organization dedicated to developing an open, multivendor Common Applications Environment (CAE) based on de facto and international standards. The CAE is a comprehensive software environment designed to provide application portability. X/Open publishes its specifications in a series of volumes called the *X/Open Portability Guide* (XPG). X/Open has over 40 member companies which include Amdahl, AT&T, Digital Equipment Corporation, Fujitsu, Hewlett-Packard, IBM, ICL, NCR, NEC, and Olivetti. Some of X/Open's objectives include portability of applications at the source code level so that application porting is a mechanical recompilation process; connectivity of applications via portable networking services that are independent of underlying protocols; and support for common protocol stacks to ensure that systems conforming to X/Open can interwork effectively. The X/Open Common Applications Environment, as defined in Issue 3 of the *X/Open Portability Guide*, is based upon the interfaces specified in the IEEE 1003.1–1988 POSIX standard, and is extended to cover the other aspects required in a comprehensive open systems environment. In 1988, X/Open introduced a trademark to act as a ready identifier for products which conform to the specifications published in the *X/Open Portability Guide*. This use of the trademark is strictly controlled by a complex licensing agreement which sets out the criteria for compliance for all types of products conforming to X/Open specifications, and establishes stringent rules on the use of the trademark. See **Common Applications Environment**.

XPG X/Open Portability Guide. See **X/Open**.

X Protocol A low-level communication standard (for client application and server software) to request and deliver requests for window manipulation under the X Window System. See **X Window System**.

X-ray A ray of electromagnetic waves whose waves are shorter than those of ultraviolet light. An X-ray has a frequency between 0.3 and 300^{18} hertz. Its invisible wavelength is between 1 and 1000 pico-

meters. If measured in microns, it lies between 0.000001 and 0.001 microns. The energy of an X-ray (electromagnetic energy) is strong enough to produce ionized gases, or deeply penetrate solids, and to destroy molecular structures such as living tissues. In computing, X-rays are used in security devices to detect the presence of firearms in luggage, because X-rays have very little attenuation (signal decay caused by friction). In medicine, they are used to produce photos of the body, particularly to see the structure of bones. This is done by transmitting X-rays through the body in transit to sensitive film which records the variation in transmission, highlighting (showing) the variation of densities within the body (shape and place of bones, in this case). They are also used to treat cancer of the skin, and internal organs. X-rays cannot be focused, reflected, nor refracted by regular methods. Because of their high energy, X-rays must always be used with care. X-rays cannot travel through highly dense substances such as bone, lead, and gold. X-rays were discovered in 1895 in Würzburg, Germany, by a professor of physics, Wilhelm Röntgen, who used the term 'X' to mean 'unknown'.

X-ray tube A tube which generates a very high energy electron beam that is concentrated onto a metal target (anode) to generate X-rays. The higher the voltage used, the smaller the wavelength of the X-ray. See **X-ray**.

XT Extended Technology. Introduced in 1983 by IBM, the PC–XT personal computer was based on the Intel 8088 microprocessor and a 16-bit data bus. The original XT models offered a clock speed of 4.77 megahertz — a speed now considered too slow for modern business and personal applications. The next generation of computers, based on the Intel 8088 microprocessor, were called 'turbo XTs', offering a 10-megahertz clock speed.

XUI X User Interface Toolkit; X Window standard services that support the development of user interfaces for any hardware that supports the X Window System.

X User Interface Toolkit X Window standard services that support the development of user interfaces for any hardware product that supports the X Window System. Abbreviation 'XUI'.

X Windows See **X Window System**.

X Window System Developed by Robert W. Scheifler and Jim Gettys at the Massachusetts Institute of Technology, the X Window System is used as the de facto industry standard to control the display of bit-mapped display devices such as engineering workstations. The purpose is to allow applications to be written independently of input/output systems such as video devices. It also provides a standard environment for application software such as computer-aided design packages and page-layout editors. It began when the two engineers needed to have a hardware-independent means for sending graphic images throughout the network, as well as to be able to use various remote applications simultaneously. The result was the 'X Window Protocol', a standard supported by a group of related manufacturers called the 'X Consortium'. The X Window System is also called 'X.11' and is defined as a distributed, network-transparent, multitasking, windowing, bit-mapped graphics protocol. In this context, 'distributed' describes the two-piece construction of the protocol. These two pieces are called the 'server' and the 'client'. The server is part of the X Window terminal, while the client is on the host computer. This client/server model allows applications to be run on any display device on the network. 'Network transparency' means that the user can use applications programs that are running on other machines scattered throughout the network as if they were running on the user's machine. This is especially useful if the user needs to connect to several different computers on a network. 'Multitasking' refers to the fact that a user can have more than one application running simultaneously on the X Window terminal. 'Windowing' describes the ability to have several individual 'screens' on one display. Each application has its own screen, and X Window provides for moving and resizing windows. 'Bit-mapped graphics' means that each pixel (dot) on the screen can be controlled individually. X Window is an open and nonproprietary windowing system that can be supported under any operating system and on any hardware. Other windowing options which compete with X Window include Microsoft Windows, Apple's own interface, and OS/2 Presentation Manager.

Yale virus A boot-sector virus that infects diskettes by moving the data in the boot sector and overwriting it to a fixed track (usually track 39 of sector 8). Although Yale is one of the earlier viruses (found in the United Kingdom), it manages to survive because it intercepts the Control-Alt-Delete sequence (known as 'interrupt 9') and fakes a re-boot by causing the monitor to blank, and the usual re-boot functions to take place, while it remains in memory to infect another diskette. Yale is sometimes called 'Alameda' or 'Merritt'. See **boot-sector virus**.

yaw angle Virtually all modern disk heads are attached to their positioners by a suspension (or 'gimble'). The gimble permits the slider to pitch, roll, and move vertically over a limited range, but not to yaw (change angle with respect to the track) or move forward, back, or sideways. Pitch, roll, and vertical motion give the slider compliance with the media surface by permitting it to maintain constant flying height over minor irregularities. Yaw angle, fore and aft motion, and sideways motion must be minimized because they change the relationship between the head and the recorded track. The gimble is usually fabricated from stainless steel for high strength and compliance, and is rigidly attached to the access arm. See **positioner**.

YModem An extension of the original XModem transfer protocol. YModem was developed by Chuck Forsburg in the early 1980s. YModem added features such as transfer of file names, multifile transfers, increased reliability of error checking, and increased data throughput. Compare **ZModem**.

YUV A color-encoding scheme for natural pictures in which luminance and chrominance are separate. The human eye is less sensitive to color variations than to intensity variations. YUV allows the encoding of luminance (Y) information at full bandwidth and chrominance (UV) information at half bandwidth.

Zapf Chancery This is a distinctive calligraphic typeface designed by Herman Zapf in 1979 for the International Typeface Corporation (ITC). The backward flourish of letters such as 'h', 'k', and 'l' firmly establishes Chancery's calligraphic heritage. The name 'Chancery' refers to the Papal Chancery of the Middle Ages, and acknowledges the art of the early scribes. **▼**

Aa	*Bb*	*Cc*	*Dd*	*Ee*
Ff	*Gg*	*Hh*	*Ii*	*Jj*
Kk	*Ll*	*Mm*	*Nn*	*Oo*
Pp	*Qq*	*Rr*	*Ss*	*Tt*
Uu	*Ww*	*Xx*	*Yy*	*Zz*
1	*2*	*3*	*4*	*5*
6	*7*	*8*	*9*	*0*

Zapf Chancery *Some of the characters that form Zapf Chancery normal.*

Zapf Dingbats A character from a font which contains ornamental symbols such as squares, arrows, and bullets, used either to decorate a page or when designing forms and coupons. Almost from the first days of printing, ornamental symbols have been used to indicate the start and end of chapters. Since most of these early ornaments were based on floral themes, they were called 'fleurons' and the name is still sometimes used even though the motifs can vary. A common dingbat font is ITC Zapf Dingbats designed in 1978 by Hermann Zapf. **▼**

zero (In data processing.) [ISO The number that when added to or subtracted from any other number does not alter the value of that other number. *Note:* Zero may have different representations in computers, such as positively or negatively signed zero (which may result from subtracting a signed number from itself) and floating point zero (in which the fixed point part is zero while the exponent in the floating point representation may vary).]

zero address instruction [ISO A machine instruction that has no address part. *Ex-*

ample: Certain instructions for a stack machine.]

zero fill [ISO To fill unused storage locations with the representation of the character denoting zero.]

040 See **Motorola 68040**.

zero suppression [ISO The elimination of non-significant zeros from a numeral.]

zero suppression function [ISO The function that allows the process by which unwanted zeros are omitted from the printed or displayed result of a calculation.]

zero-volt suspend mode See **ultra green**.

zero wait state Referring to a central processing unit which can process information at its optimal speed without having to wait for other components (such as dynamic random-access memory) to catch up. Abbreviation 'ZWS'. See **wait state**.

ZIF Zero insertion force. A ZIF socket in a PC is normally provided for the CPU chip to enable easy upgrades.

Mac-based	Standard	Shift	Option	Option/shift	Mac-based	Standard	Shift	Option	Option/shift
A	❀	✿	{	)	Y	❙	✱	⑨	➤
B	❂	✛	∫	➟	Z	■	✳	Ω	➠
C	✳	✢	}	(	`	❁	❞	❀	❁
D	❄	✤	∂	▱	|	☞	✄	②	➚
E	❆	✜	♠	♠	1	●➤	✠	♥	➜
F	❅	◆	⑤	➪	2	✓	✂	❖	➔
G	✾	✧	◆	➭	3	✔	✂	❖	→
H	✽	★	→	➫	4	✗	∞	♥	➞
I	✼	☆	↗	↗	5	✘	✿	❤	➞
J	✺	❂	∆	⇨	6	✖	☏	❦	➡
K	✱	☆	➤	➡	7	✗	©	❧	○
L	●	✩	③	⇨	8	✈	➤	➣	➡
M	○	★	µ	➡	9	✚	✈	⑥	➢
N	■	✯	➤	➤	0	✐	⌧	❼	❽
O	❏	✫	⑩	④	-	✍	✿	❼	±
P	❐	✩	π	∏	=	†	☞	≠	❿
Q	❑	✱	❻	❺	[	✱	'	⑨	→
R	❒	✲	♣	➢	]	✳	"	➔	⊃
S	▲	✶	➤	➪	;	➤	✚	⑩	③
T	▼	✷			'	✎	✿	❾	➤
U	◆	✳	①	‥	'	✏	✝	≤	↗
V	❖	✵	√	◊	.	✑	✝	≥	①
W	➤	✳	Σ	➢	/	✒	❜	÷	⑨
X	|	✳	≈	⇒	\	✱	❝	⑧	⑨
					space			❶	❶

Zapf Dingbats *Character set for Zapf Dingbats showing how different symbols can be obtained by using keyboard option keys. This particular character set applies to the Macintosh.*

ZModem A file transfer protocol developed by Chuck Forsburg in the mid-1980s. It was designed to rectify some of the limitations associated with YModem, as well as to provide support for high-speed, packet, and network communications environments.

zone punch [ISO A hole punched in one of the upper three card rows of a 12-row punch card.]

zooming 1. Enlarging or reducing images on screen. 2. [ISO Progressively scaling the entire display image to give the visual impression of movement of all or part of a display group toward or away from an observer. *Note:* The scaling value should be the same in all directions.]

ZWS Zero wait state; referring to a central processing unit which can process information at its optimal speed without having to wait for other components (such as dynamic random-access memory) to catch up. See **wait state**.

STYLE MANUAL

CORRECT USAGE
OF COMPUTER TERMINOLOGY

This appendix covers correct usage,
grammar, ambiguity, and layout.
Each of these sections is prescriptive,
offering solutions and examples to give
practical advice about the correct usage of
computer terminology.

Topics include abbreviations, acronyms,
capitalization, numbers, and word breaks.

ABBREVIATIONS

An abbreviation is a shortened form of a word (or group of words) used to represent the full version of that word.

Some abbreviations are formed through:

- omission — omitting all but the initial letter of a word, as in:

C	capacitor
D	density
e	emitter
g	gravity
p	page

- using the initial letters of the words in a phrase, as in:

CCP	command control program
CPU	central processing unit
GIS	graphic information system
PLD	programmable logic device
ULSI	ultra-large-scale integration

- the use of the first part of a word, as in:

carr.	carrier
col.	column
in.	inch
mon.	monitor
vol.	volume

- substitution — replacing words with their etymological symbol, as in:

d.	penny, from the Latin, *denarius*
e.g.	for example, from the Latin, *exempli gratia*
i.e.	that is, from the Latin, *id est*
no.	number, from the Latin, *numero*
lb	pound, from the Latin, *libra*

- contraction — shortening the form of words, as in:

can't	cannot
ESC	escape character
etc	et cetera
GND	ground
nichrome	nickel-chromium alloy

- using mathematical symbols, as in:

=	equals
<	less than
−	minus
×	multiplication
+	plus

- compound abbreviation, as in:

ABL	Atlas BASIC Language, where 'BASIC' stands for 'Beginners' All-purpose Symbolic Instruction Code'
ACL	advanced CMOS logic, where 'CMOS' stands for 'complementary metal-oxide semiconductor'
NetBEUI	NetBIOS Extended User Interface, where 'BIOS' stands for 'basic input/output system'
RBW	RISC-based workstation, where 'RISC' stands for 'reduced instruction set computing'
VAI	VAX Information Architecture, where 'VAX' stands for 'Virtual Access Extension'

- combination — standard abbreviations and agreed symbols are used with nonstandard abbreviations, as in:

GB	gigabit
kb	kilobyte
Mb	megabyte, where 'mega' is an agreed metric prefix which means 1 000 000, whereas 'byte' is a contraction of 'binary digit eight'
MBPS	megabits per second, where 'bit' stands for 'binary digit'
Tb	terabyte

NOTES

i)   The shortened form is sometimes used as the standard symbol, as in:

cm	centimeter
m	meter
MHz	megahertz
mm	millimeter
V	volt

ii) The shortened form sometimes becomes a standard colloquialism, as in:

co-op	cooperative
demo	demonstration
exam	examination
plane	airplane
rep	representative

iii) Sometimes the shortened form becomes a standard word in common usage and is used more frequently than the original form. Such words include:

bra	brassière
bus	omnibus
flu	influenza
fridge	refrigerator
phone	telephone

CONFUSION

Although it is generally agreed that abbreviations can take various forms, there is little accord as to how they should be written. The use of the full stop within abbreviations is widely debated, and American texts and authoritative dictionaries contradict each other. Further complications arise when British texts are consulted.

This text endorses the argument that the full stop should not be used when abbreviating words which end with the same letter as the original version of the word (called a 'contraction' rather than an 'abbreviation'), and therefore, this text states that the shortened form of 'doctor' does not need a full stop after 'Dr' because both 'Dr' and 'doctor' end in 'r'. Other such words would include 'mister' (Mr), 'Limited' (Ltd), and 'street' (St).

CORRECT USAGE

There are several factors to take into account before a favored house style can be implemented. Although the English language offers flexibility in parts, it must also demand accuracy in certain areas.

The following highlight common applications, and offer examples of correct usage.

1) Use abbreviations only when it is absolutely necessary. When dealing with words or phrases which are better known by their abbreviated version, show the full version in brackets after the first mention of the abbreviation, but note that this rule (which is contrary to normal English standards) should only be applied if the abbreviation is used more than the full version.

CORRECT

A proposed industry-standard interface between an application and the user is called 'FIMS' (Forms Interface Management System). This was proposed by CODASYL (Conference on Data System Languages), and supported by ANSI (American National Standards Institute) and ISO (International Organization for Standardization). In 1959, CODASYL introduced COBOL (Common Business-Oriented Language).

1.1) Or, if the full version is the term most frequently used, but an abbreviation is used in order to simplify the text, then place the abbreviated form in brackets *after* the term first appears.

EXAMPLE

. . . these initiatives include significant reductions in charges for long-term commitments for domestic and regional use, and the introduction of transponders for unrestricted use (TUU). TUUs allow the use of Intelsat capacity for a mix of domestic and international traffic with the goal of enhancing telecommunications . . . The year also witnessed the implementation of digital circuit multiplication equipment (DCME) . . .

2) Use abbreviations when the long form is cumbersome to write and hard to read, and when the target readers are well versed in the technical terminology. It is advisable to include a glossary of terms with all documentation which uses abbreviations and shortened forms. Compare the two examples that follow.

AVOID

Using the carrier sense multiple access with collision detection method, a device first checks that the cable is free from other carriers and then transmits, while continuing to monitor the presence of another carrier. Local area networks not exceeding 40 nodes work particularly well with carrier sense multiple access with collision detection. In a carrier sense multiple access local area network without collision detection, all stations have the ability to sense traffic on the local area network. One weakness in carrier sense multiple access (without collision detection) is that two stations may sense a clear channel at the same time and transmit simultaneously, resulting in a collision. The Institute of Electrical and Electronics Engineers network management standard number 802.3 carrier sense multiple access with collision detection bus access method offers high transmission speeds of up to 10 megabits per second.

CORRECT

Using the CSMA/CD method, a device first checks that the cable is free from other carriers and then transmits, while continuing to monitor the presence of another carrier. LANs not exceeding 40 nodes work particularly well with CSMA/CD. In a CSMA LAN without collision detection, all stations have the ability to sense traffic on the LAN. One weakness in CSMA (without collision detection) is that two stations may sense a clear channel at the same time and transmit simultaneously, resulting in a collision. The IEEE 802.3 CSMA/CD bus access method offers high transmission speeds of up to 10 megabits per second.

3)   Only use the full stop in an abbreviation when it is absolutely necessary. Remember that too many punctuation marks can clutter a sentence.

AVOID

C.C.I.T.T. is an advisory committee established under the U.N., within the I.T.U., to recommend worldwide standards. Draft recommendations are drawn up for approval by the C.C.I.T.T. Approved recommendations are classified by a letter and a number published in the C.C.I.T.T. book. The letter relates to a series of recommendations. C.C.I.T.T. is a permanent group of the I.T.U. The other two permanent groups of the I.T.U. are the C.C.I.R., which deals with the coordination of long-distance radio telecommunications; and the I.F.R.B. which regulates the allocation of radio frequencies.

4) Full stops must be used to differentiate two similar words, where one is abbreviated and one is not, but it is better to re-write to avoid the ambiguity.

EXAMPLE 1

AVOID

The Ocean Seafood Company recently announced the availability of a new program designed to calculate the cost of freight for fish. The program is available for c.o.d clients. At this stage, the program cannot cater for cod.

CORRECT

The Ocean Seafood Company recently announced the availability of a new program designed to calculate the cost of freight for fish. The program is available for clients who wish to pay cash on delivery. At this stage, the program cannot calculate freight for the cod variety of fish.

INCORRECT

The Ocean Seafood Company recently announced the availability of a new software program designed to calculate the cost of freight for fish. The program is available for cod clients. At this stage, the program cannot cater for cod.

EXAMPLE 2

AVOID

The salary calculations for Jan. were accidentally deleted from the disk and it was found that on the backup file the salary for Jan was incorrect.

CORRECT

The salary calculations for January were accidentally deleted from the disk and it was found that on the backup file the salary for Miss Jan Smith was incorrect.

INCORRECT

The salary has been completely erased for Jan and it was found that on the backup file the salary was incorrect for Jan.

ACRONYMS

An acronym is a shortened form of a group of words. It is always pronounced as a word in itself, and is used to represent the full version of that group of words.

Some acronyms are formed through:

- using the initial letters of the words in a phrase, as in:

CAD	computer-aided design
LIPS	logical inferences per second
MOS	metal oxide semiconductor
RAM	random-access memory
ROM	read-only memory

- using the initial letters of the words in a product name or trade name, as in:

CICS	Customer Information Control System — pronounced 'kicks'
EDVAC	Electronic Discrete Variable Automatic Computer — pronounced 'ed-vack'
ENIAC	Electronic Numeric Integrator and Calculator — pronounced 'any-yak'
ISIS	Intelligent Scheduling and Information System — pronounced 'eye-siss'

- using the initial letters of the words in a name of an organization or corporation, as in:

ANSI	American National Standards Institute — pronounced 'an-see'
GOSIP	Government Open Systems Interconnection Profile — pronounced 'goss-sip'
NASA	National Aeronautics and Space Administration — pronounced 'nass-sa'
SIM	Society for Information Management — pronounced 'sim'
SPEC	Systems Performance Evaluation Cooperative — pronounced 'speck'

- using a combination of initial letters and parts of words in a phrase, as in:

ARPANET	Advanced Research Projects Agency Network — pronounced 'are-pa-net'
COBOL	Common Business-Oriented Language — pronounced 'coe-boll'
CODASYL	Conference on Data System Language — pronounced 'coe-da-sil'
CODEC	coder-decoder — pronounced 'coe-deck'
COMSAT	Communications Satellite Corporation — pronounced 'com-sat'

- using a combination of initial letters and parts of words in a phrase, where the acronym is not written using only capital letters, as in:

Co-Com	Coordinating Committee
laser	light amplification by stimulated emission of radiation
radar	radio detecting and ranging
sonar	sound navigation ranging
telco	telephone company

Sometimes the words used to form the acronym are selected with the intention of making the acronym sound catchy or interesting, as in:

CATCH	Computer-Assisted Terminal Criminal Hunt
OSCAR	Orbital Satellite-Carrying Amateur Radio
PILOT	Programmed Inquiry Learning or Teaching

Some acronyms are formed from a combination of other acronyms and abbreviations, as in:

FACOM	Fujitsu Automatic Computer, where the word 'Fujitsu' is an acronym for Fuji Tsushinki Seizo Limited, and the work 'Fuji' is an acronym derived from Furukawa and Jimens.

Although most acronyms are pronounced as one word, such as RAM and ROM, some are pronounced using a combination of initials, as in:

GFLOP	giga floating point operations per second — pronounced 'gee-flop'
MFLOP	mega floating point operations per second — pronounced 'em-flop'

Some acronyms are written in a way that is totally different to the sequence of words from which they are derived, as in:

pixel	picture element — pronounced '<u>picks</u>-el'
UNIX	uniprogrammed version of Multics — pronounced '<u>you</u>-nicks'

Some shortened forms may appear to be acronyms but they are not generally pronounced as a word. For example:

IT	information technology, used as an abbreviation — pronounced 'eye-tea'
MUX	multiplexer, used as an abbreviation — pronounced 'em-you-ex'
TI	Texas Instruments, used as an abbreviation — pronounced as 'tea-eye'
UPS	uninterruptible power supply, used as an abbreviation — pronounced 'you-pea-es'

Some acronyms are not pronounced the way they appear. For example:

DEC	Digital Equipment Corporation — pronounced 'deck' (not 'dess' as in decimal)
SCO	Santa Cruz Operation — pronounced 'skoe'. (It may also be pronounced as an abbreviation '<u>es</u>-sea-owe'.)
SCSI	small computer system interface — pronounced '<u>skuzzy</u>'

AMBIGUITY

In written and spoken English, ambiguity can lead to frustration and misunderstanding. When using shortened forms or words otherwise common to the computer industry, ensure that the meaning of each sentence is clear and concise.

1) **AVOID**

> Before you connect the printer to the computer port, make sure that it is turned off.

Such a sentence is ambiguous because one cannot tell which item should be turned off — the printer or the computer.

CORRECT

> Before you connect the printer to the computer port, make sure that the printer is turned off.

2) **AVOID**

> The first artificial satellite called 'SPUTNIK I' was launched in 1957 by the USSR.

From this statement, it is difficult to ascertain whether SPUTNIK I was the first-ever satellite to be launched, or if SPUTNIK I was the first satellite *with such a name* to be launched.

CORRECT

> The first artificial satellite, called 'SPUTNIK I', was launched in 1957 by the USSR.

3) **AVOID**

> The decision by the Japanese 'fifth-generation' committee to work with Prolog has given it a temporary lead in the industry.

It is unclear if Prolog was given the advantage, making it the popular product, or if the committee was leading due to the fact that Prolog was being used.

CORRECT

The decision by the Japanese 'fifth-generation' committee to work with Prolog has given Japan a temporary lead in the industry.

4) **AVOID**

This CAD package allows engineers to easily sketch complex three-dimensional designs then rotate and view them from any angle.

It could be suggested that the engineers physically rotate, not the drawing on the screen.

CORRECT

The CAD package allows engineers to easily sketch complex three-dimensional designs then rotate the designs so that they can be viewed from any angle.

CAPITALS

Shortened forms such as abbreviations and acronyms are often written using capital letters. For this reason, the use of capital letters in sentences may create confusion if the shortened form no longer stands out for the reader to recognize, and/or if the word or symbol changes its value when it is capitalized.

If, for some reason, capital letters must be used throughout a sentence, either re-write the entire sentence to ensure that it is clear and accurate, or modify the use of abbreviations to ensure they are clearly marked and identified.

1) **AVOID**

THIS COLLEGE TRIED TO OFFER PRIVATE PILOT COURSES IN FRANCE. HOWEVER, THE DEPARTMENT REFUSED TO OFFER US PERMITS.

Sentences written using capital letters can lead to even greater confusion because in this case, one cannot tell if 'PILOT' refers to the 'one who is licensed to fly an aircraft', or is an acronym for 'Programmed Inquiry Learning or Teaching'. Also, 'US' could mean 'United States', or the objective case of 'we'.

CORRECT

THIS COLLEGE TRIED TO OFFER PRIVATE P.I.L.O.T. COURSES IN FRANCE. HOWEVER, THE DEPARTMENT REFUSED TO ISSUE US WITH PERMITS.

or

THIS COLLEGE TRIED TO OFFER 'PROGRAMMED INQUIRY LEARNING OR TEACHING' (PILOT) COURSES IN FRANCE, BUT WE WERE UNABLE TO OBTAIN PERMITS FROM THE DEPARTMENT OF EDUCATION IN PARIS.

2) **INCORRECT**

IN COMPUTING TERMS, THE ABBREVIATION MB (MEGABIT) REFERS TO 1 048 576 BITS, WHEREAS THE ABBREVIATION MB (MEGABYTE) REFERS TO 1 048 576 BYTES.

When special symbols are used in a capitalized sentence, ensure that all symbols are accurately represented. In the previous example, it is obvious that megabit and megabyte cannot have the same abbreviated form.

CORRECT

IN COMPUTING TERMS, THE ABBREVIATION MB (MEGABIT) REFERS TO 1 048 576 BITS, WHEREAS THE ABBREVIATION Mb (MEGABYTE) REFERS TO 1 048 576 BYTES.

Some organizations use their company's name as part of the product name. To differentiate between the company and the product, some organizations print corporate style-manuals asking their staff to use capital letters when referring to the product. This is incorrect.

English grammar dictates that of the four types of nouns (common noun, proper noun, abstract noun, and collective noun), capital letters may be used only for proper nouns. The use of capitals for proper nouns is restricted to the first letter of the name of a particular person or thing (such as New York, October, and Monday; not NEW YORK, OCTOBER, and MONDAY).

When unfamiliar words are used, some people tend to assume, incorrectly, that capitalization is necessary. Cache (pronounced 'cash') is from the French word *cacher*, meaning 'to hide'; for this reason, it should be treated just like other words (such as budget, from the French *bougette*, which means 'bag' or 'wallet').

INCORRECT

CACHE memory can enhance your database application.

CORRECT

Cache memory can enhance your database application.

Some trademarks and service marks may appear as capitals, but only when there is not an English equivalent.

NUMBERS

DENOMINATIONS ABOVE ONE MILLION

Avoid the use of denominations over one million (the words 'billion' and above) in any document that may be circulated internationally. For an explanation, refer to the entry in the dictionary under 'exponent'.

1) Do not use the term 'billion' when multiples of 'million' will suffice.

   AVOID

   This city houses 6 billion people.

   PREFERRED USAGE

   This city houses 6000 million people.

2) When denominations above one million are used extensively throughout a document, always note the value of the number in powers of ten.

   INCORRECT

   The processing speed starts at 1 million hertz, then expands to 1 billion hertz. Optional equipment can enlarge your system to transfer at 1 trillion hertz.

   AVOID

   The processing speed starts at 1 million (10^6) hertz, then expands to 1 billion (10^9) hertz. Optional equipment can enlarge your system to transfer at 1 trillion (10^{12}) hertz.

   PREFERRED USAGE

   The processing speed starts at 1 megahertz (10^6 Hz), then expands to 1 gigahertz (10^9 Hz). Optional equipment can enlarge your system to transfer at 1 terahertz (10^{12} Hz).

3) When denominations above one million are used extensively throughout a document, and numbers are derived from a base of 2, always note the value of the number in powers of two. The reason for this is that $2^{10} = 1024$, which

is sometimes rounded to 1000 or 10^3. Similarly, 2^{20} = 1024 x 1024 or 1 048 576, so the error in rounding to 1 000 000 or 10^6 is almost 5%.

INCORRECT

This computer can hold **800 million bytes** of information. An optional optical storage unit can give you access to **6 billion bytes.**

AVOID

This computer can hold **800 megabytes** of information. An optional optical storage unit can give you access to **6 gigabytes.**

or

This computer can hold **800 megabytes** (800 x 10^6) of information. An optional optical storage unit can give you access to **6 gigabytes** (6 x 10^9).

PREFERRED USAGE

This computer can hold **800 megabytes** (800 x 2^{20}) of information. An optional optical storage unit can give you access to **6 gigabytes** (6 x 2^{30}).

All this may seem trivial, but consider the person who purchases an industry-standard personal computer. The brochure suggests that the computer contains an 800-megabyte hard disk, but upon installation of the operating system the user is told by the installation program that only 760 megabytes are available. This is a common problem which not only causes inconvenience, but may pose legal problems as well. In this example, the brochure reported 800 megabytes, using the decimal numbering system (base 10), while the installation program counted in binary (base 2).

NUMBERS — LAYOUT

Where the use of very large numbers becomes cumbersome, use a combination of words and figures. For example:

    two thousand million
    2400 million
    three million million
    450 million million

Decimal factors should be used in technical publications. For example:

2 000 000 000	$= 2 \times 10^9$
2 400 000 000	$= 2.4 \times 10^9$
3 000 000 000 000	$= 3 \times 10^{12}$
450 000 000 000 000	$= 4.5 \times 10^{14}$

NUMBERS — PUNCTUATION

Unless they form part of a table of numbers, figures below 9999 should not be separated by a comma nor space. For example: 4097, not 4,097 nor 4 097.

1) When numbers form part of a table, it is permissible to use a space to break up numbers above 999 so that columns line up, but only if numbers above 9999 are used in that same table.

CORRECT

8 743.88
3 989.00
45.55
434 654.77
3 989.00
4 922.17

641.77
2121.99
21.87
2462.00
8643.51
3.12

INCORRECT

8 743.88
3989.00
45.55
434 654.77
3989.00
4922.17

641.77
2121.99
21.87
2 462.00
8643.51
3.12

2) Commas should not be used to break up large numbers.

CORRECT

0.000 001	0.000 02	0.0003
100 000	20 000	3000

INCORRECT

0.000,001	0.000,02	0.000,3
100,000	20,000	3,000

3) Always examine numbers very carefully lest they be ambiguous, leading to error.

AVOID

Most industry-standard personal computers can store 256, 512 or 1024 kilobytes of information.

In this example, it can be taken that computers can store either '256 512' kilobytes or '1024' kilobytes.

SUGGESTED USAGE

Most industry-standard personal computers can store 256 or 512 or 1024 kilobytes of information.

Note that in Europe, the comma is used instead of the decimal point, and vice versa.

NUMBERS AND COMPUTER PROCESSING

Numbers used to represent part numbers (including item numbers) in catalogs may need to be expressed as long figures. This may be due to the software that processes the information. A space or a comma in some software may not be acceptable. For such reasons, it may be necessary to express part numbers and characters in the following ways:

ILAB5ZNS2138   2311912112JB   1801932112CB

NUMBERS AND DATES

With the introduction of electronic data interchange (EDI), it has become necessary to standardize how dates can be expressed in data systems. The International Organization for Standardization tables a system in 'ISO 2711'. This standard uses the year followed by the number of the day (from 1 to 365 — or 366 in a leap year).

For example, 11 December 1999 will be written as 1999345, because 11 December is the 345th day of the year.

Two digits instead of four may be used for the year (99345).

When writing dates in the United States, it is common to place the month, day, then year (12-11-99). The British system places the day, month, then year (11-12-99). These two systems have created much confusion. For this reason, the International Organization for Standardization issued an all-numeric form of writing dates under standard 'ISO 2014–1976'. This standard requires that dates be set out in year (using all four digits), month, and day.

EXAMPLE

19991211   or   1999-12-11

In formal correspondence, the easiest and most logical way to set out dates is:

11 December 1999

When several dates are used in a sentence, follow these examples:

The conference on database management will commence 11 December 1999 and continue on the 12th and 13th.

Conference papers will be printed daily to coincide with seminars held 11, 12, and 13 December. Special technical committee meetings will be held 9, 11, 12, and 18 January 2000.

NUMBERS — RANGE

When using a range of numbers to express page numbers or tolerances, clarity is important.

INCORRECT	USE
322–6	322–326
10–1	10–11
16–7	16–17

INCORRECT	USE
78–7 BC	78–77 BC
1977–8	1977–78
1982–985	1982–85
4.5–6	4.5 to 6.0
5.5–7	5.5 to 7.0
5.5–7.5	5.5 to 7.5
–2.1–1	–2.1 to 1.0
4––2.5	4.0 to –2.5
11.12–1	11.12 to 1

NUMBERS AND SYMBOLS

For clarity, a space is required between a number and its unit.

AVOID	USE
256Mb	256 Mb
33cm	33 cm
9mm	9 mm
1920km	1920 km

Some symbols must not be separated from their numbers.

AVOID	USE
2 nd	2nd
3 rd	3rd
90 %	90%
18 °C	18°C

NUMBERS — AS WORDS

When using numbers ranging from one to (and including) ten, the figures should be spelled out unless they are used in tables, special scientific expressions, or technical specifications.

Large numbers used as approximate measures may be spelled out, but large complex numbers used for accurate expression should be written in full using Arabic numerals.

INCORRECT	We set up 15 personal computers, 5 of which had 560 Mb hard disks. We also had 5 60 Mb disks fitted to the other 10.
USE	We set up 15 personal computers, five of which had 560-Mb hard disks. We also had five 60-Mb disks fitted to the remaining ten.
INCORRECT	In television, the aspect ratio is three to four, and in high-density television, the recommendation is nine to sixteen.
USE	In television, the aspect ratio is 3:4, and in high-density television, the recommendation is 9:16.
INCORRECT	Over 386 486 computers were sold last month.
USE	Of the computers based on the Intel 486 microprocessor, over 386 were sold last month.
INCORRECT	In 1994 350 units were sold, but in 1995 200 units were returned for repair.
USE	In 1994 this company sold 350 units, but 200 units were returned for repair in 1995.
INCORRECT	B is the hexadecimal symbol for binary one zero one one (which is equal to the decimal number 11).
USE	The letter 'B' is the hexadecimal symbol for binary 1011 (which is equal to the decimal number eleven).
INCORRECT	The profit on 12 inch monitors is low.
USE	The profit on 12-inch monitors is low.

Where possible, do not use numbers to open a sentence.

AVOID

56 hard disks were damaged in the storm.

USE

The storm damaged 56 hard disks.

Where possible, do not use numbers to close a sentence unless they represent years or currency.

AVOID

The number of phone calls we received was 89.

We saw a dramatic increase in sales in nineteen-sixty-five.

USE

We received 89 phone calls.

We saw a dramatic increase in sales in 1965.

Avoid ending a sentence with a decimal point.

AVOID

His score was 43.50.

USE

He scored 43.5 in his examinations.

NUMBERS AND CURRENCY

The same misunderstanding that may result between the American and British usage of the word 'billion' may occur with the misuse of numbers and currency.

Since the introduction of satellite news services and the proliferation of syndicated news items from around the world, it has become difficult to discern between local and foreign reports. In particular, reports of foreign investment or fraud may be misleading unless they articulate the currency being used.

When there is a chance of ambiguity, write:

US$4500.20	not	$4500.20
US$50¢	not	0.50¢ nor US$0.50
A$500	not	$500
¥30 000	not	Y30 000
UK£15	not	£15 nor L15

DECIMAL POINT

Note that in some European countries, the decimal point is used as the 'unit separator'. For example, in the United States, US$1 000 000.00 is written with one decimal point to show where the 'cents' commence, whereas in Italy, the same amount would be written US$1.000.000,00 — the comma is used to separate 'cents' and the point used to separate the units.

Avoid showing a figure below one without using the full decimal expression.

AVOID

We were .5 kg over the limit.

USE

We were 0.5 kg over the limit.

CONTRACTED FIGURES

It is permissible to shorten a large figure. For example, US$1 750 000 may be written as US$1.75 million. However, where more than two decimal places would be needed, it is recommended that the full amount be used.

AVOID

US$1.3472 million

USE

US$1 347 200

WORD BREAKS

Although comprehensive advice about word breaks can be sought from an English dictionary or text, it is important to highlight some of the problems associated with incorrect hyphenation.

The English language cannot offer strict rules for every situation, but the following guidelines should address most of the areas and offer helpful suggestions. Note that some hyphens are necessary to join two words together, while others are used at the end of lines to break words that would not fit on that line.

1) A word may be divided between its syllables only if the word is made up of more than five letters, and either side of the hyphenation contains at least three letters.

WORD	INCORRECT	CORRECT
passing	pa-ssing	pass-ing
dancing	danci-ng	danc-ing
swimmer	swimm-er	swim-mer
moving	mo-ving	mov-ing

2) Do not hyphenate a word if it can lead to incorrect pronunciation:

WORD	INCORRECT	CORRECT
omnipotent	omni-potent	omnipo-tent
mothers	mot-hers	moth-ers
coincidentally	coin-cidentally	coinci-dentally
humorous	hum-orous	humor-ous
therapist	the-rapist	ther-apist

3) Do not hyphenate a word at a point where each side of the hyphen forms a complete word.

WORD	INCORRECT	CORRECT
hottest	hot-test	hott-est
redraw	red-raw	re-draw
reallocate	real-locate	re-allocate

4) Note that the inclusion or omission of a hyphen can change the meaning of a word. For example:

I must re-cover the chair with new material to match the carpet.

I must recover that file from the system.

Computer games for children offer good recreation.

Police suggested that a re-creation of the incident might reveal additional clues.

I did re-lay the carpet.

My son won the relay race.

AVOID

A membrane keyboard is a pressure sensitive two dimensional keyboard covered with dust and dirt proof plastic sheets.

Such a statement can be ambiguous. First, it suggests that the keyboard is covered with dust, then the keyboard is covered with a protective plastic sheet. Also, if this statement is read over the radio using a monotone voice, listeners may be confused about the use of 'two', and may understand it to mean that the keyboard is 'sensitive to' keyboards covered with dust . . .

USE

A membrane keyboard is a pressure-sensitive two-dimensional keyboard, covered with dust-proof and dirt-proof plastic sheets.

5) Some word combinations must be hyphenated only when they appear before a noun. For example:

	IBM is a well-known computer manufacturer.
But:	As a computer manufacturer, IBM is well known.
	He is a part-time programmer.
But:	This programmer works part time.
	This is an out-of-date filing system.
But:	This filing system is out of date.

6) Unless forced by the page layout, do not hyphenate:

(a)   a shortened form including an abbreviation, acronym, or contraction (such as FORTRAN)

(b)   numbers or figures (such as '128 186 375')

(c)   words of one syllable (such as 'strength')

(d)   a word that already contains a hyphen (such as 'on-line') unless it breaks at the hyphen

(e)   a word at a prefix that does not contain three or more letters unless:

- the prefix precedes a proper noun (such as 'un-American' or 'pro-Christianity')

- the root word begins with either a 'w', 'y', or a vowel letter (such as 'de-emphasize' or 'co-worker')

FIGURES AND SYMBOLS

The use of hyphens between numbers and symbols may change the meaning of statements. A hyphen should only be used if the number is distanced from the subject by an additional symbol or unit of measure.

1)   **INCORRECT**

The new computer from Fujitsu offers 22 megabyte flash memory cards from Intel.

The introduction of Intel's 1-megabyte flash-memory cards makes this statement ambiguous because the reader could assume that the new computer arrives with 22 separate cards, each capable of storing 1 megabyte. Also, if this statement were read over the radio, the listener may assume that the computer arrives with 20 separate cards, each capable of storing 2 megabytes of memory.

AVOID

The new computer from Fujitsu offers 22-megabyte flash-memory cards from Intel.

USE

Using Intel flash-memory cards, the XYZ computer from Fujitsu allows the user to store a maximum of 22 megabytes of data on each card.

2) AMBIGUOUS

Joseph Jacquard used 80 column cards in the late 1950s. He used 96 column cards in 1969.

USE

Joseph Jacquard used 80-column cards in the late 1950s. He used 96-column cards in 1969.

The pairs shown below illustrate why a hyphen is not required if the number relates and refers directly to the unit of measure that is written to the right of it. In contrast, the second example in each pair requires a hyphen to group together the number and the symbol (or unit of measure) because the number relates to a subject other than the unit of measure.

The processor operates at 80 nanoseconds.

But: This is an 80-nanosecond processor.

The 68030 central processing unit runs at 40 MHz.

But: It runs a 40-MHz central processing unit.

A compact disk only 4.7 inches in diameter can store 700 megabytes of data.

But: The 4.7-inch compact disk can store 700 megabytes of data.

The Intel Pentium microprocessor operates at clock speeds reaching 150 MHz.

But: The 150-MHz Pentium microprocessor is available from Intel Corporation.

AVOID

The personal computer from Apple was designed with a 16 megahertz 68030 Motorola processor. It came with six built in ports for connecting a wide range of peripherals, plus an optional 40 megabyte hard disk drive. It also offered a 3½ inch Apple SuperDrive floppy disk drive which could read, write, and format MS DOS and OS/2 disks.

USE

The personal computer from Apple was designed with a 16-megahertz 68030 Motorola processor. It came with six built-in ports for connecting a wide range of peripherals, plus an optional 40-megabyte hard disk drive. It also offered a 3½-inch Apple SuperDrive floppy disk drive which could read, write, and format MS–DOS and OS/2 disks.

LANGUAGE

Despite the many debates about which version of English is more correct, or which is easier to use, or which is more popular or dominant, it is important to observe the following simple rules.

1) Regardless of nationality, a writer must observe the writing style of the country wherein the document is written, or the country from which the document was commissioned (or original copyright will be held).

   For example, an American working in London is obliged to use the British system when communicating with the British people, and would therefore spell 'colour' instead of 'color'.

   Conversely, a person from London working in New York is obliged to use 'meter' instead of 'metre', despite the many debates about the correct usage. (It is interesting to note that Americans had at one time used 'metre' as the standard, but Webster decided to follow popular usage and make 'meter' the standard in his dictionaries.)

2) A writer must observe the style dictated by the dictionary that is recognized by the local government. For example, the *Oxford* is the standard in England; the *Macquarie* is used in Australia; and the *Merriam-Webster* is used in the United States.

3) Regardless of nationality or preferred style, names of organizations, registered trade names, and service marks must not be changed to suit a house style. Similarly, professional titles must remain unchanged.

CORRECT

Association Française de Normalisation
International Organization for Standardization
Color Graphics Adapter
Distribution Programme Manager
ACOMPLIS (A Computerised London Information Service)

INCORRECT

Association Francaise de Normalization
International Organisation for Standardisation
Colour Graphics Adaptor
Distribution Program Manager
ACOMPLIS (A Computerized London Information Service)

OUR WORDS ARE OUR DEFINITION;
THEY DETERMINE OUR THOUGHTS.
WE ARE WHAT WE THINK,
WE THINK WHAT WE KNOW,
AND WE KNOW WHAT WE CAN ARTICULATE.

ILLUSTRATIONS

*Most of the diagrams and photographs used in this publication
were provided courtesy of the organizations listed below.*

*The entry under which the item can be found is listed first,
followed by the copyright owner.*

access time	*International Organization for Standardization*
A/D converter	*Pioneer Communications of America, Inc*
Adobe Illustrator	*NeXT Computer, Inc*
Apple Computer Corporation	*Apple Computer, Inc*
ATM	*NCR Computer Corporation*
Autodesk	*Autodesk*
AZERTY	*Compaq Computer Corporation*
backup	*Compaq Computer Corporation*
BallPoint mouse	*Microsoft Corporation*
bar code scanner	*NCR Computer Corporation*
Boolean operation	*International Organization for Standardization*
bubble memory	*Fujitsu Limited*
buffer	*Intel Corporation*
cache	*Intel Corporation*
CAD	*Evolution Computing*
CADD	*Xerox Corporation*
caddy	*Apple Computer, Inc*
calculator	*Texas Instruments*
cathode-ray tube	*Apple Computer, Inc*
CD–ROM	*Pioneer Communications of America, Inc*
circuit	*Digital Equipment Corporation*
circuit board	*Compaq Computer Corporation*
clip art	*NeXT Computer, Inc*
compact disk	*Acer, Inc*
computer	*Compaq Computer Corporation*
computer graphics	*Silicon Graphics*
computer system	*Digital Equipment Corporation*
CPU	*Intel Corporation*
Data General	*Data General Corporation*
Dell, Michael S.	*Dell Computer Corporation*

density	*IBM Archives*
desktop computer	*Compaq Computer Corporation*
desktop publishing	*Apple Computer, Inc*
digital signal processor	*Texas Instruments*
digitizer	*GTCO Corporation*
disk drive	*Compaq Computer Corporation*
distributed transaction processing	*Digital Equipment Corporation*
docking station	*Compaq Computer Corporation*
dot matrix printer	*Intel Corporation*
dumb terminal	*Compaq Computer Corporation*
dyadic (N-adic) Boolean operation	*International Organization for Standardization*
Earth station	*Overseas Telecommunications Commission*
EasyCAD2	*Evolution Computing*
electrothermal printer	*Technical Computing and Graphics*
emulate	*Hewlett–Packard Company*
error correction code	*Digital Equipment Corporation*
ExCA	*Intel Corporation*
expansion board	*Compaq Computer Corporation*
expansion slot	*Compaq Computer Corporation*
facsimile	*Fujitsu Limited*
FastCAD	*Evolution Computing*
faxmodem	*Intel Corporation*
fiber optics	*Overseas Telecommunications Commission*
fingerprint sensor	*Fujitsu Limited*
first generation	*IBM Archives*
fixed disk	*Compaq Computer Corporation*
FORTRAN	*IBM Archives*
Gates, William H	*Microsoft Corporation*
geostationary satellite	*Overseas Telecommunications Commission*
Go-Screen	*Go Man Go Productions*
green technology	*Acer Computer Australia*
growth in depth	*Digital Equipment Corporation*
hand-held scanner	*Logitech*
hard disk	*Hewlett–Packard Company*
HEMT	*Fujitsu Limited*
Hewlett, William R.	*Hewlett–Packard Company*
hierarchical database	*Digital Equipment Corporation*
Hollerith, Herman	*IBM Archives*
hologram scanner	*Fujitsu Limited*
human brain	*Fujitsu Limited*
hypermedia	*NeXT Computer, Inc*

IBM	*IBM Archives*
iCOMP	*Intel Corporation*
icon	*Apple Computer, Inc*
IDE	*Acer Computer Australia*
impact printer	*Intel Corporation*
Indeo	*Intel Corporation*
ink-jet printer	*Hewlett–Packard Company*
integrated circuit	*Texas Instruments*
Intel 80486	*Intel Corporation*
interface	*Compaq Computer Corporation*
internal modem	*Compaq Computer Corporation*
Jobs, Steven P.	*NeXT Computer, Inc*
keyboard	*Advanced Micro Devices*
Kilby, Jack St. Clair	*Texas Instruments*
laptop computer	*Compaq Computer Corporation*
laser	*Hewlett–Packard Company*
laser disk	*Pioneer Communications of America, Inc*
laser printer	*Canon Australia Pty Ltd*
LaserWriter	*Apple Computer, Inc*
light-emitting diode	*Hewlett–Packard Company*
light pen	*Technical Computing and Graphics*
Lisa	*Apple Computer, Inc*
look aside cache	*Intel Corporation*
Macintosh	*Apple Computer, Inc*
magnetic core	*IBM Archives*
magnetic tape	*IBM Archives*
mainframe	*Compaq Computer Corporation*
Marconi, Guglielmo	*Overseas Telecommunications Commission*
Maxis	*Maxis*
McNealy, Scott	*Sun Microsystems*
MIDI	*NeXT Computer, Inc*
minicomputer	*Digital Equipment Corporation*
monitor	*Wyse Technology*
morphing	*Silicon Graphics*
MOS	*Intel Corporation*
multiprocessing	*Wyse Technology*
network interface card	*3Com Corporation*
neurocomputer	*Fujitsu Limited*
Newton MessagePad	*Apple Computer, Inc*
non-return-to-zero recording	*International Organization for Standardization*
Norton Utilities	*Symantec Pty Ltd*
notebook	*Canon Australia Pty Ltd*
numeric keypad	*Apple Computer, Inc*

OHP	*Apple Computer, Inc*
operating system	*Microsoft Corporation*
optical disk	*Pioneer Communications of America, Inc*
OSI reference model	*Intel Corporation*
OS/2	*Microsoft Corporation*
OverDrive	*Intel Corporation*
Packard, David	*Hewlett–Packard Company*
paint program	*XTree Corporation*
paperless office	*Apple Computer, Inc*
PC board	*NeXT Computer, Inc*
PCI	*Intel corporation*
PCMCIA	*New Media Corporation*
Pentium	*Intel Corporation*
personal computer	*Compaq Computer Corporation*
phase modulation recording	*International Organization for Standardization*
Pick	*Pick Systems*
plotter	*Technical Computing and Graphics*
p-n Junction	*NCR Corporation*
polarized return-to-zero recording	*International Organization for Standardization*
portable computer	*Compaq Computer Corporation*
punched card	*IBM Archives*
QWERTY	*Apple Computer, Inc*
radio wave propagation	*Overseas Telecommunications Commission*
relational database	*Digital Equipment Corporation*
resonant-tunneling effect	*Fujitsu Limited*
RISC	*Silicon Graphics*
robotics	*Texas Instruments*
router	*SynOptics Communications, Inc*
satellite transmission	*Overseas Telecommunications Commission*
scanner	*Hewlett–Packard Company*
screen saver	*Maxis*
sector interleaving	*Intel Corporation*
Shih, Stan	*Acer, Inc*
silicon	*Texas Instruments*
Simulation	*Silicon Graphics*
SMT	*Digital Equipment Corporation*
speech recognizer	*Fujitsu Limited*
spreadsheet	*NeXT Computer, Inc*
storage hierarchy	*Digital Equipment Corporation*
supercomputer	*Intel Corporation*
tape drive	*Olivetti Systems*

telecomputing	*Toshiba (Australia) Pty Limited*
thin film head	*Fujitsu Limited*
tightly-coupled multiprocessing	*Wyse Technology*
track	*Intel Corporation*
transaction processing	*Digital Equipment Corporation*
transistor	*IBM Archives*
ultra green	*Acer, Inc*
UNIX	*Digital Equipment Corporation*
unscheduled down-time	*Digital Equipment Corporation*
UPC	*Fujitsu Limited*
vacuum tube	*IBM Archives*
VAX	*Digital Equipment Corporation*
video conferencing	*Toshiba (Australia) Pty Limited*
virtual reality	*Virtual World Entertainment*
voice-output device	*Texas Instruments*
WIMP	*Light Source*
Winchester	*Fujitsu Limited*
Windows NT	*Microsoft Corporation*
Wozniak, Stephen	*Apple Computer, Inc*
WYSIWYG	*NeXT Computer, Inc*

BACK COVER

Apple Computer, Inc
Hewlett–Packard Company
IBM Archives
Overseas Telecommunications Commission
Texas Instruments

END PAPERS

In addition to the photographs acknowledged above, other material was provided courtesy of the following organizations:

Acer, Inc
Apple Computer, Inc
Compaq Computer Corporation
Hewlett–Packard Company
Intel Corporation
Overseas Telecommunications Commission
Silicon Graphics

INVITATION

READER REGISTRATION COUPON

Prentice Hall would like to keep you informed about future editions of this book. To register, please complete this coupon and post it to:

Prentice Hall Australia, PO Box 151, Brookvale NSW 2100, Australia.

Your name _____

Job title _____

Full address _____

_____

Zip code _____ Country _____

Phone ( ) _____ Fax ( ) _____

YOUR COMMENTS AND SUGGESTIONS

Your comments about this book, and your suggestions, would be welcomed. If you know of a word that should be included, please write to the address below and enclose any information or illustrative material you feel is appropriate.

- ✂

TO THE PUBLIC RELATIONS DEPARTMENT

If you work in a computer-related field, please forward this notice to your Public Relations Department.

The Author of *Prentice Hall's Illustrated Dictionary of Computing* invites you to place him on your mailing list to receive regular information about your company. Please send press releases, corporate reports, photographs, and diagrams to:

Jonar C. Nader
PO Box 15
Pyrmont NSW 2009
Australia